CONTENT

To the world, to society, and sadly, to most individuals, the perception of professional art and artists is a terribly skewed one. Popular culture's depiction has become obsolete. The notion that an artist is a hedonistic, scatter-brained idealist, who blithely sits around waiting for mood or inspiration to strike, is at best, naive. Like any job, creation is work, often hard work, which demands contemplation, direction, and a clearly defined goal. As Andy Warhol once said, "Why do people think artists are special? It's just another job." Of all the artistic mediums and genres, this fact is best illustrated by the design artist. In no other field of creativity are concept, contemplation and planning more essential than in design.

Throughout human history, the artist has sought to evoke a response in her audience—goal-driven creation is nothing new. But we abide in a time and place altogether different than our forebears', dominated by corporate advertising and the truly global reach of media communications. As such, in this budding 21st century, design has become paramount. The designer is the new Rembrandt, on the frontline of what society is exposed to and what people are offered. The designer has access to the largest audience in the history of art, for today, her work truly has the chance to reach everybody.

As a general principle, that is precisely her job; attracting the audience is no longer a casual consideration, as perhaps with painters or sculptors of days yore. It is now the only consideration, and so the work must be set upon with a strict agenda and, when an artist has been hired on assignment, a mandate. The designer cannot simply throw paint onto canvas in dripping, random fashion, as might a Jackson Pollock. Nor would her still life any longer be a random selection of objects. Nor can she any longer, if success is desired, sculpt, paste, or sketch on the whim of utter fancy. Rather, she must be ever-considerate of her aim or her client's aim in creating, in designing—what is the piece trying to convey? Whom is it trying to reach, and in many cases, what is it trying to promote? This is the art world of today.

Consider: a postcard, a rock concert flyer, a travel magazine featurette, a soft drink's ad campaign, a book's packaging and presentation—each one is trying to attract you, to reach out and speak to you. And each one is the work of an artist. When you peruse the shelves of any retailer, looking at the wide array of available products, every item you see was at one point or another in the hands of a design artist. Any advertisement, be it on television, in a magazine, or on the world wide web, originated in the mind of...yep, you guessed it: the design artist. It seems an awful lot of power and influence for one genre to have over the art world at large.

But then again, this is where design steps outside the boundaries of traditional art. Design is not a genre in the typical sense or definition of the word because it encompasses all genres, all mediums, and at times, it shifts between genres multiple times in one work! It can be

ZOOM IN ZOOM OUT

An exploration from design concept, format to visual impact

viction:ary™

ZOOM IN ZOOM OUT

An exploration from design concept, format to visual impact

Published and distributed in Europe
and Latin America by

INDEX BOOK

Index Book S.L.
Consell De Cent 160 Local 3 08015 Barcelona Spain
Phone: +34 93 4545547 / +34 93 4548755 Fax: +34 93 4548438
Email: ib@indexbook.com URL: www.indexbook.com

viction:ary™

Published and distributed for
the rest of the world by viction:workshop ltd.

Room2202 22nd Floor, Kingsfield Centre
18-20 Shell Street, North Point, Hong Kong
URL: www.victionary.com Email: we@victionary.com

Concept & art direction by Victor Cheung
Book design and produced by viction:design workshop
Preface by Shawn D. Roberts
Edited by viction:ary

ISBN 84-96309-77-0
Printed and bound in China

Acknowledgements

We would like to thank all the designers and companies who made a
significant contribution to the compilation of this book. Without them this
project would not have been possible.

We would also like to thank all the producers for their invaluable
assistance throughout. Its successful completion also owes a great deal to
many professionals in the creative industry who have given us precious
insights and comments. We are also very grateful to many other people
whose names do not appear on the credits but have made specific input
and continuous support the whole time.

Future Editions

If you would like to contribute to the next edition by Victionary, please
email us your details to submit@victionary.com

painted, silk-screened, sketched, photographed, cut n' pasted, welded, sculpted in Earth's every material; it can be multimedia, digital, analog; the designer's arsenal lists as long as does the reckoning of all man's creations.

However, despite the seeming endlessness of possibility, limitations yet exist. Aside from essential concerns like target audience, the desired effect or mood of the piece, and originality of theme or approach, she does face some of the more mundane hang-ups one might suffer in any pursuit, namely, the allotted budget. This in turn effects every rung on the ladder of process: materials, research capabilities, medium, and size (also known as range).

In Zoom In Zoom Out, Victionary presents designs from artists the world over, herein broken down and presented according to three core components and provisions—Format, Concept, and Visual. In so doing, Victionary aspires to not only showcase the skill and versatility of our best modern-day designers, but also, to examine the very building blocks of this wholly creative field, by both it's expansive and restrictive elements. Of course, the assignment—and therefore the agenda—will certainly dictate how wide or narrow the creative margin is, as well as all other aforementioned rudiments. But because design is so all-inclusive a field, the fluctuations are nearly endless, despite any special client stipulations.

Take Airside's proposal for a Coca-cola summer ad campaign on the theme "refreshment". Two potential hang-ups come to mind: originality (since Coke's been advertising for decades) and imaging (the Coke bottle must appear in the image to get their message across and reveal the product itself).

Airside chose a very simple approach. They write, "the ads show the traditional glass bottles with the logo replaced by the word 'Love', written Coke-style. Surrounding the bottles are beautiful, bold-coloured patterns emanating like flowers, reminiscent of the 70s Coke campaigns." Here, they circumvent the originality dilemma by going retro and appealing to an older generation. As for the image restriction, Airside used the familiar cursive lettering on the bottle's label to reveal a fetching concept: that "Coca-Cola" is synonymous with "Love."

Another concept-minded design is Kinetic's direct mailer promotion for Lorgan's, the Retro Store. This original concept is an actual letter, sent to actual people at actual addresses, which looks like it was mailed in the Seventies. This is sure to intruige, and thus inspire a peek inside. There, the recipient will find products available at Lorgan's which remind the individual of the lasting importance and relevance of the products. This is a concept, a message the designer communicates—it says, "rediscover your youth." It says, "we're still here." It's inviting, nostalgic, and original—cleverly arousing reminiscence, and appealing to those long gone days of old.

Often, rather than a promotion, the assignment is to create the product itself or a piece of that product. Captivating the desired audience is still the destination, sure, but how best to arrive there—that is, which way to drive a project—often varies. Many times with product design, the overall visual takes precedence over any communicated concept or physical format.

In "Big Upstate," a feature for an issue of BIG Magazine, John Codling and Darren Crawforth of The Fold headed to my neck of the woods: upstate New York. They approached and described it thus: "Upstate is an idea, not a place. A state of mind, not of geography, that seduces with possibilities of escape, wildness, timelessness." Making their depiction of the upstate locale accessible to everyone's personal perception was crucial, to inspire a longing for vacation, for recreation. The Big Magazine spread captivates, simultaneously developing a sense of distance and closeness in the viewer. It's ingenius, at once accomplishing both a promotion and the related packaging.

Milkxhake's designers set about designing a magazine for FABRICA of Italy, to be titled simply FAB magazine. The visual concept is aimed at instilling a sense of the creative flow and free association, both in image and words. Since the magazine is not for sale, (circulates among creative industry professionals) this is an interesting look at the way design agendas can become narrow, as opposed to the usually broad appeal of ad campaigns and product salability.

Our third grouping is based on Format, or the makeup and layout of a piece. This was the main focus of a project by Base of New York, done for La Casa Encendida. The assignment was to create a book—which would then be a promotional gift for the company's clients—featuring artists' work exhibited by La Casa Encendida during the previous year. This was the only requirement.

Since the art was already finished, and therefore the appearance rendered, the designers had to consider how best to arrange it all into presentable form—that's format. The Base chose "to work with the physical materials and textures the original artists used in their own projects in the exhibition," according to the lead designer. The format, the very makeup of the book, becomes an extension of the original artists' color schemes and structural identities—basically, it's an anthology of mini-re-creations. It was Base's consideration of this atypical format which rendered the other artists so well.

 Format isn't necessarily just physical quality. Martin Woodtli contributed his silk-screened promotion posters for a Swiss museum. Notice the way he creates the illusion of physical matter, in the lettering and the background imagery—the colors lunge off the page, revealing a whole world inside just a few basic colors. The work attempts to reel in new fans of the design and experimental art fields.

This volume contains dozens more examples from the three categories, all sharing the same ends, though the means will vary. That's the beauty of design: a common goal with an infinite number of ways to achieve it. The design all-star and industry pro, April Greiman, sums up the temperament of this shared end—the common goal: "Design must seduce, shape, and perhaps more importantly, evoke emotional response." It is the imperative of extraordinary design to grab the audience—in scrutinizing the work and the surrounding circumstances of the designs in Zoom in- Zoom out, consider the obstacles an artist must hurdle in meeting this essential challenge.

The title, Zoom In Zoom Out, means looking from different perspectives; from the format, then closer to the visual, and finally, to the heart of the concept. Victionary focuses on these three categories by looking closer. We ask, "How will this design reach the hearts and minds of the people? How will this design overcome the restrictive shackles integral to the task? Whether packaging, promotion, or product, where must this design's energies be focused? By the communication of concept, the attraction of visual, or the appreciation of format; The possibilities are endless. So look inside—the cutting edge of 21st century art awaits you.

By Shawn D. Roberts
Utica, New York
February 26, 2006

Our structure selections key on format, shape, complexity, layout and systems — elements of the actual creation of a work. These designs nonetheless run the full range of artistic assortment. Structure is paramount in how a piece is composed, how it is rendered. Such a piece might share general concepts and intentions with its design contemporaries in the message and look sections, but things like materials, size and shape take absolute precedence in a structurally-focused display.

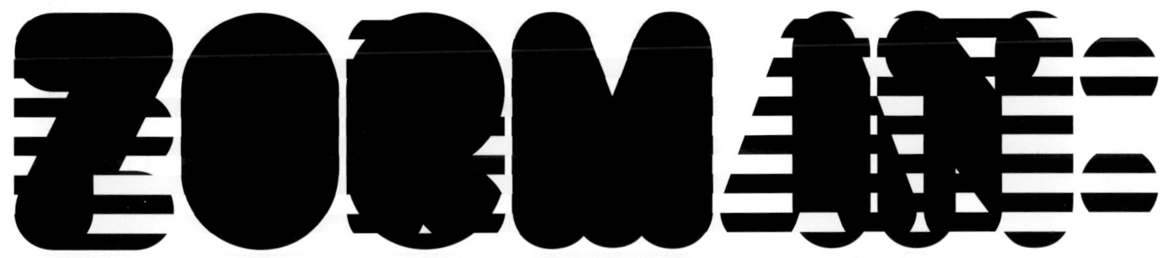

Julia H●ffmann

New York, USA

Title: Space
Type of work: Magazine
Client: -
Design: ad, d// Julia Hoffmann
Year: 2002

This was a large semester project at the School of Visual Arts, which assigned students to create a magazine from start to finish - from the idea of 'name about what' to the articles, photos and execution. Space Magazine deals with all aspects of space: living space, public space or even outer space. It looks at space in a more philosophical way. A special font for the drop caps based on the logo was also designed.

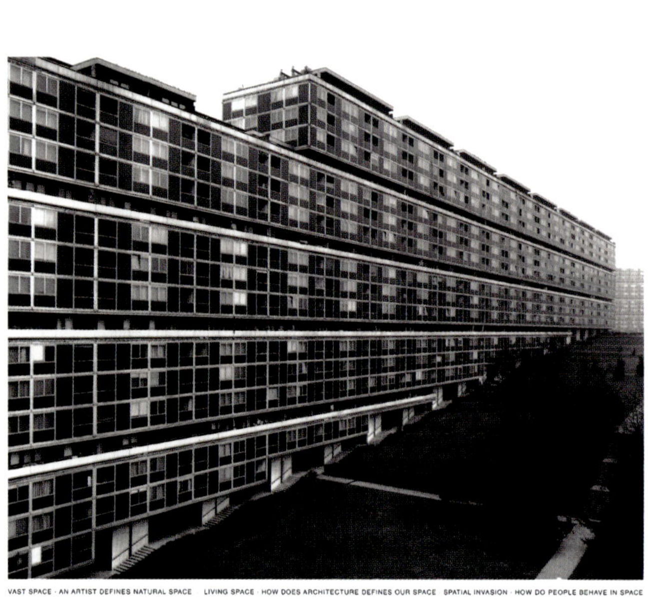

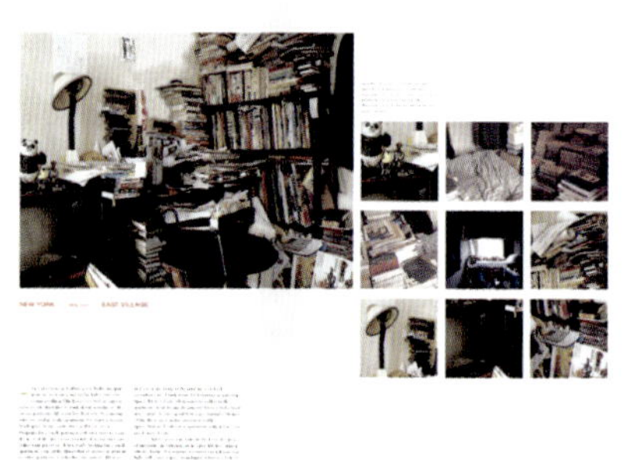

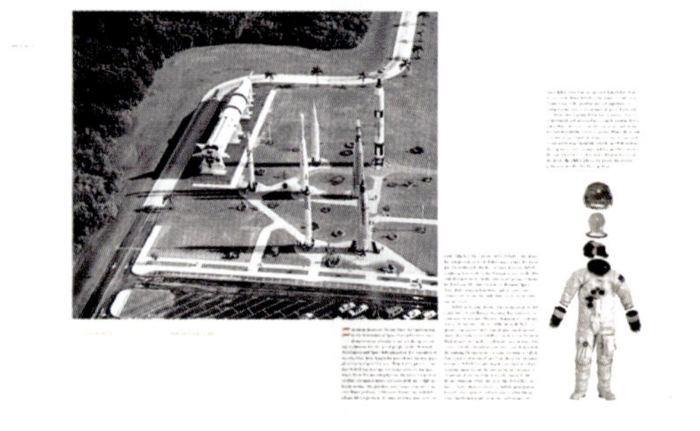

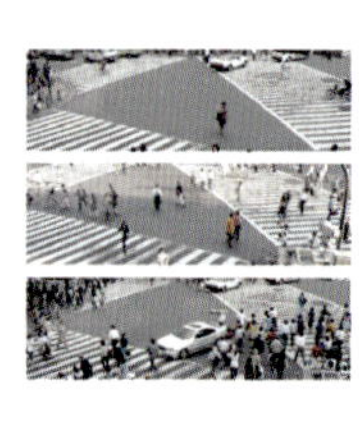

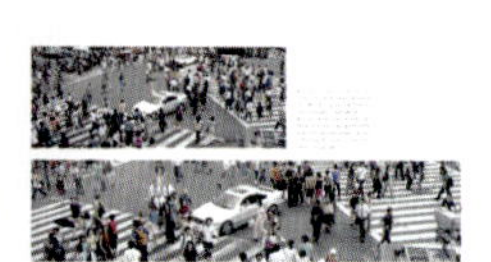

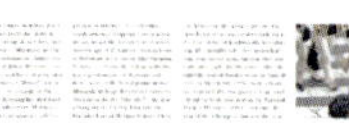

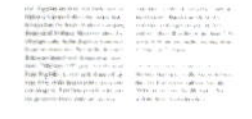

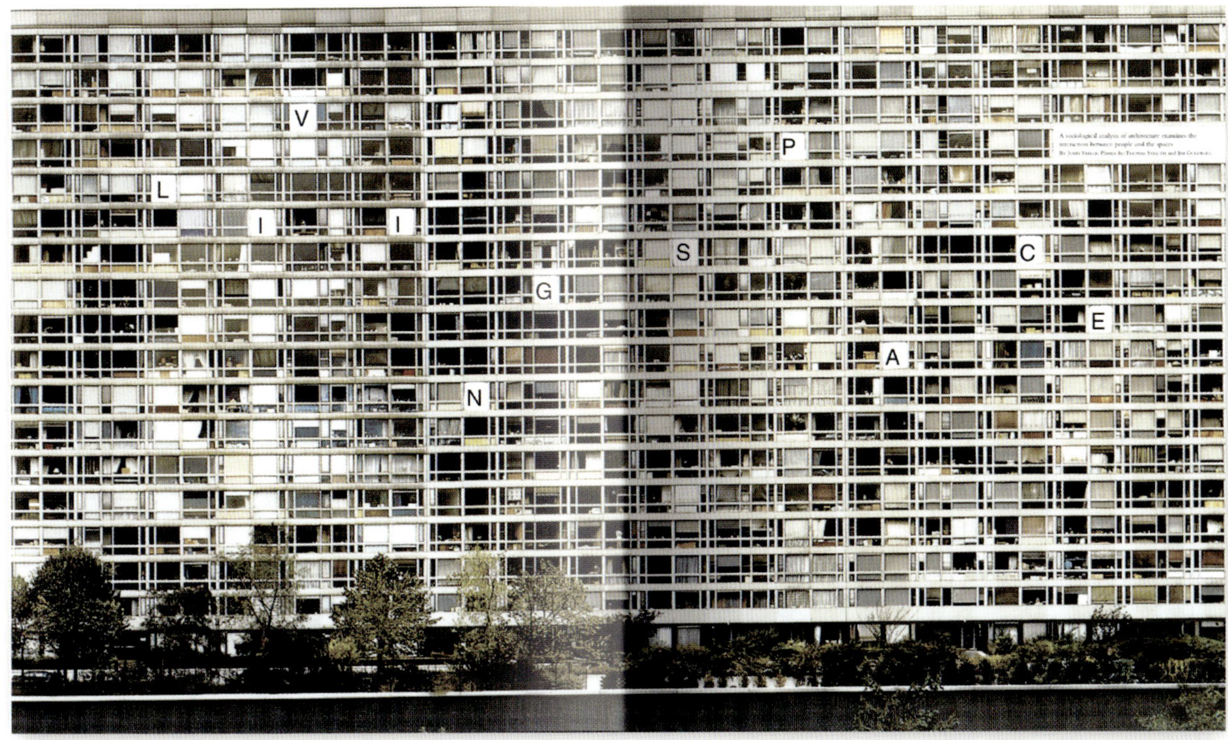

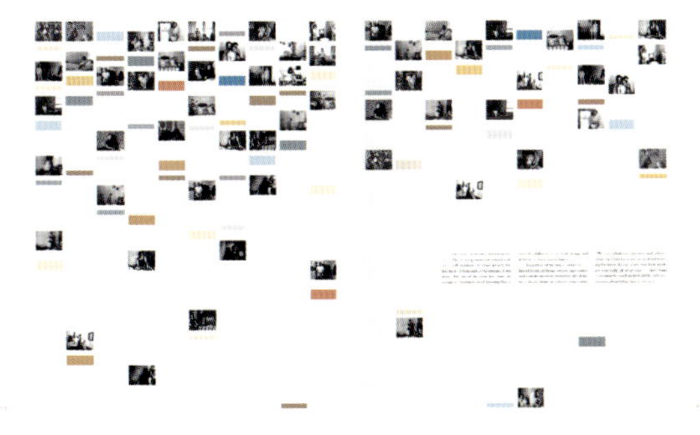

THERE IS A FORMULA OF OBSCURE ORIGIN THAT A MAN IN A CROWD REQUIRES AT LEAST TWO SQUARE FEET. THIS IS AN ABSOLUTE MINIMUM AND APPLIES, ACCORDING TO ONE AUTHORITY, TO A THIN MAN IN A SUBWAY. A FAT MAN WOULD REQUIRE TWICE AS MUCH SPACE OR MORE. JOURNALIST HERBERT JACOBS BECAME INTERESTED IN SPATIAL BEHAVIOR WHEN HE WAS A REPORTER COVERING POLITICAL RALLIES. HIS FORMULA IS THAT CROWD SIZE EQUALS LENGTH X WIDTH OF THE CROWD DIVIDED BY THE APPROPRIATE CORRECTION FACTOR DEPENDING UPON WHETHER THE CROWD IS DENSE OR LOOSE.

SPATIAL INVASION

personal space

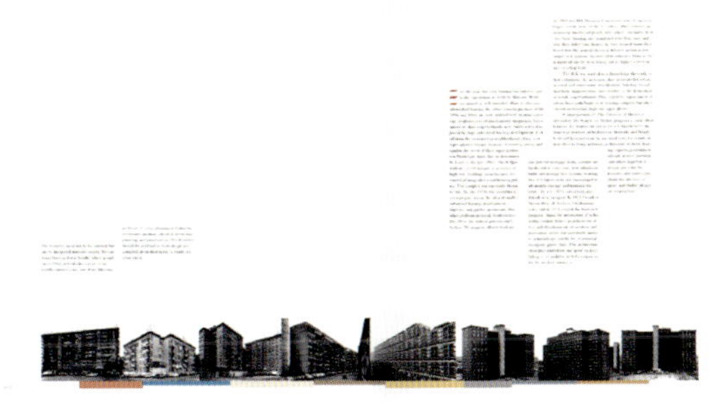

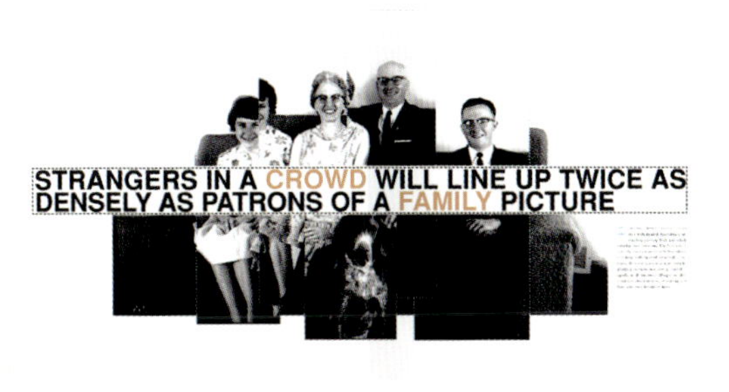

Julian Morey

London, UK

Title: Comic Sans Poster
Type of work: Magazine cover, poster
Client: *Creative Review*
Design: ad, d// Julian Morey
Year: 2004

The designers were commissioned to interpret the typeface Comic Sans into the form of a poster for an article on the history of Comic Sans. This design also became the cover design for the issue.

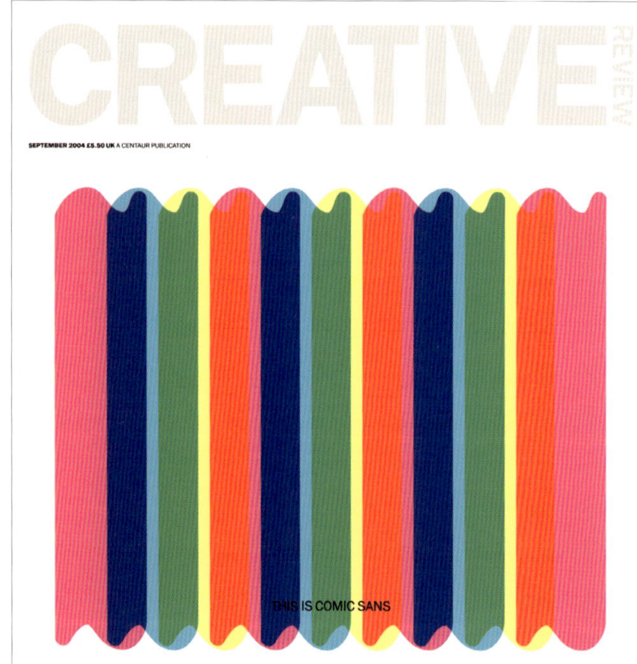

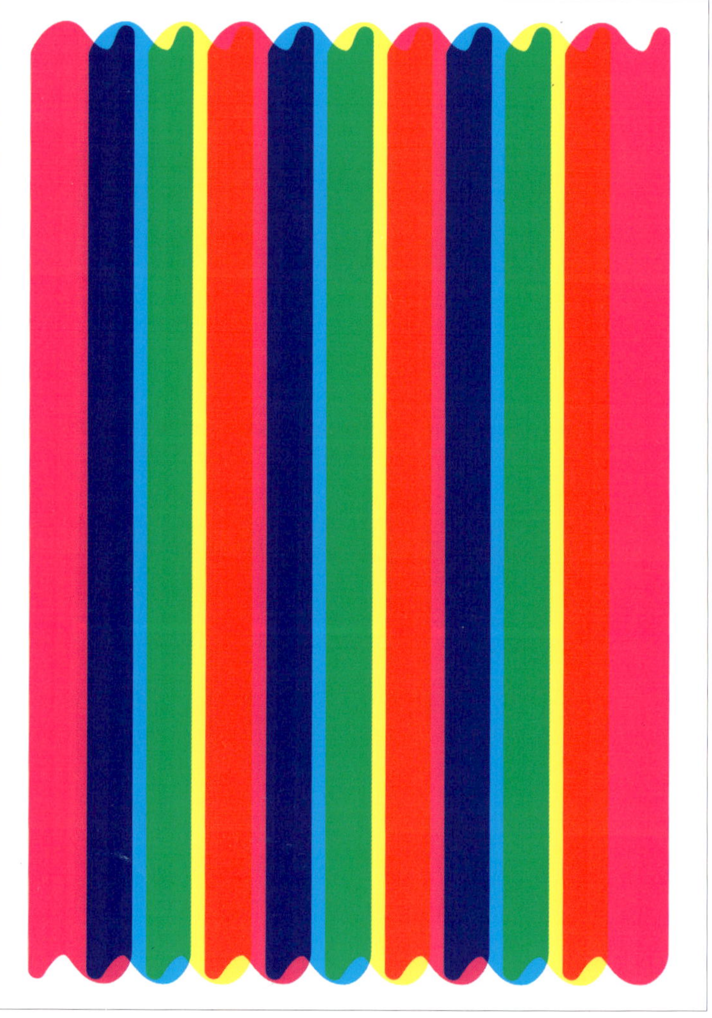

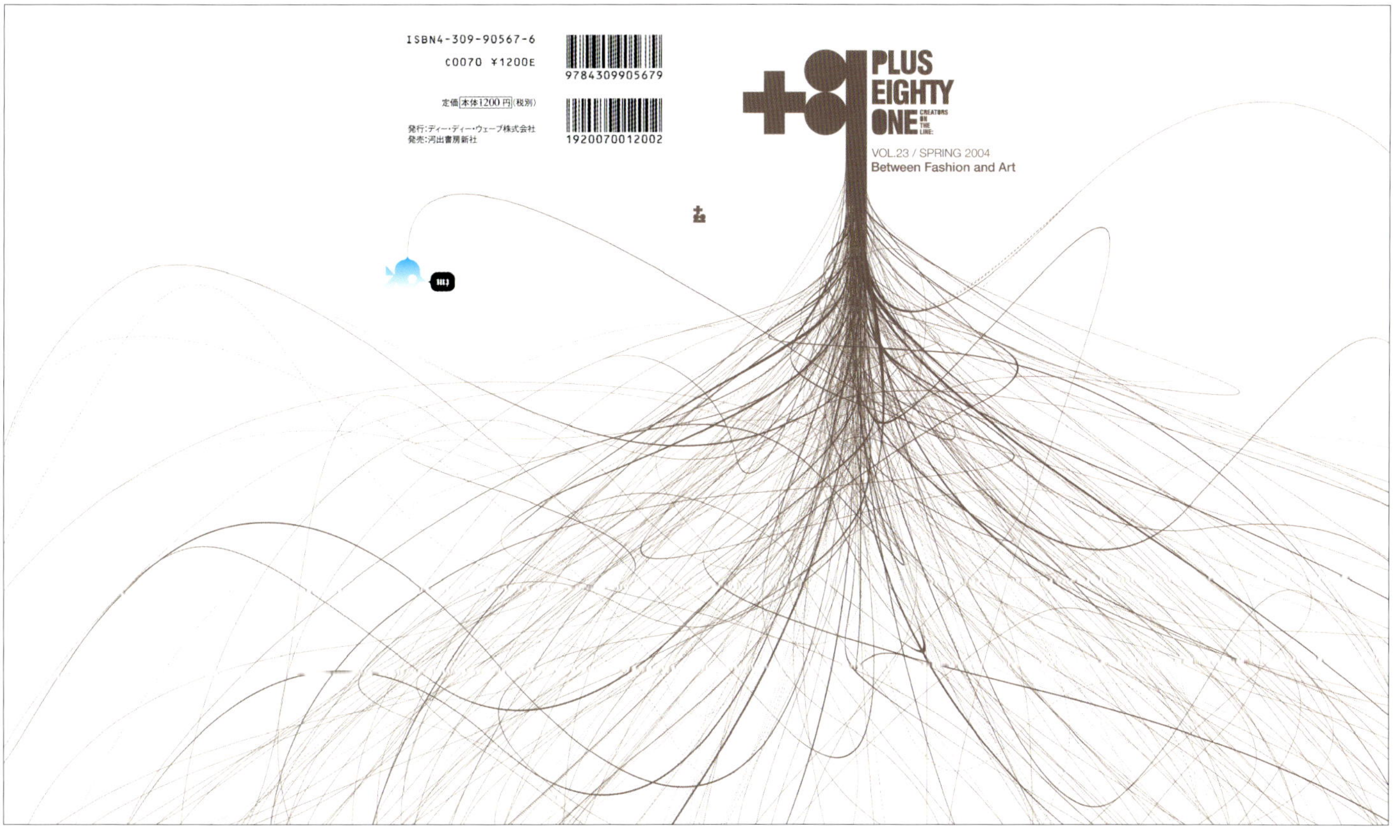

Build

London, UK

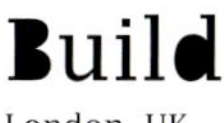

Title: +81 cover
Type of work: Magazine cover
Client: *+81* Japan
Design: ad, d// Michael C. Place
Year: 2004

This piece is an organic logo adaptation corresponding to growth, renewal, photo-synthesis, life giving and energy.

Base

New York, USA

Title: La Casa Encendida
Type of work: Book, catalogue, brochure
Client: La Casa Encendida
Design: ad, d// Base
Year: -

The designer was asked to design a book for La Casa Encendida's first anniversary to give to their clients. The only requirement was the content. They wanted to include the work of the artists that exposed permanently that year. So they started working on it and thought to work with the fisical materials and textures the artists used in their own projects in the exhibition. The idea was accepted by the client immediately. The quality, the variety of materials and the book binding made a nice and special book, which pleased everybody.

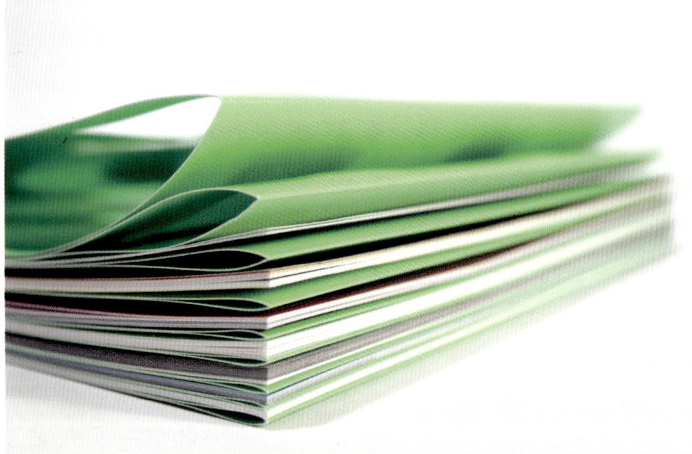

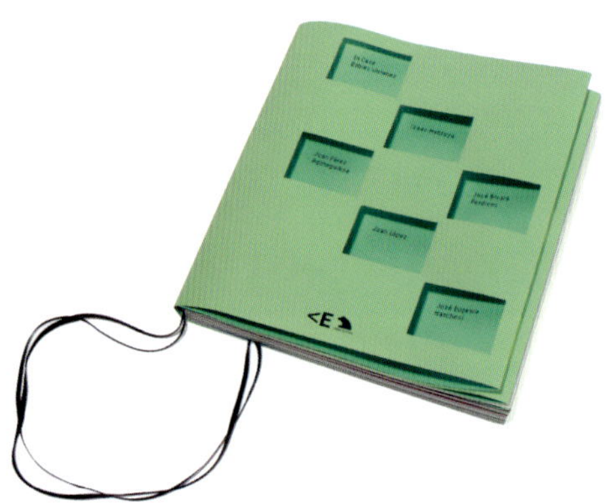

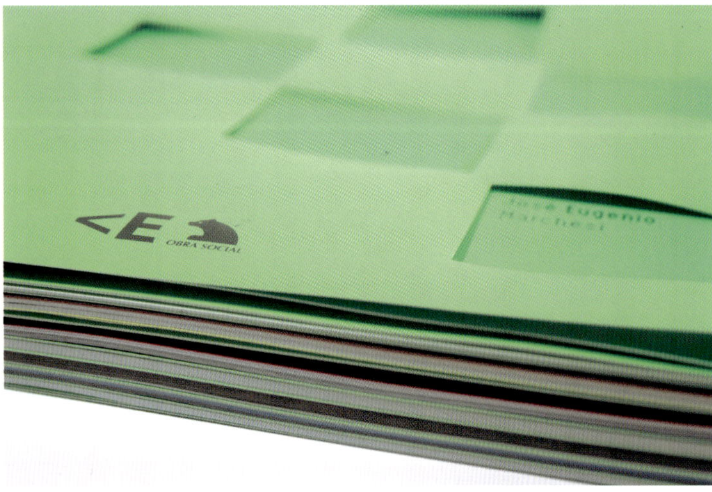

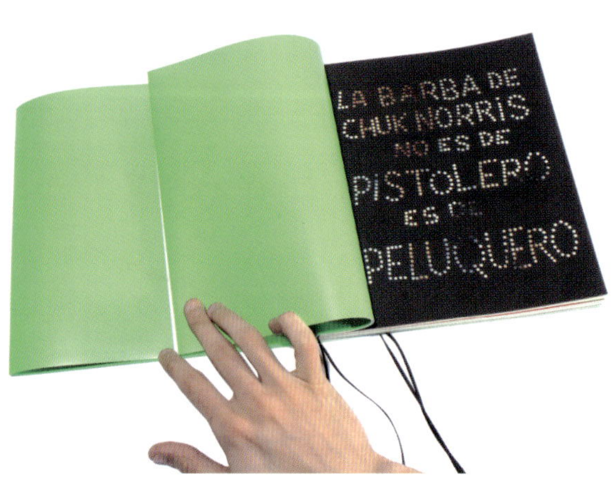

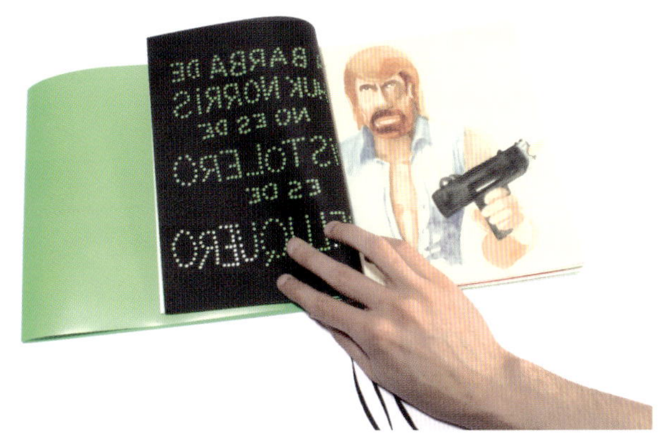
BARBA DE
UK NORRIS
NO ES DE
STOLERO
ES DE
GUCRO

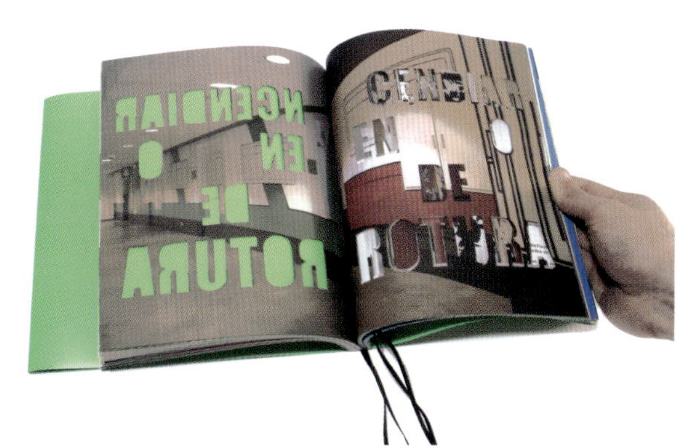
NCENDIAR
EN
DE
ROTURA

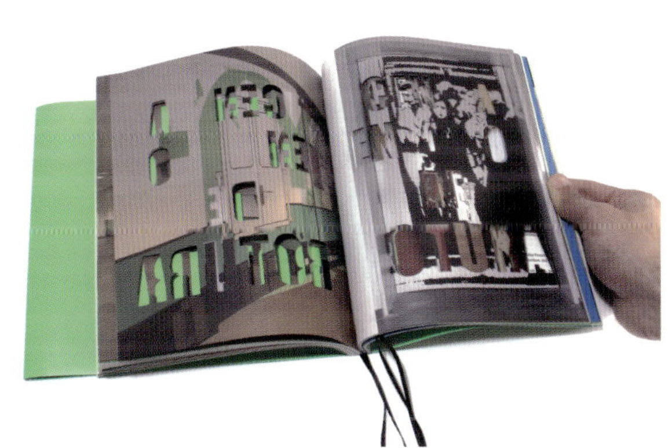
CEN
EN
BOT RA

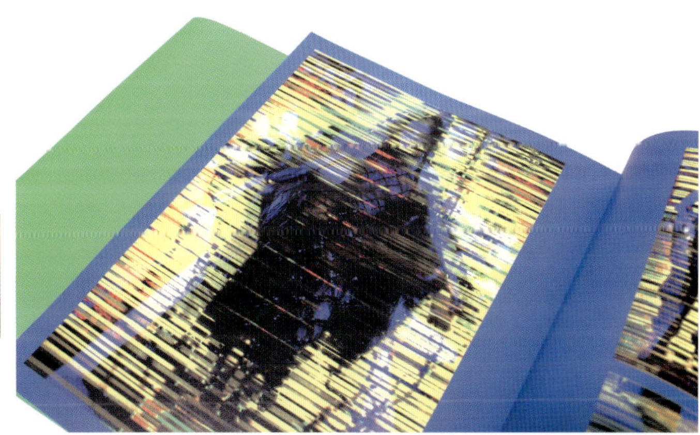

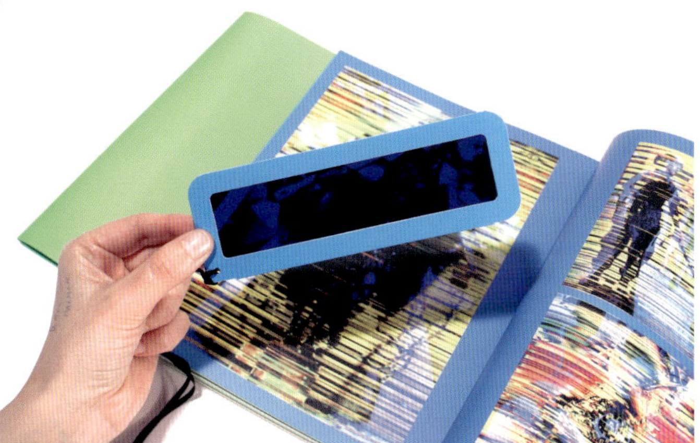

Toxic Design Studio

Rome, Italy

Title: Doc/atene.Gemine.Muse
Type of work: Catalogue
Client: Documenta
Design: ad, d// Fabio Lattanzi Antinori
Year: 2005

It is a personal visual research aiming to find a link between people and the way they imagine and represent themselves. People who is willing to participate to the project are interviewed, scanned and represented through symbols for their relationship with the surroundings. Documents have been made in Rome, Brussels, Toronto, Monaco, Milano and Athens. The catalogue has been released recently in occasion of the designer's last exhibition in Rome. It had to be quite small in order to be included with an Italian magazine.

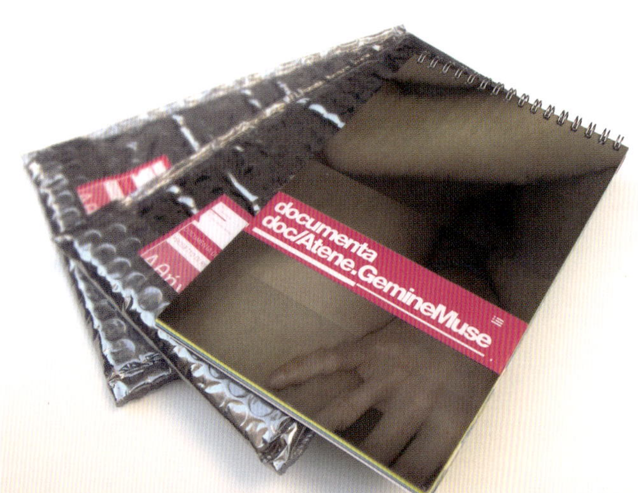

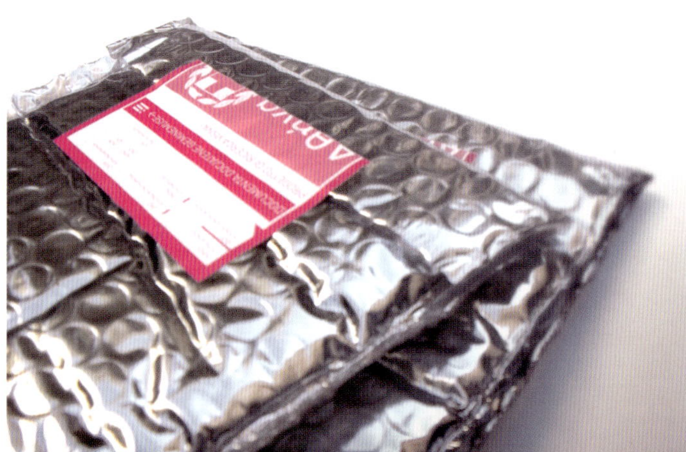

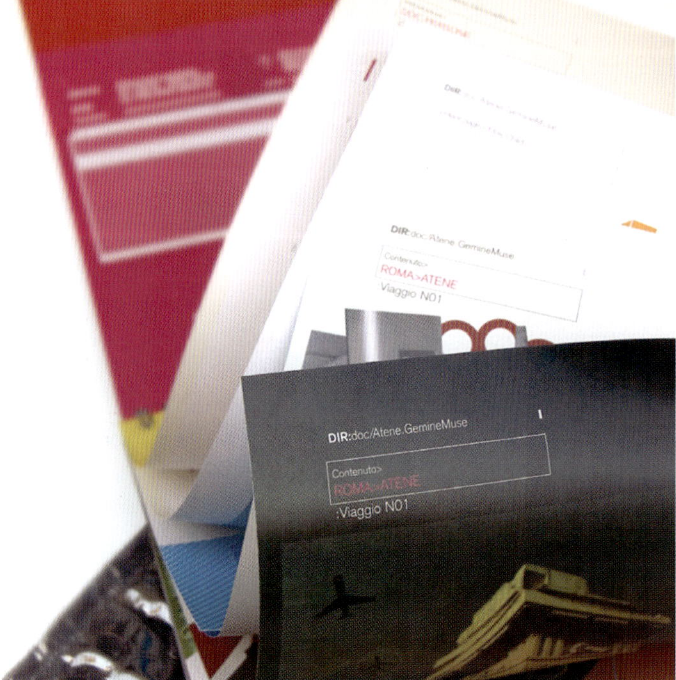

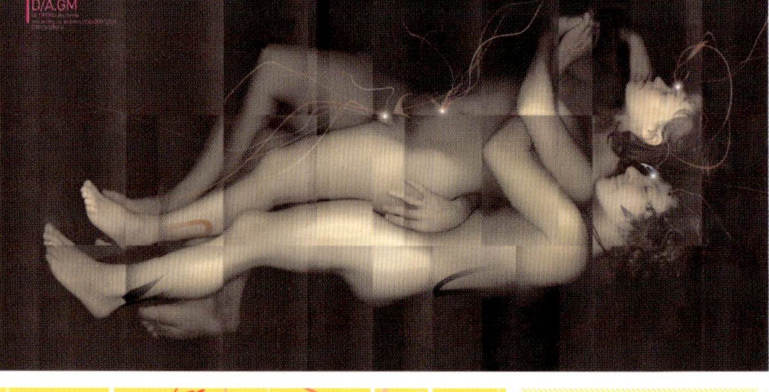

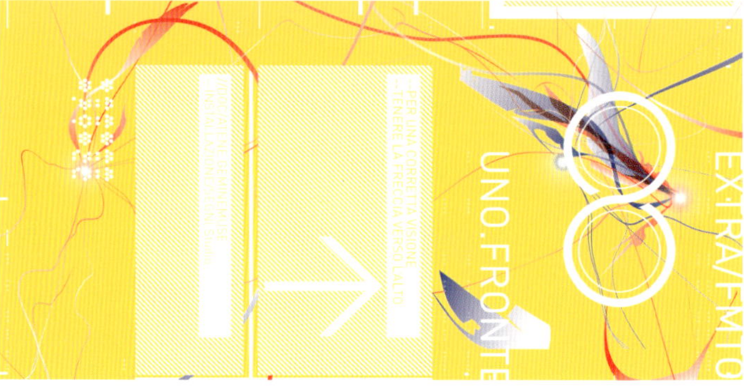

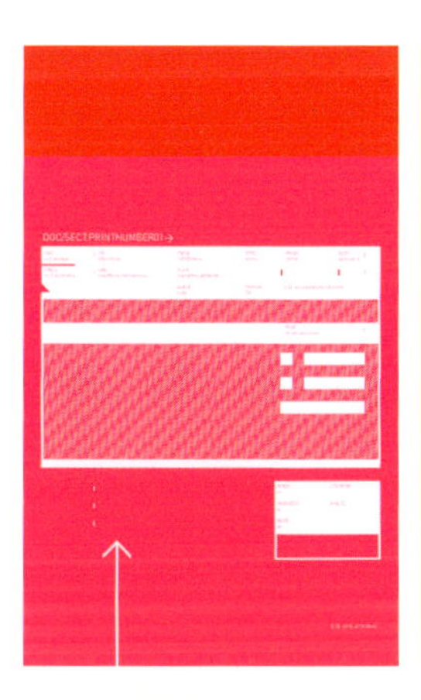
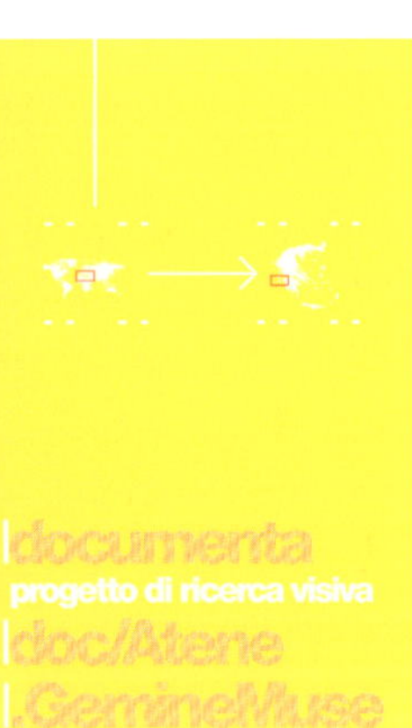
documenta
progetto di ricerca visiva
doc/Atene
GemineMuse
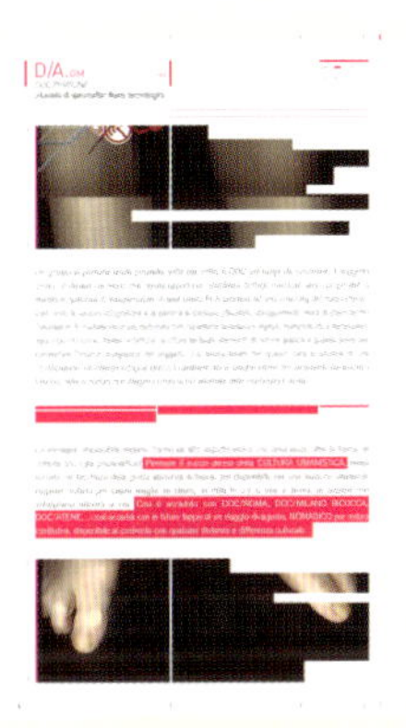
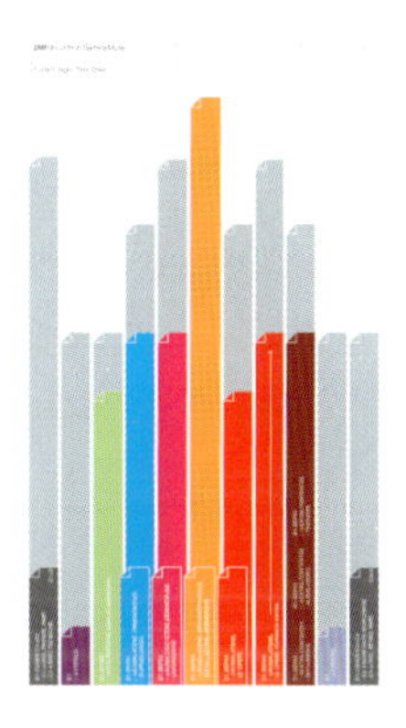
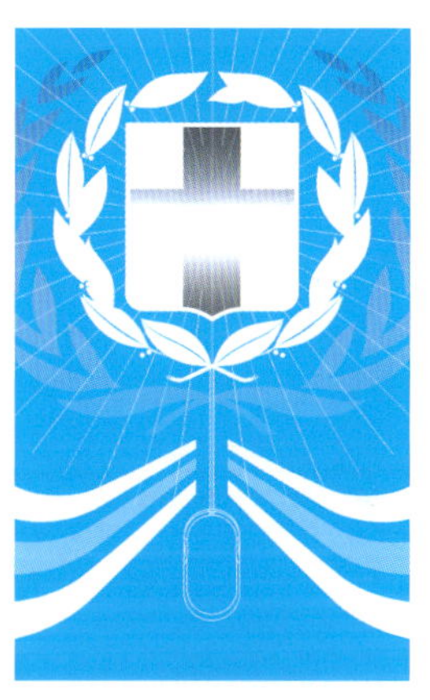
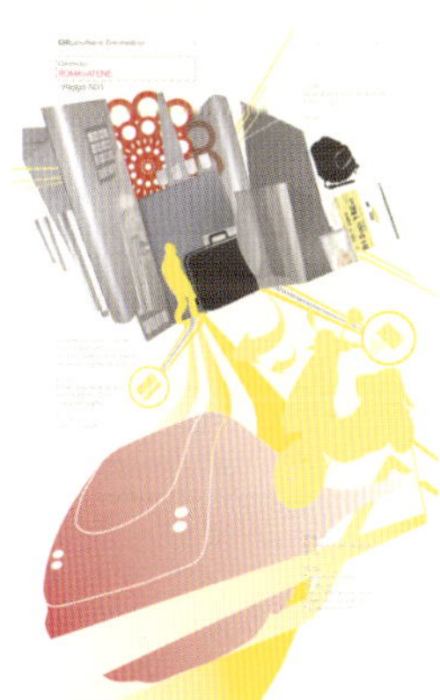
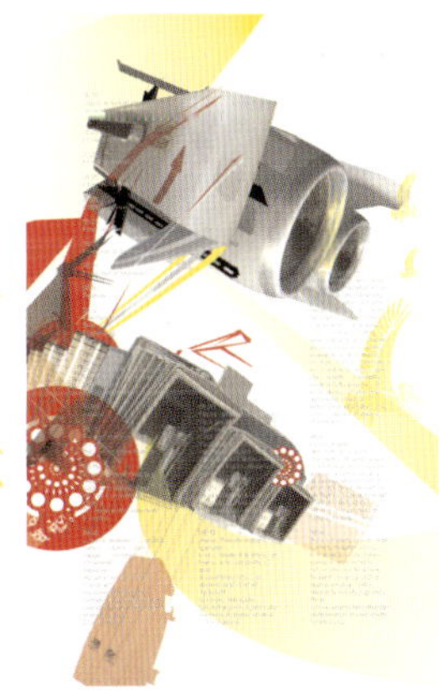
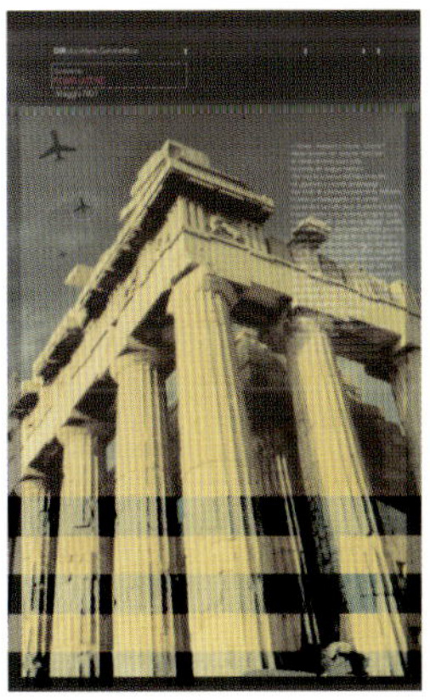
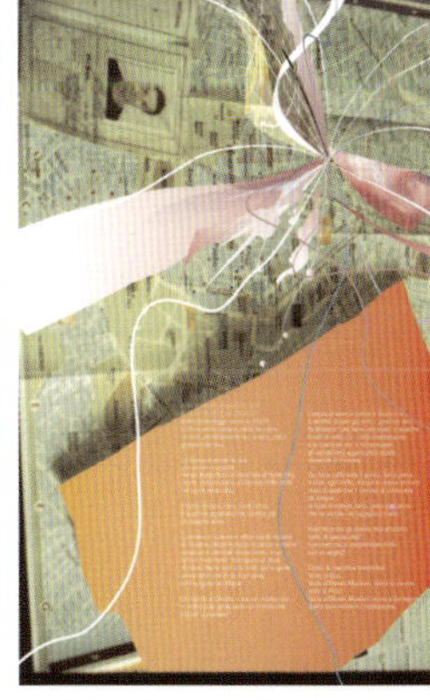
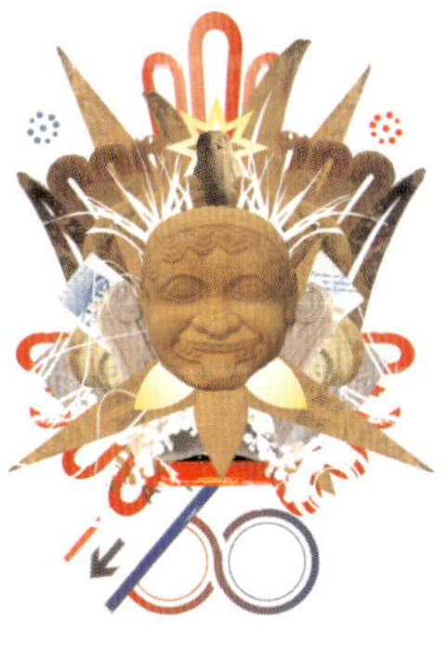
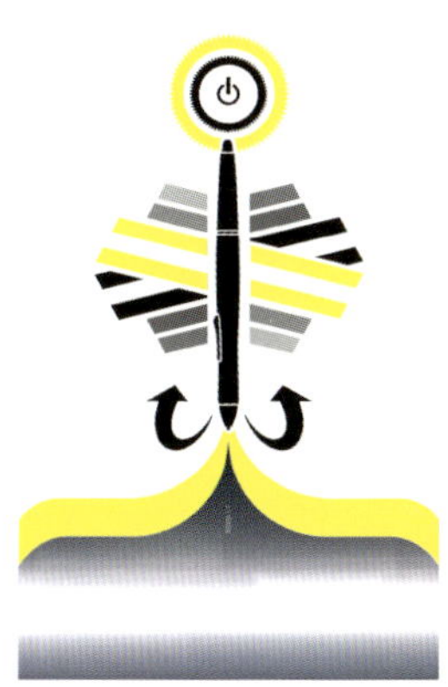
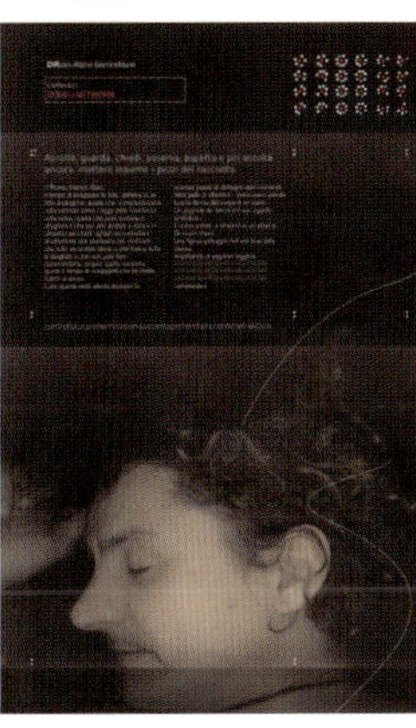
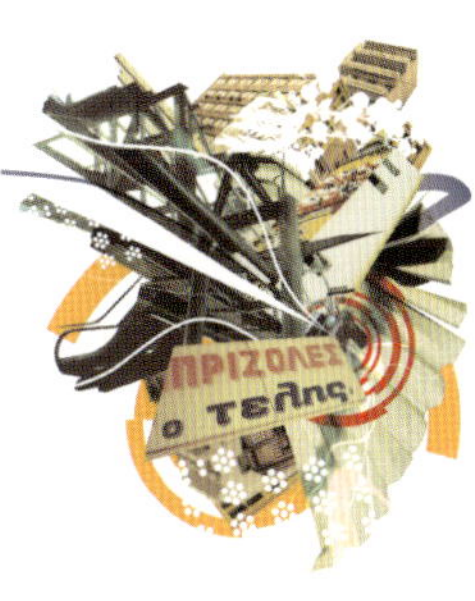
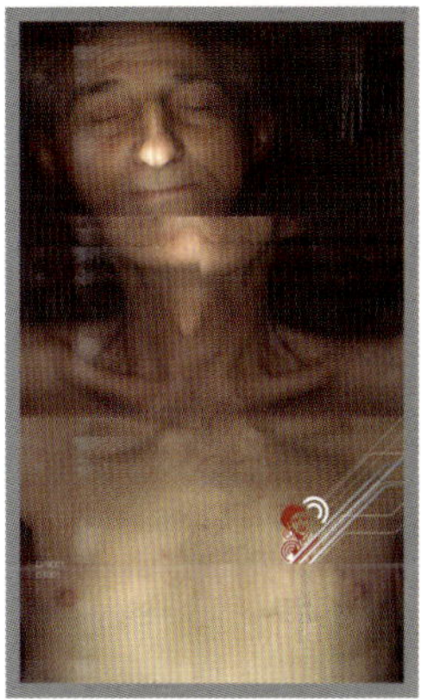
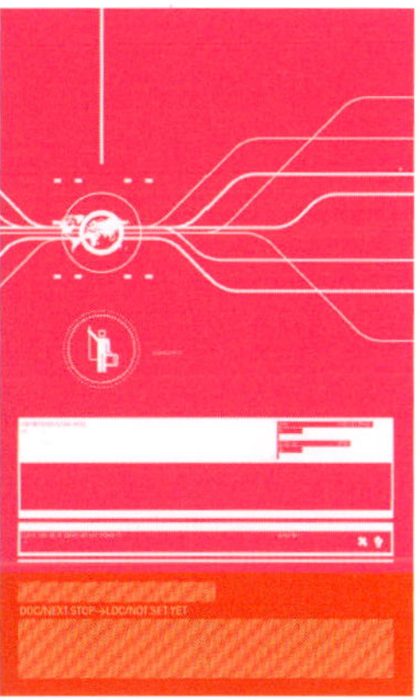

Kinetic

Singapore

Title: Discover
Type of work: Annual report
Client: Amara Holdings Ltd
Design: ad, d// Jonathan Yuen, Roy Poh, Pann Lim
Year: 2004

The concept of the annual report was to rediscover the new Amara Hotel that has just went through a new facelift. French folded pages are left blank and readers have to tear to open the perforated pages to 'discover' what it is inside.

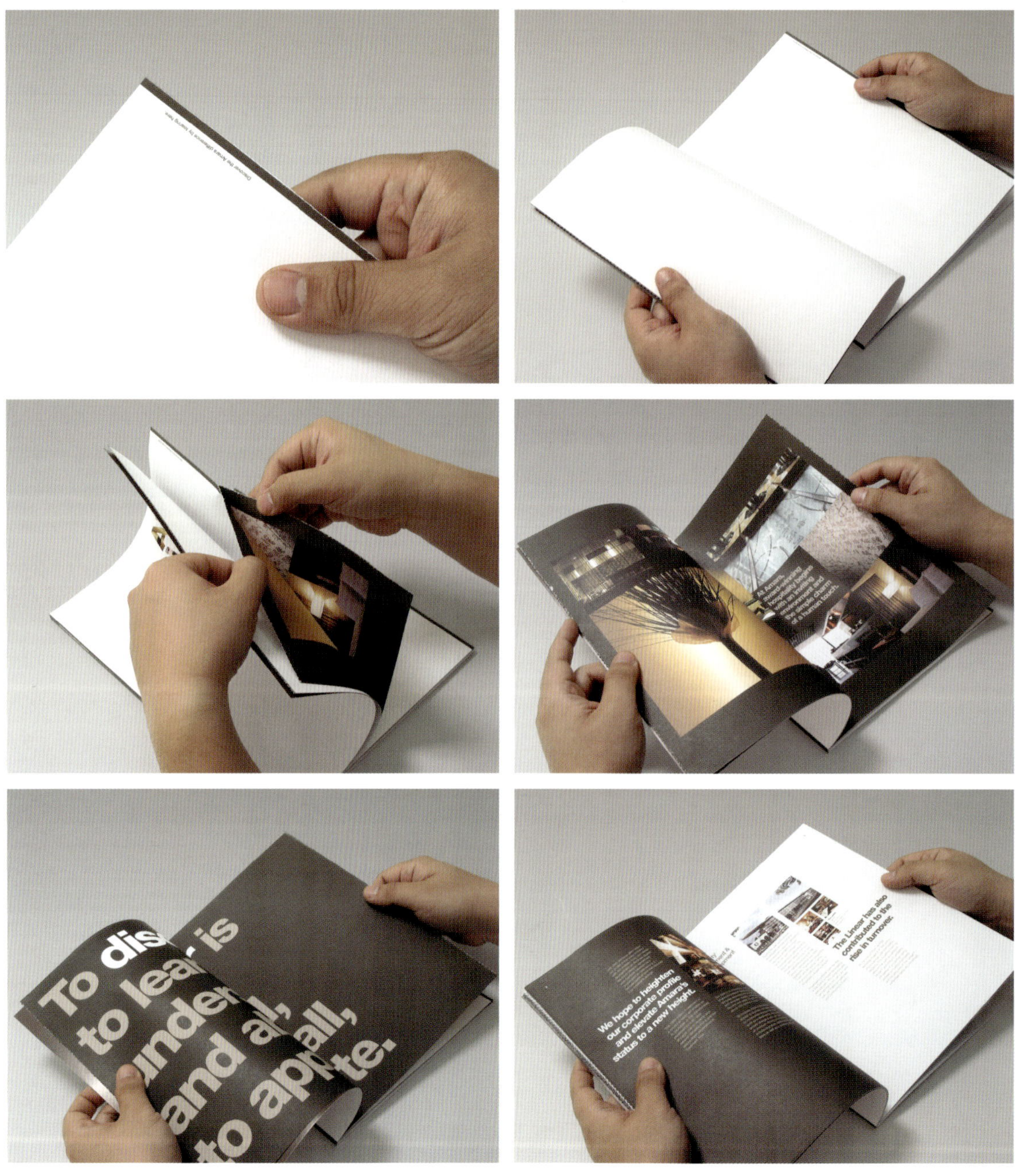

tess Giberson

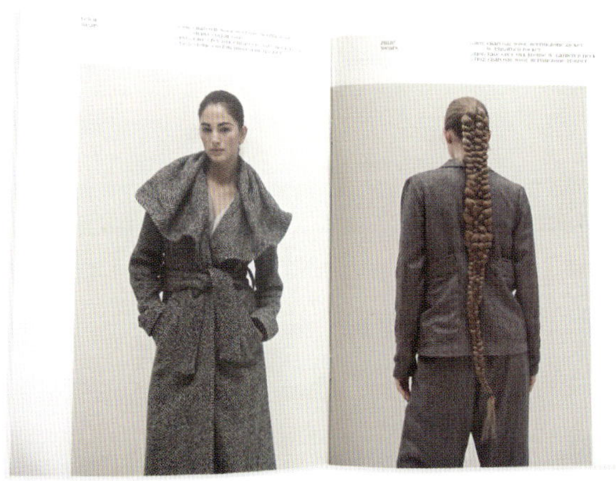

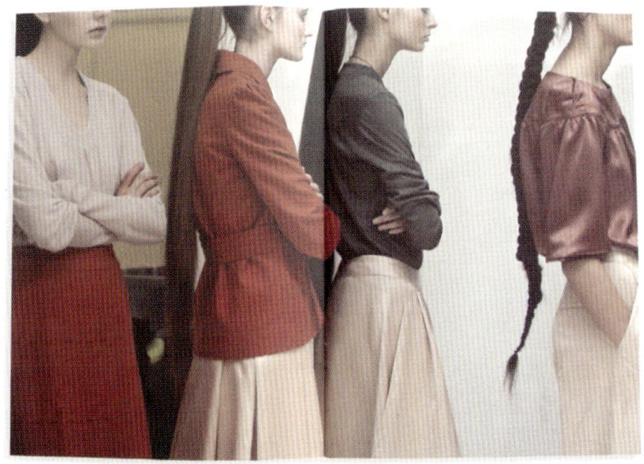

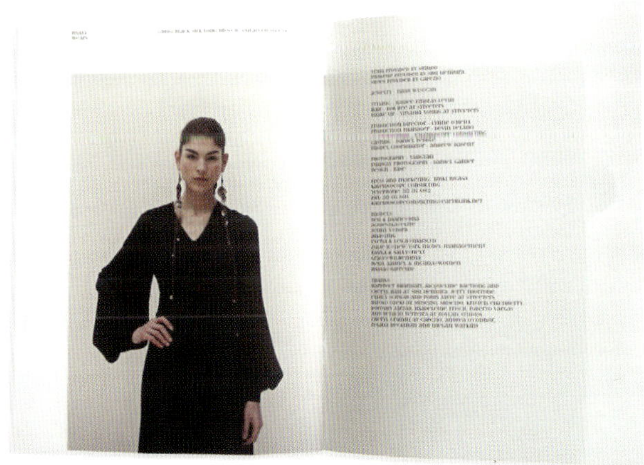

Base

New York, USA

Title: –
Type of work: Brochure
Client: Tess Giberson
Design: ad, d// Base p// Yang Tan
Year: 2005

This image book for the fall/winter '05 collection of the New York-based women's fashion house, Tess Giberson, that uses the photos from the runway and backstage of their fashion show. They also designed their new logo and brand identity.

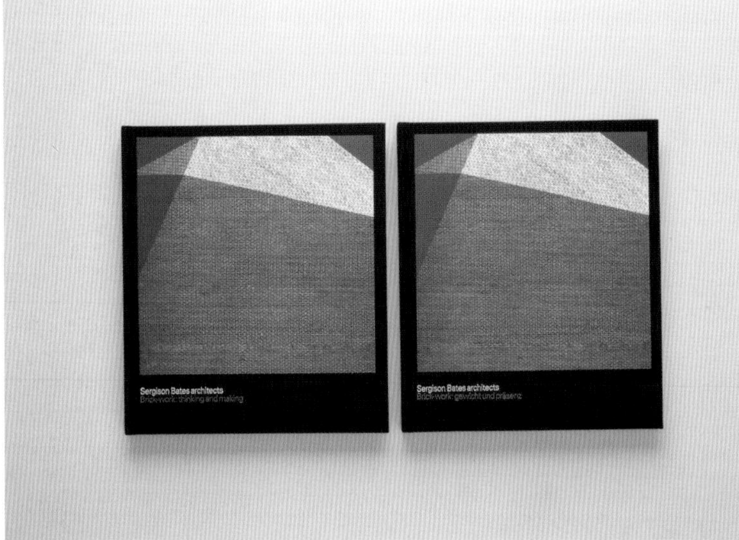

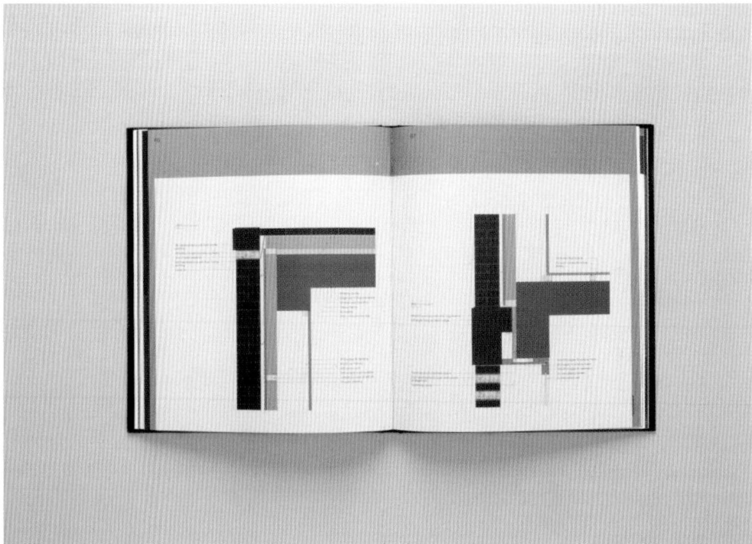

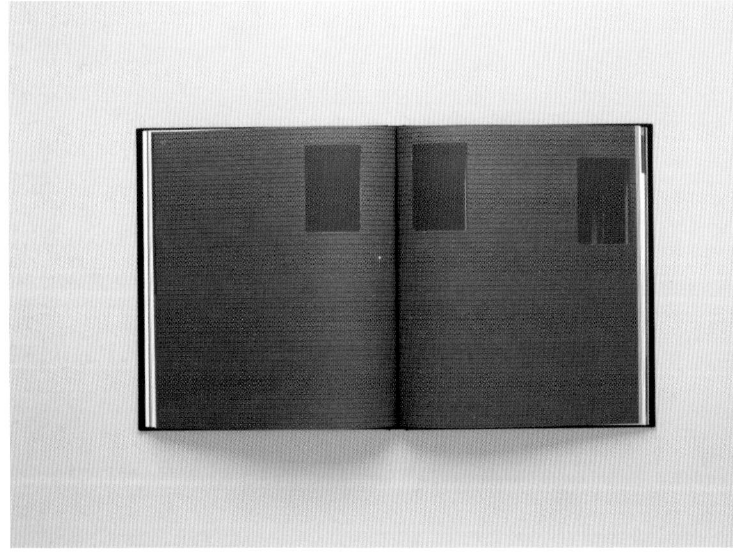

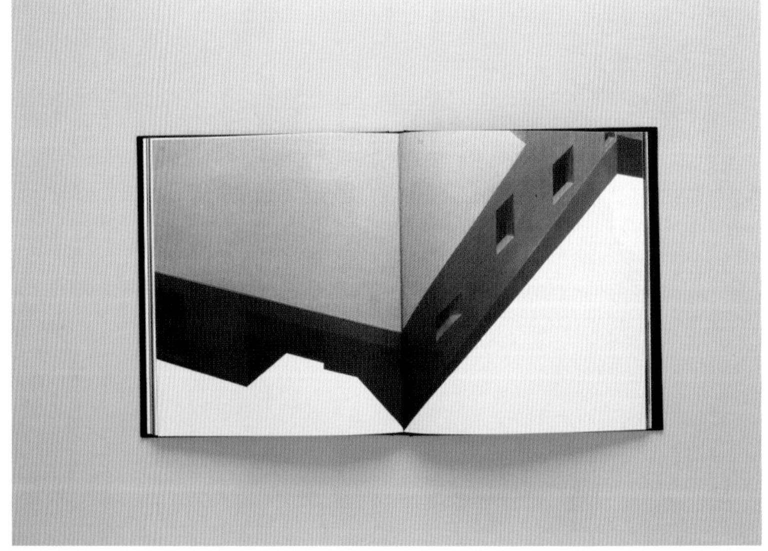

Cartlidge Levene

London, UK

Title: Brick-work: thinking and making
Type of work: Book
Client: Sergison Bates Architects
Design: Cartlidge Levene
Year: 2005

A book examining Sergison Bates architects' use of bricks in their buildings which, although traditionally, is an unfashionable material in contemporary architecture. The book contains three essays on the subject and eight case studies consisting of model photographs and construction drawings. It has been kept very simple using only two colours - black and grey. A navigational device was created through the use of short pages that divide chapters and separate the constructional drawings from the photographs. The book is a hard working document aimed at architectural students and is intended as an antidote to the 'glossy monograph'. It was published by GTA, Institute for the History and Theory of Architecture, ETH Zürich.

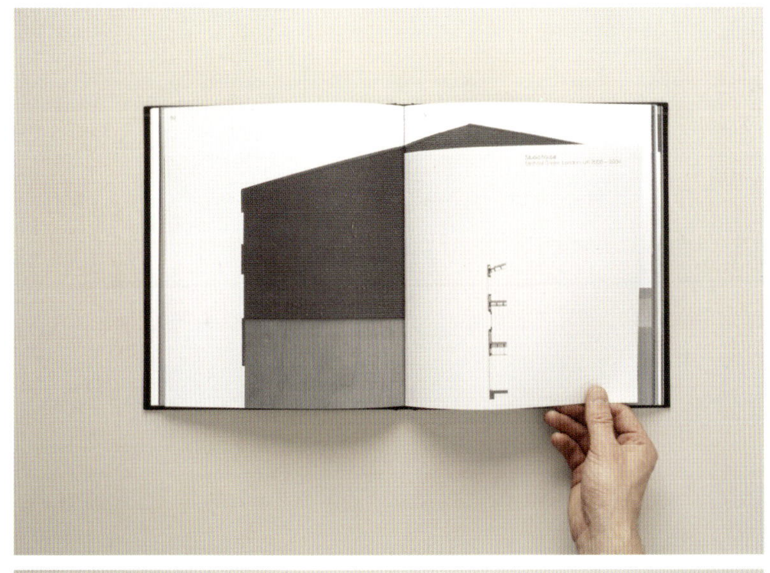
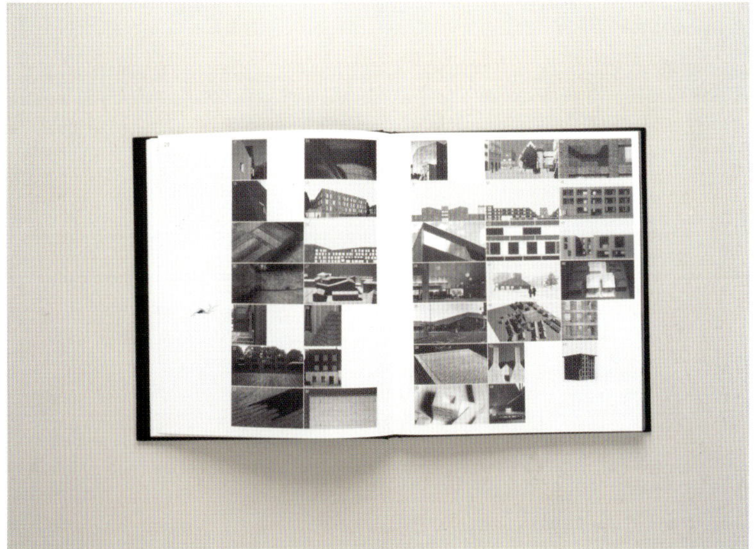
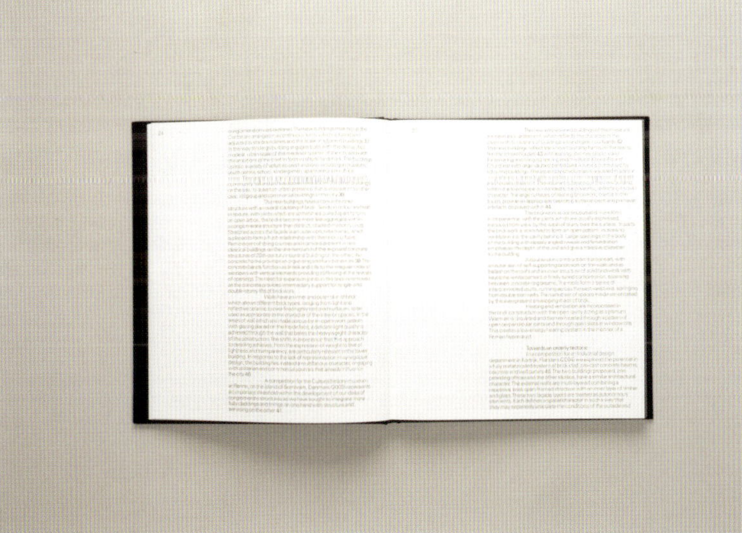
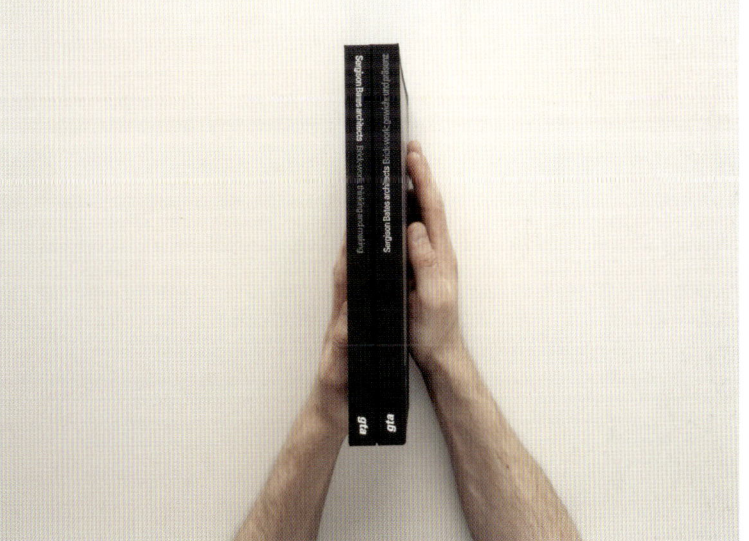

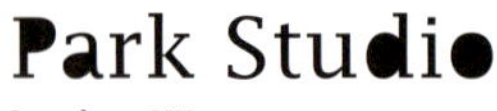

Park Studio

London, UK

Title: Architecture & Design Team's Newsletter
Type of work: Newsletter
Client: British Council
Design: ad, d// Linda Lundin, Nina Nägel
Year: 2004-05

The concept is based on each spread where subject has its own identity. Folded paper backdrops sit behind each spread and each has its own typeface, as an expression of the content of the spread. The cover functions as a content page with the eccentric typefaces that creates an immediate strong visual impact. To add an extra dimension to the cover, the title is printed on a separate yellow flap.

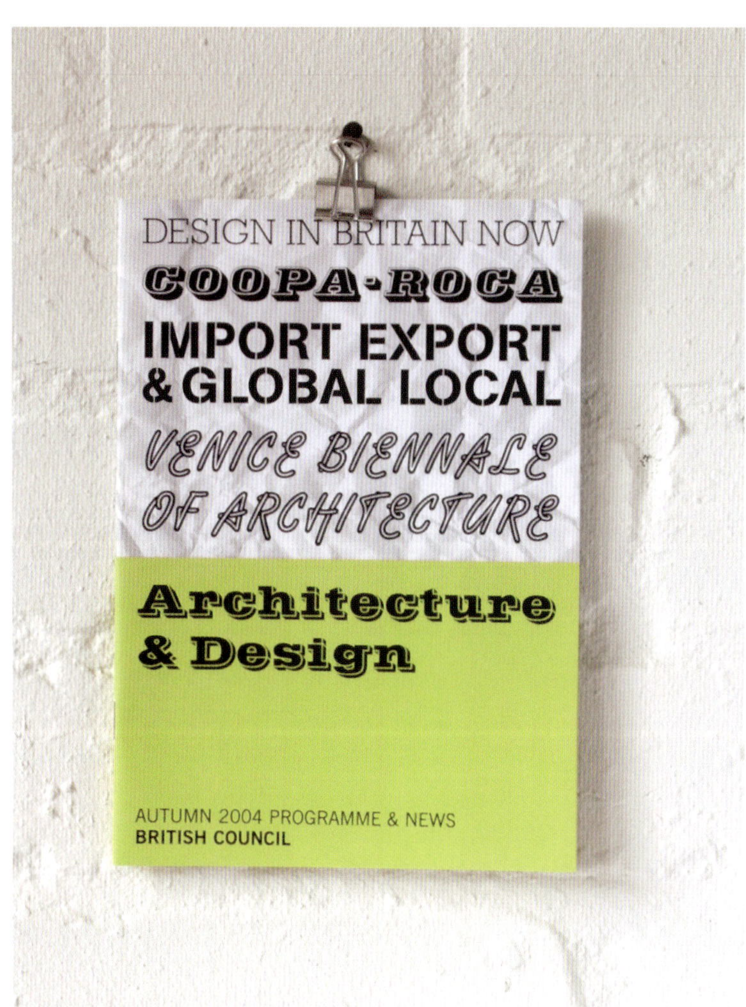

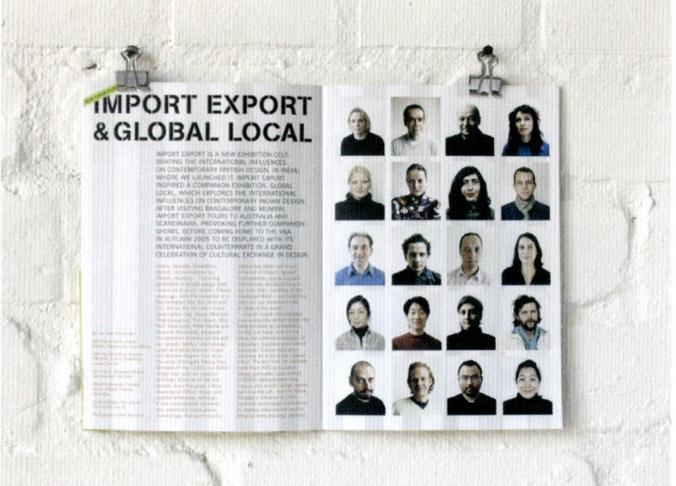

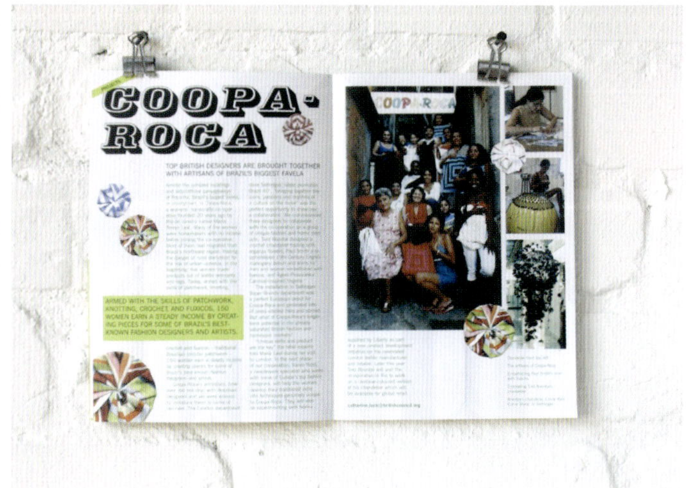

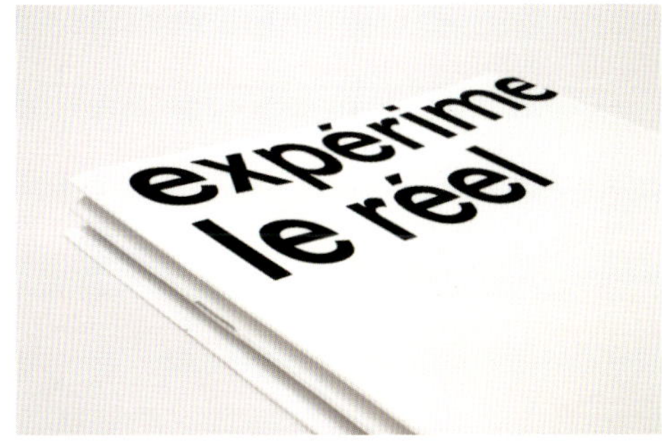
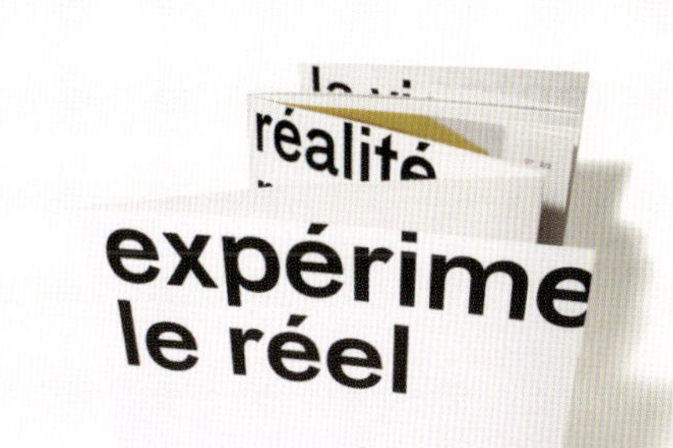
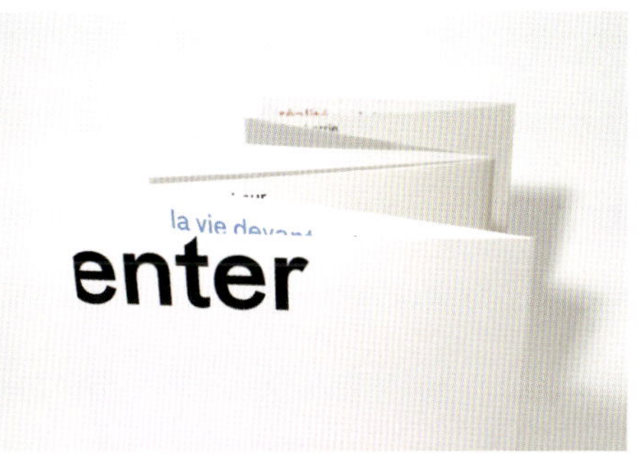
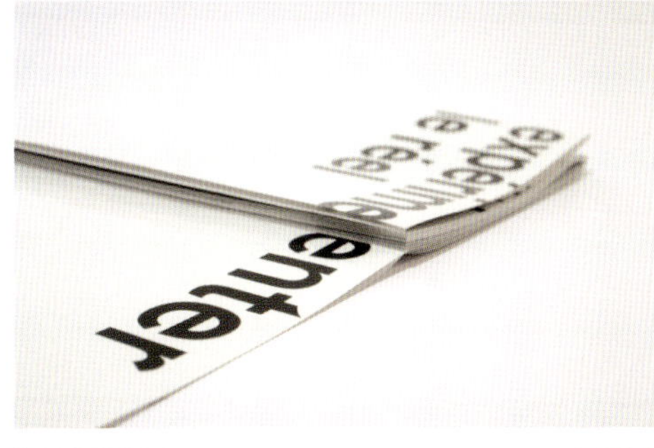
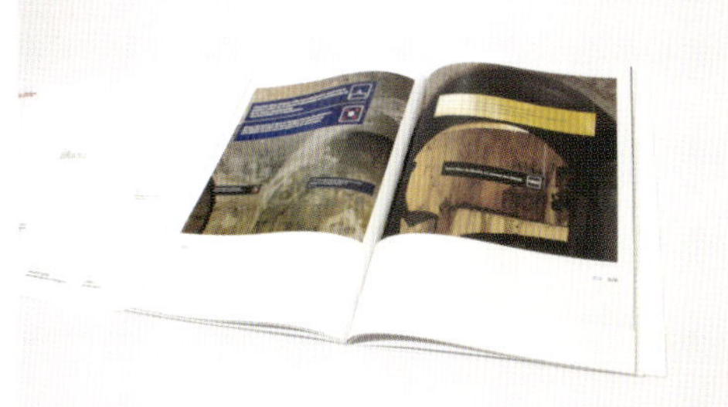
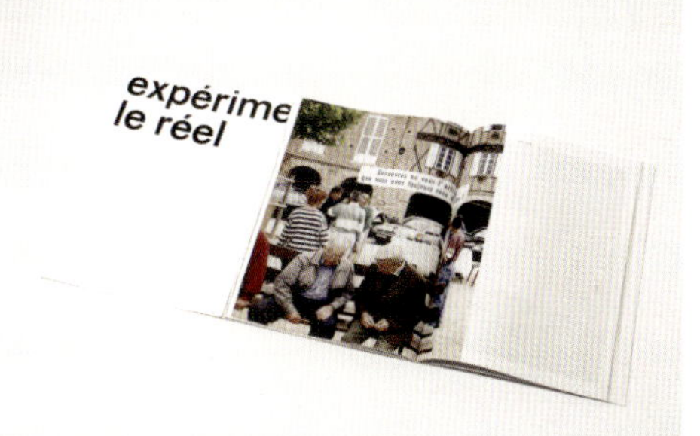
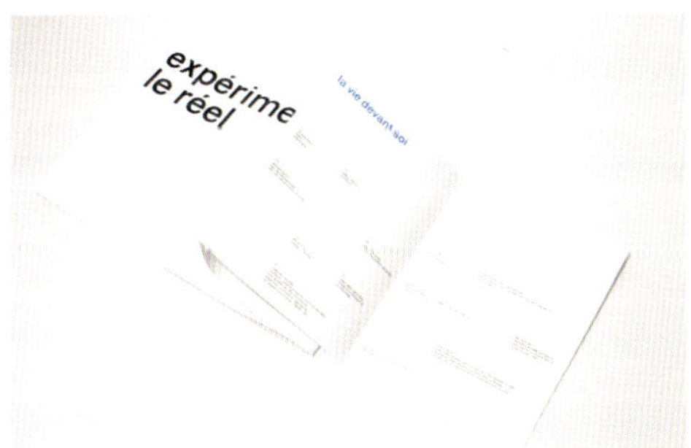
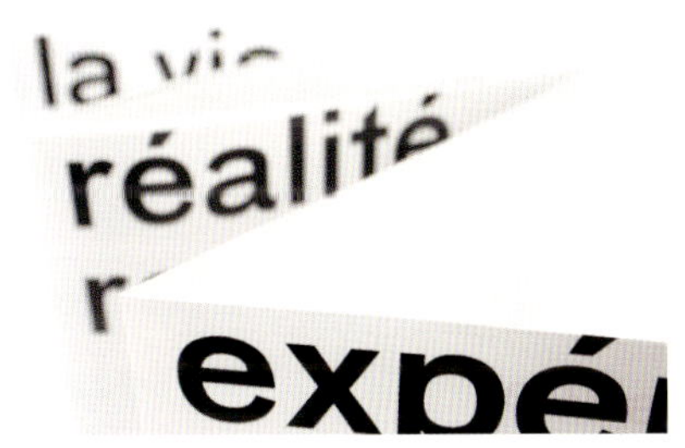

Base

New York, USA

Title: Éxperimenter le Réel
Type of work: Catalogue
Client: Cimaise et Portique (Contemporary Art Center)
Design: ad, d// Base
Year: 2004-05

Base designed this catalogue by dividing it into two parts as in an art exhibition. The book can be read from both sides, cover or back cover, where you find one or the other part of the exhibition. There is a common part in the middle of the book for the text. The artists had to work from something daily, real for the exhibition and Base wanted to transfer this idea on the book, so they chose a thin and glossy paper with staples trying to imitate a magazine since it is a daily object.

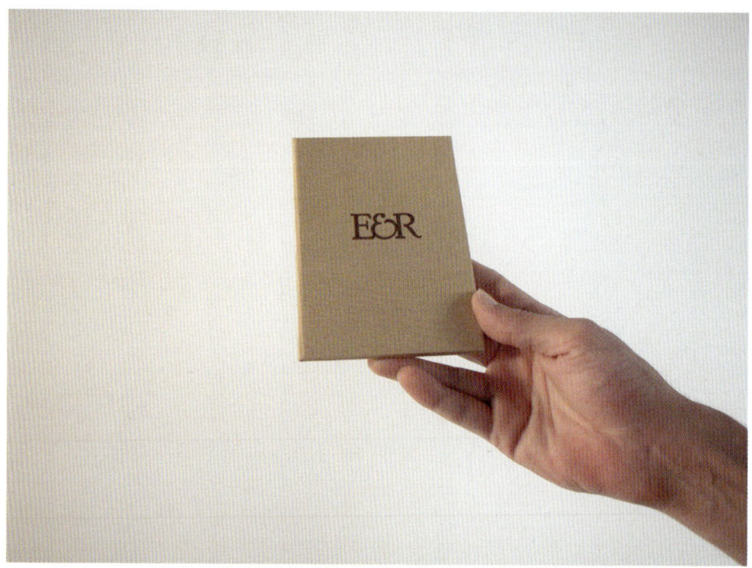

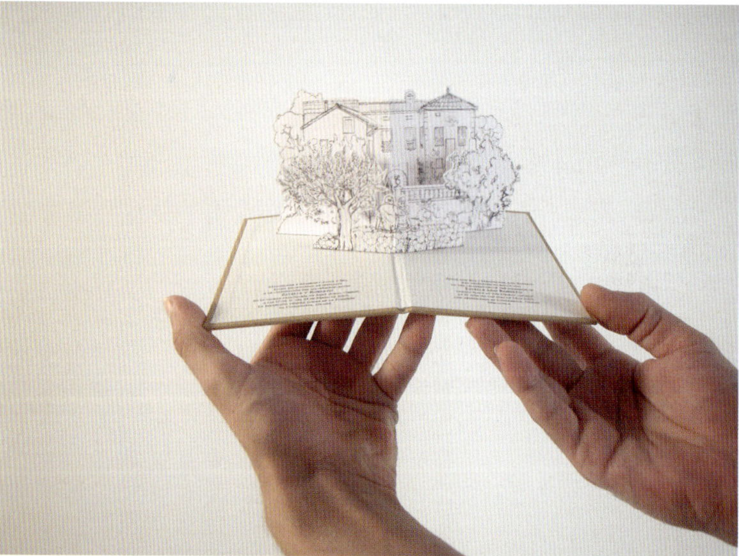

Fundición Gráfica

Illes Balears. Spain

Title: Stelle&Roberto
Type of work: Invitation Card
Client: Stelle&Roberto
Design: ad, d// David Robles, Juan Chito
Year: 2005

A special invitation card for the designer's friend's wedding, for which they thought that the classic pop-up books could be a good idea. They did many tests and started printing and hand cutting the drawings. For the covers, they ordered 100 small handmade hardcover and paperback lined in fabric. The drawings were hand glued one by one. Finally the covers were screen printed with 'E&R' as the title of that event.

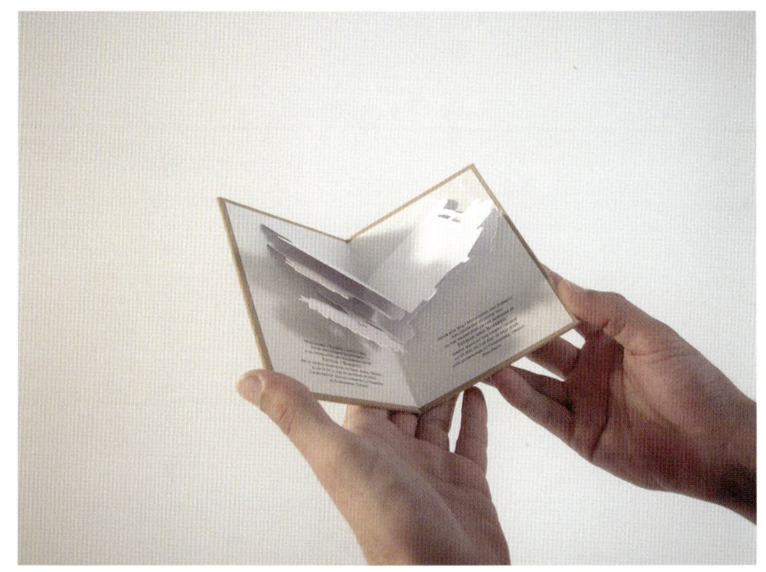

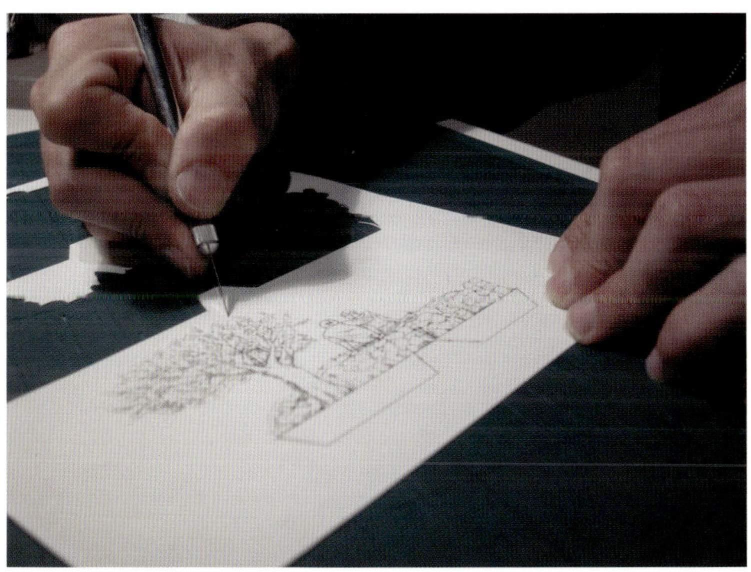

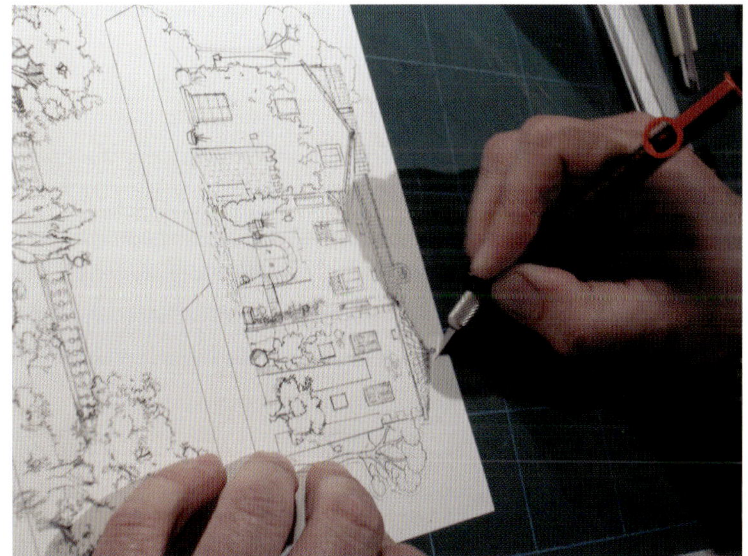

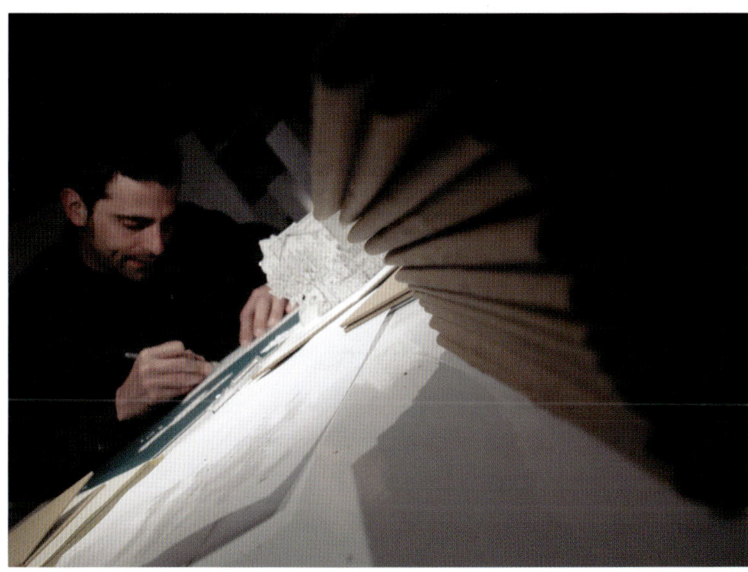

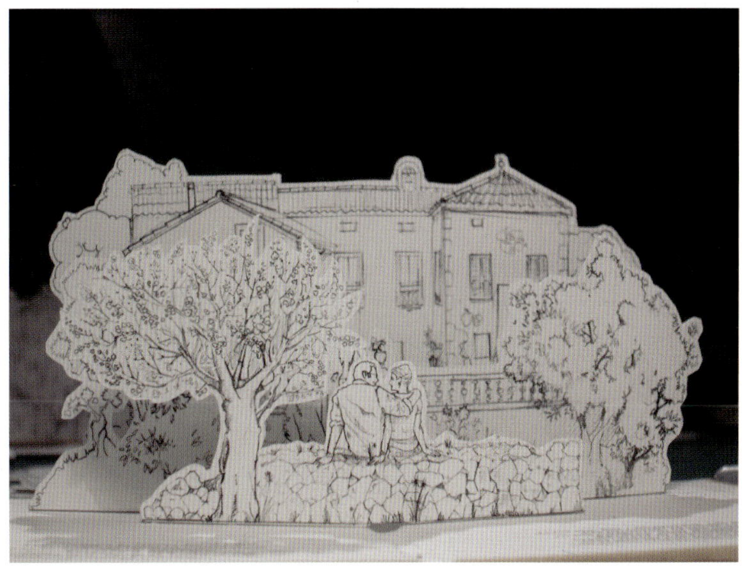

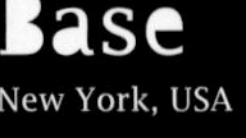

Base

New York, USA

Title: Blanc Kelly
Type of work: Poster
Client: Blanc Kelly
Design: ad. d// Base
Year: 2005

This set of posters is designed with elements of a shirt, mainly the collar and the chest where buttons can be spread. It is very simple with only 3 colours on each poster, either black and white, pink and white and even plain white. A 3-dimensional effect is added by folding the poster.

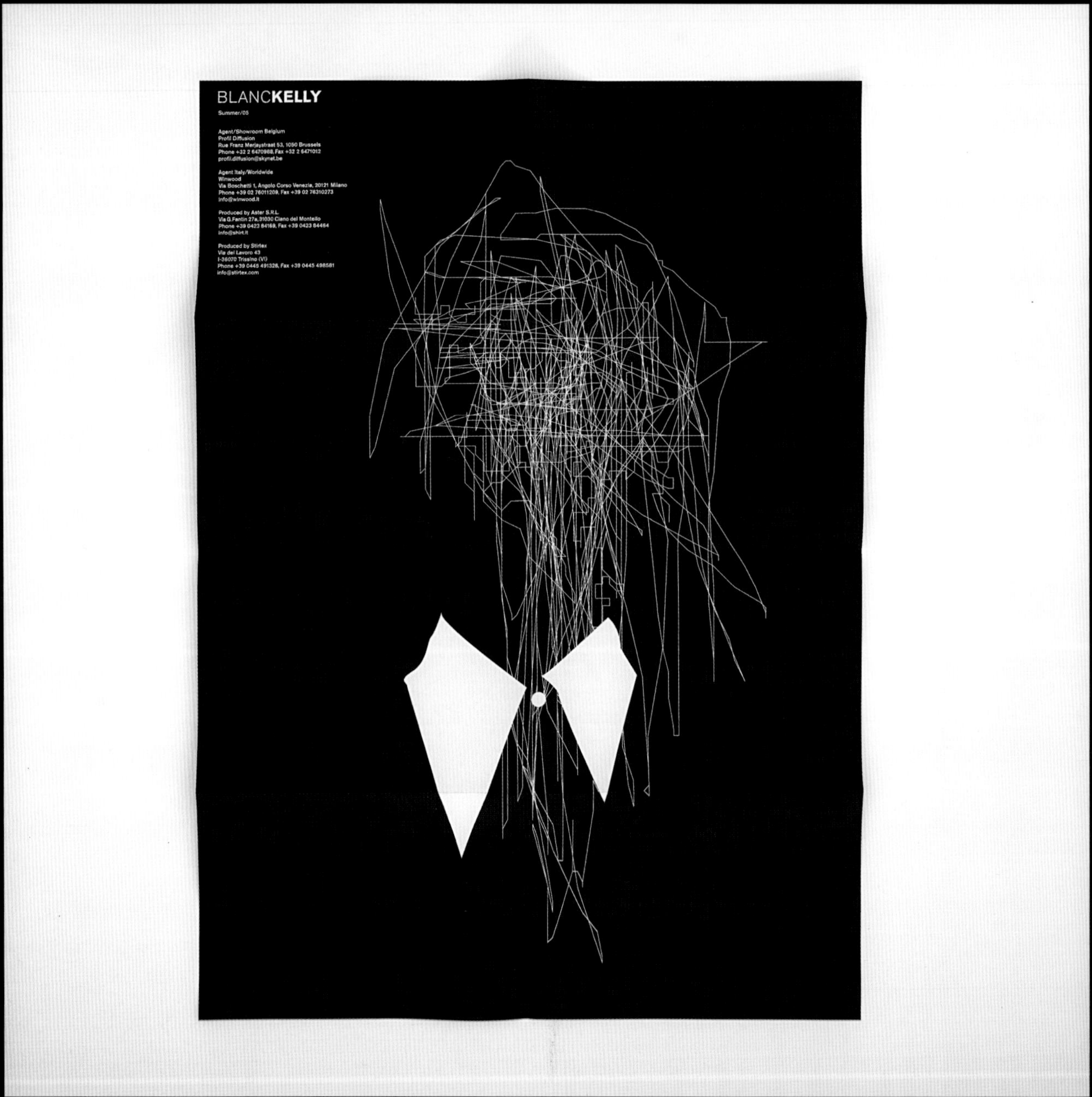

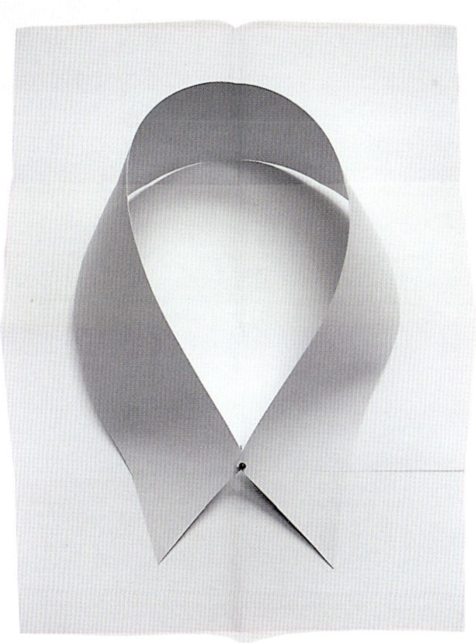

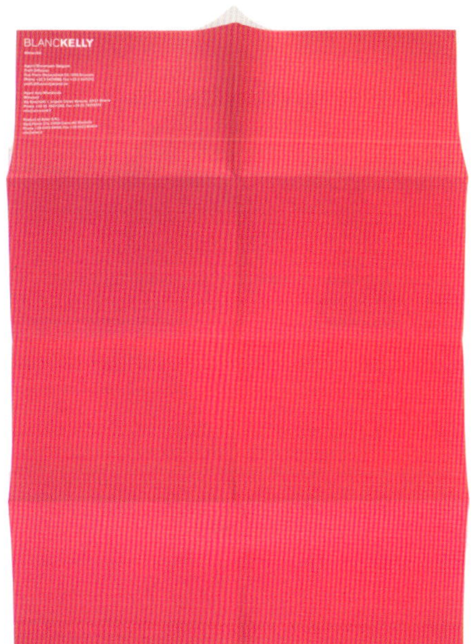

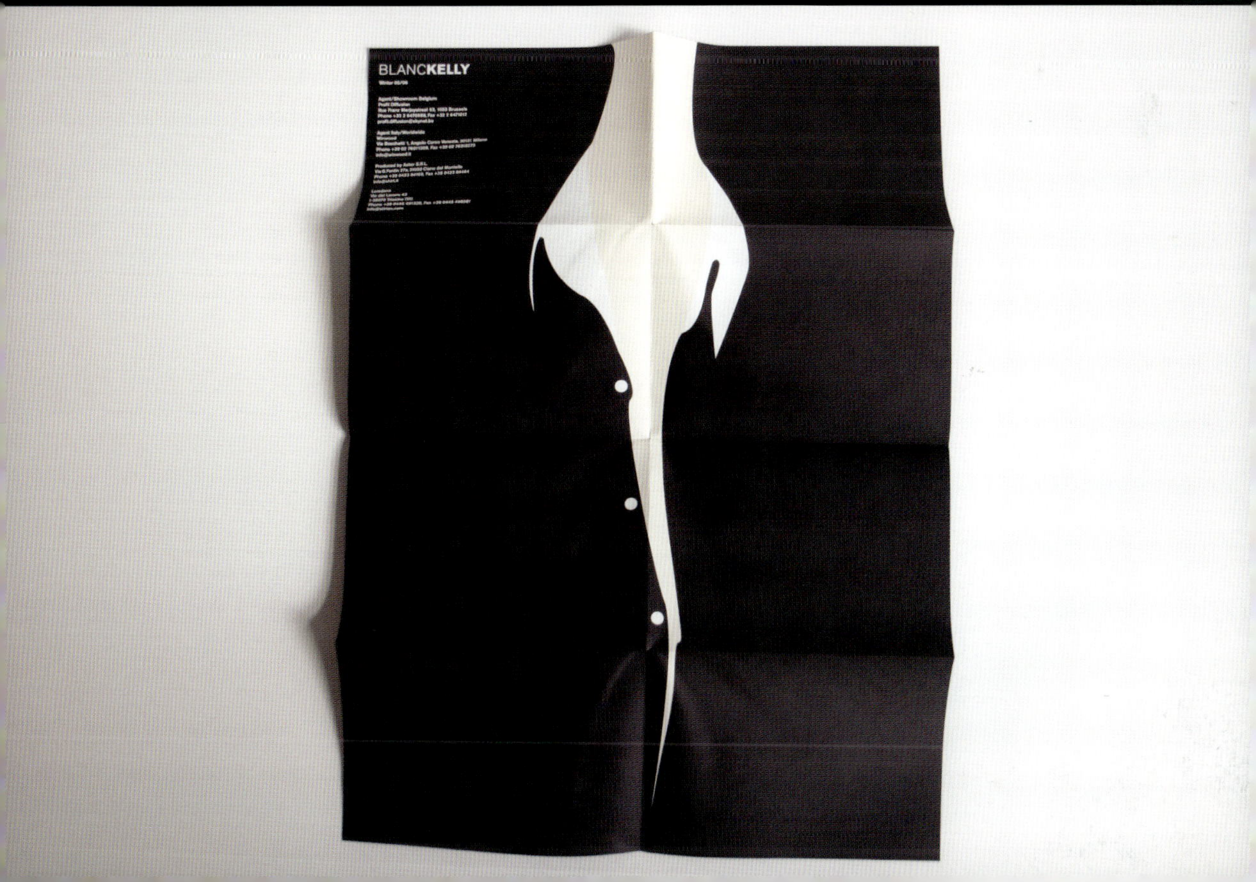

BLANCKELLY

DesignArbeid

Amsterdam, The Netherlands

Title: CABK promotional items
Type of work: Brochure, poster
Client: CABKartez Zwolle, The Netherlands
Design: d// DesignArbeid, Theo Ruys, Eva Blaak, Robert Slotman
Year: 2004-05

These promotional material for the Artschool CABKartez shows all the symbols of the complex world we are living in as patterns. During your studies you are supposed to take a stand in relation to theses symbols, whether it's CNN or Buddha, you have to find your way. The school's main goal is that the students define their own patterns.

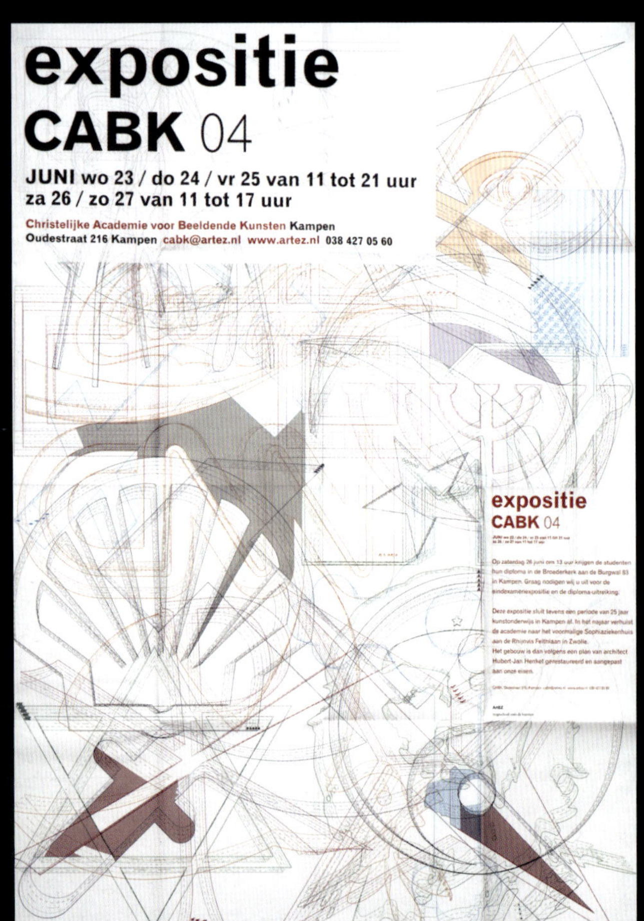

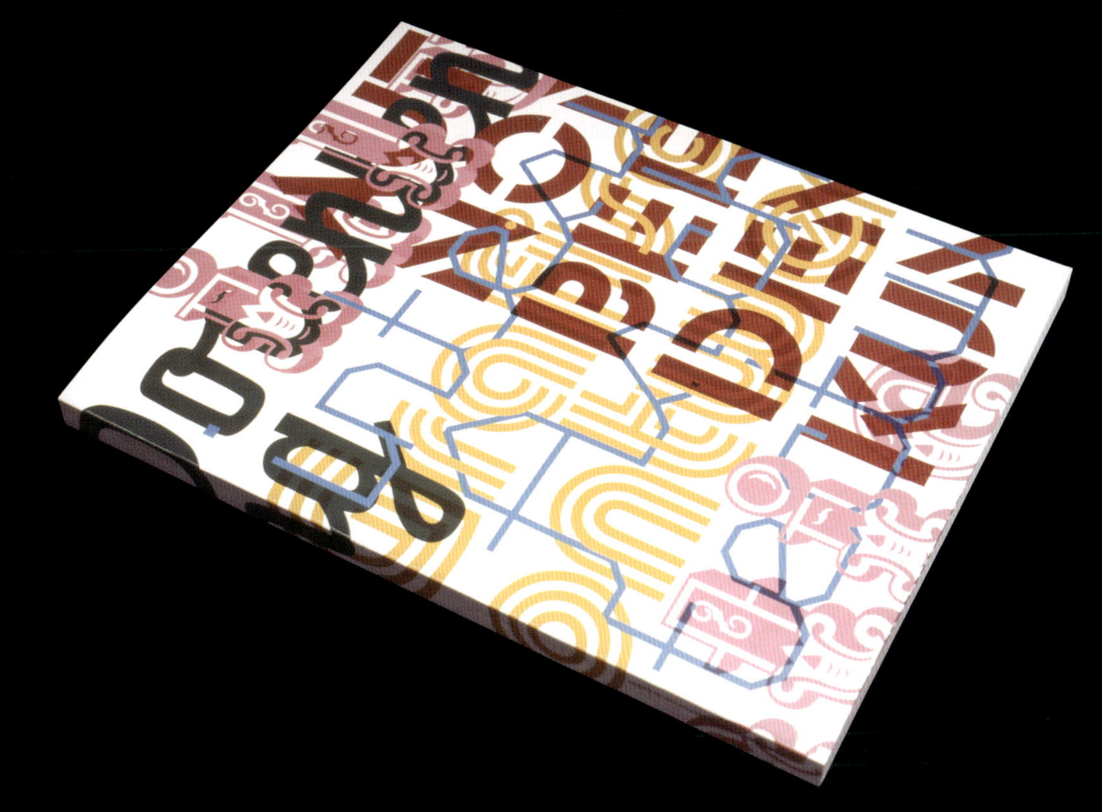

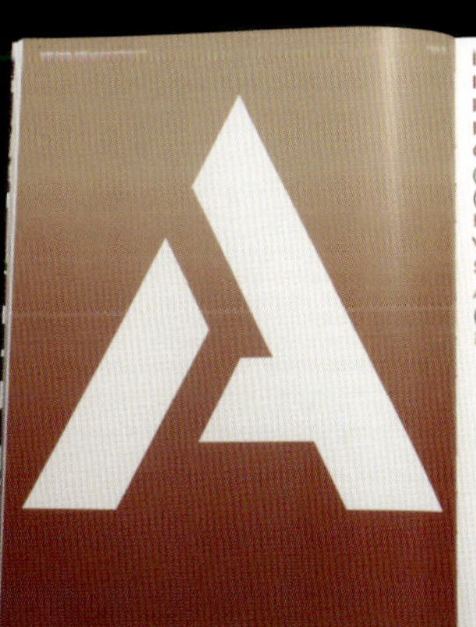
HANNEKE BLOEMEN (14)
LINDA BRUINEKOOL (16) JAN DERKS (18)
PETER EHRMANN (20) JOLIEN FORMER (22)
RICK FRATERMAN (24) ELEANOR KATLEEN
GROOTOONK (26) JURRIAN VAN DEN HAAK
(28) KARIN HILVERTS (30) FEDDE DE JONG
(32) JOHAN DE JONGE (34) WANDA VAN
KONINGSVELD (36) MANNIE KRAK (38) NIELS
VAN DER KUUR (40) ERNST PANSIER (42) CINDY
SCHRIEKENBERG (44) LEONIE STELLEMA (46)
AUKJE VERSENDAAL (48) MACHIEL VISKAAL
(50) REMCO VISSER (52) DIEUWKE WIJMA (54)
MAAIKE WIJMENGA (56)

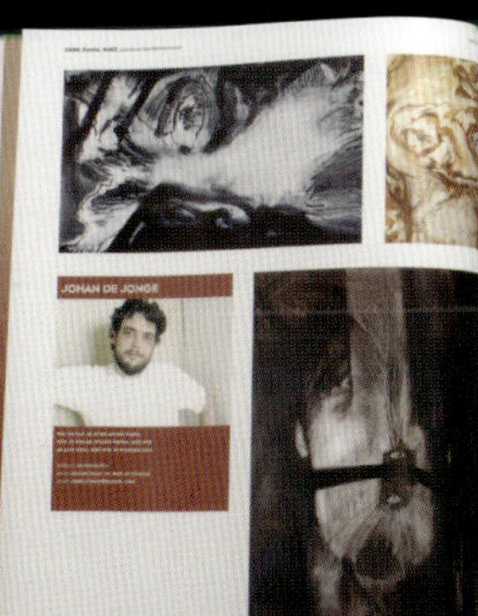

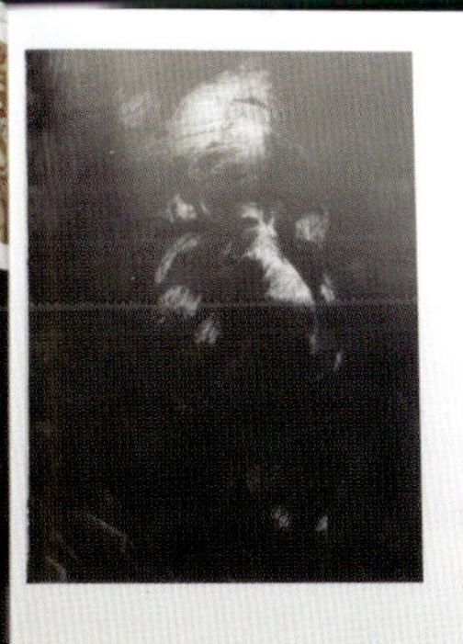

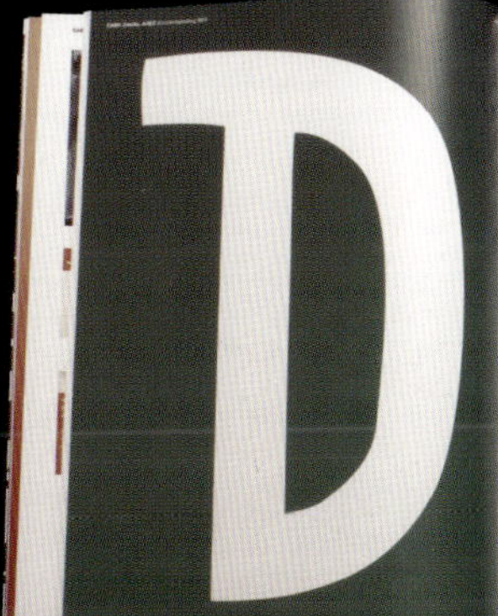
Suzanne Groeneweg (60)
Jan Heerens (62) Jacqueline van
Hoevelaken (64) Alina Hoving (66)
Deja Meinen (68) Dana Olde Nordkamp
(70) Martine Ruiter (72) Marije Schot
(74) Jedidjah Slagter (76) Maikel van
Vilsteren (78) Jorieke Wessels (80)

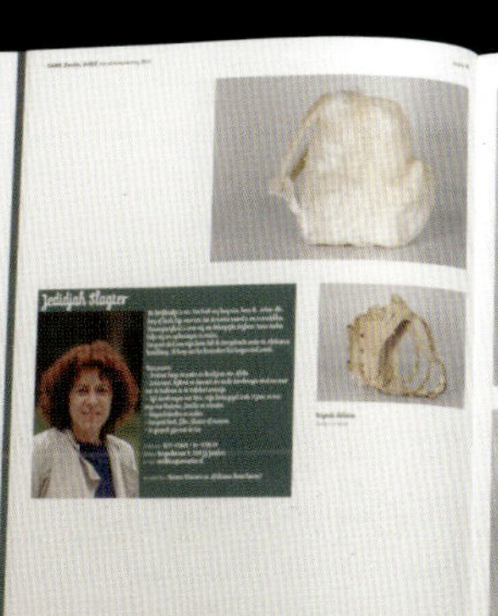

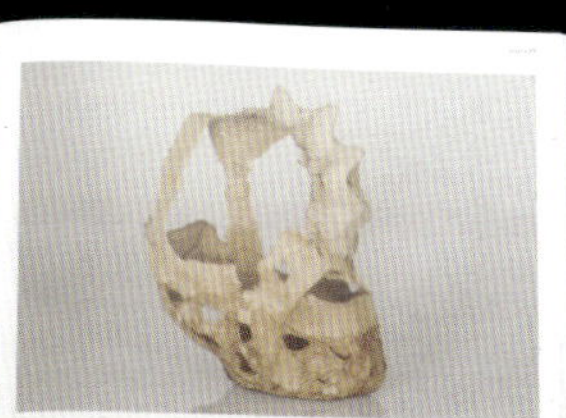

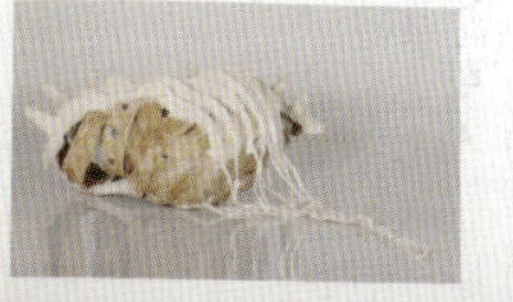

Base

New York, USA

Title: Open Process
Type of work: Book
Client: Hangar
Design: ad, d// Base
Year: 2004

A project designed for a center of artistic production, which celebrates throughout the year 'Processos Oberts', a series of artistic events in which the most important thing is the process behind the final result. The graphic idea is based on unfinished materials focusing on the process concept.

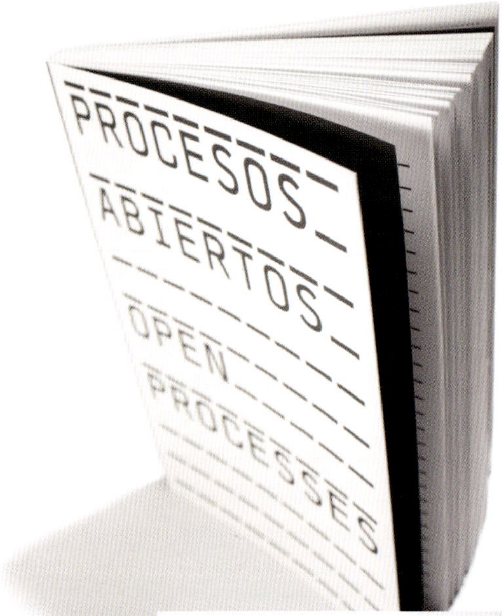

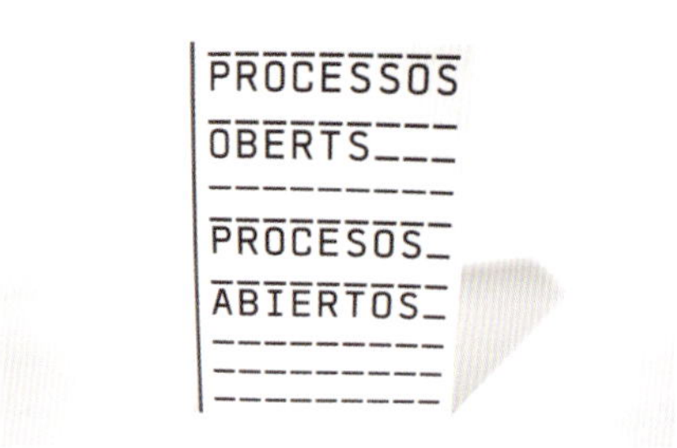

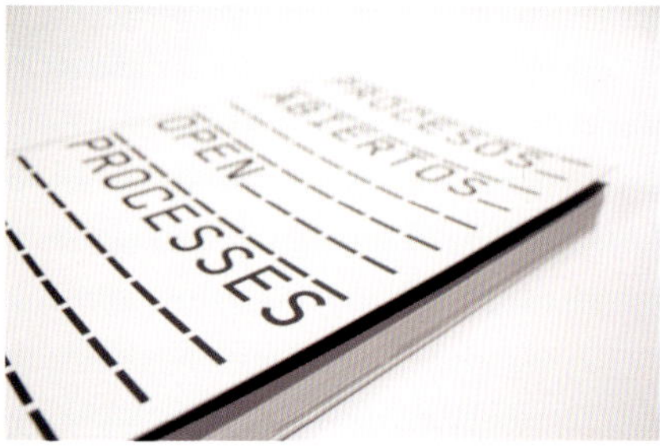

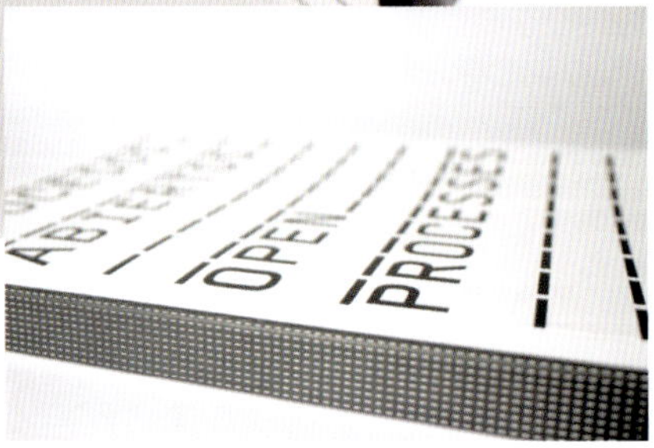

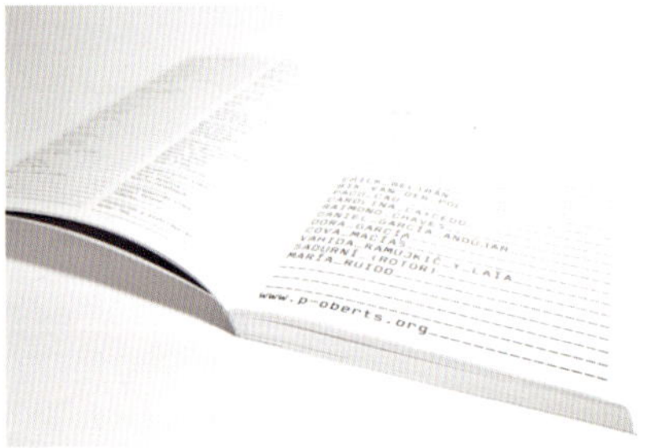

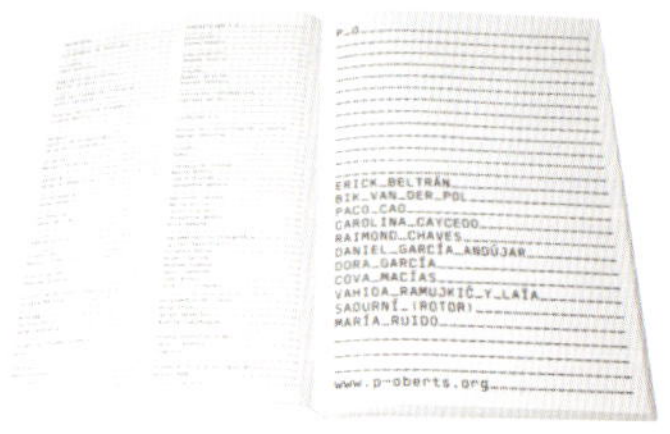

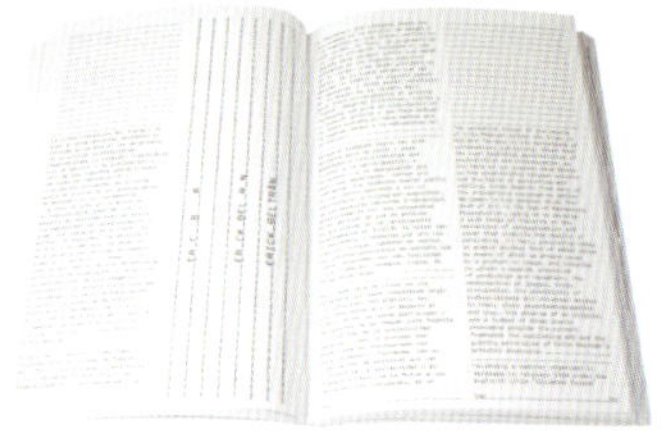

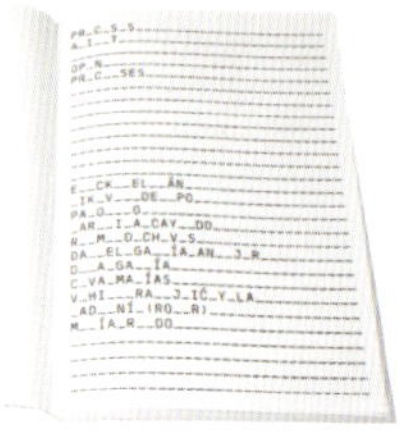

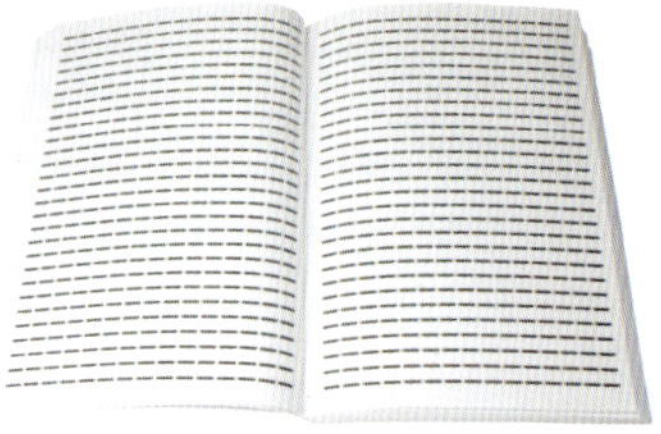

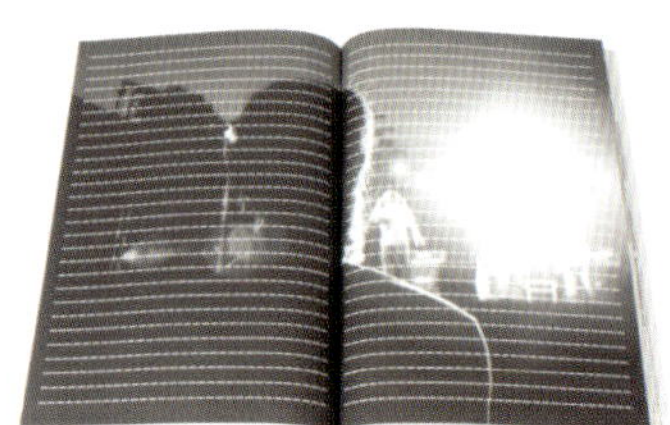

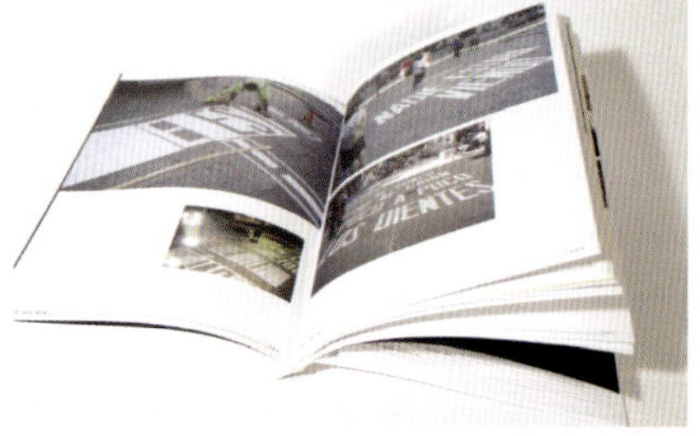

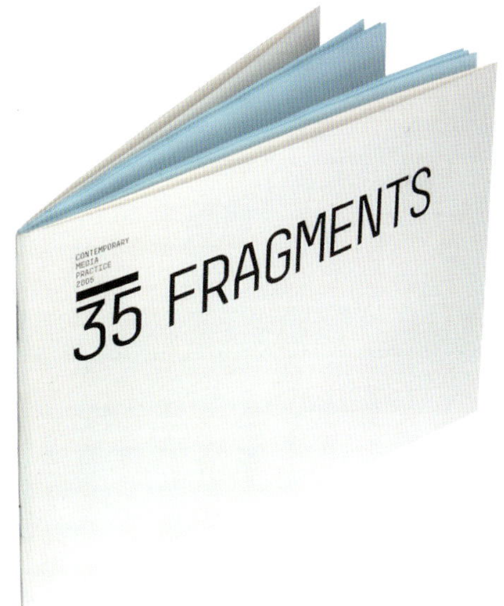

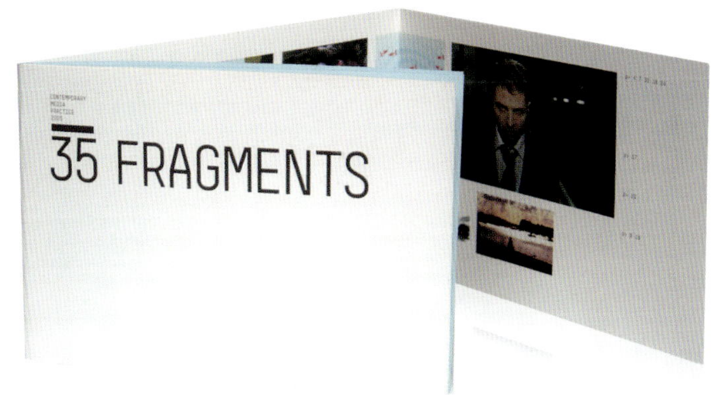

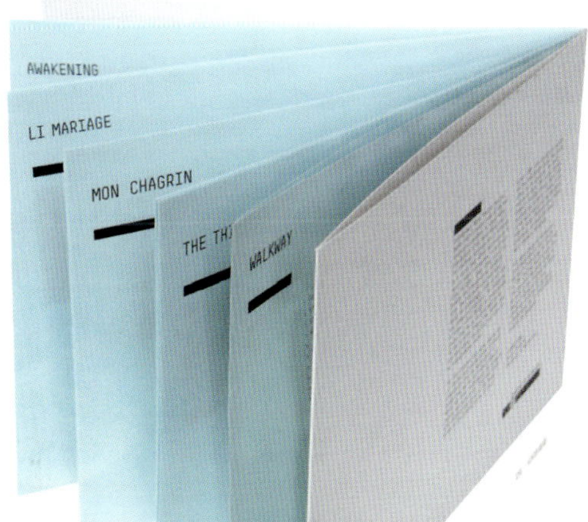

PAGE	TITLE	PAGE	TITLE
p› 2	A Plastic Toy Dinosaur	p› 20	Loneliness in London
p› 3	A Vision of Hope	p› 21	Missed Connections
p› 4	A Woman's Phallacy	p› 22	Mon Chagrin
p› 5	Absent Trace	p› 23	Narcissism
p› 6	All and Nothing	p› 24	O - Circle
p› 7	Animal Magic	p› 25	Peacehaven
p› 8	Awakening	p› 26	Race for the Price
p› 9	Bouquet	p› 27	Reversion
p› 10	Scum, More Than Just a City	p› 28	Scent of Roses
p› 11	De Arranged Marrige	p› 29	Silly Games
p› 12	"Fetch!"	p› 30	The Condition of Bernard Cross
p› 13	Framed Emotions	p› 31	The Orange
p› 14	Hidden Fears	p› 32	The Third Team
p› 15	In/visible	p› 33	Three Thousand Five Hundred and Sixty Feet
p› 16	Infinite Space	p› 34	Untitled 2005
p› 17	Kismat	p› 35	Urban Footprints
p› 18	Li Mariage	p› 36	Walkway
p› 19	Light Wash		

Design: Emmi Salonen › www.emmi.co.uk

Emmi Sal●nen

New York, USA

Title: University of Westminster Degree Show Catalogue
Type of work: Booklet
Client: Emmi Salonen
Design: ad, d// Emmi Salonen
Year: 2005

This is an end of year catalogue designed for the Contemporary Media Course which has 60 students. Some students did not have work ready to show in the catalogue and some had very low resolution. However the clients wanted 'unity' and to avoid having someone's work/page shining over others. In the final solution, the high res full colour images are printed on a white matt card around the cover, which then folds in on the front and back, giving more room to the images. The inside pages with the information of the projects and contact details are printed on 100g blue papers in one colour black. Some of them have images, some not, some have their image only on the inside page as resolution is not high enough for the cover. In this way, the catalogue ended presenting a group in a solid and equal manner.

Base
New York, USA

Title: –
Type of work: Logo, catalogue, advertising, art direction
Client: nuala
Design: ad, d// Base
Year: 2004

Each page of this Catalogue is designed in different sizes to enhance the romantic feel of the foggy images for the label 'nuala'. The logo of 'nuala' here is made simple but stylish, matching with the designer's clothes.

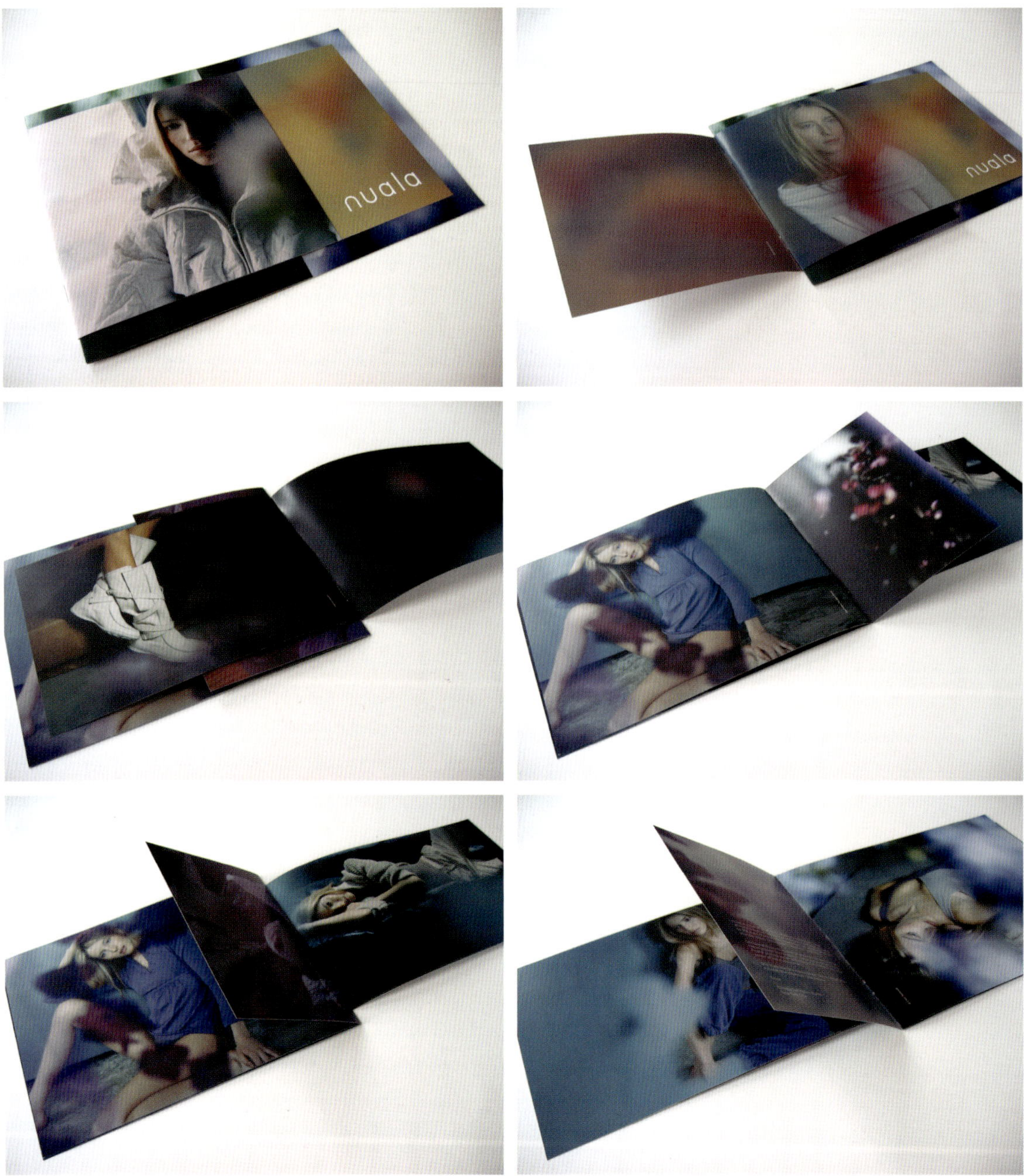

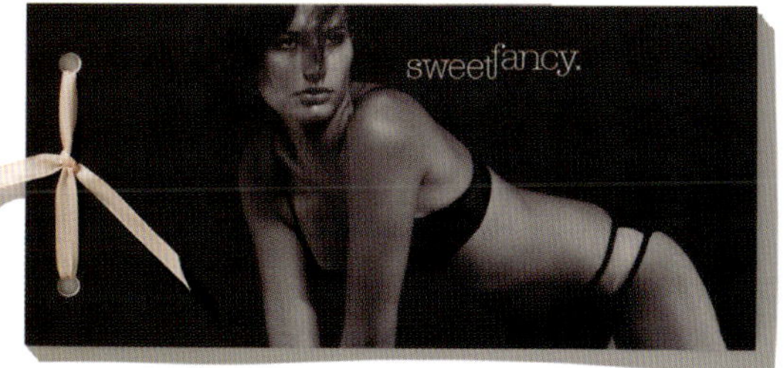

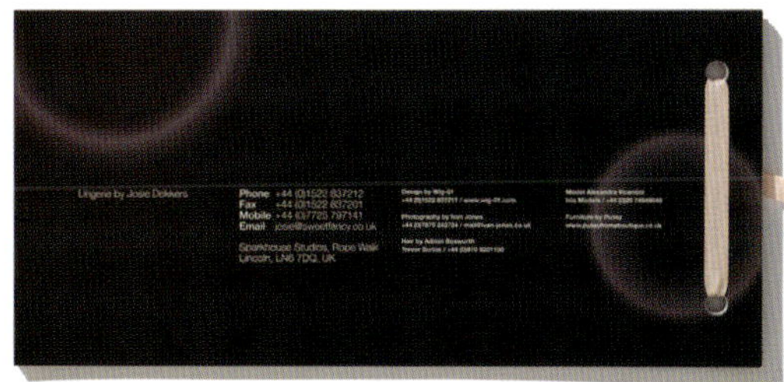

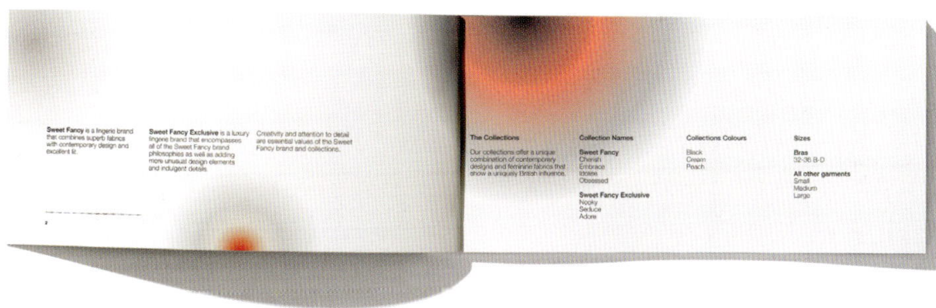

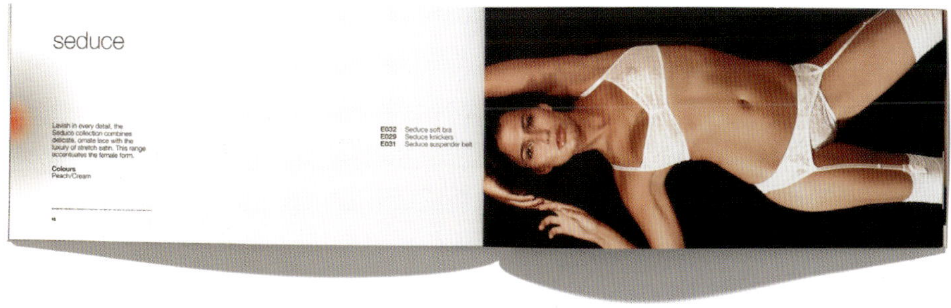

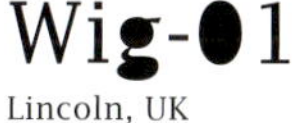

Wig-01

Lincoln, UK

Title: Sweet Fancy
Type of work: Look book
Client: Sweet Fancy
Design: ad, d// Wig-01
Year: 2005

This Look book is made of 3 main colours: Black to represent secretness, pink to represent sexiness and white to represent innocent. The pinky circles, look like soap bubble that is transparent itself but makes the images behind to be foggy, enhance the mysterious feel from the black background while the ribbons can lead you to think of underwears, their products.

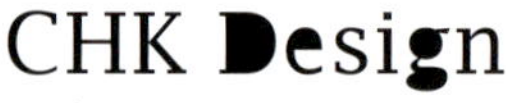

CHK **D**esign

London, UK

Title: 'Miser & Now' Magazine (issues 3, 4 and 5)
Type of work: Magazine
Client: Keith Talent Gallery
Design: ad, d// Christian Küsters
Year: –

Spreads in *'Miser & Now'*, a new contemporary culture magazine, based in London. The slightly unusual name is based on an anagram formed of the two first names of the founders of the gallery. The logo design is based on the English pound notes and refers visually to the word 'Miser'. Issues 3 to 5 were theme-based in which the design reacts strongly to each issue's theme.

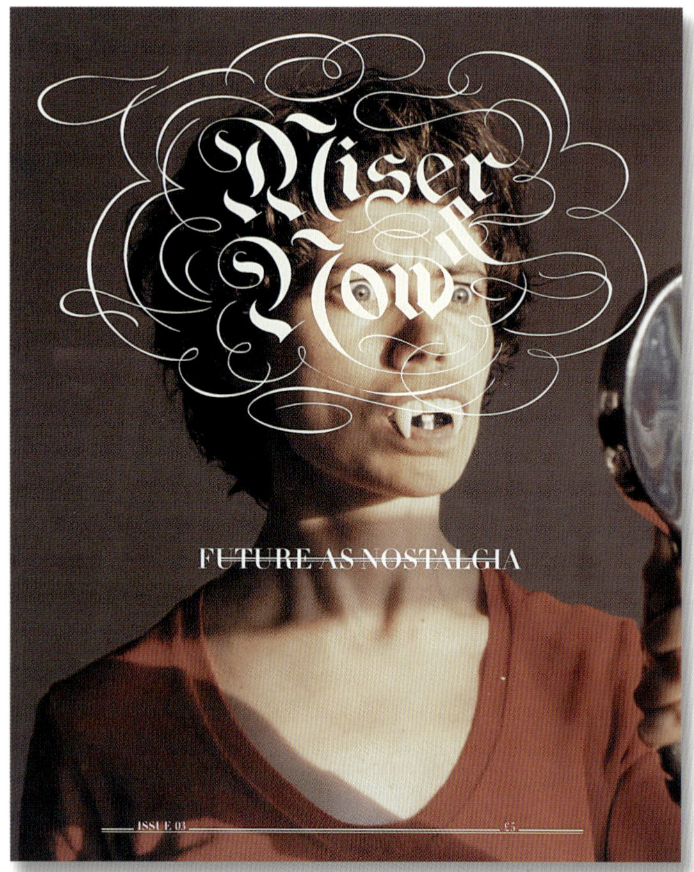

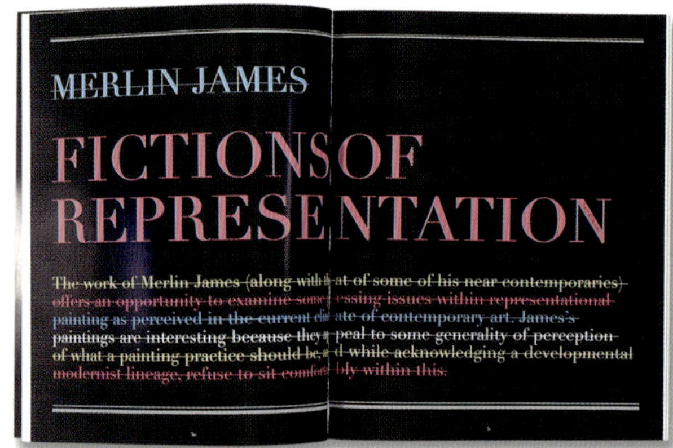

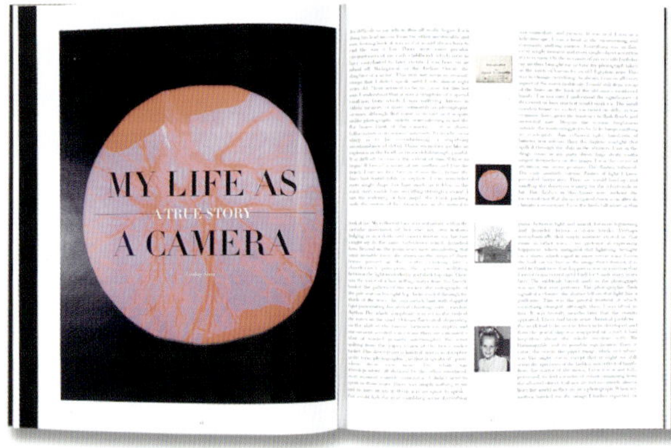

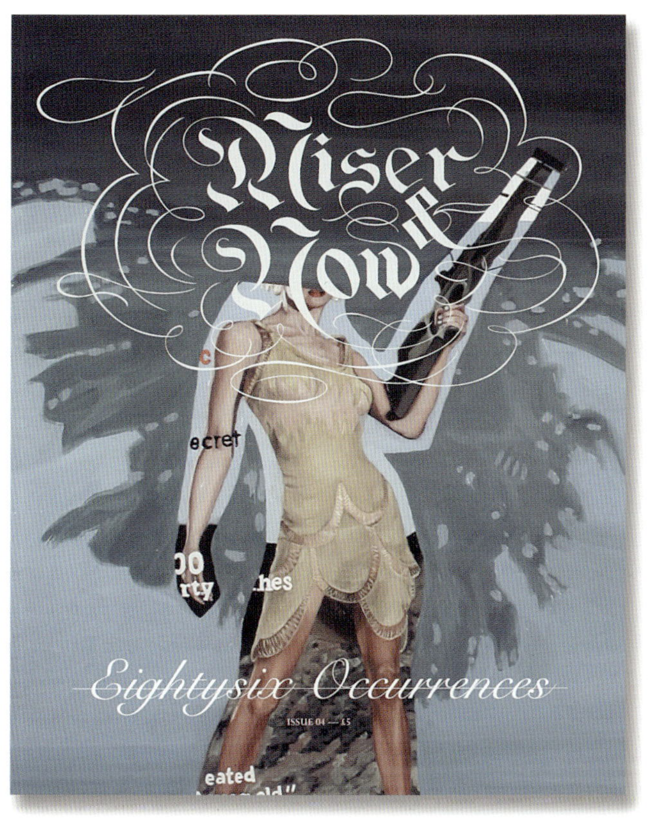

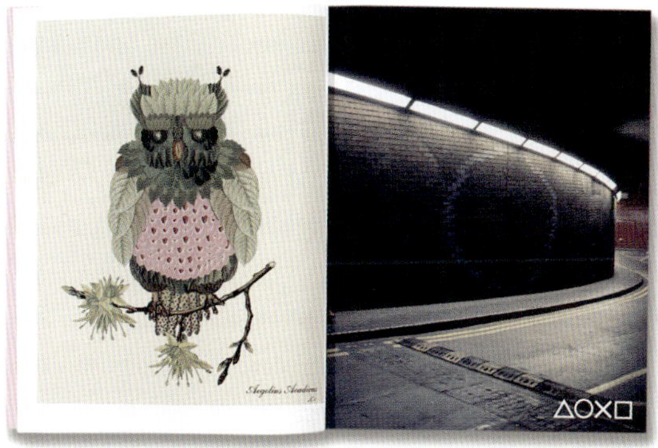

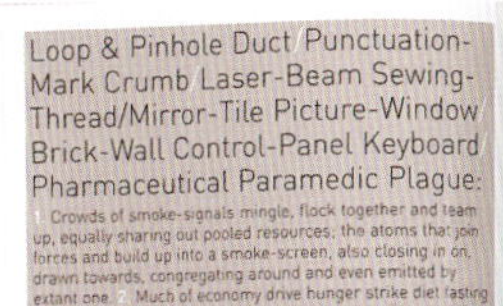
Loop & Pinhole Duct Punctuation-Mark Crumb Laser-Beam Sewing-Thread/Mirror-Tile Picture-Window Brick-Wall Control-Panel Keyboard Pharmaceutical Paramedic Plague:

1 Crowds of smoke-signals mingle, flock together and team up, equally sharing out pooled resources; the atoms that join forces and build up into a smoke-screen, also closing in on, drawn towards, congregating around and even emitted by extant one. 2 Much of economy drive hunger strike diet fasting smoke-screen will roll up, fold flat, crumple inwards, straighten out, cut apart and tear down; parting company, broken and split giving birth to many more free-lance smoke-signals, while exhaling and recruiting others. 3 Certain smoke-signals take it in turns and are selected for guarding the remainder of smoke-screen, performing sentry-duty patrol tasks. 4 Protectively sheltering smoke-screen is hide-out sanctuary safe-house drop-in-centre refuge, where like-minded smoke-signals find safety-in-numbers. 5 Itinerant courier messenger homing pigeon smoke-signals are dispatched from smoke-screen, sent out on their assigned missions. 6 Centralised smoke-screen is head-office base, reported back to by secret-agent smoke-signals, returning laden with findings of news, plunder and bounty to deliver and receive further such briefings.

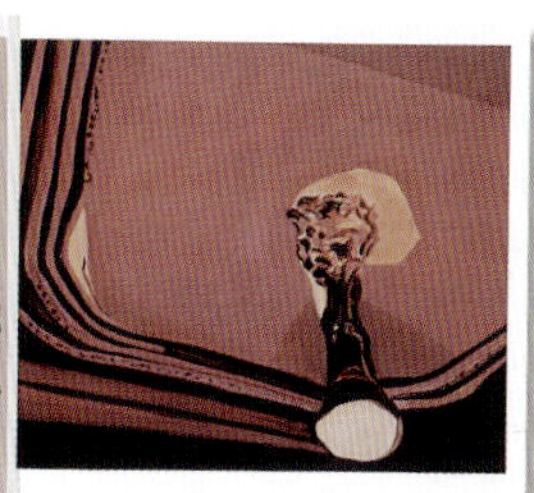

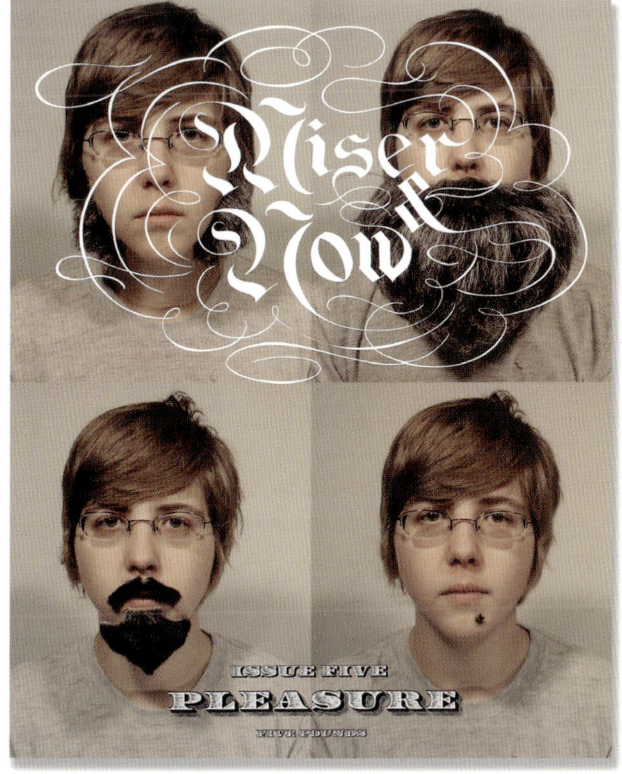

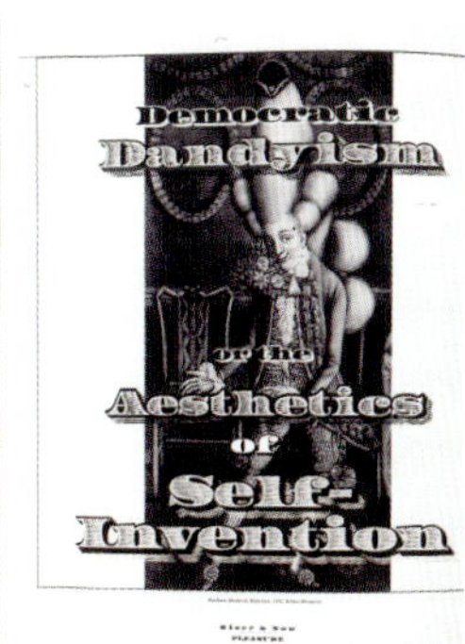

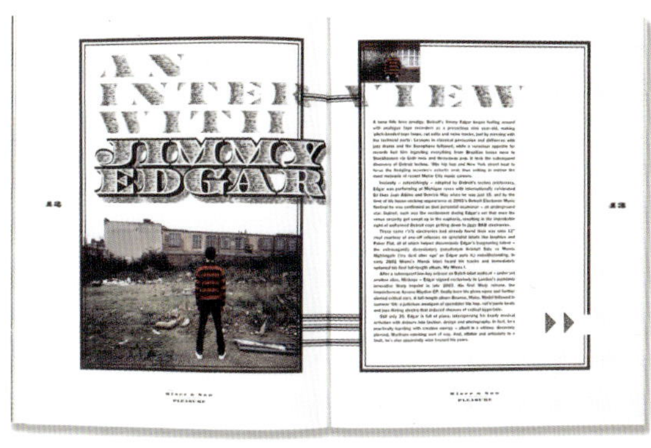

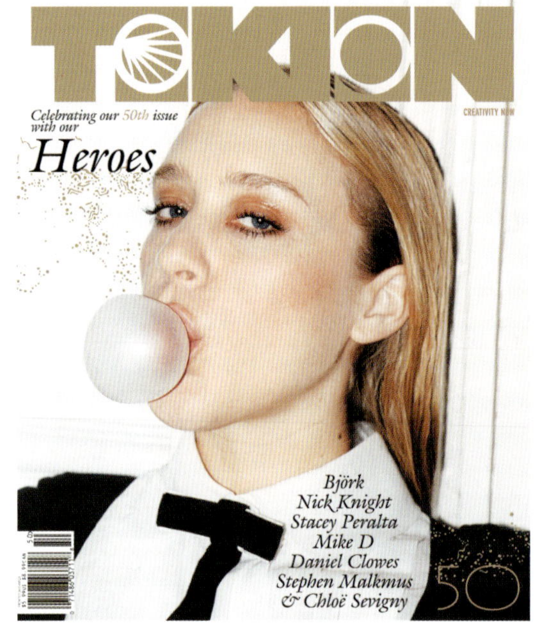

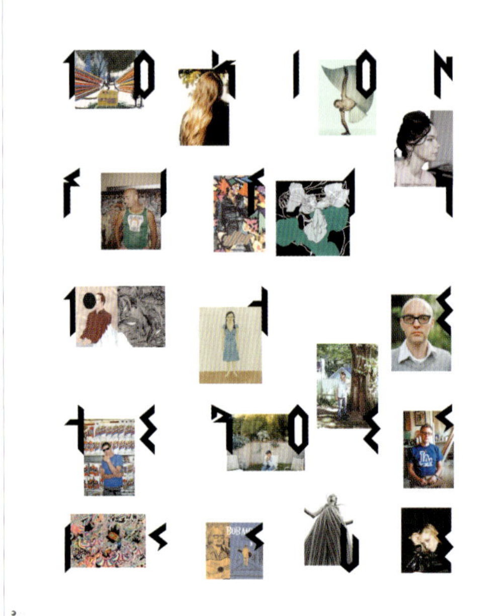

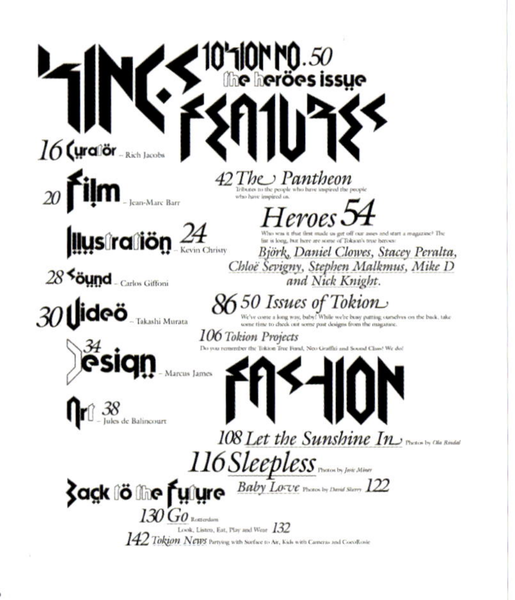

Deanne Cheuk

New York, USA

Title: Tokion Magazine Issue #50
Type of work: Editorial art direction
Client: *Tokion Magazine*
Design: ad, d// Deanne Cheuk
p// 1,2: Kenneth Cappello 3: Josie Miner
Year: 2005

Black and white is the main colours of this maga-zine design. Breathing space (i.e. white area) is largely reserved to give simple and clear layout specially putting together with lots of small imag-es and typo-graphics. It is also useful when plac-ing with a full-page B/W photograph, to enhance the feel of comfortness and laziness.

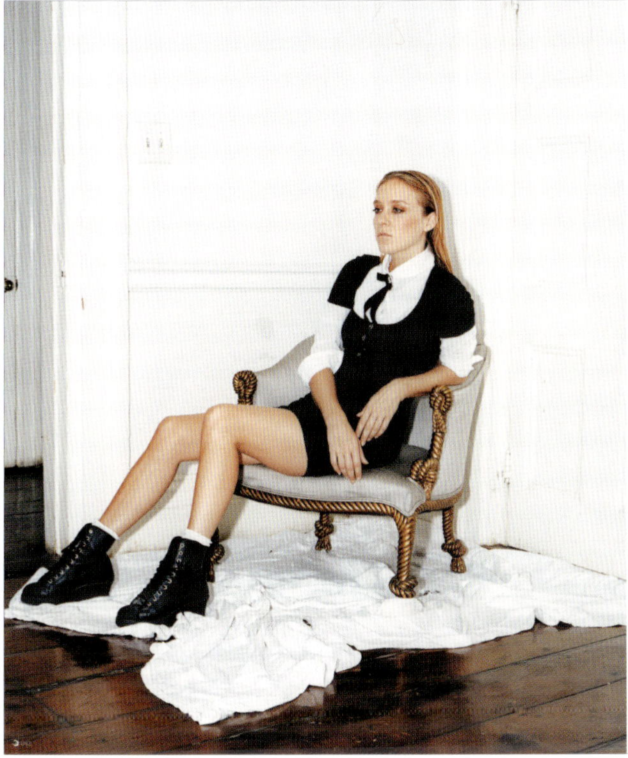

text | KEN MILLER ~ photos | KENNETH CAPPELLO ~ thanks | DOLCE & GABANNA

CHLOË SEVIGNY

Chloë Sevigny has appeared in films directed by the great filmmakers of our time—Lars von Trier, Jim Jarmusch and Woody Allen, to name just a few. She has gained notoriety for taking roles in controversial films ranging from *Kids* to *Boys Don't Cry* to *Brown Bunny*. Yet it seems she's still struggling in some ways to gain the respect she deserves as an actor. Maybe she's too accessible? To dressed up or dressed down? Too inaccessible and 'hip'? Whatever the reason, parts in the upcoming HBO series *Big Love* (about a family of bigamists) and the David Fincher film *Zodiac* will get the rest of the world's priorities in order.

WHERE ARE YOU RIGHT NOW?
CHLOE SEVIGNY: I'm on my lunch break, upstate (in New York).

I THOUGHT YOU WERE IN SAN FRANCISCO SHOOTING ZODIAC?
CS: Yeah, I was. I took the red eye last night.

WHAT ARE YOU SHOOTING UPSTATE?
CS: It's called *Lying*. It's with Jena Malone and Leelee Sobieski. It's about a bunch of girls. It is very much inspired by Robert Altman's *3 Women*, and Peter Weir's *Picnic at Hanging Rock*. I play this girl who is a compulsive liar who doesn't really have that many friends. She's also an artist, and she has these girls who she works with, and she convinces them to come upstate with her and convinces them that it is her house, but it is really her parents' house. She says her parents are dead, and she tells them all these tall tales. They are up here trying to figure her out. But... I'm not really sure that it really goes anywhere. (*Laughs.*) I shouldn't really say that! I'm sure it will be really beautiful. The director is kind of a protégée of Gus Van Sant. I don't know... You've got to try it. You can't just sit around.

MAKING A TV SHOW IN LA, A MOVIE IN SAN FRANCISCO AND A MOVIE IN UPSTATE NEW YORK, ALL IN THE SAME WEEK... IT SEEMS LIKE AT THIS POINT MAYBE YOU SHOULD BE SITTING AROUND MORE.
CS: You think? (*Laughs.*) You think that I should sit around and stop doing all these crappy indies?

I DON'T KNOW ABOUT THAT. BUT MAYBE YOU SHOULD TAKE A DAY OFF.
CS: I do need a day off. But I just wrapped this TV show, and I am so afraid that if it becomes successful, I will end up only being that character. And that would be really unfortunate. So I want to try and get in as many movies as possible before the show comes out.

BUT DOESN'T IT GET KIND OF SCHIZOPHRENIC? YOU'VE PLAYED THREE CHARACTERS IN THREE WEEKS...
CS: Yeah, sometimes it is hard to focus. The environment and the wardrobe and the makeup help a lot with that.

SINCE YOU'RE MAKING THIS INDIE MOVIE UPSTATE... HOW IS IT THAT YOU HAVE FOUND SOME OF THE

FIRST TIME DIRECTORS THAT YOU HAVE WORKED WITH, LIKE (BOYS DON'T CRY DIRECTOR) KIMBERLY PIERCE OR (SHATTERED GLASS DIRECTOR) BILLY RAY OR THIS DIRECTOR YOU'RE WORKING WITH NOW?
CS: Well, with Kimberly, it was because of the script. Harmony (Korine) and I had actually been following the story about Teena Brandon—all of the different stories that had come out in *The New Yorker* and *Playboy* and everything. Harmony had actually toyed around with the idea of writing a script of her life. When I heard through the trades or somewhere that someone else had written a script, I decided I had to meet (the director). Christine (Vachon) produced that film, and she also produced *Kids*. With Billy Ray, he had me in mind and approached me. Almost every movie I've done, people have approached me. I'm pretty lucky so far...

WHEN YOU'RE DECIDING WHAT TO TAKE, IS IT MORE BASED ON THE CHARACTER OR IS IT BASED ON MEETING THE PERSON?
CS: It depends. In the case of *Dogville*, it obviously wasn't the character—I wasn't much of a character! (*Laughs.*) But it was Lars von Trier, so it was just based on the director. In the case of *Shattered Glass*, I was intrigued by the character and the story. Not the character I played, but the main character. And it was also an opportunity for me to play a mainstream, bright girl who is just kind of competent. So that was more based on characters. It really actually varies.

I'M WONDERING WHAT YOU MIGHT BE TYPECAST AS?
CS: I'm usually the sympathetic character. Like *American Psycho*...

YOU'RE PRETTY MEAN IN DEMONLOVER.
CS: Do you think so?

YOU SELL CONNIE NIELSEN INTO A BROTHEL IN THE DESERT! THAT'S PRETTY MEAN!
CS: I guess I was! In that case, it was the director. I was a big fan of Olivier Assayas' other films. (With *Demonlover*), I didn't understand the script

Sleepless

Photography by JOSIE MINER
Styling by MEGHAN SCOTT

Model: CAROL SIPPEL @ NY models | Hair: RAMONA @ Bumble & Bumble | Make-up: JILLIAN CHASTIN for Tarte | Casting: CASTING BY US

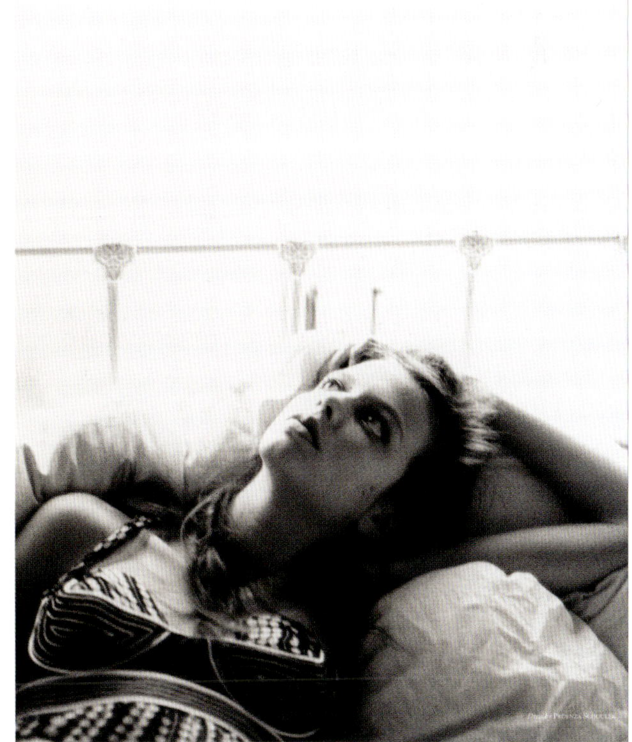

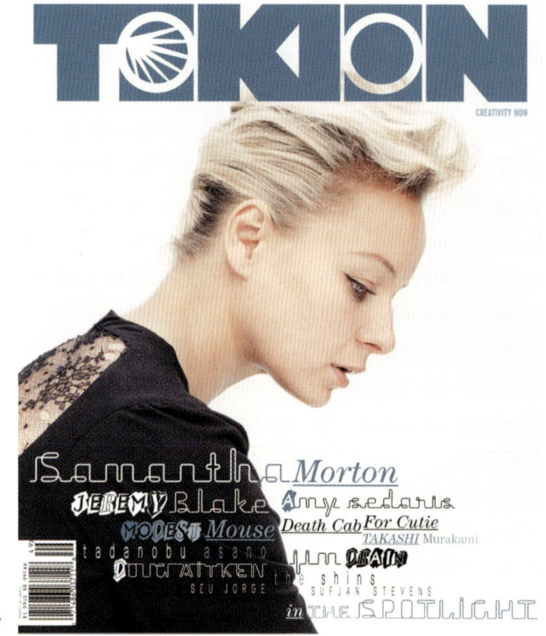

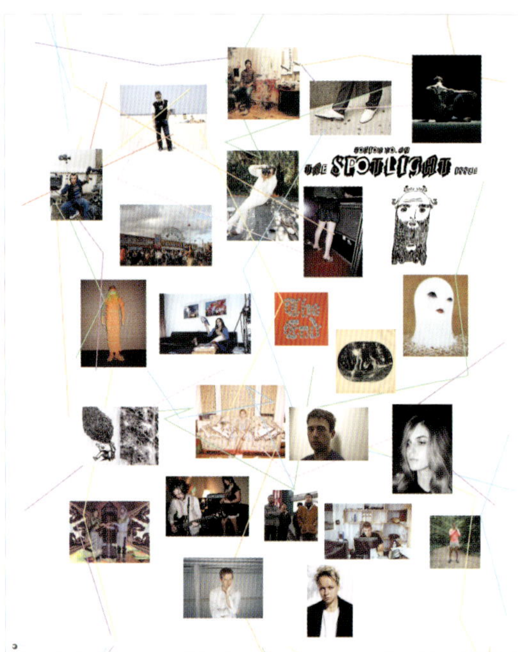

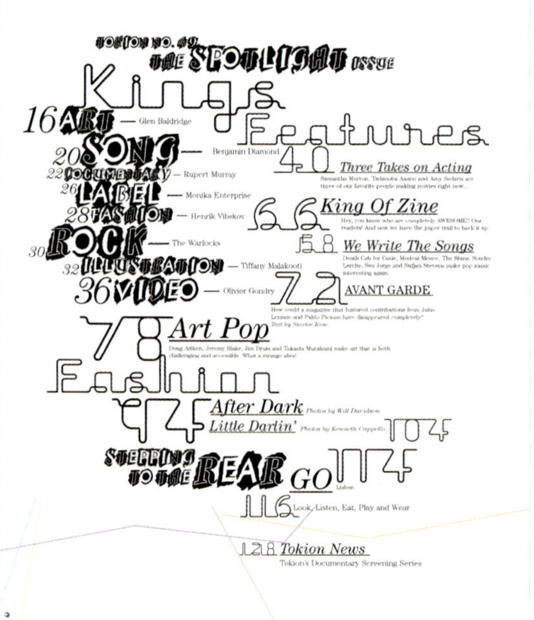

Deanne Cheuk

New York, USA

Title: Tokion Magazine Issue #49
Type of work: Editorial art direction
Client: *Tokion Magazine*
Design: ad, d// Deanne Cheuk p// 1,2: Benjamin
Alexander Huseby 3: Jason Nocito 4: Leigh Ledare
5: Kenneth Cappello 6: Will Davidson
Year: 2005

A coloured net is added between images and
spreading the net to different pages gives consis-
tency to the design. Here, photographs and body
copies are placed in square blocks with black and
white as the theme colour.

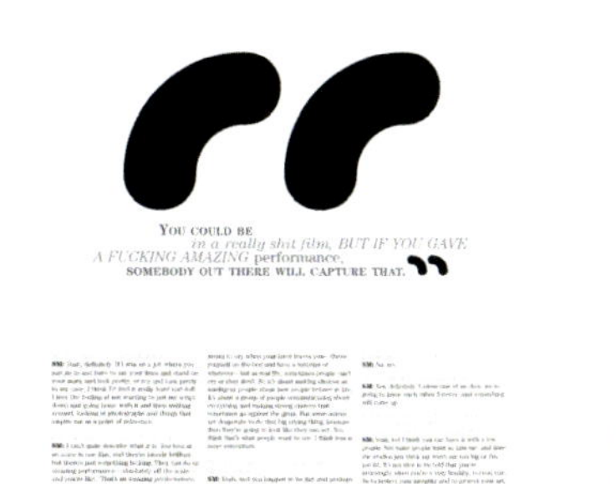
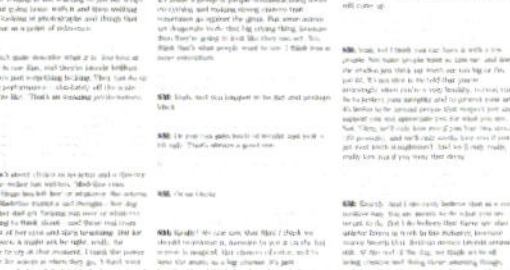

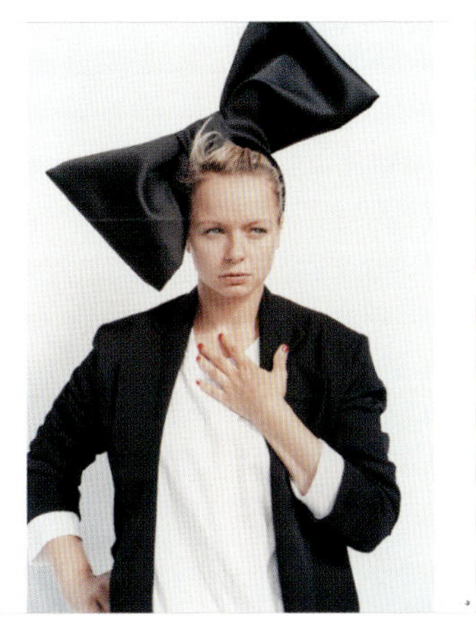

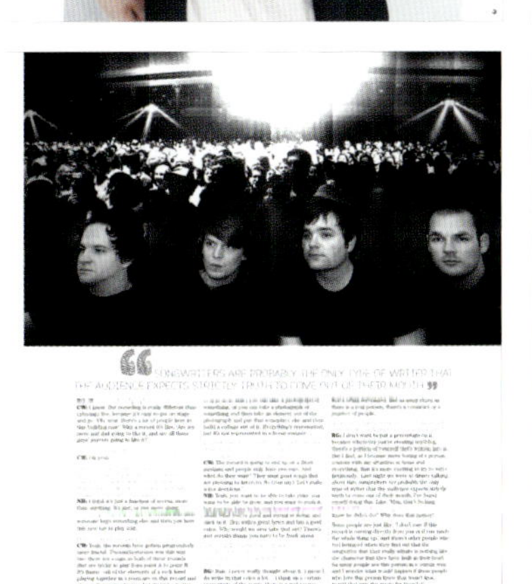

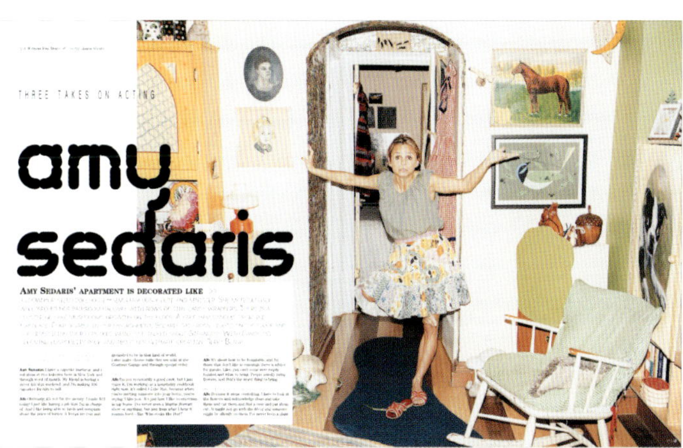

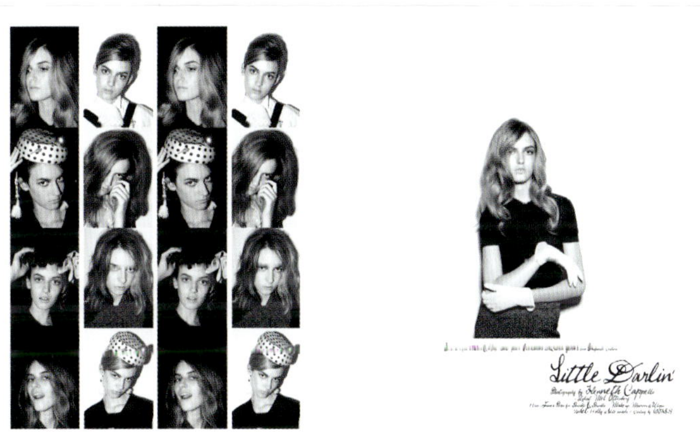

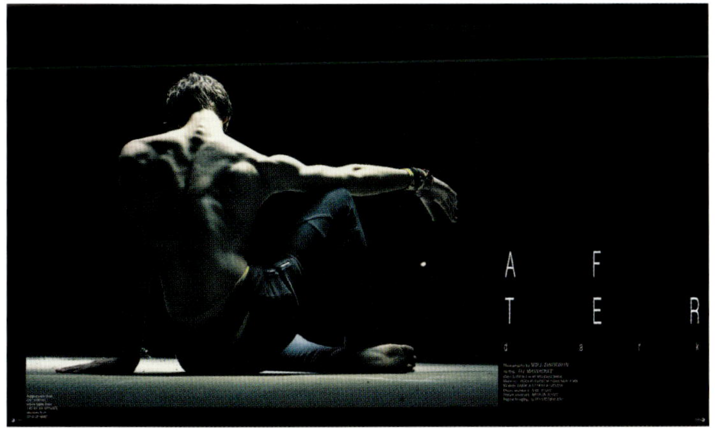

You could be in a really shit film, BUT IF YOU GAVE A FUCKING AMAZING performance, SOMEBODY OUT THERE WILL CAPTURE THAT.

In movie trailers, soundtracks and TV, indie rock has become the new pop...
DEATH CAB FOR CUTIE
WE RECENTLY SAT DOWN WITH THE WELL-MANNERED GENTLEMEN

THREE TAKES ON ACTING
amy sedaris
AMY SEDARIS' APARTMENT IS DECORATED LIKE

Little Darlin'

A F T E R

2.//   3.//
4.//   5.//
6.//

Cartlidge Levene
London, UK

Title: Bruce Nauman: Raw Materials
Type of work: Book
Client: Tate Modern
Design: Cartlidge Levene
Year: 2004

A book which documents a show for Tate Modern, in which the installation consists entirely of sound where Nauman would fill the vast Turbine Hall with audio. The designer's approach was to document the audio works as beautiful typographic pieces, evoking the rhythm of the delivery and capturing nuances and inflections of the spoken words. The book therefore becomes an essential guide to the installation and the only documentation of the experience that will live on afterwards. The design of the book sets a visual representation of the show.

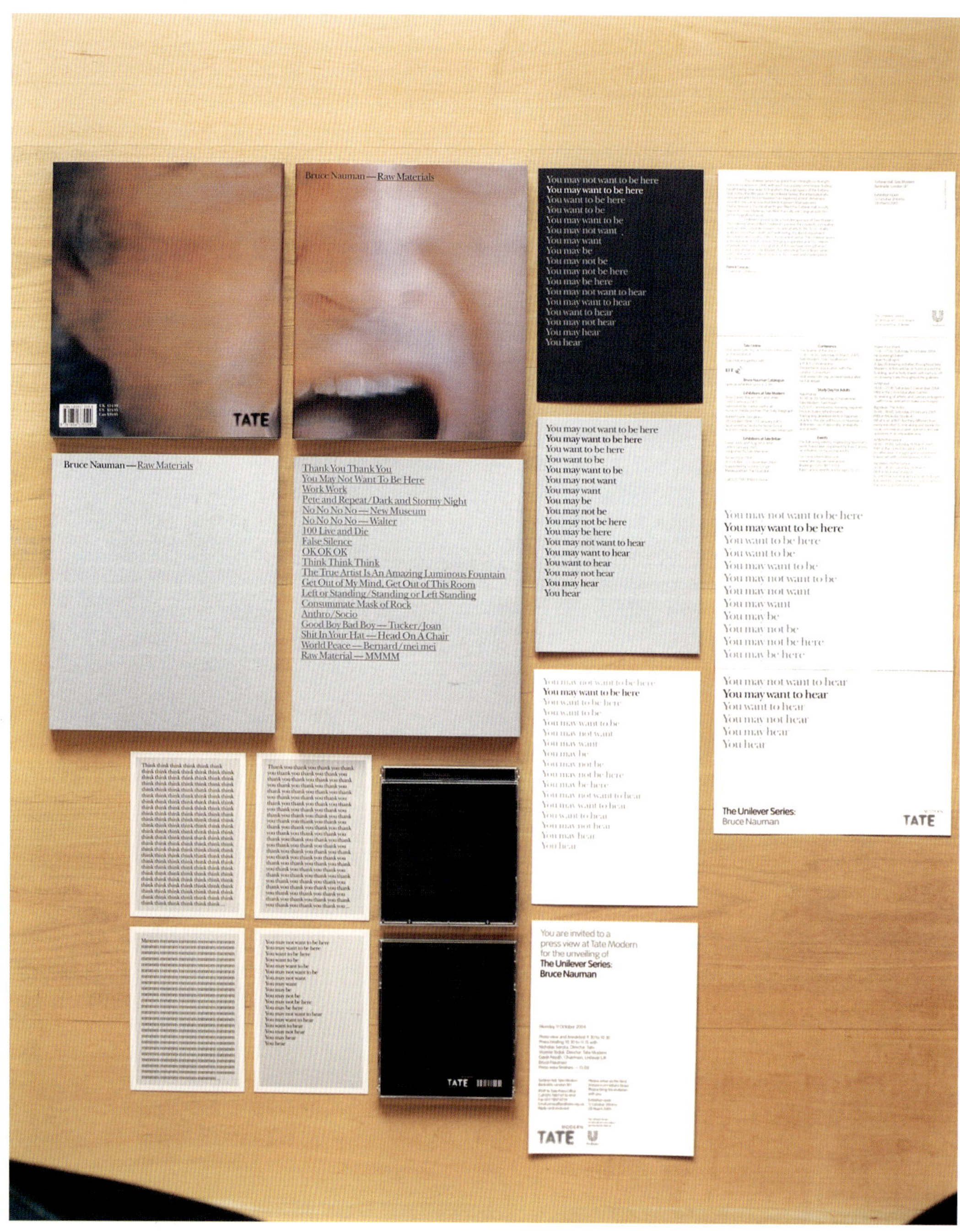

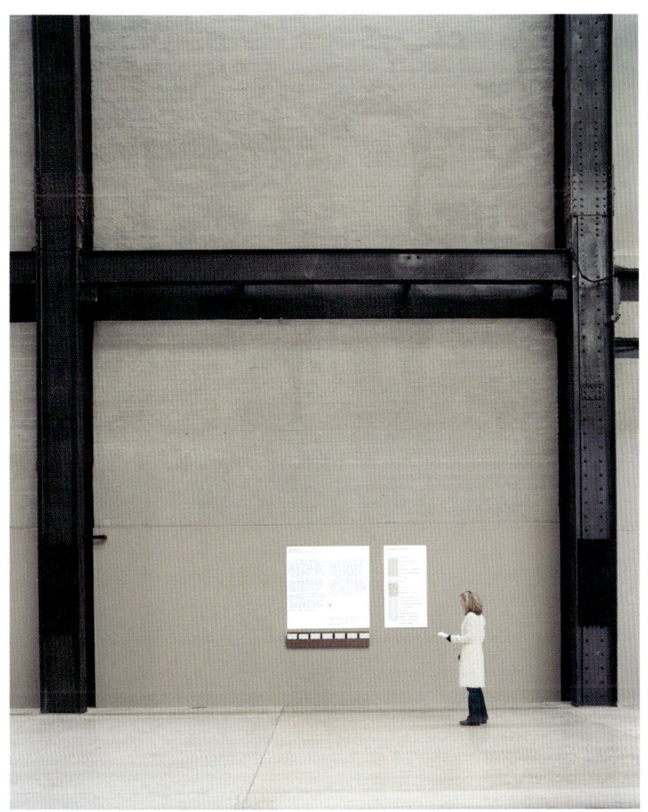

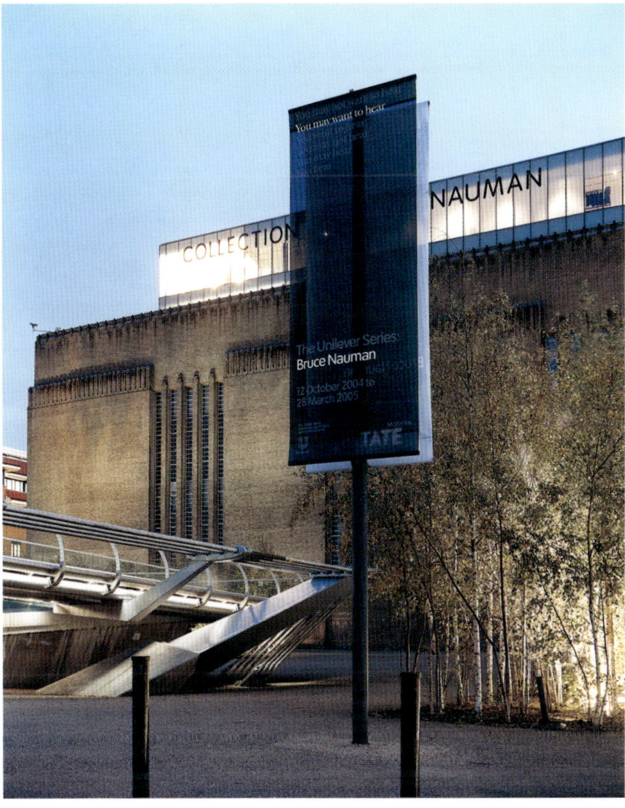
You may want to hear
COLLECTION
NAUMAN
The Unilever Series:
Bruce Nauman
12 October 2004 to
28 March 2005
TATE

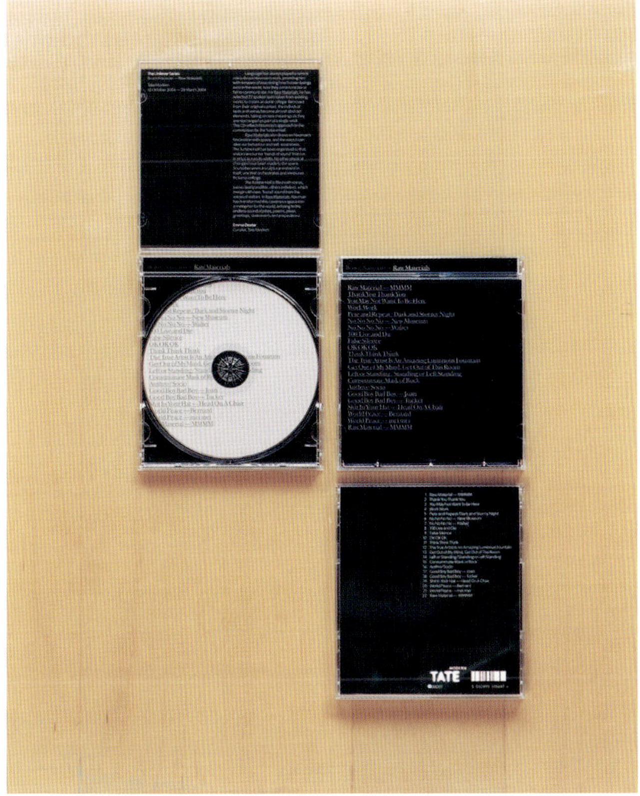

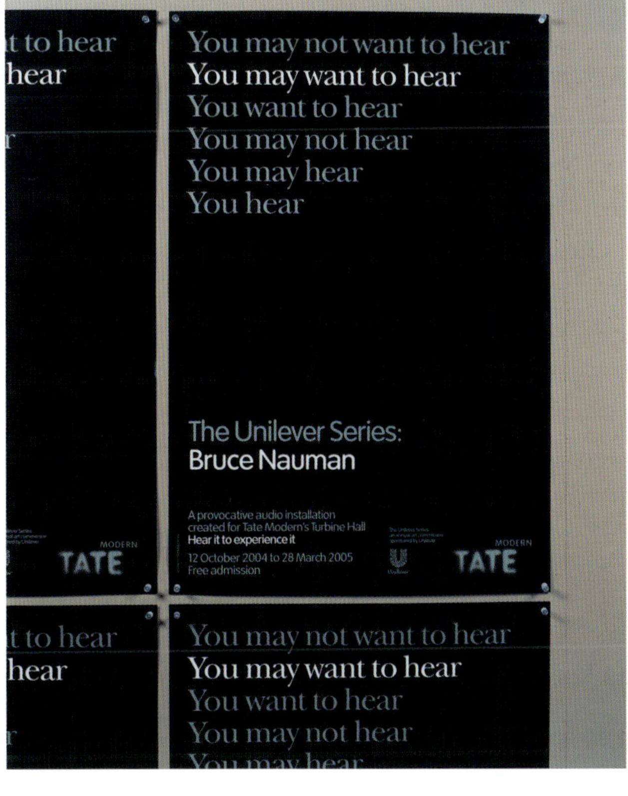
t to hear
hear
You may not want to hear
You may want to hear
You want to hear
You may not hear
You may hear
You hear
The Unilever Series:
Bruce Nauman
A provocative audio installation
created for Tate Modern's Turbine Hall
Hear it to experience it
12 October 2004 to 28 March 2005
Free admission
MODERN TATE
MODERN TATE
Unilever
t to hear
hear
You may not want to hear
You may want to hear
You want to hear
You may not hear
You may hear

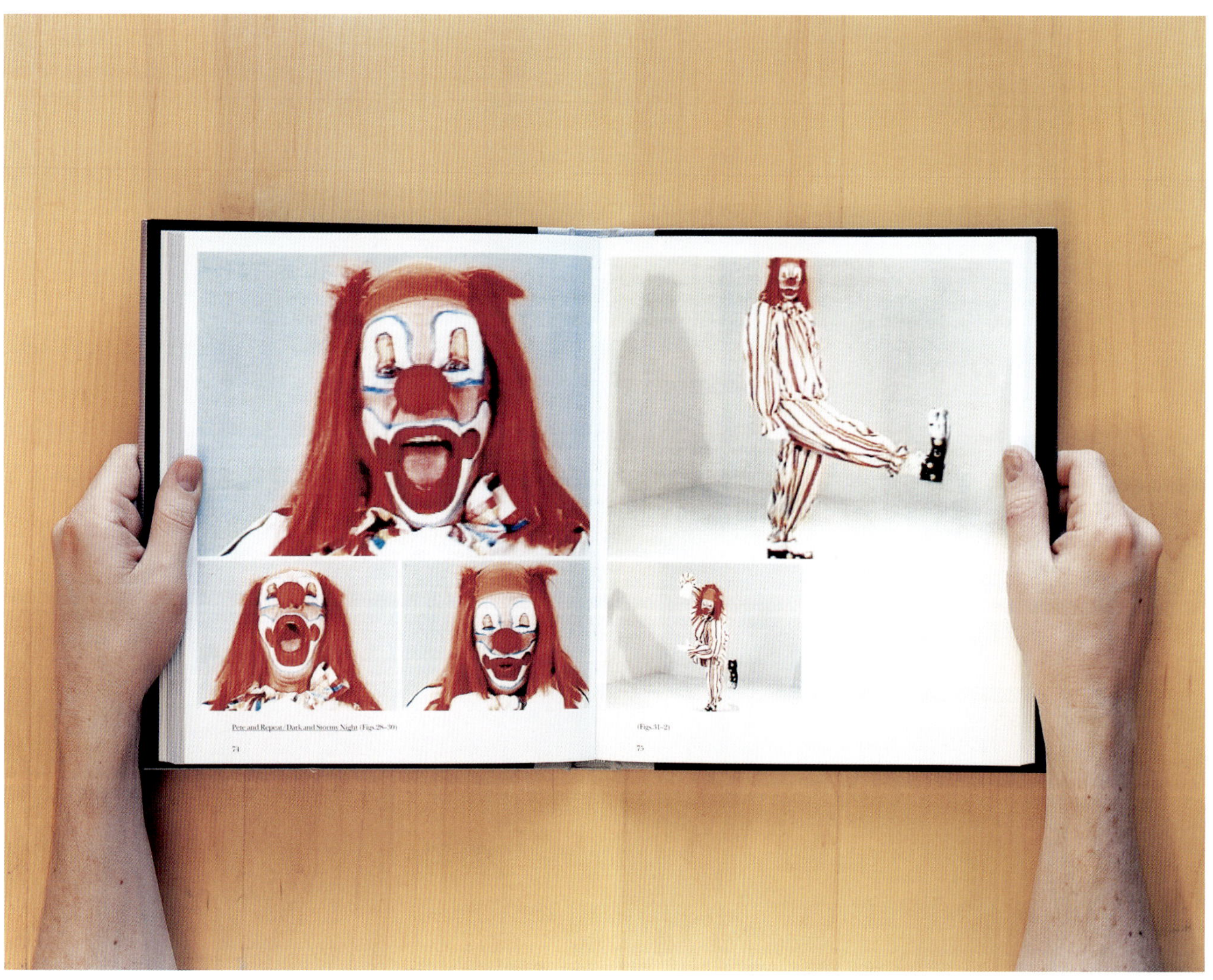
Pete and Repeat/Dark and Stormy Night (Figs.28–30)
74
(Figs.31–2)
75

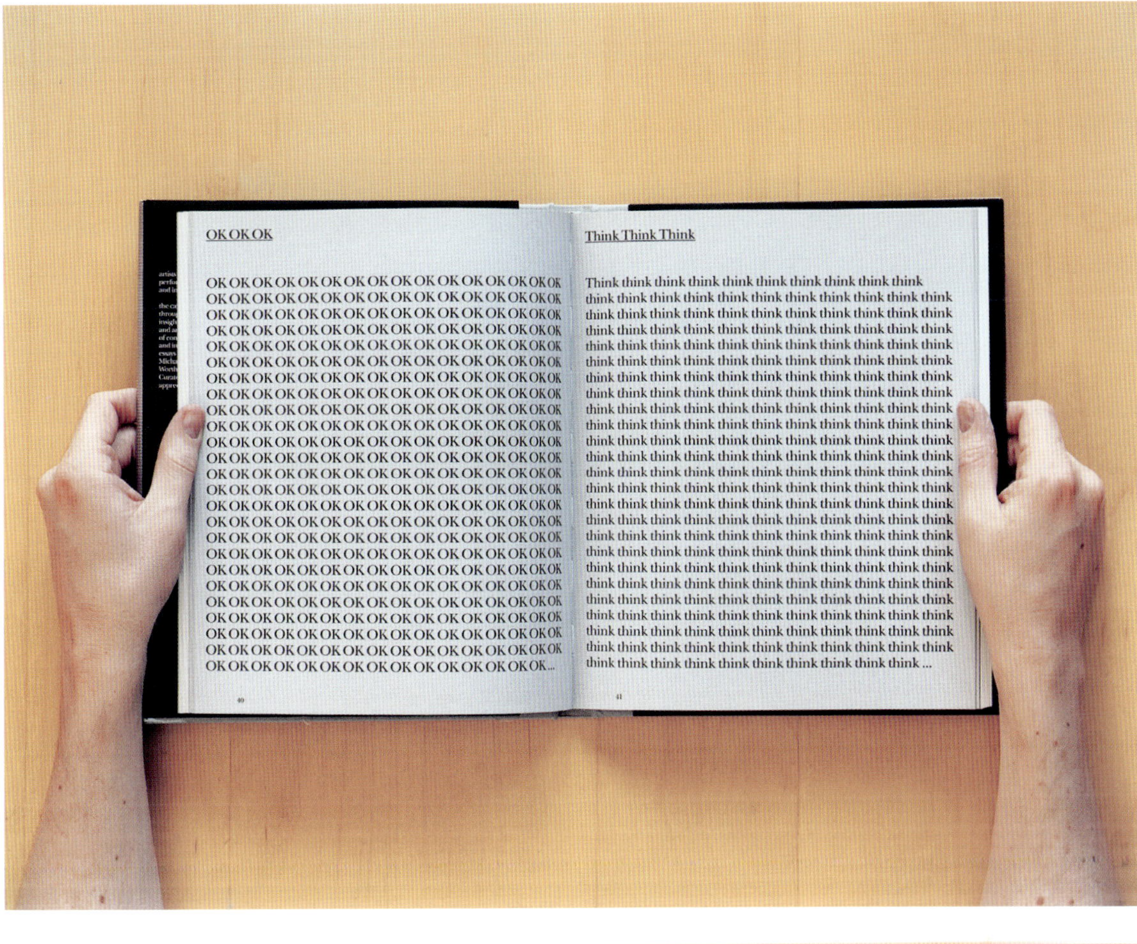

OK OK OK

OK OK OK OK OK OK OK OK OK OK OK OK OK OK OK OK
OK OK OK OK OK OK OK OK OK OK OK OK OK OK OK OK
OK OK OK OK OK OK OK OK OK OK OK OK OK OK OK OK
OK OK OK OK OK OK OK OK OK OK OK OK OK OK OK OK
OK OK OK OK OK OK OK OK OK OK OK OK OK OK OK OK
OK OK OK OK OK OK OK OK OK OK OK OK OK OK OK OK
OK OK OK OK OK OK OK OK OK OK OK OK OK OK OK OK
OK OK OK OK OK OK OK OK OK OK OK OK OK OK OK OK
OK OK OK OK OK OK OK OK OK OK OK OK OK OK OK OK
OK OK OK OK OK OK OK OK OK OK OK OK OK OK OK OK
OK OK OK OK OK OK OK OK OK OK OK OK OK OK OK OK
OK OK OK OK OK OK OK OK OK OK OK OK OK OK OK OK
OK OK OK OK OK OK OK OK OK OK OK OK OK OK OK OK
OK OK OK OK OK OK OK OK OK OK OK OK OK OK OK OK
OK OK OK OK OK OK OK OK OK OK OK OK OK OK OK OK
OK OK OK OK OK OK OK OK OK OK OK OK OK OK OK OK
OK OK OK OK OK OK OK OK OK OK OK OK OK OK OK OK
OK OK OK OK OK OK OK OK OK OK OK OK OK OK OK OK
OK OK OK OK OK OK OK OK OK OK OK OK OK OK OK OK
OK OK OK OK OK OK OK OK OK OK OK OK OK OK OK OK
OK OK OK OK OK OK OK OK OK OK OK OK OK OK OK OK
OK OK OK OK OK OK OK OK OK OK OK OK OK OK OK OK
OK OK OK OK OK OK OK OK OK OK OK OK OK OK OK OK
OK OK OK OK OK OK OK OK OK OK OK OK OK OK OK OK...

40

Think Think Think

Think think think think think think think think think think
think think think think think think think think think think think
think think think think think think think think think think think
think think think think think think think think think think think
think think think think think think think think think think think
think think think think think think think think think think think
think think think think think think think think think think think
think think think think think think think think think think think
think think think think think think think think think think think
think think think think think think think think think think think
think think think think think think think think think think think
think think think think think think think think think think think
think think think think think think think think think think think
think think think think think think think think think think think
think think think think think think think think think think think
think think think think think think think think think think think
think think think think think think think think think think think
think think think think think think think think think think think
think think think think think think think think think think think
think think think think think think think think think think think
think think think think think think think think think think think
think think think think think think think think think think think
think think think think think think think think think think think
think think think think think think think think think think think ...

41

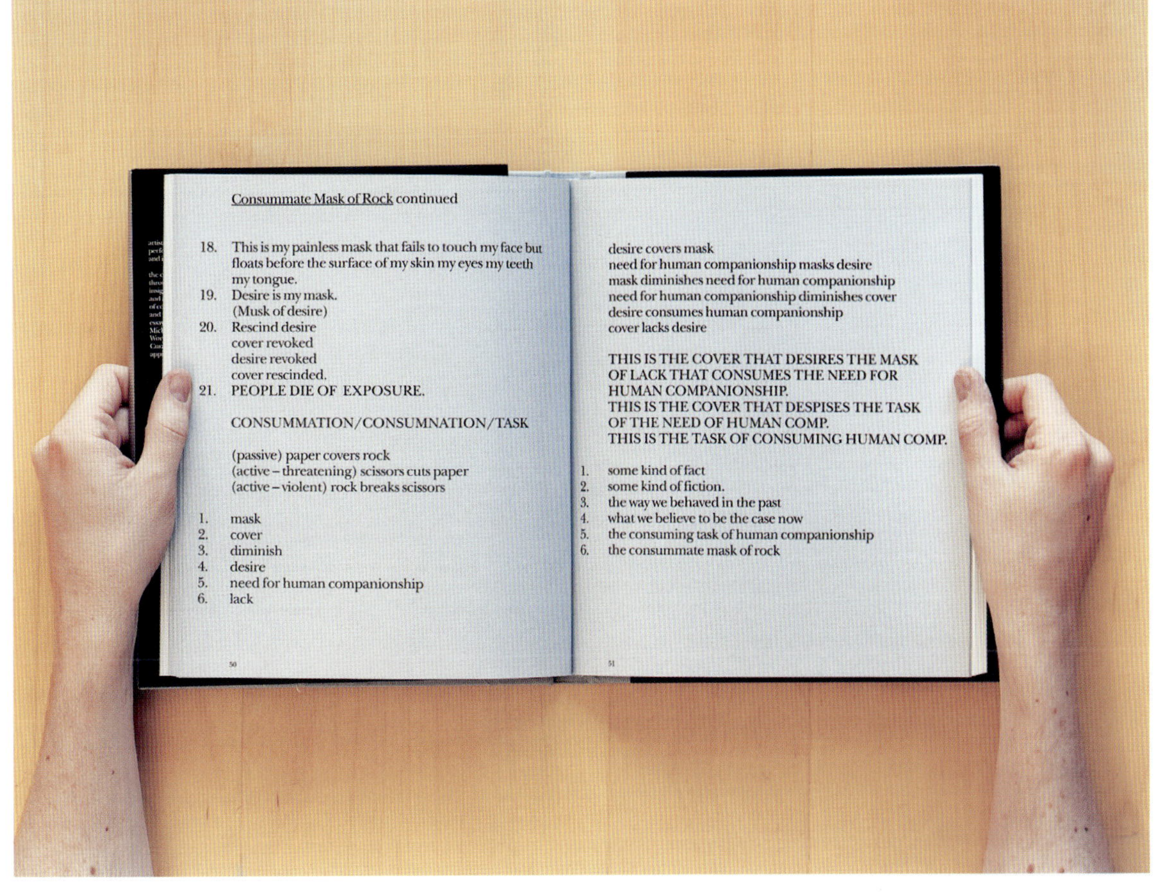

Consummate Mask of Rock continued

18. This is my painless mask that fails to touch my face but
     floats before the surface of my skin my eyes my teeth
     my tongue.
19. Desire is my mask.
     (Musk of desire)
20. Rescind desire
     cover revoked
     desire revoked.
     cover rescinded.
21. PEOPLE DIE OF EXPOSURE.

CONSUMMATION/CONSUMNATION/TASK

(passive) paper covers rock
(active – threatening) scissors cuts paper
(active – violent) rock breaks scissors

1. mask
2. cover
3. diminish
4. desire
5. need for human companionship
6. lack

50

desire covers mask
need for human companionship masks desire
mask diminishes need for human companionship
need for human companionship diminishes cover
desire consumes human companionship
cover lacks desire

THIS IS THE COVER THAT DESIRES THE MASK
OF LACK THAT CONSUMES THE NEED FOR
HUMAN COMPANIONSHIP.
THIS IS THE COVER THAT DESPISES THE TASK
OF THE NEED OF HUMAN COMP.
THIS IS THE TASK OF CONSUMING HUMAN COMP.

1. some kind of fact
2. some kind of fiction.
3. the way we behaved in the past
4. what we believe to be the case now
5. the consuming task of human companionship
6. the consummate mask of rock

51

All art direction/
photography/
typography made in Build.

DESIGNBYBUILD.COM FOR,

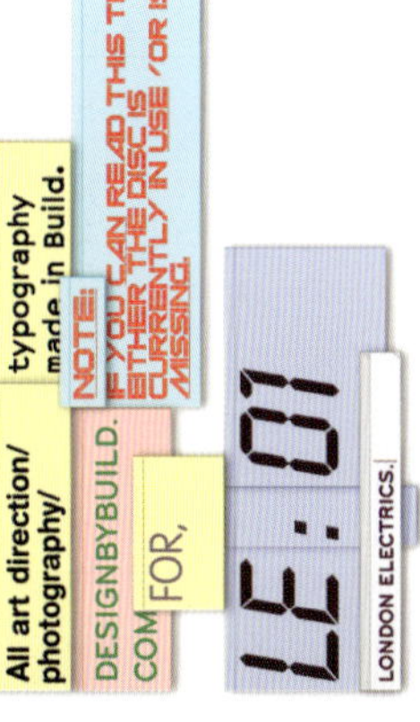

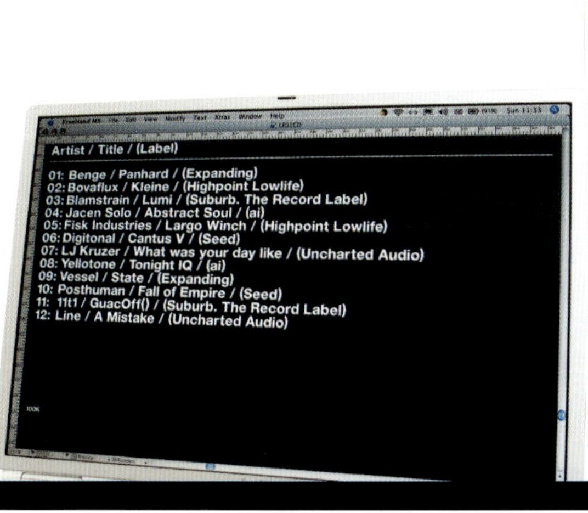

Tracks 01-09 P 2005 Expanding Records. C 2005 Expanding Records. Tracks 02-05 P 2005 Highpoint Lowlife Records. C 2005 Highpoint Lowlife Records. Tracks 03-11 P 2005 Suburb The Record Label. C 2005 Suburb The Record Label. Tracks 06-10 P 2005 Seed Records. C 2005 Seed records. Tracks 07-12 P 2005 Uncharted Audio. C 2005 Uncharted Audio. Tracks 04-08 P 2005 Ai Records. C 2005 Ai Records.

All tracks: P 2005 London Electrics. C 2005 London Electrics. LE01CD. All rights of the producers and of the owner of the recorded work reserved. Unauthorised copying, public performance, broadcasting, hiring or rental of this recording prohibited. www.londonelectrics.co.uk

disc
COMPACT   LOGO
DIGITAL AUDIO

0 66601 71198 23

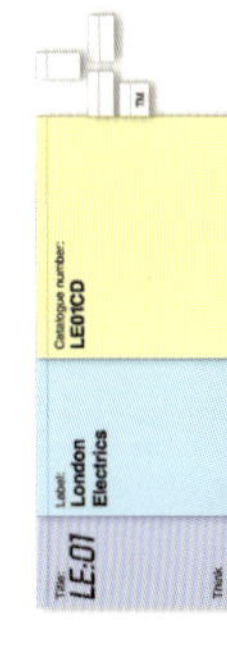

Build

London, UK

Title: LE:01
Type of work: Music packaging
Client: London Electrics
Design: ad, d// Michael C. Place
Year: 2005

This piece is a non vector artwork cover, in which the concept of 'Photography as Typography' and 'Screenshots as Typography' is used. It is made of consumer electrical items, household items and office hardware.

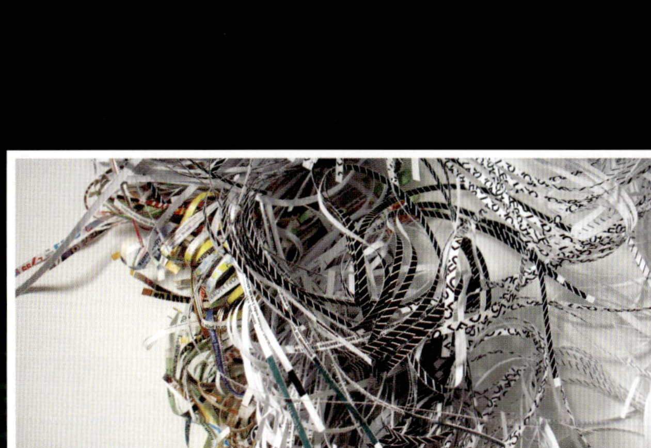

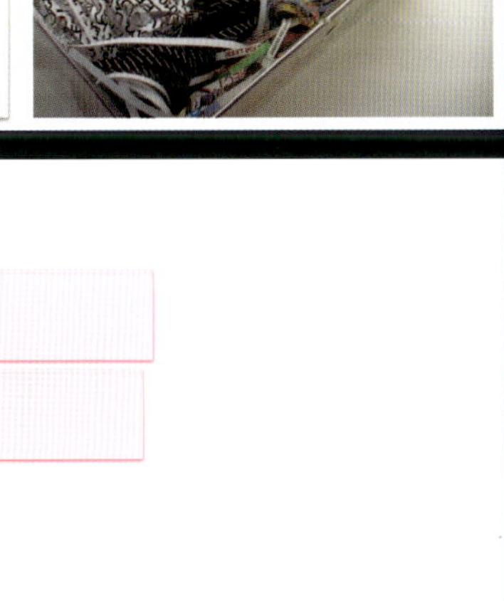

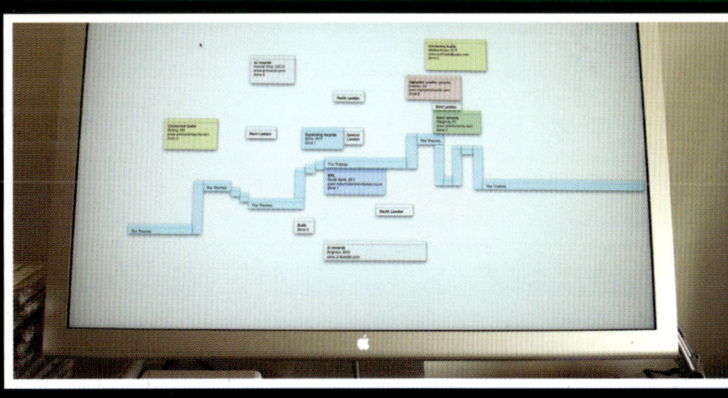

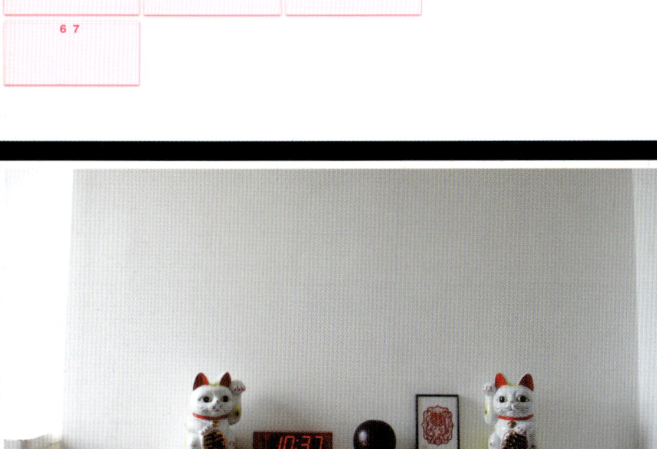

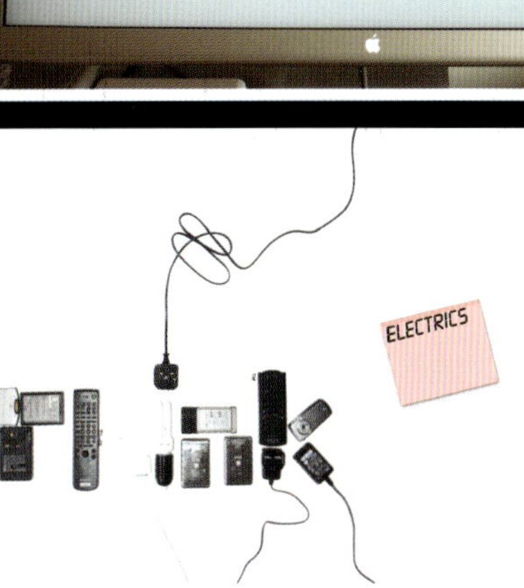

Traffic

London, UK

Title: EMI Autumn Invite
Type of work: Invitation
Client: EMI Records
Design: ad// Jeremy Plum d// Barry Smith
Year: 2005

The EMI Autumn presentation showcases the artists on all the individual labels within EMI. They needed a design that has an autumnal feel, in which there were no limits to production although the design had to fit within a DL sized envelope. Avoiding the clichés of falling leaves, the designer developed a typographic response that was based around the concentric circles of wood grain. To give the design its autumnal feel, the designer chose a 560 gsm Claret coloured stock and had the design foil blocked in copper foil onto both the front and the reverse of the invite. The finished product has a very luxurious feel that reflects the prestige of the EMI Company.

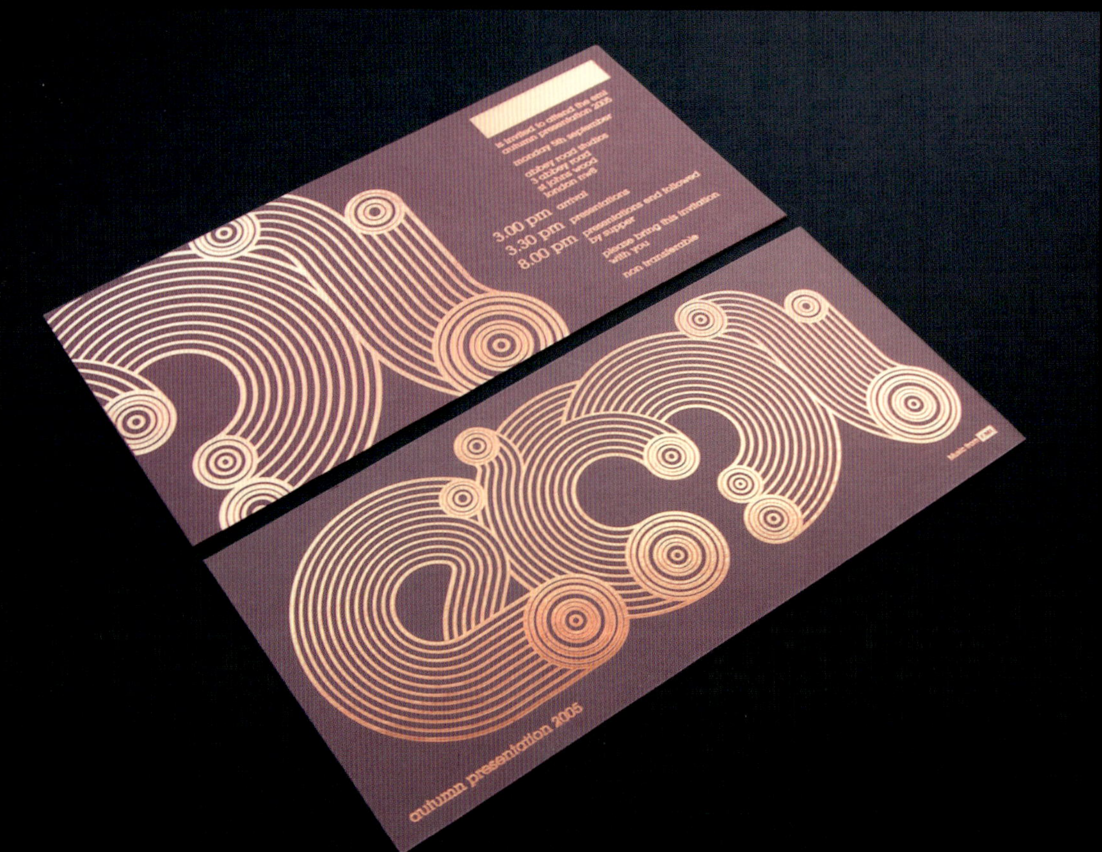

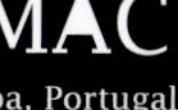

RMAC

Lisboa, Portugal

Title: Lux – 6th Anniversary Invitation
Type of work: Invitation
Client: Lux Frágil
Design: ad// Ricardo Mealha, Ana Cunha
d// Ana Cunha
Year: 2004

An invitation commemorating the 6th anniversary was designed for the Lux/Fragil, the hippest nightclub in Portugal situated in the port zone of Lisbon, overlooking the Tagus River (River Tejo). The concept is focused on both the color and shape which reminds of Japanese Origami and a pop-up map.

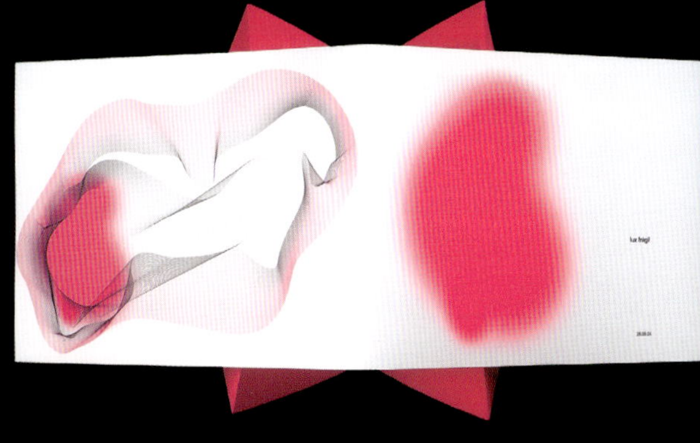

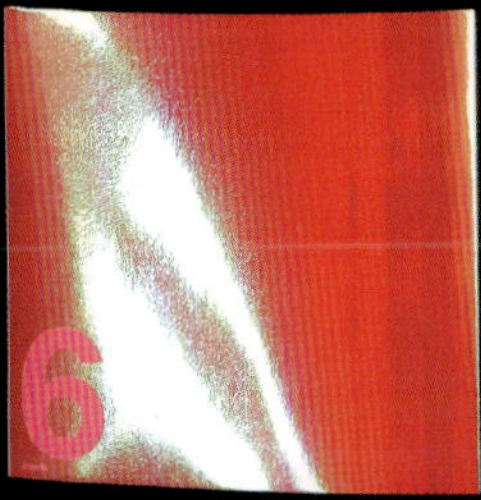

Design People Studio

Madrid, Spain

Title: Winter is Red Red
Type of work: Self promotional items
Client: Design People Studio
Design: ad, d// Maria Monferrer, Alejandro Cañada
Year: 2005

The set of self promotional items includes microsite, cards, business card, poster, letterhead, envelope, t-shirts and pins. A theme and the same colour scheme is used throughout different items on different materials.

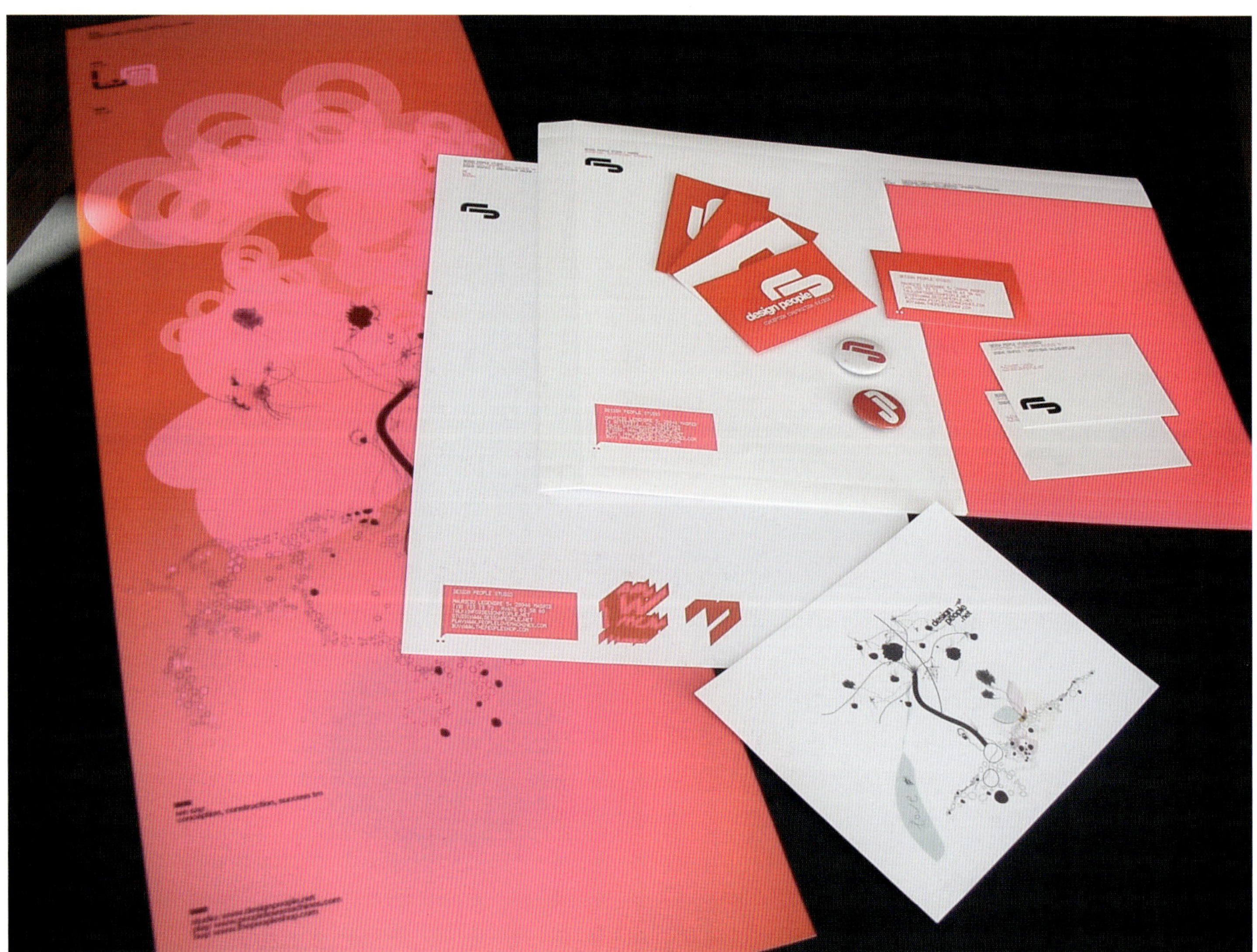

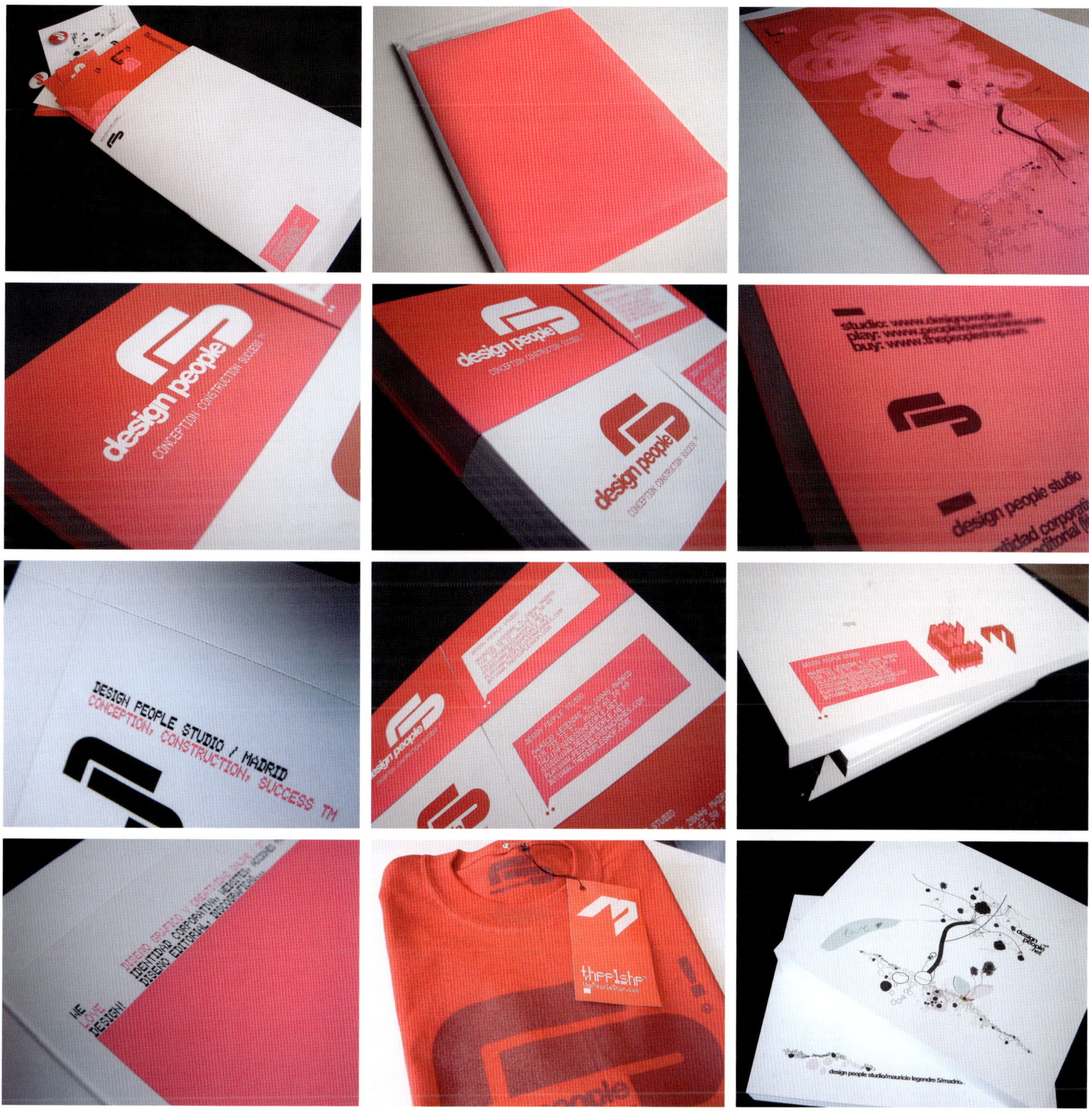

Design People Studio

Madrid, Spain

Title: -
Type of work: Packaging
Client: The People Shop
Design: ad, d// Maria Monferrer, Alejandro Cañada
Year: 2005

A set of self promotional items includes clothes tags, stickers and delivery boxes were designed for The People Shop. This is a simple and neat design. Similar colour scheme from pink to red to brown is used throughout different items on different materials.

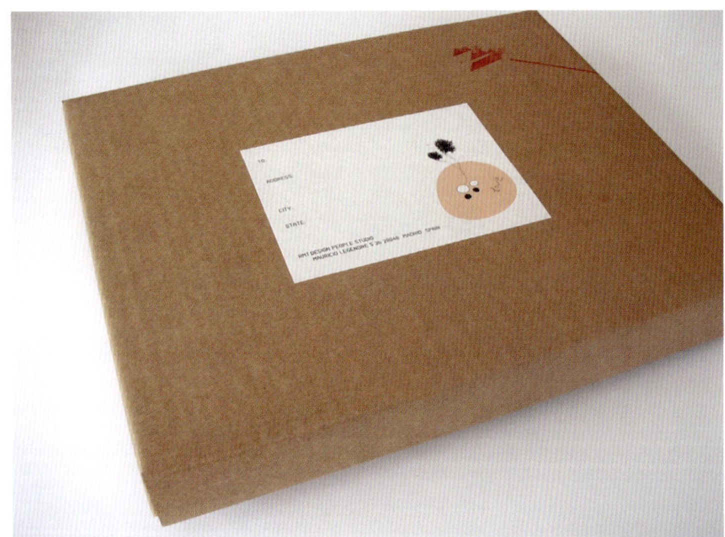

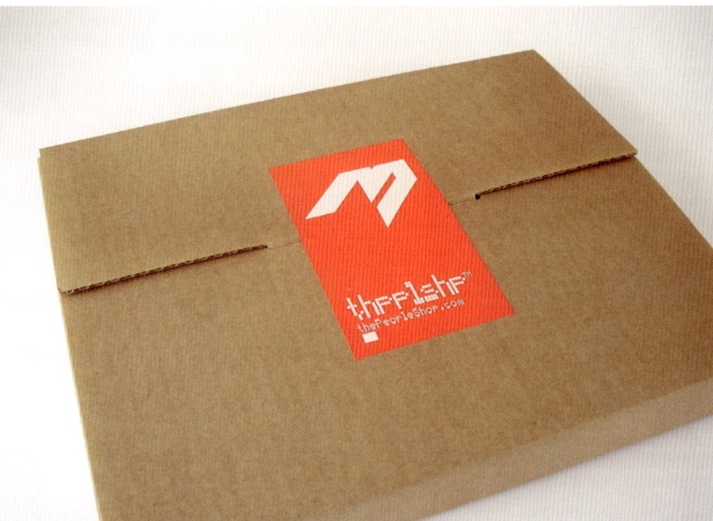

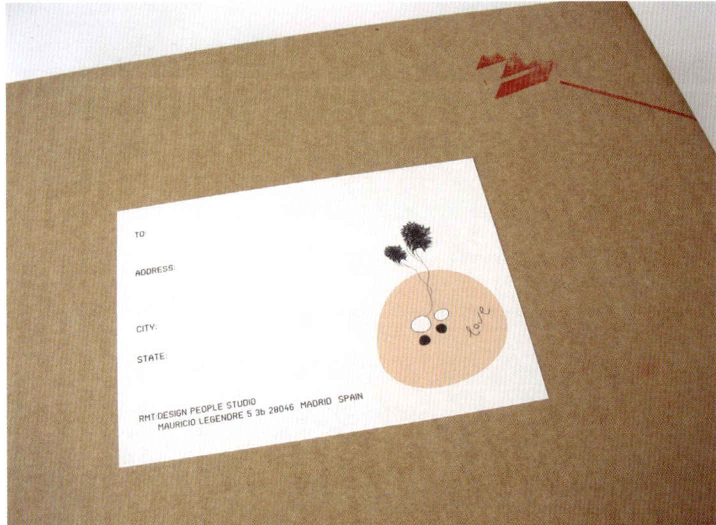

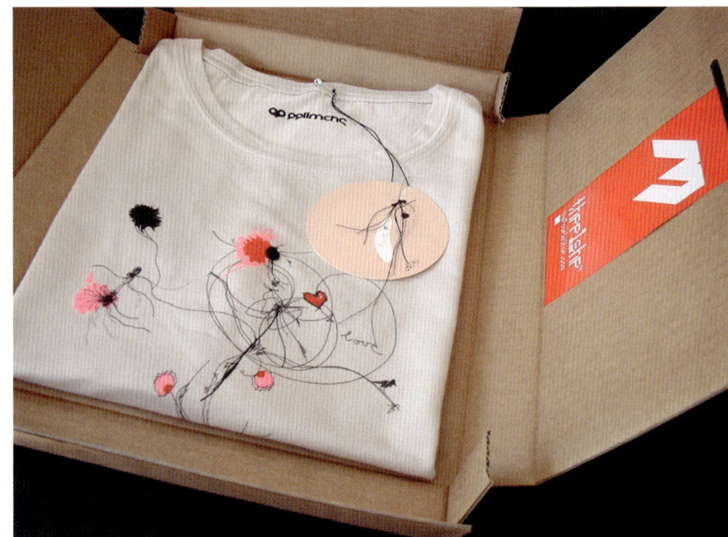

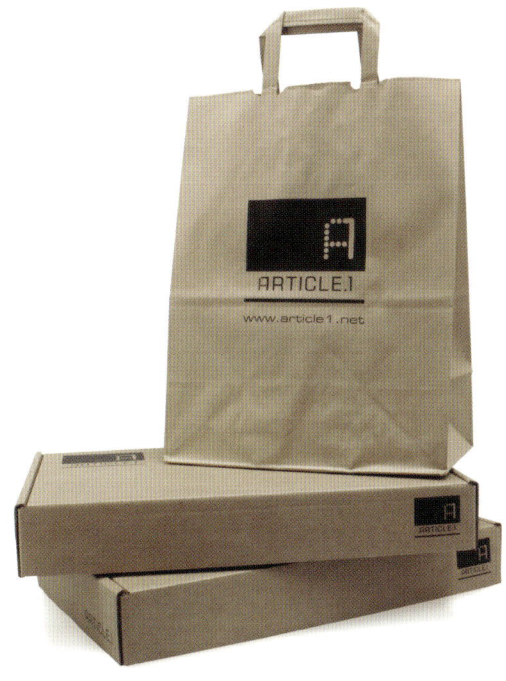

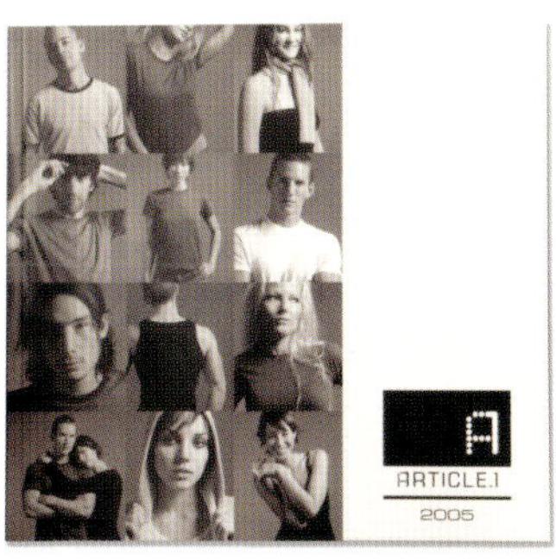

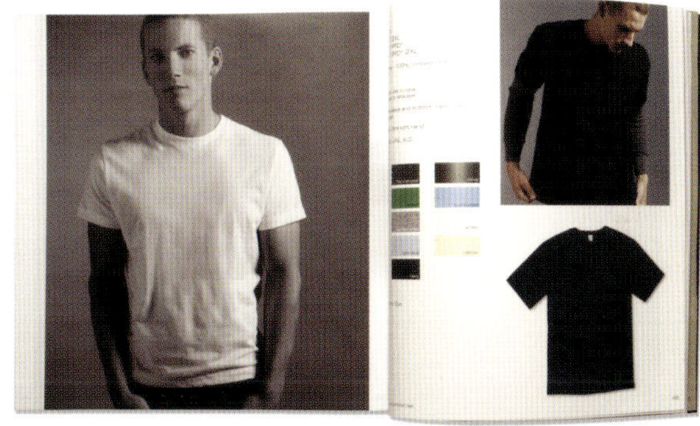

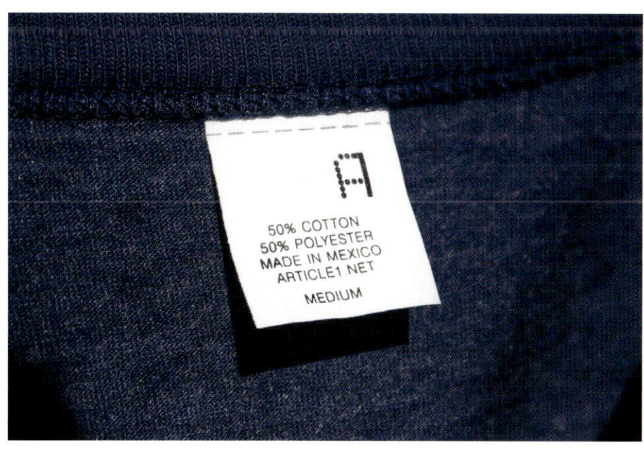

J3 Productions

California, USA

Title: Article 1
Type of work: Corporate identity, collateral
Client: Article 1
Design: ad// Jonathan Lo
Year: 2005

The concept behind all the pieces for Article.1, that produces high end stock apparel, was all about the concept of 'basics'. The color story has been stripped down to basic black/white, natural or recycled papers, and sepia toned photography. All design elements were intentionally 'under designed' to convey pure functionality, and to enhance the idea that Article.1's products can act as a 'blank canvas'.

Stiletto

New York, USA

Title: As Four
Type of work: Label, tag, poster, invitation, packaging
Client: As Four
Design: ad, d// Stiletto
Year: 2004-05

A set of items designed for the design clothing label 'As Four', in which only black and white is used to create a consistent look and feel. Rubber band is used for the label as well as on the perfume package. A decorative floral shape is also used throughout the identity.

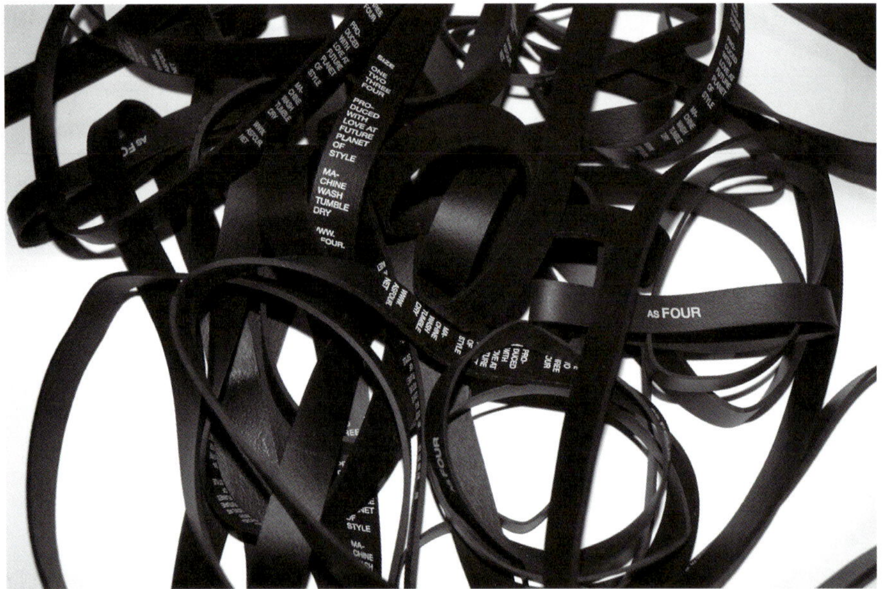

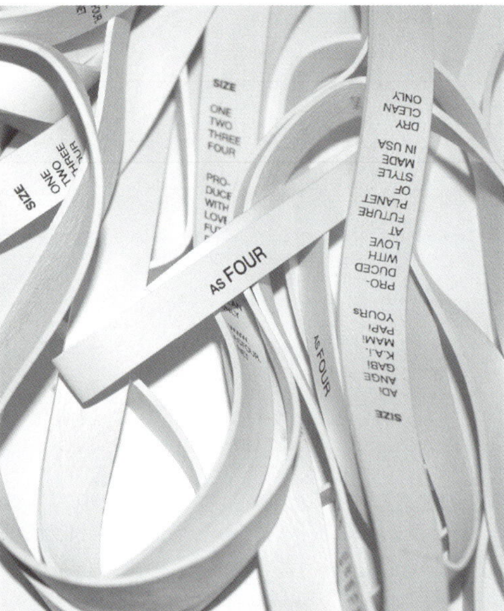

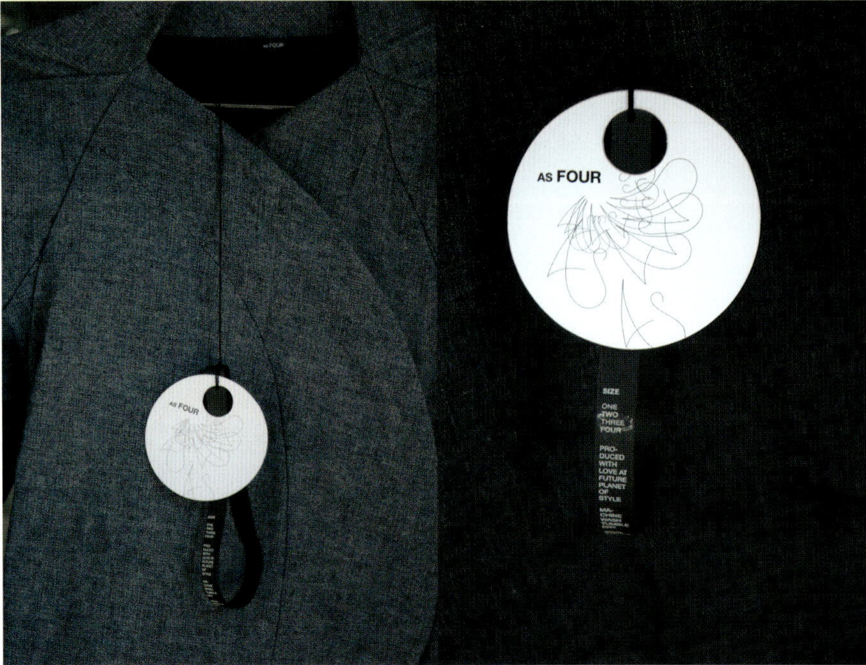

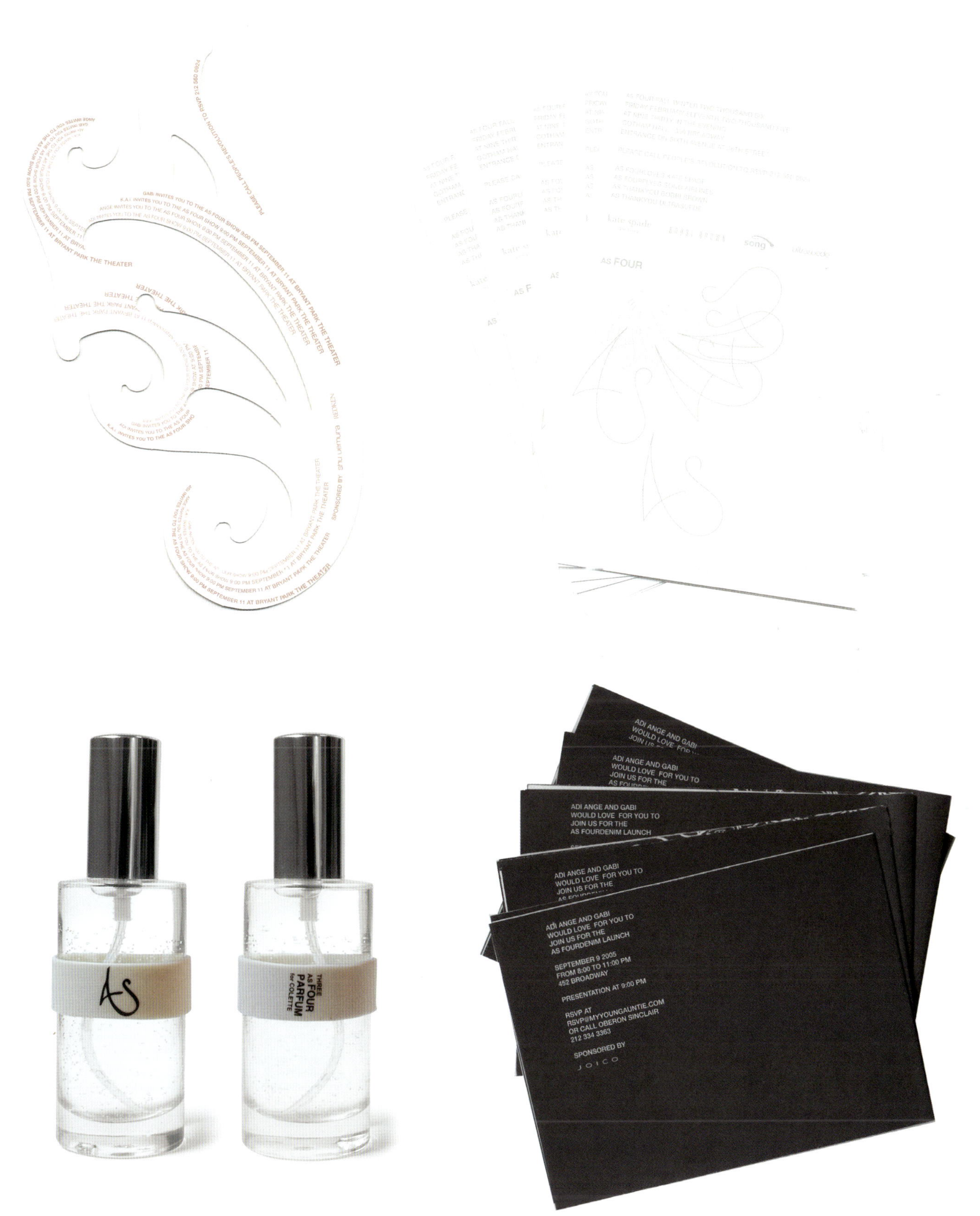
ADI ANGE AND GABI
WOULD LOVE FOR YOU TO
JOIN US FOR THE
AS FOURDENIM LAUNCH

SEPTEMBER 9 2005
FROM 8:00 TO 11:00 PM
452 BROADWAY

PRESENTATION AT 9:00 PM

RSVP AT
RSVP@MYYOUNGAUNTIE.COM
OR CALL OBERON SINCLAIR
212 334 3363

SPONSORED BY
JOICO

THREE
AS FOUR
PARFUM
for COLETTE

AS

Airside

London, UK

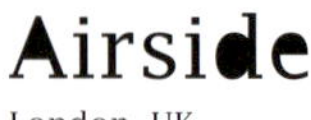

Title: Crafts Council Knit2Together Exhibition
Type of work: Exhibition, promotional materials
Client: The Crafts Council, London
Design: ad, d// Airside
Year: 2005

This piece was designed to negate the normal stark space in exhibition and stand out from the dark walls. The furniture in the show is made purposely simple to make no distraction to any exhibit, no matter to accentuate form and scale or to rest. However, to continue the theme of the show, the plinths is made interlocked and akin to knitted yarn thereby. The graphics for the marketing material is set to convey the theme of the exhibition, so a 'knitted' poster is created. ALso, to have the same tune of the exhibition, the graphics on the poster are modern and abstract, which is a contrast to the idea that knitting is a traditional and homely craft.

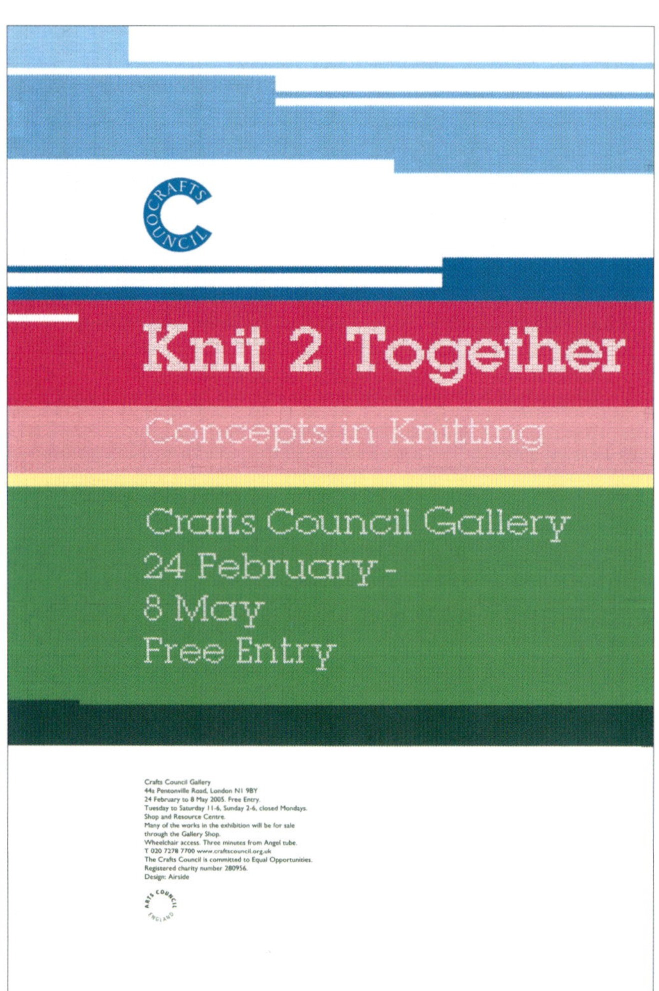

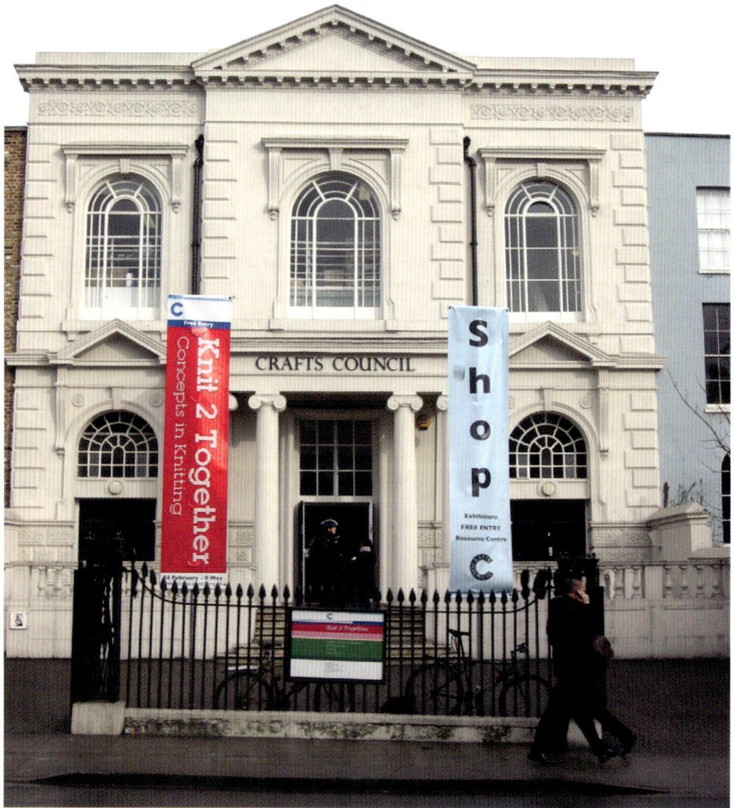

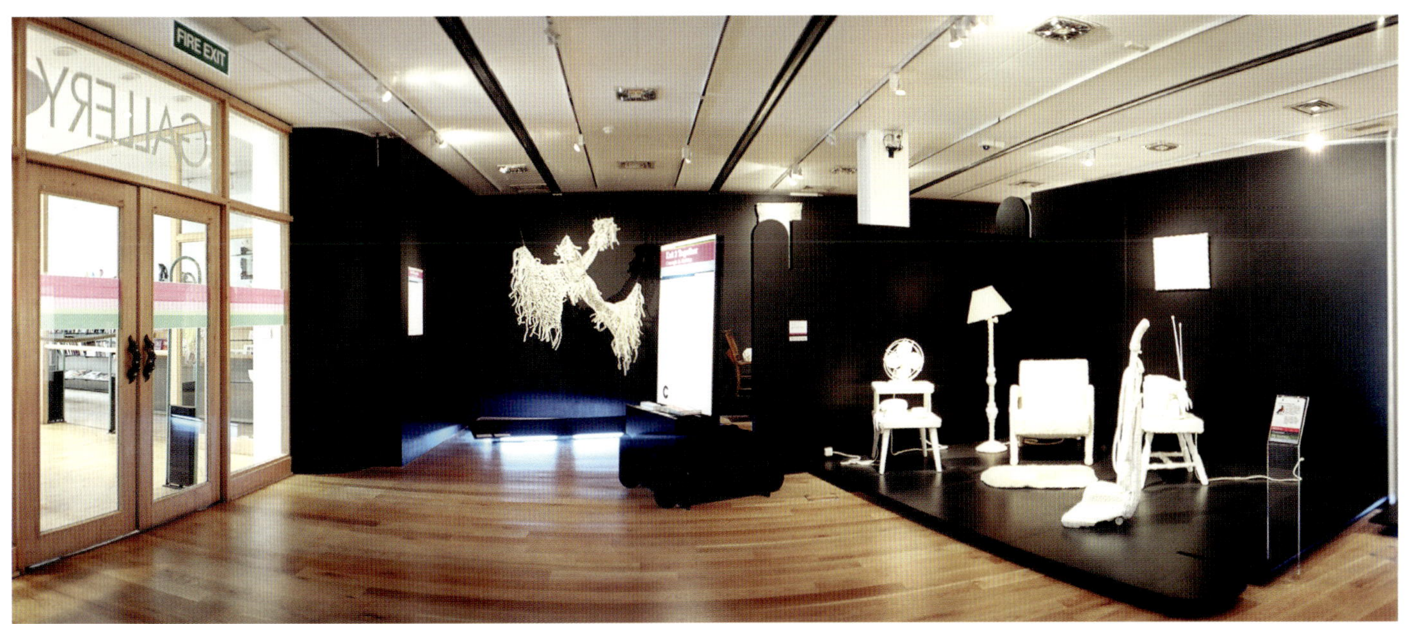

FIRE EXIT
GALLERY

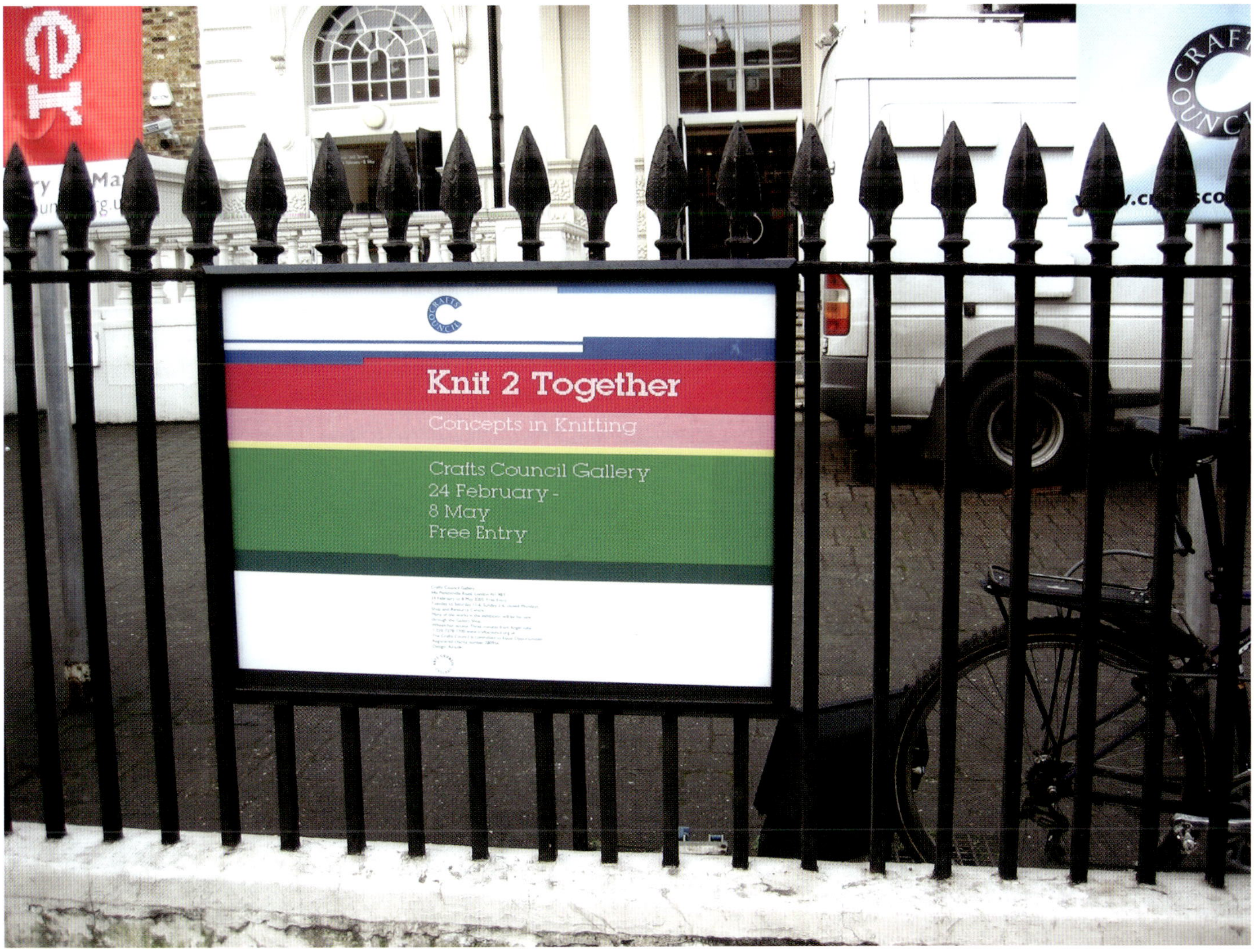

Knit 2 Together
Concepts in Knitting
Crafts Council Gallery
24 February –
8 May
Free Entry

Stiletto

New York, USA

Title: Rick's Picks
Type of work: Identity, promotional items
Client: Rick's Picks
Design: ad, d// Stiletto
Year: 2005

An identity created for a food brand that is carried through the food packaging, labels, promotional items such as stickers, cards, T-shirts and client's web site.

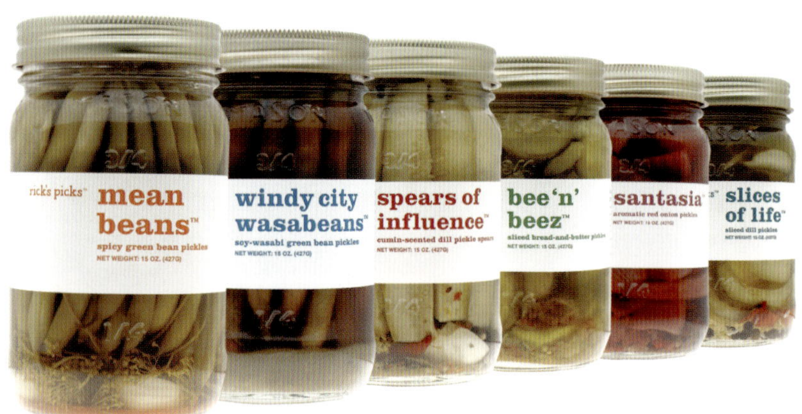

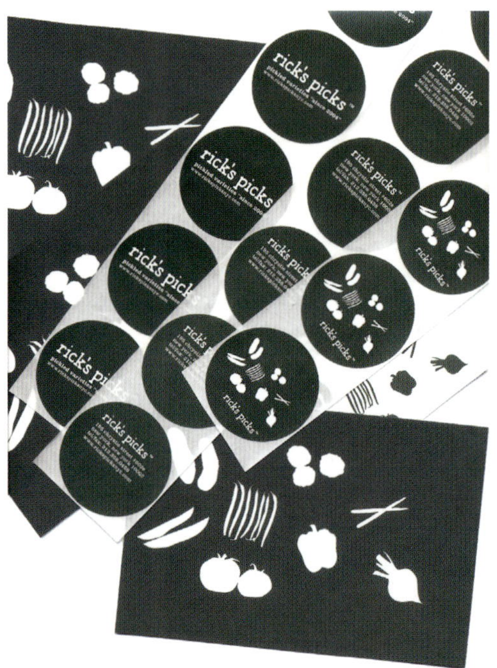

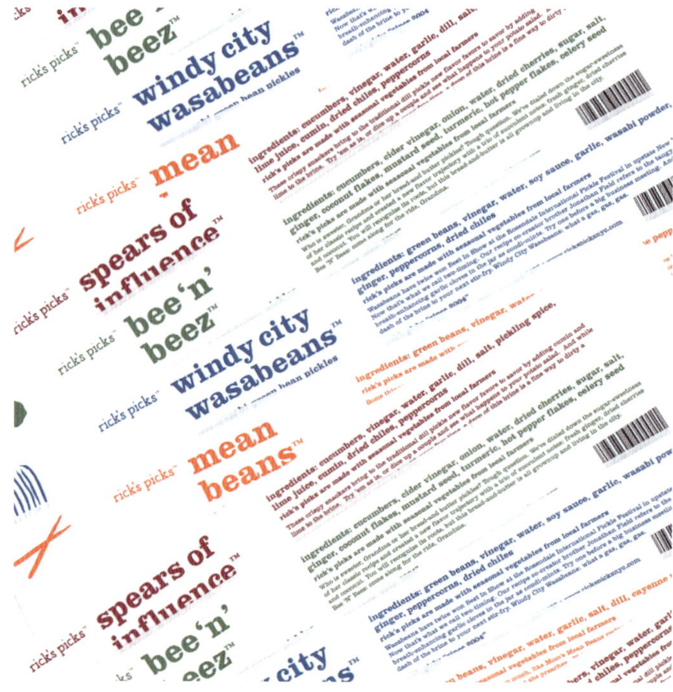

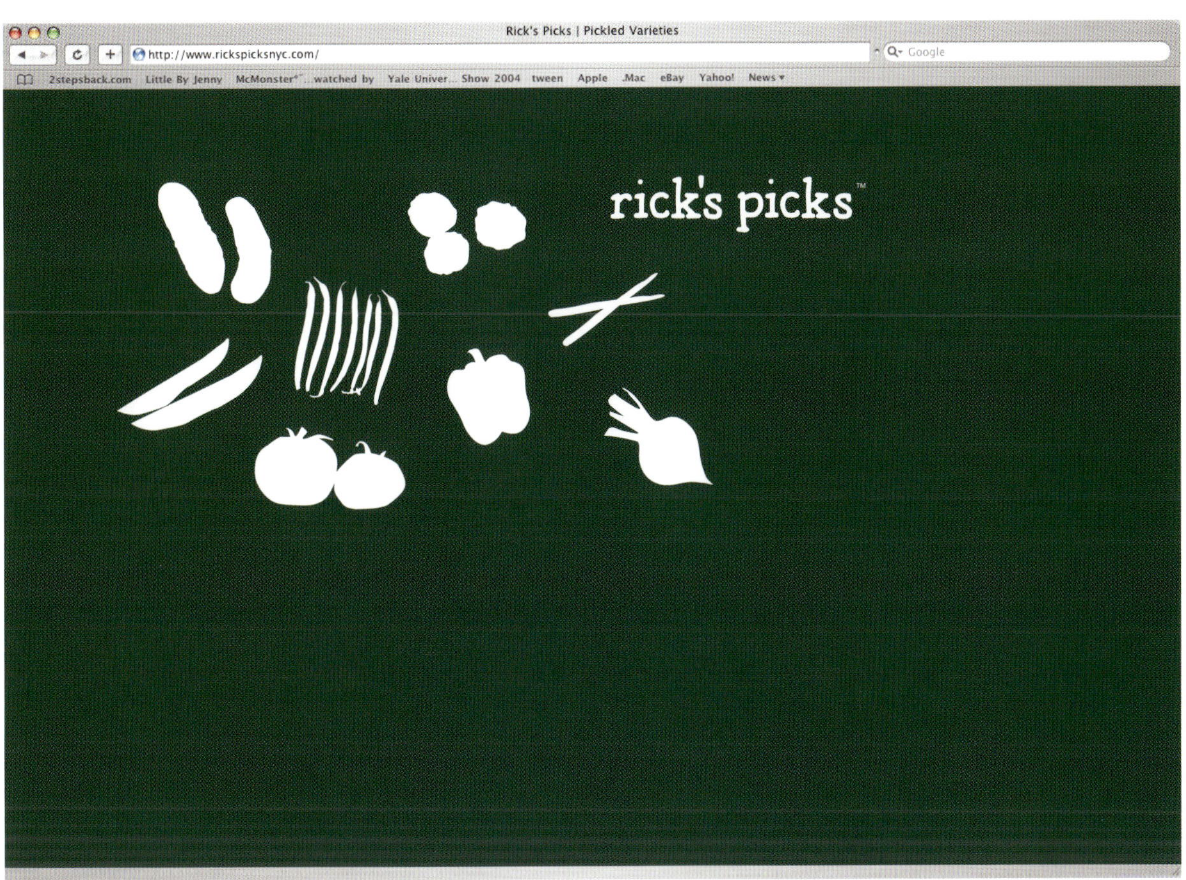

Rick's Picks | Pickled Varieties
http://www.rickspicksnyc.com/
2stepsback.com   Little By Jenny   McMonster*   ...watched by   Yale Univer...   Show 2004   tween   Apple   .Mac   eBay   Yahoo!   News
rick's picks™

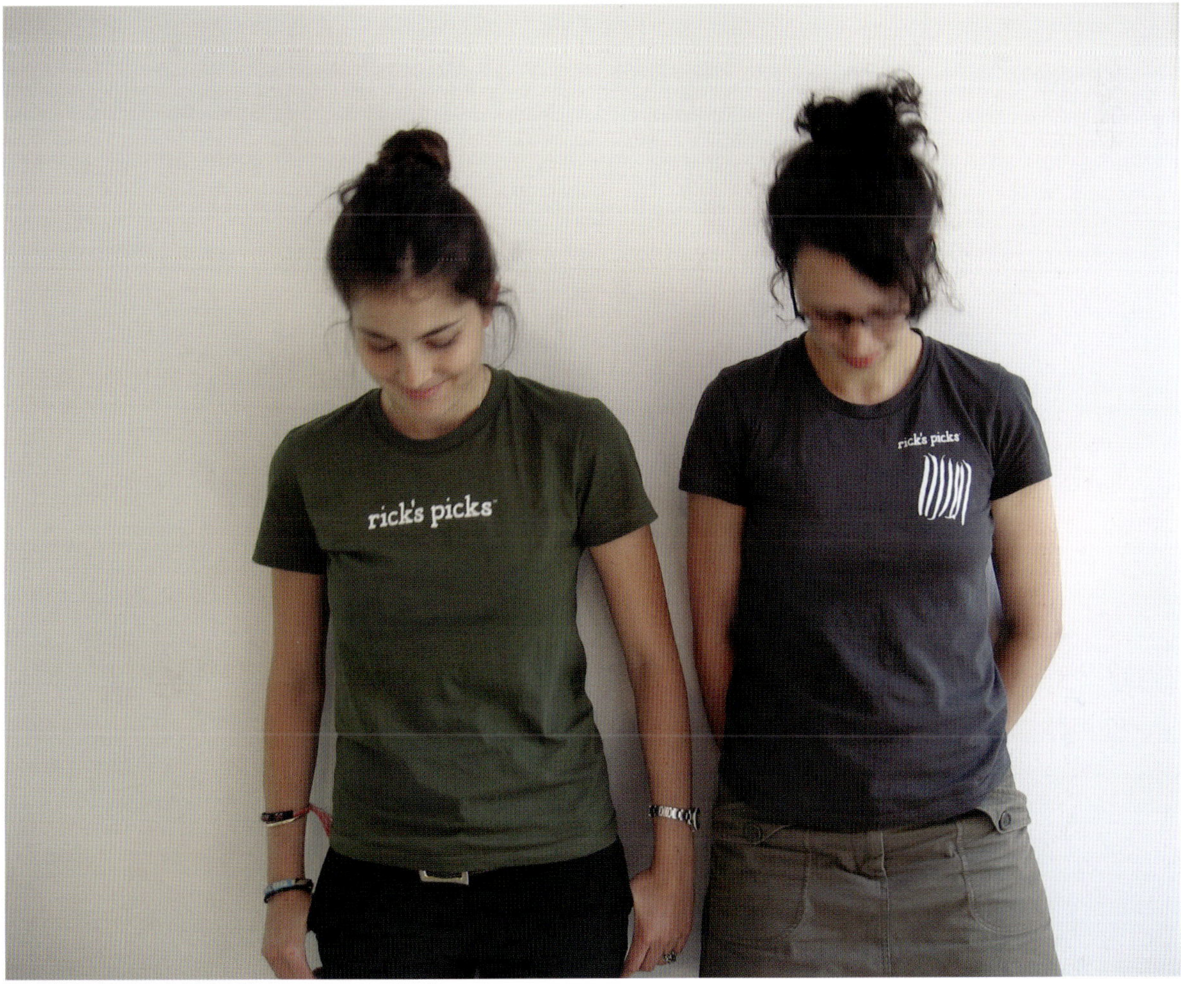

rick's picks™
rick's picks

Trafik

France

Title: Le Voxx
Type of work: Visual identity
Client: Le Voxx
Designers: Trafik
Year: 2003-04

The letter 'V' in the client's name 'Le Voxx' is used as the main idea of this visual identity. An arrow-liked icon is created thereby and it is now used on different items and materials such as table cloth, window blind and doors.

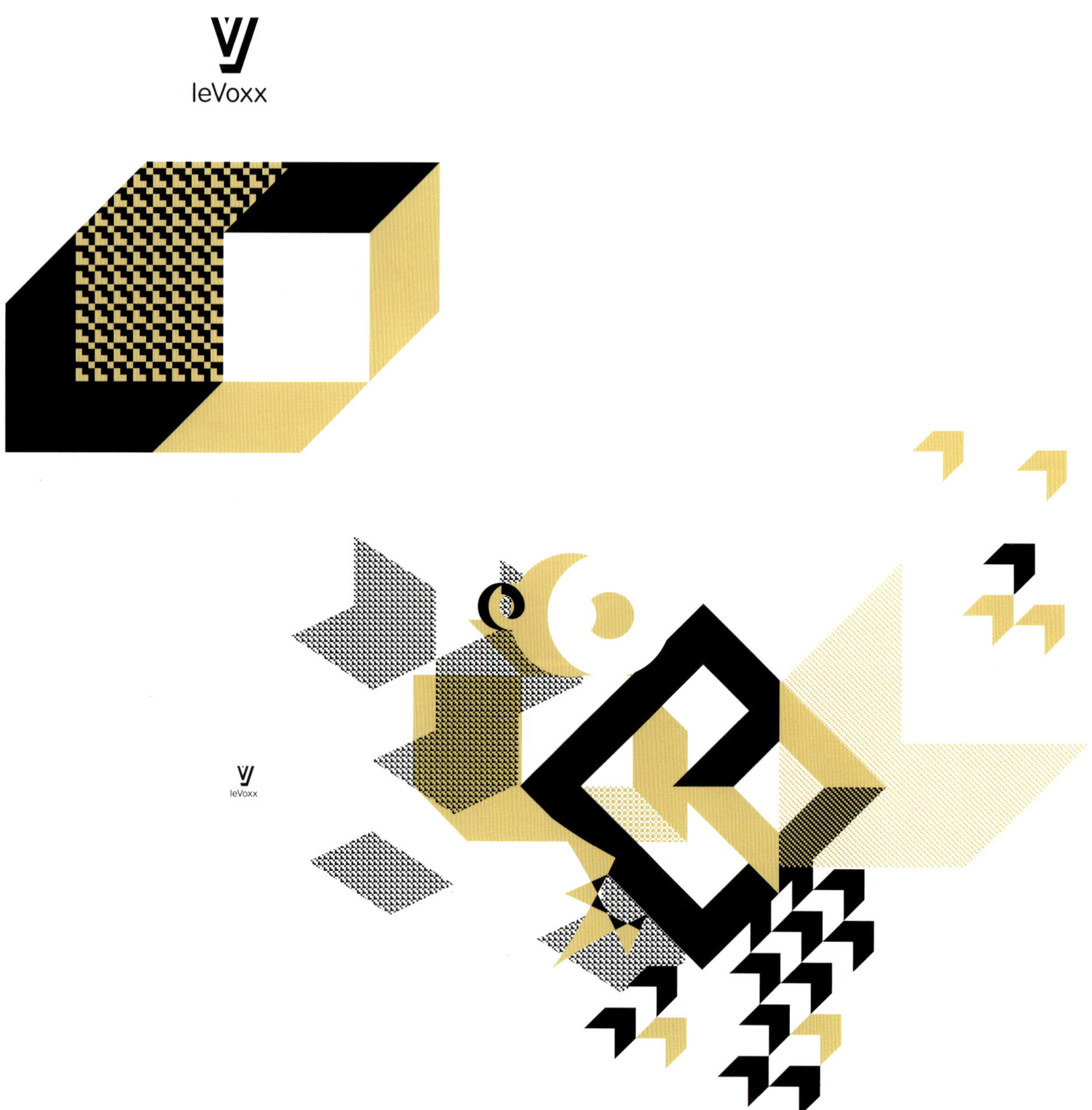

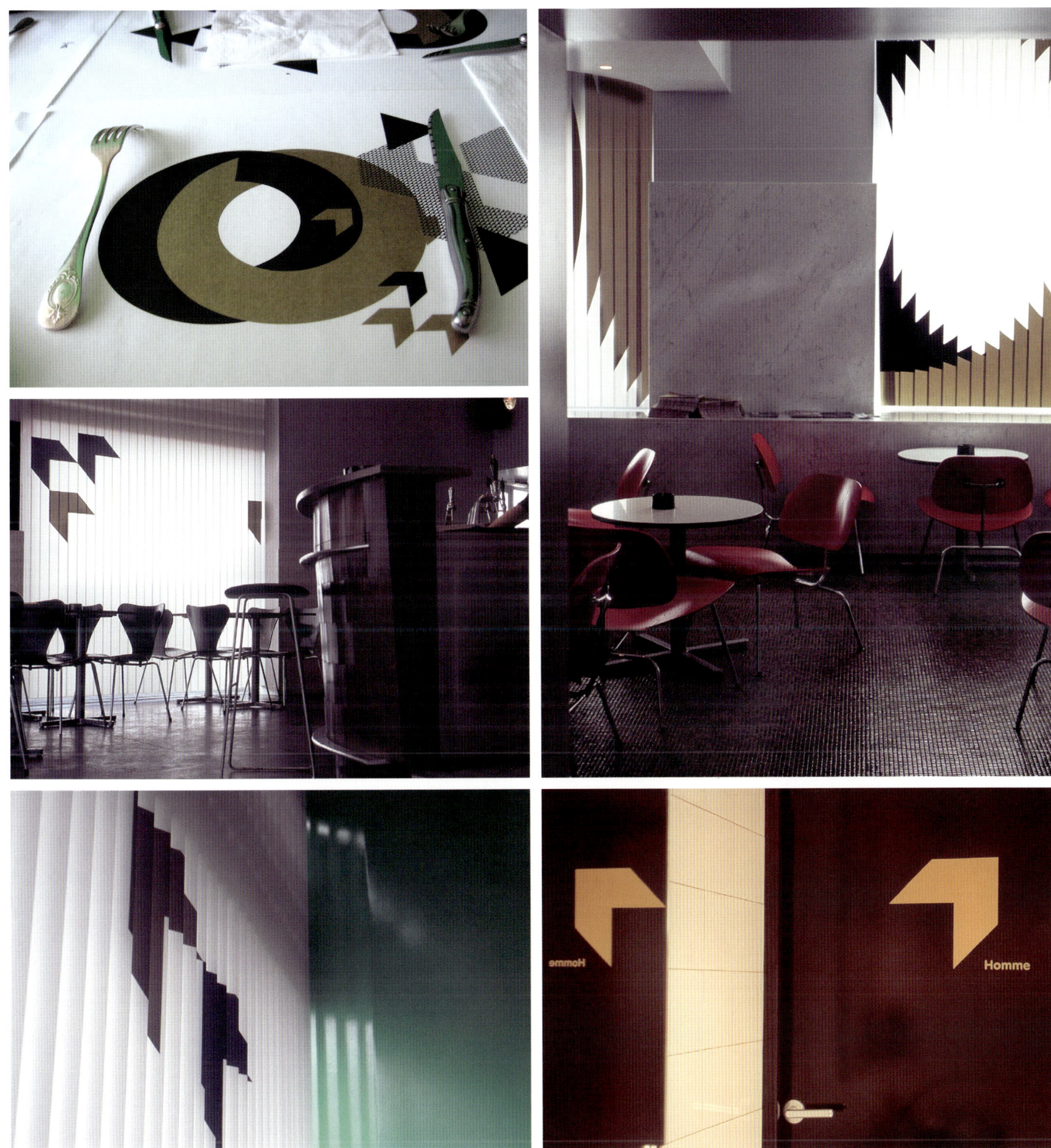

Homme
Homme

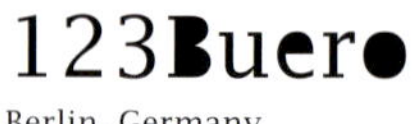 123Buero

Berlin, Germany

Title: 1.// 123naiv 2.// 123sweater
Type of work: 1.// Type design 2.// Sweater design
Client: Selfinitiated Project
Design: ad, d// Timo Gaessner
Year: 2005

1.// 123naiv is a grotesk rounded with script elements in four weights. 2.// 123sweater is a presentation for the two typedesigns: 123naiv and 123queen. Both sweaters are in two colours all over silk screen prints. They were made in an edition of 20 pieces.

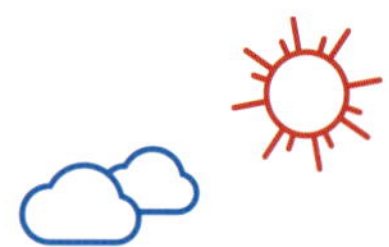

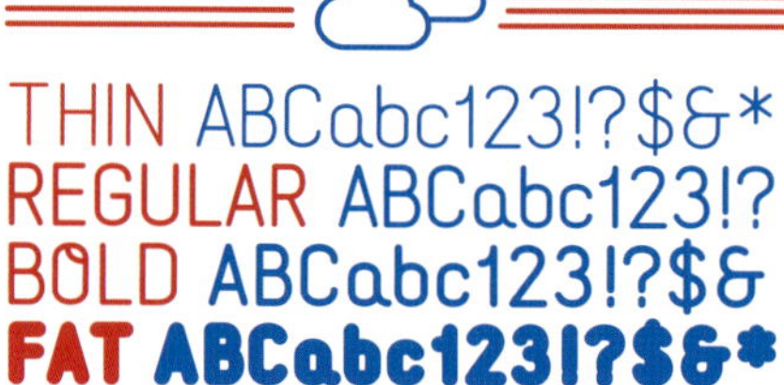

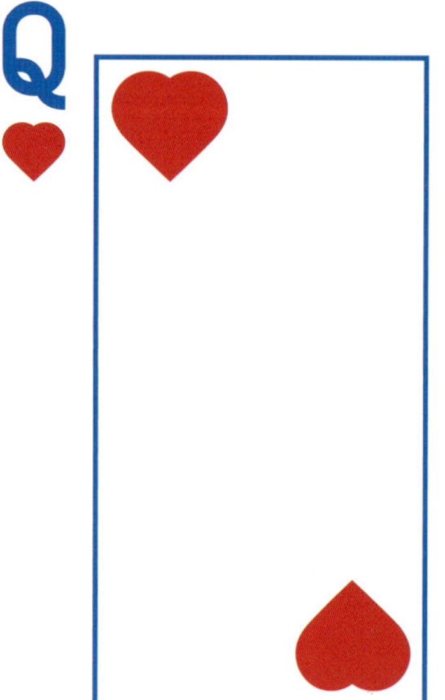

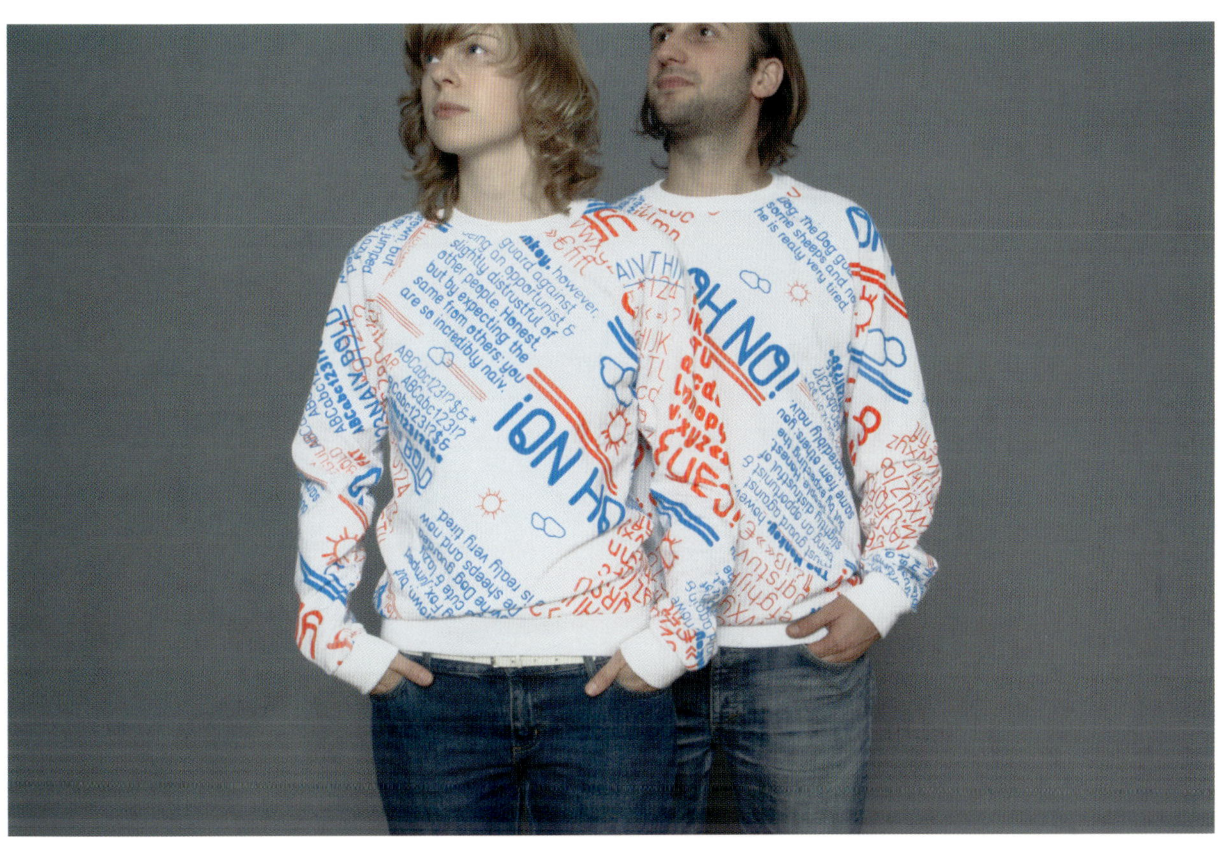

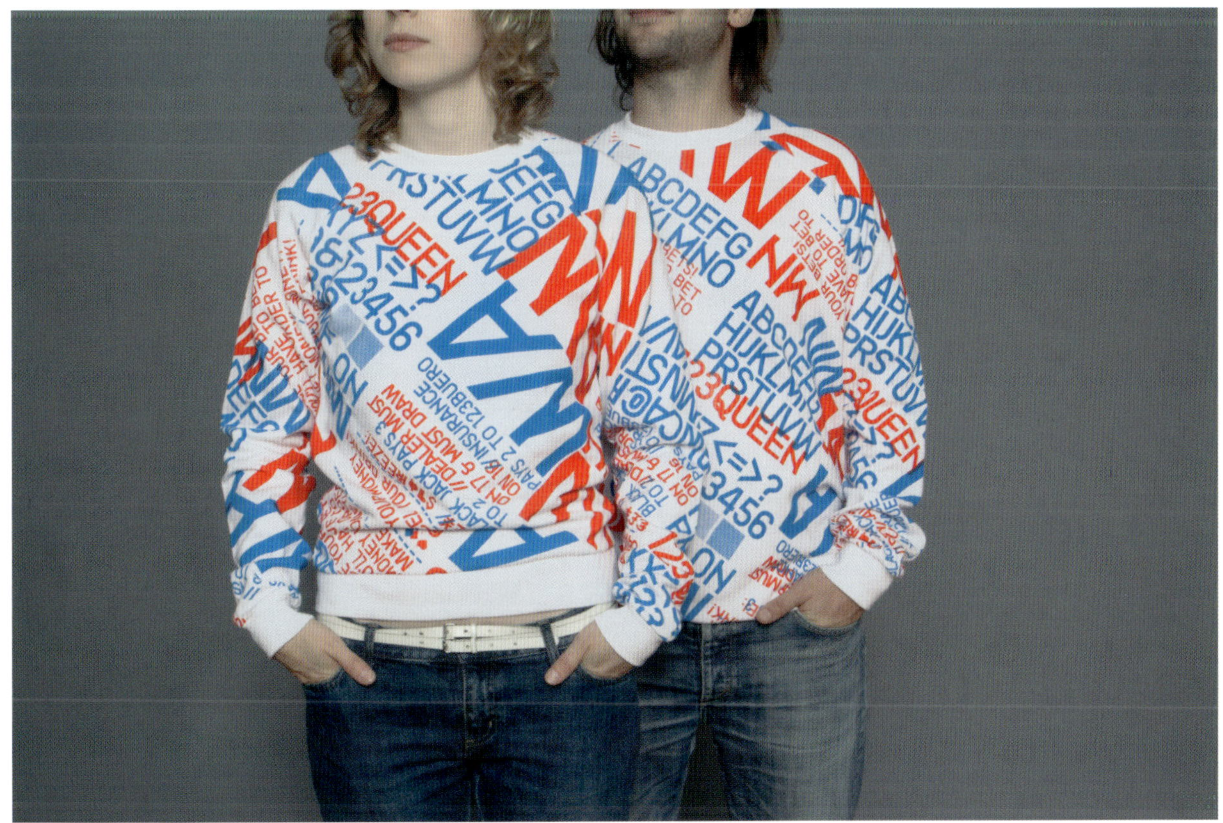

T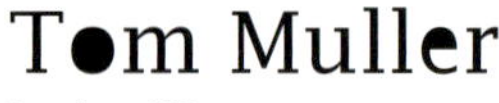m Muller

London, UK

Title: Mam Tor™ Event Horizon / Mam Tor™ Publishing
Type of work: Logo, book
Client: Mam Tor™ Publishing
Design: ad, d// Tom Muller
Year: 2004-05

The logo is made with bolded letters in black and white only. It gives a strong and solid feel. The design of the book is also designed in black and white to match the tone of the logo while the use of red adds excitement and enhances the solid feel.

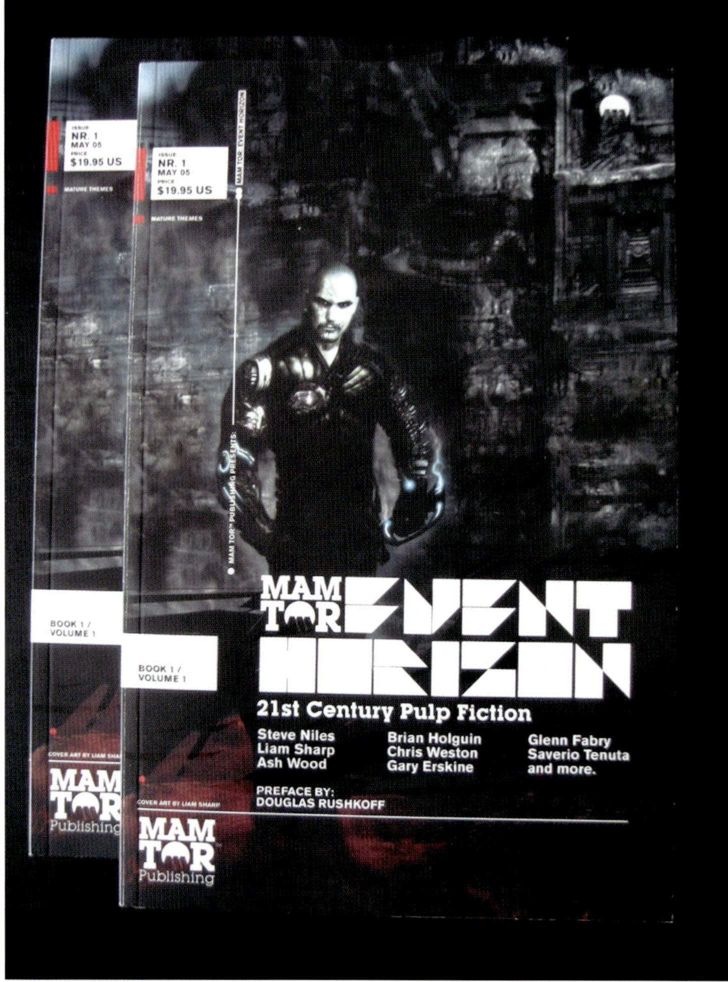

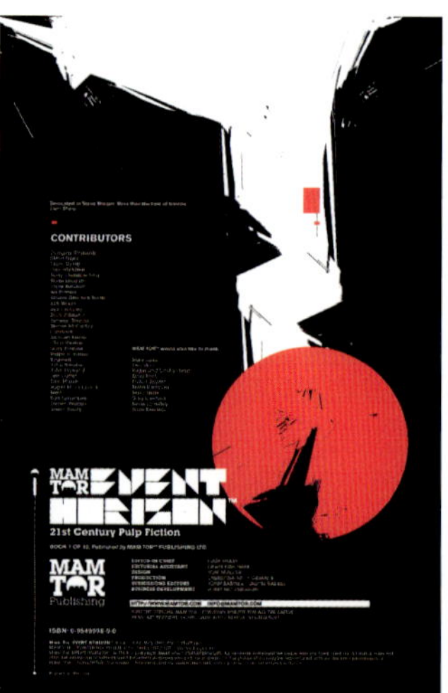

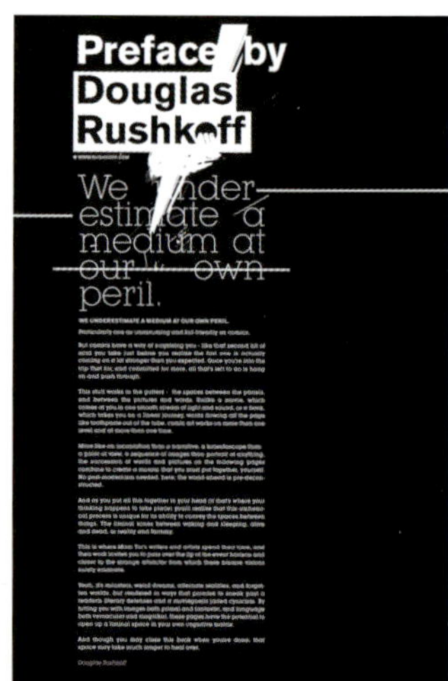

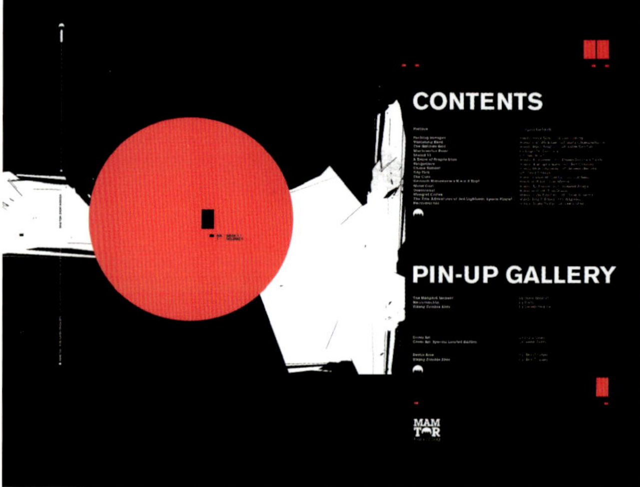

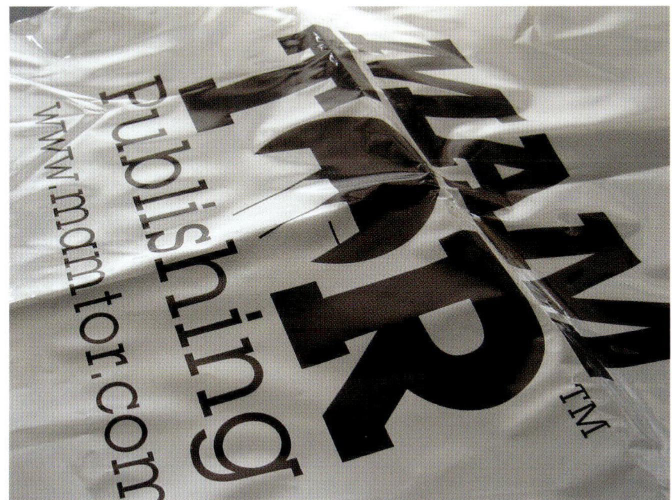

MAM
TOR
Publishing
www.mamtor.com
TM

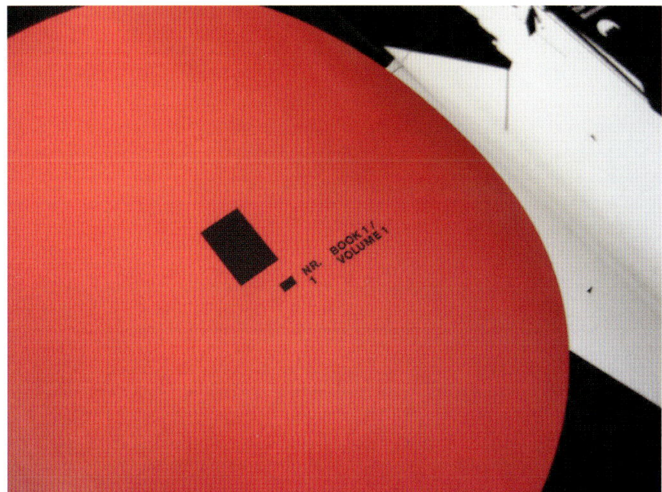

NR. BOOK 1 /
1 VOLUME 1

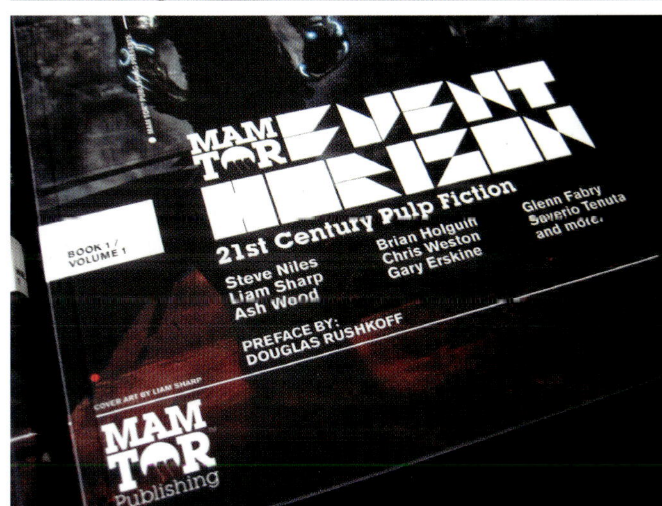

MAM EVENT
TOR HORIZON
21st Century Pulp Fiction
BOOK 1 /
VOLUME 1
Steve Niles
Liam Sharp
Ash Wood
Brian Holguin
Chris Weston
Gary Erskine
Glenn Fabry
Saverio Tenuta
and more.
PREFACE BY:
DOUGLAS RUSHKOFF
COVER ART BY LIAM SHARP
MAM
TOR
Publishing

Preface by
Douglas
Rushkoff
We under-
estimate a
medium at
our own
peril.
WE UNDERESTIMATE A MEDIUM AT OUR OWN PERIL.

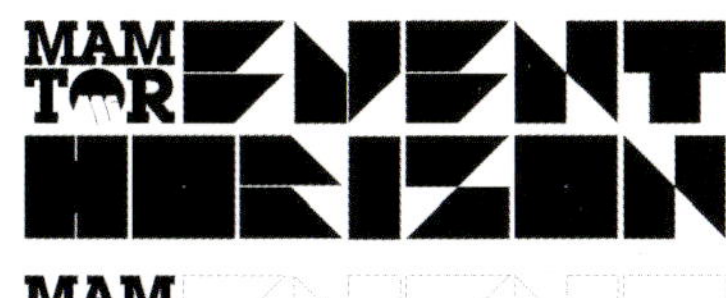
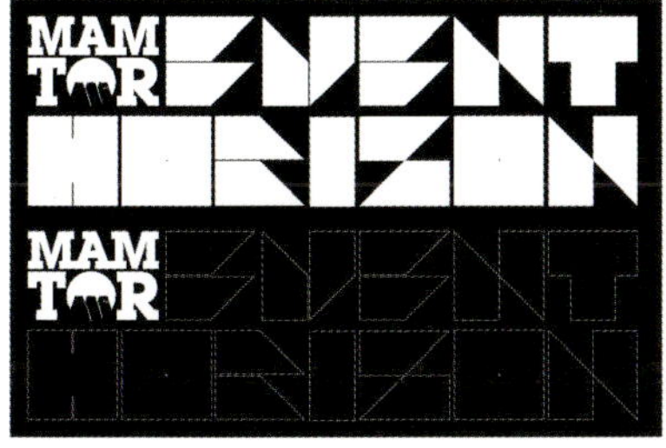
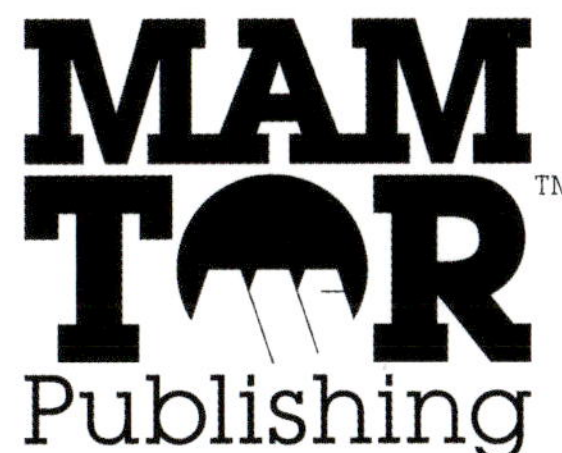
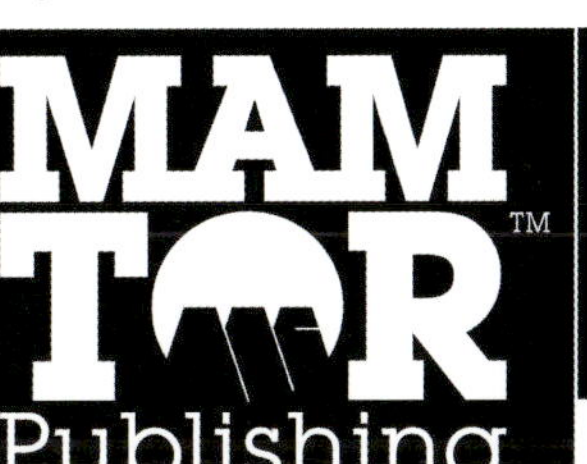
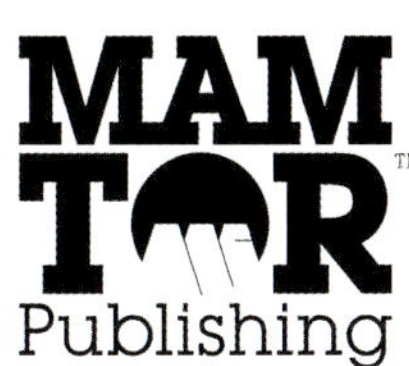
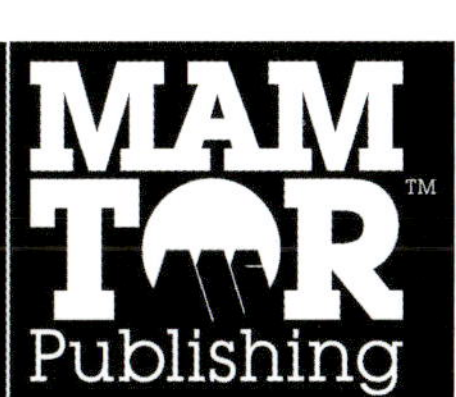
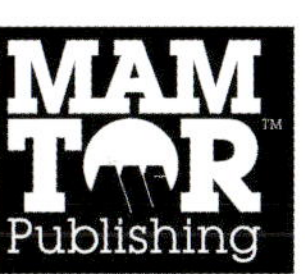

Beng

Amsterdam, The Netherlands

Title: Drillem
Type of work: Identity, campaign
Client: Drillem
Design: ad, d// Jan Willem van den Ban
Year: 2004-recent

An identity for Drillem, a Dutch electro-pop duo band who has become successful in The Netherlands, Belgium and in the UK over the past 2 years. The art work Beng designed for the band has helped to establish their image in the media and evoked a lot of very positive response from their audience and loads of T shirt sales.

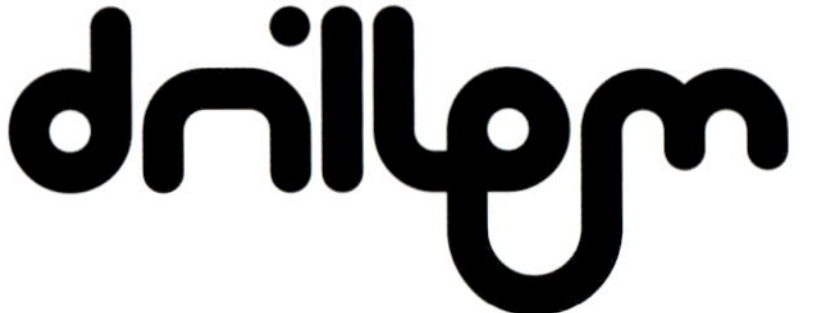

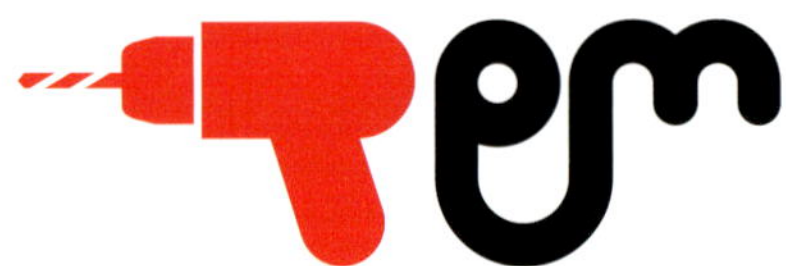

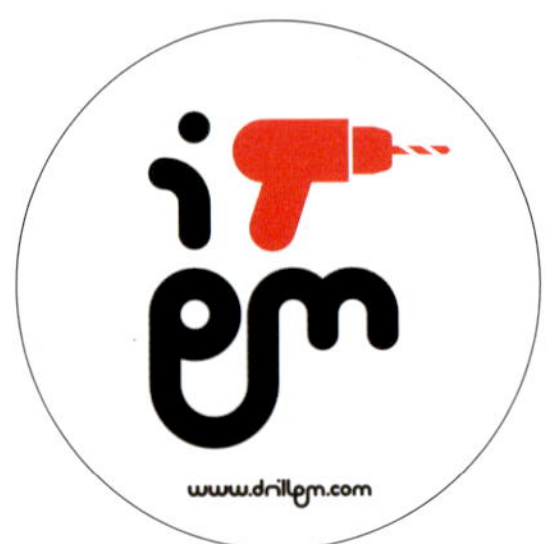

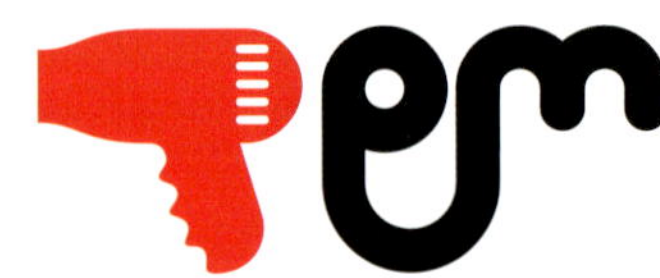

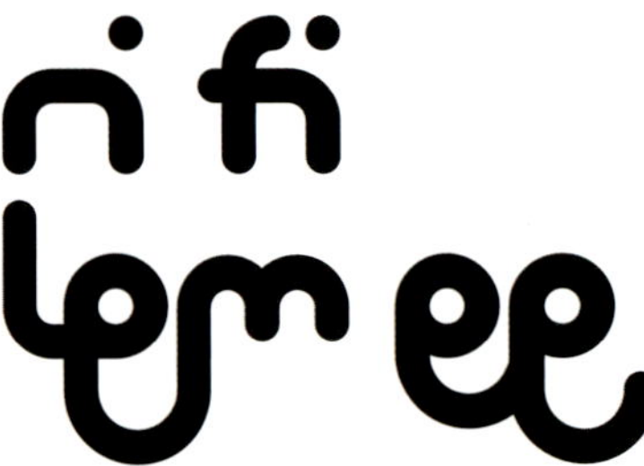

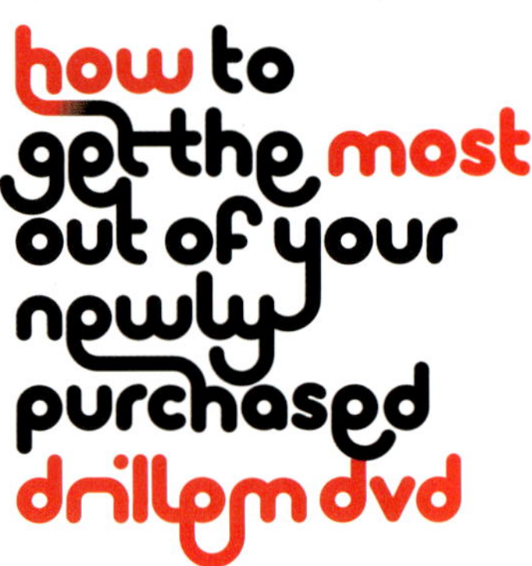

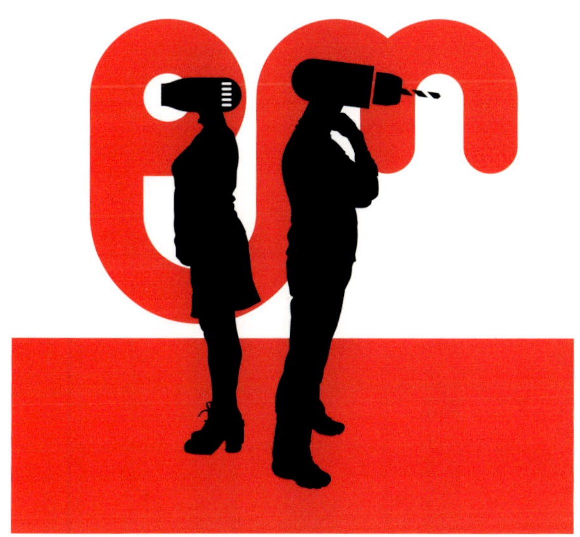

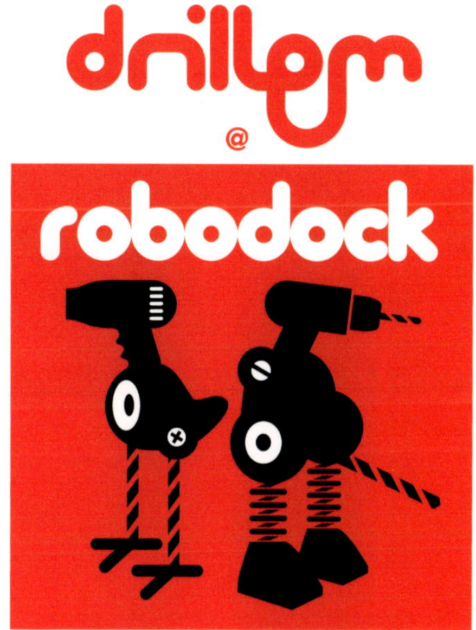

drillem
@
robodock
drillem@robodock | 25 sept | ADM terrein | A'dam

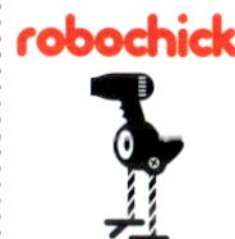

robochick

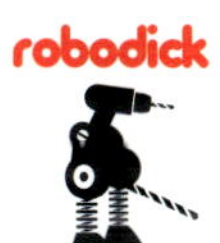

robodick

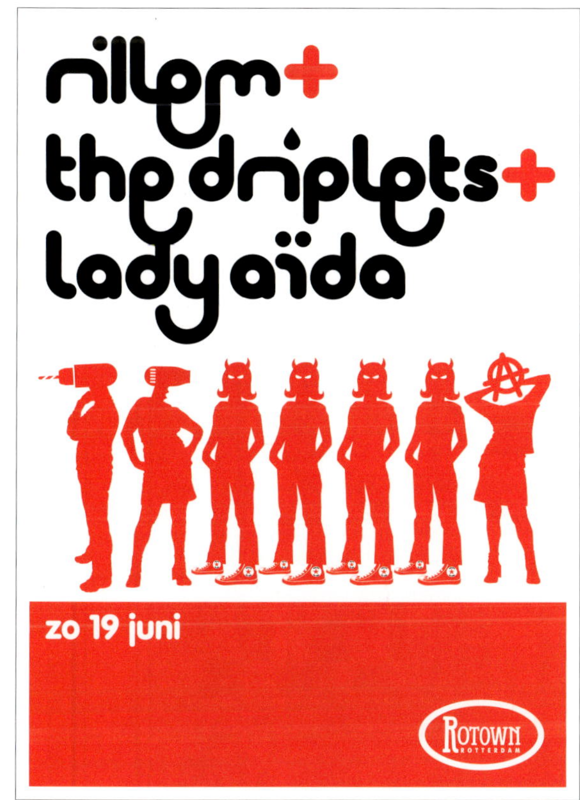

drillem+
the driplets+
lady aïda
zo 19 juni
ROTOWN
ROTTERDAM

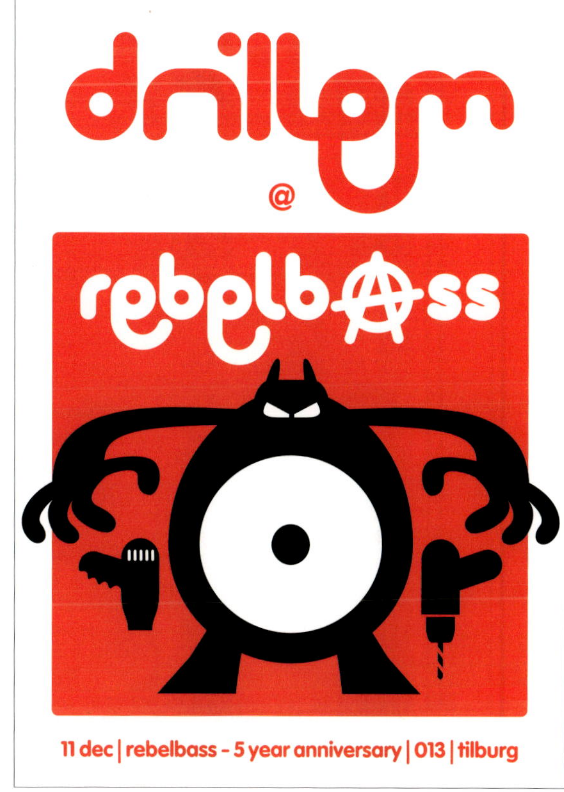

drillem
@
rebelbass
11 dec | rebelbass - 5 year anniversary | 013 | tilburg

Beng

Amsterdam, The Netherlands

Title: Drillem
Type of work: Identity, campaign
Client: Drillem
Design: ad, d// Jan Willem van den Ban
Year: 2004-recent

An identity for Drillem, a Dutch electro-pop duo band who has become successful in The Netherlands, Belgium and in the UK over the last 2 years. The art work Beng designed for the band has helped to establish their image in the media and evoked a lot of very positive response from their audience and loads of T shirt sales.

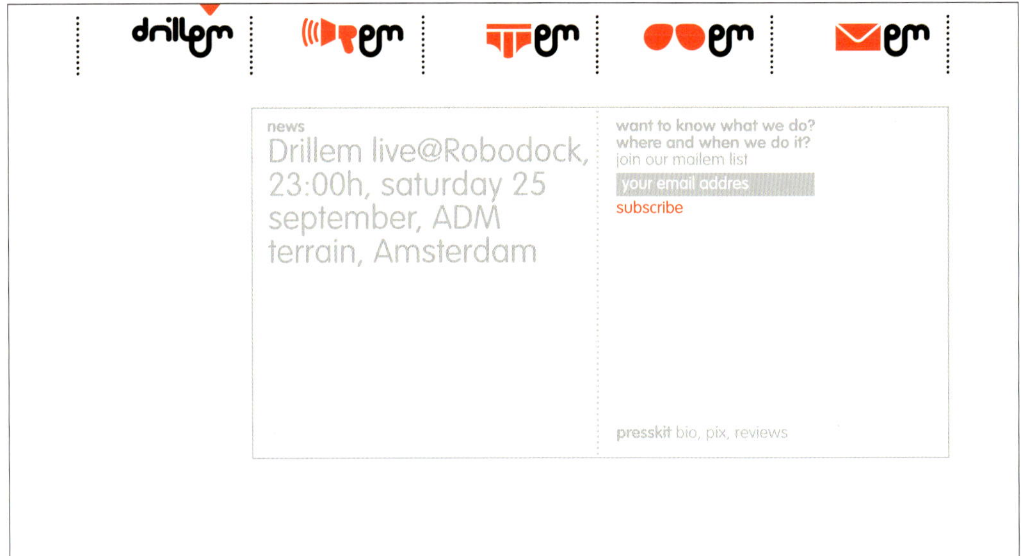

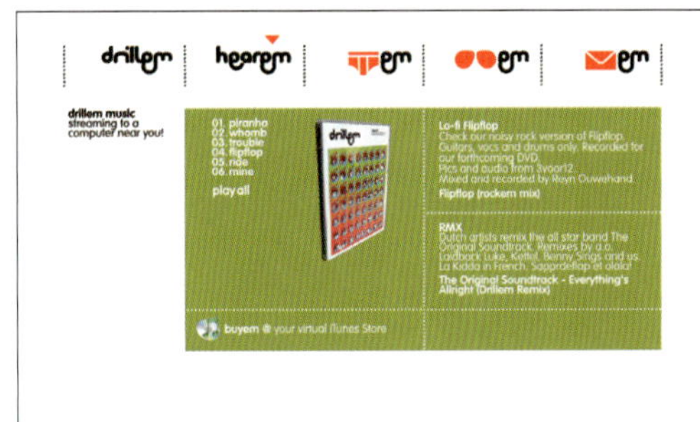

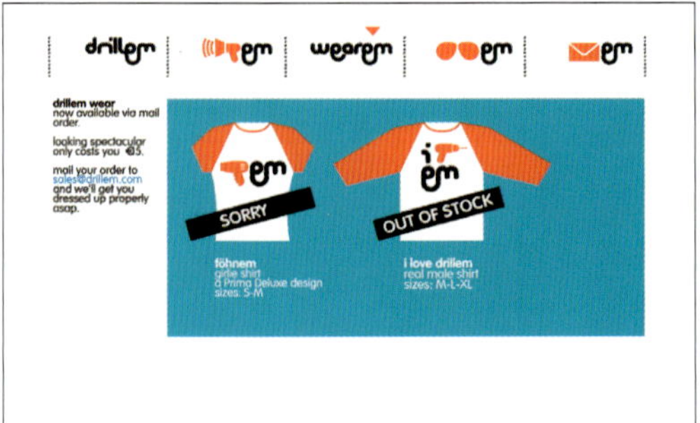

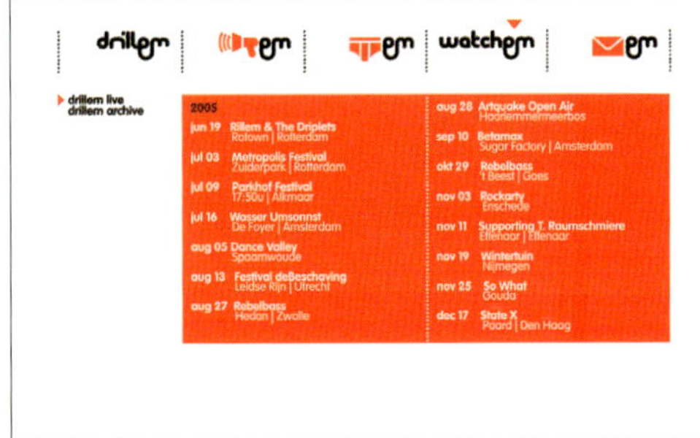

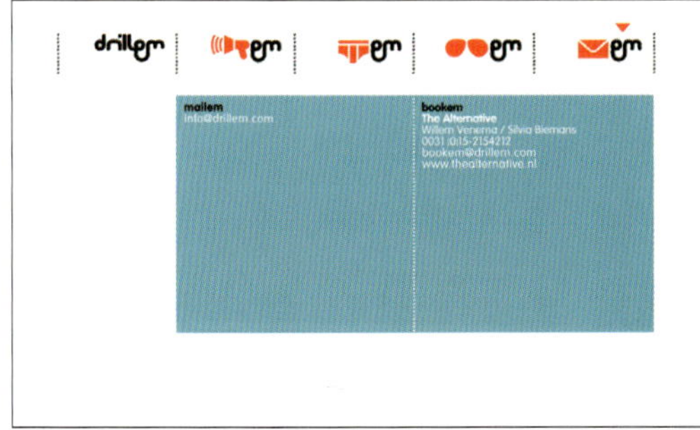

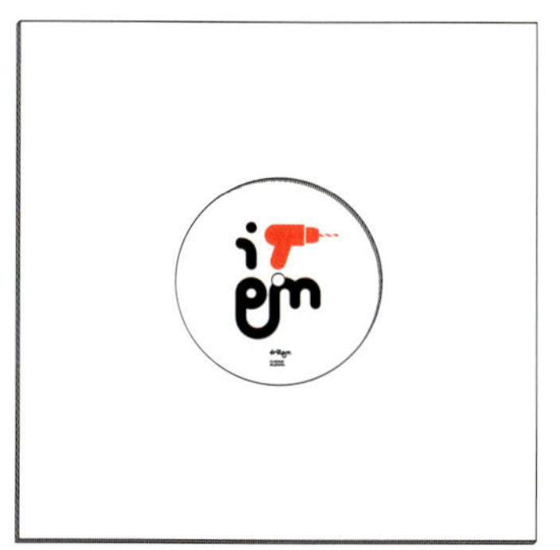
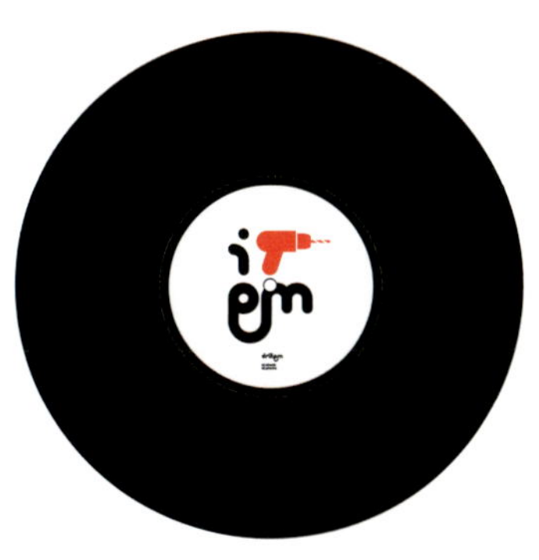
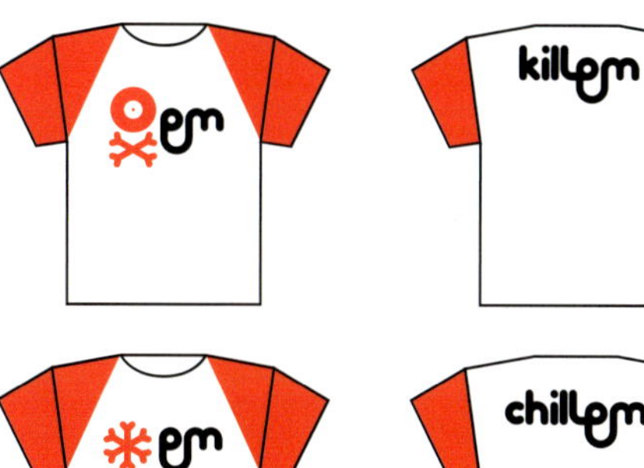

killem

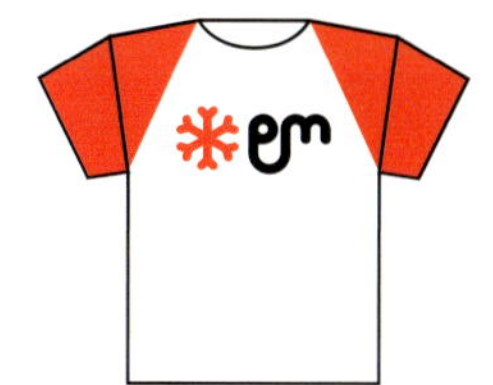

chillem

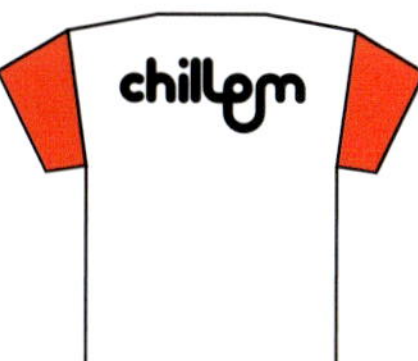
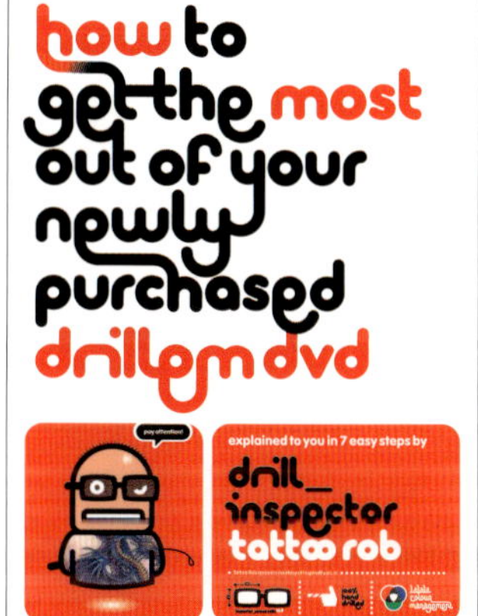

how to get the most out of your newly purchased drillem dvd
explained to you in 7 easy steps by
drill_
inspector
tattoo rob

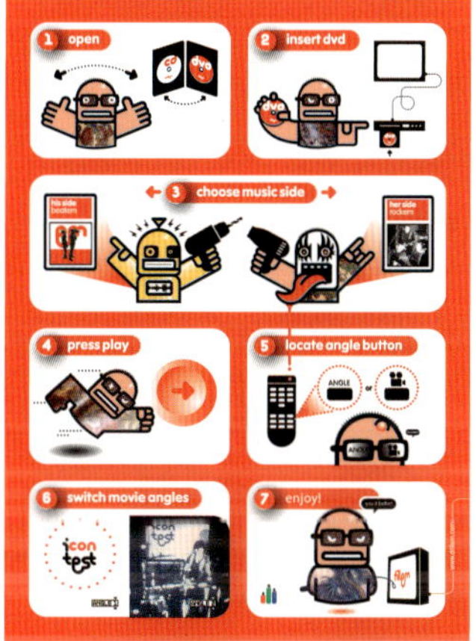

1 open
2 insert dvd
3 choose music side
4 press play
5 locate angle button
6 switch movie angles
7 enjoy!

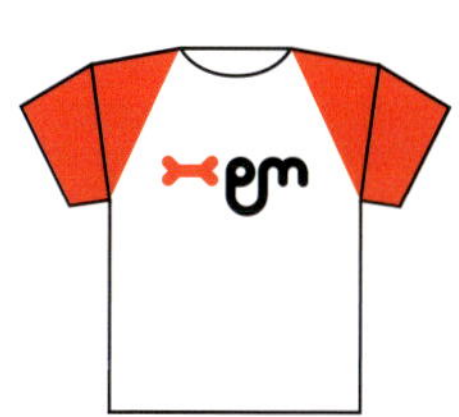

bonem

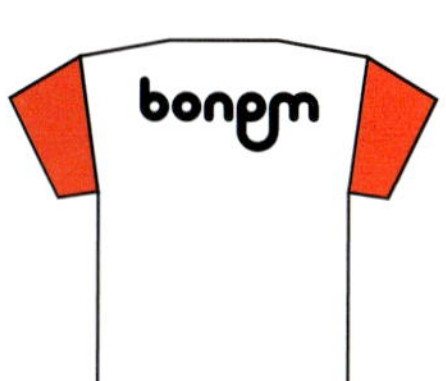

clonem

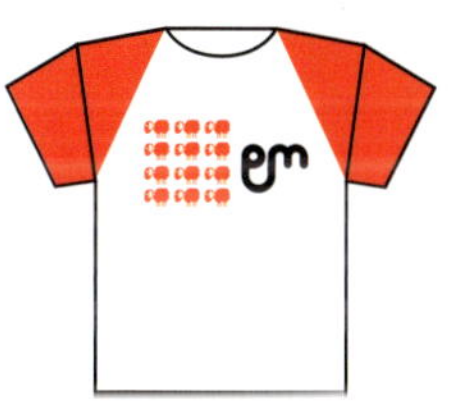
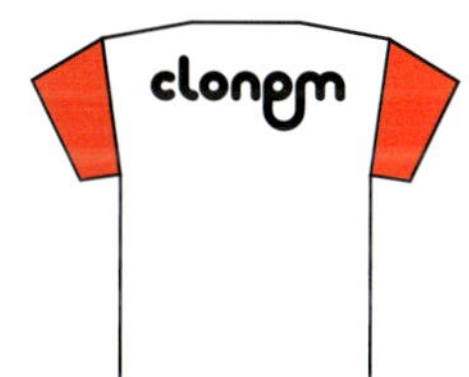
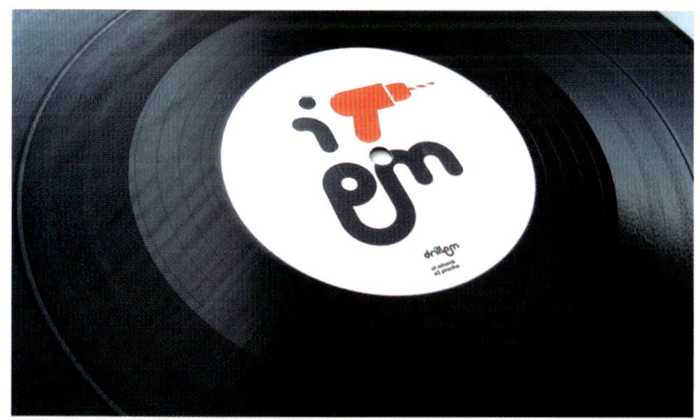
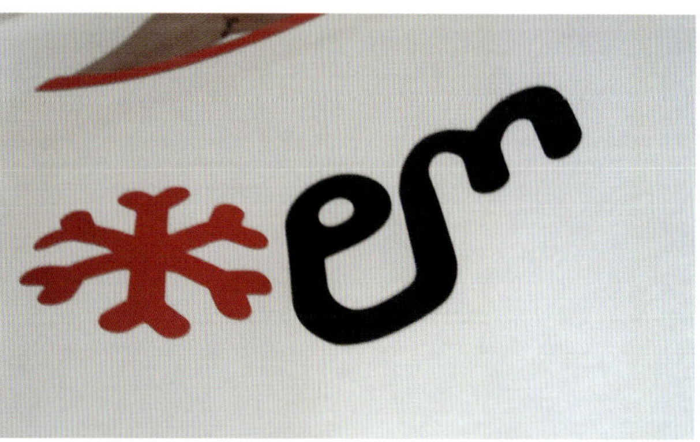
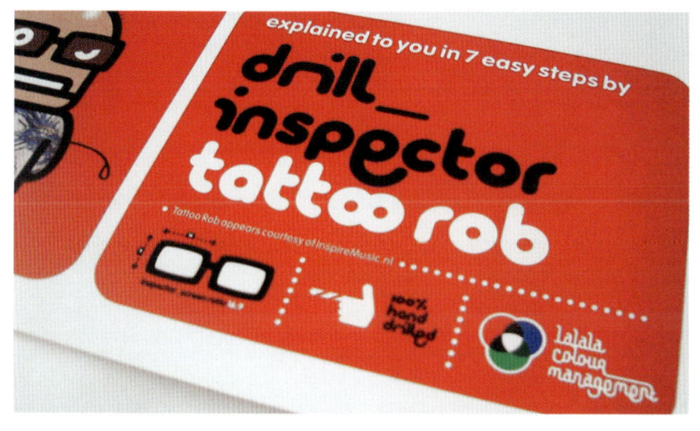

explained to you in 7 easy steps by
drill_
inspector
tattoo rob
* Tattoo Rob appears courtesy of InspireMusic.nl
100% hand drilled
lalala
colour
management

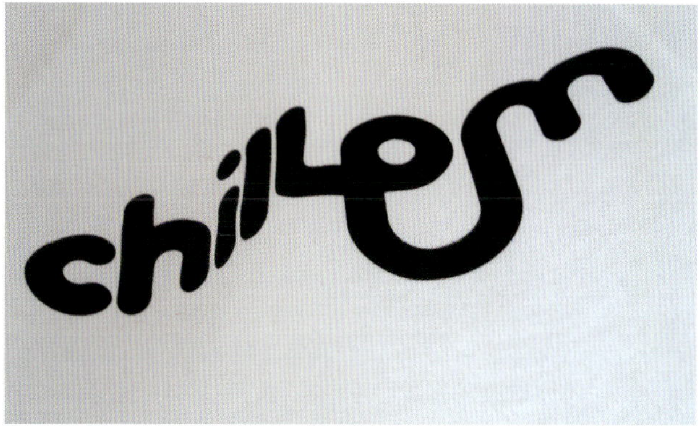

chillem

Zion Graphics

Stockholm, Sweden

Title: Bisse Bengtsson
Type of work: Invitation card
Client: Bisse Bengtsson
Design: ad, d// Ricky Tillblad
Year: 2005

This invitation card for Bisse Bengtsson is designed mainly with typographics. A simple but grand design that it is, contains a dark green background and shinny light green words.

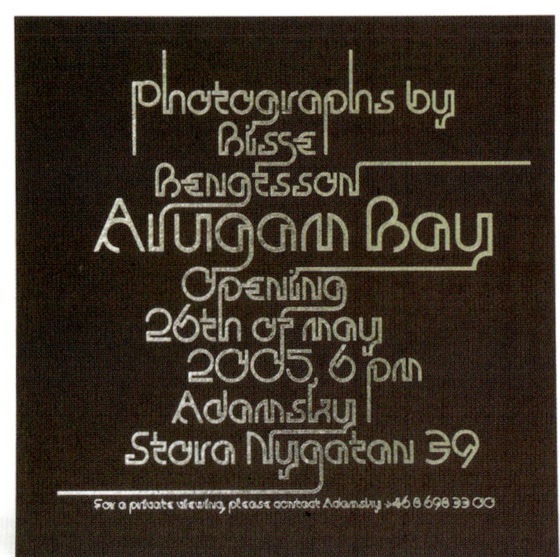

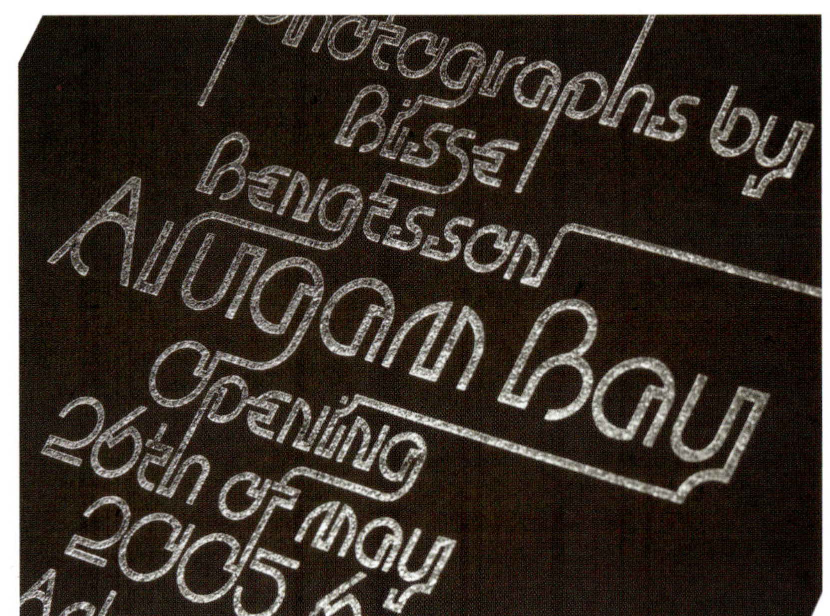

C1●●

Munich, Germany

Title: Fantastik Plastik
Type of work: Flyer
Client: Plastik Jugganots
Design: ad, d// Christian Hundertmark
Year: 2005

Playing with the name of project title 'Fantastik Plastik' that shown on the flyer, there is no images nor pictures but words only. The name is once again mentioned in pink at the flyer's bottom, but this time, it is in a rather formal type face.

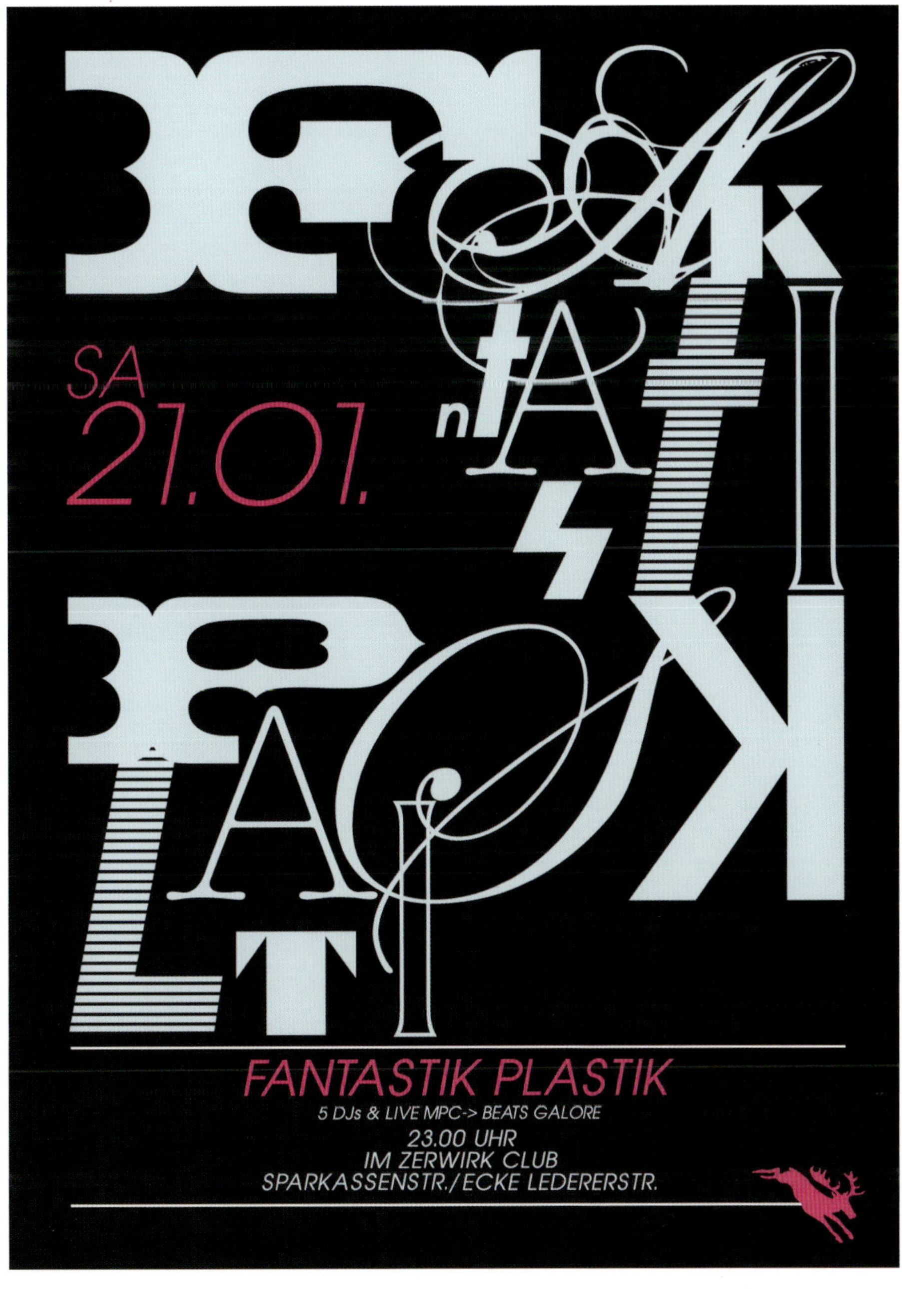

Grandpeople

Bergen, Norway

Title: Trollofon
Type of work: Promotional effects
Client: Pilota FM
Design: ad, d// Grandpeople
Year: 2005

This piece was designed for Trollofon 2005, which had a scientific approach and a large focus on the exhibition of strange objects from the natural historic museum of Bergen. The profile was reflected by a partly imaginary, pseudo-scientific object from an old tree root. Small details were added for extra pleasure and effects.

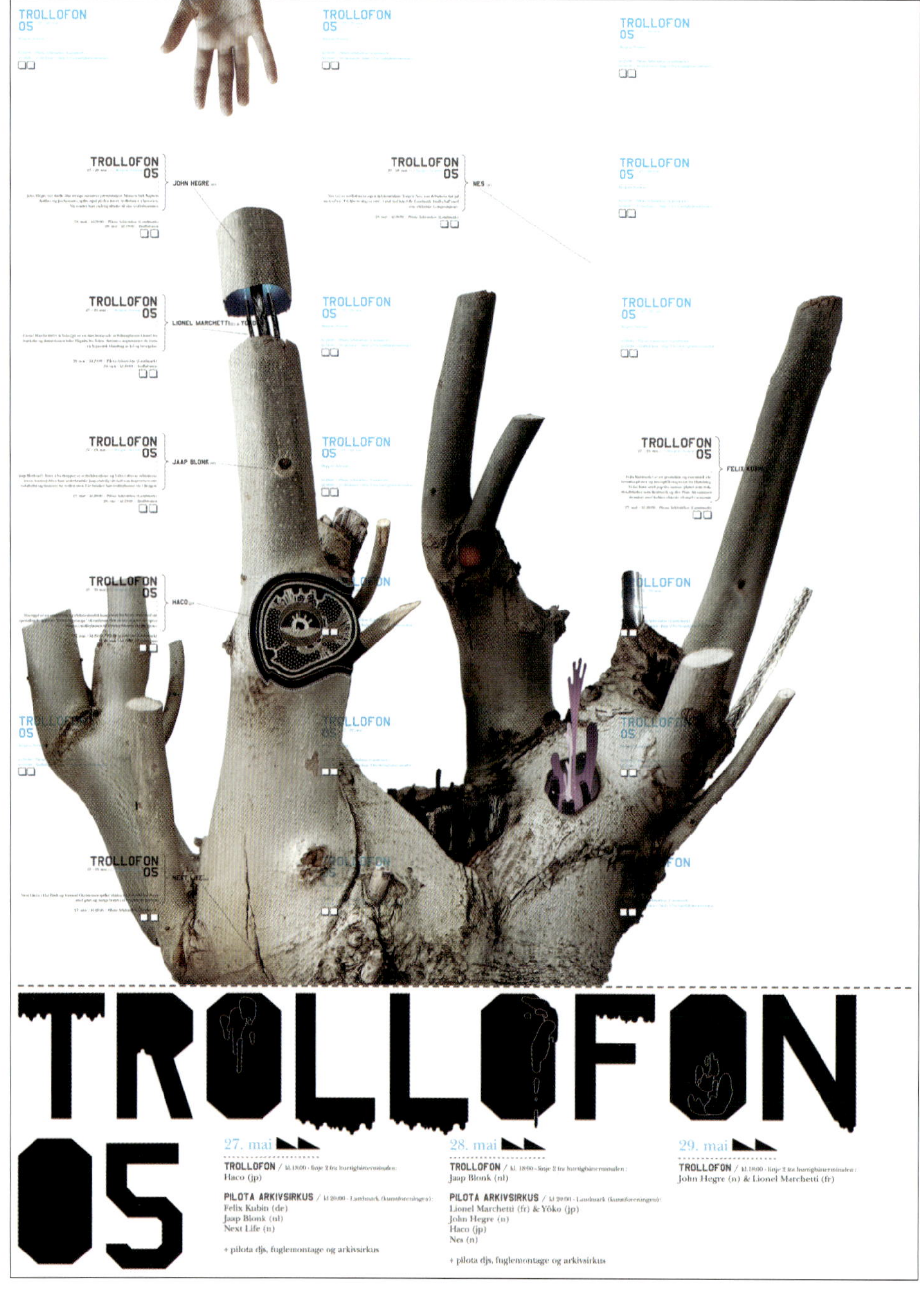

+−

Julia H●ffmann

New York, USA

Title: Act French
Type of work: Poster
Client: The French Embassy in New York
Design: ad// Paula Scher d// Julia Hoffmann
Year: 2004

Warm and romantic colours is used for this poster of The French Embassy in New York. Font for detailed information is in rather old-fashion style to bring out the classic feeling of France, which matches with the slogan of 'Act French', to discover French tradition and custom and act like French!

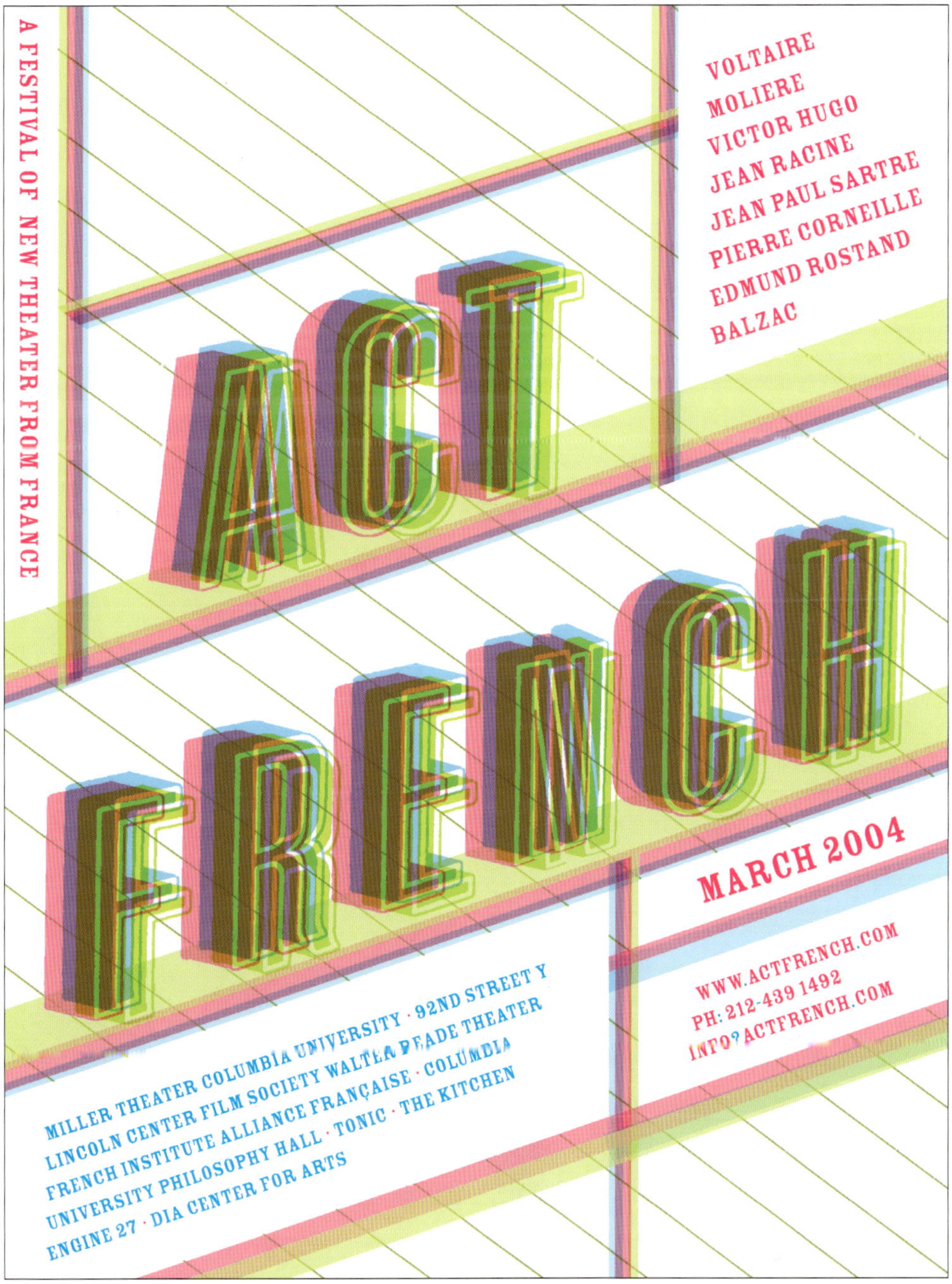

DESIGN ✶ MARTIN WOODTLI   SERIGRAPHIE ✶ ULDRY
MUSEUM FÜR GESTALTUNG ZÜRICH
SPORT
DESIGN
13. NOVEMBER 2004–13. MÄRZ 2005
DI–DO 10–20h / FR–SO 11–18h / 24.12., 31.12., 11–16h / MONTAGS SOWIE 25.12., 1.1. GESCHLOSSEN / AUSSTELLUNGSSTRASSE 60, 8005 ZÜRICH

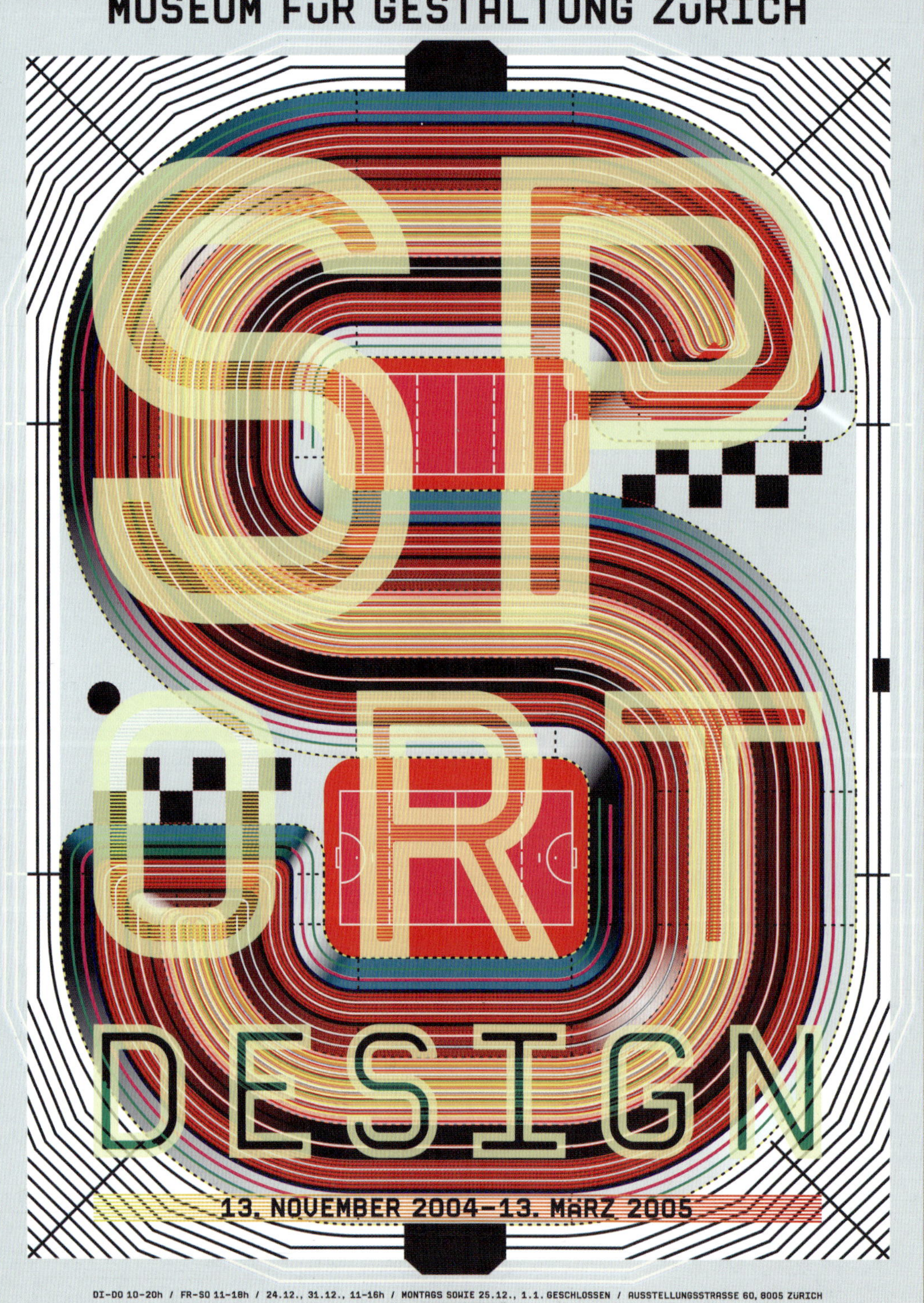

1.//

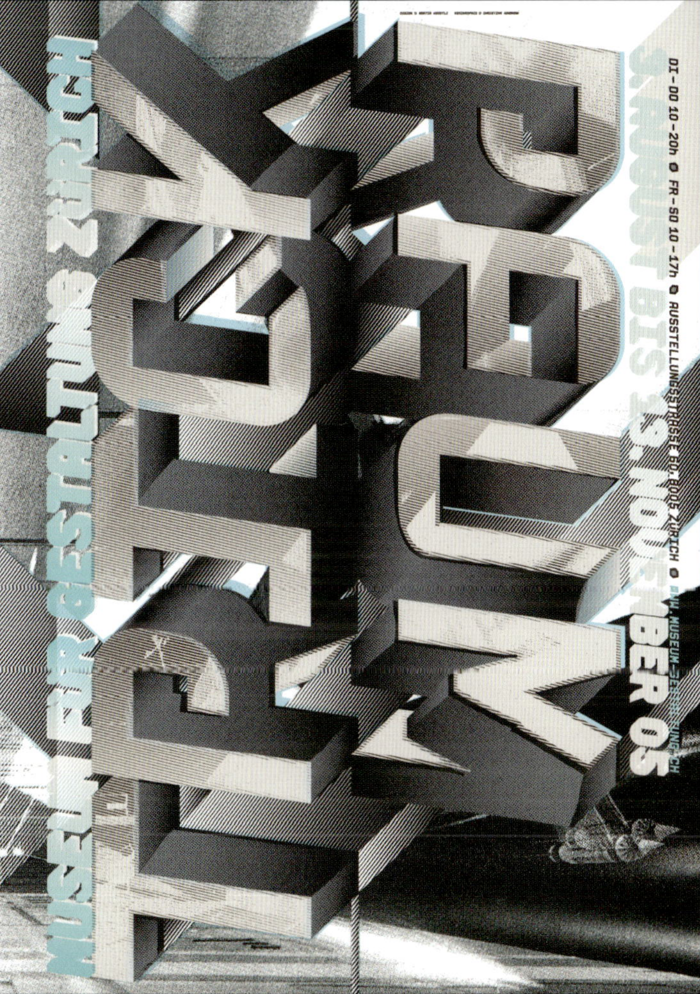

2.//

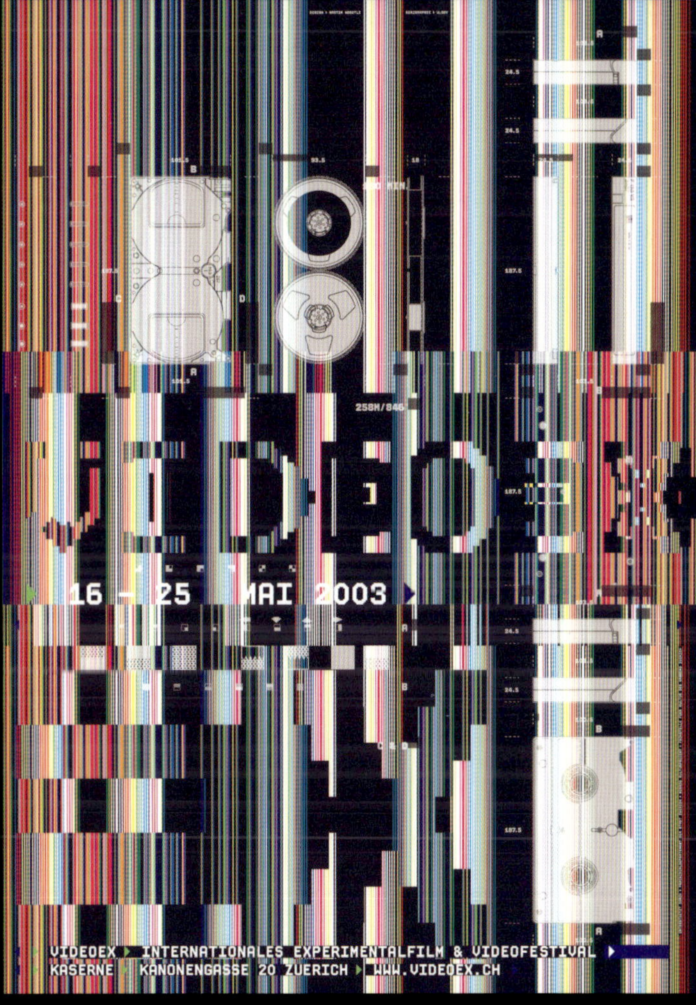

3.//

Martin Woodtli

Zürich, Switzerland

Title: 1.// Sportdesign 2.// Trickraum
3.// VideoEx
Type of work: Poster
Client: 1,2.// Museum für Gestaltung Zurich
3.// Patrick Huber, Kunstraum Walcheturm
Design: ad, d// Martin Woodtli
Year: 1.// 2004 2.// 2005 3.// 2003

An artwork to play with typography and colours
that it is, they are designed for different clients.
However, similar tone and manner that you can
find from these 3 posters is the mixture of coloured background and 3-dimensional type face.

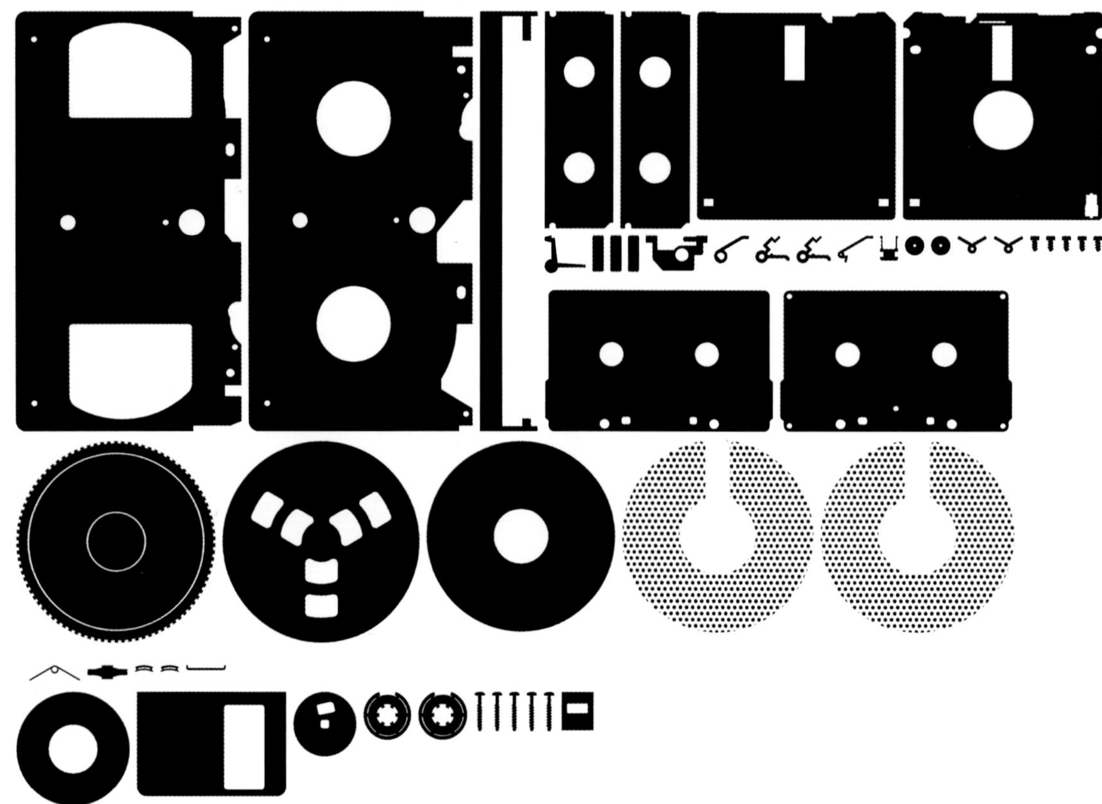

2xPoster set.

Limited Edition Print. Non-standard paper size: 700x1000

**Components: Compact Audio Cassette: Philips, 1963 / Video Home System Cassette: JVC, 1976 /
3.5" High-Density Floppy Diskette: Sony, 1981.
Graphic Design by Build, 2003.**

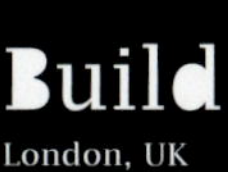

Build

London, UK

SONY® like.no.other™

Title: Sony™
Type of work: Advertising
Client: Fallon/Sony™
Design: ad, d// Michael C. Place
Year: 2005

This piece is about microtechnology versus macrotypography; interacting elements, new worlds, new environments, and scale.

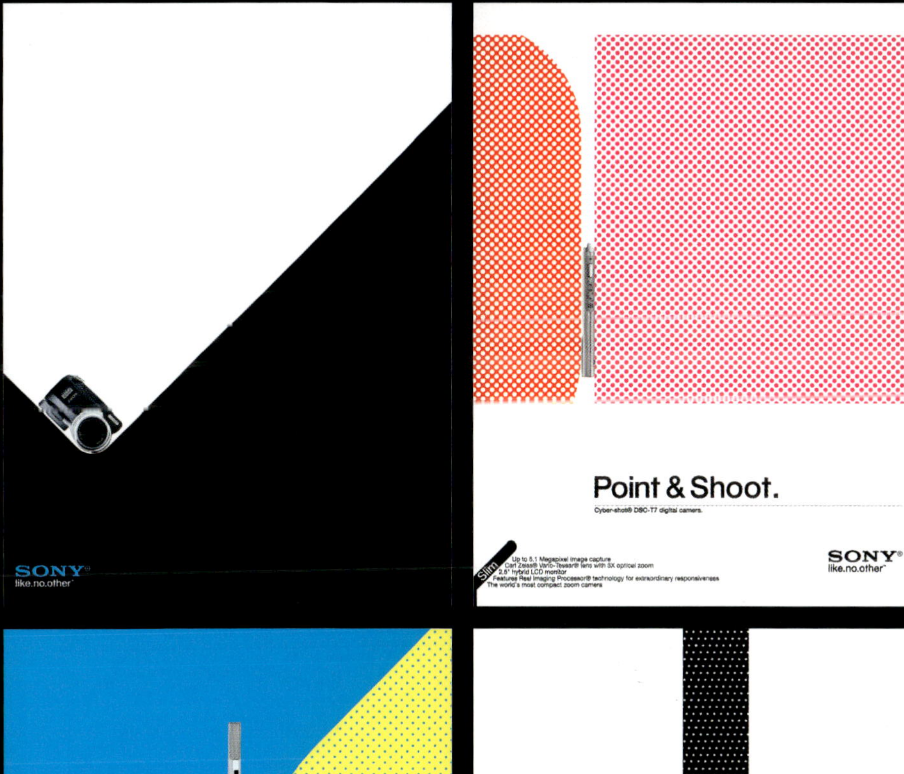

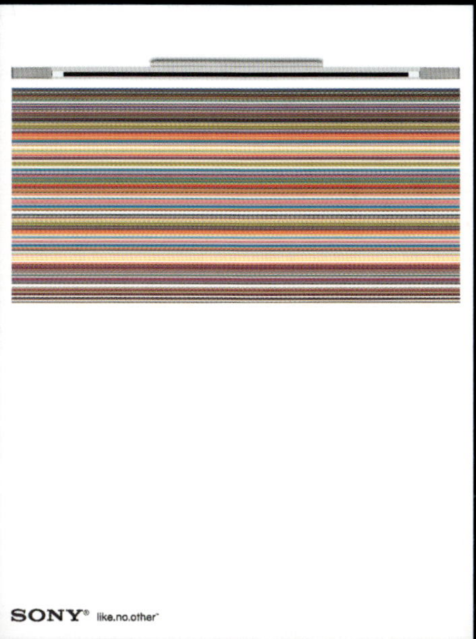

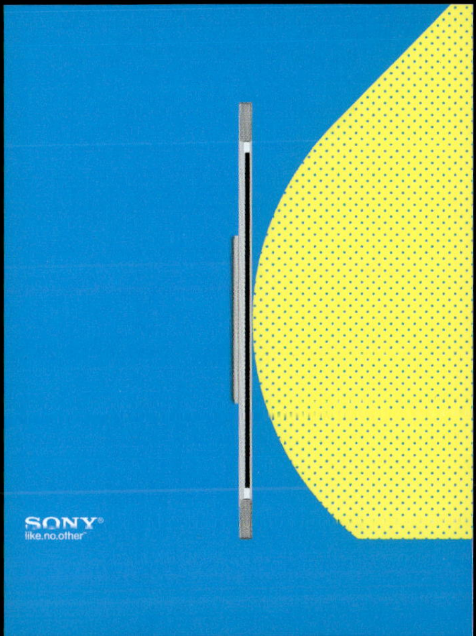

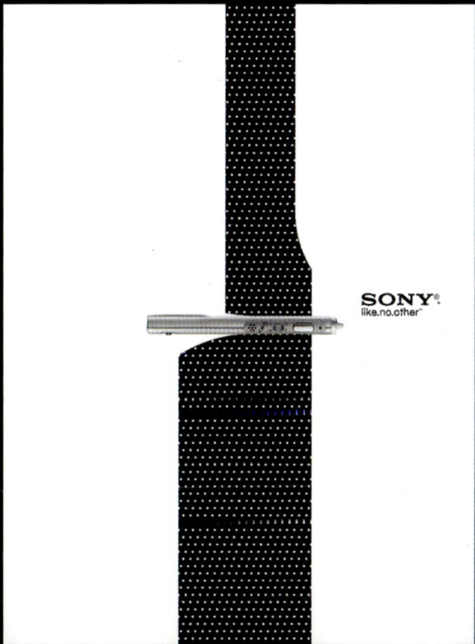

SONY® like.no.other™

Julian Morey

ndon, UK

Title: 1.// POP 2.// Rock and Roll 3.// Club-21
Type of work: 1,2.// Postcard 3.// Greeting Card
Client: 1.// London Cardguide 2,3.// Fontworks UK
Design: 1,3.// ad, d: Julian Morey 2.// ad: Julian Morey d: Julian Morey, François Lefranc
Year: 1.// 2000 2.// 2002-03 3.// 2002

1.// Postcard design from a series for the London Cardguide. 2.// A series of greeting cards published by Editions Eklektic in black, gold and sliver. The design was again published in 2003 as a limited edition silk-screen print. 3.// Poster to promote Club-21's digital typefaces, which uses an animal alphabet illustrattion with ascii art drawn by Joan Stark.

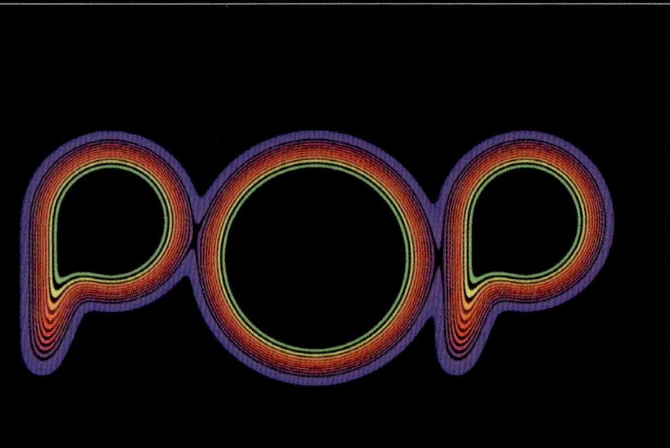

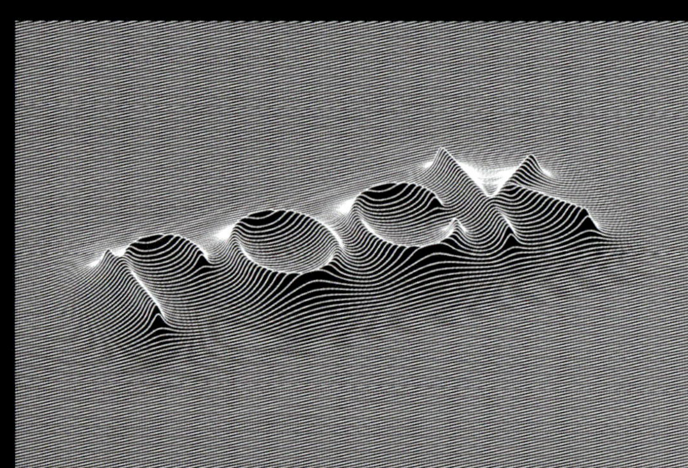

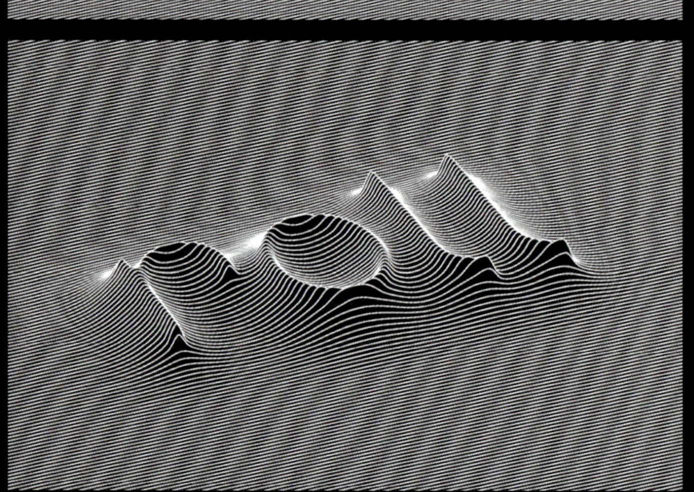

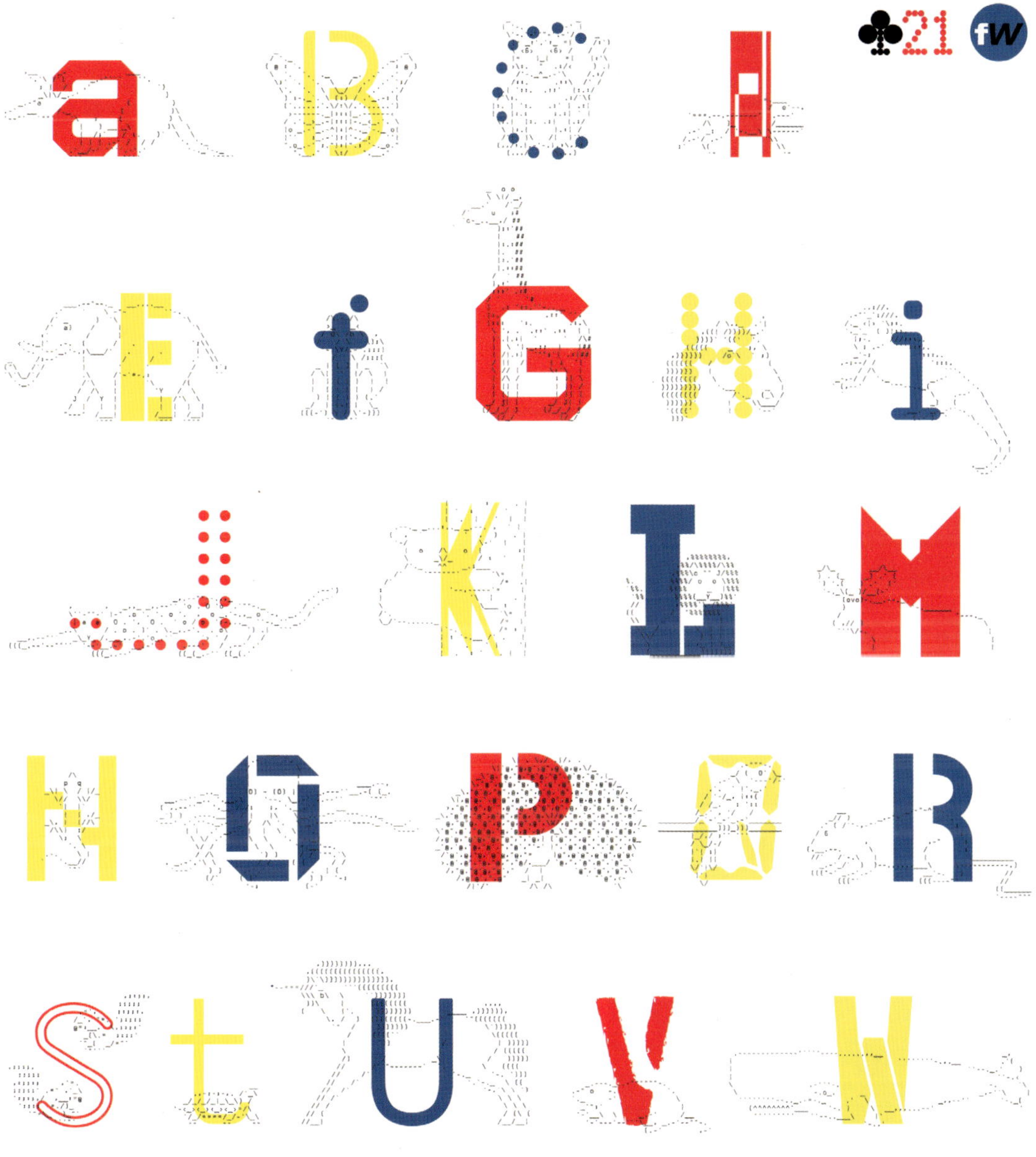

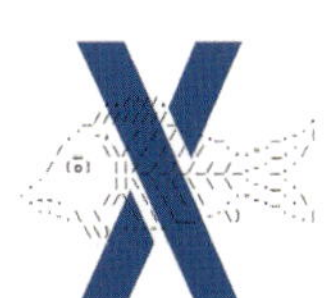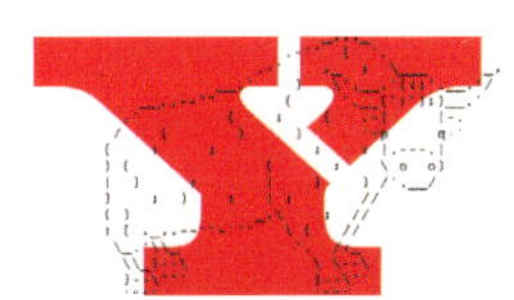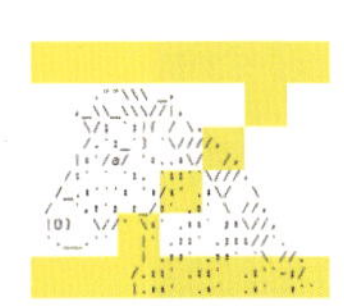

A is for Aardvark (Alpine)
B is for Butterfly (Skye)
C is for Cat (Frieze Bold)
D is for Dog (Electro)
E is for Elephant (Portfolio)
F is for Fox (Kathode)
G is for Giraffe (Pacific Bold)
H is for Horse (Checkout)
I is for Iguana (Typogram)
J is for Jaguar (Checkout Extended Ultra-Light)
K is for Koala (Spacer)
L is for Lion (Jakarta)
M is for Moose (VMR)
N is for Newt (Preset-F)
O is for Octopus (Octago)
P is for Peacock (Brassplate)
Q is for Quetzal (Liquid-D)
R is for Rat (Roadworks)
S is for Squirrels (Skye Outline)
T is for Turtle (Simpson Typewriter)
U is for Unicorn (Thompson Typewriter)
V is for Vole (Paintworks)
W is for Whale (Greenwich)
X is for X-Ray Fish (Signplate)
Y is for Yak (Ionia)
Z is for Zebra (Zexon)

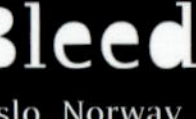

Oslo, Norway

Title: Poster for TIFF 05
Type of work: Poster
Client: TIFF, Tromsø International Film Festival
Design: ad, d// Erik Hedberg, Eirik Seu Stokkmo
Year: 2005

This 4+1 colours on recycled, matt paper poste[r]
was designed for TIFF, which is a film festival
showing more underground and alternative film
rather than the Hollywood block busters. It is
located in Tromsø Norway in the north of Norw[ay]
above the artic circle.

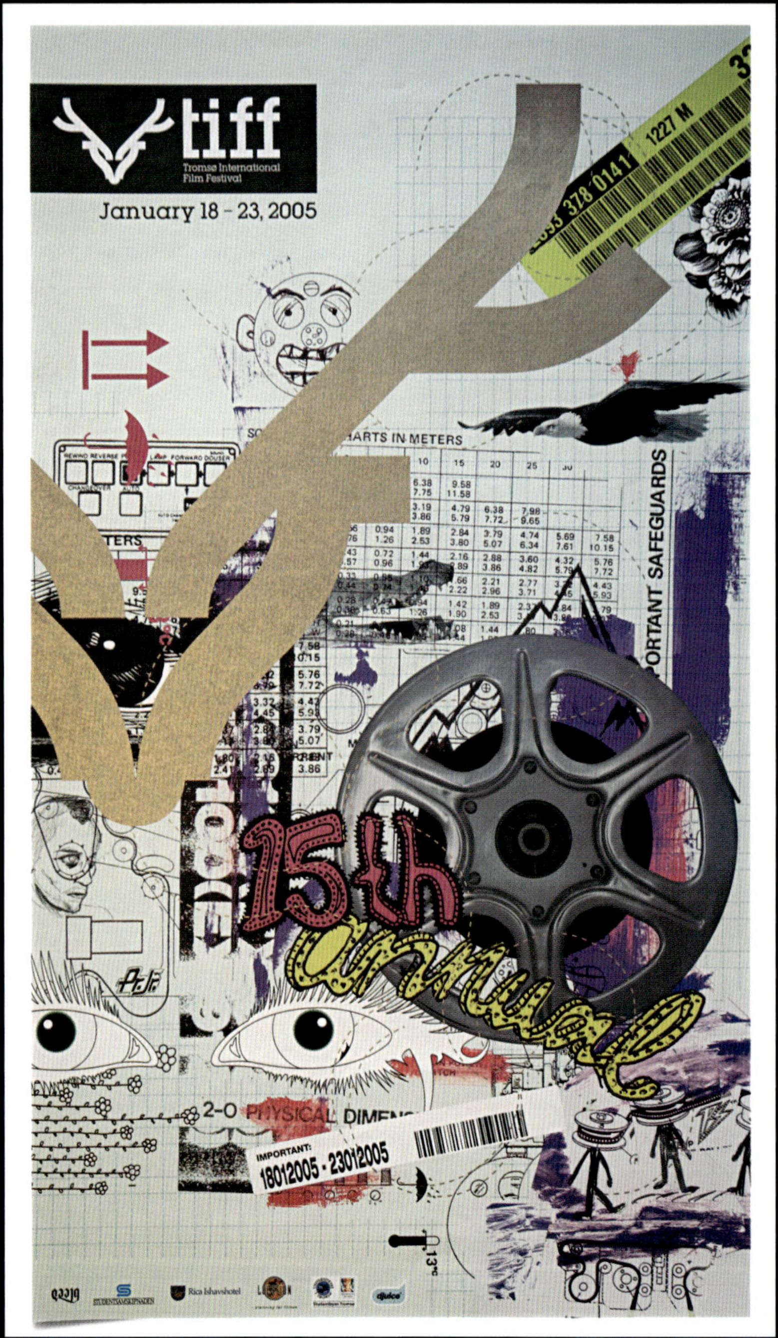

Gud
og
Klem

Grapórar-
buskapen
í rustam
gamalla
gilda

Primö-
turnor

Um (mynd)
Lux eda
An ferils

Heimer,
sagore,
gludman

RMAC

Lisboa, Portugal

Title: 1.// Lux- 7th Anniversary Invitation
2.// 25th Edition Modalisboa: Desire
Type of work: Invitation
Client: 1.// Lux Frágil 2.// Associação ModaLisboa
Design: 1.// ad: Ricardo Mealha and Ana Cunha d: Ana Cunha 2.// ad: Ricardo Mealha and Ana Cunha d: Ricardo Mealha
Year: 2005

1.// This was designed commemorating the 7th anniversary of Lux/Fragil, the hippest nightclub in Portugal situated in the port zone of Lisbon, overlooking the Tagus River (River Tejo). The concept is about the colour, shape, and the mysterious.

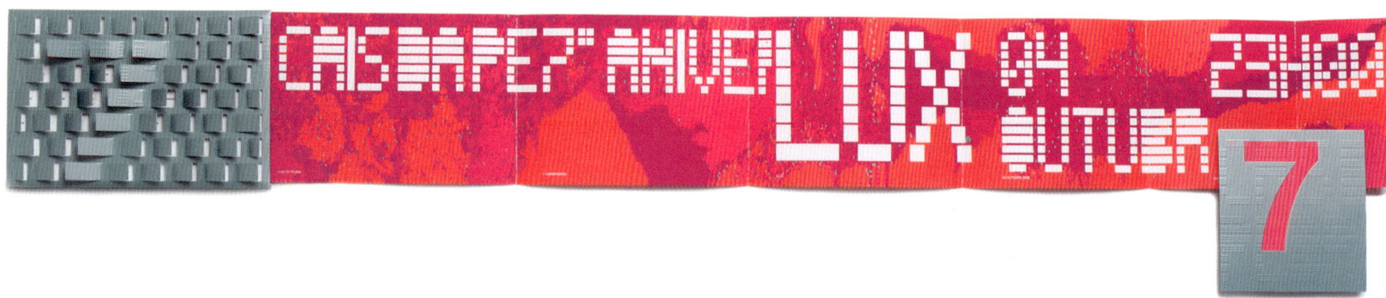

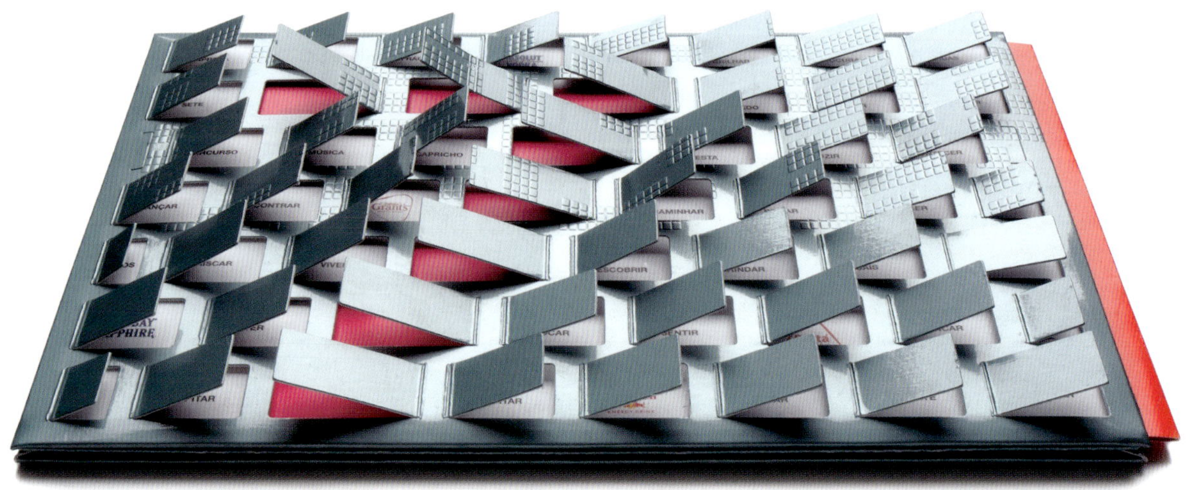

1.//

Desire
MODAliSBOA
25
LION OF
PORCHES
Presented by
SEAT
auto emoción
Sexta 14.10.05
22h15 LisboaFashionWeek
13/14/15/16 Outubro 2005
25ª Edição Verão/Summer 06
Armazém 23/Cais da Matinha
2005 2088

Desire
MODAliSBOA
25
Aleksandar
Protich
Presented by
SEAT
auto emoción
Sexta 14.10.05
19h00 LisboaFashionWeek
13/14/15/16 Outubro 2005
25ª Edição Verão/Summer 06
Lab Armazém 23/Cais da Matinha
2005 2058

Desire
MODAliSBOA
25
Maria
Gambina
Presented by
SEAT
auto emoción
Sábado 15.10.05
20h00 LisboaFashionWeek
13/14/15/16 Outubro 2005
25ª Edição Verão/Summer 06
Armazém 23/Cais da Matinha
2005 2140

Válido para 1 pessoa.
Não dá acesso à sala de desfiles.
Para sua comodidade vá de táxi.
Desire
MODAliSBOA
25
Área social
Presented by
SEAT
auto emoción
LisboaFashionWeek
13/14/15/16 Outubro 2005
25ª Edição Verão/Summer 06
Armazém 23/Cais da Matinha

Desire
MODAliSBOA
25
Ricardo
Dourado
Presented by
SEAT
auto emoción
Quinta 13.10.05
19h15 LisboaFashionWeek
13/14/15/16 Outubro 2005
25ª Edição Verão/Summer 06
Lab Armazém 23/Cais da Matinha
2005 2027

Desire
MODAliSBOA
25
Lara
Torres
SEAT
auto emoción
Sábado 15.10.05
15h00 LisboaFashionWeek
13/14/15/16 Outubro 2005
25ª Edição Verão/Summer 06
Lab Armazém 23/Cais da Matinha
2005 2095

Válido por 1 dia.
Este convite tem que ser validado na recepção.
Para sua comodidade vá de táxi.
Desire
MODAliSBOA
25
Sponsor VIP
Nome:
LisboaFashionWeek
13/14/15/16 Outubro 2005
25ª Edição Verão/Summer 06
Armazém 23/Cais da Matinha
SEAT
auto emoción

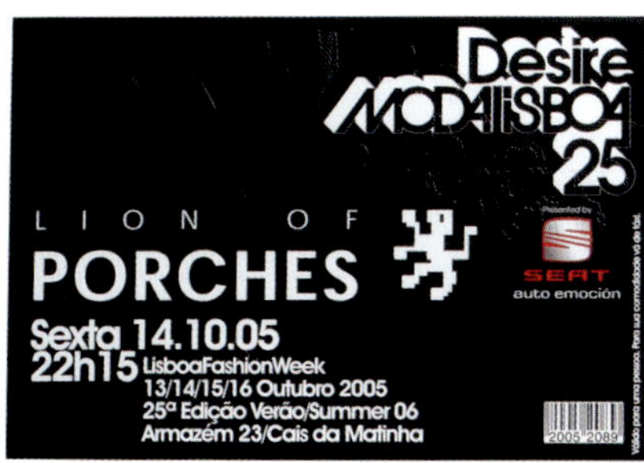

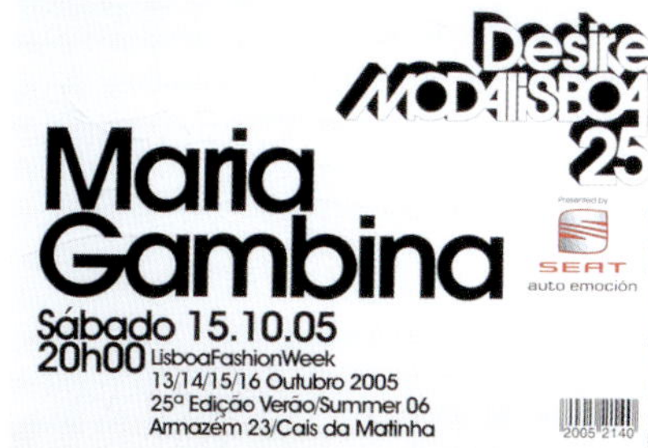

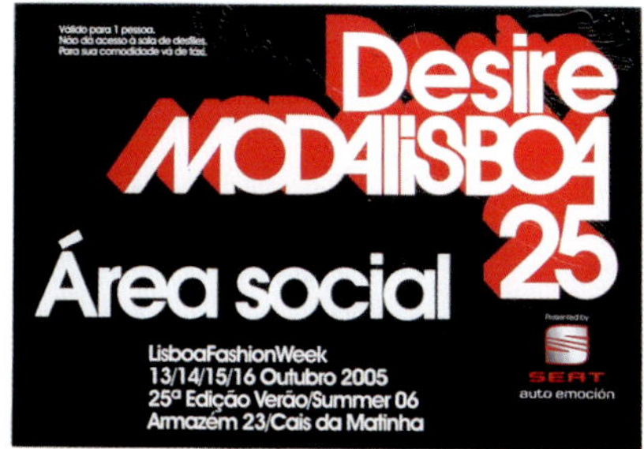

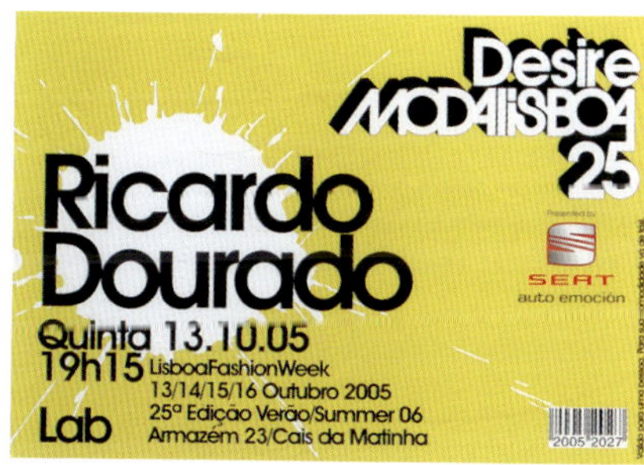

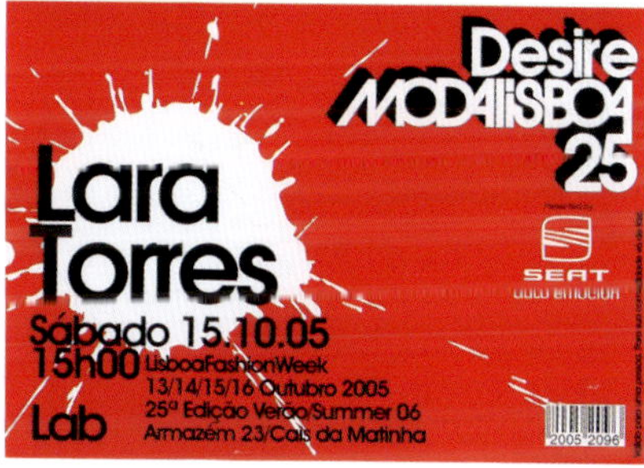

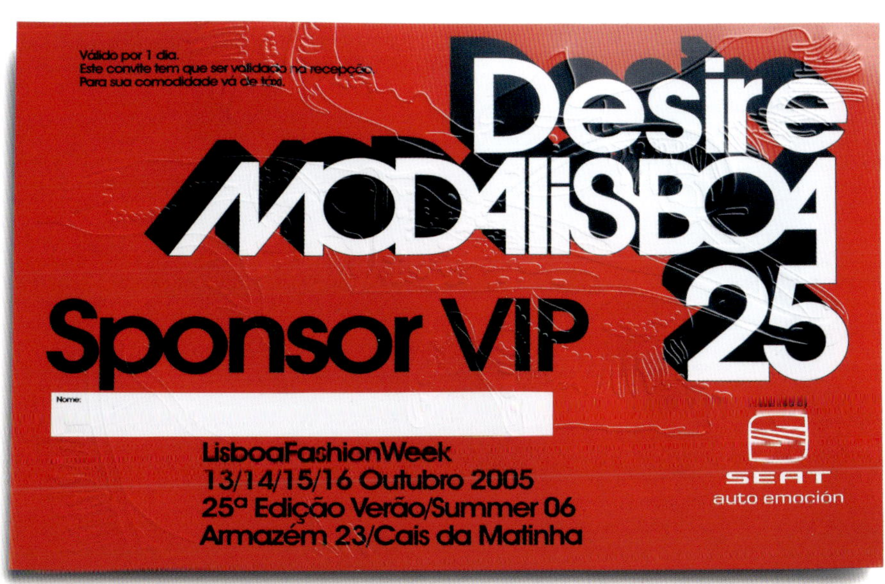

2.//

RMAC

Lisboa, Portugal

Title: Absolux
Type of work: Invitation Card
Client: Lux Frágil
Design: ad, d// Ricardo Mealha and Ana Cunha
Year: 2004

The main elements behind this party invitation card were the Absolut Vanilia Vodka bottle and the flavour behind the drink – vanilla. They played with different shades of white and the contrast of glossy vs. matt inks and varnishes that convey lightness, transparency and sophistication. The materials and techniques employed consisted of a large sheet, silk screen printed in white of transparent vinyl sticker, a hard-stock transparent vinyl sheet silk screened in white and a large sheet of mirror-like paper containing images of vanilla beans offset-printed in four colours.

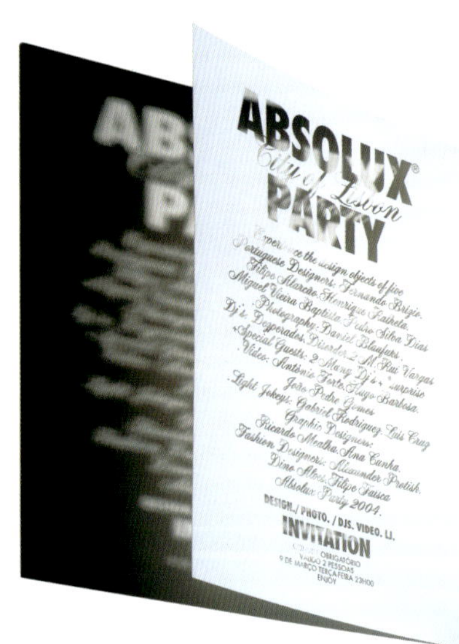

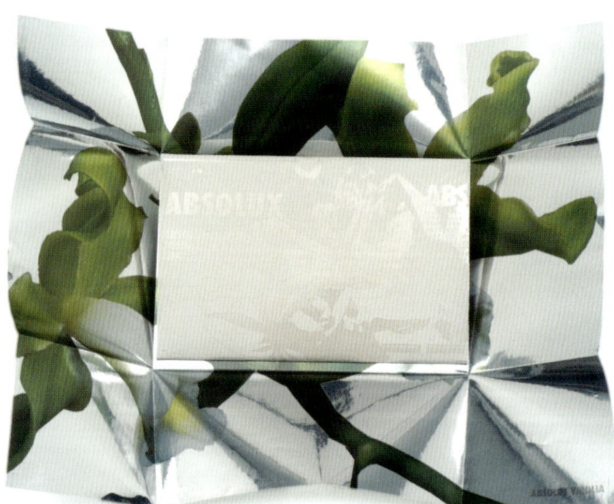

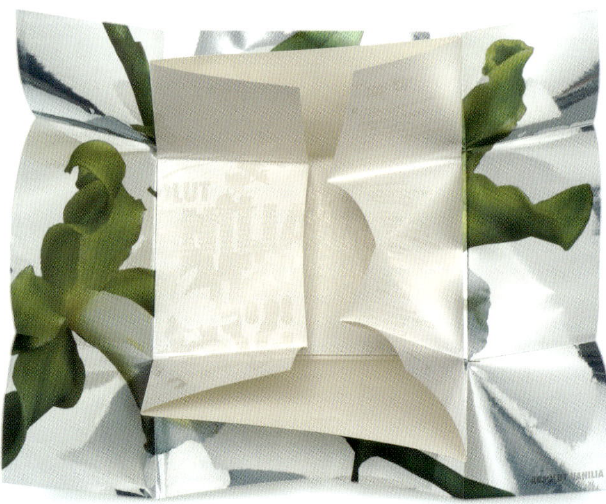

Alice Chan

Hong Kong, China

Title: Postcard design for Asteria Company
Type of work: Postcard
Client: Asteria
Design: ad, d// Alice Chan aka Asteria
Year: 2005

This set is a combination of stickers and post-cards with images that are not duplicate. The designer had to create and design a distinctive cute but naughty iconic image for the use on Asteria product, so she chose a red plastic bag that brings out a feeling of sharpness. Also, two badges which were made by foam were made to emphasize the thickness and layer.

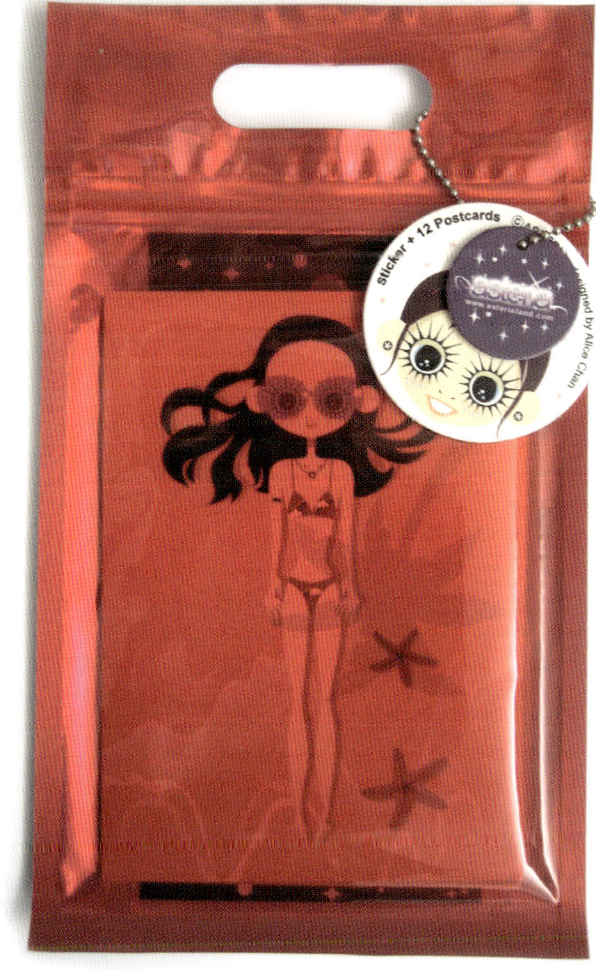

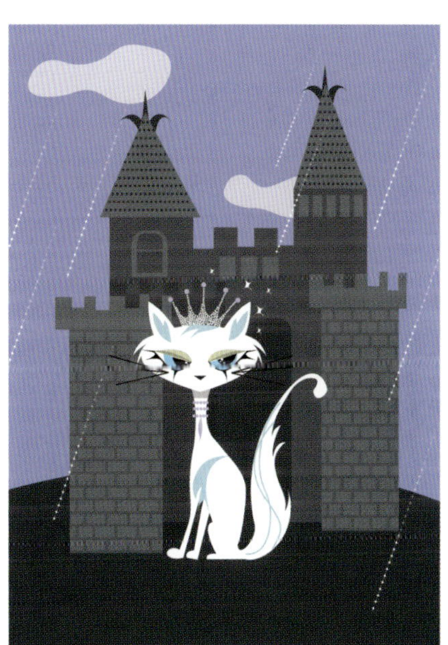

Aloof Design

Sussex, UK

Title: Georgina Goodman Autumn Winter 2005 Show Invitation
Type of work: Invitation Card
Client: Georgina Goodman
Design: ad// Sam Aloof d// Andrew Scrase
Year: 2005

This invitation card is designed to entice customers and press to the international fashion buying season of Georgina Goodman, a couture and ready to wear shoe designer. The show acts as an introduction to the season, so the design has to be unique, eye-catching, and informative.

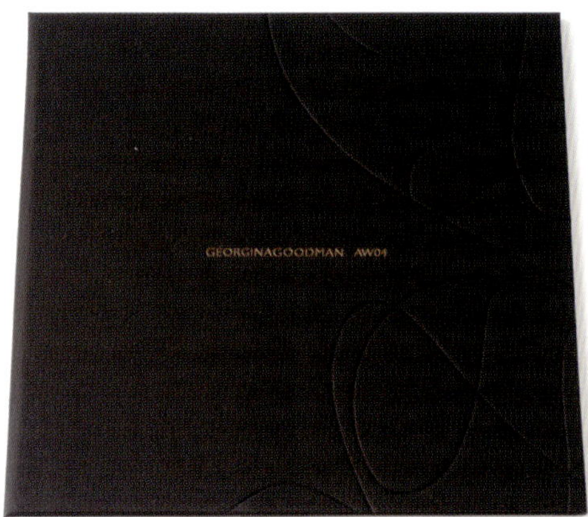

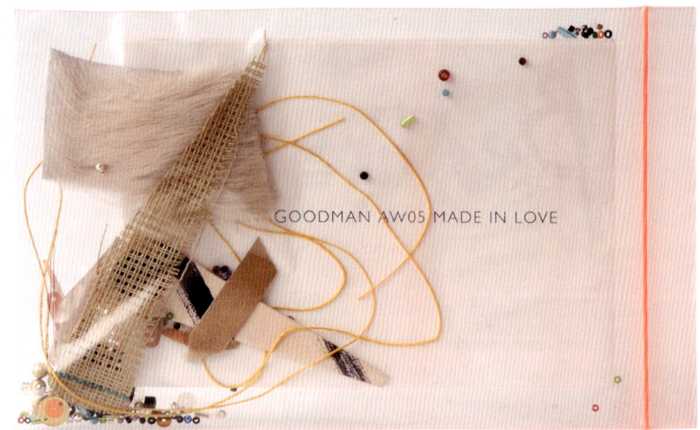

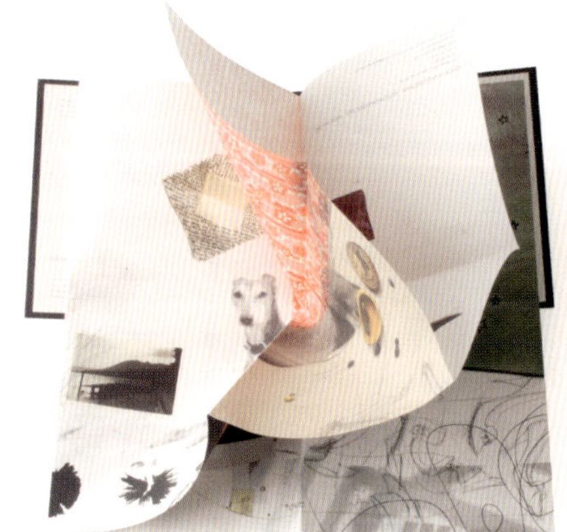

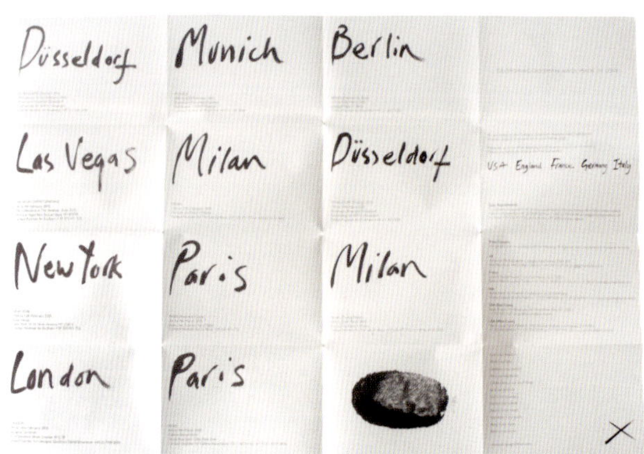

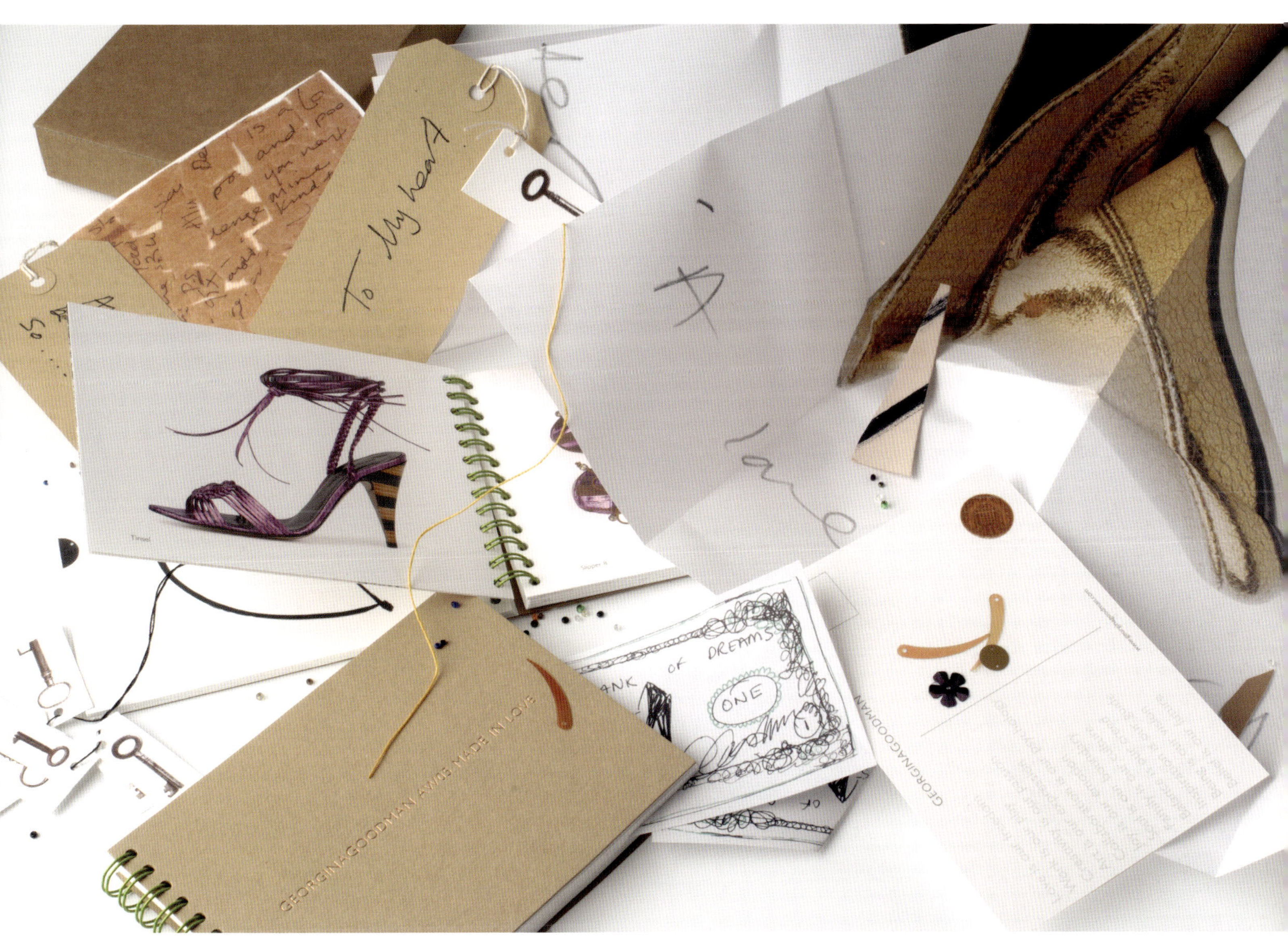
To My Heart
Tassel
GEORGINA GOODMAN AW05 MADE IN LOVE
BANK OF DREAMS
ONE
GEORGINAGOODMAN

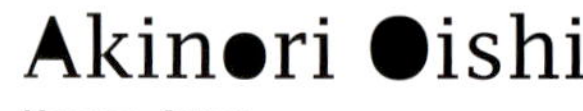

Akin●ri ●ishi

Nagoya, Japan

Title: Le Petit Bonhomme
Type of work: Flyer
Client: YCAM (Yamaguchi Center for Arts and Media)
Design: ad, d// Akinori Oishi, YCAM
Year: 2005

This flyer is designed for the exhibition 'Le Petit Bonhomme', meaning small people like beans in French. The concept was carried out through the format, layout and graphics of the promotional items. This flyer is also used as a 'stamp rally' catelogue in which visitors collect a stamp after visiting each exhibited work, so that they do not miss any of them and at the same time they can have fun with the exhibition. It is designed in a unique long horizontal format to correspond with the drawings in the exhibition.

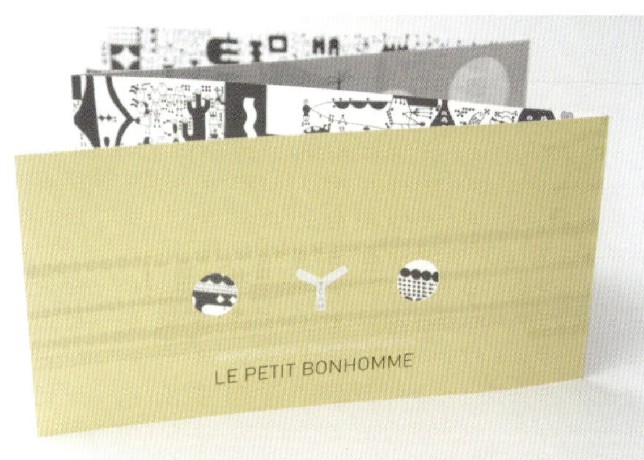

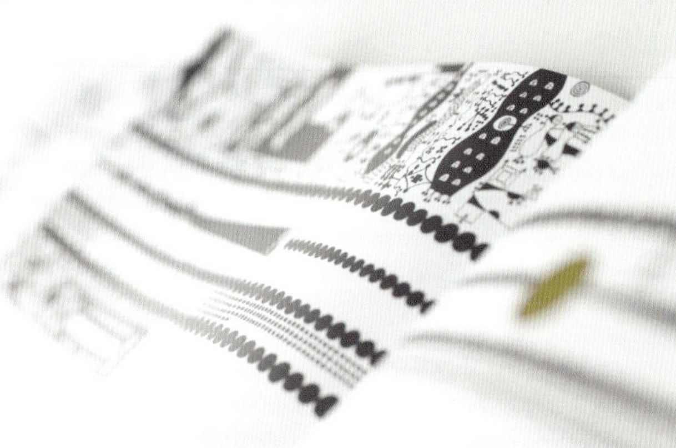

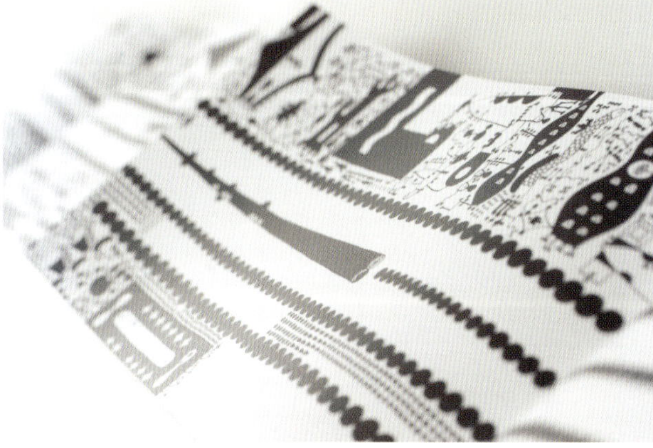

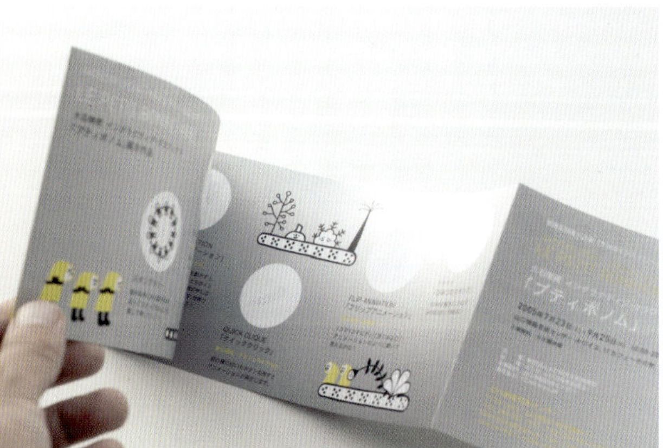

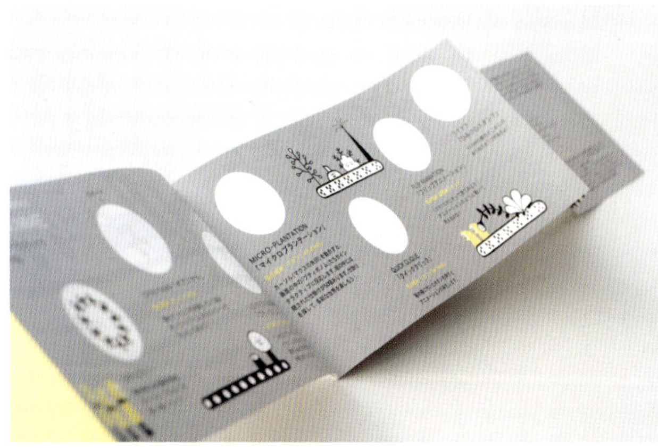

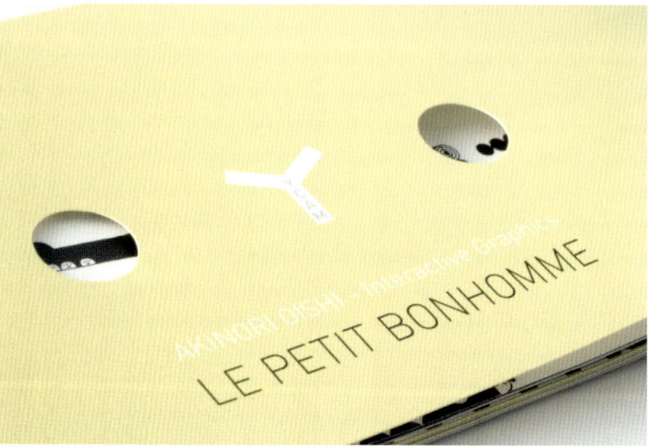

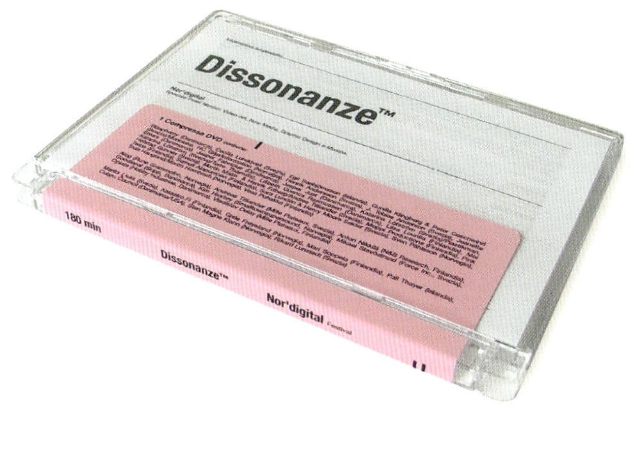

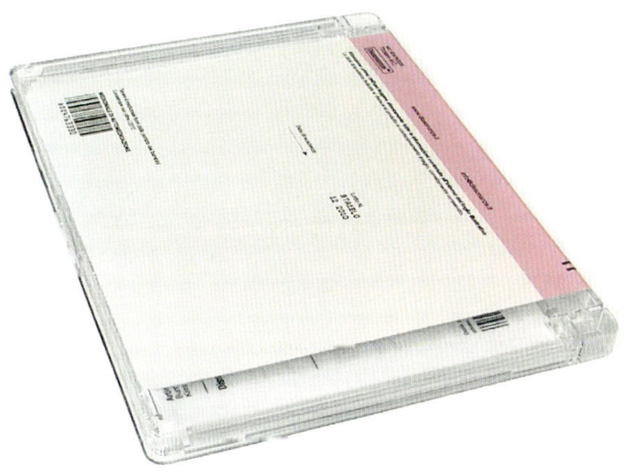

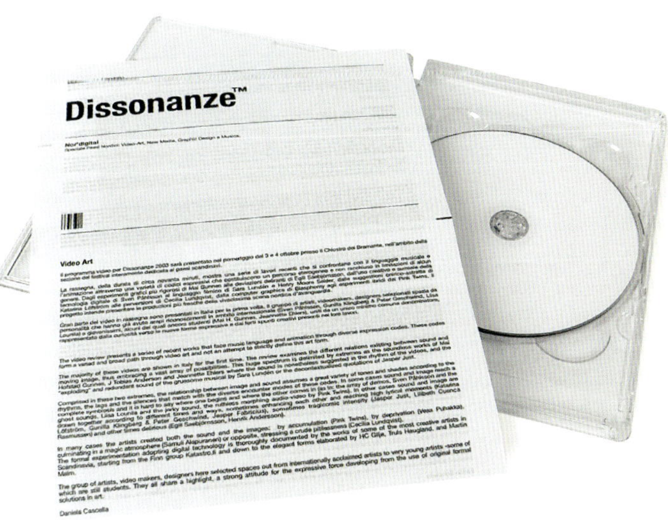

Studio Volk

Rome, Italy

Title: Dissonanze DVD
Type of work: DVD Packaging
Client: Dissonanze
Design: ad, d// Volk, Enrico Bonafede
Year: 2004

A simple, clean but informative design for this DVD packaging of Dissonanze DVD, is made with white and pink only, with no images but words only.

Brighten the Corners

London, UK / Stuttgart, Germany

Title: DAAD Information Pack
Type of work: Cards
Client: DAAD (German Academic Exchange Service)
Design: ad, d// Billy Kiossoglou, Frank Philippin
Year: 2004

These eight cards in 100x150 mm were designed for The DAAD (German Academic Exchange Service), which provides scholarship programmes for the UK and distributes publications on study, research and scholarship opportunities in Germany. In order to illustrate the organisation's role, a series of characteristically British and German images were chosen and then overprinted. The resulting composite highlights both the similarities and differences between Britain and its continental neighbours and the organisation's positioning between them.

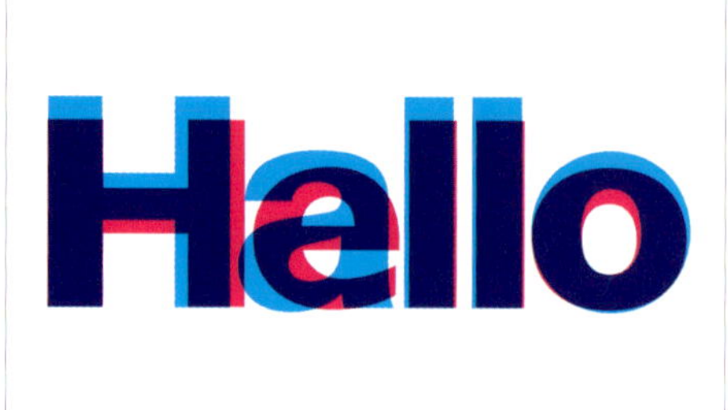

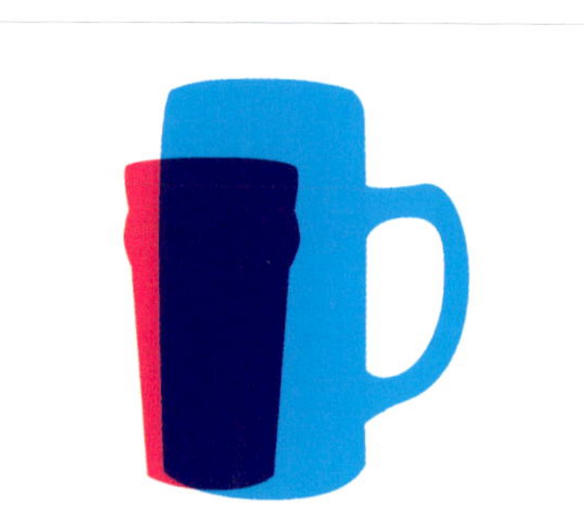

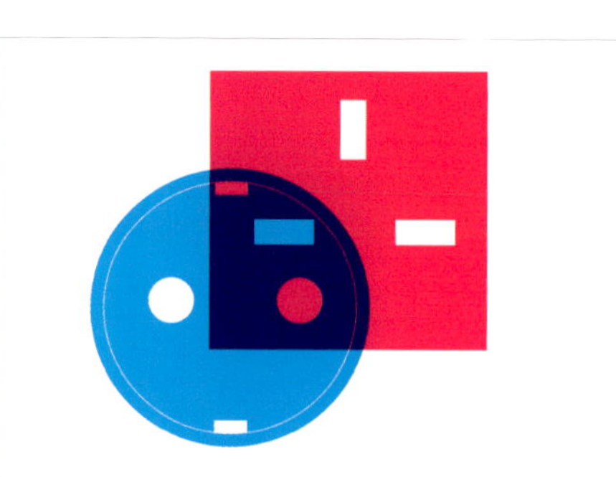

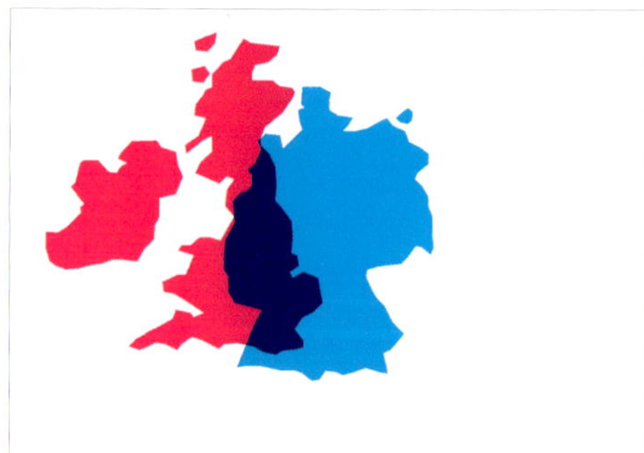

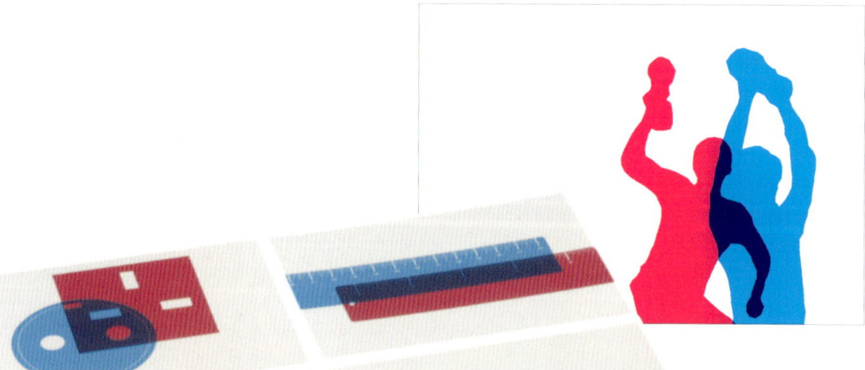

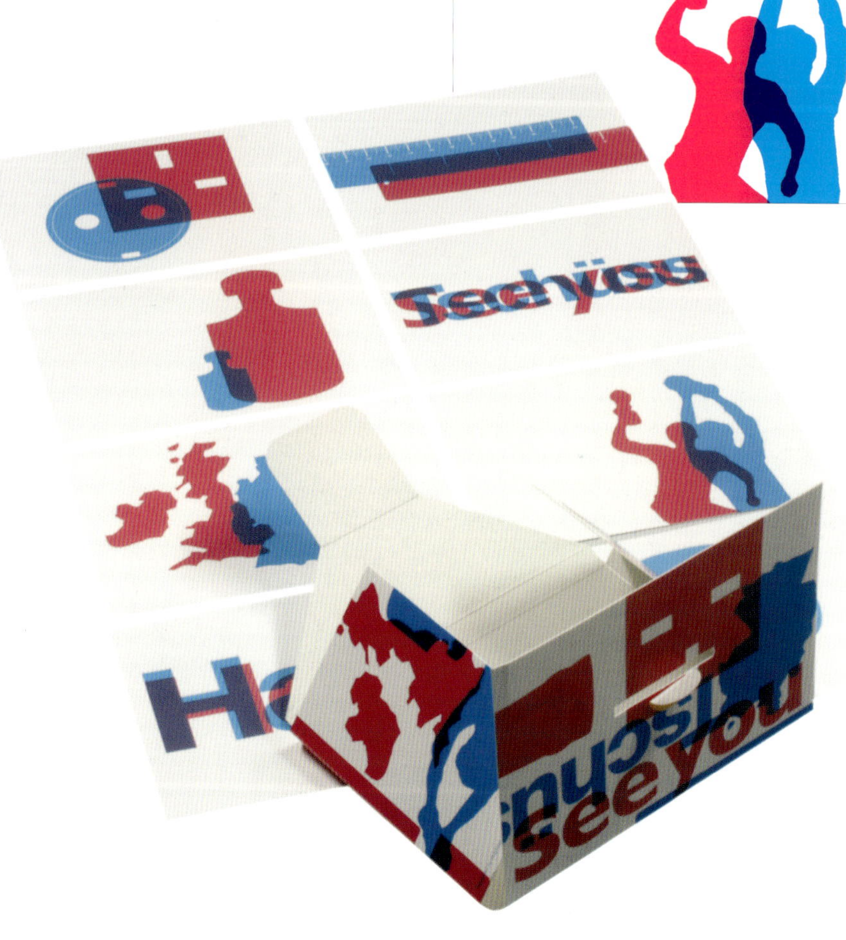

J3 Productions

Irvine, USA

Title: Storybook Sugar 'Kalidescope'
Type of work: Packaging
Client: Sugar Cosmetics
Design: ad// Jonathan Lo, Garrison Smet
d// Garrison Smet
Year: 2005

This is the second design in a series of 'storybook sugar' make up sets. Each set contains a limited edition palette of lip-glosses and eye-shadows.

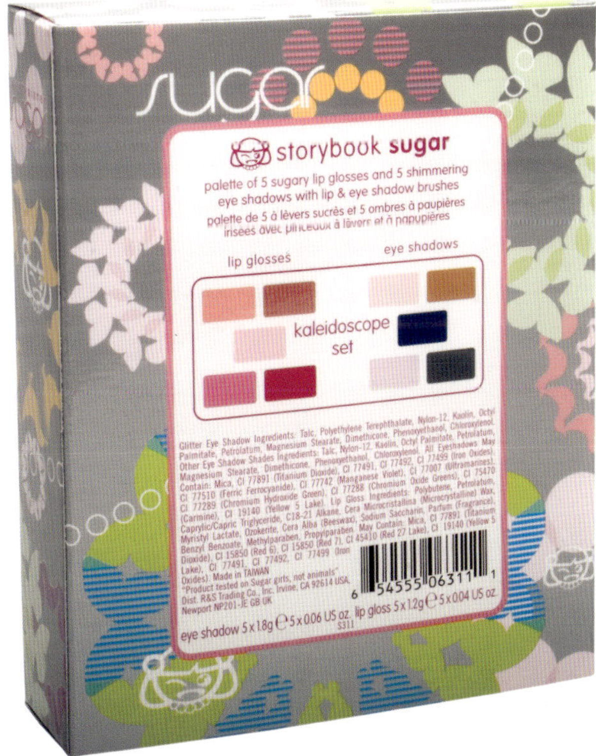

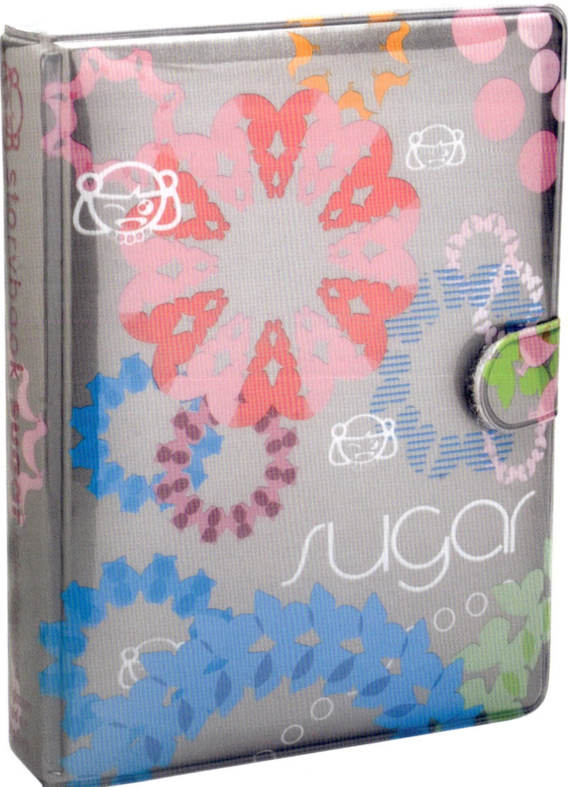

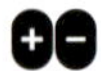

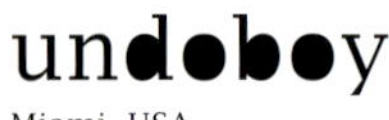
un**do**boy

Miami, USA

Title: 1.// COOP 2.// Wearable Bag
Type of work: 1.// Fashion Packaging 2.// Bag
Client: -
Design: 1.// ad, d: undoboy & Ryan Meis
2.// ad, d: undoboy
Year: 1.// 2005 2.// 2004

1.// A collaboration project that was designed to bring happiness to people. It is a fashion brand that tells our friendship and stories. It comes with a secret gift in the package when people buy a T-shirt. 2.// The case symbolizes the transformation from school bag to office briefcase. The designer's idea was to break the society's rules in our life.

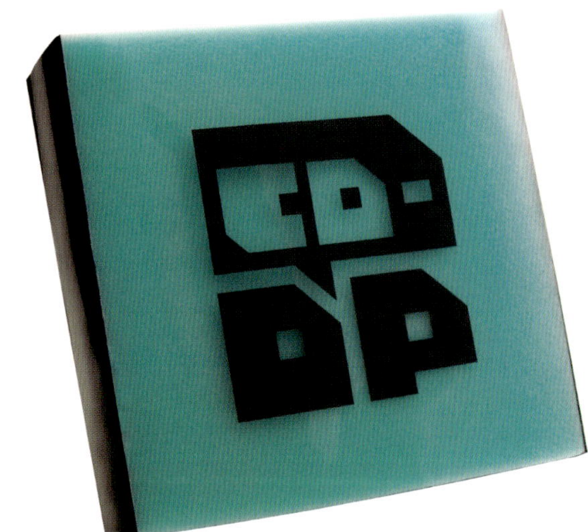

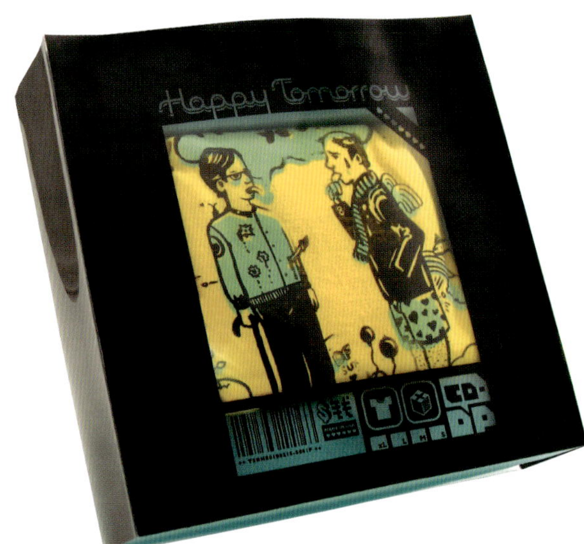

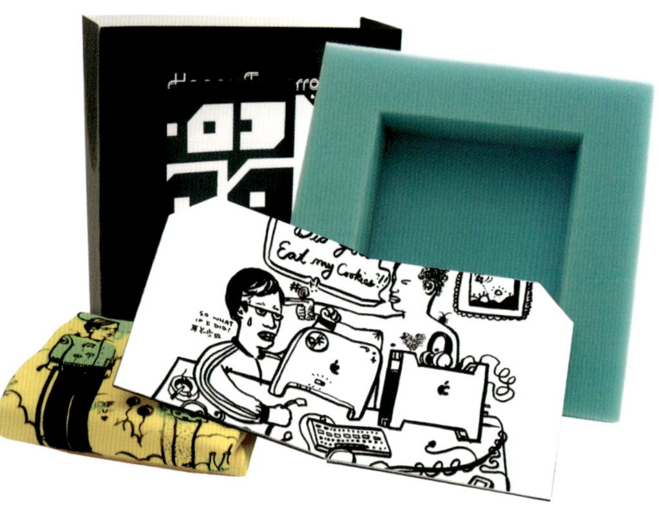

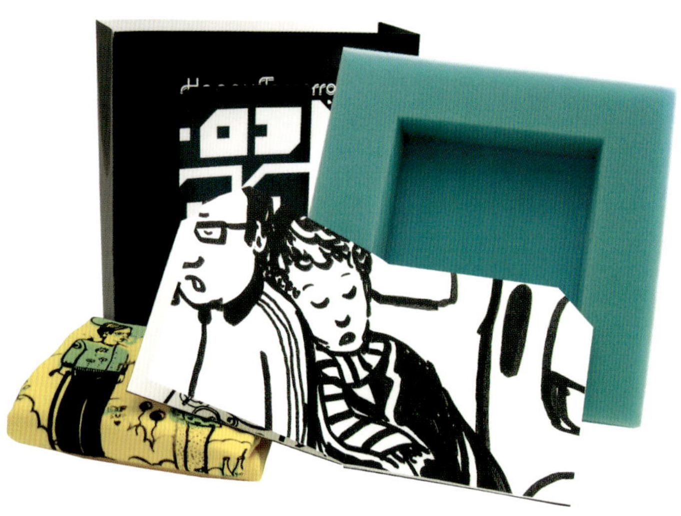

1.//

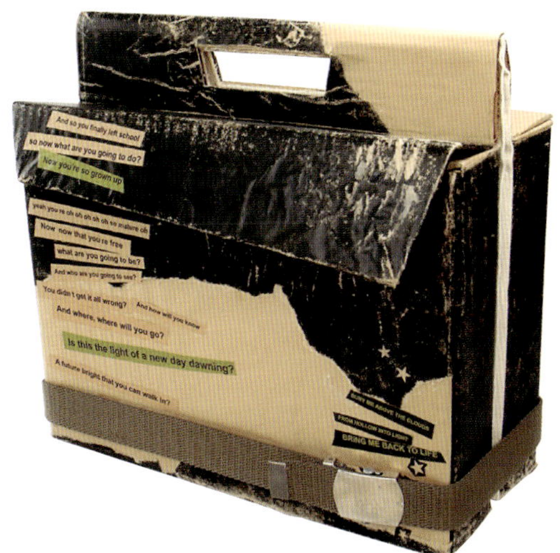

And so you finally left school
So now what are you going to do?
Are you're so grown up
yeah ya oh oh oh oh oh oh so mature oh
Now now that you're free
what are you going to be?
And who are you going to see?
You didn't get it all wrong? And how will you know?
And, where, where will you go?
Is this the light of a new day dawning?
A future bright that you can walk in?
BURY ME ABOVE THE CLOUDS
FROM HOLLOW INTO LIGHT
BRING ME BACK TO LIFE

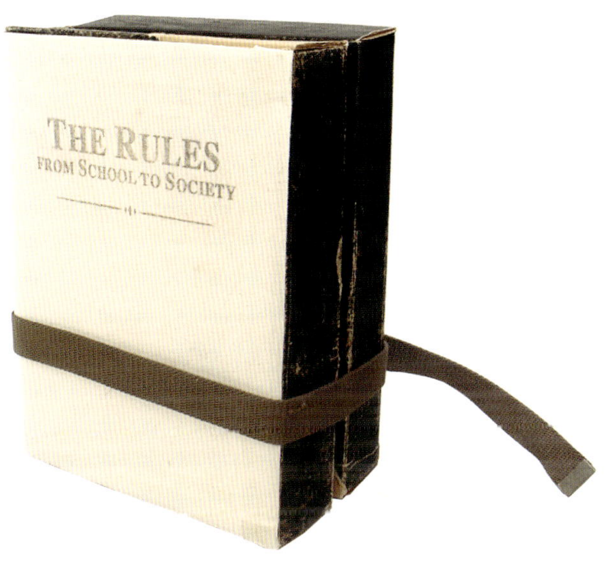

THE RULES
FROM SCHOOL TO SOCIETY

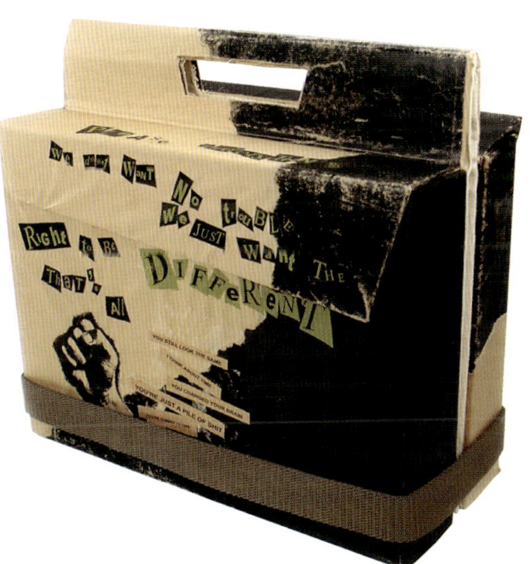

We just want No trouble
We just want The
Right to Be different
That's all
DIFFERENT

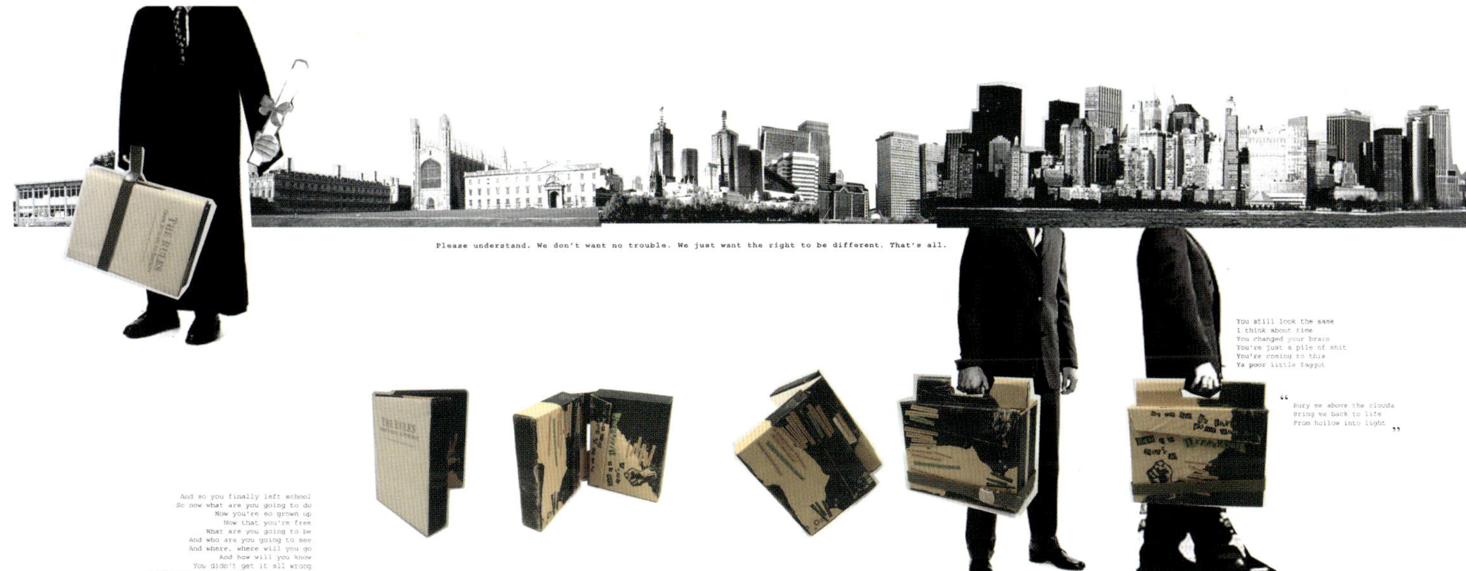

THE RULES
Please understand. We don't want no trouble. We just want the right to be different. That's all.
You still look the same
I think about time
You changed your brain
You're just a pile of shit
You're coming to this
Ya poor little faggot
" Bury me above the clouds
Bring me back to life
From hollow into light "
And so you finally left school
So now what are you going to do
Now you're so grown up
Now that you're free
What are you going to be
And who are you going to see
And where, where will you go
And how will you know
You didn't get it all wrong
Is this the light of a new day dawning
A future bright that you can walk in

"What is it telling me about?" This is a question you might ask when looking at a design. In the following pages, the central message—that is, what the artist or client wants to tell their prospective audience, to you—is the key ingredient. Sometimes the statement is obvious, bludgeoning the senses and demanding you to take notice; at other times, the statement is subtle. When viewed as a whole, you'll notice a stark similarity in all the message: they are trying to motivate you to one end or another. Take a look at how these artists harness the power of suggestion.

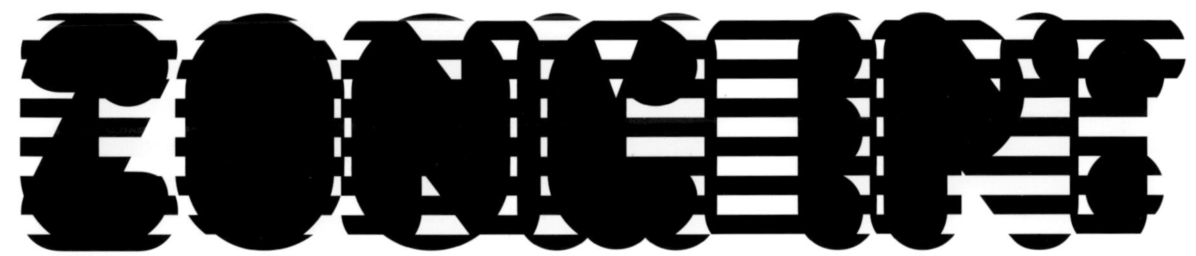

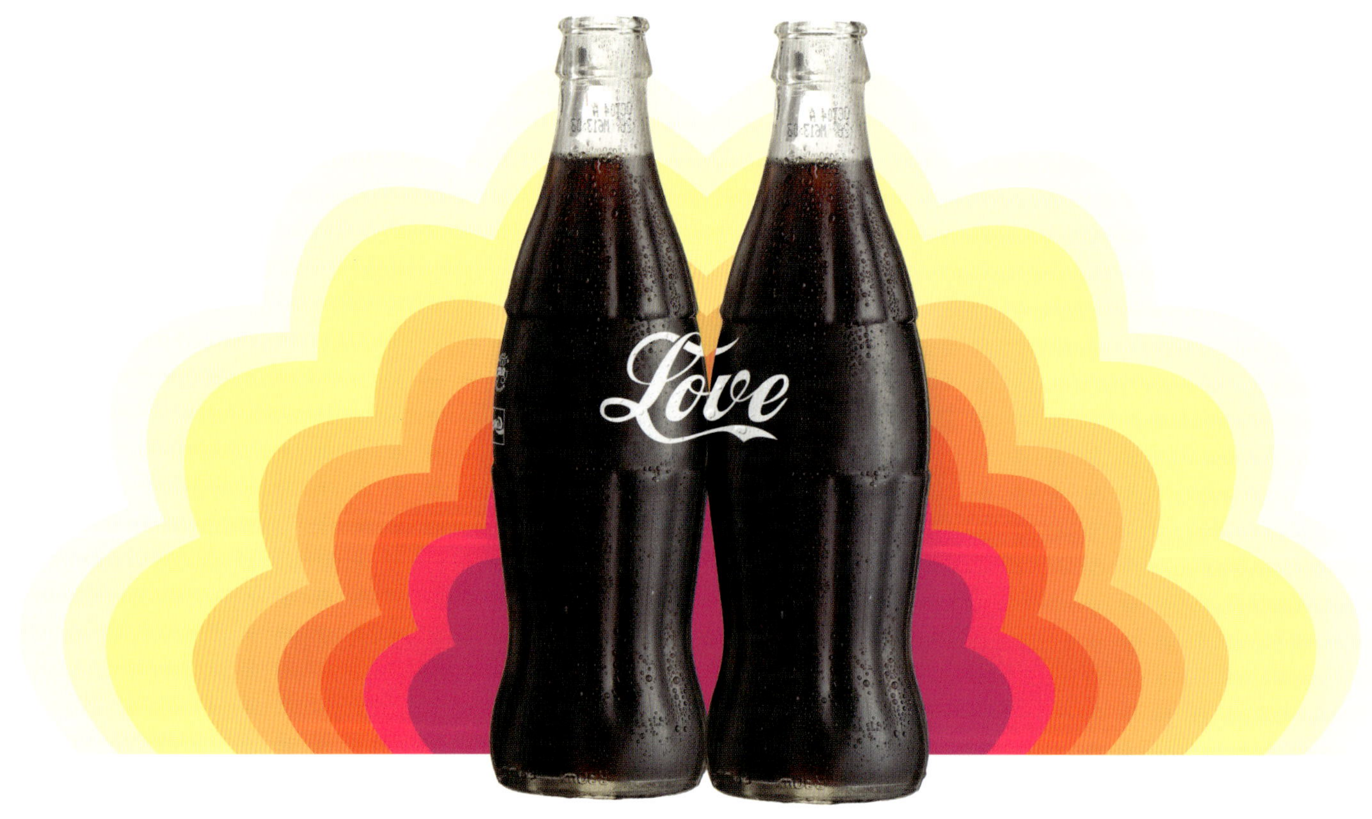

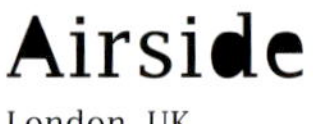

Airside

London, UK

Title: Coca-Cola
Type of work: Billboards and bus advertising illustrations
Client: Coca-Cola, Mother London
Design: ad// Airside, Mother d// Airside
Year: 2005

A Coca-Cola print ad campaign for 2005 summer on a theme of 'refreshment'. Commissioned by Mother, conceived and executed by Airside, the ads show the Coca-Cola traditional glass bottles with the logo replaced by the word 'Love', written in Coca-Cola style. Surrounding the bottles are beautiful bold coloured patterns emanating like flowers as reminiscent of the 70s Coca-Cola campaigns. The ads appeared on buses and billboard sites throughout the whole July, same year.

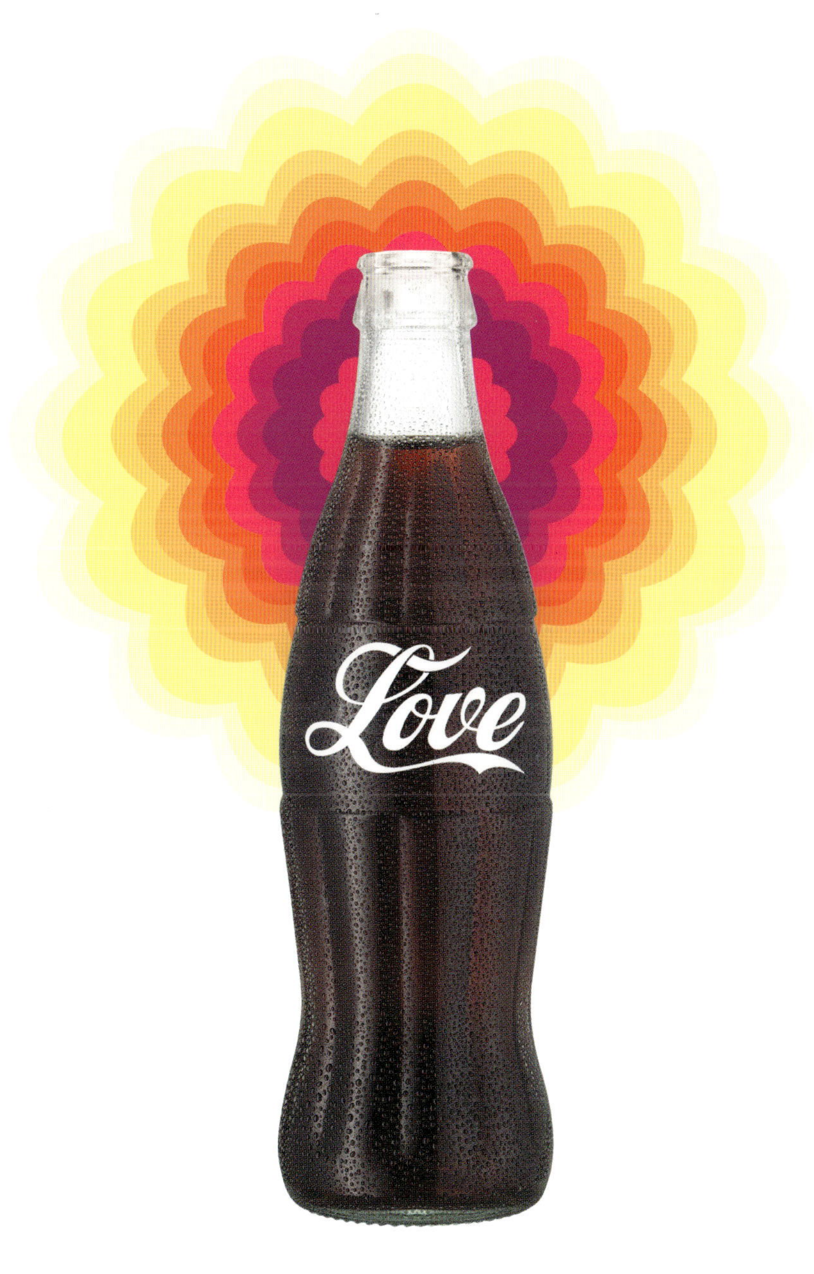
Love

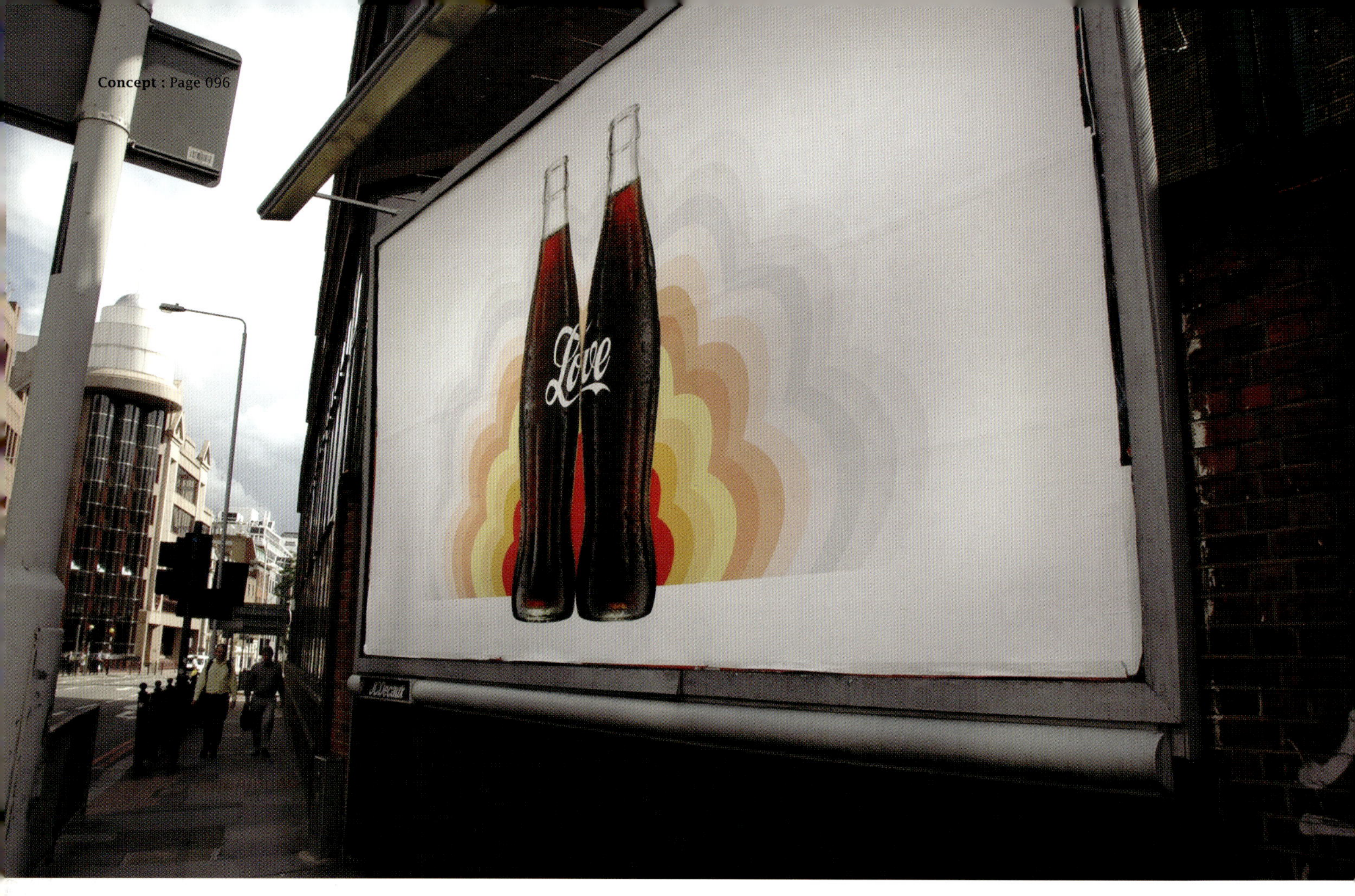
Love

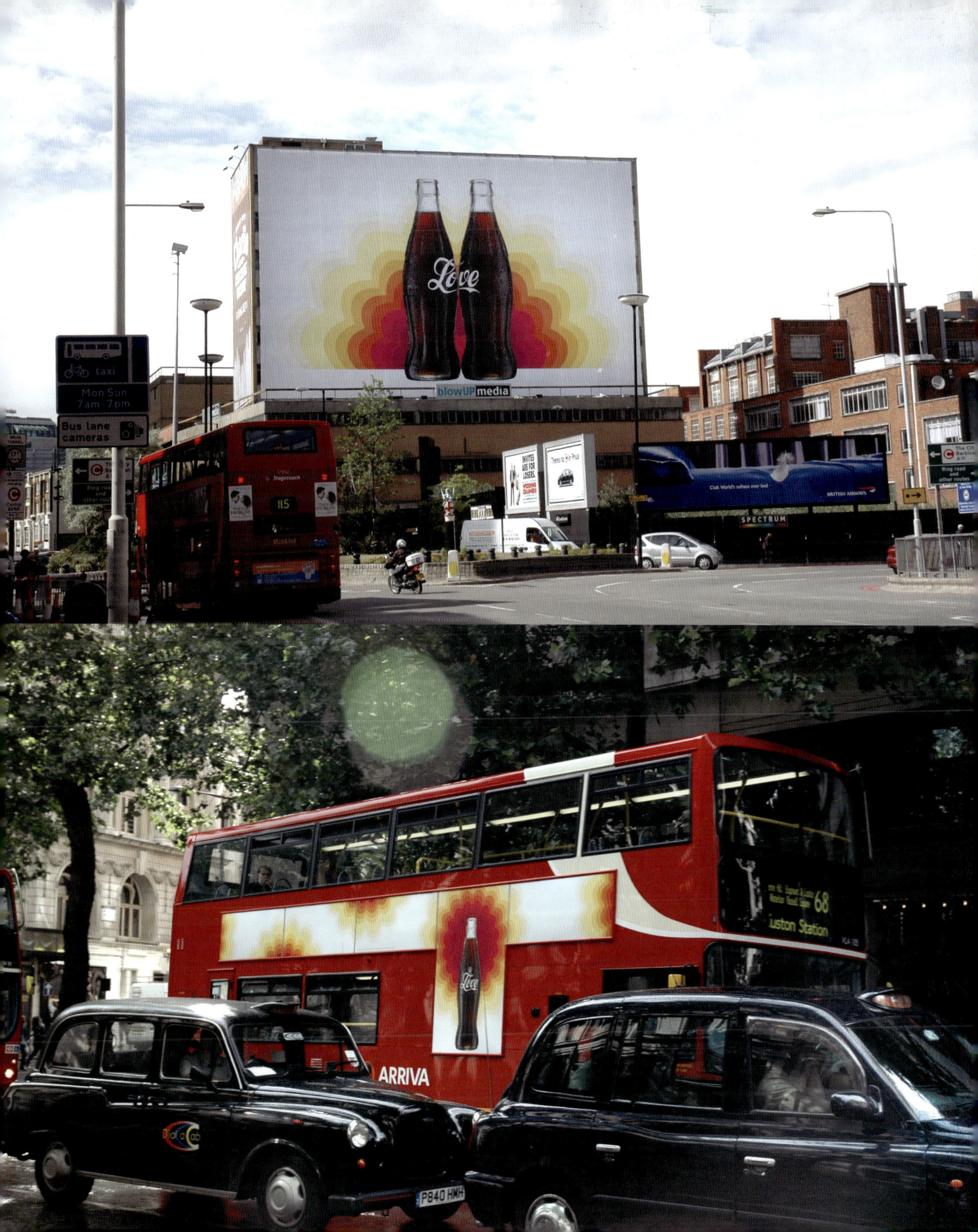
Love
blowUP media
115
Stagecoach
taxi
Mon Sun
7am - 7pm
Bus lane
cameras
INVITES ARE FOR LOSERS.
Club World's softest ever bed
BRITISH AIRWAYS
SPECTRUM
68
Euston Station
ARRIVA
Love
P840 HMH

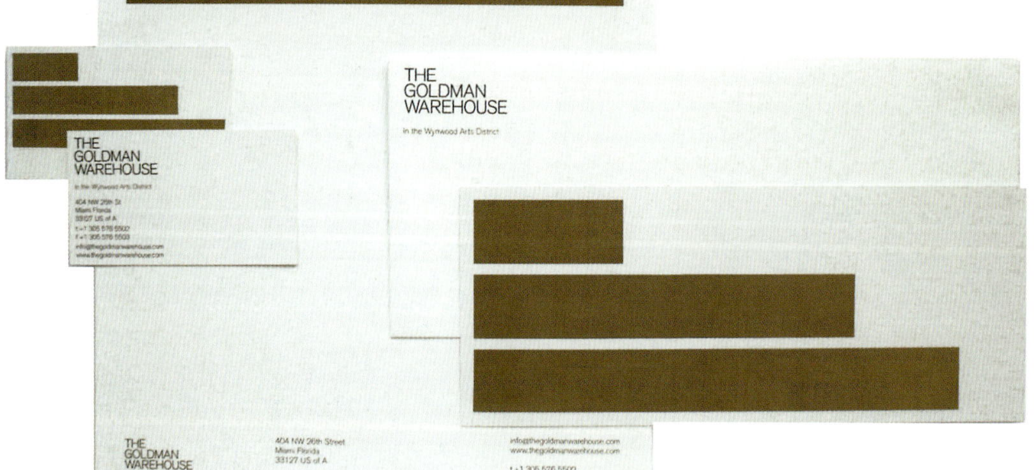

Emmi Sal●nen

London, UK

Title: –
Type of work: Identity
Client: Tony Goldman
Design: ad// Jan Wilker d// Emmi Salonen
p// Simon Hare Photography
Year: 2005

This identity for a gallery was designed by Emmi Salonen at Karlssonwilker Inc., NY. The gallery exhibits private collections of abstract art, so the identity needed to look trustworthy and smart. The solution was to echo the idea that whilst the paintings were hanging at the exhibition, they were missing from someone's home, leaving marks on the wall where something is supposed to be and has been there for years. The identity reflects this by marking the area of an enlarged logotype with bold golden stripes. On technique-wise, the logo is gilded on the building.

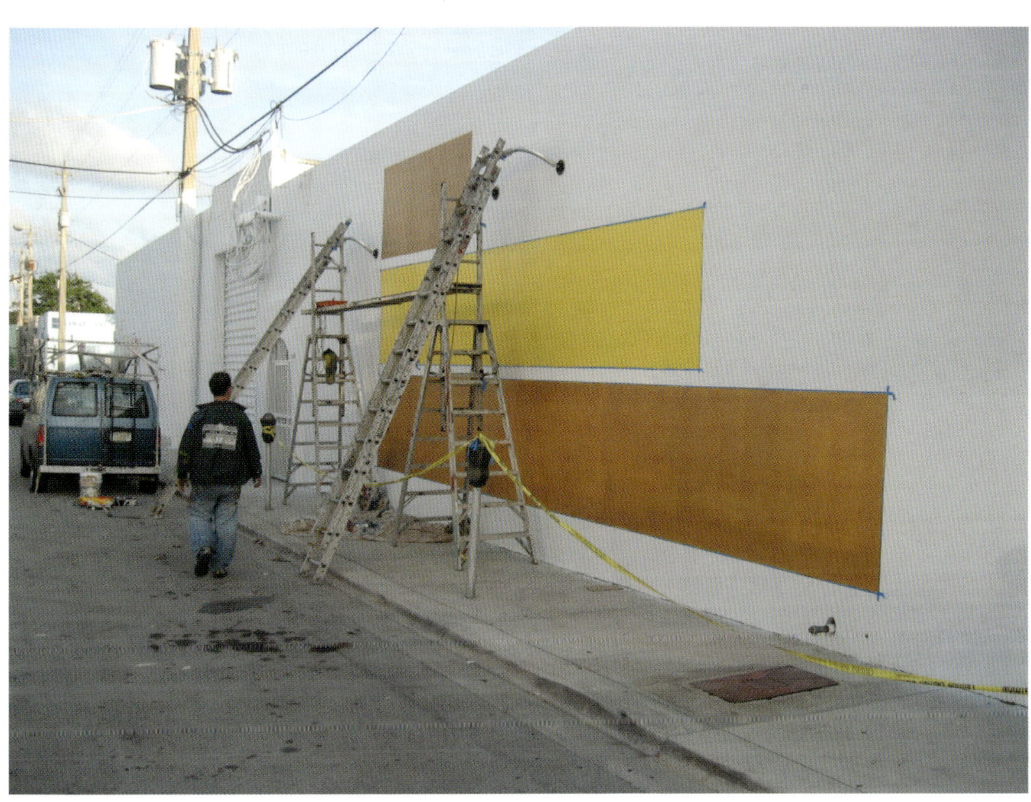

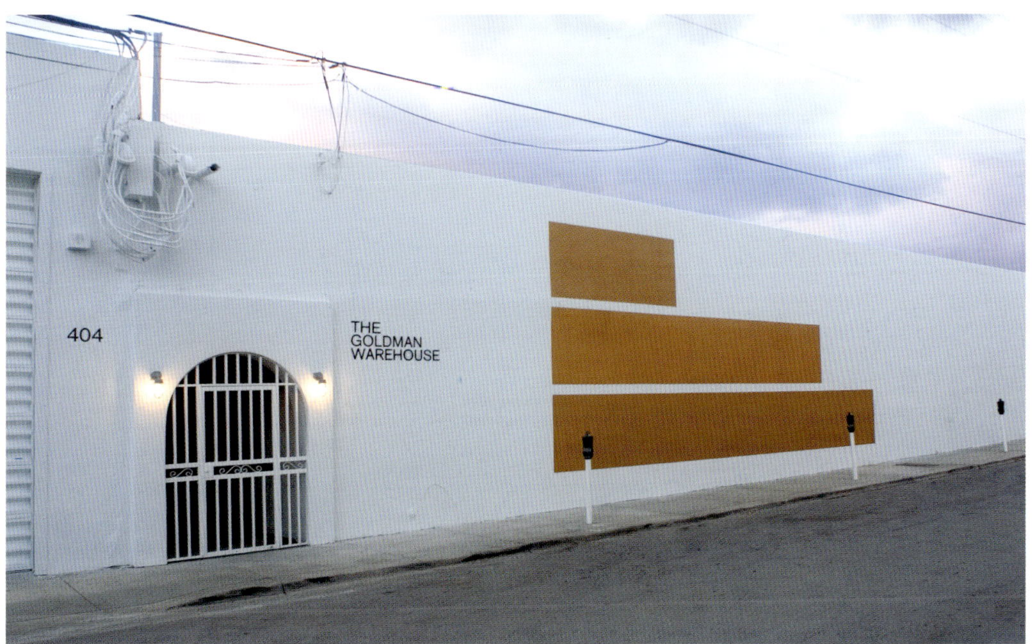
404
THE
GOLDMAN
WAREHOUSE

Al**o**of **D**esign

London, UK

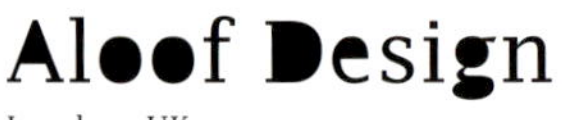

Title: Mulberry Notesbook
Type of work: Invitation, notebook
Client: GFSmith
Design: ad, d// Sam Aloof
Year: 2005

An alternative press give-away to coincide with Mulberry's Spring/Summer Men's Wear Collection fashion show in Florence. An all-paper 'notes' book for use throughout Fashion Week was created and was inspired by Mulberry's iconic Leather Agenda. The 8pp cover is made from a single sheet of card, die cut and debossed with a custom drawn pattern. The text pages are bound to the back cover and the closure tab can also be used as a page marker.

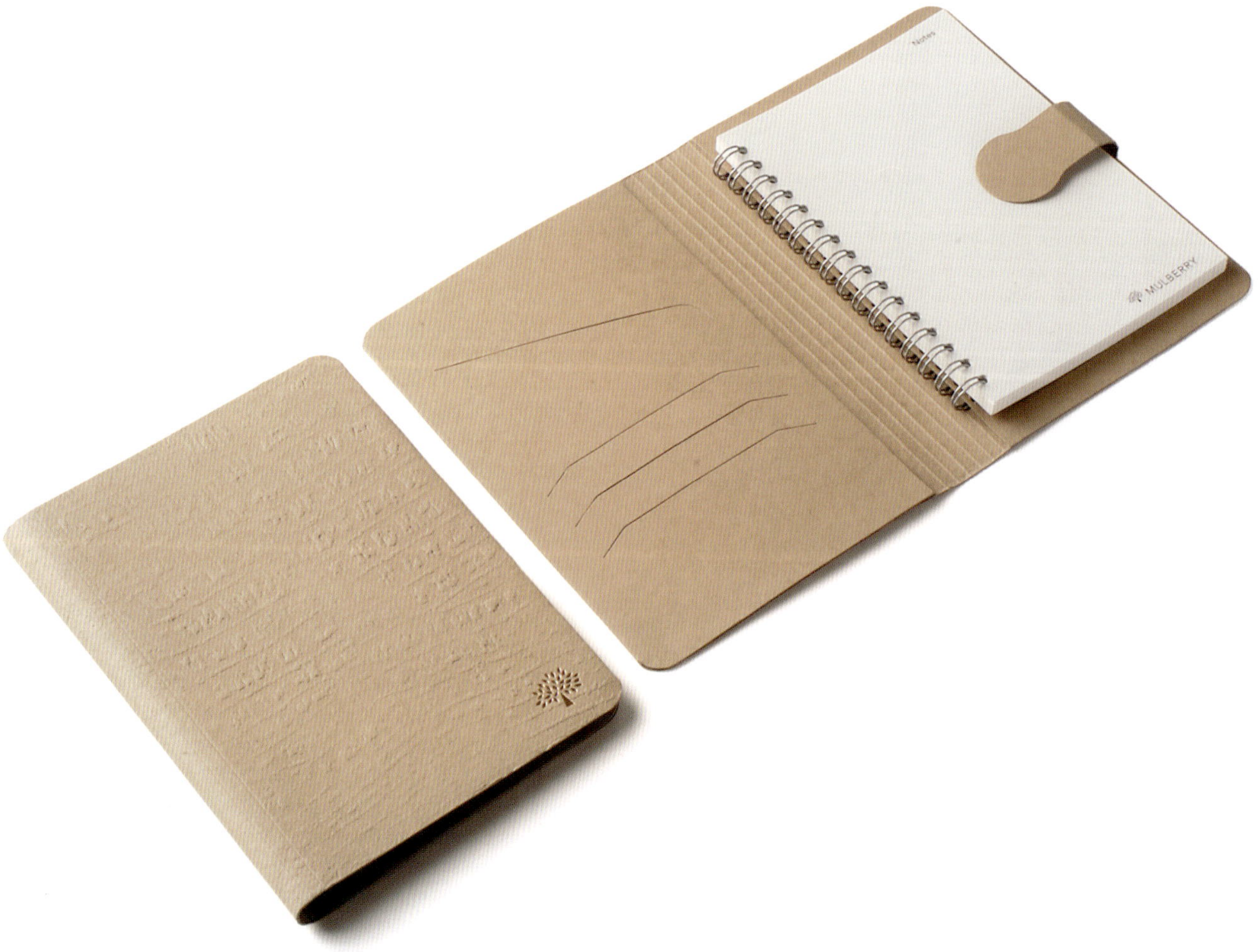

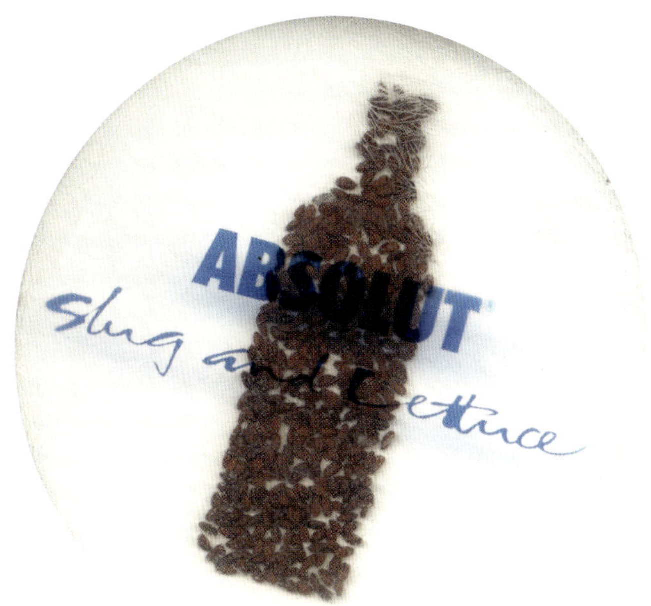

1.//

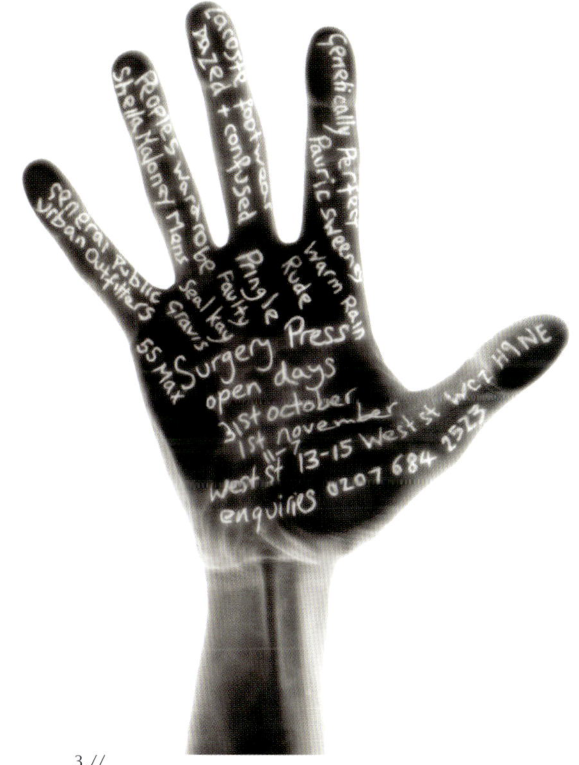

3.//

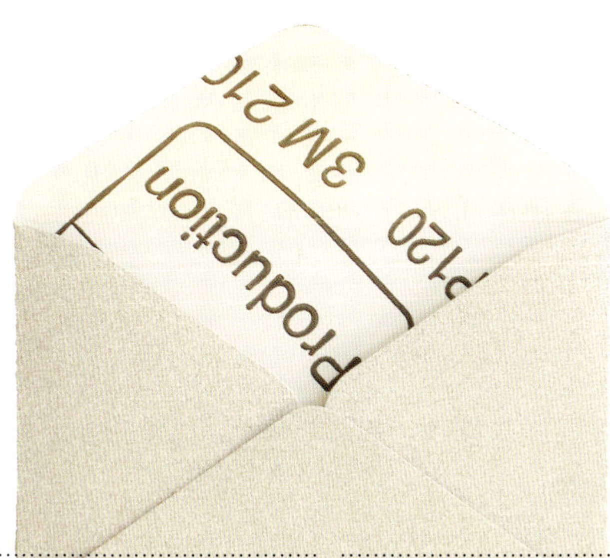

2.//

Warmrain

London, UK

Title: -
Type of work: 1.// Marketing Campaign
2.// Bill Folder 3.// Invitation
Client: 1.// Absolut Vodka 2.// sketch
3.// Surgery Public Relations
Design: ad// Mark Lawson Bell d// Warmrain
Year: 1,2.// 2005 3.// 2004

1.// A design of a series of drink mats for the bars, Slug and Lettuce, which uses a petri dish containing blotting paper and a stencil of grass seed in the shape of the Absolut bottle. 2.// These envelopes are made from sandpaper, sponsored by 3M, make even the simplest request of 'bill please', an unforgettable sensory experience. 3.// Highlighting the details of the press event as well as the PR companies client list, this invitation recalls those times when writing a reminder on anything but our hand just wasn't an option. The copy was written on the Creative Directors hand, scanned and printed life size onto A3 translucent paper.

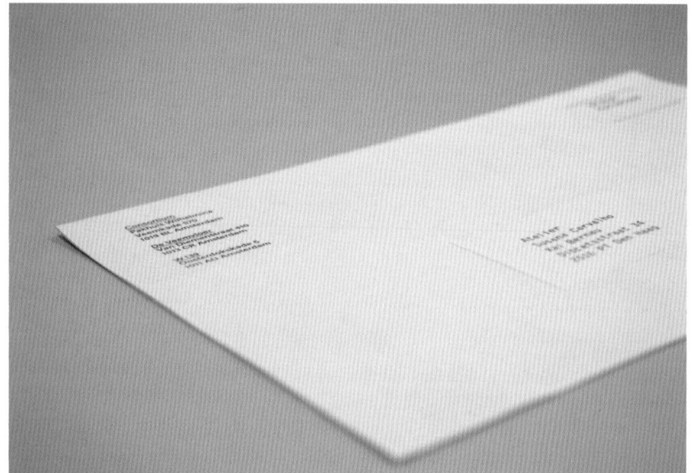

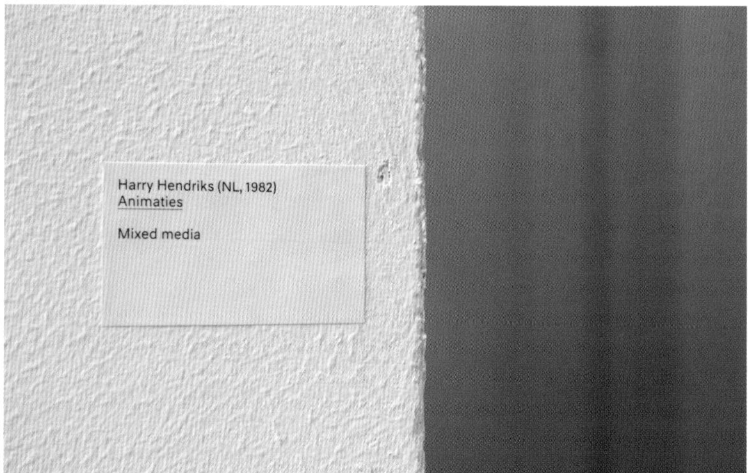

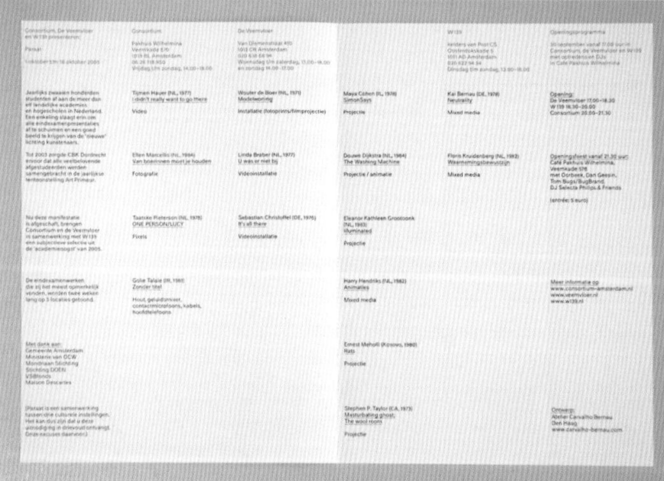

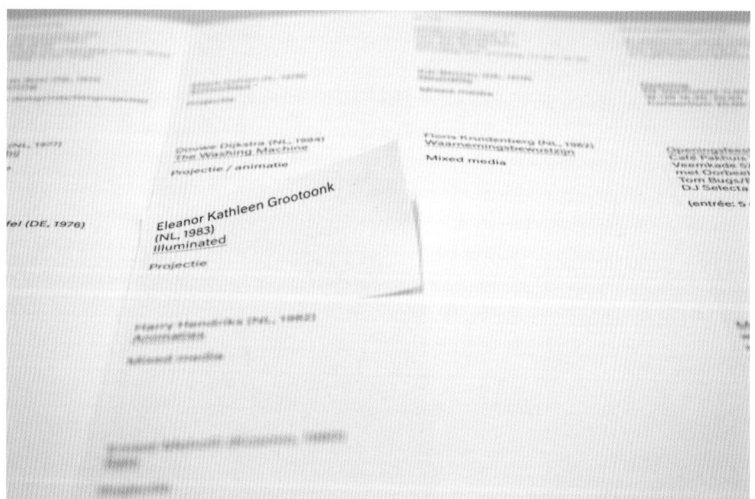

Atelier Susana Carvalho Kai Bernau

Hague, The Netherlands

Title: W139 / Paraat
Type of work: Invitation
Client: W139, Amsterdam
Design: ad, d// Susana Carvalho, Kai Bernau
Year: 2005

An invitation for an exhibition of graduated students from Fine Art Academies in The Netherlands. Despite of severe restrictions in time and budget, they wanted to give the invitations an extra value: The invitation is printed on an A4 format adhesive paper with a custom grid half-cut. The individual stickers are in a grid of slits that orders the information on the page; the stickers can be used as captions for the individual artworks, as address stickers for the galleries or as reminders of the opening programme.

RMAC

Lisboa, Portugal

Title: Spring/ Summer Collection 06 – Invitation
Type of work: Promotion
Client: Alves/Gonçalves
Design: ad// Ricardo Mealha, Ana Cunha
d// Ricardo Mealha
Year: 2005

This invitation card designed for Spring/Summer Collection 06 of Alves/Gonçalves is delighted by the handcrafted-liked patterns in white with a baby blue background. It is as sophisticated and simple as its ready-to-wear designs.

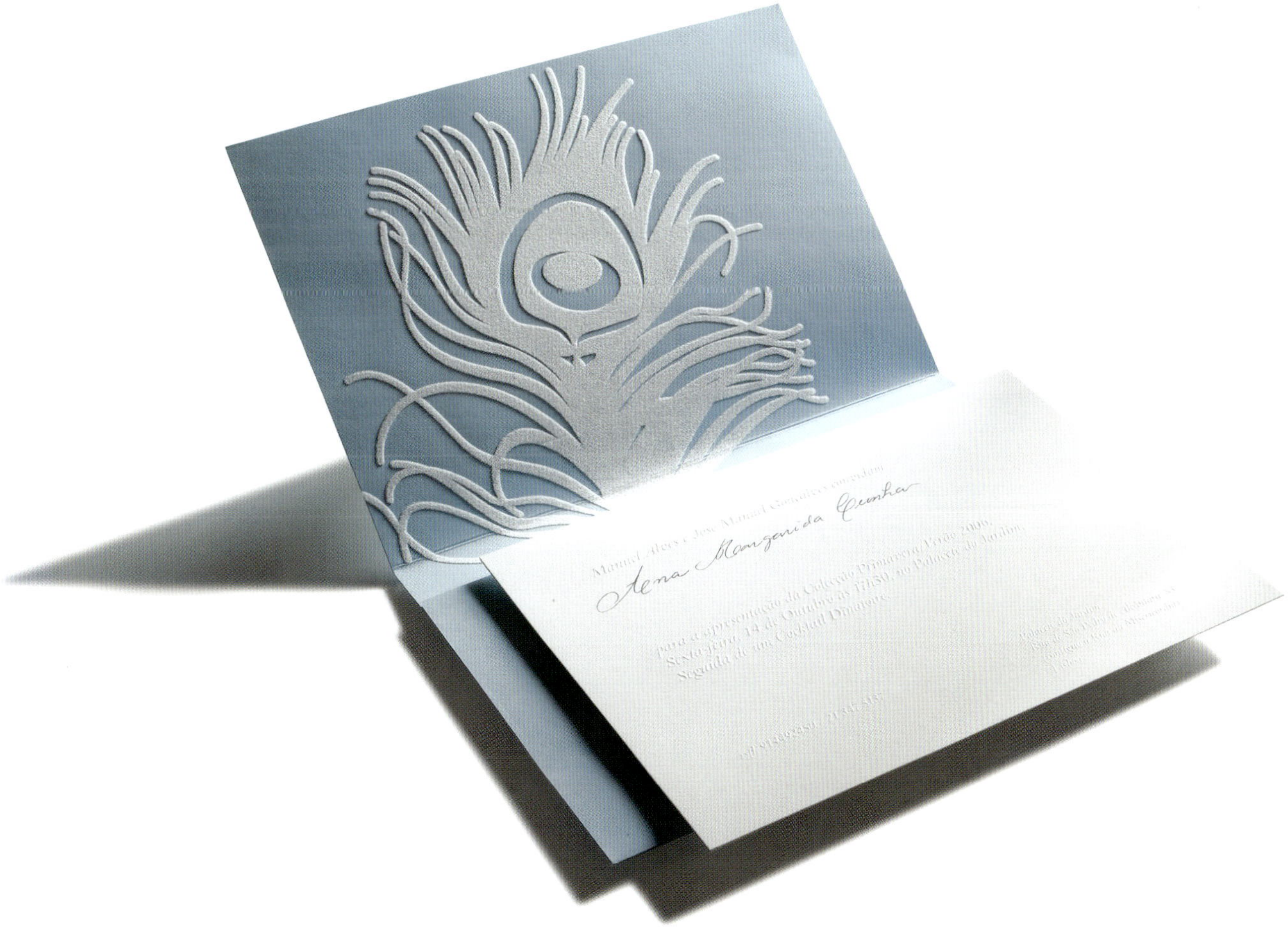

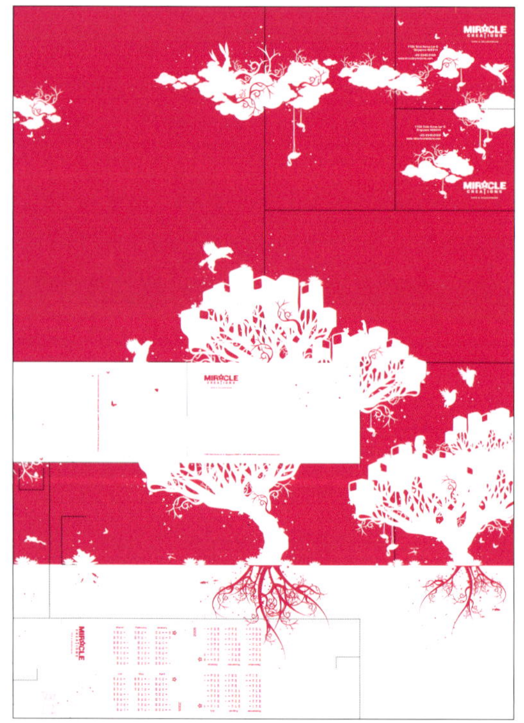

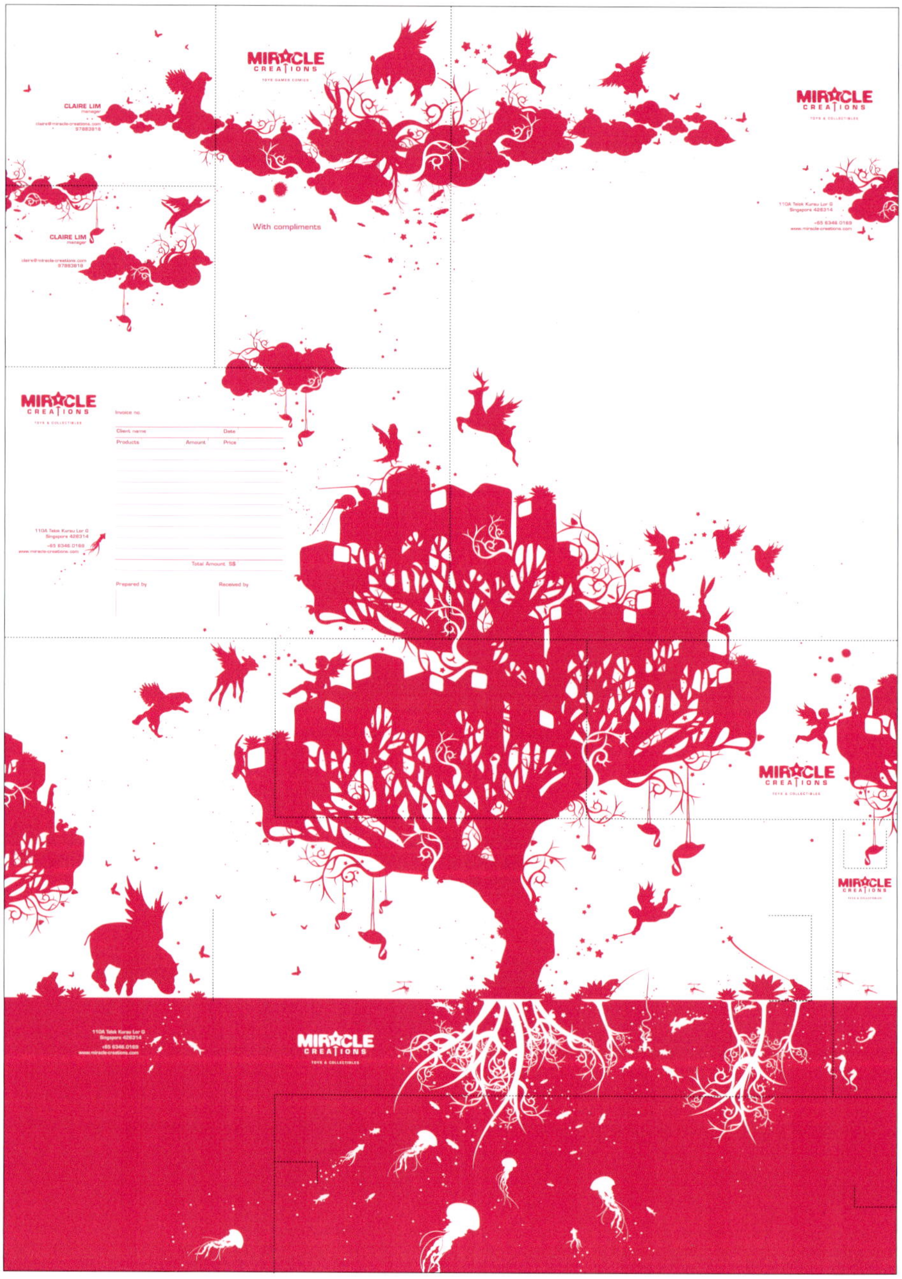

Kinetic

Singapore

Title: Miracle Creations
Type of work: Corporate Identity
Client: Miracle Creations
Design: ad, d// Jonathan Yuen, Roy Poh, Pann Lim
Year: 2004

For this project, cost efficiency is the key as the client is a SOHO dealing in toys and collectibles. The design addresses the issue with an all-in-one poster, parts of which can be detached to work as an amazing array of stationery: name card, 'with compliments' note, letterhead, invoice, postcard, CD sleeve, bookmark, or even a calendar!

Stephen Layfield

Sydney, Australia

Title: The Shirt Company
Type of work: Direct mail letterhead
Client: The Shirt Company
Design: ad, d// Stephen Layfield
Year: 2005

This piece as a direct mail, is the primary piece of communication for The Shirt Company's to express what they did. It is required to be memorable and stand out from the crowd.

Stephen Layfield

Sydney, Australia

Title: John's Birthday Invite
Type of work: Invitation
Client: John Stilgoe
Design: ad, d// Stephen Layfield
Year: 2004

An invitation for Birthday drinks at The Queen's Head, simply represented by placing a UK stamp with the Queen's face corresponding to the restaurant's sign.

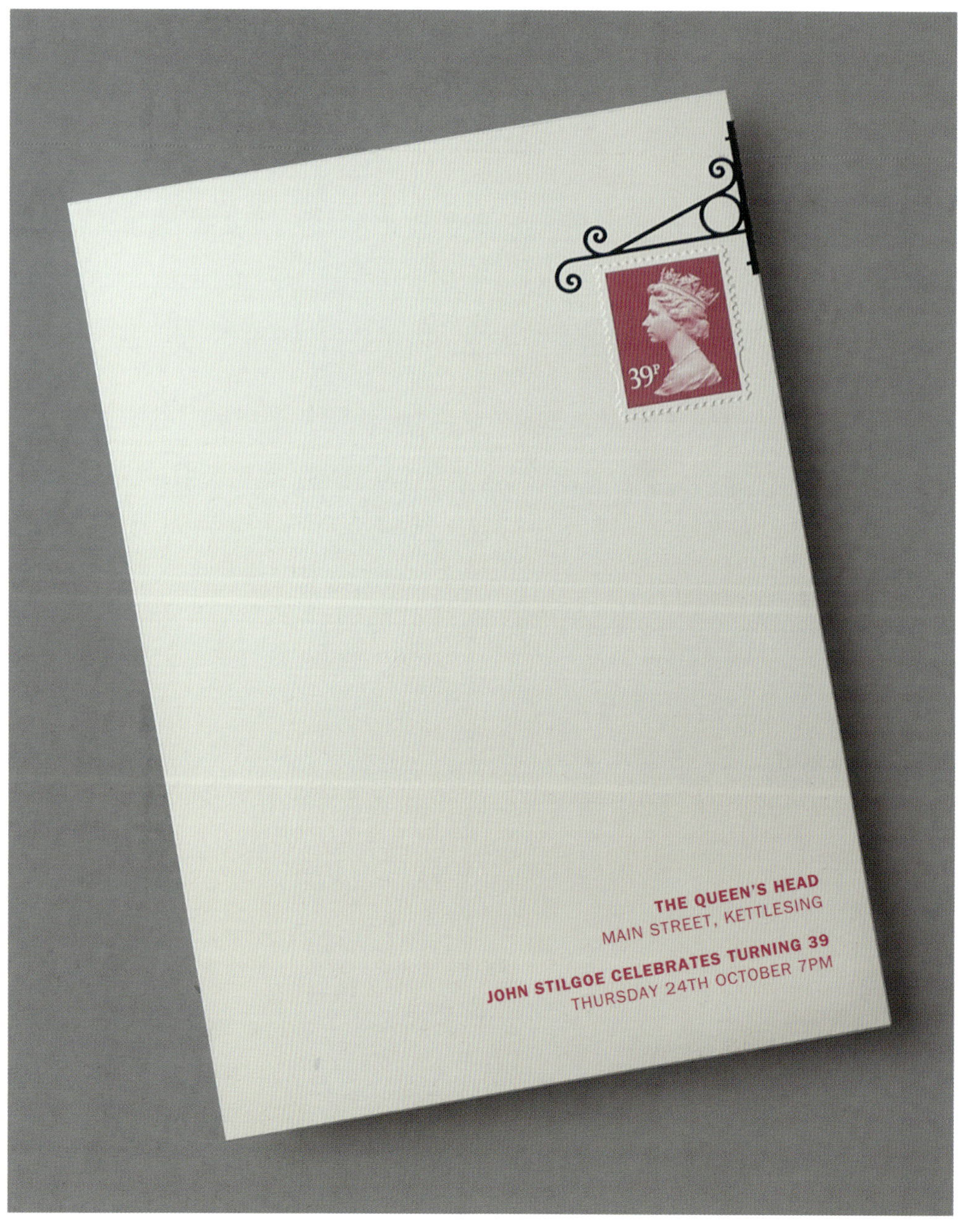

Stephen Layfield

Sydney, Australia

Title: Daniel's Birth Announcement
Type of work: Birth announcement
Client: Steven & Julie Swires
Design: ad, d// Stephen Layfield
Year: 2004

The solution of the design for this birth announcement came from turning the envelope upside down to create a nappy, completed with a safety pin foil blocked in shiny silver.

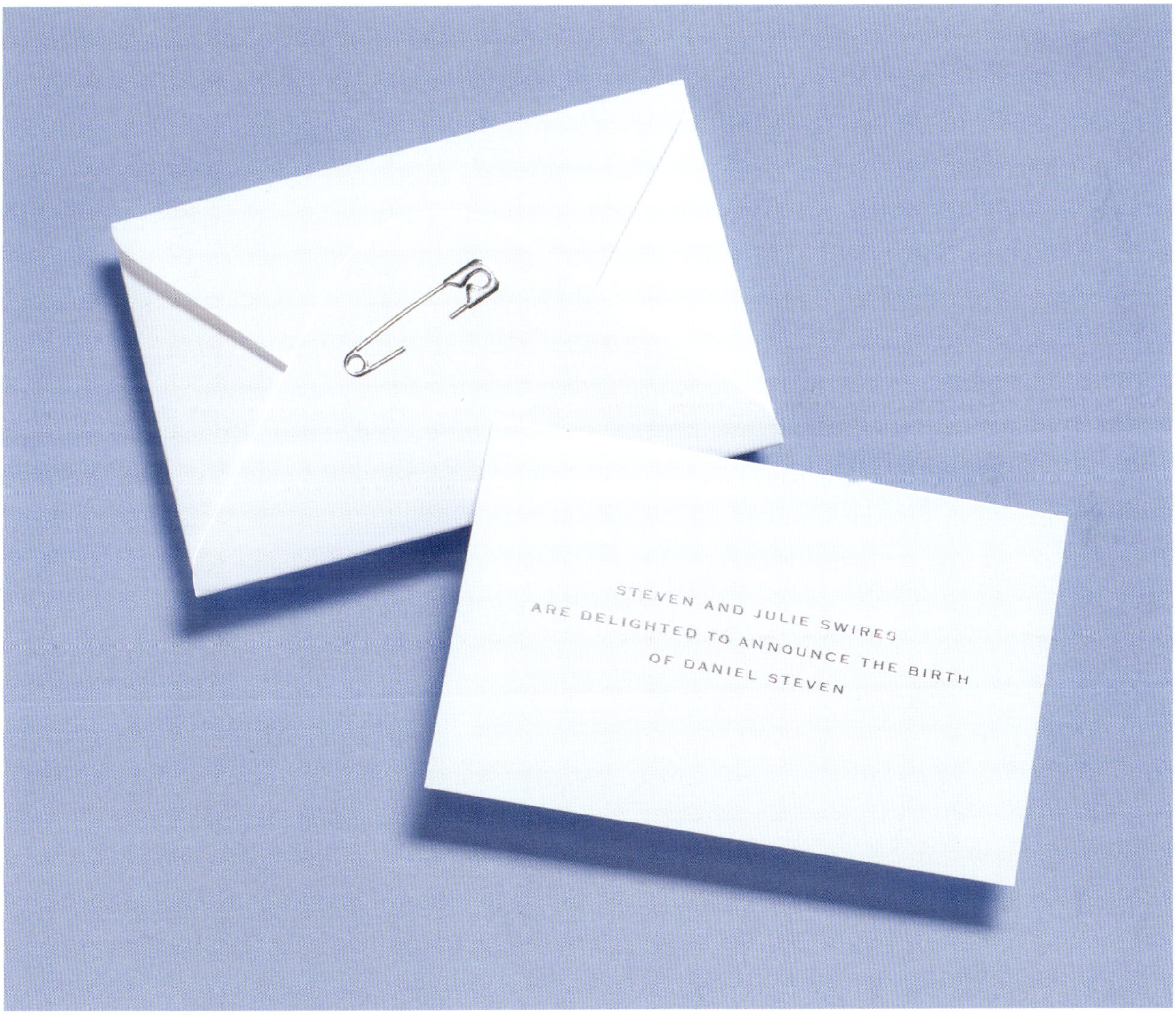

Maiko Gubler

Berlin, Germany

Title: avec
Type of work: Identity
Client: avec
Design: ad, d// Maiko Gubler
Year: 2005

An identity for an artist management studio based in Paris. The requirement included teeny-weeny budget, flexible artists & products and an address soon to be changed. To avoid double printing costs, the logo is embossed and printed respectively on plain material. The client is provided with a normal stamp as well as with an embossed stamp of the logo to enhance the feel of standard stationary material.

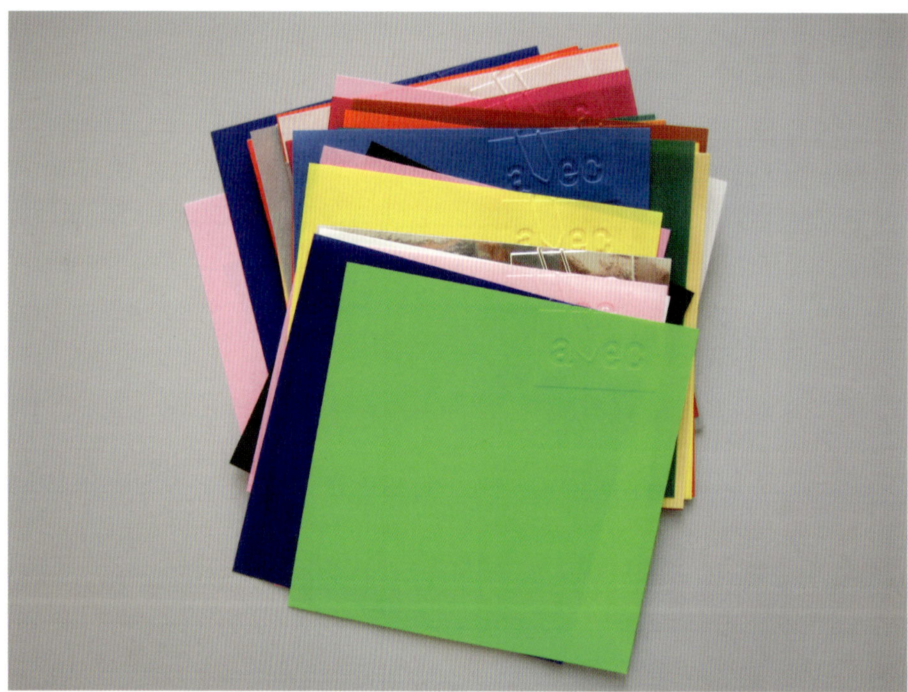

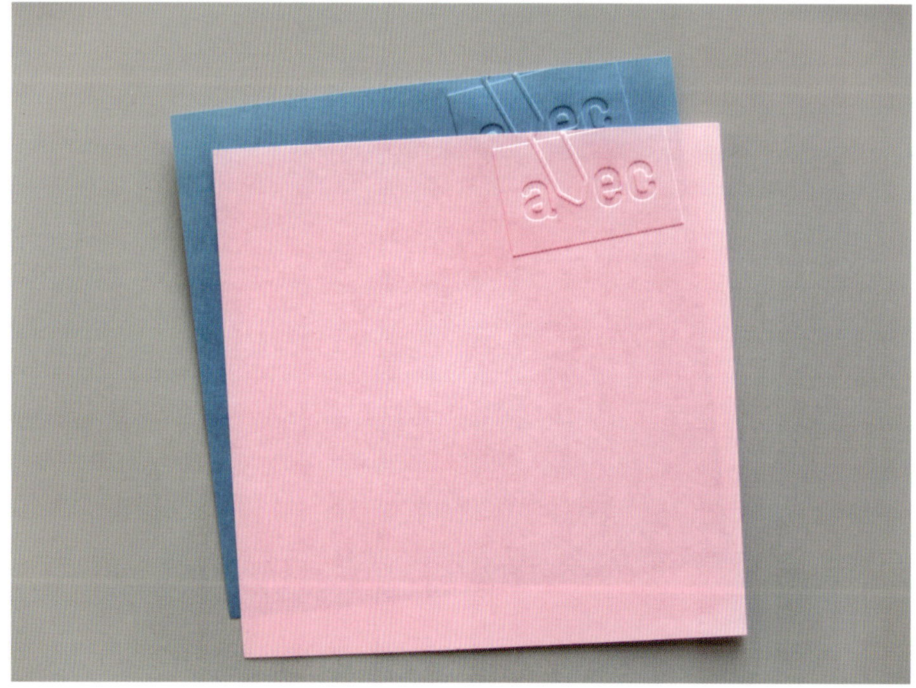

Serial Cut™

Madrid, Spain

Title: –
Type of work: Identity, record sleeves
Client: Urbana Recordings
Design: ad, d// Sergio del Puerto
Year: 2004

Identity design for David Penn´s electronic music label. The concept for the record sleeves was the contrast between black and white on each side, with the stickers having a different colour for each release. The only typeface used was Helvetica, which is never out of date. The first double CD compilation –My Rules– used the same design concept. The only exception was Deux´s release 'Sun Rising Up', which used pink on the cover and the Avantagarde® typeface.

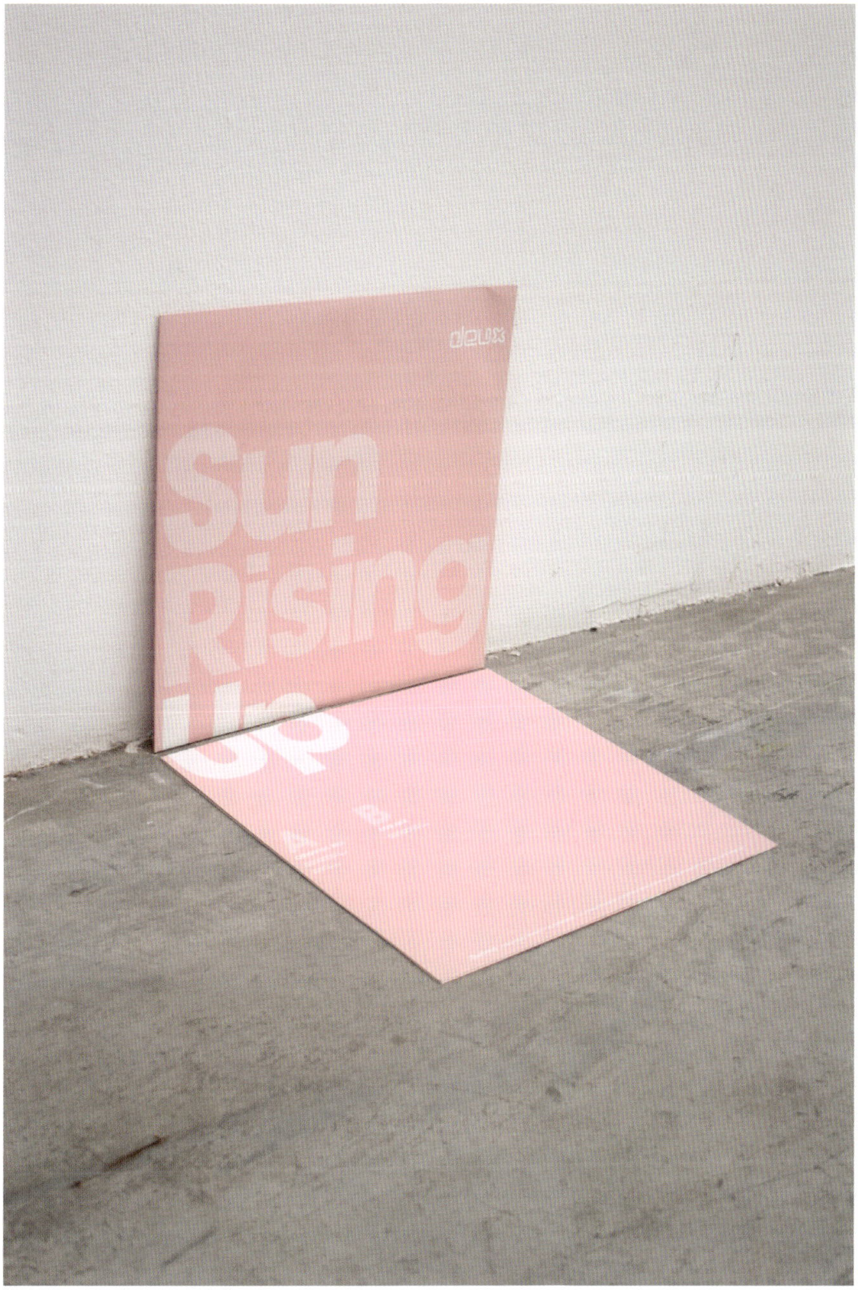

CAFÉ TRÊS ™

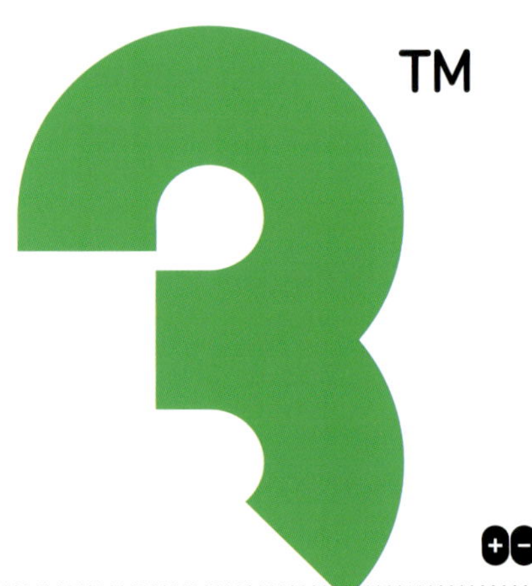

RMAC

Lisboa, Portugal

Title: Café 3
Type of work: Logo, stationary
Client: Café 3
Design: ad// Ricardo Mealha and Ana Cunha
d// Ana Cunha
Year: 2004

An identity for Café 3, which is a space where the decoration, the concept, the summary and the environment contribute for one same end: to feel good and eat well. It is a restaurant with attention to details and elegant decoration, in bright colours, mainly green. The designers developed the logotype and stationary with special attention in the choice of the materials for production.

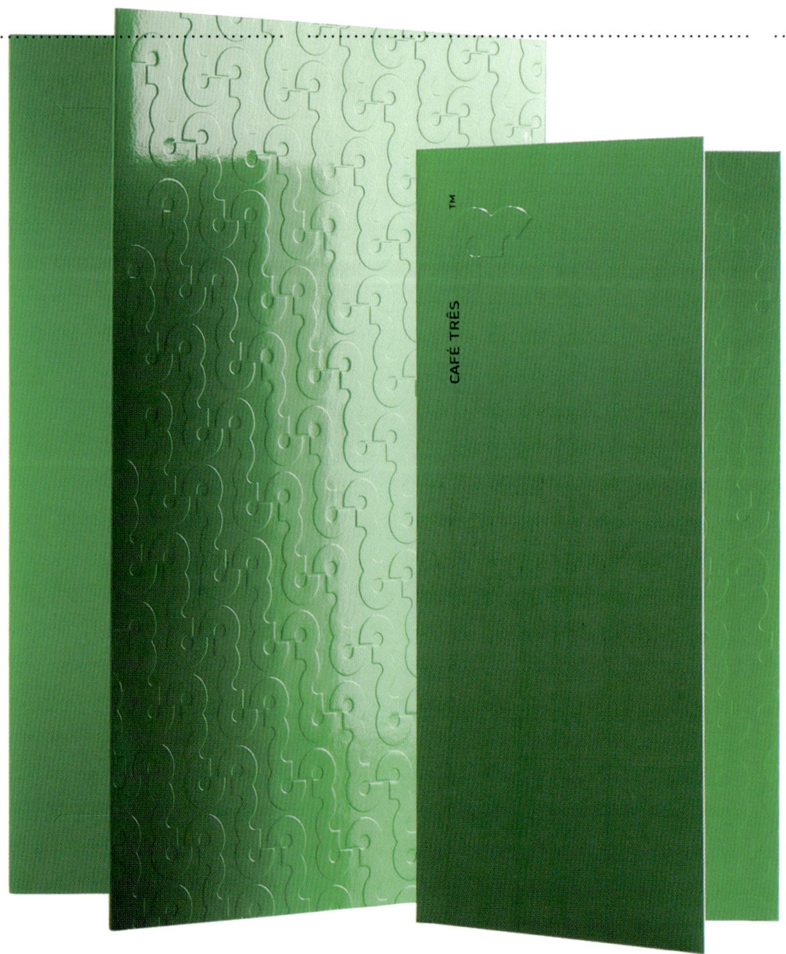

Elmw●●d

Melbourne, Australia

Title: X-ray Wedding Invite
Type of work: Wedding invitation
Client: Mr. & Mrs. Kitching
Design: ad// Richard Scholey d// Graham Sturzaker, Paul Sudron
Year: 2003

A wedding invitation for male and female nurses who met at medical school. The line 'in sickness and in health' was combined with an x-ray of a wedding cake. The style of the outer folder was in the style of a medical appointment. Outer invite was printed in one colour on silver, and x-ray in one colour on plastic film.

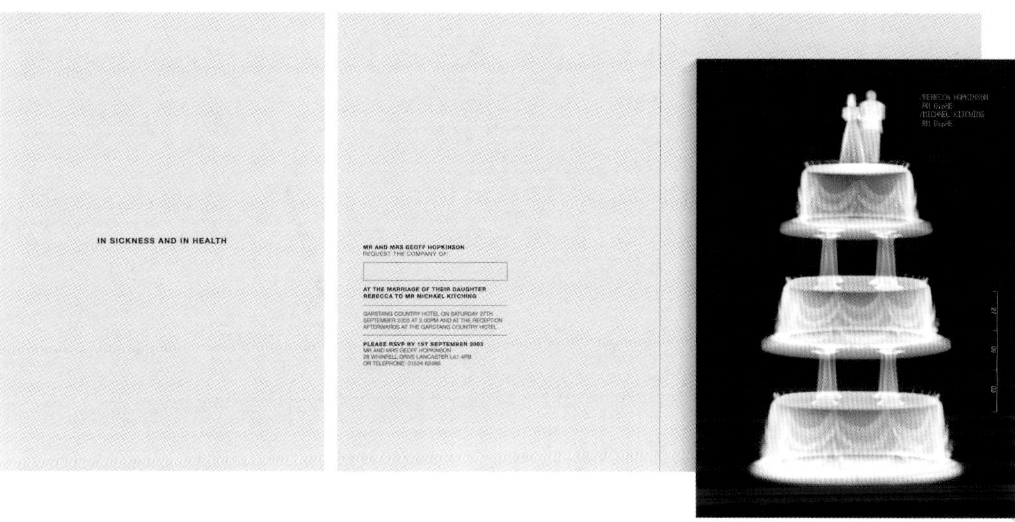

F●rm®

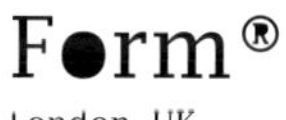

London, UK

Title: Form® New Year Card
Type of work: Self promotional direct mailer
Client: Form®/UniForm®
Design: ad// Paul West, Paula Benson d// Andy Harvey
Year: 2003/2004

A New Year message of self promotional direct mail from the two companies; Form® and Uni-Form® was designed under a limited budget, but in a sophisticated and minimalist way. The solution was to laser die cut a mirror-board stock, resulting in a matt white on the outer, and reflective silver on the inner of the card. They designed a sans serif, geometric font that was as thin as the laser-cut would allow, and had no isolated counters. This design allowed the light to shine through the type to reflect on the silver inside, giving the card a tactile quality.

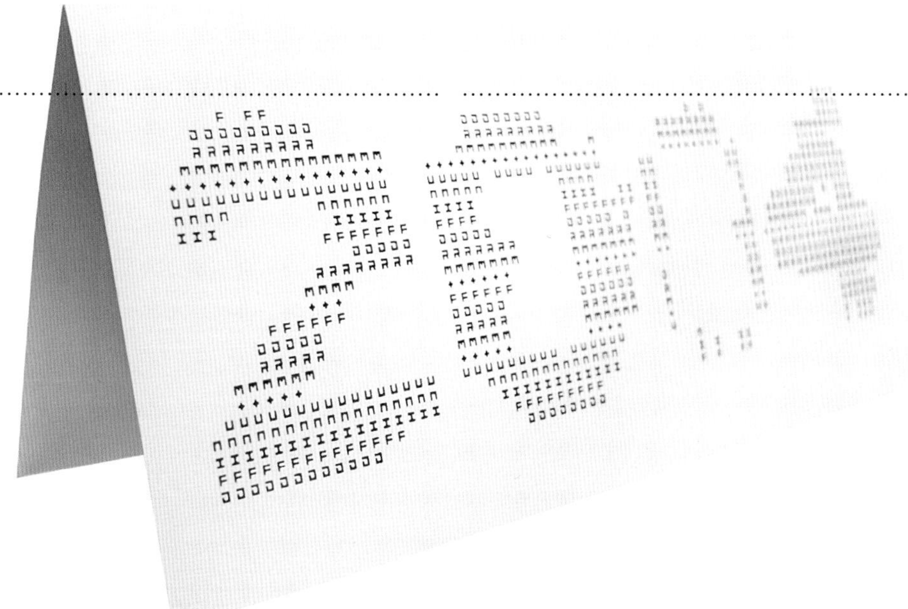

Kinetic

Singapore

Title: Sushi Delivery
Type of work: Direct mailer
Client: Nagano Sushi
Design: ad, d// Roy Poh, Pann Lim
Year: 2004

A set of 'wind-up sushi toy' direct mailer cum menu is delivered to offices and residential areas around Valley Point Shopping Centre, where the client's restaurant is located, to inform them of its new delivery service.

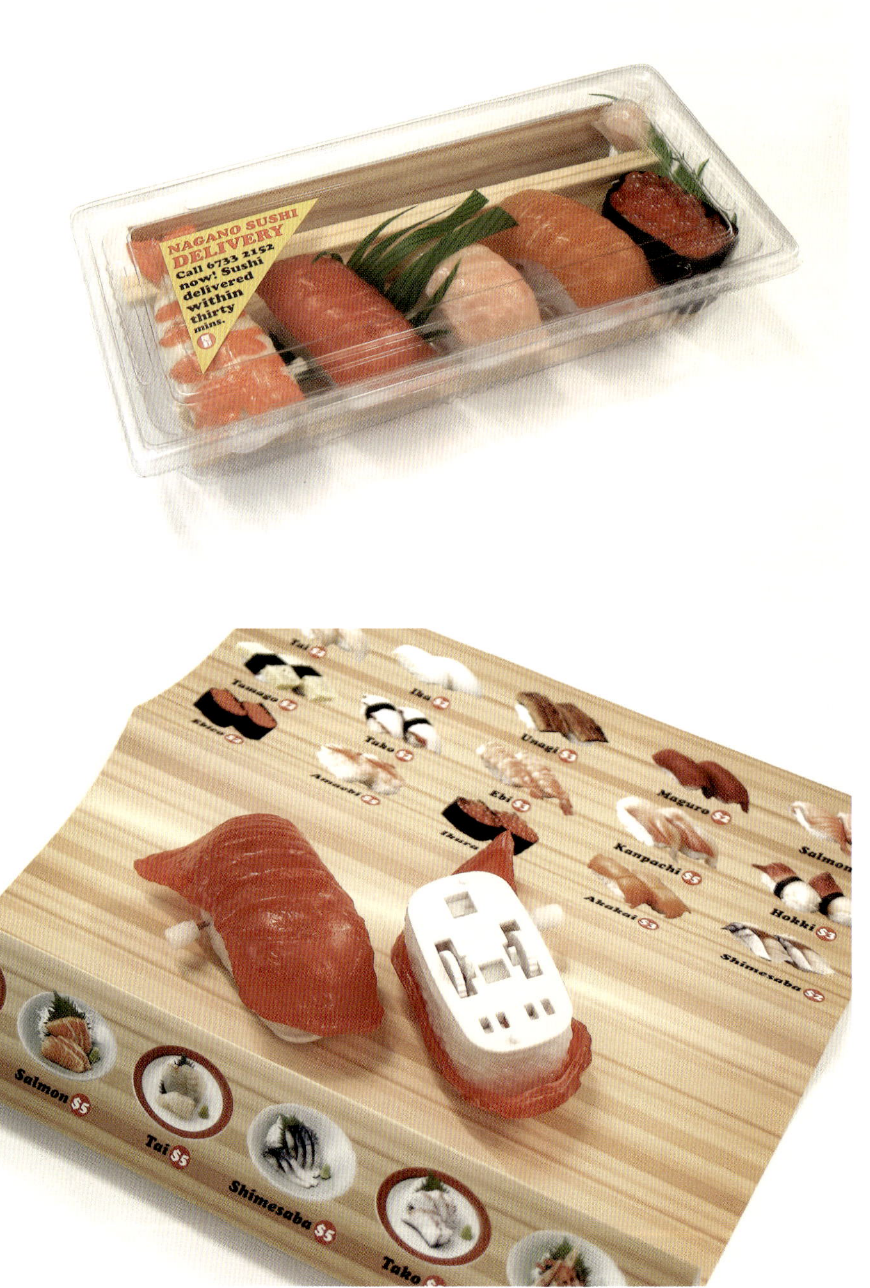

Stephen Layfield

Sydney, Australia

Title: Louise's Moving Card
Type of work: Card
Client: Louise Leffler
Design: ad, d// Stephen Layfield
Year: 2005

The idea for this moving card was inspired by the many ball-bearing puzzles the designer had as a child. Louise's new home is marked by a debossed red circle and the object is to get the ball-bearing into it's 'home.'

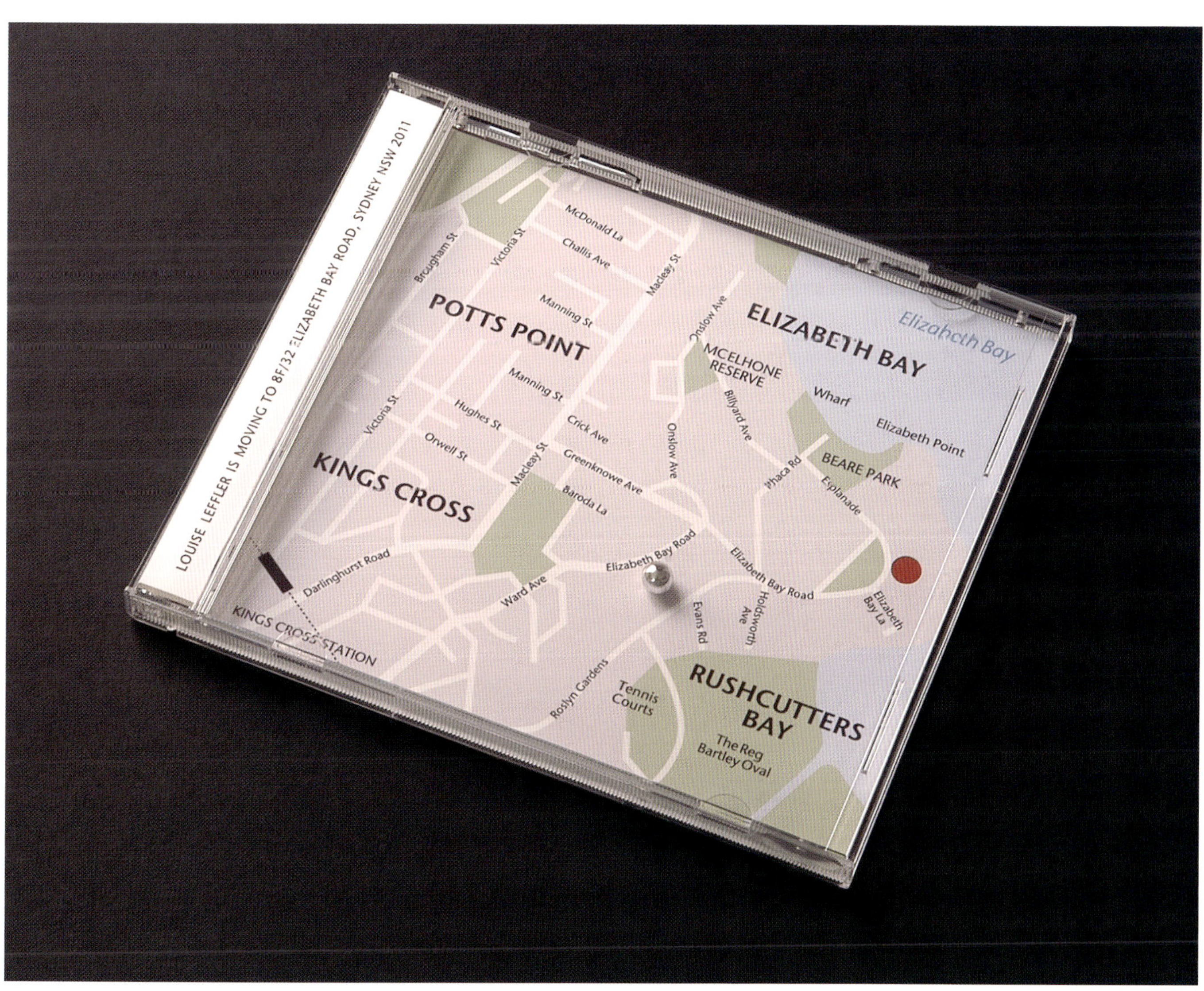

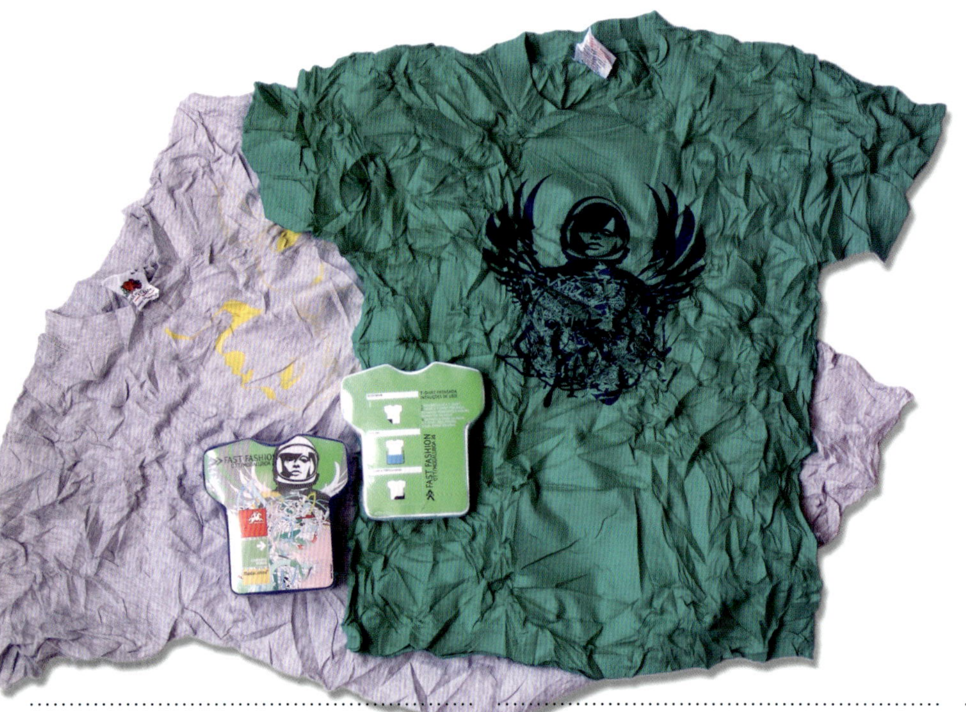

RMAC

Lisboa, Portugal

Title: 1.// T-shirts ModaLisboa 2.// Modalisboa Fast Forward 24th Edition
Type of work: 1.// T-shirts 2.// VIP invitation
Client: 1.// CTT 2.// Associação ModaLisboa
Design: ad// Ricardo Mealha, Ana Cunha d// 1.Patrick Goor, Diogo Potes 2.Ana Cunha, Diogo Potes
Year: 2005

1.// An original way to sell t-shirts from a vending machine: compressed t-shirts with irreverent illustrations allusive to the edition of 'ModaLisboa Fast Forward' show's theme. 2.// For this invitation the subject was 'Fast-forward': speed cars and technology. The picture base of this edition is a composite illustration for allusive elements – the speed, modernity and auto-roads. In the Vip invitation is a 3D illustration that pops up from the paper when the red/blue glasses are put on.

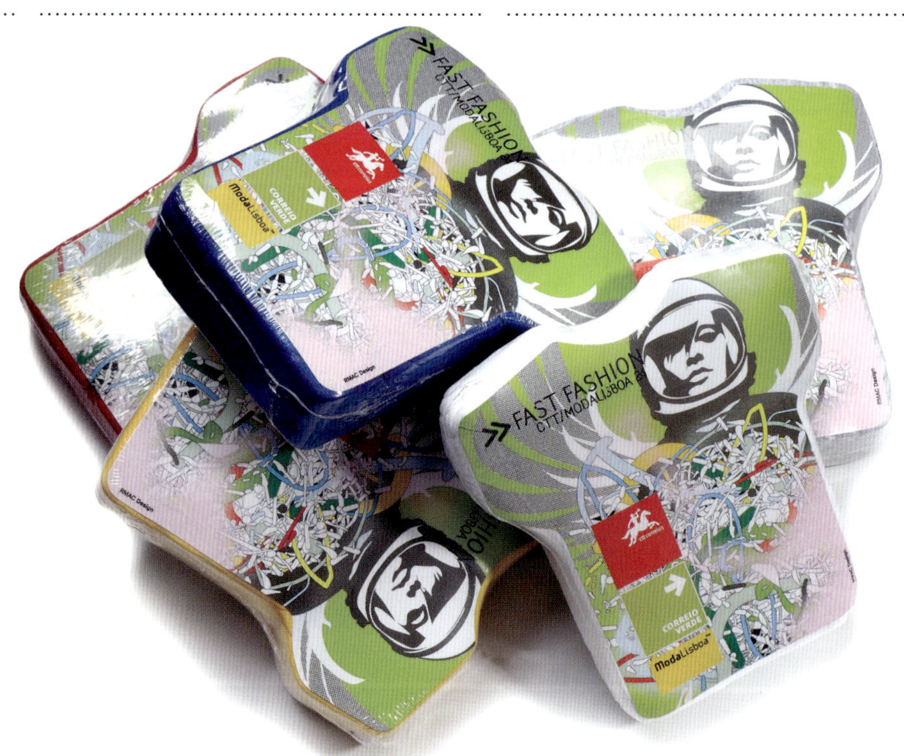

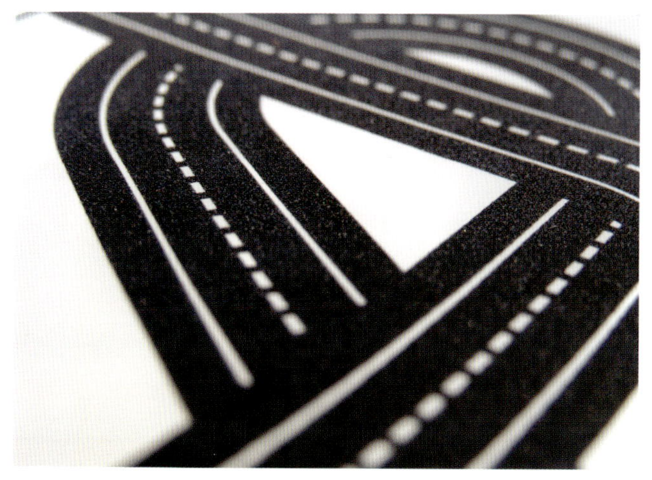

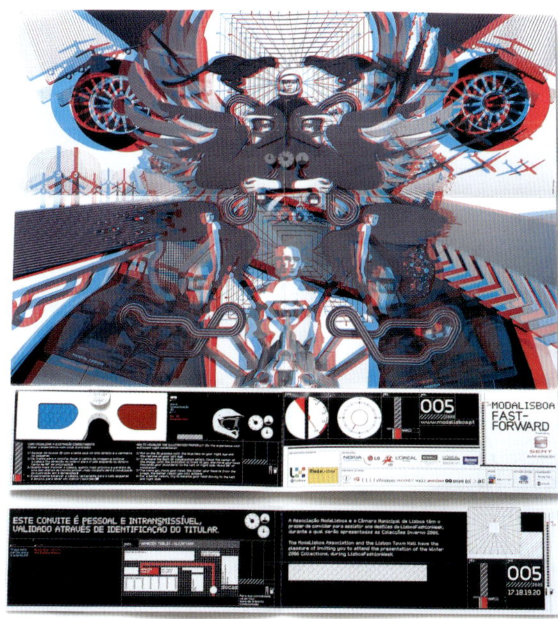

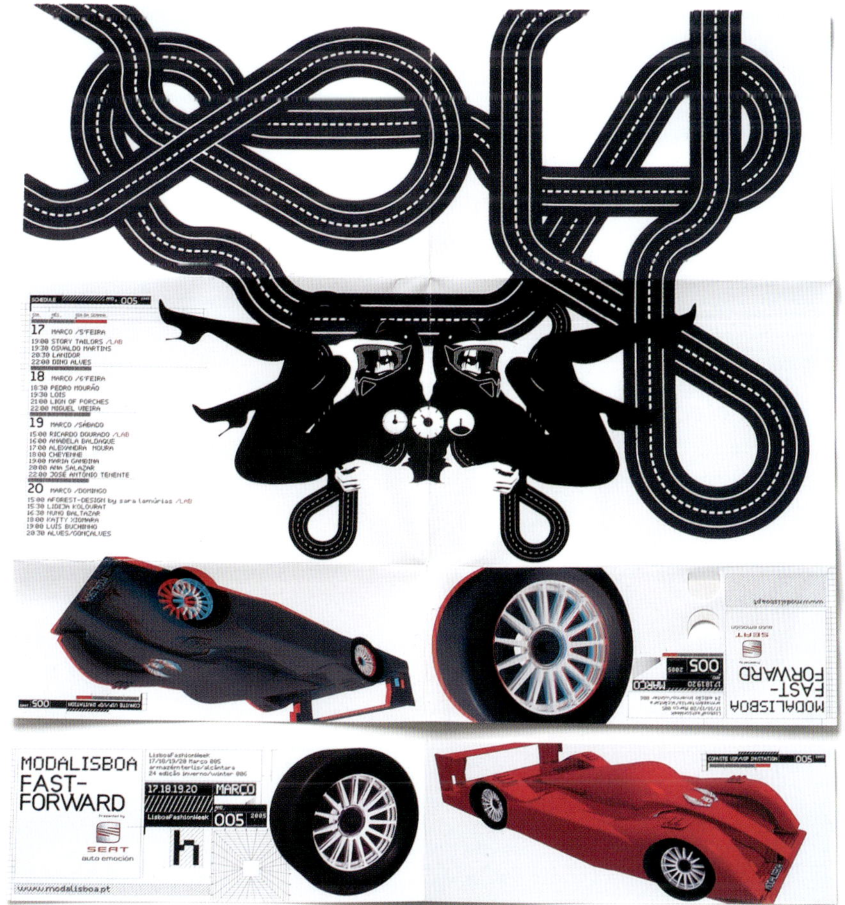
MODALISBOA
FAST-
FORWARD
SEAT
auto emoción
17.18.19.20 MARCO
005 2005
LisboaFashionWeek
www.modalisboa.pt

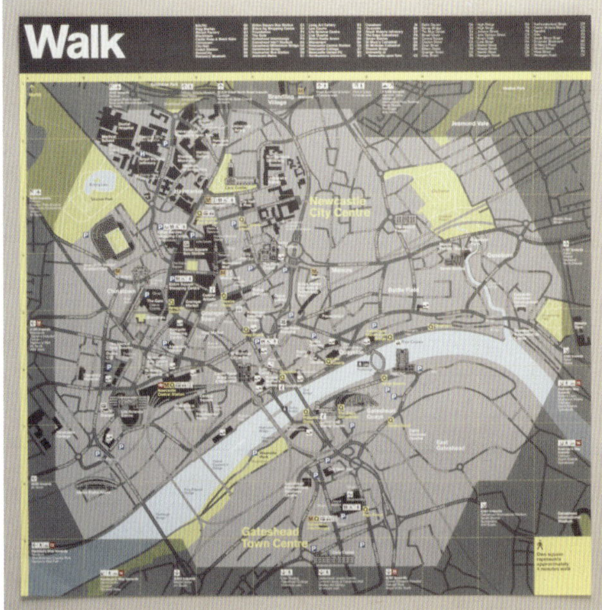

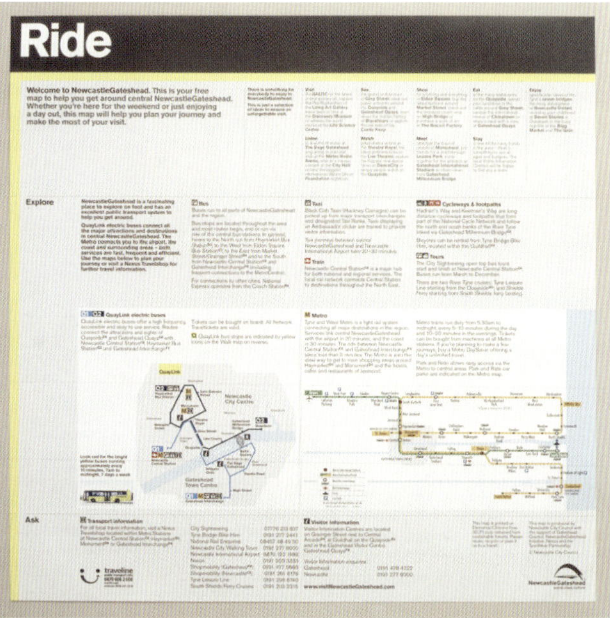

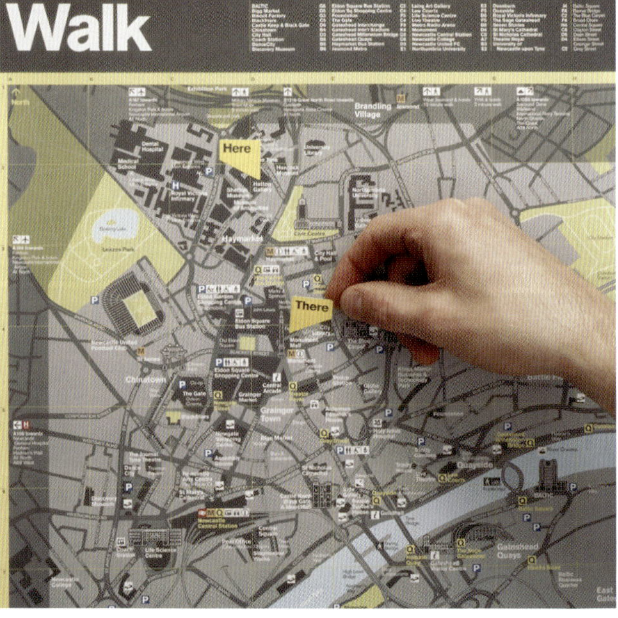

Cartlidge Levene

London, UK

Title: WalkRide Newcastle Gateshead map
Type of work: Map
Client: Newcastle City Council, Gateshead Metropolitan Borough Council
Design: Cartlidge Levene, City ID
Year: 2005

An identity and map for Newcastle Gateshead that seamlessly combines information for both pedestrians and public transport users in the city. For the pedestrian 'Walk' map, careful editing of information and a simple typographic hierarchy provides a balance between richness and legibility that helps make it approachable and friendly. Illustrated landmarks are used as engaging elements to draw the user in. On the reverse 'Ride' side of the map transport information is presented in a clear, simple manner to make the information as useful and digestible as possible. 'Here' and 'There' stickers were produced as a tool for use by Visitor Information Centre staff to point out destinations and routes to visitors.

Nun● Martins

Portugal

Title: Expo Erasmus
Type of work: –
Client: Faculdade de Belas Artes Universidade do Porto
Design: Nuno Martins, Leonardo Pereira, Marta Madureira
Year: 2003

The idea of this design is come from the suitcase flip when we travel by plane. Simple put theexpo name in bolded font on the top, plus the receiver's name in bold again in white on a black background.

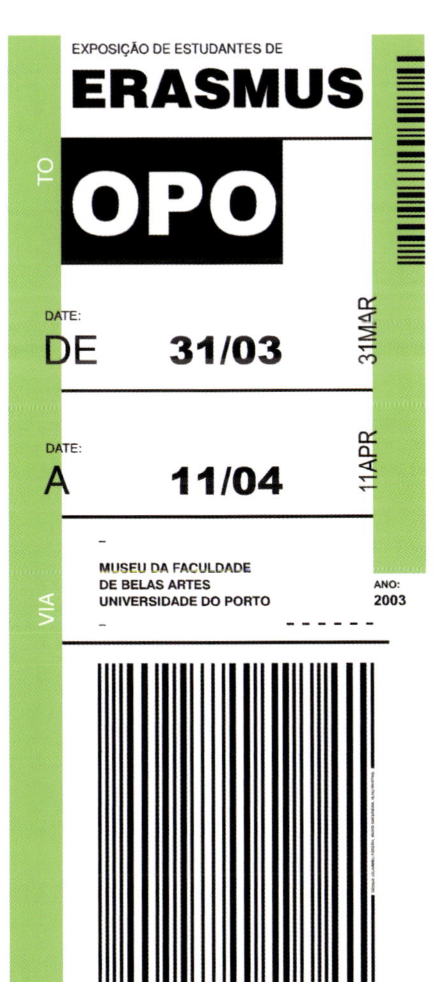

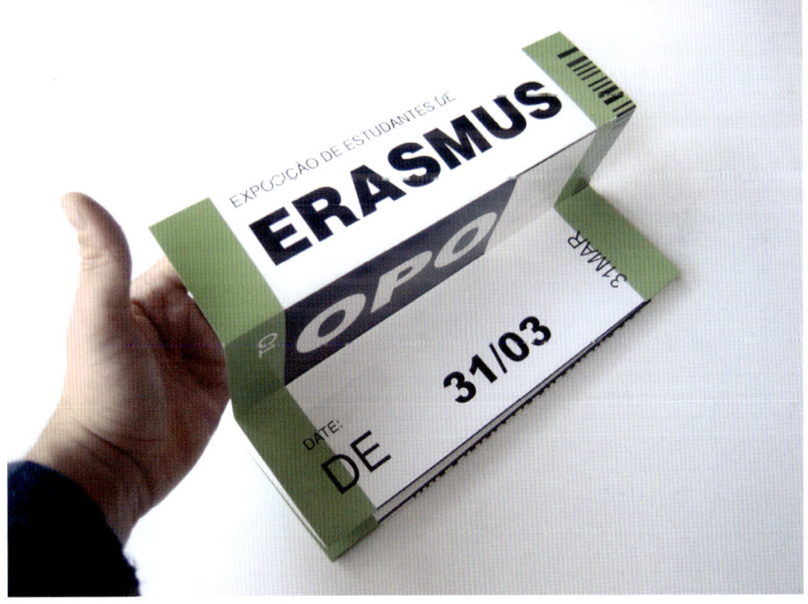

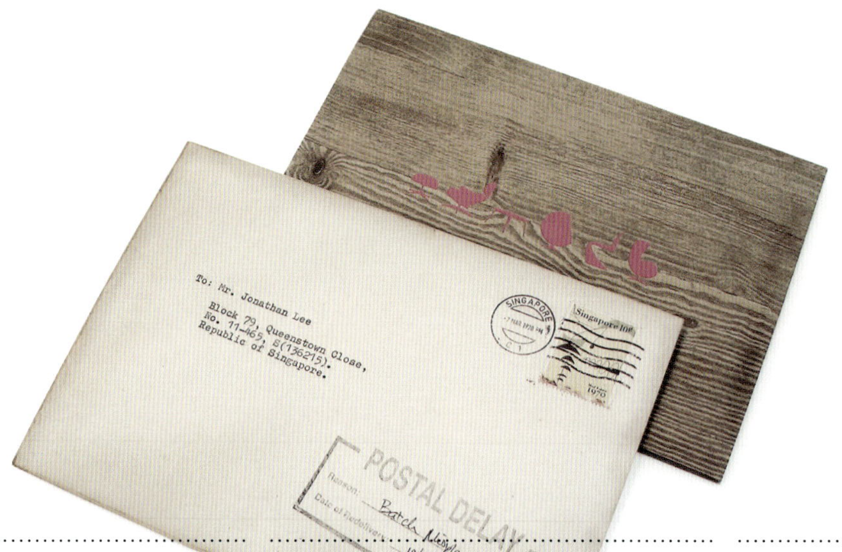

Kinetic

Singapore

Title: Postal Delay
Type of work: Direct mailer
Client: Lorgan's The Retro Store
Design: ad// Roy Poh, Pann Lim d// Roy Poh
Year: 2005

This piece is like a blast from the past in which intriguingly, the addresses receive a letter from the seventies, whose delivery has been delayed. In the meantime, a retro-styled mailer announces 'new' arrivals at Lorgan's. The takeaway, although 35 years late, the wares advertised in the mailer still have appeal today – after all, they are time-lessly classic.

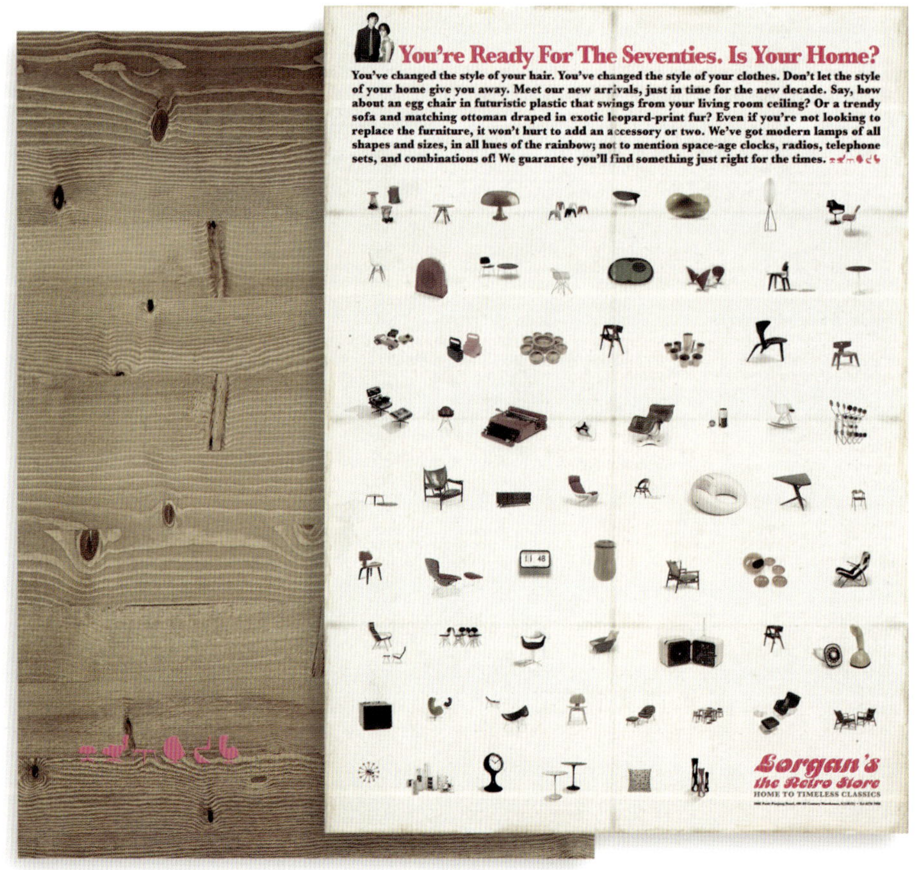

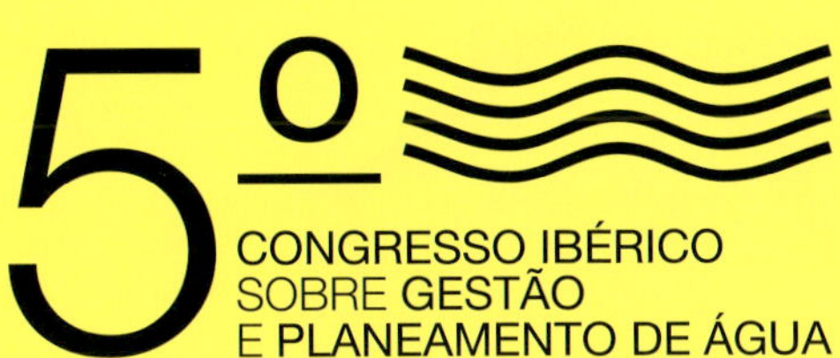

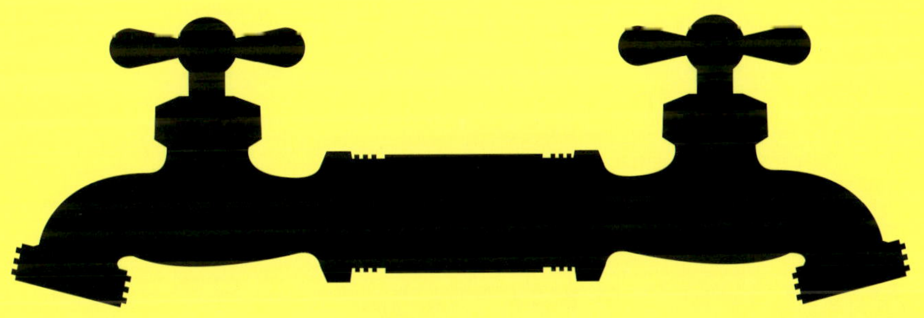

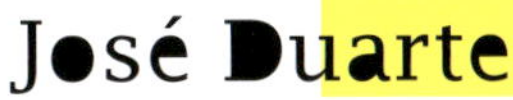

José Duarte

Covilhã, Portugal

Title: -
Type of work: -
Client: Águas do Algarve
Design: ad, d// José Duarte
Year: 2006

Proposal of a graphic image to an Iberic Conference about water management and sustainability. The aim of this work was to create a direct and easy reading message, what has determinated the use of vectorial language. Deliberately was chosen an improbable colour for an event related to water.

Enric Aguilera

Barcelona, Spain

Title: 18:30
Type of work: Calendar
Client: Enric Aguilera Asociados
Design: ad// Enric Aguilera d// Màrius Zorrilla
Year: 2004-05

The idea of this project, in which the same person was photographed against the same background with the same light and at 6:30 p.m. on the 24th of each month, was to explain the passing of time in a subtle way, little by little, unhurriedly.

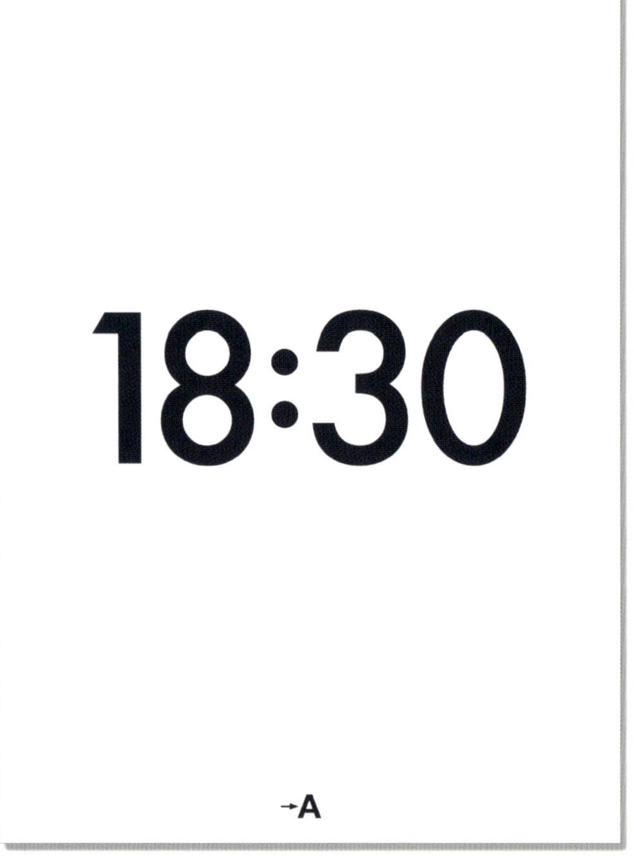

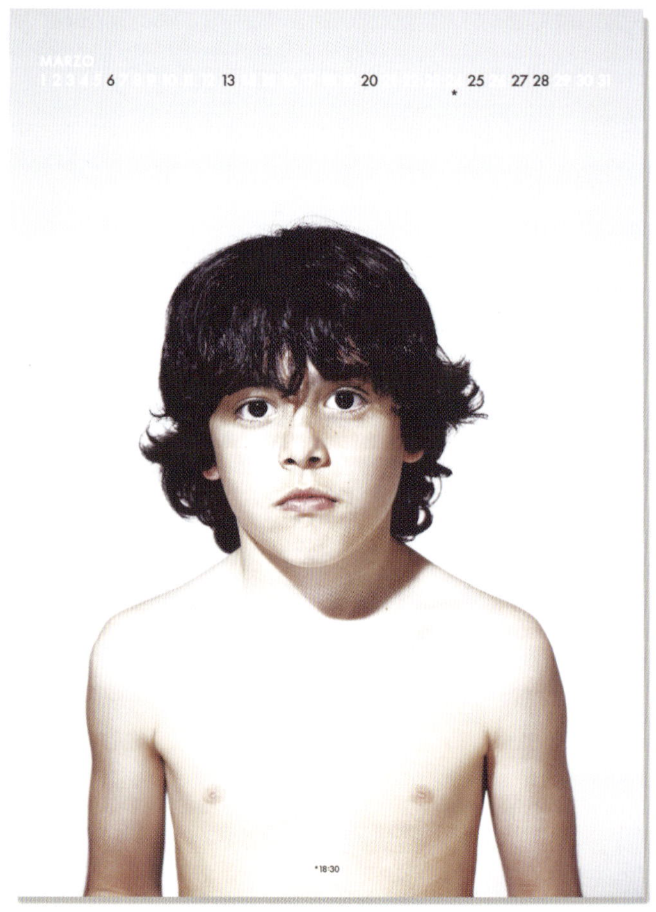

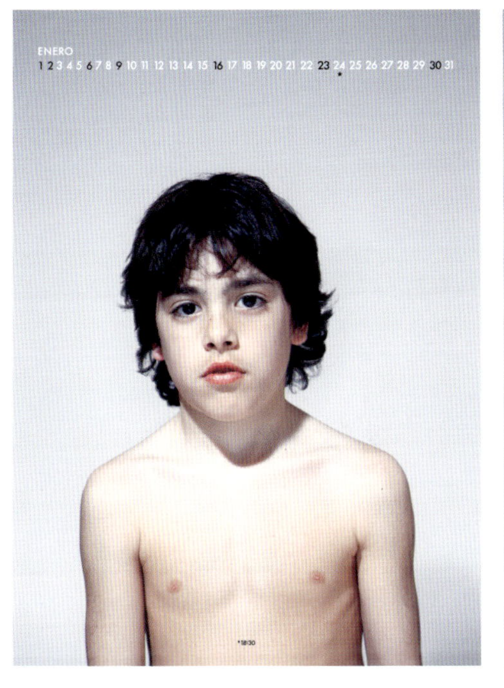
ENERO
1 2 3 4 5 6 7 8 9 10 11 12 13 14 15 16 17 18 19 20 21 22 23 24 25 26 27 28 29 30 31

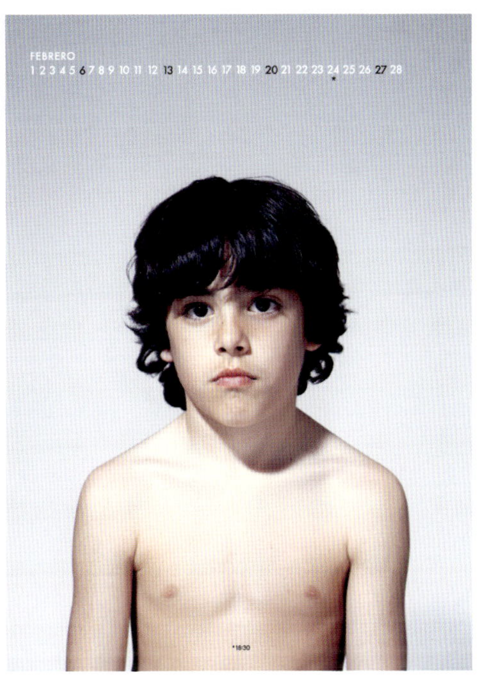
FEBRERO
1 2 3 4 5 6 7 8 9 10 11 12 13 14 15 16 17 18 19 20 21 22 23 24 25 26 27 28

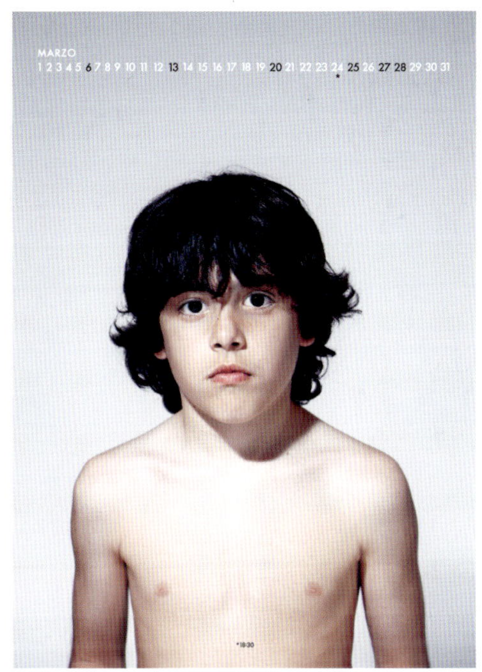
MARZO
1 2 3 4 5 6 7 8 9 10 11 12 13 14 15 16 17 18 19 20 21 22 23 24 25 26 27 28 29 30 31

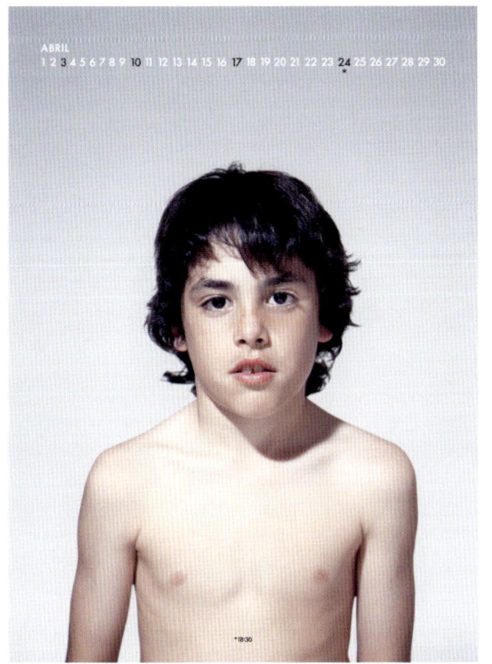
ABRIL
1 2 3 4 5 6 7 8 9 10 11 12 13 14 15 16 17 18 19 20 21 22 23 24 25 26 27 28 29 30

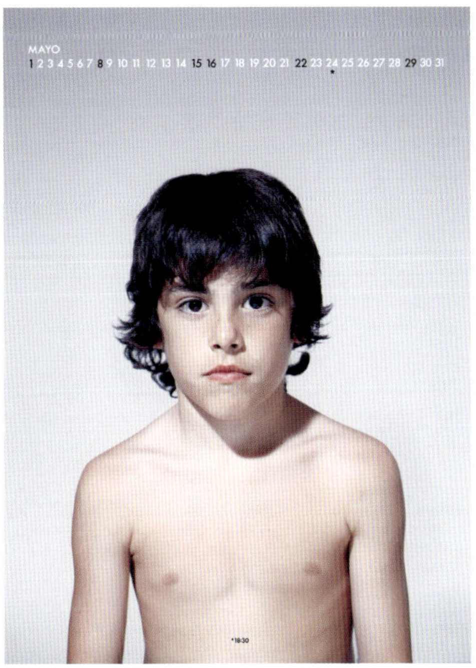
MAYO
1 2 3 4 5 6 7 8 9 10 11 12 13 14 15 16 17 18 19 20 21 22 23 24 25 26 27 28 29 30 31

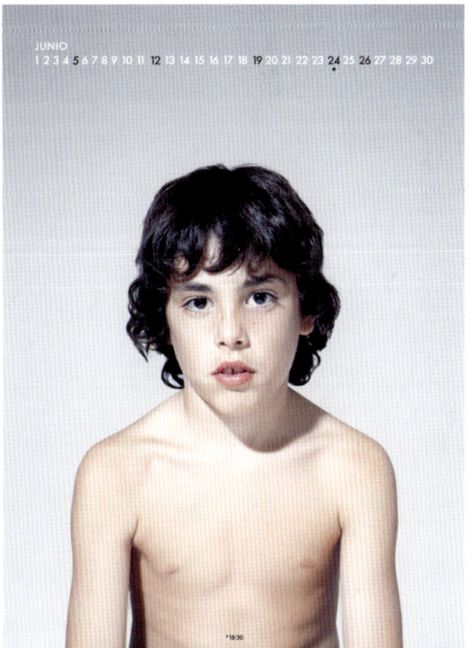
JUNIO
1 2 3 4 5 6 7 8 9 10 11 12 13 14 15 16 17 18 19 20 21 22 23 24 25 26 27 28 29 30

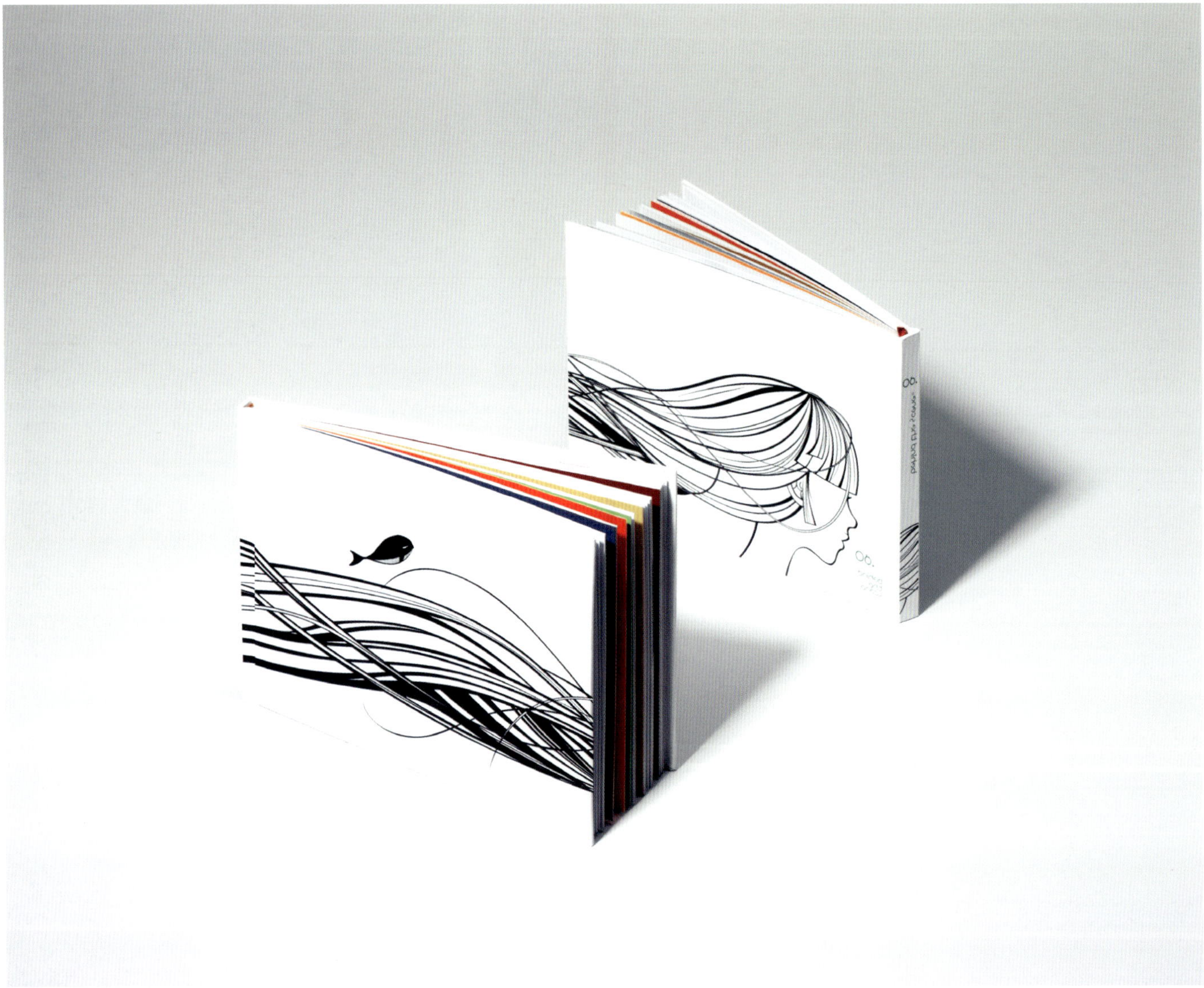

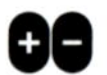

Chillichilly

Hong Kong, China

Title: Behind The Scene
Type of work: Sketchbook
Client: Chillichilly
Design: ad// Arthur Yung, Clement Cheung
d// Arthur Yung, Clement Cheung i// Bon Leung
Year: 2005

A series of eight sketchbooks. The story of each uniquely illustrated sketchbook unfolds upon turning over to the back. When eight sketchbooks are lined up together, the spine connects and makes a picture. The eight different front and back cover designs of each sketchbook also has a story of its own. Upon turning over the sketchbook, it reveals an amusing and sometimes surprising story.

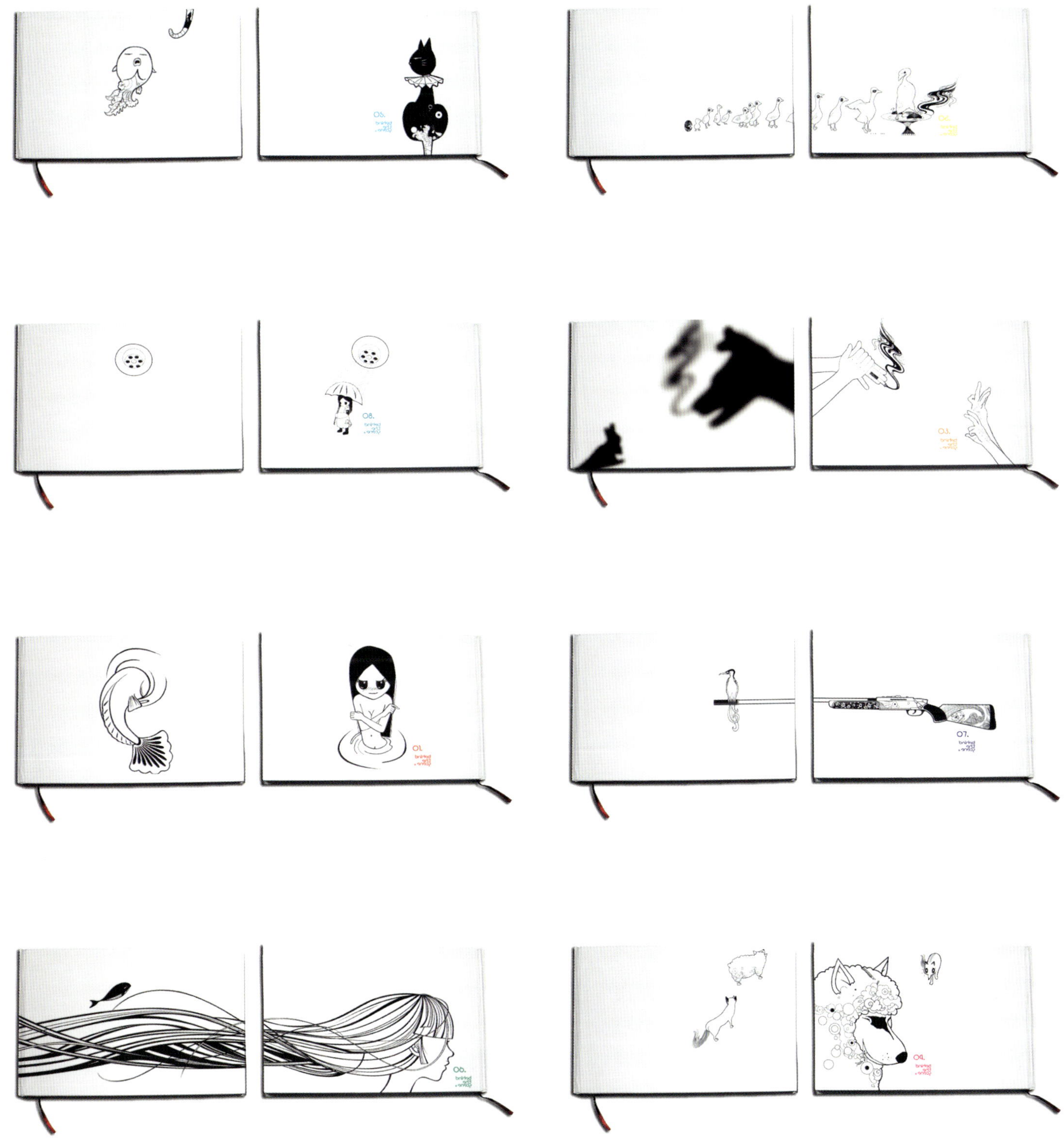

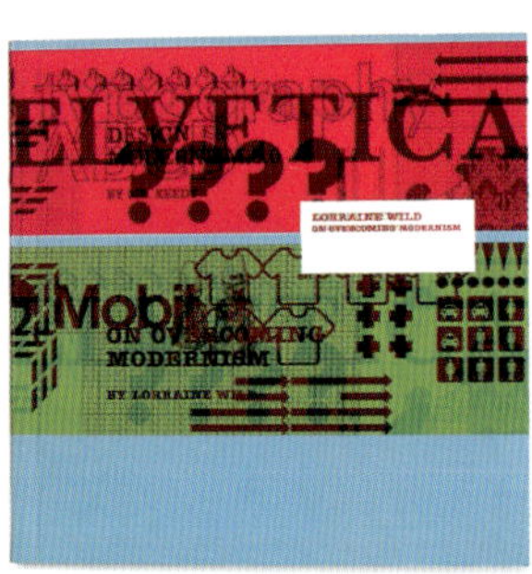
HELVETICA
???
DESIGN
Mobil
ON OVERCOMING
MODERNISM
BY LORRAINE WILD
LORRAINE WILD
ON OVERCOMING MODERNISM

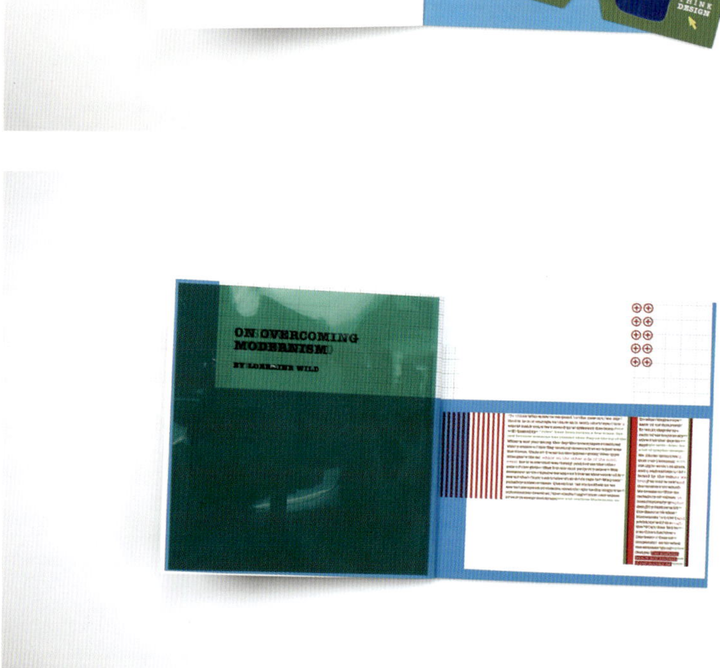
READ
LORRAINE WILD
THINK DESIGN

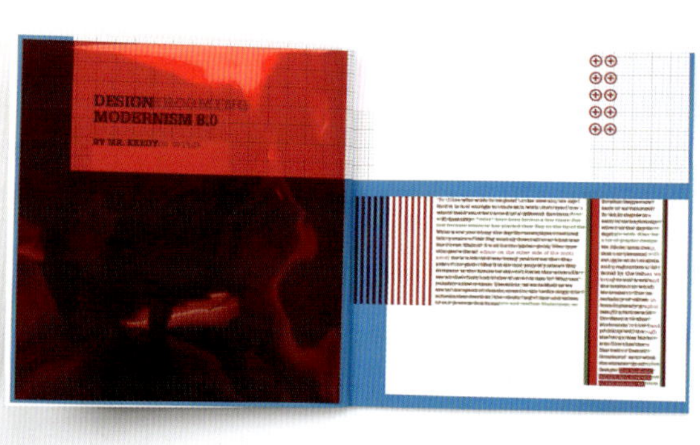
DESIGN
MODERNISM 8.0
BY MR. KEEDY WILD
ON OVERCOMING
MODERNISM
BY LORRAINE WILD

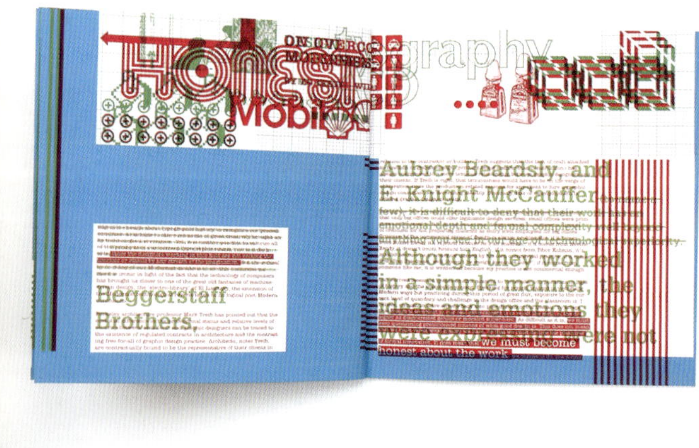
HONEST
ON OVERCOMING MODERNISM
Mobil
Aubrey Beardsly, and
E. Knight McCauffer
Although they worked
in a simple manner, the
ideas and emotions they
we must become
honest about the work
Beggerstaff
Brothers

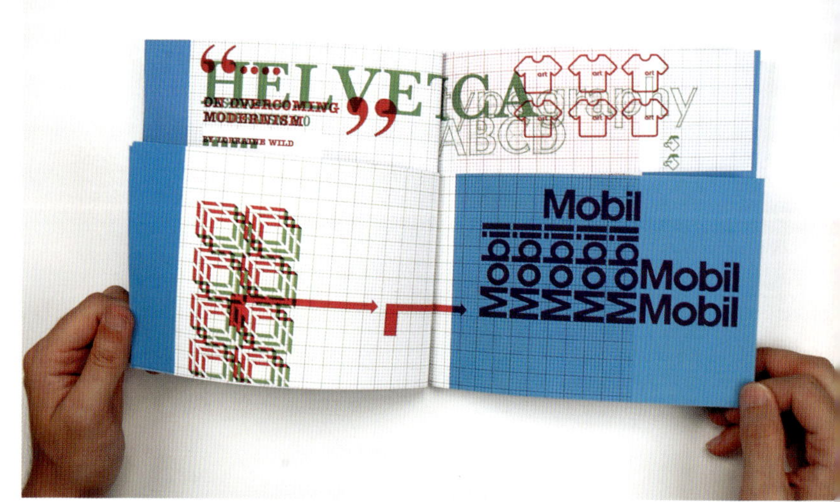
"...HELVETICA"
ON OVERCOMING
MODERNISM MO
LORRAINE WILD
ABCD
Mobil
Mobil
Mobil
Mobil
Mobil
Mobil

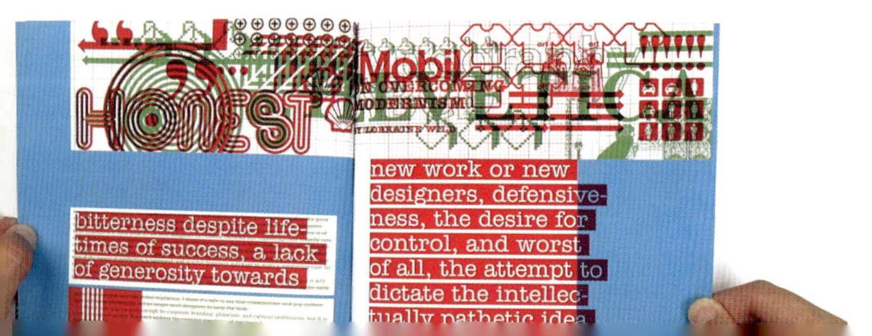
Mobil
HONEST
HELVETICA
ON OVERCOMING MODERNISM
BY LORRAINE WILD
bitterness despite life-
times of success, a lack
of generosity towards
new work or new
designers, defensive-
ness, the desire for
control, and worst
of all, the attempt to
dictate the intellec-
tually pathetic idea

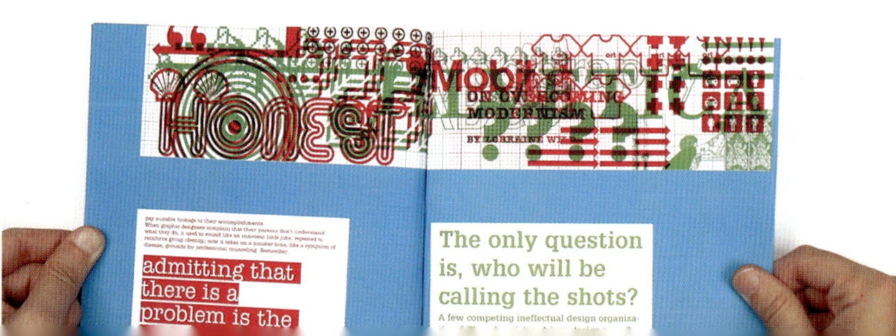
Mobil
ON OVERCOMING
MODERNISM
BY LORRAINE WILD
HONEST
admitting that
there is a
problem is the
The only question
is, who will be
calling the shots?

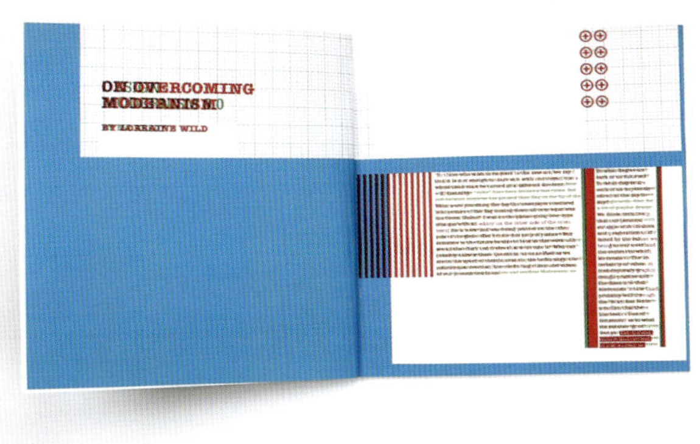

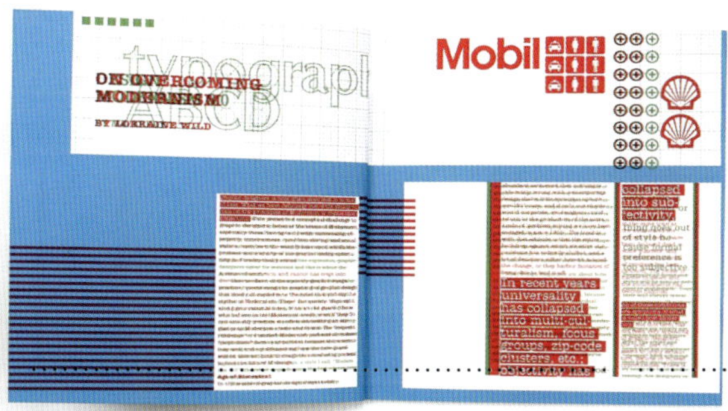

un**do**boy

Miami, USA

Title: Micro/Macro
Type of work: Book
Client: –
Design: ad, d// undoboy
Year: 2004

The designer used colour filters and overlapping type to hold two opposing essays, one is talking about font type Helvetica while the other one is about mobil company Shell.

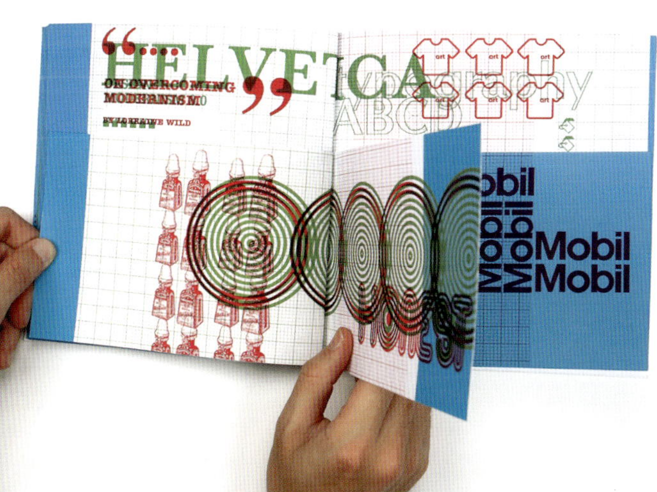

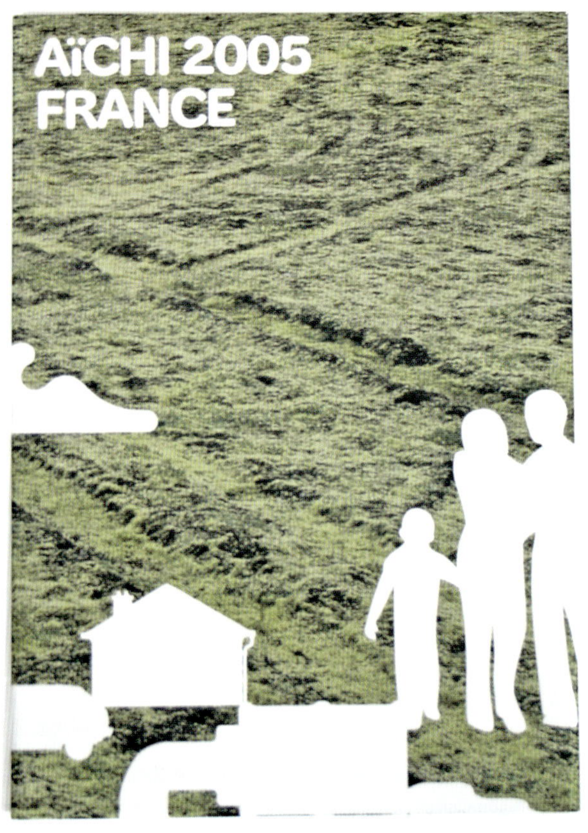

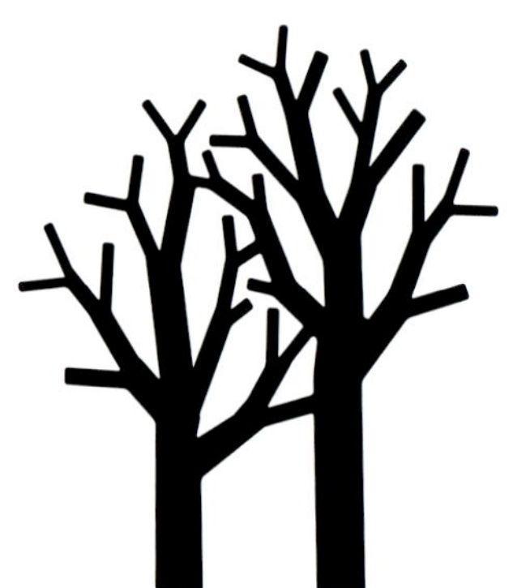
AICHI 2005
France

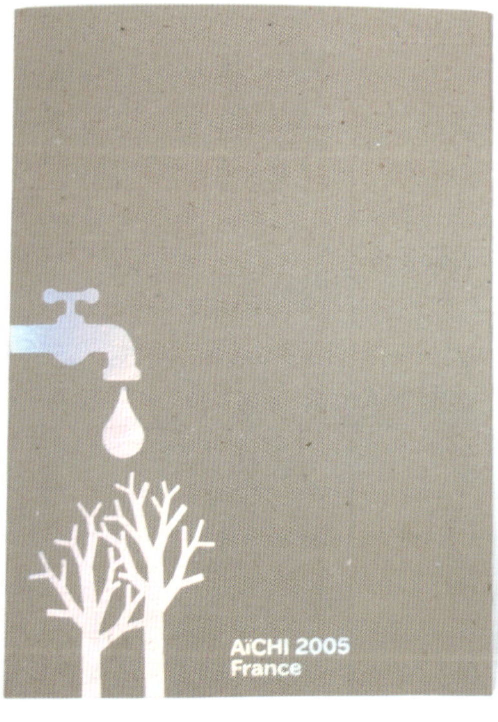
AïCHI 2005
France

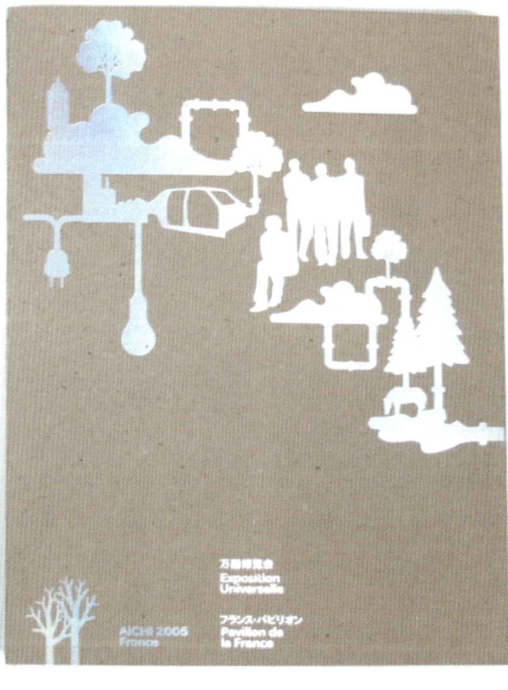
万国博覧会
Exposition
Universelle

AïCHI 2005
France

フランス・パビリオン
Pavillon de
la France

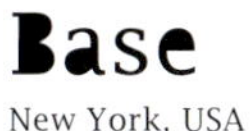Base

New York, USA

Title: Aichi 2005/ Universal Exhibition, Japan/ French Pavilion
Type of work: Exhibition
Client: Ministère de la Culture, France
Design: ad, d// Base
Year: 2005

This project was designed for The World's Fair 2005, which took place in Aïchi, Japan. France and Germany decided to make a statement by sharing a pavilion at the exposition. Base won the commission to design the identity system for the French half. Working with the exposition's theme of 'sustainable development' and France's theme of 'global communication,' Base developed a graphic system that encompassed everything from the environment to T-shirts to communications materials to catalogues and signage.

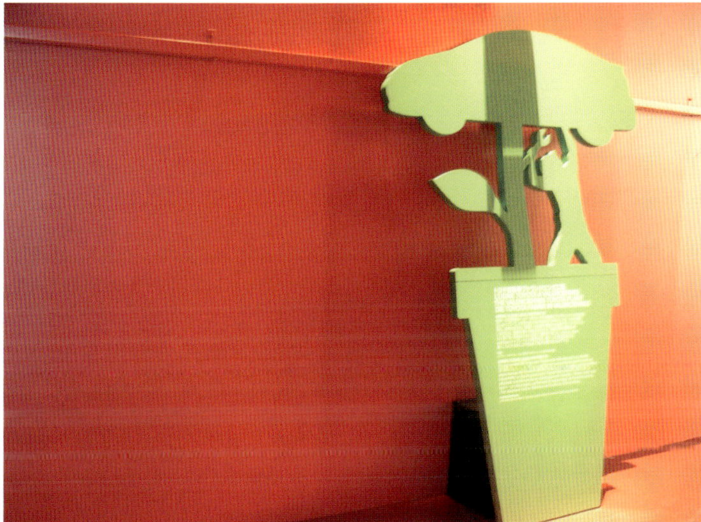

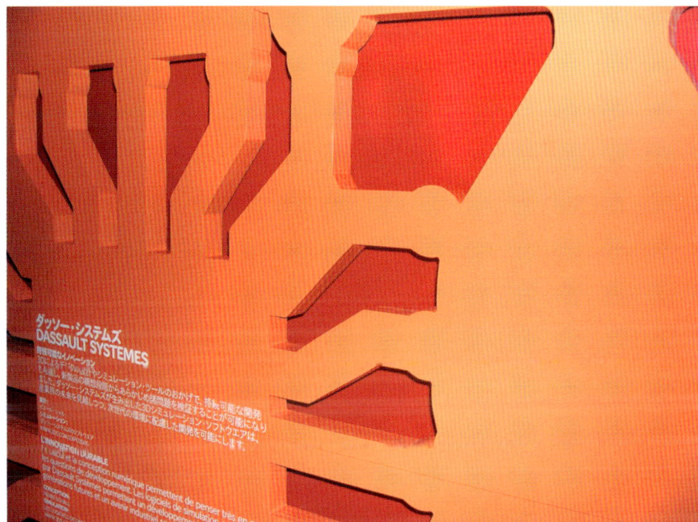

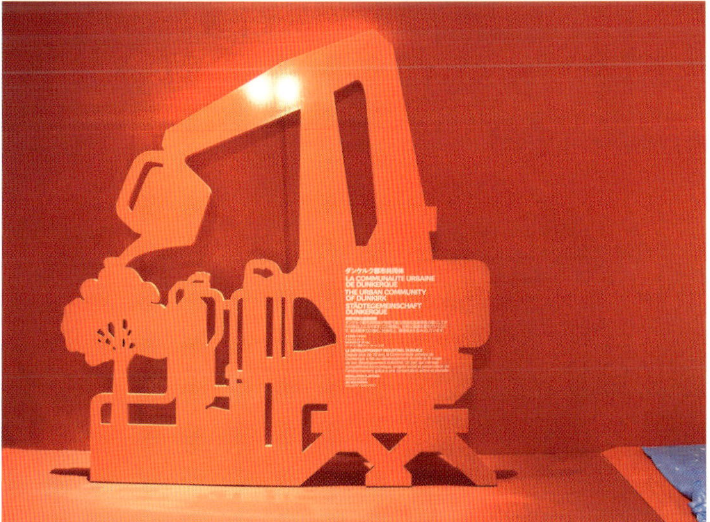

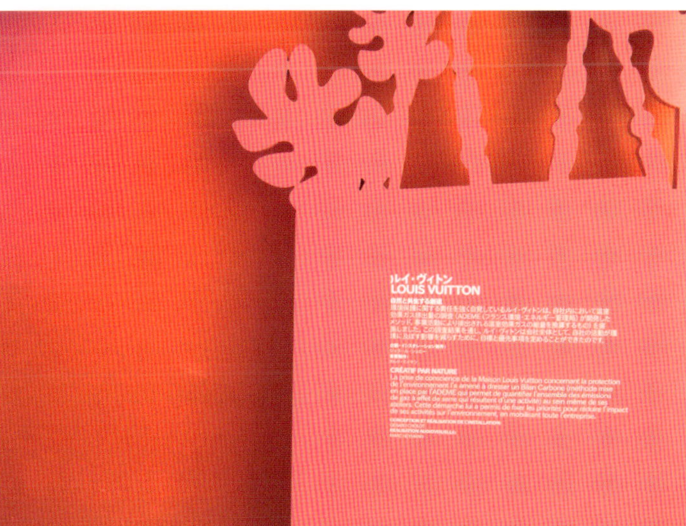

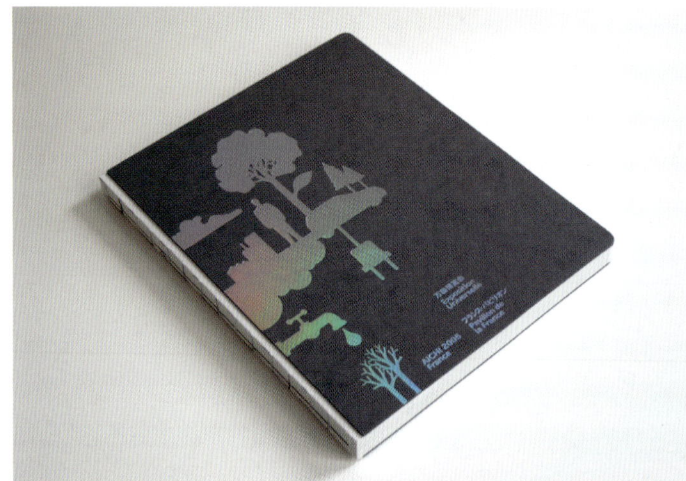

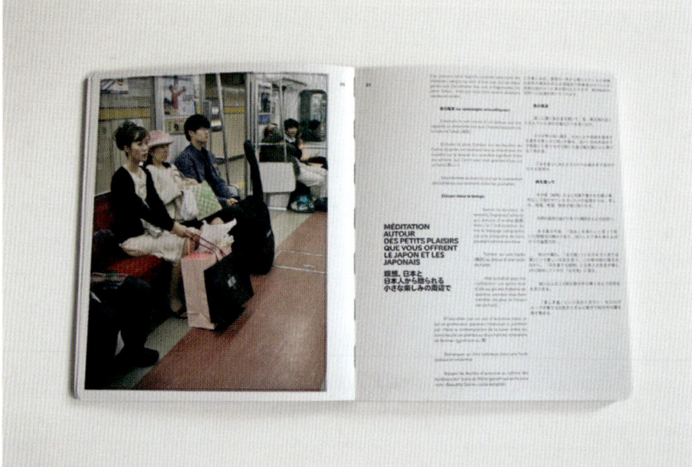

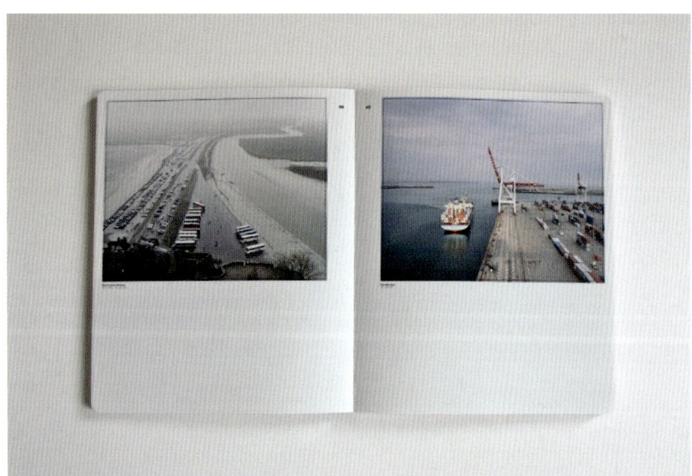

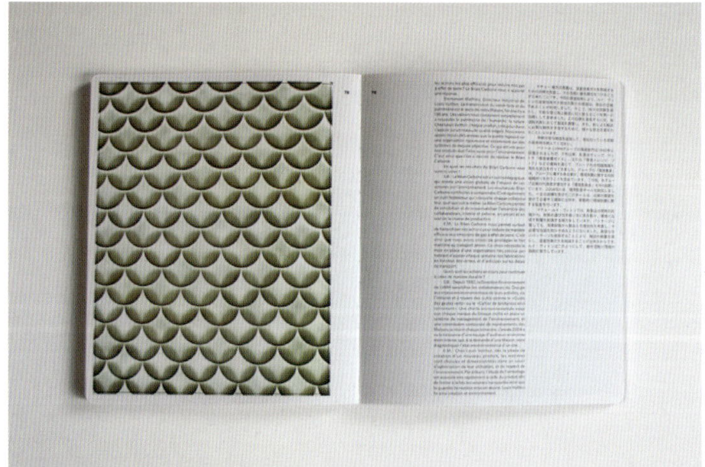

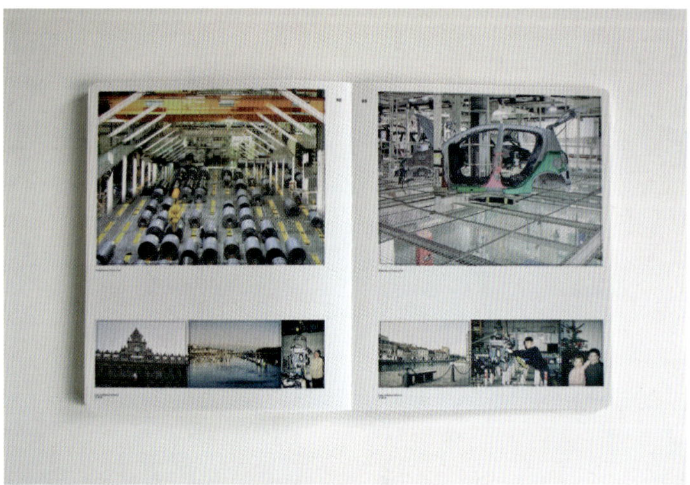

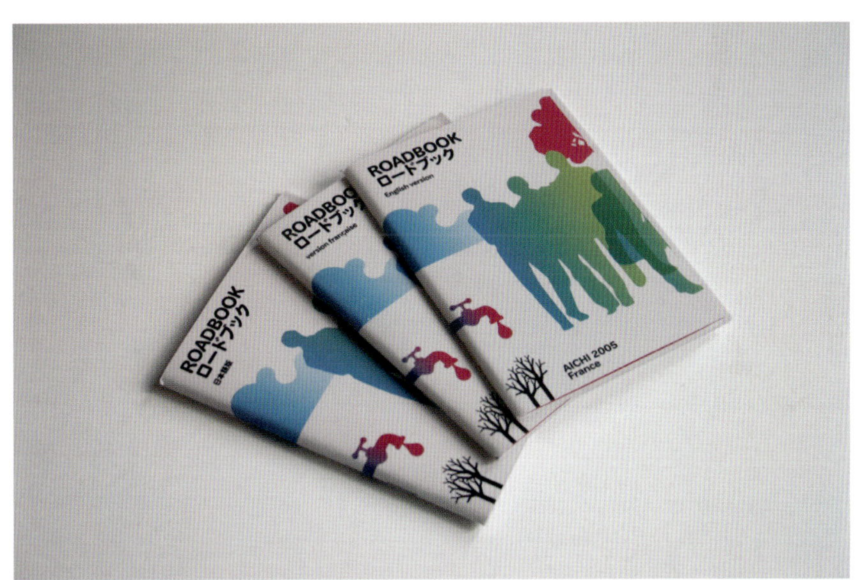

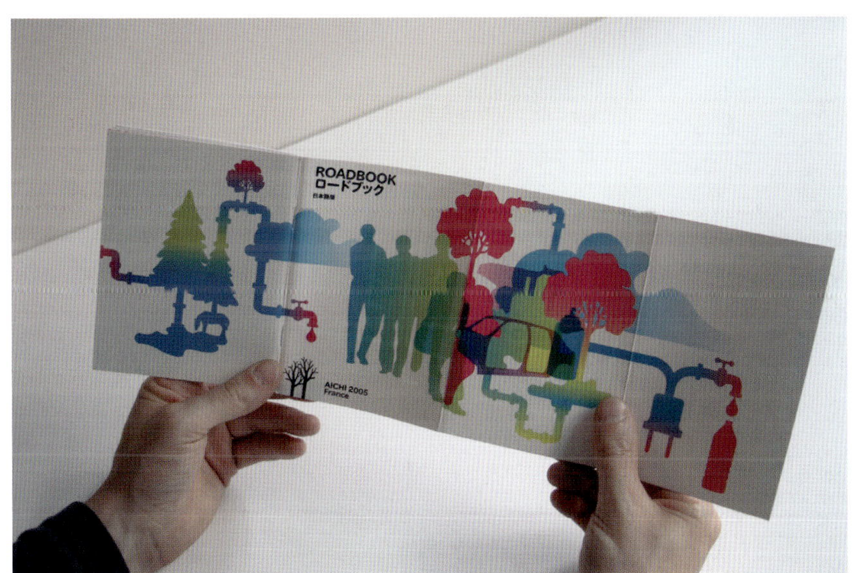

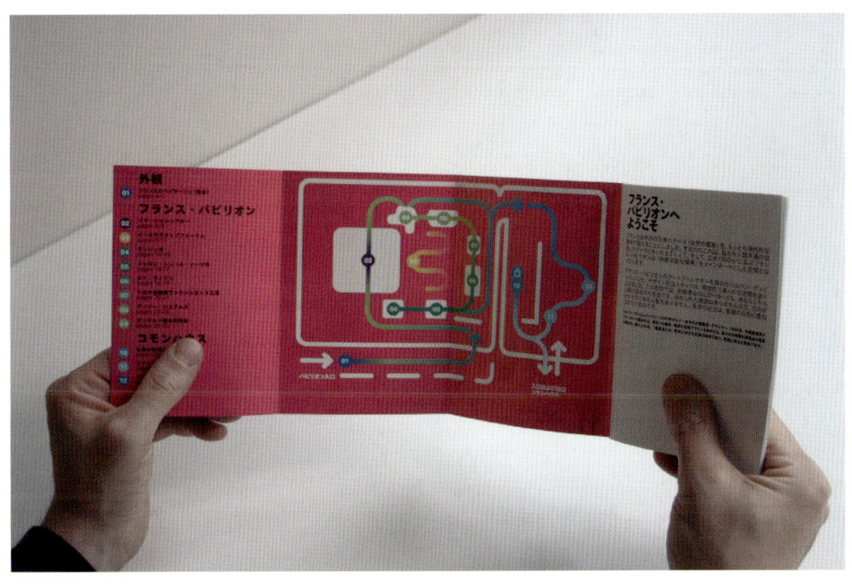

IS SUS- TAINABLE DEVELOP- MENT A REALISTIC GOAL?

The concept of sustainable development first received official recognition in 1987, when the United Nations General Assembly adopted the Brundtland report entitled "Our Common Future."

The definition of development "which meets current needs without compromising the capacity of future generations to meet theirs" has now been adopted definitively.

It is no longer just an aim. It has become a major personal and collective wager. The questions that it raises are applicable to us all. And it is precisely the multitude of issues surrounding the subject that constitutes its wealth.

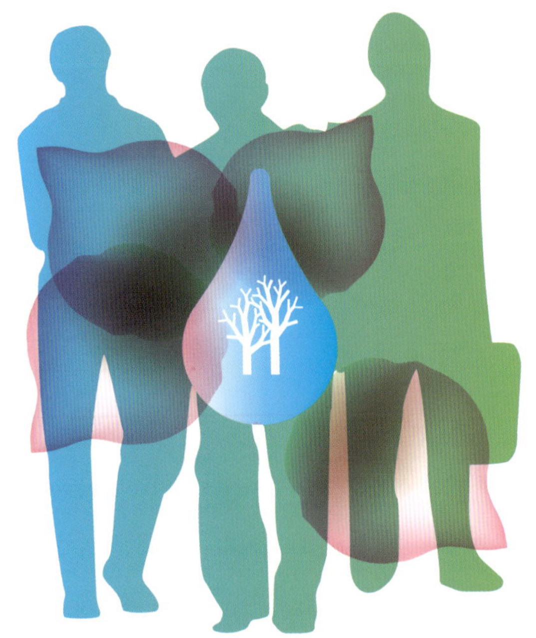

持続可 能な開 発とは？

持続可能な開発という概念は、国連総会が「我ら共有の未来」と題するブルントラント報告書を採択した1987年に初めて公式に認められるようになりました。

「将来の世代が自らの欲求を充足する能力を損なうことなく、現代の世代の欲求を満たす」というこの定義は、今日ではもはや取りざたされることはなくなっています。

「持続可能な開発」は、単なる目標ではなく、集団レベルと同じぐらい個人レベルでも途方もない挑戦になっています。「持続可能な開発」が投げかけている疑問点のどれもが、私たち人間に対して投げかけられているものなのです。そして、この増え続ける疑問点こそが、「持続可能な開発」を豊かなものにしています。

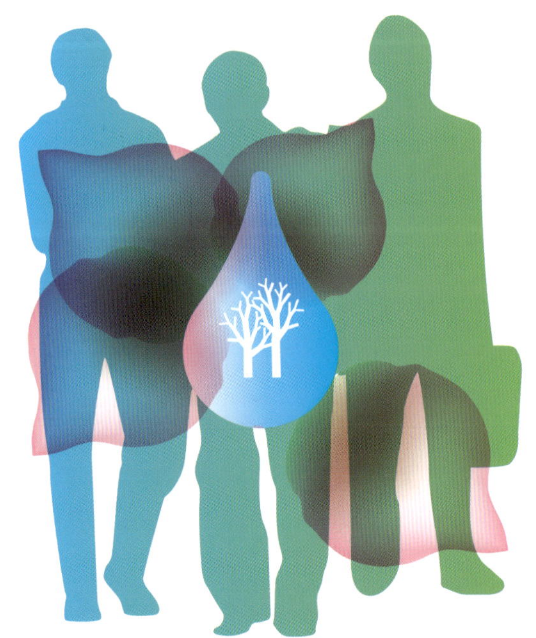

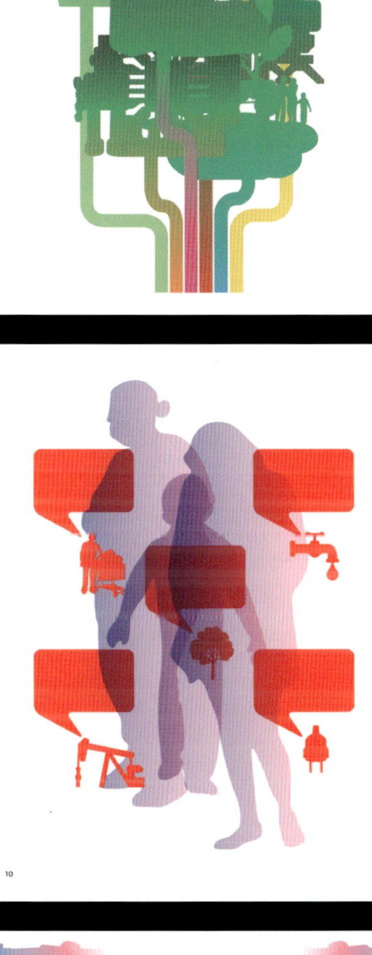
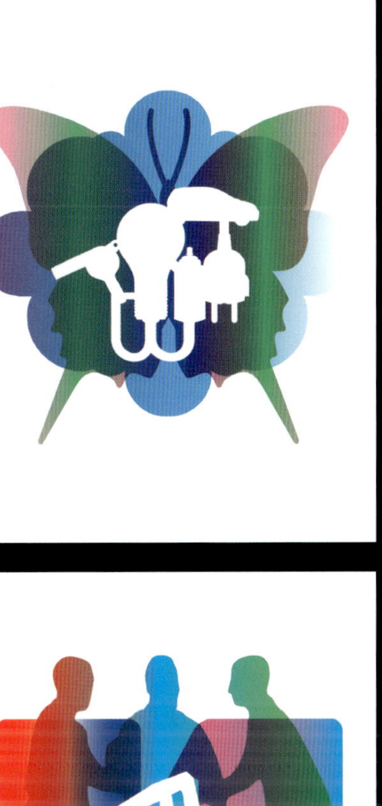
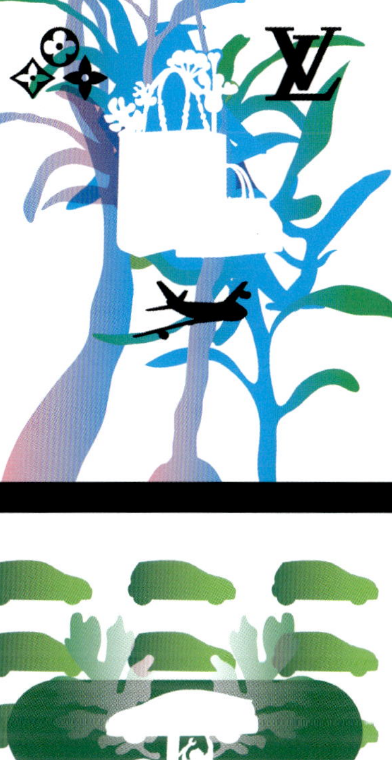
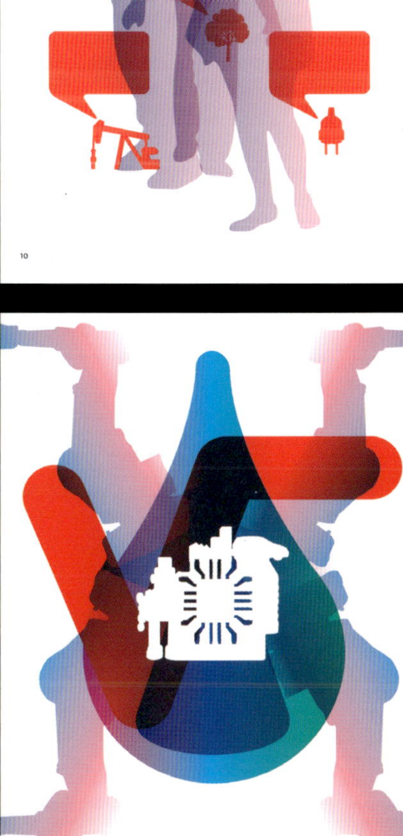
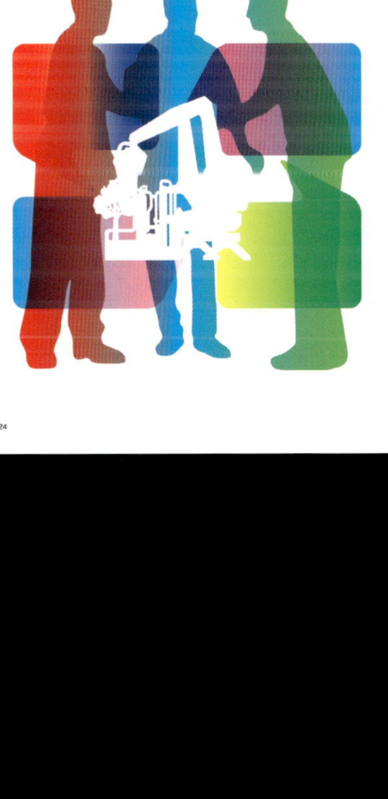
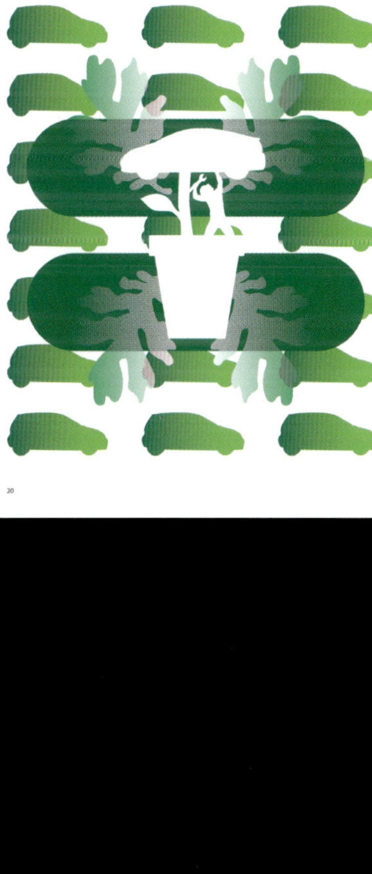

Mark Boyce

London, UK

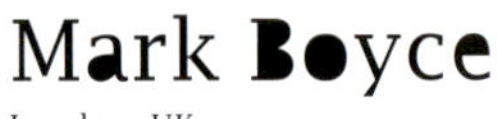

Title: The Malagarba Works
Type of work: Book
Client: Will Alsop, Bruce McLean, Wiley Academy
Design: ad, d// Mark Boyce
Year: 2003

A book published on the occasion of the exhibition 'Bruce Mclean & William Alsop, Two Chairs, The Malagarba Works' held at the MK Gallery in Milton Keynes. 140mm x 210mm. 240pp. The original intention for this book was for it to be brick-like in size but restrictions inflicted on the design by the publisher prevented this. Rather than compensating for this by making the book larger in width and height we opted to edit the work to show only a select number of pieces and showing only one painting, drawing or photograph per page. In essence this book is 10 years of collaborative works condensed into 240 pages.

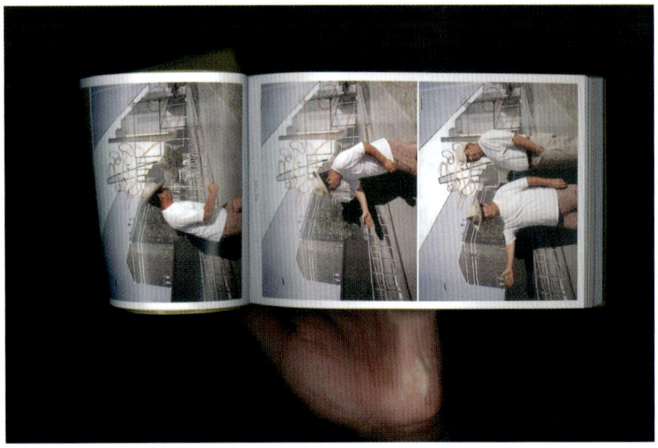

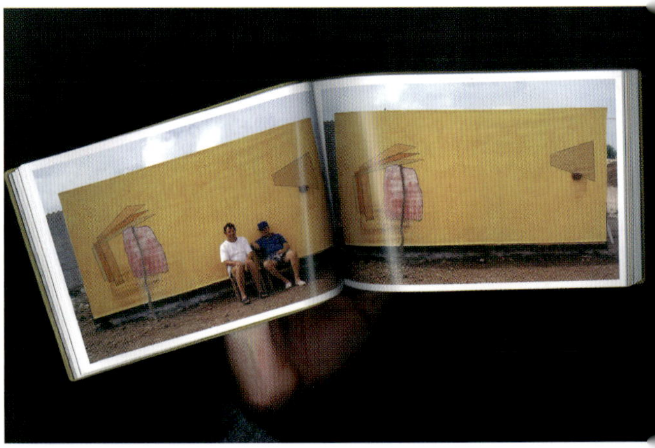

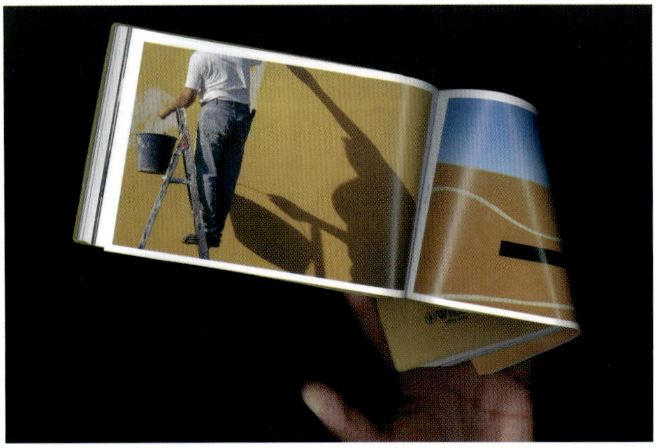

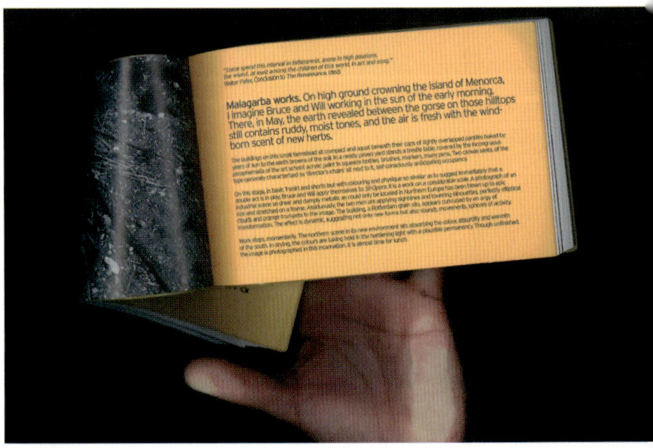

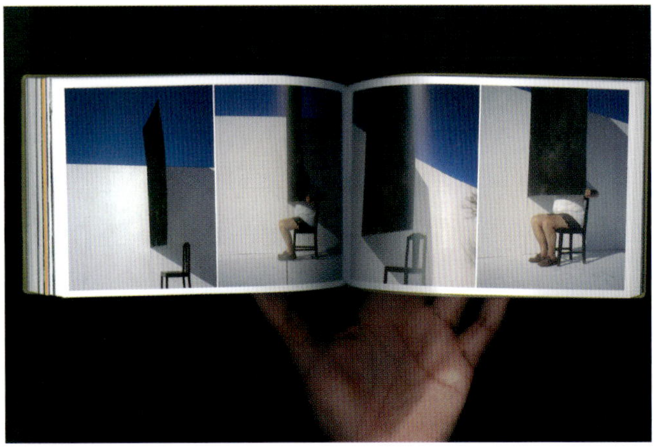

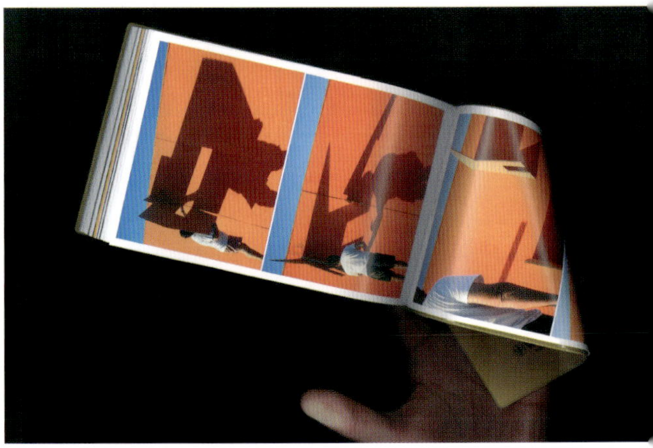

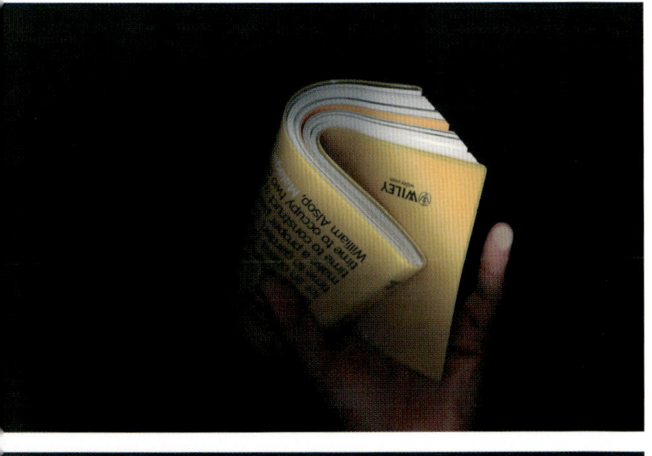

WILEY
William Alsop
time to occupy two

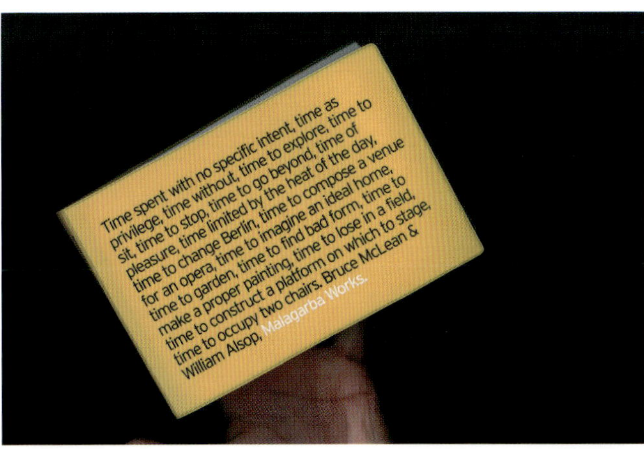

Time spent with no specific intent, time as
privilege, time without, time to explore, time to
sit, time to stop, time to go beyond, time of
pleasure, time limited by the heat of the day,
time to change Berlin, time to compose a venue
for an opera, time to imagine an ideal home,
time to garden, time to find bad form, time to
make a proper painting, time to lose in a field,
time to construct a platform on which to stage,
time to occupy two chairs. Bruce McLean &
William Alsop, Malagarba Works.

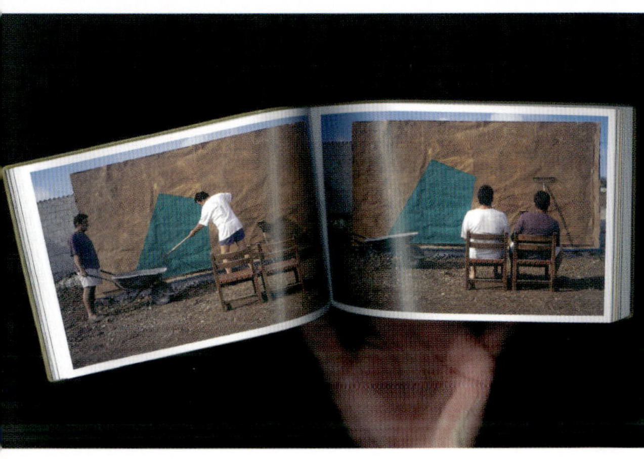

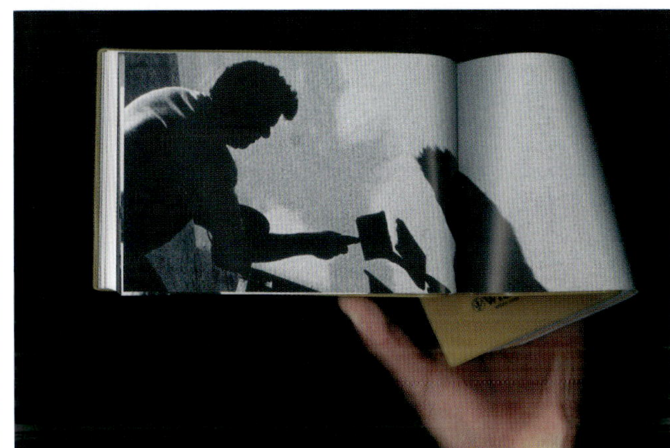

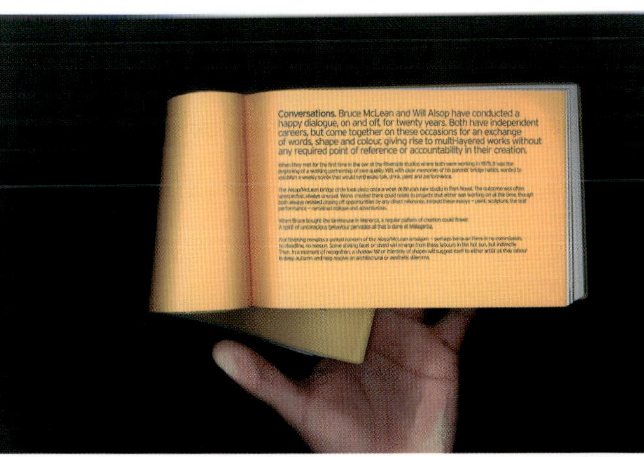

Conversations. Bruce McLean and Will Alsop have conducted a
happy dialogue, on and off, for twenty years. Both have independent
careers, but come together on these occasions for an exchange
of words, shape and colour, giving rise to multi-layered works without
any required point of reference or accountability in their creation.

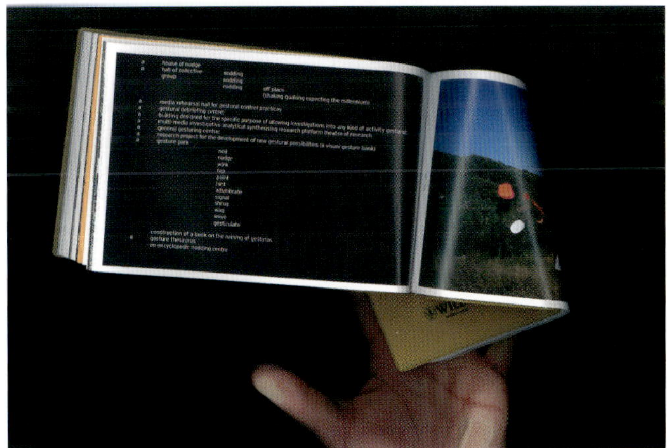

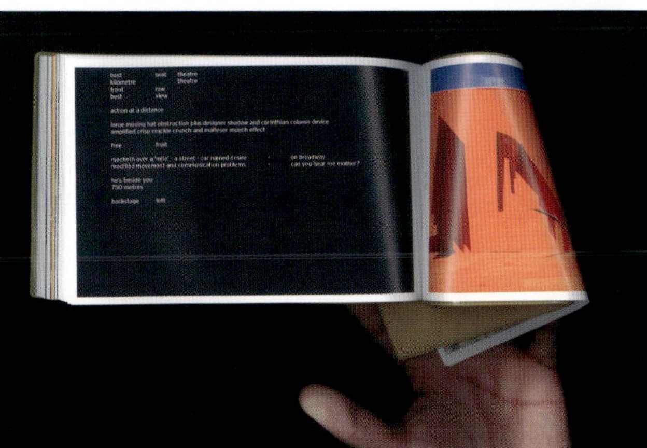

Made

Oslo, Norway

Title: CMYK Book 05
Type of work: Book
Client: Lloyd & Associates, Germany
Design: ad// Made, Kimberly Lloyd d// Made
Year: 2005

This is designed for an independent magazine festival held in Barcelona. The book features some of the festivals' contributors but is at the same time an independent publication showcasing the best magazine the world has to offer. The book has contributions from several well-known writers, photographers, designers and artists. It is a 350-page project designed with 15 stocks of paper, and several special printing techniques.

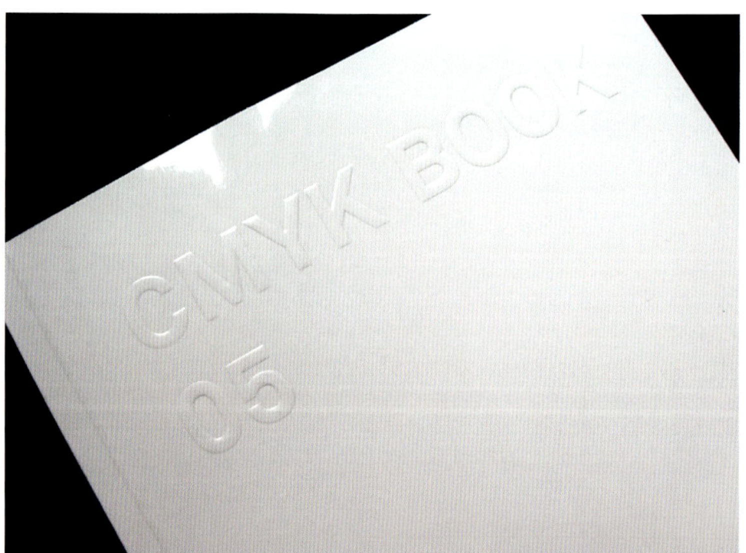

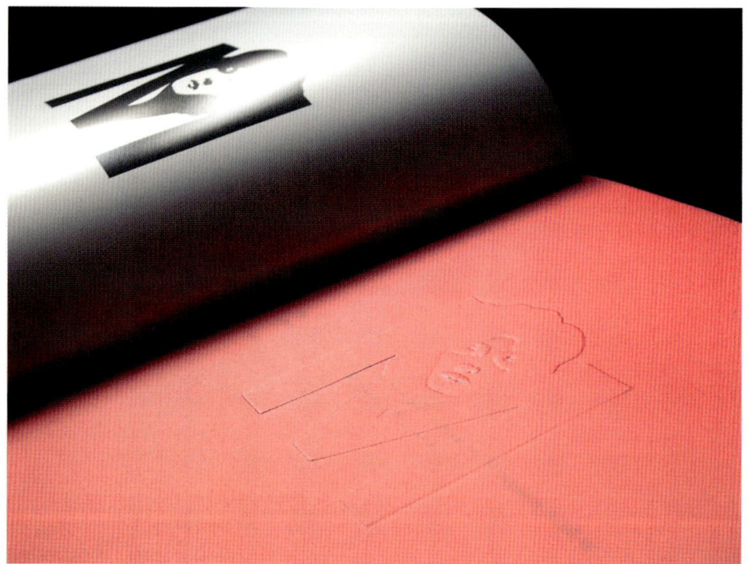

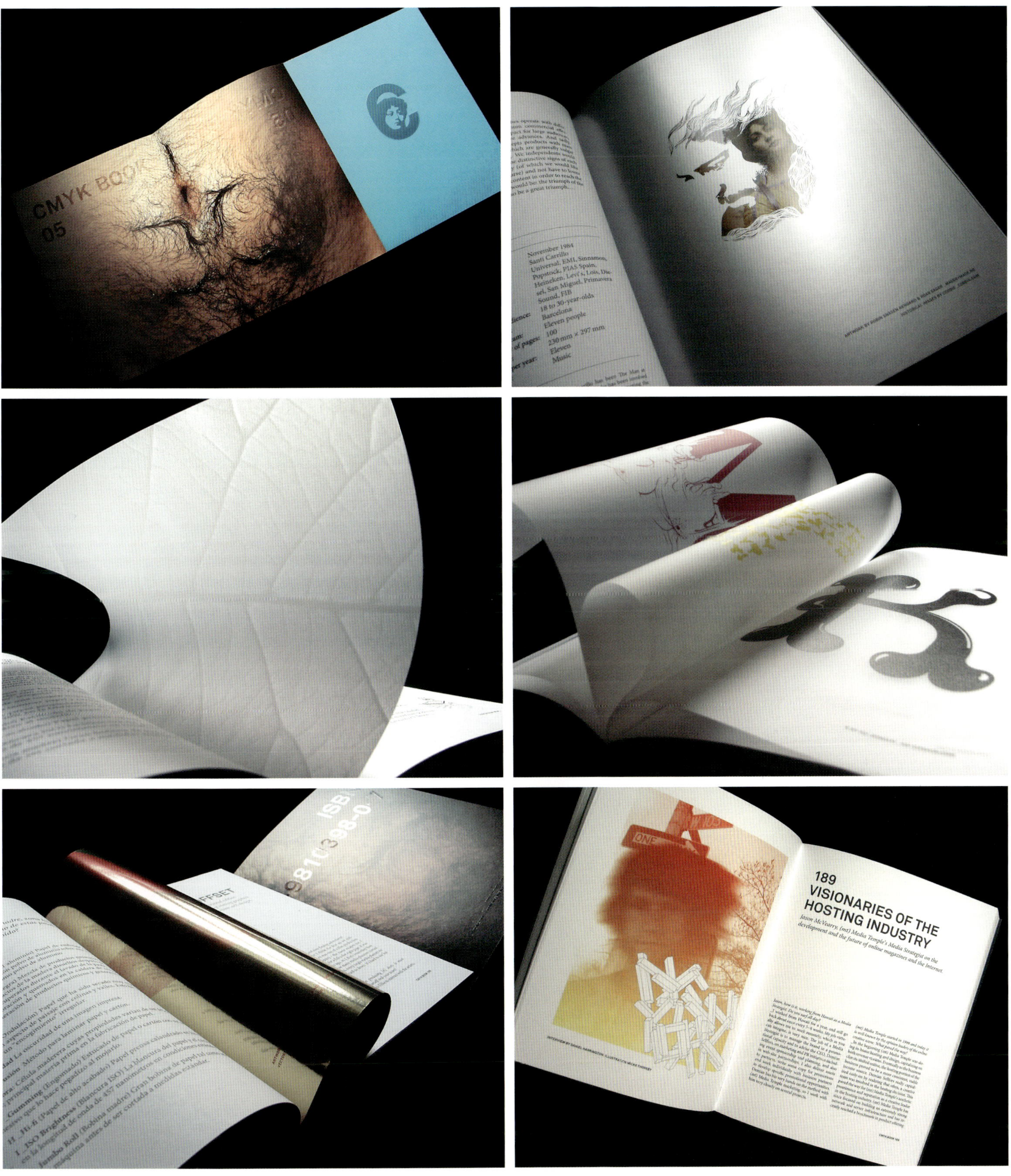

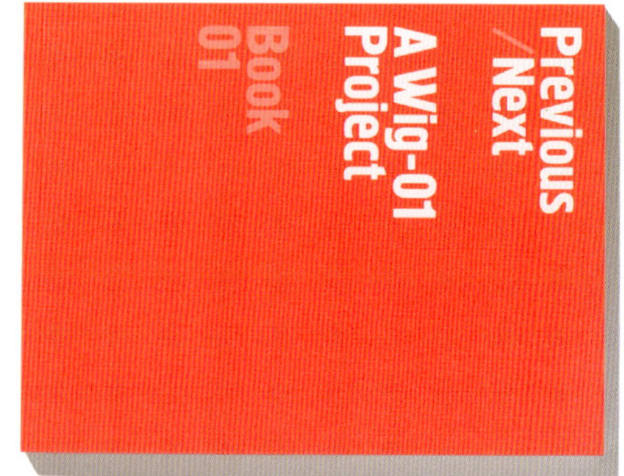

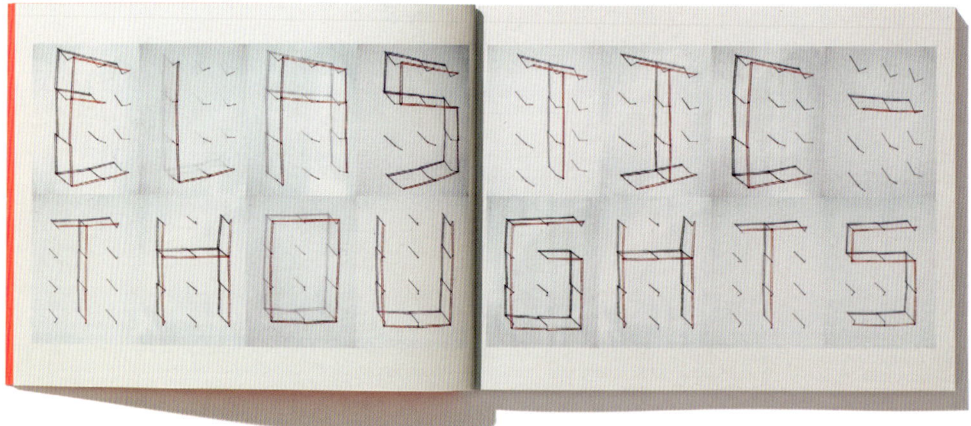

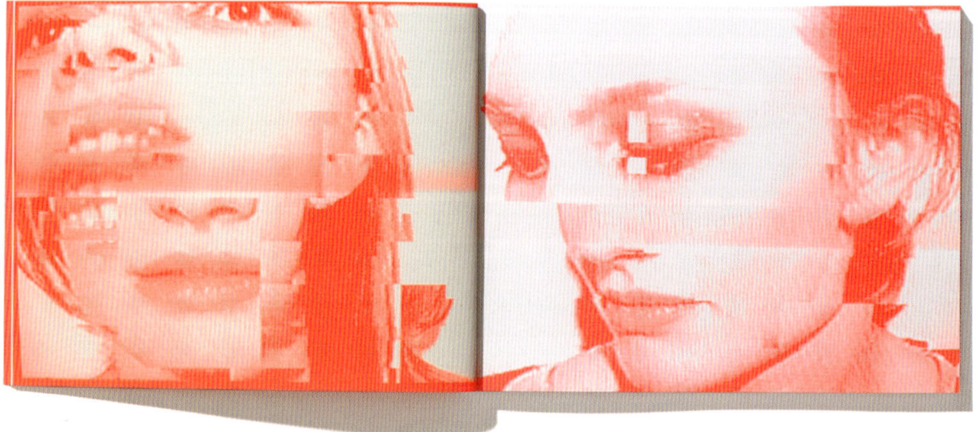

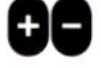

Wig-01

Lincoln, UK

Title: Previous/Next: A Wig-01 Project
Type of work: Book
Client: Wig-01
Design: ad, d// Wig-01
Year: 2005

Contains 68 pages in perfect bound, Previous/
Next is a collection of experiments and projects by
multi-disciplinary design studio Wig-01 based.

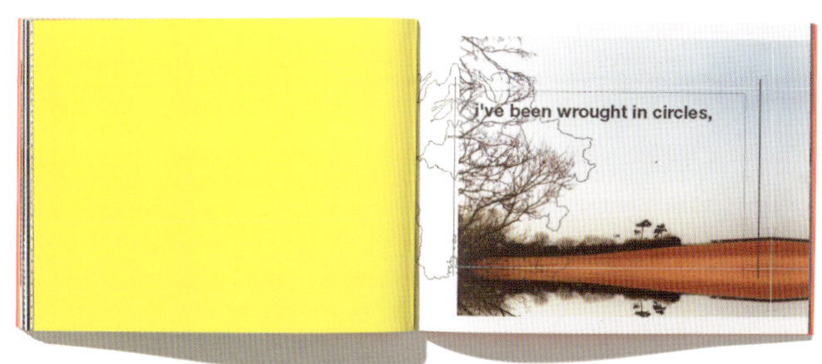

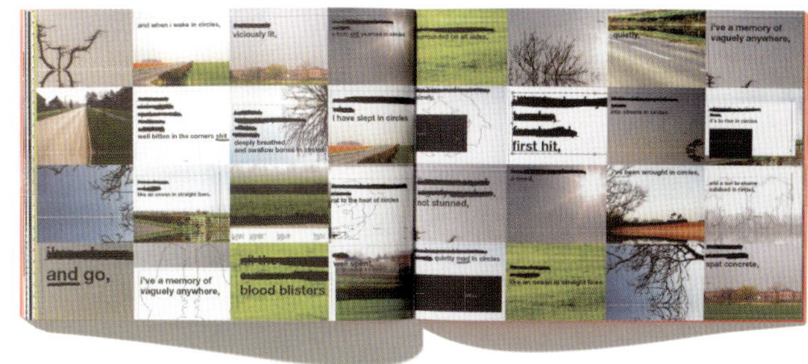

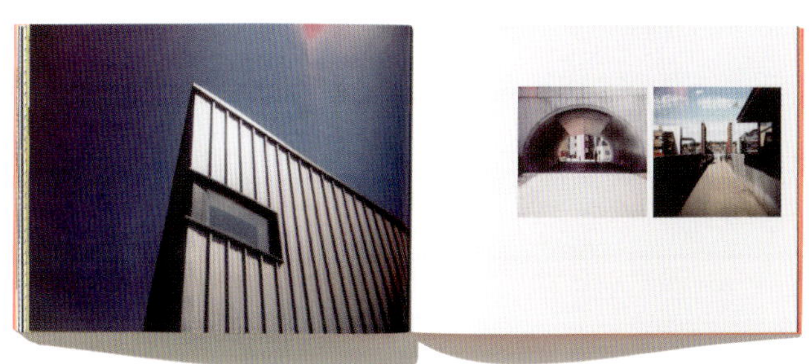

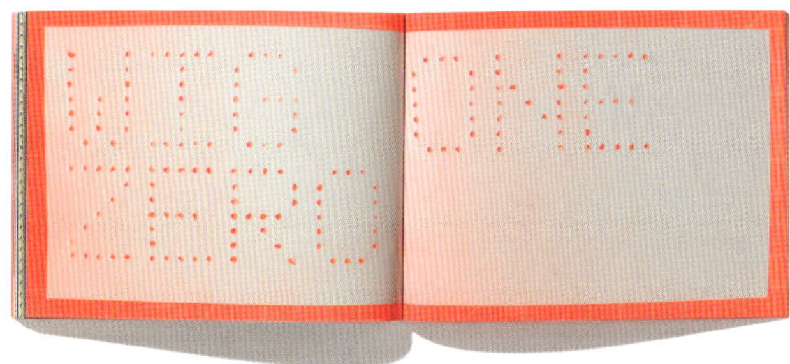

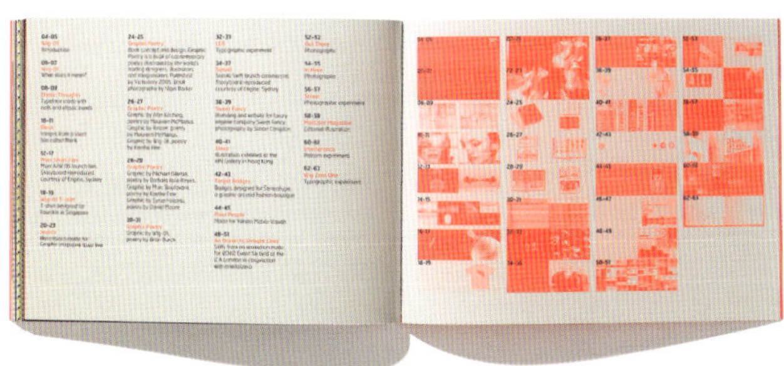

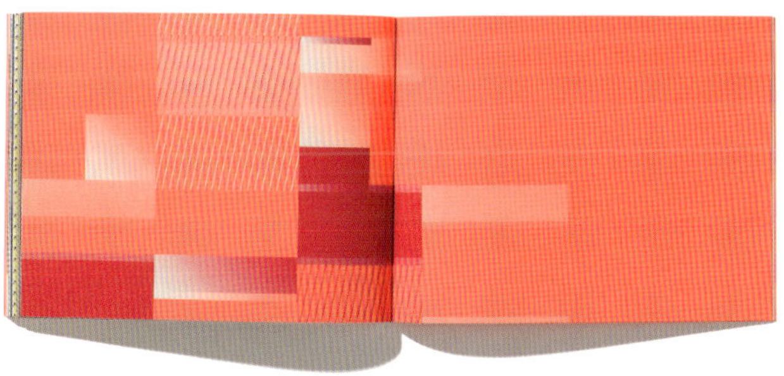

Cartlidge Levene

London, UK

Title: Mapping (Live Work Social Visit Listen)
Type of work: -
Client: Cartlidge Levene
Design: Cartlidge Levene
Year: 2004

A self generated piece consists of maps from different areas of the North of Scotland and texts listing activities over the last five years. The maps were stripped down to basic outline shapes and overprinted in sections to abstract them from information into simple graphic textures. The list of activities were also reduced into single words, without context, to act as mental prompts for the five year period. Printed with Evelyn Pottie at art.tm screenprinting workshop. The book and posters were shown at the 'Filesharing' Gallery in Berlin in 2004.

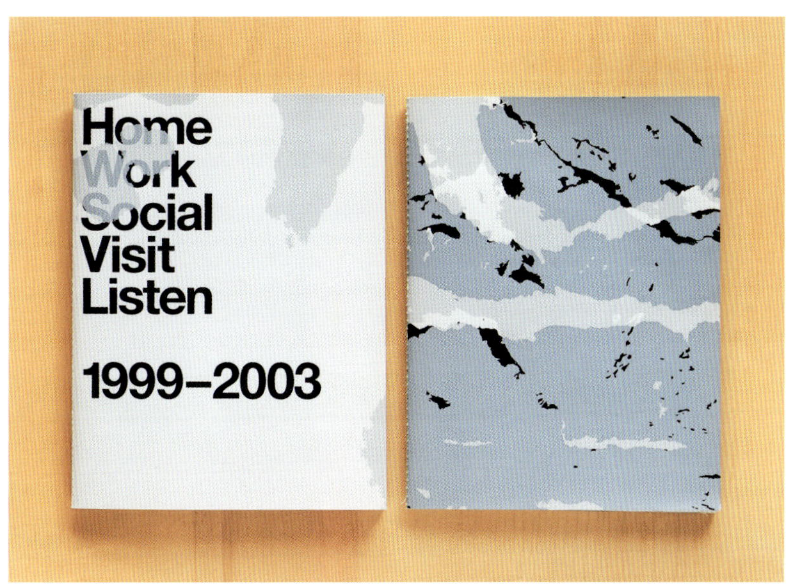

Home
Work
Social
Visit
Listen

1999–2003

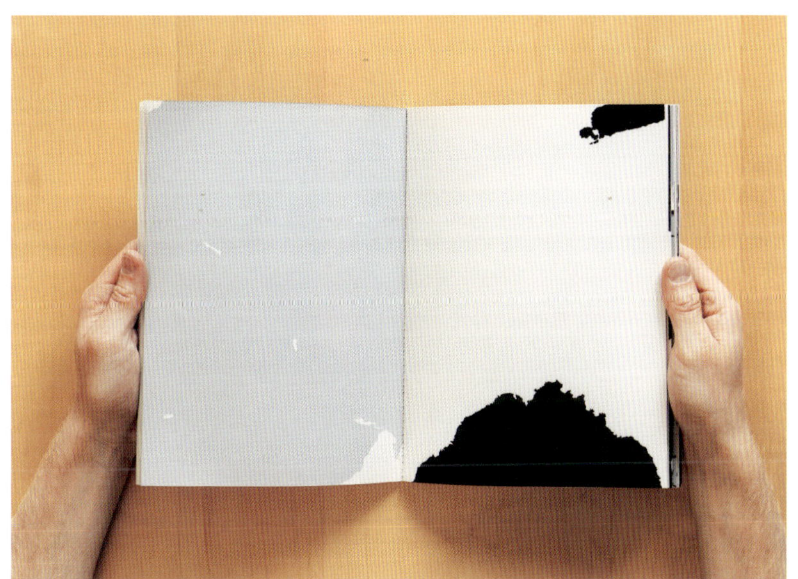

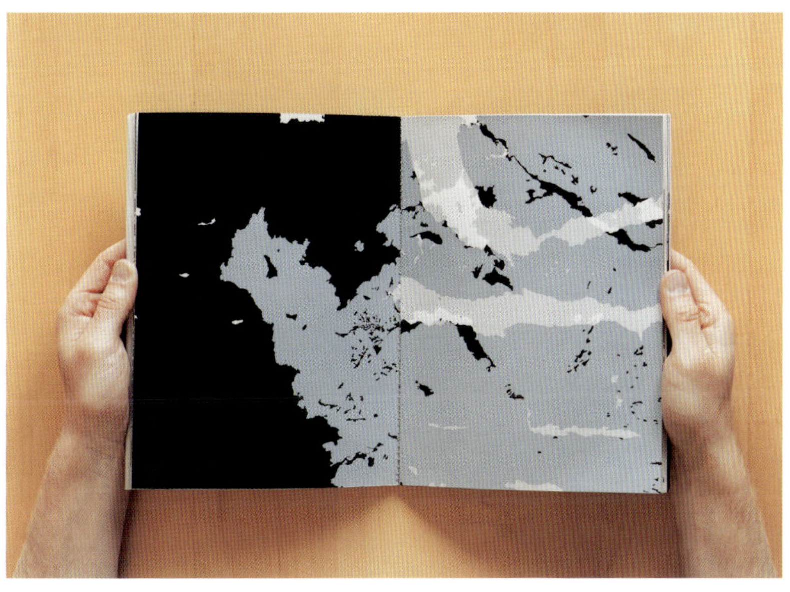

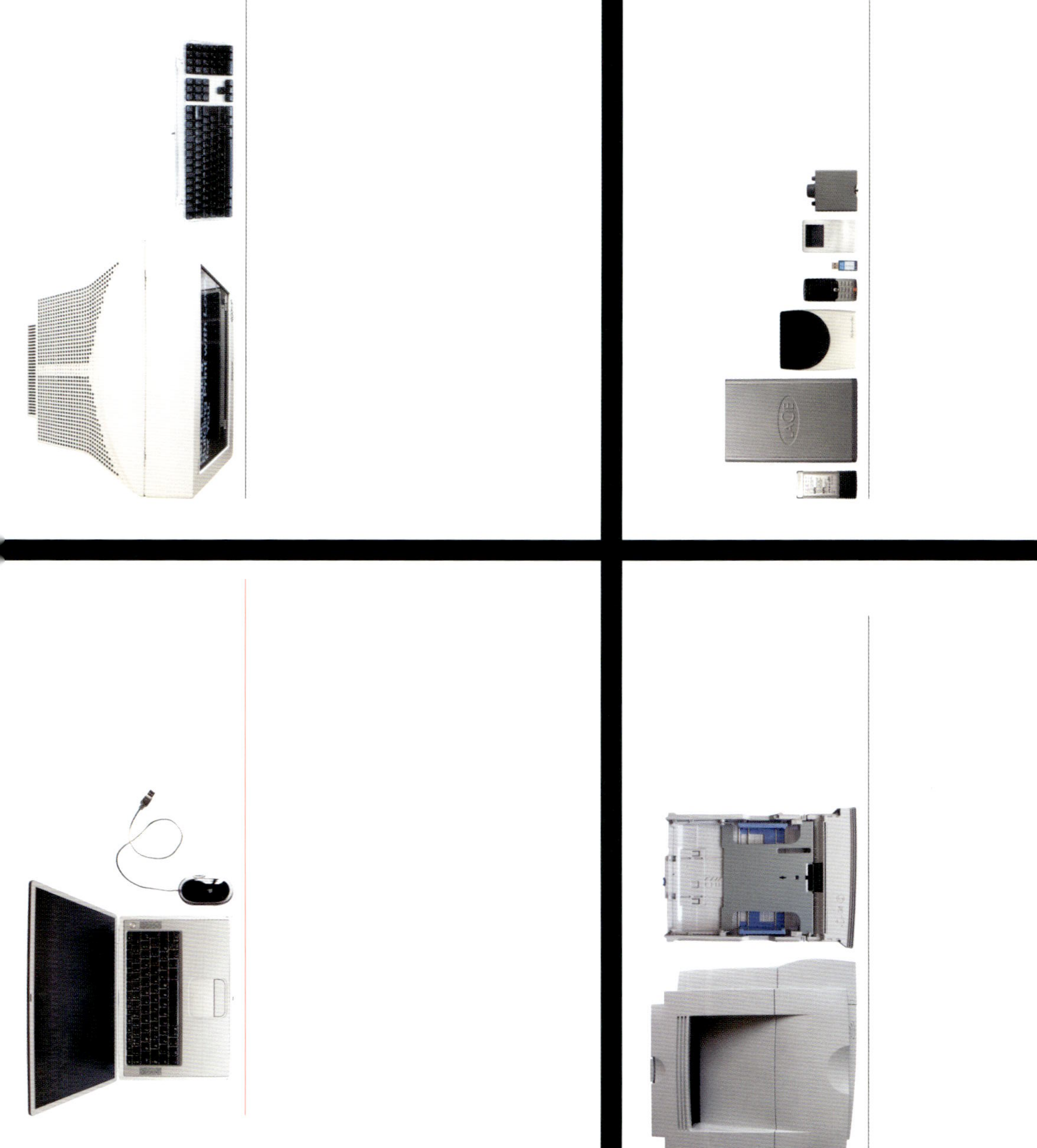

●Build Printed Office [Input/Output devices].
●Cover: Apple Macintosh Powerbook, Apple Pro-Mouse. ●Pg2: Sony Multiscan E500, Apple Extended Keyboard. ●Pg 3: Hewlett Packard Laserjet 2300d. ●Pg 4: PCMCIA Card, Lacie CD-Writer, Wiredshuttle DSL, Sony Ericsson T610, D-Link Bluetooth adapter, Apple iPod [30GB], Tivoli Audio PAL.
●Print with Love™

Refill. Issue 4, set in 12pt ATÖur Bodoni Medium type.

Build

London, UK

Title: Think™ [Creative Review cover]
Type of work: Magazine, editorial
Client: *Creative Review* magazine
Design: ad, d// Michael C. Place
Year: 2005

The idea of this cover is 'photography as typography' and using arrangements of consumer electrical items in a recognizable and readable form to replace text.

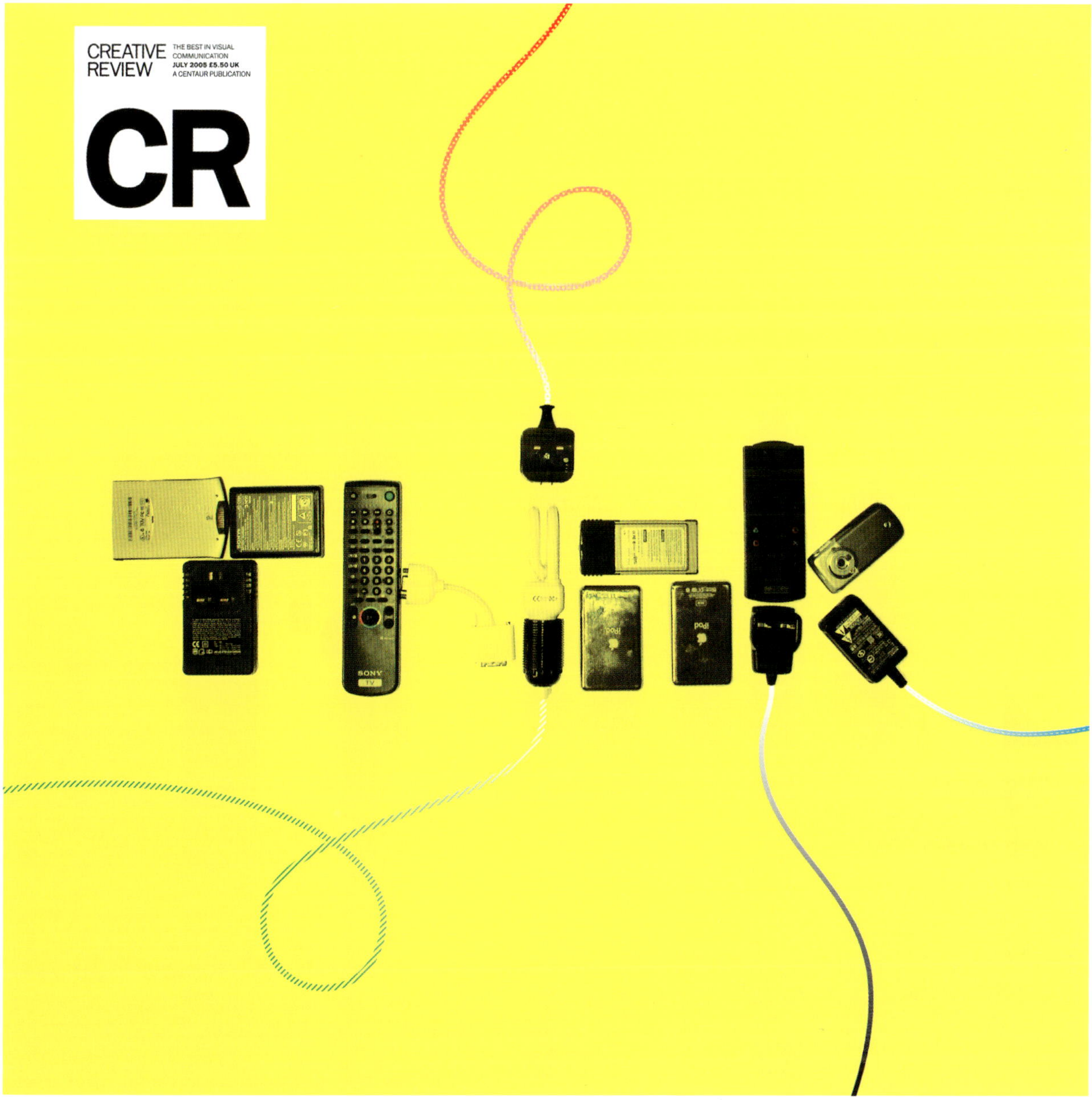

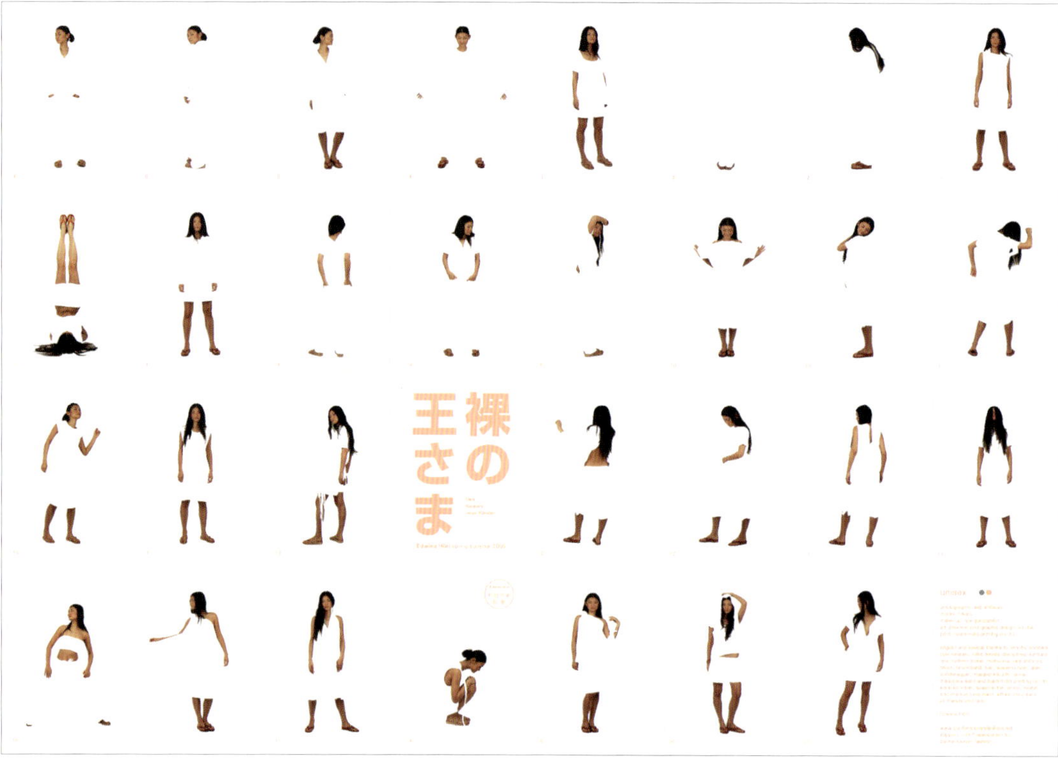

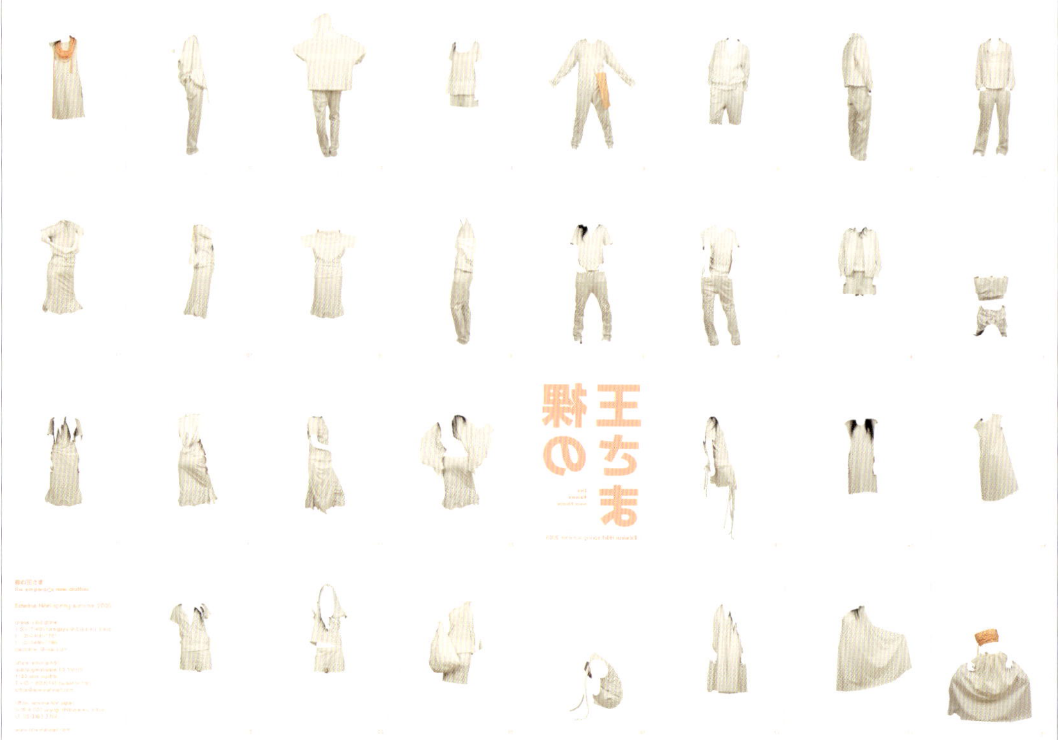

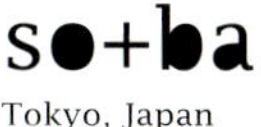

so●+ba

Tokyo, Japan

Title: Edwina Hörl Fashion Design Promotion
Type of work: Poster catalogue
Client: Edwina Hörl promotion
Design: ad, d// so+ba
Year: 2005

'Hadaka no osama' meaning the emperors new cloth, is the name of the 'Summer / Autumn collection 05' by Edwina Hörl, a Tokyo based Austrian fashion designer. The poster works with the fact, that the emperor didn't wear any clothes. On the backside only clothes are printed while on the front side, there are only body parts of models. However, by looking at the poster against the light, the model with the cloth is now visuable.

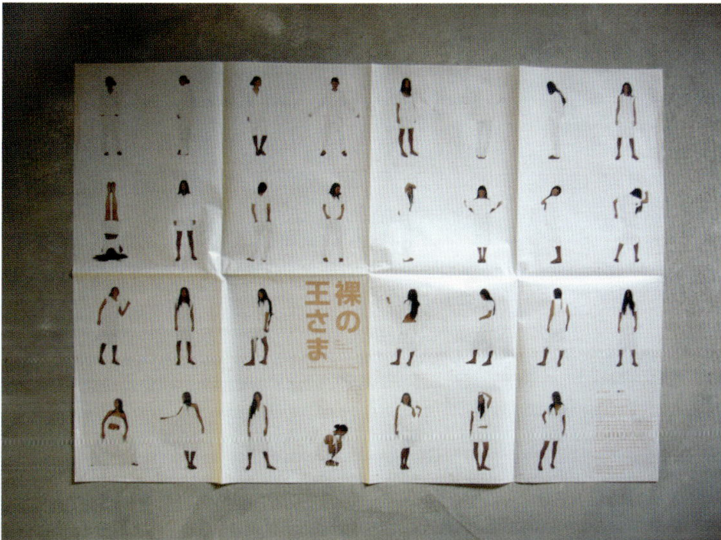

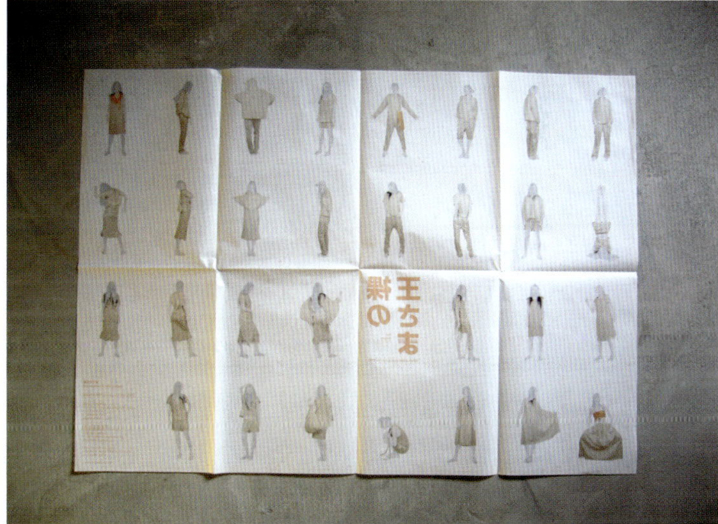

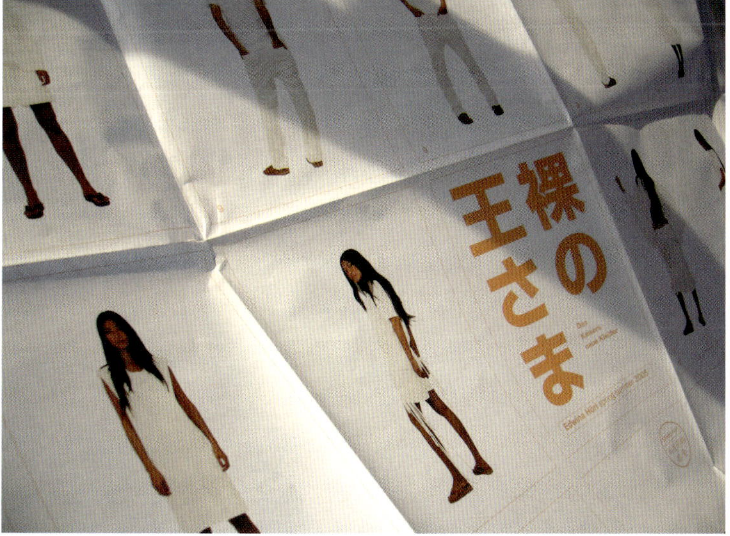

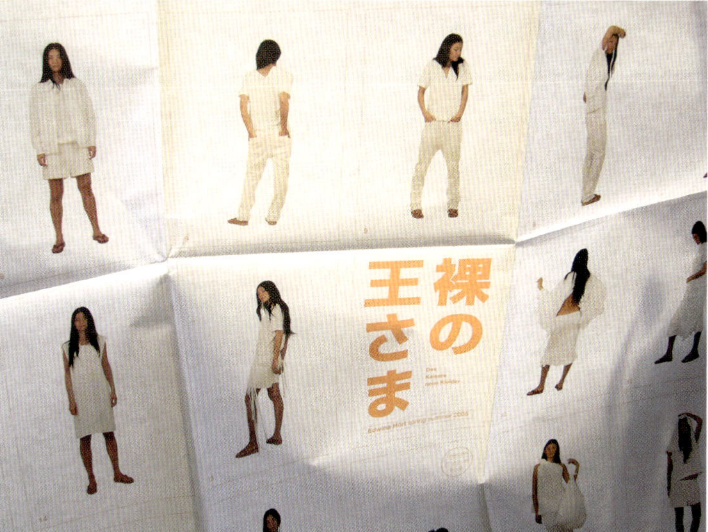

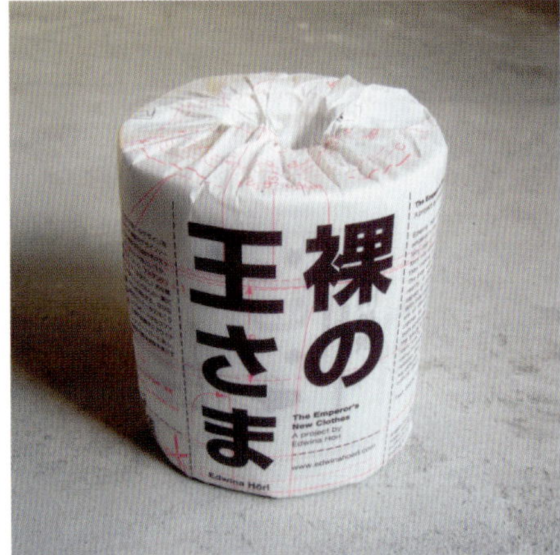

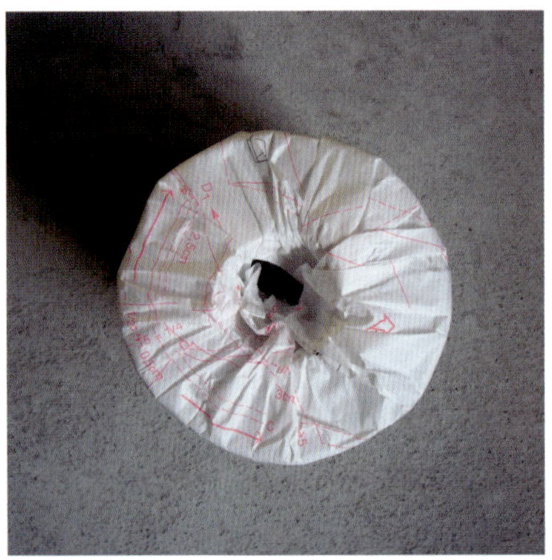

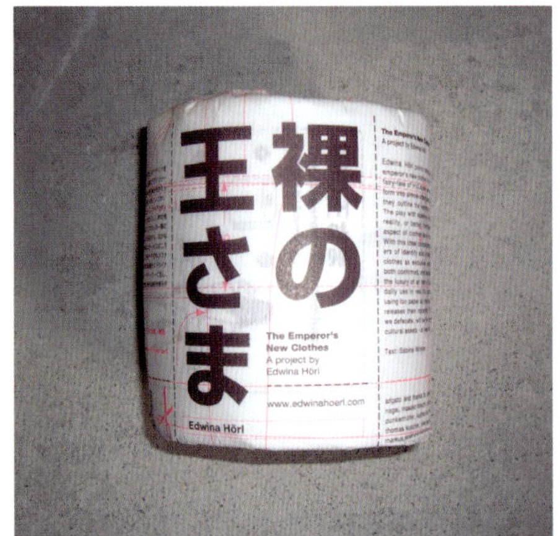

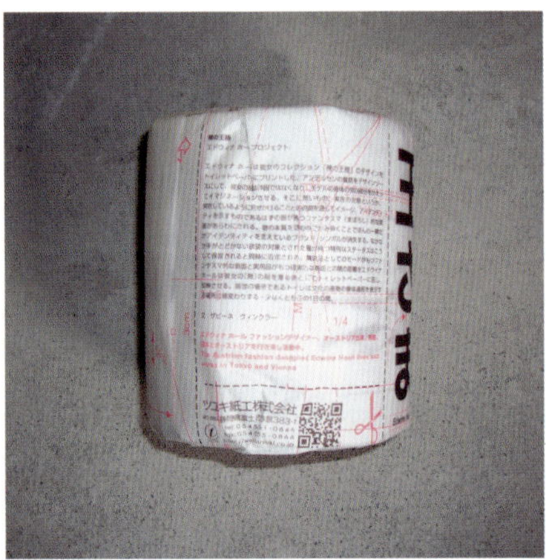

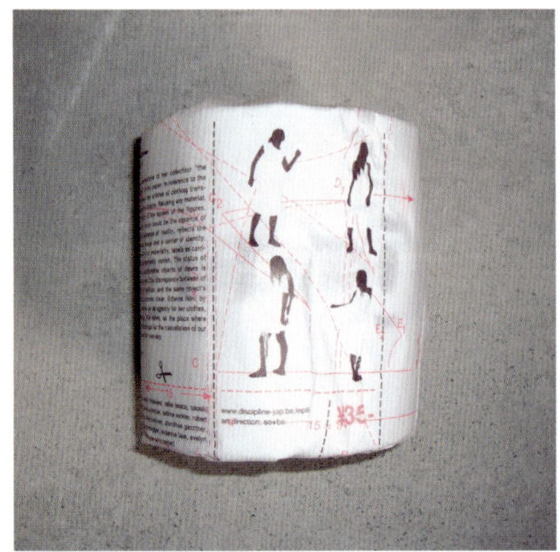

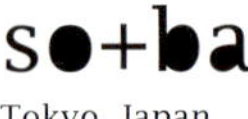

Tokyo, Japan

Title: Edwina Hörl Fashion Design Promotion
Type of work: Toilet paper
Client: Edwina Hörl promotion
Design: ad, d// so+ba
Year: 2005

'Hadaka no osama' meaning the emperors new cloth, is the name of the 'Summer / Autumn collection 05' by Edwina Hörl, a Tokyo based Austrian fashion designer.

For the world-exhibition, so+ba designed a toilet paper for the collection. An installation was created with the printed toilet paper in the Austrian pavilion. Now the paper is available for ¥350 in various museum shops in Japan.

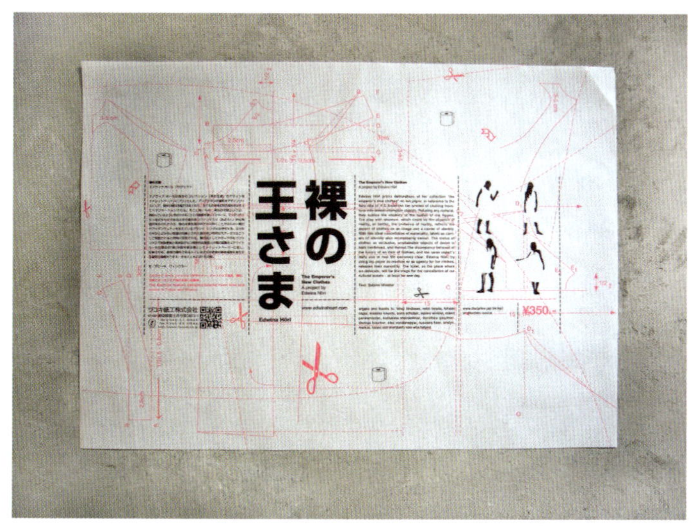

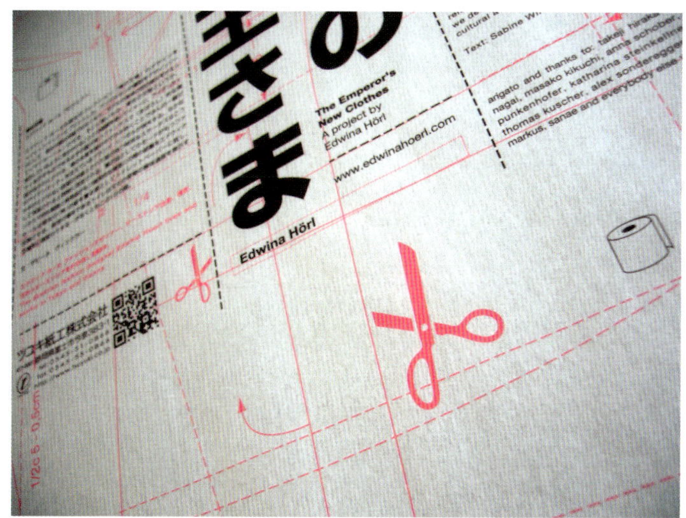

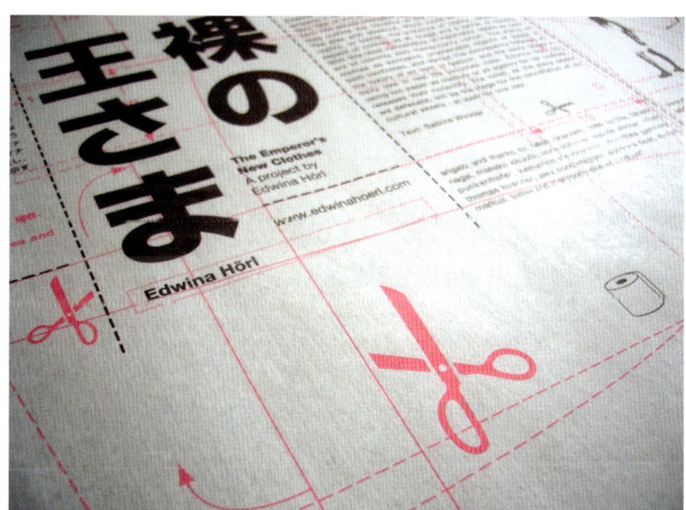

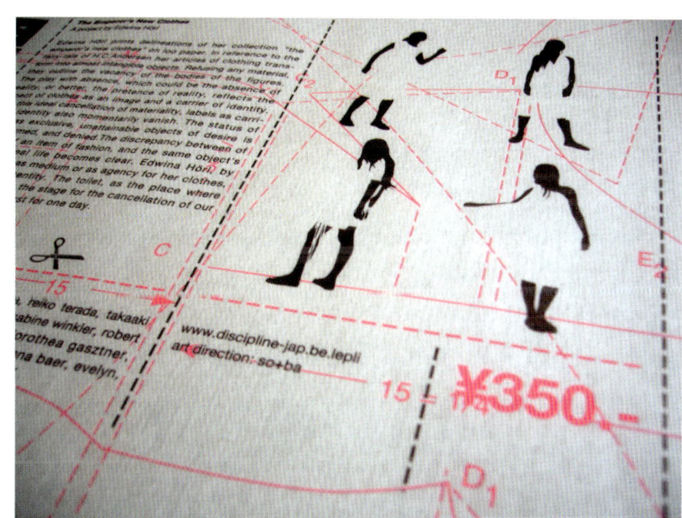

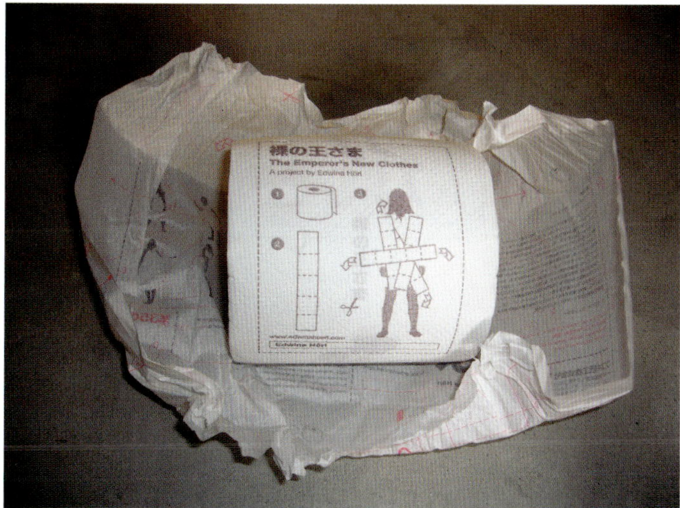

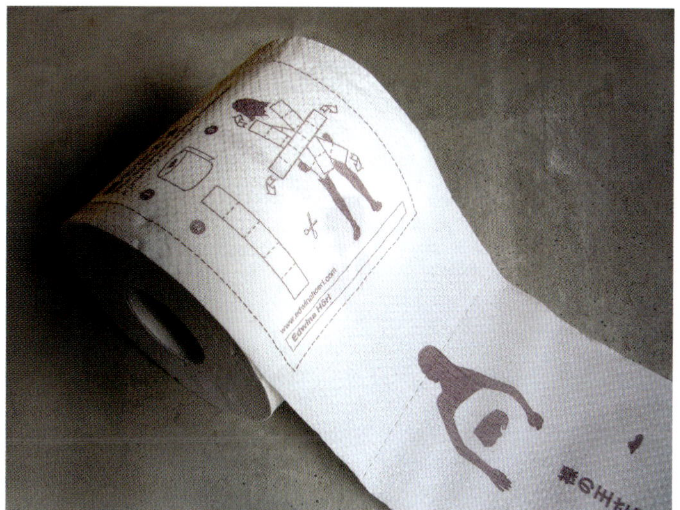

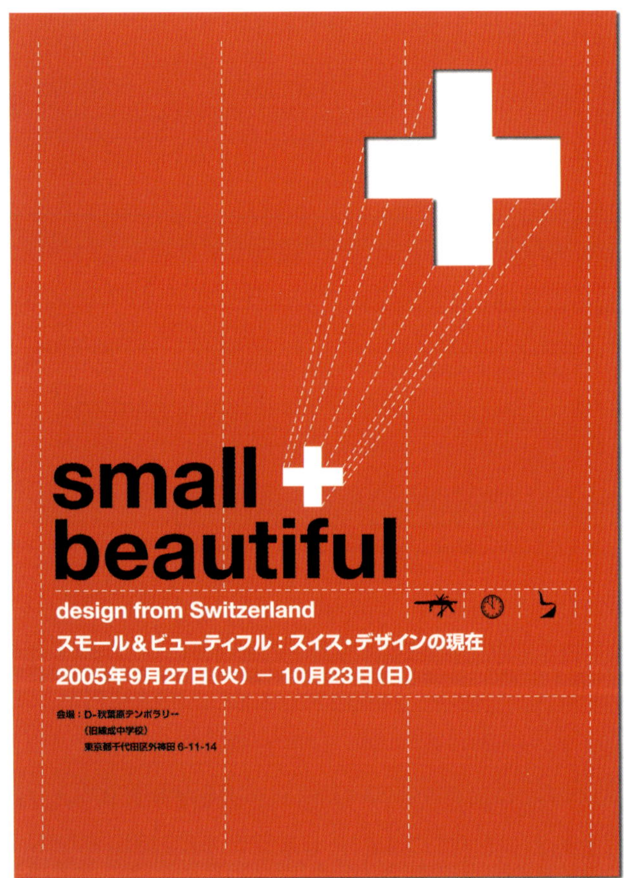

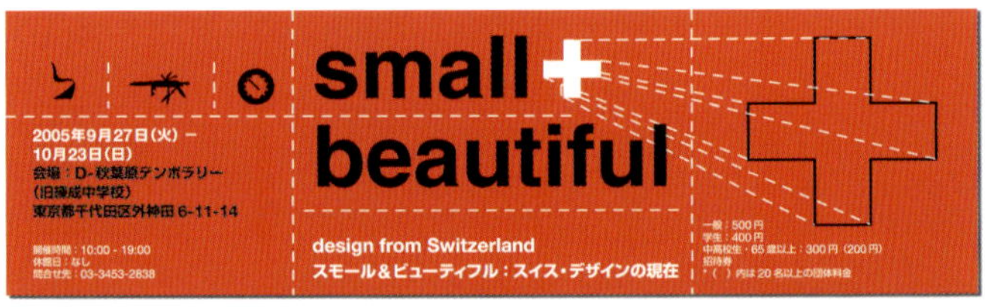

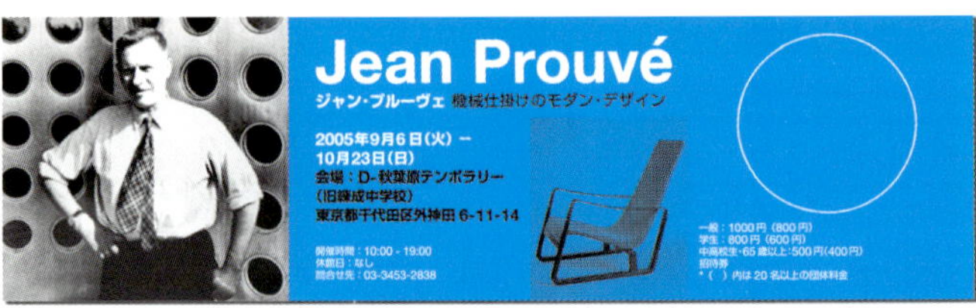

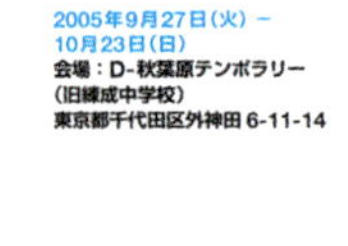

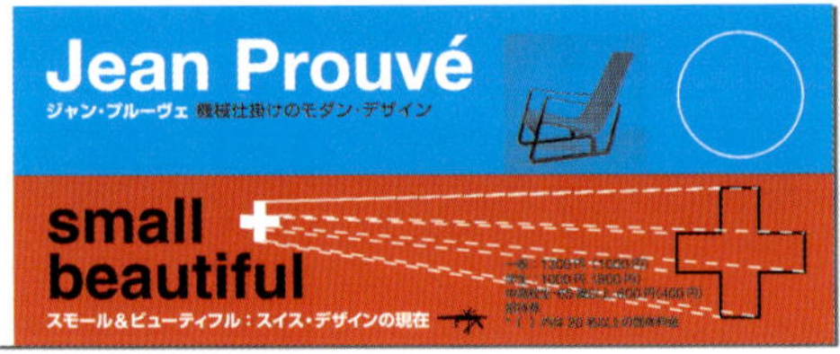

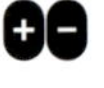

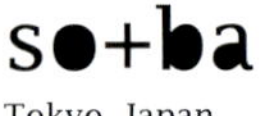

so+ba

Tokyo, Japan

Title: small+beautiful
Type of work: Exhibition flyer, ticket and poster
Client: -
Design: ad, d// so+ba
Year: 2005

'small + beautiful' is a Swiss design exhibition, first started in Switzerland and traveling around the world. From October 2005 until the end of year 2006, 'small + beautiful' travelled throughout Japan. The design concept 'get an inside view of Switzerland' is visualized with cut out crosses on all the promotional matterials.

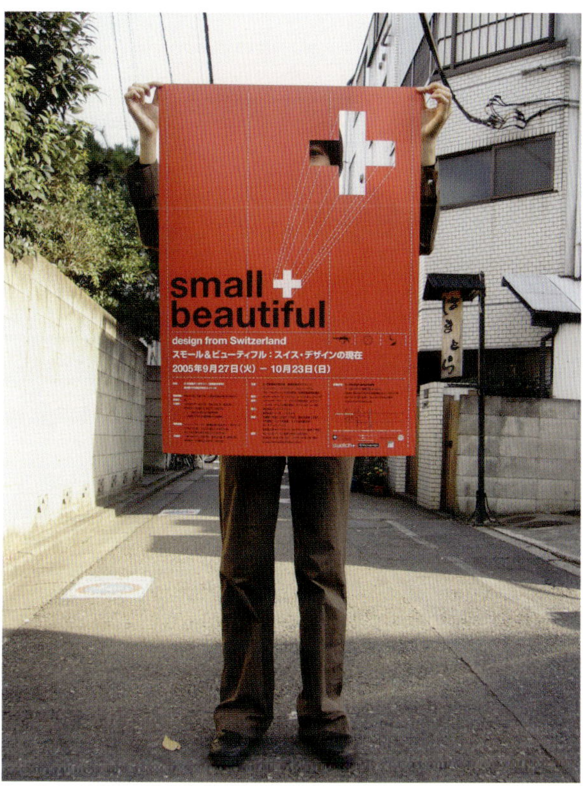

small +
beautiful
design from Switzerland
スモール＆ビューティフル：スイス・デザインの現在
2005年9月27日（火） － 10月23日（日）

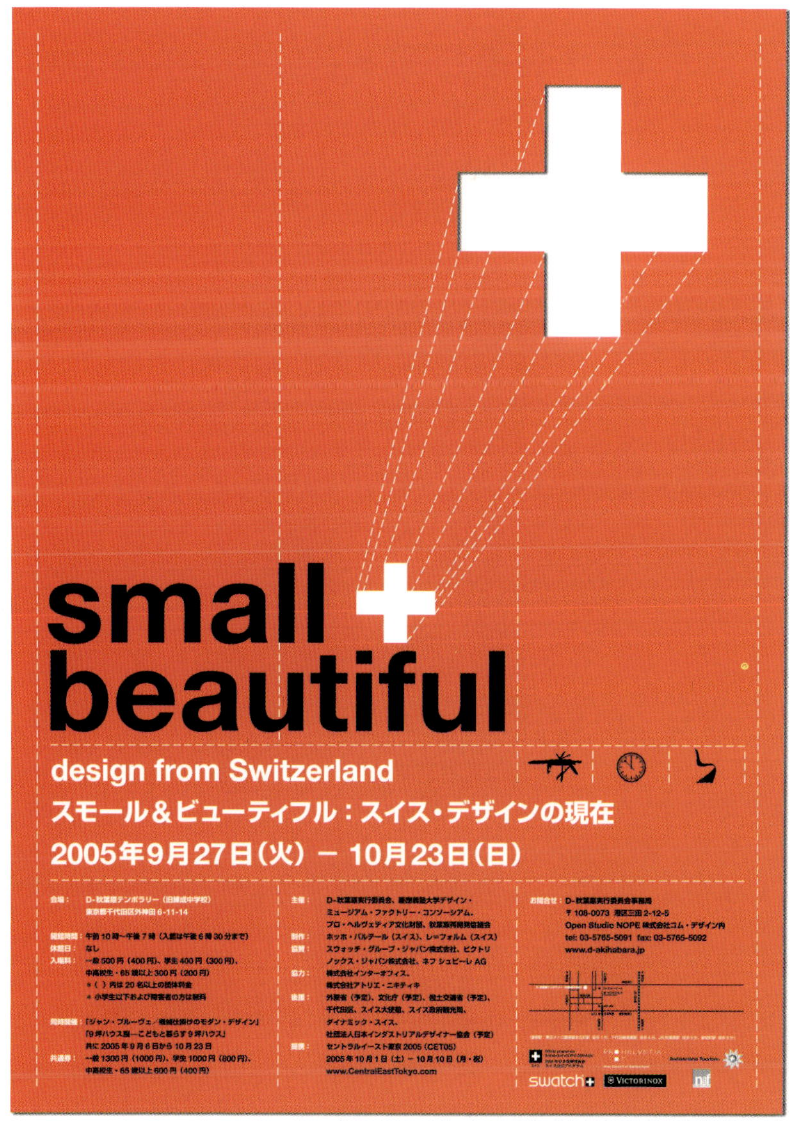

small +
beautiful
design from Switzerland
スモール＆ビューティフル：スイス・デザインの現在
2005年9月27日（火） － 10月23日（日）

会場： D-秋葉原テンポラリー（旧練成中学校）
東京都千代田区外神田 6-11-14
開館時間： 午前10時－午後7時（入館は午後6時30分まで）
休館日： なし
入場料： 一般500円（400円）、学生400円（300円）、
中高校生・65歳以上300円（200円）
＊（ ）内は20名以上の団体料金
＊小学生以下および障害者の方は無料

同時開催：「ジャン・プルーヴェ：構築詩におけるモダン・デザイン」
「9坪ハウス展—こどもと暮らす9坪ハウス」
共に2005年9月6日–10月23日
共通券： 一般1300円（1000円）、学生1000円（800円）、
中高校生・65歳以上600円（400円）

主催： D-秋葉原実行委員会、慶應義塾大学デザイン・
ミュージアム・ファクトリー・コンソーシアム、
プロ・ヘルヴェティア文化財団、秋葉原究明特殊協議会
製作： ネッホ・バルチール（スイス）、レ フォルム（スイス）
協賛： スウォッチ・グループ・ジャパン株式会社、ビクトリ
ノックス・ジャパン株式会社、ネフ シュピーレ AG
協力： 株式会社インターオフィス。
株式会社アトリエ・ニキティキ
後援： 外務省（予定）、文化庁（予定）、国土交通省（予定）、
千代田区、スイス大使館、スイス政府観光局、
ダイナミック・スイス。
社団法人日本インダストリアルデザイナー協会（予定）
関連： セントラルイースト東京 2005（CET05）
2005年10月1日（土）– 10月10日（月・祝）
www.CentralEastTokyo.com

お問合せ： D-秋葉原実行委員会事務局
〒108-0073 港区三田 2-12-5
Open Studio NOPE 株式会社コム・デザイン内
tel: 03-5765-5091 fax: 03-5765-5092
www.d-akihabara.jp

swatch +   VICTORINOX   nef

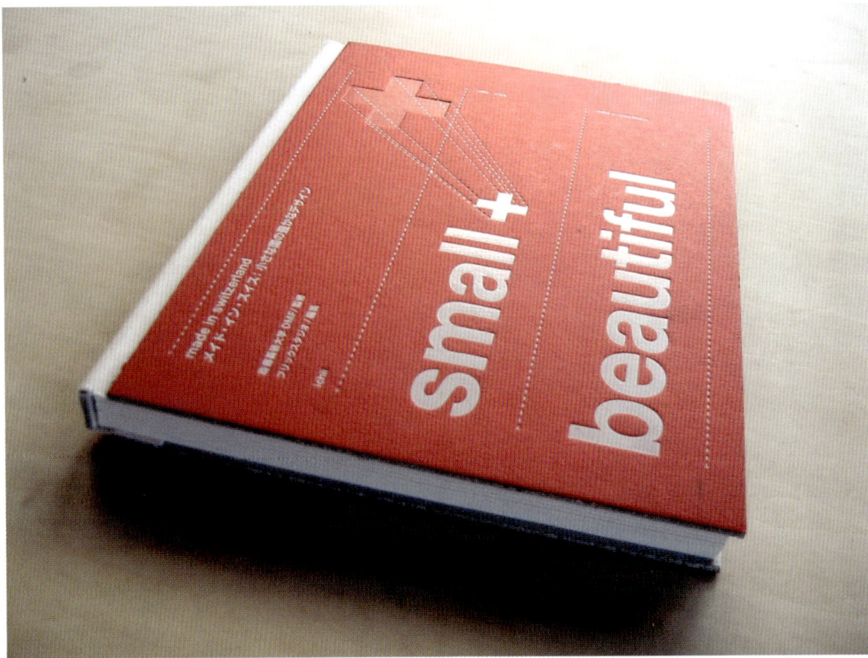

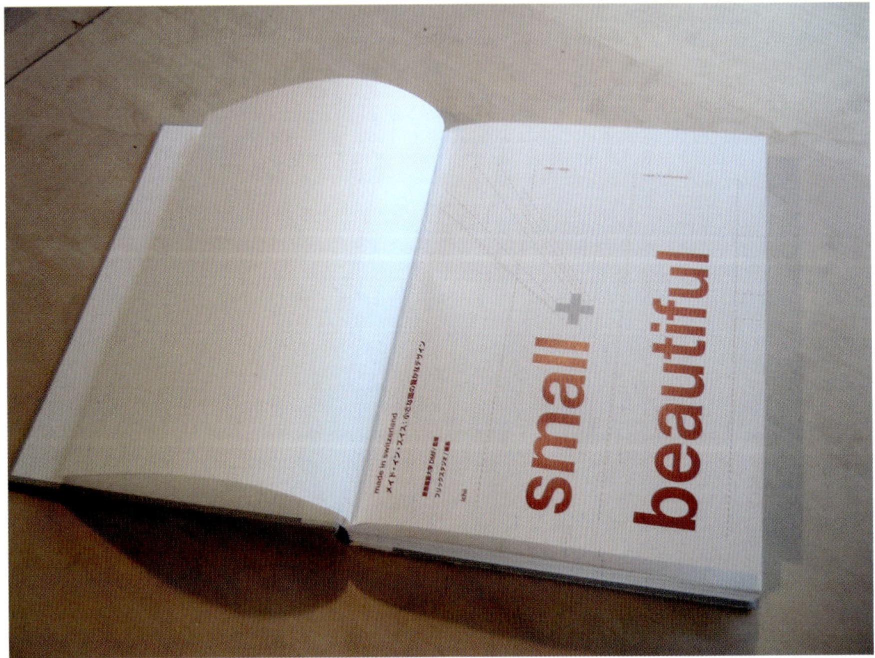

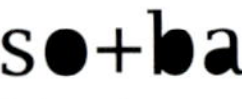

so+ba

Tokyo, Japan

Title: small+beautiful
Type of work: Exhibition catalogue
Client: -
Design: ad, d// so+ba
Year: 2005

'small + beautiful' is a Swiss design exhibition, first started in Switzerland and traveling around the world. From October 2005 until the end of year 2006, 'small + beautiful' travelled throughout Japan. The design concept 'get an inside view of Switzerland' is visualized with cut out crosses on all the promotional matters.

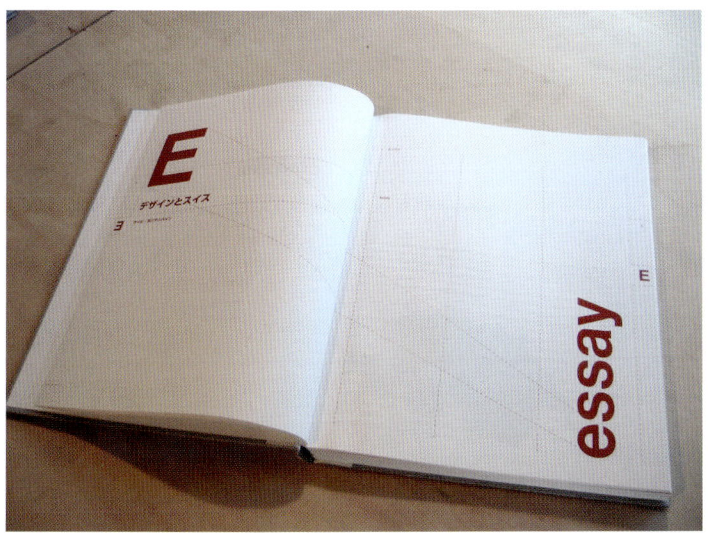
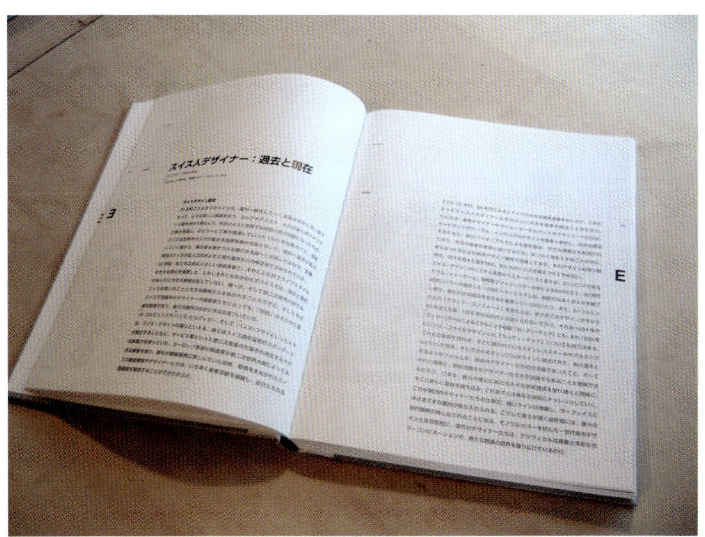
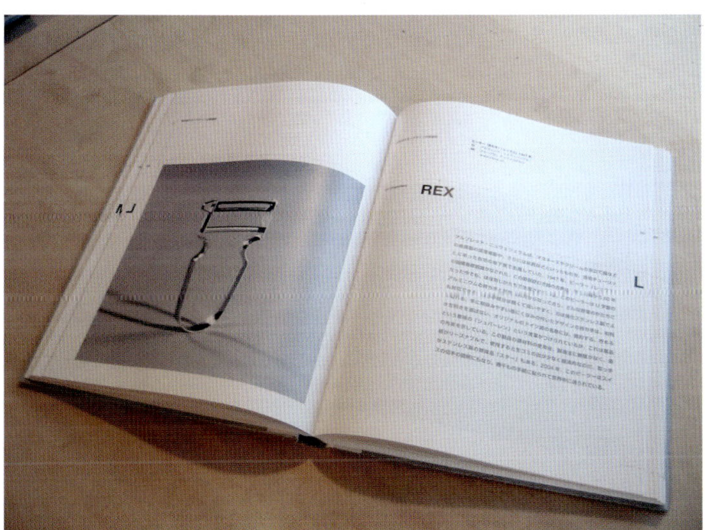
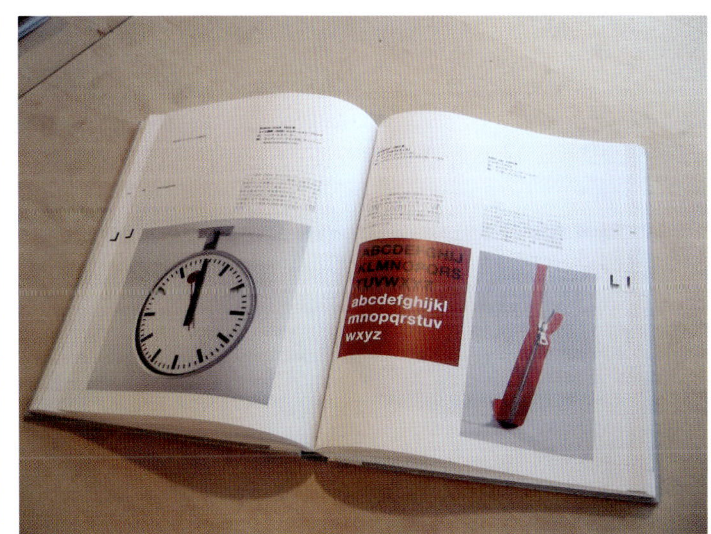
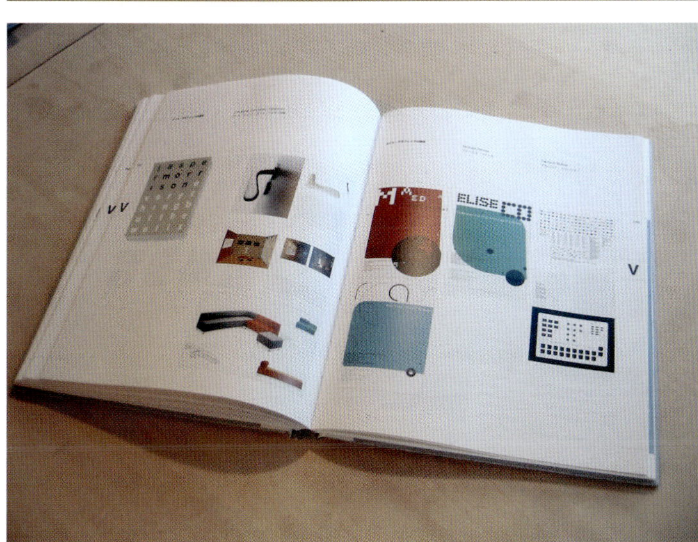
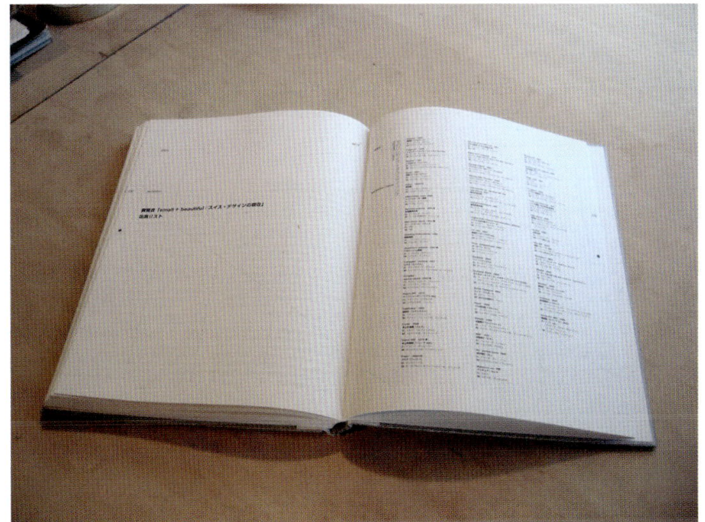

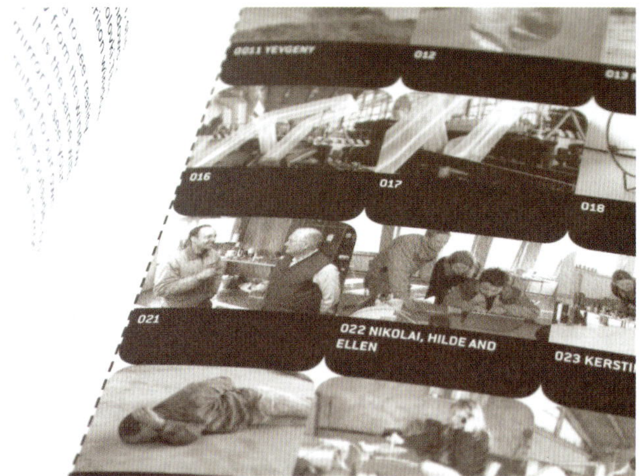

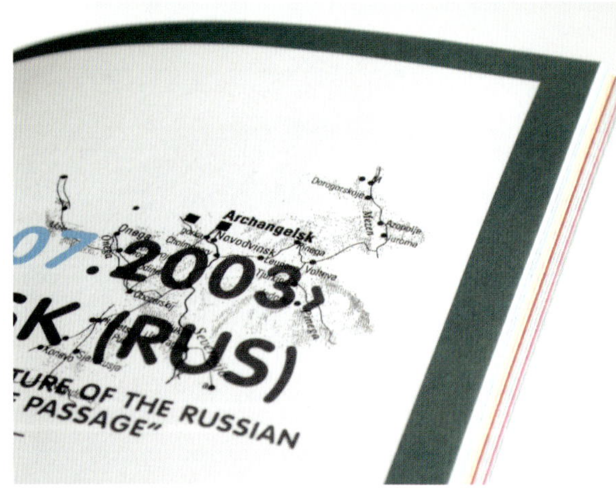

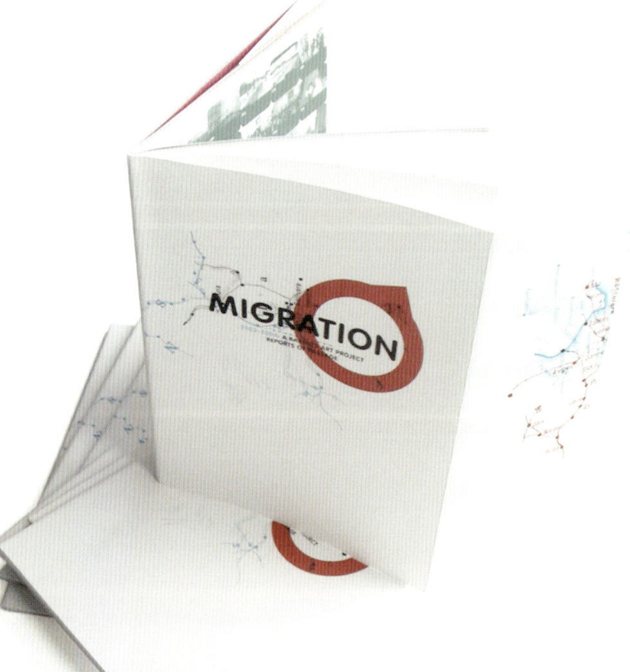

Gra**nd**people

Norway

Title: Migration
Type of work: Catalogue
Client: Pikene På Broen
Design: ad, d// Grandpeople
Year: 2004

This was an art collaboration between artists from Norway, Sweden, Finland and Russia, including seminars and exhibitions in different cities and communities in the Barents region. This catalogue, which was mainly for documentary and internal use, is the first project that Grandpeople did in collaboration with the art collective Pikene På Broen in Kirkenes.

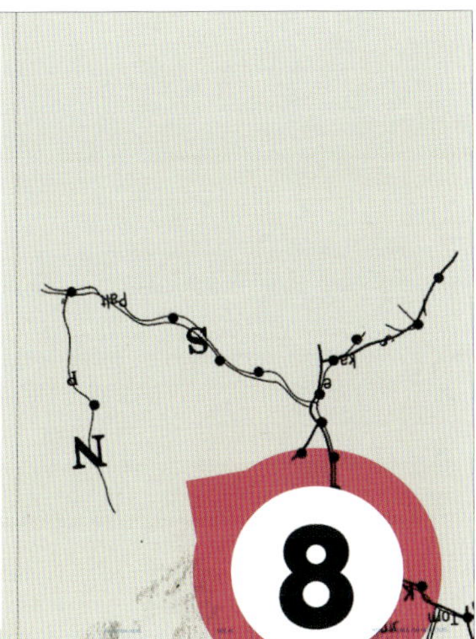

SEARCHING FOR SLOWNESS

by Jaakko Heikkilä, Kokkola, Finland

It is as if the lilac eye shadow or through the air staggering plane is closing down the eyes of the lady sitting next to me, the Swedish newspaper on her lap is wide open. I'm switching the channels of the radio. How the clouds below are sympathetic. And the sea between them. The lady opens her colourful eyes and changes her pose.
- Sweden is dark and black.
She speaks about the four hour moment of light in the middle of the day. And the rest is pure night.
- I can't live in Sweden. I try to think about the whole universe.
I nod my head in approval.
- I am homeless, she says
- I have a home. I finally open my mouth.
- My home is slowness. Or searching for it.
I tell her that I would like to live as lava, like the main character in the novel of Torgny Lindgren.
- You are Swedish, do you happen to know Lindgren? I ask.
But the lady shakes her head and tells that she doesn't know the Swedish literature.
- You look happy, she continues. Could one be homeless and be happy?
- Borders make me happy, I answer. I search for slowness from there. Worlds are greeted on the borders.
I think for a moment and then look at the lady whose eyes are twinkling in attention. I try to deepen my words as the restless hum of the plane comes down on us.
- At the border I am away and at the same time in the centre of everything. Where the borders are far away, people swell into each other like water without oxygen.
- It's possible to find slowness on the borders, I add, when the plane hits an air pocket.
- You look absent. She says.
- Searching for slowness makes absent, I answer.
And then I notice we have come to the point of discussion where it starts to fade. I look at her and I am about to say that maybe homelessness is a state where you can feel home. I turn to look out of the window instead without speaking my thoughts and I see the capital city of Faeroes, Torshav, which is now on the left side of the plane. I am imagining that its streets are washed by harsh winds. And its border, towards the other world is a dangerously humble, swelling sea. There I could find some slowness filled by the sea winds.

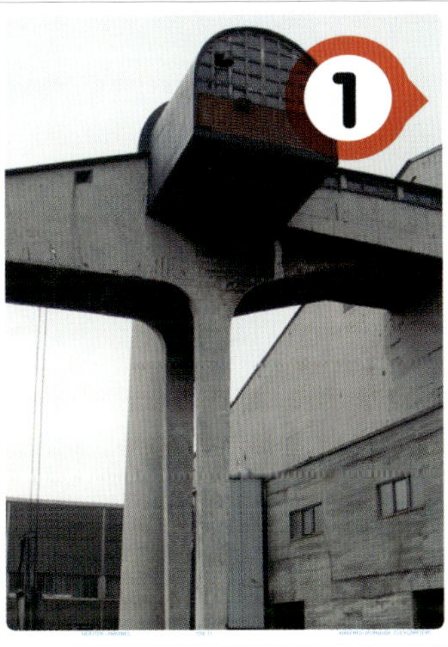

SEMINAR THOUGHTS

KIRKENES CHANGES

One aspect of the seminar was to focus on the changes of Kirkenes during the last decades. For almost a century, the people of the community have lived off the mining company A/S Sydvaranger, which, of course, had an enormous importance and influence on the society. The company took care of people, painted their fences and gave the workers apples for Christmas. People lived here, close to the border to Russia and the cold war, well aware of the strategic aspect of it. It was important for Norway, and the West, that someone actually lived here.

After the cold war ended and the borders between Norway and Russia opened up, A/S Sydvaranger closed down and people had to manage on their own.

Morten A. Strøksnes grew up in Kirkenes and was invited to talk about the changes he could see. Being the son of a NATO-officer, Strøksnes remembers the realities of the cold war very well.

- Growing up next to a border that I never crossed and with air raid alarms being tested "all the time" really does something to you. On the other side of the fence we could see Russian soldiers patrolling. It was an absolute, kafkaesque border. It marked the difference between heaven and hell, and gave the impression of an unbridgeable cleavage between "us" and "them", he told the audience at the seminar.

Then in January 2003, Strøksnes had returned to Kirkenes for the first time in fifteen years. The borders were opened, the cold war was over, and the mining factory was closed down. Having been away for so long, the changes were clear and striking and Strøksnes found a new kind of energy in the town.

- Kirkenes had changed from being the last station squeezed into a cold corner of the world, into the beginning of something new and exciting. It had changed from being the end of the line, into a place for transition; from being militarised to civilised. From being nationalised into being an international place, regionalised and even globalised. From static to dynamic, from masculine to feminine, closed to open, from monocultural to multicultural. Kirkenes had become a real bordertown, with trade and movement across the borders. Kirkenes had become a laboratory for a new time.

FROM INDUSTRIAL CULTURE TO CULTURE INDUSTRY*

Can art and culture give new energy to a local community, thereby transforming it from an industrial culture to a culture industry? Phil Wood knows a lot about this kind of transformation, and he has learned the hard way. Wood was part of a team that helped change Huddersfield from a disaster area of closed factories and coal mines and into the expanding place it is today.

- In the 1800s and the beginning of the 1900s Huddersfield was one of the richest cities in England. The wealth of the city came from industry, particularly the production of fine cotton fabrics. Then, during Margareth Thatcher's time in the middle of the 1980s both the coal and cotton industries collapsed. (...) no security or time for changing the structure of the community.

There are several similarities between Kirkenes and Huddersfield. Industrial culture dominates both places strongly. However, Huddersfield has changed its production to fit the new knowledge based economy. Keywords are design, creativity and cultural promotion and innovation. The identity of Kirkenes is still very much connected to the industry - these days to the building of ships, and maintenance and supply related to the

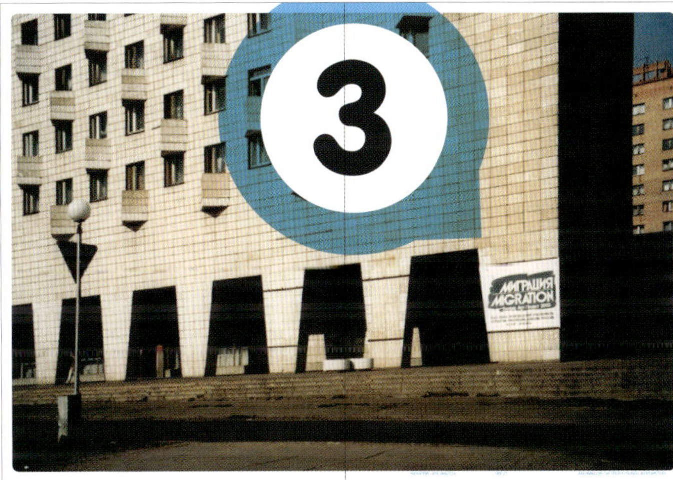

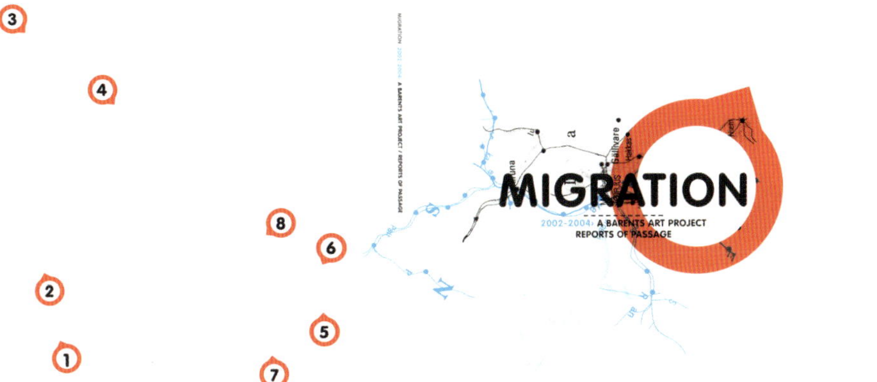

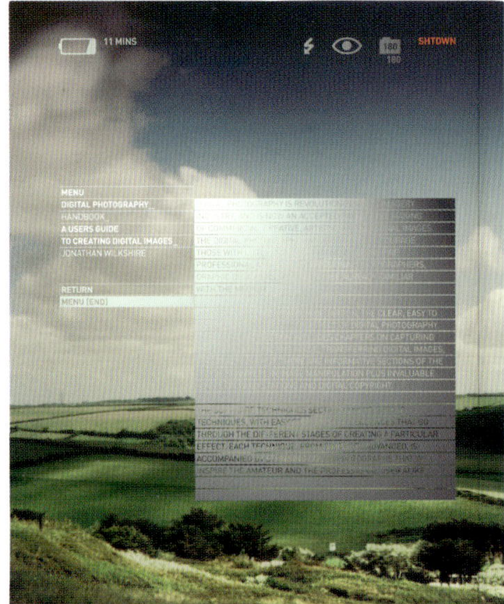

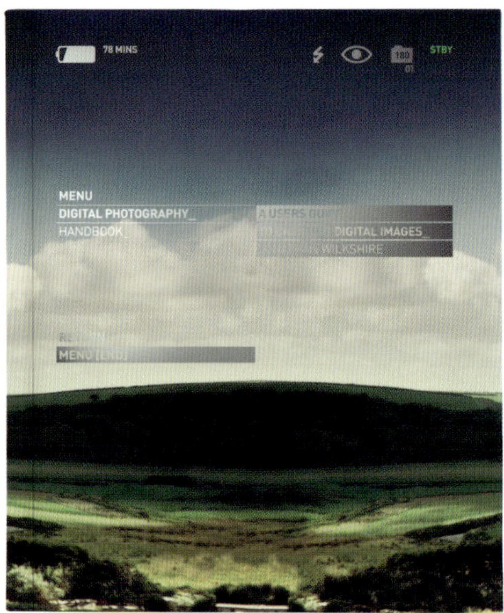

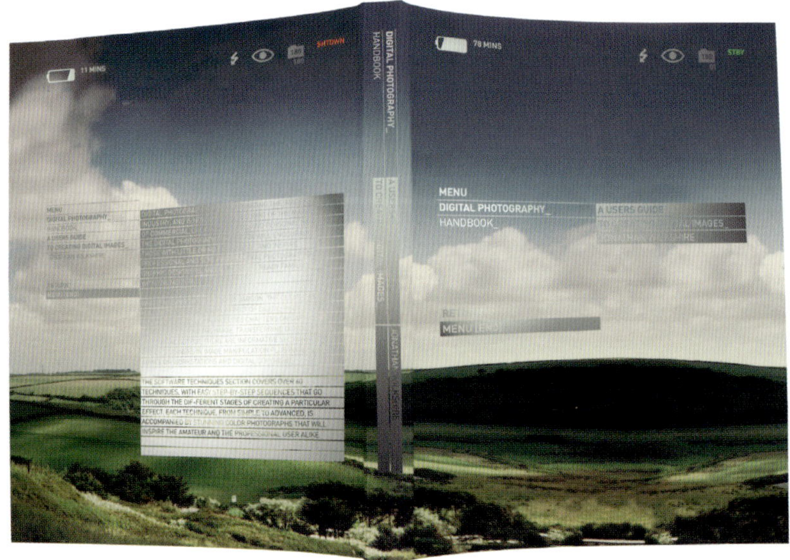

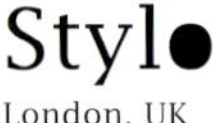

Stylo

London, UK

Title: Digital Photography
Type of work: Book
Client: Philip Xavier Publishing
Design: ad, d// Tom Lancaster
Year: 2003

A book covering all aspects of digital photography. The design concept is based on the iconography and menu systems of digital cameras. Silver ink was used throughout the whole book for text to bring out the feel of technology.

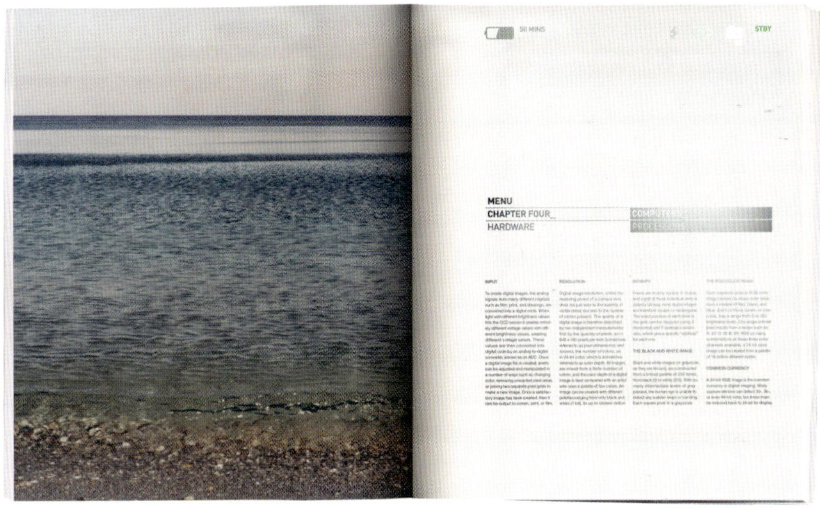

50 MINS
STBY
MENU
CHAPTER FOUR_
HARDWARE
COMPUTERS
PROCESSORS
INPUT
RESOLUTION
BITMAPS
THE RGB COLOR IMAGE
THE BLACK AND WHITE IMAGE

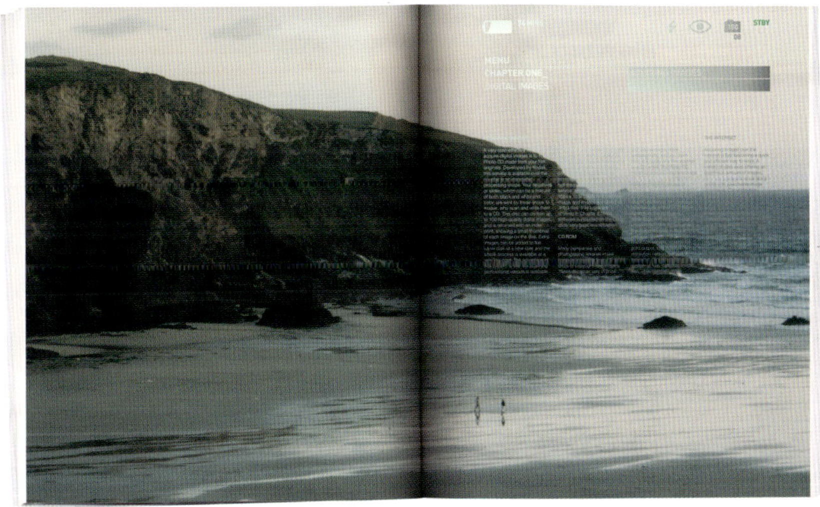

STBY
MENU
CHAPTER ONE
DIGITAL IMAGES
CD-ROM

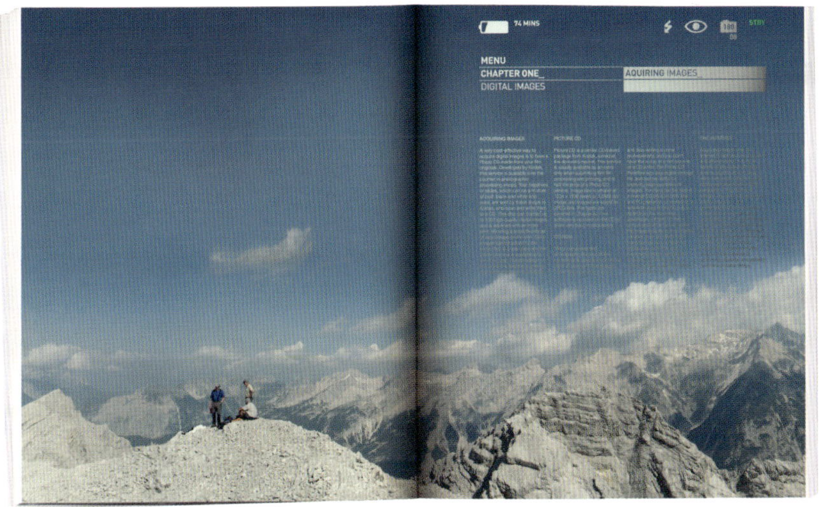

74 MINS
STBY
MENU
CHAPTER ONE_
DIGITAL IMAGES
AQUIRING IMAGES
ACQUIRING IMAGES
PICTURE CD

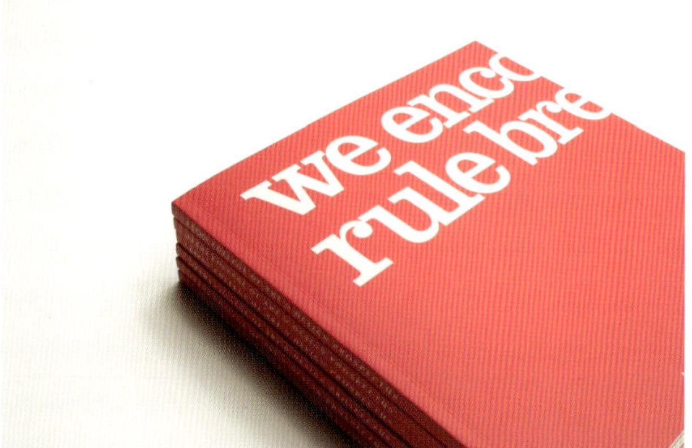

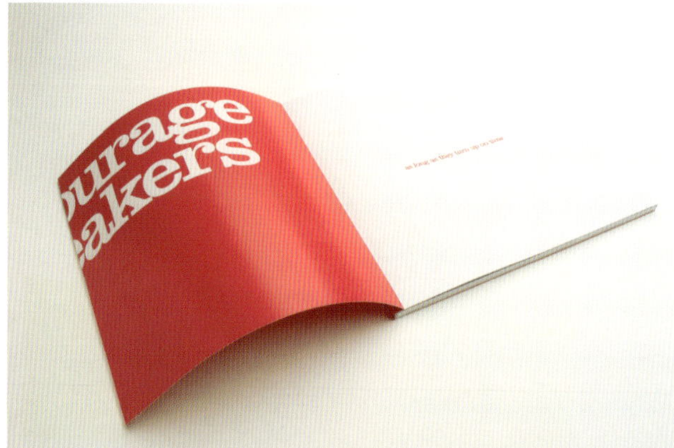

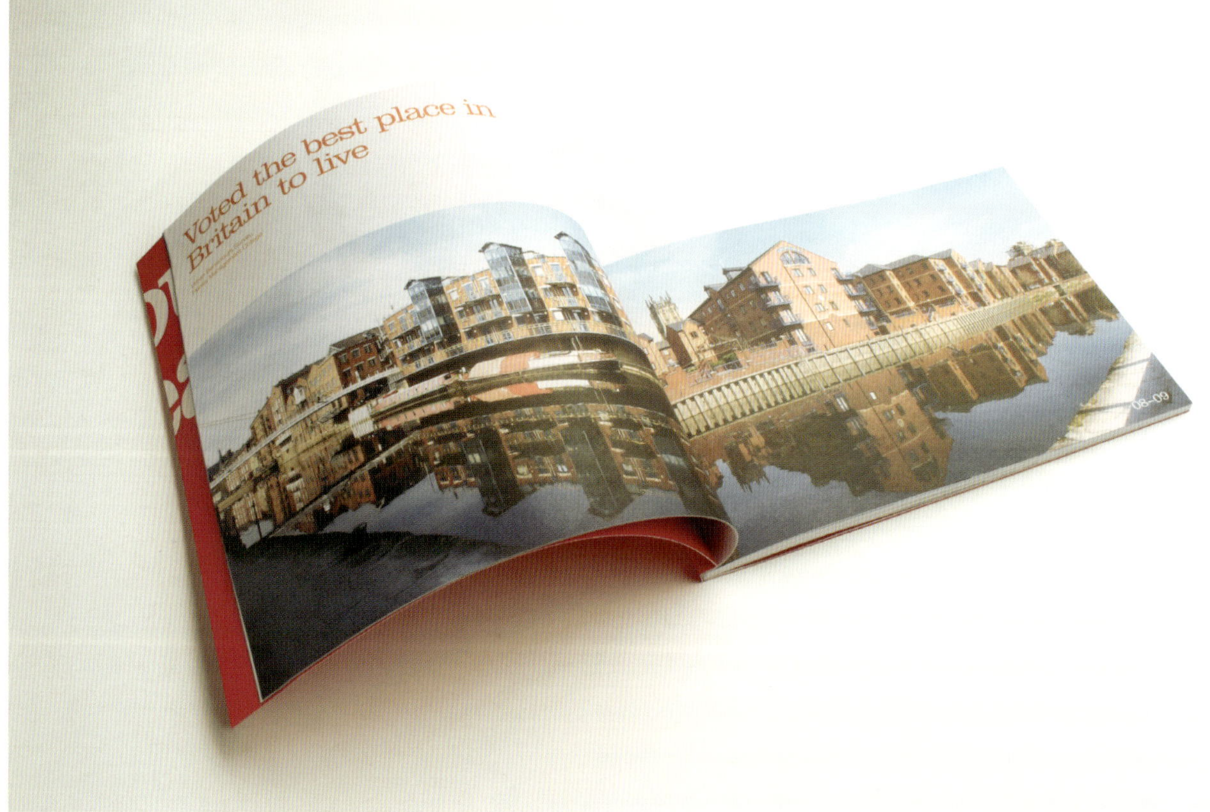

The C●nsult

Leeds, UK

Title: Leeds College of Art & Design prospectus
Type of work: Prospectus
Client: Leeds College of Art & Design
Design: ad// Alex Atkinson d// John-Paul Warner
Year: 2005

This design goes with a bold typographical treatment coupled with a magenta that was double hit for maximum depth of colour. The statement 'We encourage rule breakers' cheekily breaks around into the inner cover to meet the 'as long as they turn up on time' on the opposite page. Content was broken down into colour coded sections with full bleed pages between the end of one and the start of another. The final section is the further information section on fees and finance, which the Consult dubbed it as 'The not so interesting but very important bit'.

Paul Swagerman

Rotterdam, The Netherlands

Title: Sound Architecture
Type of work: Record sleeve
Client: Sound Architecture
Design: ad, d// Paul Swagerman
Year: 2004

The catalogue number is the image in this design. The essence of techno; 'beats', math and numbers is used to generate an alternative sign language. The first release has one square, the 4th has 4 squares and makes the number 4. A very simple but effective solution, materialized by white screenprint on cardboard.

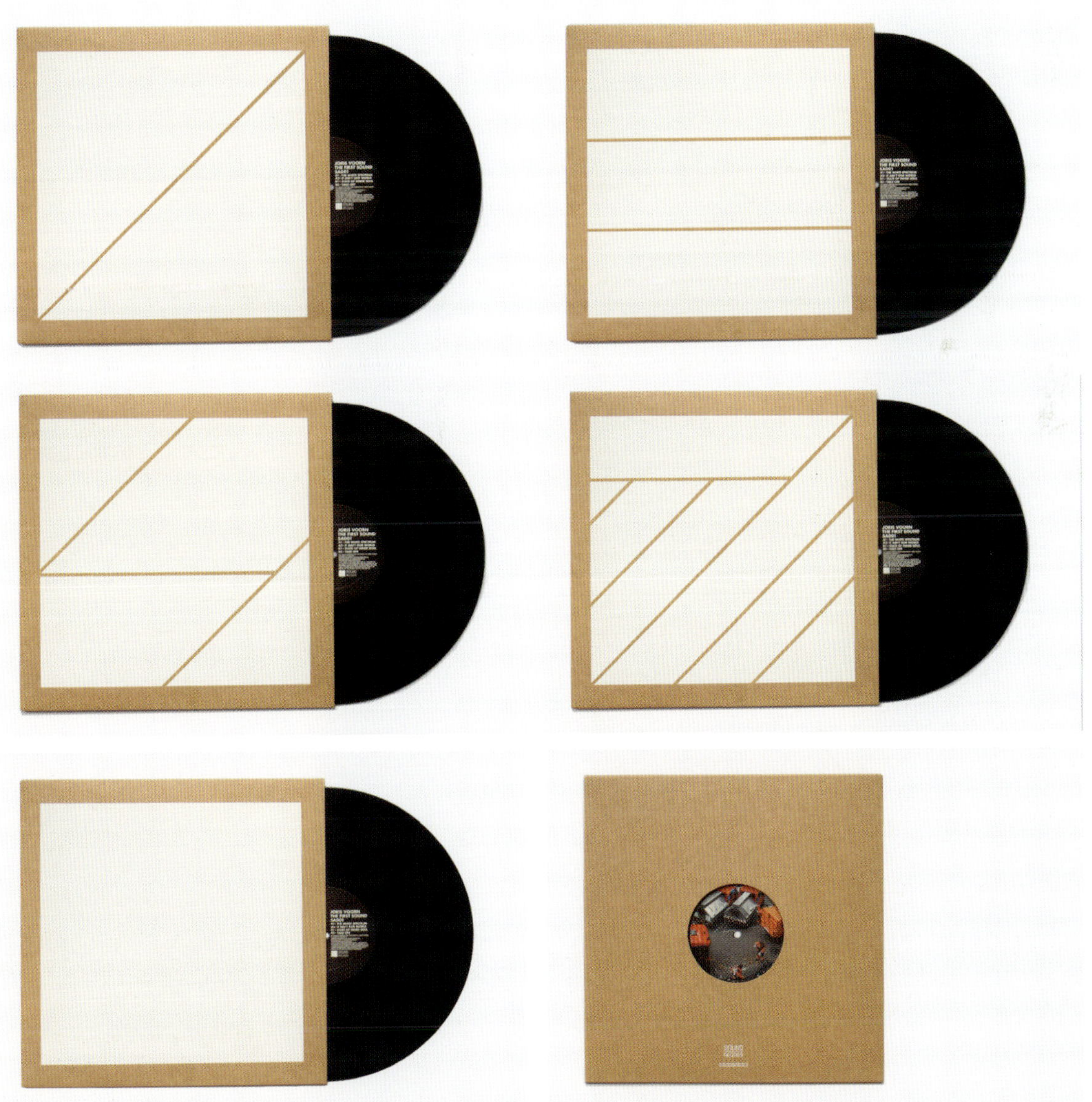

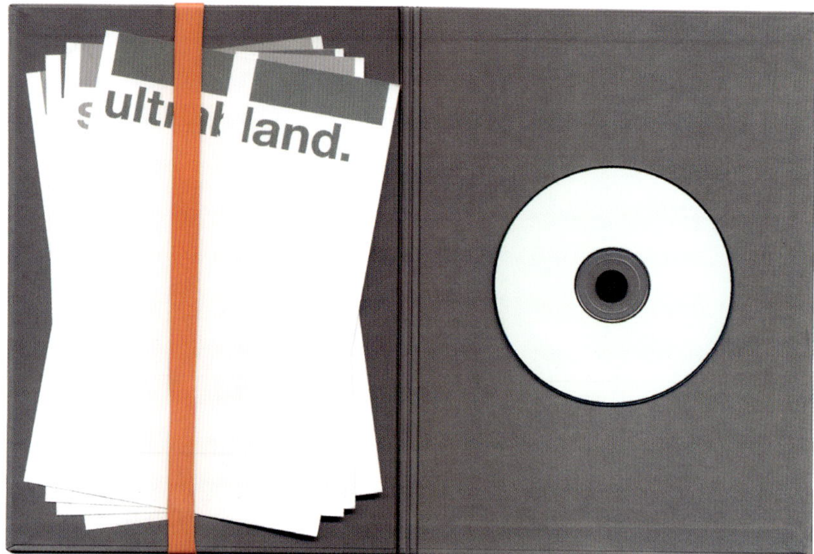

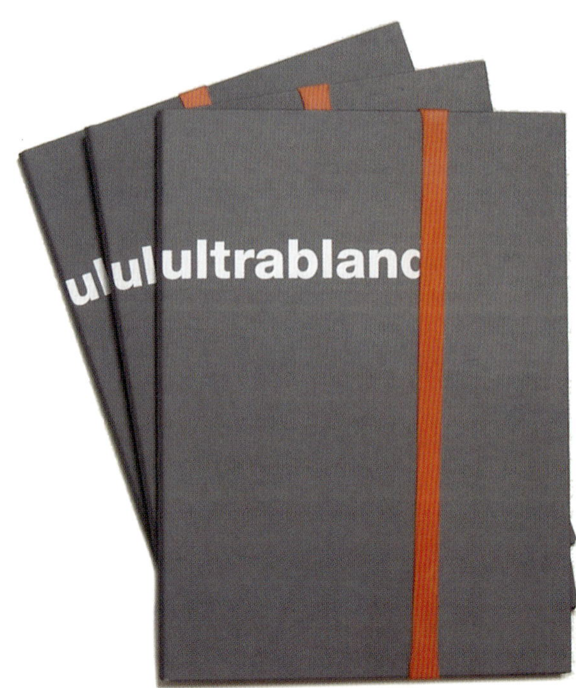

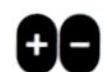

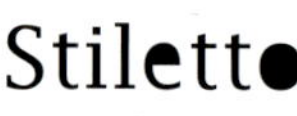

Stiletto

New York, USA

Title: Ultrabland Mailer
Type of work: Press Kit, card
Client: Ultrabland
Design: ad, d// Stiletto
Year: 2004

This press kit design is simple and user friendly with a red band tightening business cards or papers you received from others or you prepared for others.

Kinetic

Singapore

Title: The Observatory
Type of work: CD package
Client: The Observatory
Design: ad, d// Leng Soh, Pann Lim, Roy Poh
Year: 2004

This design is conceptually tied back to the album's name - 'Time of Rebirth'. The torn pages in the booklet represent the tearing away of the earlier chapters of the musicians' lives and the start of a new musical chapter for these veterans. Scribblings, drawings and random musings by the band's frontman provide an 'authentic' look and feel, one that resembles that of a diary. The CD itself features what appears to be a marker scribbling to complete the personal, honest touch.

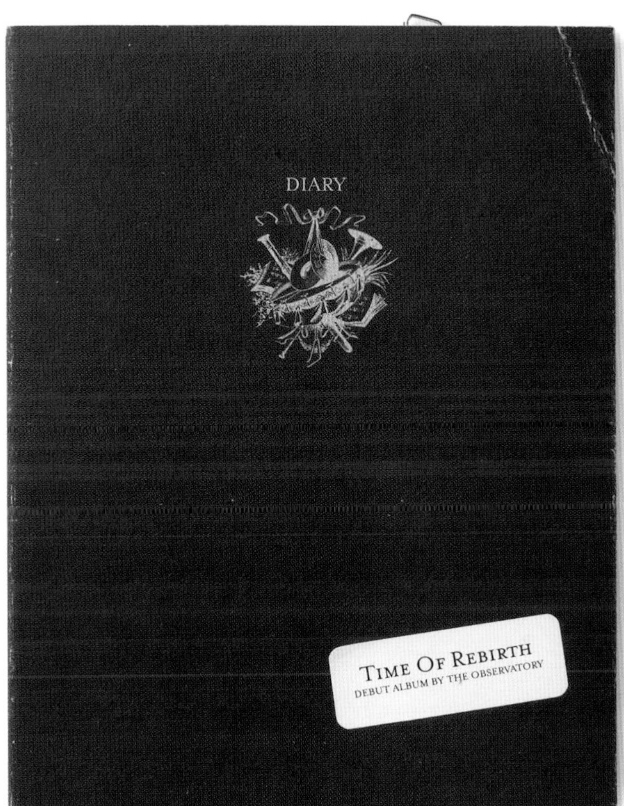

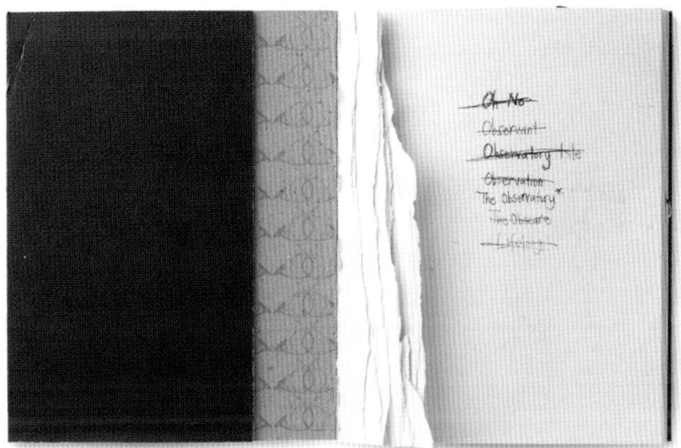

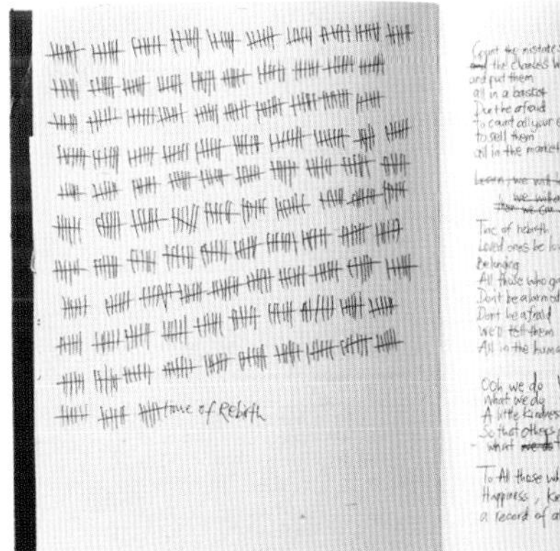

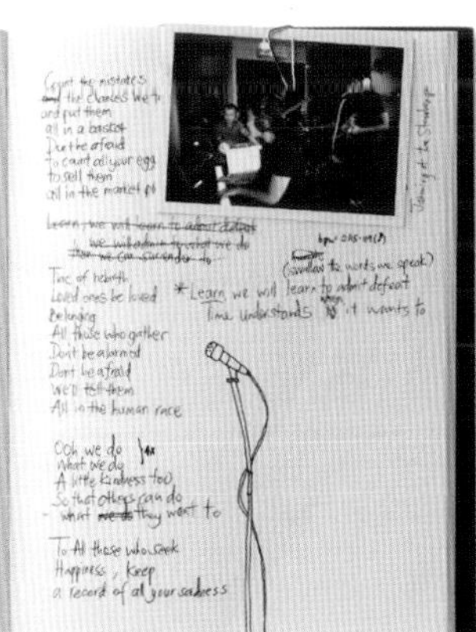

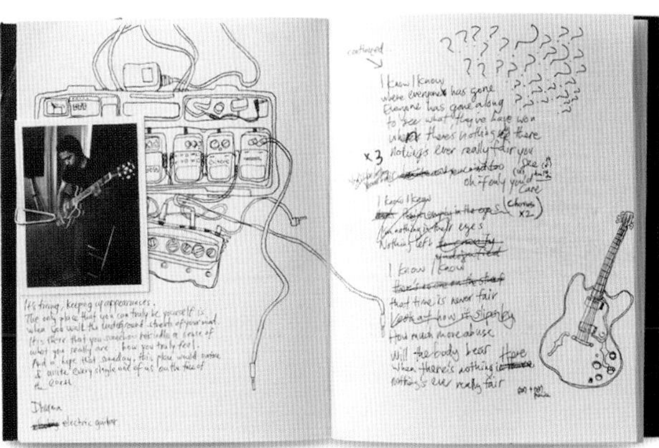

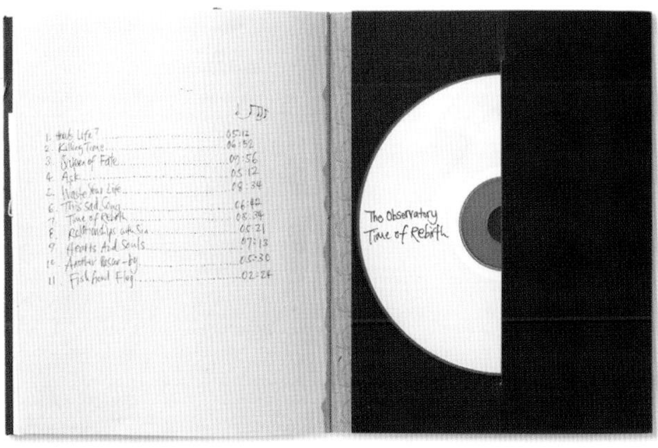

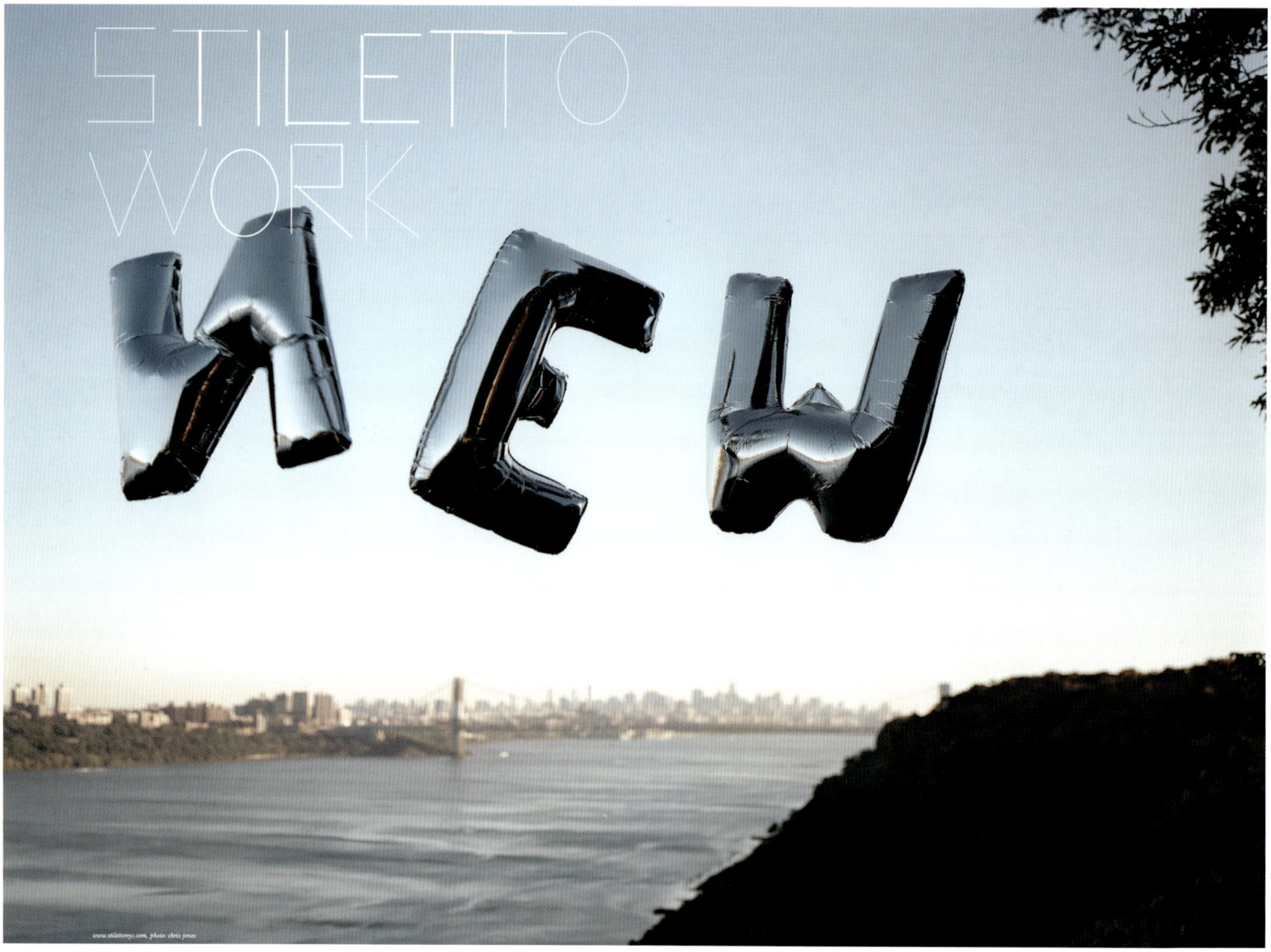

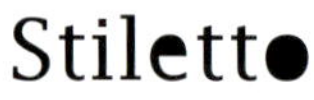

Stiletto

New York, USA

Title: Stiletto Self Promotion
Type of work: Poster, DVD packaging, mailer
Client: Stiletto
Design: ad, d// Stiletto
Year: 2005

A set of self promotion series of Stiletto includes poster, DVD packacging and the DVD cover, name cards and stationery, is simply designed with its logo, text in same type face as its logo in dark purple.

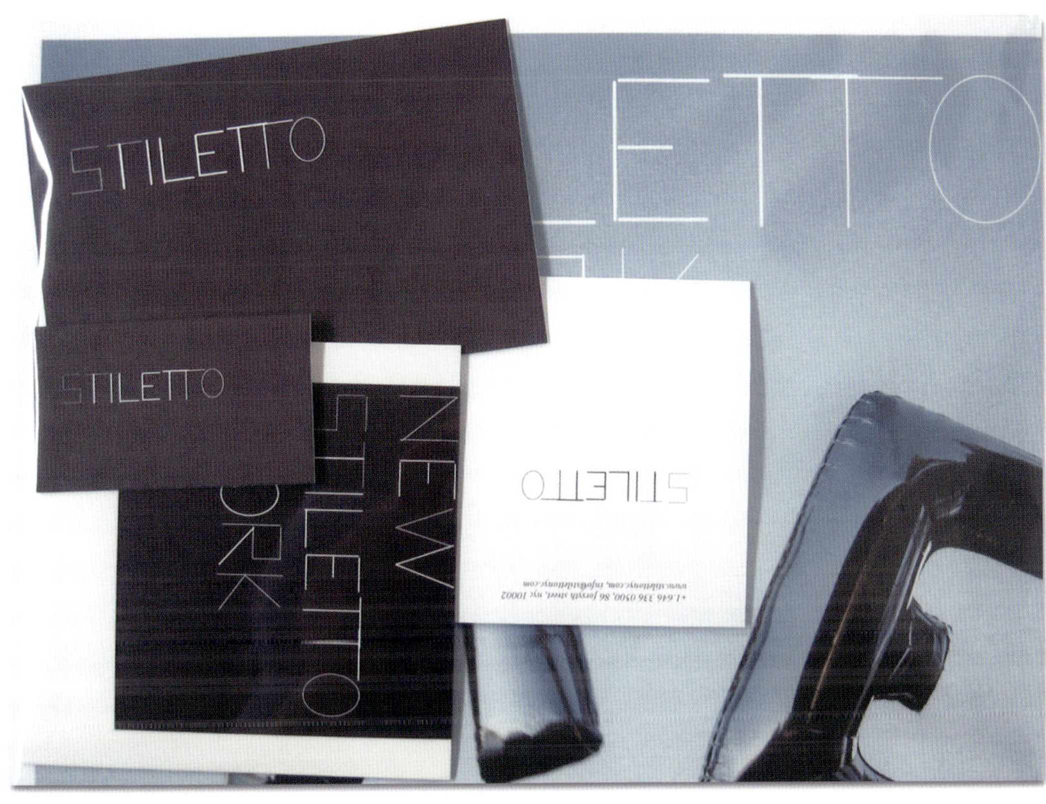

STILETTO
STILETTO
STILETTO
NEW STILETTO WORK
STILETTO
+1.646 336 0500, 86 forsyth street, nyc 10002
www.stilettonyc.com, info@stilettonyc.com

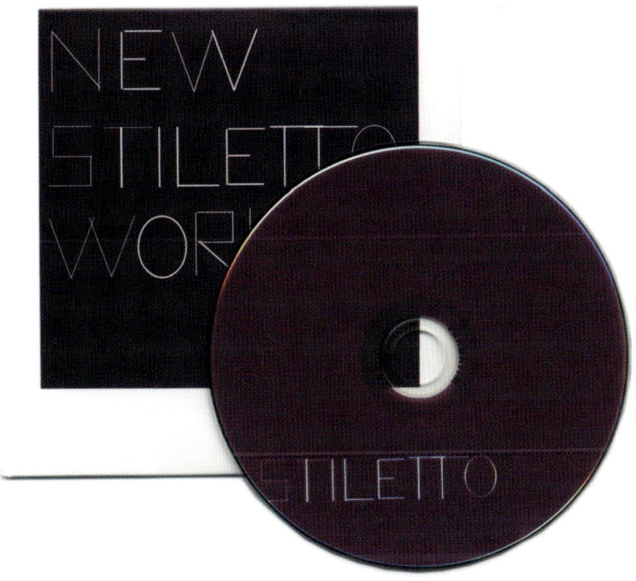

NEW
STILETTO
WORK
STILETTO

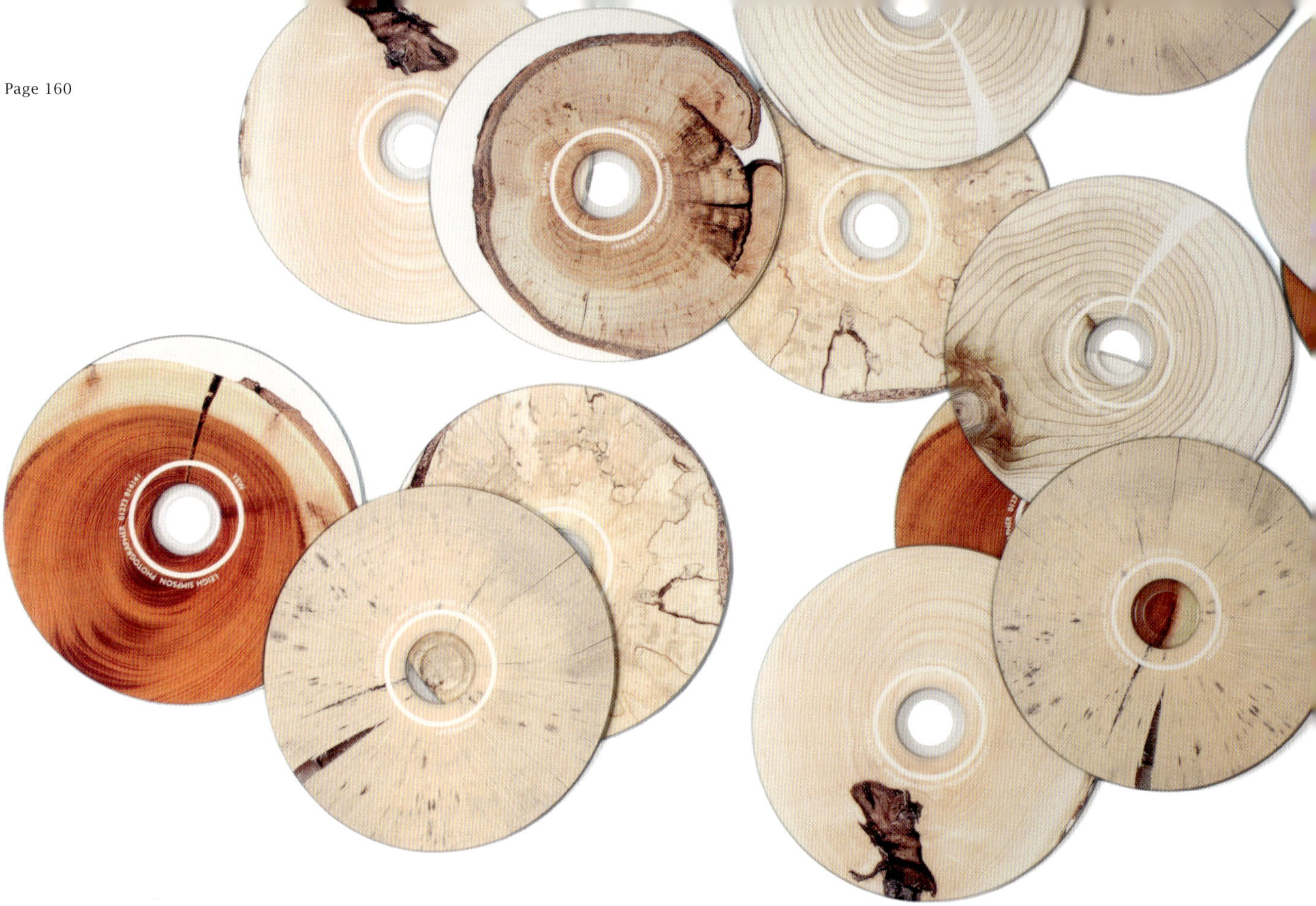

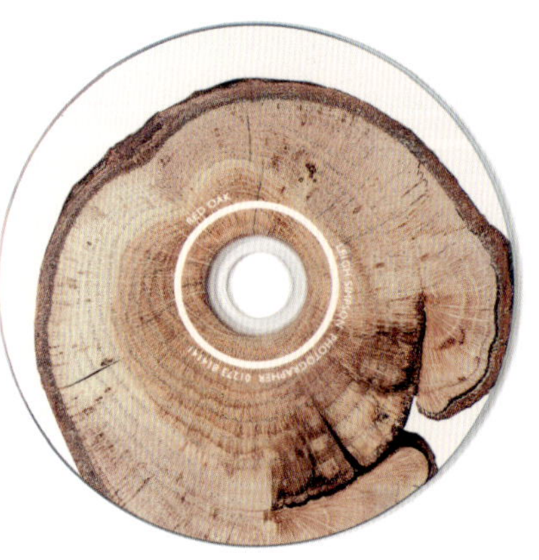

Al**oo**f **D**esign

New York, USA

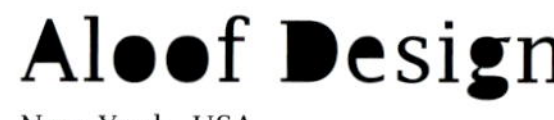

Title: Leigh Simpson Printed CDs
Type of work: Printed recordable CDs
Client: Leigh Simpson Photographer
Design: ad, d// Sam Aloof
Year: 2004

The designers were asked to come up with a way of ensuring these CDs to become more memorable and to challenge people's preconceptions, finding their inherent value exceeded that of the average unprinted recordable CD.

The first collection features six species of tree represented by their cross sections. Samples of trees with a CD sized circumference were taken from a local managed woodland, scanned and then printed onto the CDs at scale 1:1 with the center of each tree section being carefully aligned with the center of each CD.

Joseph Magliaro

New York, USA

Title: Protekshun
Type of work: Product design and packaging
Client: Es Gibt
Design: ad, d// Joseph Magliaro
Year: 2002 prototype, 2005 final edition

The series is an expression of the designer's interest in the way that fear and the need for security informs and structures our choices in daily life. There are a total of 16 unique illustrations in the series of 50 sets of 4 hand silkscreened felt discs, each one representing a system or object that purports to protect us in some way from the many 'dangers' that we are constantly told that are threatening us. Felt discs were chosen because they can double as drink coasters - another item in our everyday lives that we use to assuage our fears of ruining our valuable furnishings. Each set was individually vacuum-sealed which further stressing on how ubiquitous the idea of 'protection' is in our daily lives.

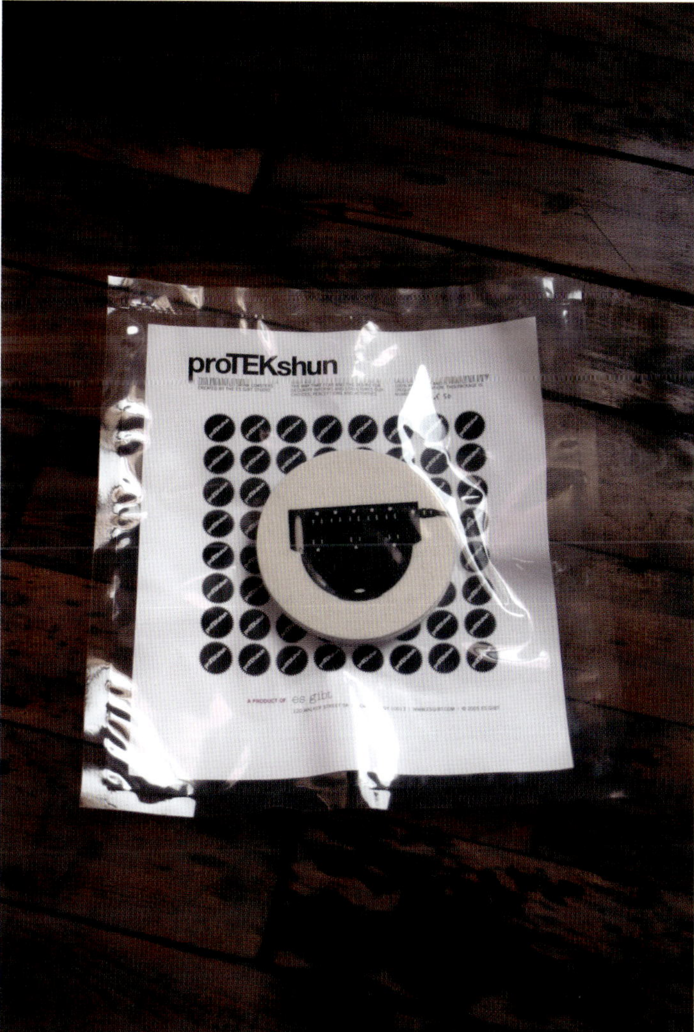

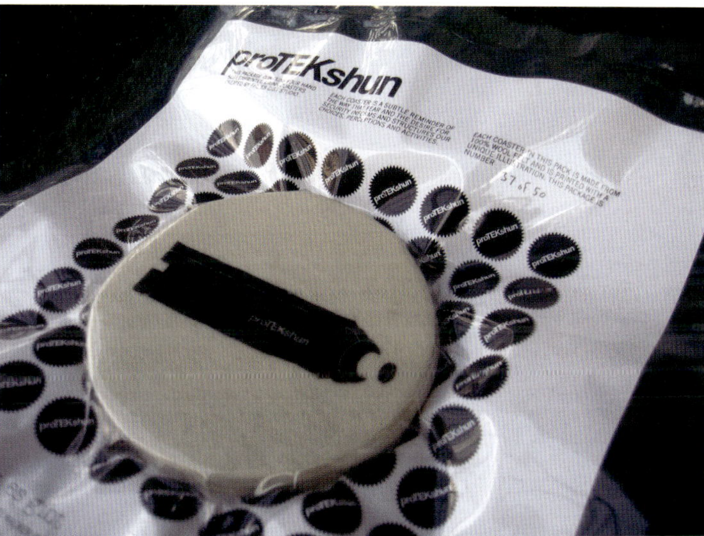

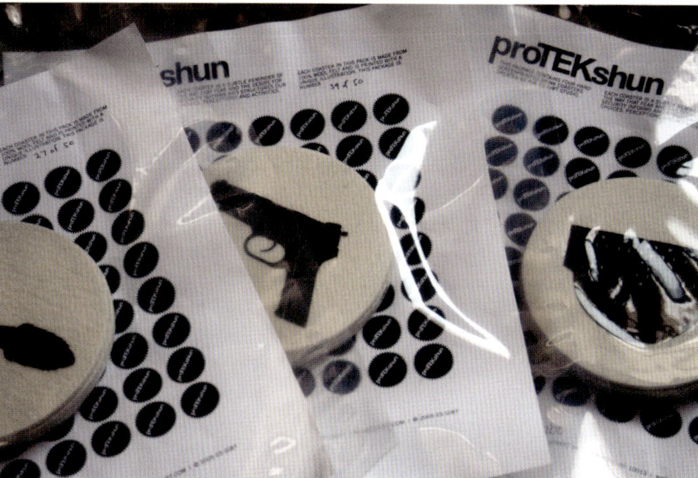

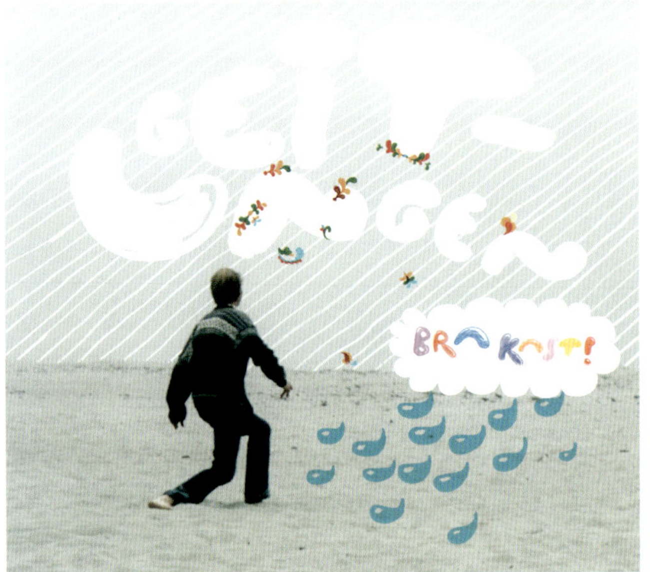

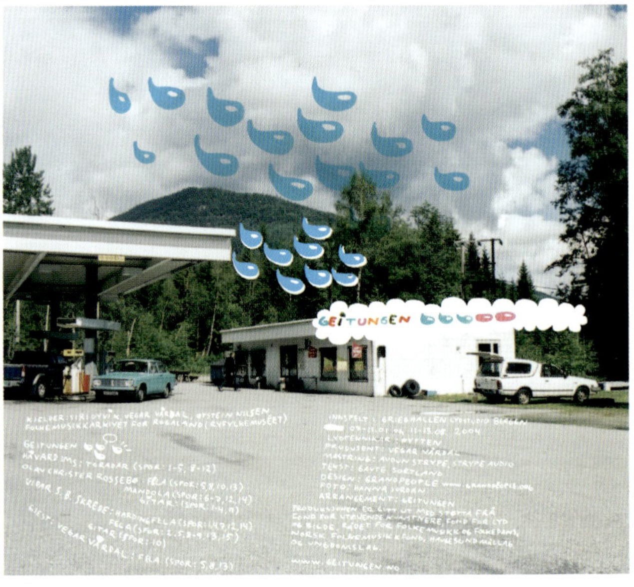

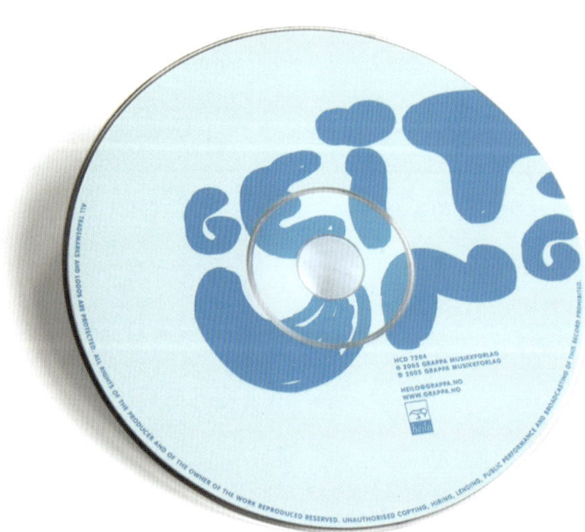

Gra**ndp**eople

Norway

Title: Geitungen – Bra Kast
Type of work: CD sleeve design – digipak
Client: Grappa
Design: ad, d// Grandpeople
Year: 2005

The designers were asked by a Norwegian folk music band, Geitungen, to design the sleeve for their second release 'Bra Kast!'. As most of the tracks were traditional tunes from the county Rogaland, on the western coast of Norway, the designers wanted to emphasize this in the design. To do this, Hanna Jordan's photographs of horses on open plains and slacker-sport on the rainy beaches of Jæren helped them a lot.

Zion Graphics

Stockholm, Sweden

Title: The Virtues
Type of work: Album cover
Client: Zip Records
Design: ad, d// Jonas Kjellberg
Year: 2005

A colourful album cover is here designed for a Swedish band called The Virtues. Requested by Zip Records, Zion Graphics understands that the band is described as wonderful Swedish pop tradition which gives familiar and friendly sound, which gave them the base of this final design.

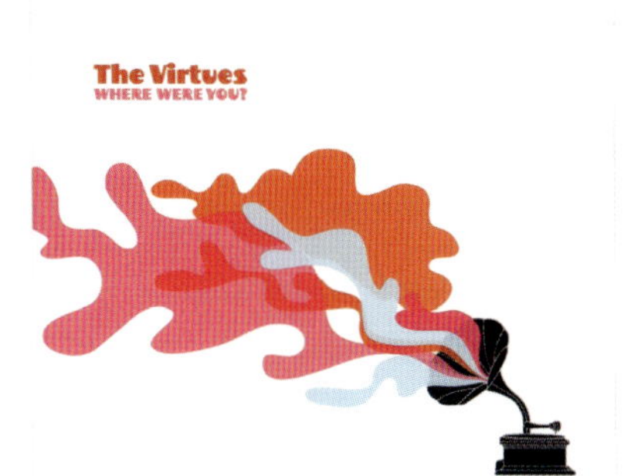

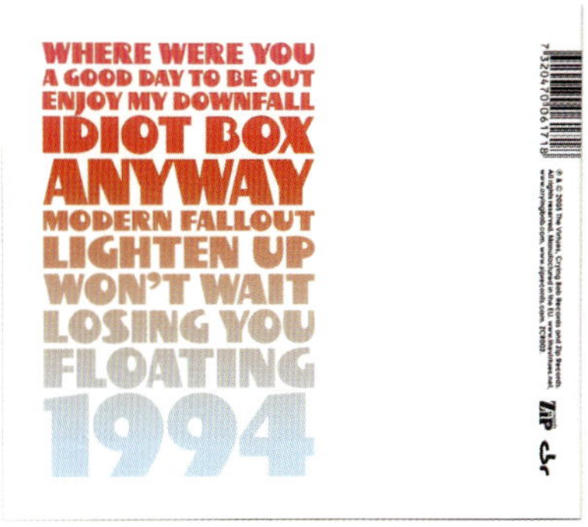

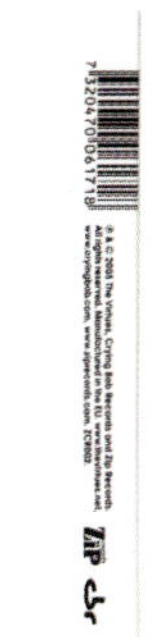

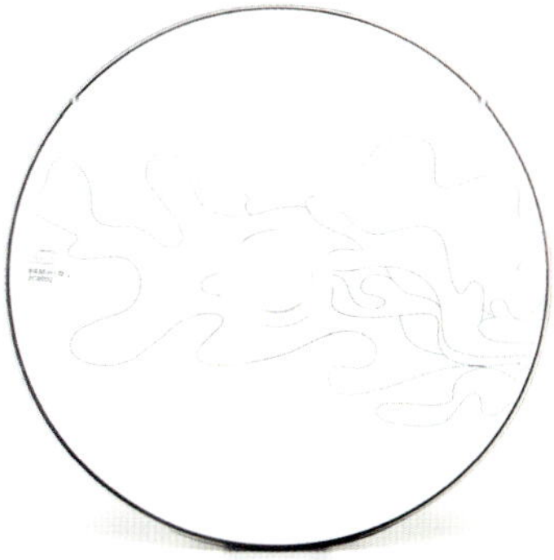

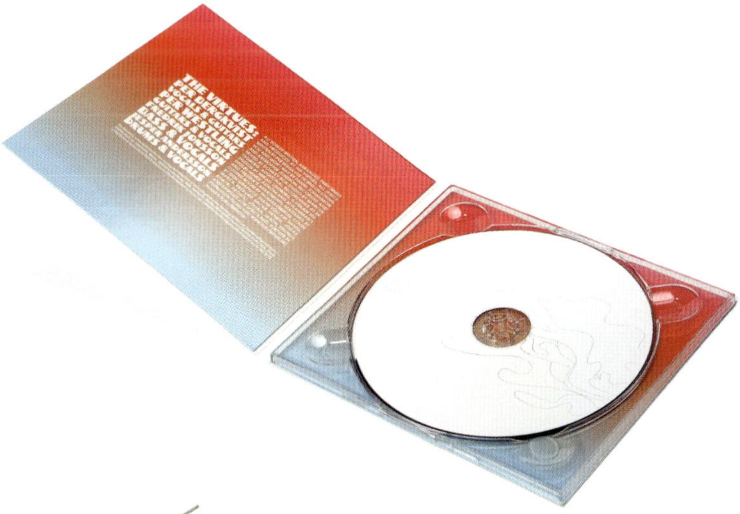

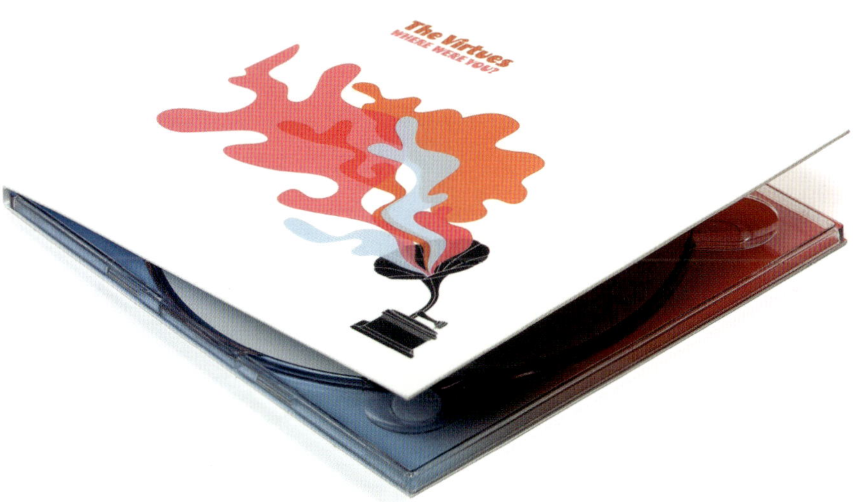

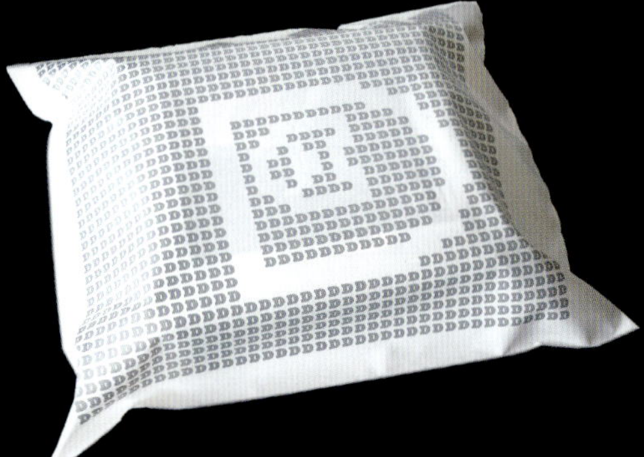

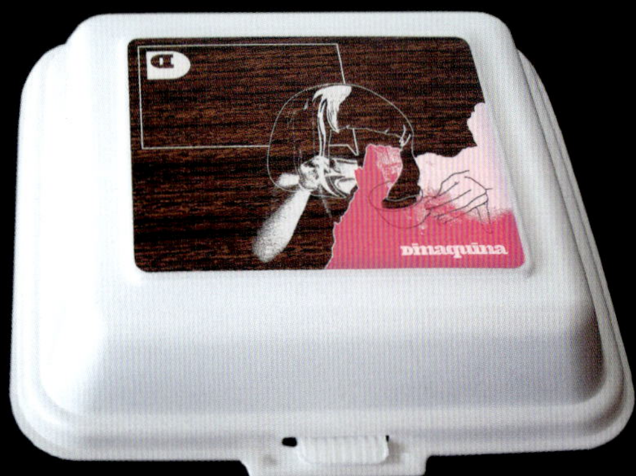

Dimaquina

Rio de Janeiro , Brazil

Title: Dimaquina Kit
Type of work: Self promotional kit
Client: Dimaquina
Design: ad, d// Antônio Pedro, Daniel Neves, Nako
Year: 2005

The designers have looked for readymade package for this project due to the small number of kits to be produced (150 units). The polystyrene box was the starting point for the kit´s design, where everything looks disposable and artificial. Besides the box, the plastic bag, the sticker and the photograph are used to fix this concept of plasticity.

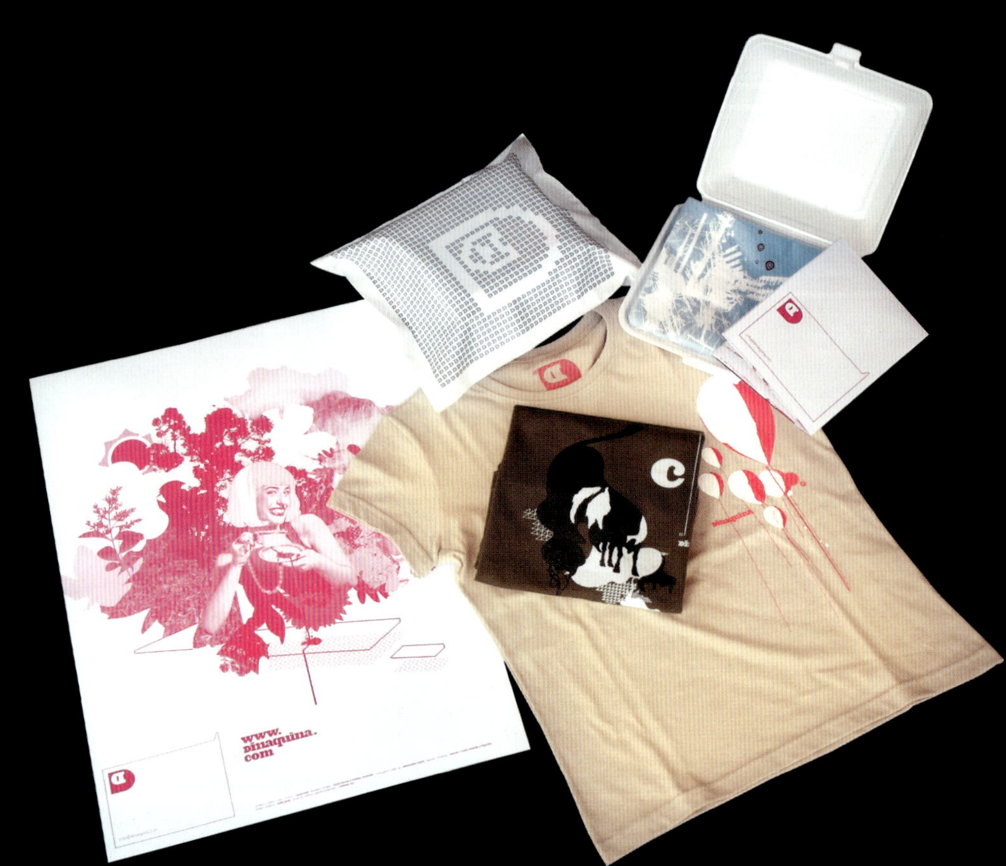

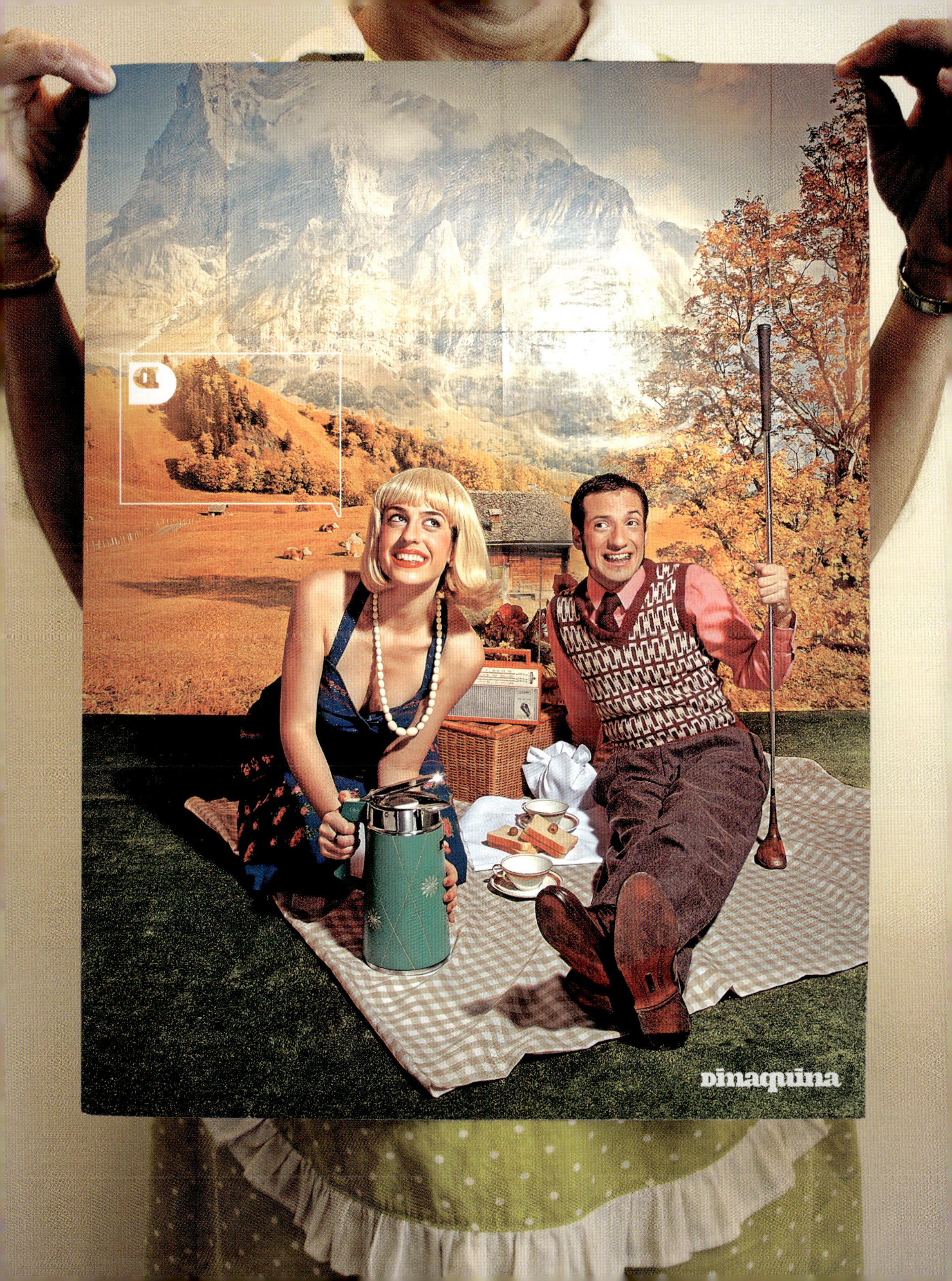

pinaquina

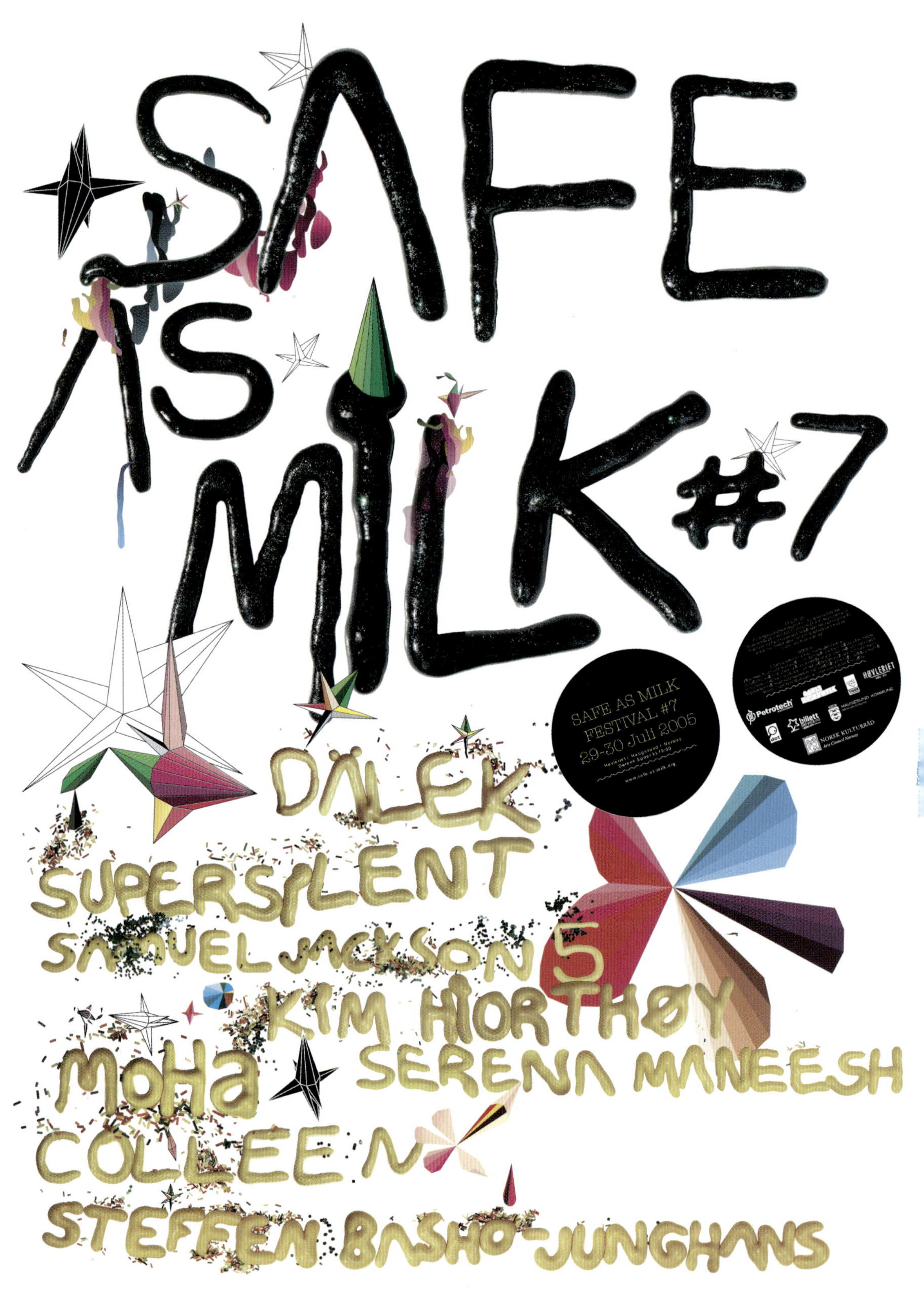

SAFE AS MILK #7
SAFE AS MILK
FESTIVAL #7
29-30 Juli 2005
Høvleriet / Haugesund / Norway
Dørene åpner kl.19:00
www.safe-as-milk.org
Petrotech
billett
HAUGESUND KOMMUNE
HØVLERIFT
dot
NORSK KULTURRÅD
Arts Council Norway
DÄLEK
SUPERSILENT
SAMUEL JACKSON 5
KIM HIORTHØY
MOHA
SERENA MANEESH
COLLEEN
STEFFEN BASHO-JUNGHANS

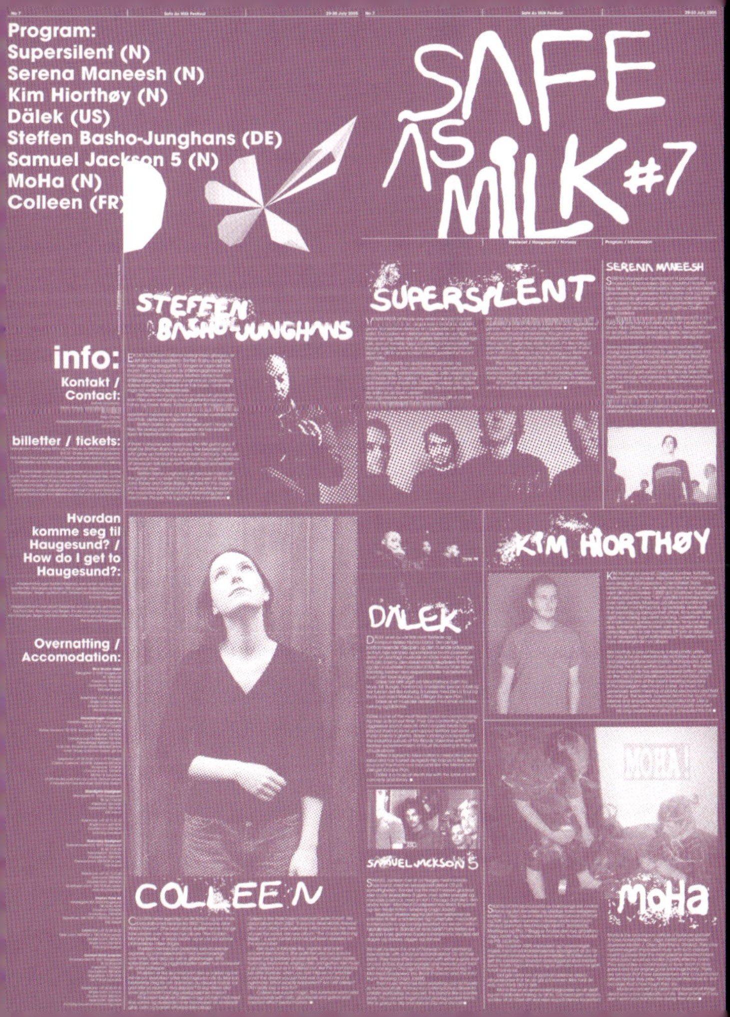

No 7 — Safe As Milk Festival — 29-30 July 2005

Program:

- Supersilent (N)
- Serena Maneesh (N)
- Kim Hiorthøy (N)
- Dälek (US)
- Steffen Basho-Junghans (DE)
- Samuel Jackson 5 (N)
- MoHa (N)
- Colleen (FR)

SAFE AS MILK #7

info:

Kontakt / Contact:

billetter / tickets:

Hvordan komme seg til Haugesund? / How do I get to Haugesund?:

Overnatting / Accomodation:

STEFFEN BASHO-JUNGHANS

SUPERSILENT

SERENA MANEESH

KIM HIORTHØY

DÄLEK

SAMUEL JACKSON 5

COLLEEN

MoHa

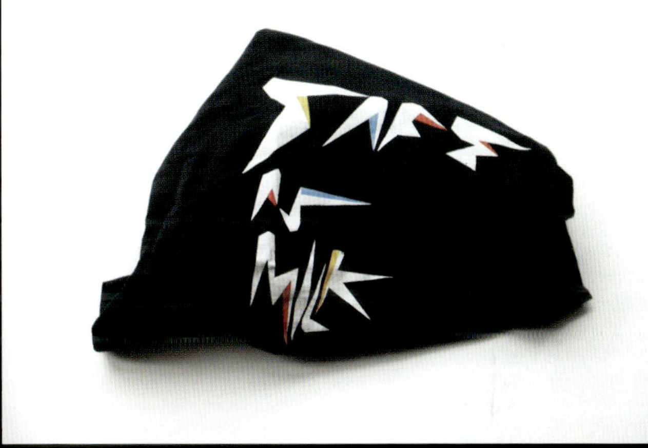

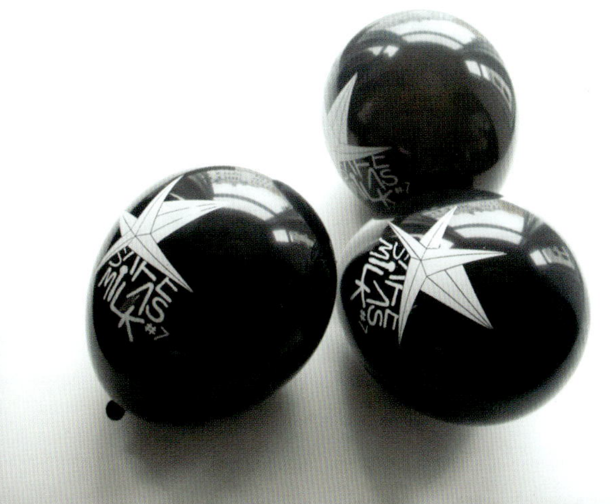

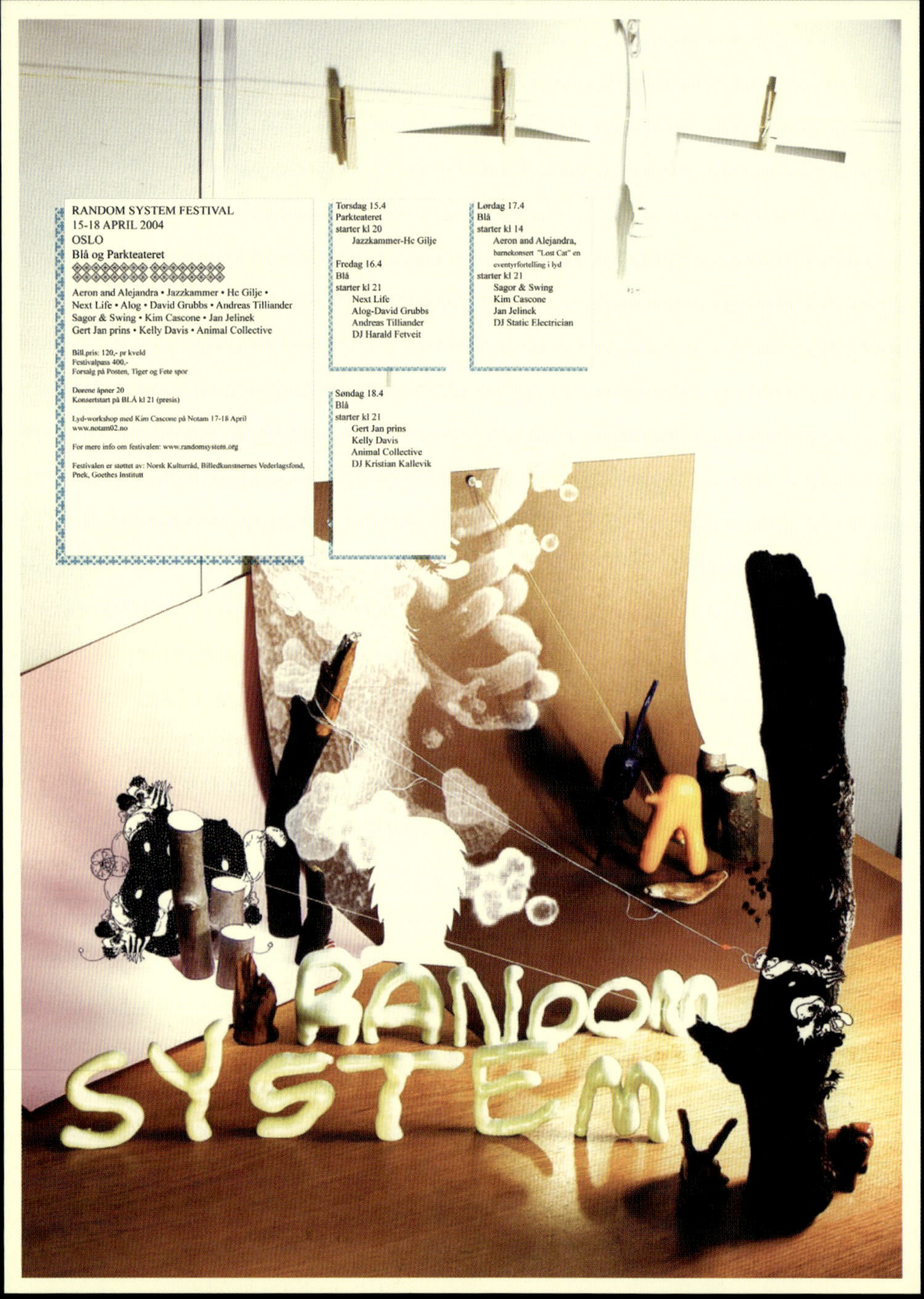

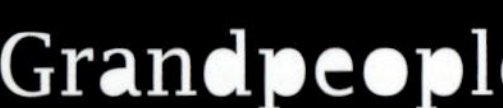

Grandpeople

Norway

Title: Random System
Type of work: Promotional effects and stage decor
Client: Random System
Design: ad, d// Grandpeople
Year: 2004

The designers were hired by Alexander Rishaug and Andreas Meland for this project. They were asked to make scene decorations at Blaa in Oslo, where the event would take place. So in this case the visuals came out based on the scenographic idea. With the valuable help from photographer Magne Sandnes, the designers constructed a theatrical tableau which they finally printed on a yellow

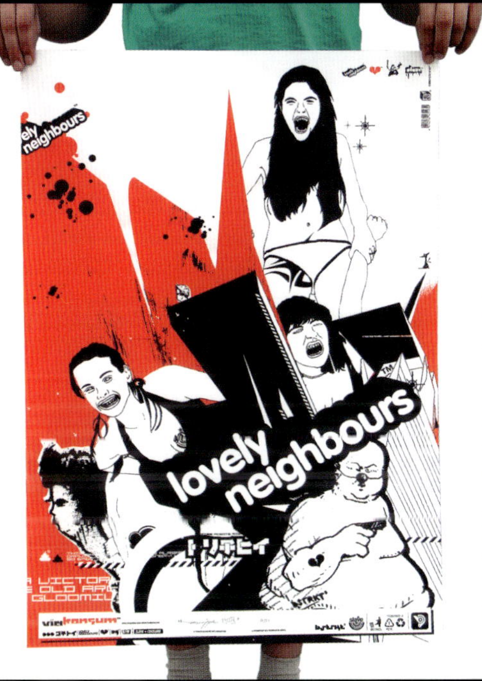
lovely
neighbours
lovely neighbours

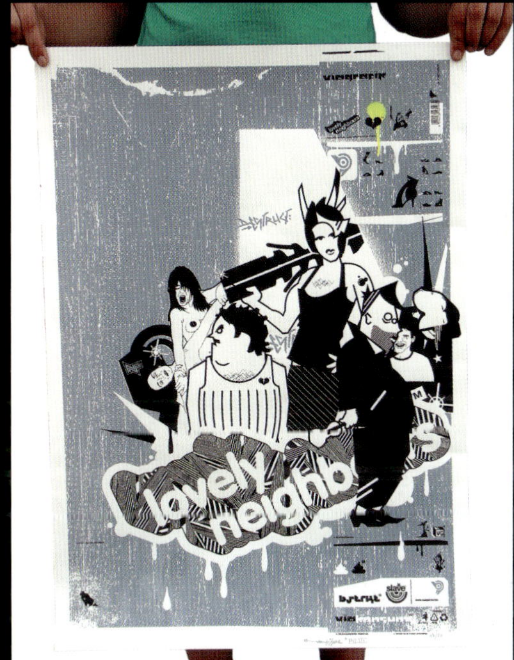
lovely
neighb

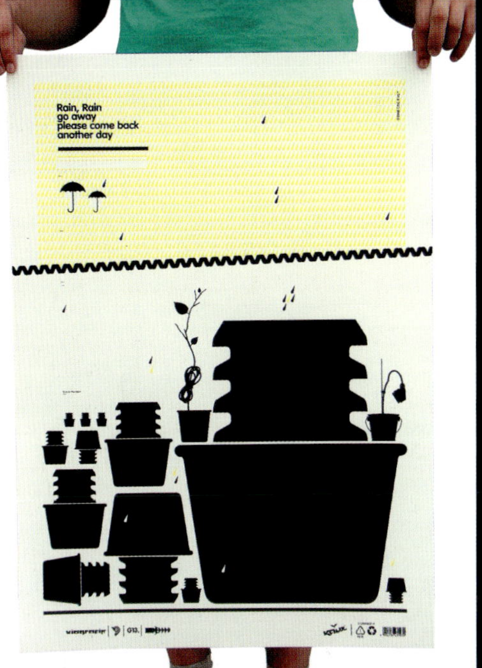
Rain, Rain
go away
please come back
another day

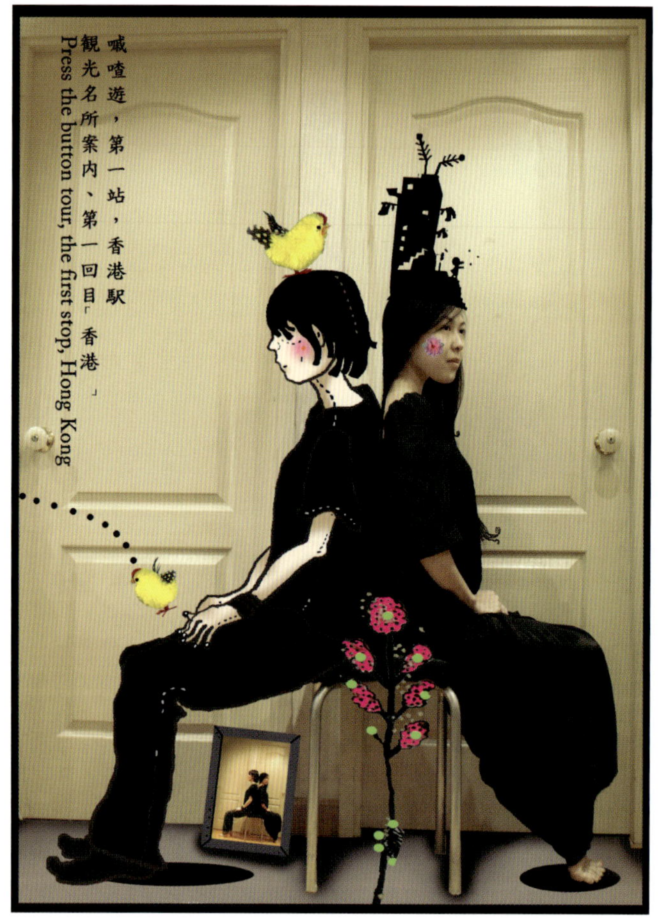

兩個神奇女子，花坊（日本）與二犬十一咪（香港），結伴相遊，計劃
踏足各個城市的旅遊景點，拍下景致回來創作，香港就是第一站。

粉紅盒子，滿載甜溜溜的感覺，她的心思被那 '喊喳' 一聲攝進了…
文字作起點，攝影為橋樑，裝置得出結果，每個城市是前行的小休地。

Two extraordinary girls, Kabo (Japan) and seemanho (Hong Kong),
are going to travel the tourist spots in every city together. They will
capture all the interesting things in photos during the journey and
will rework on them for the exhibition. Hong Kong is the first stop.

A pink box contains all the sweetest sensations of her. Her thoughts
have been captured when the button of the camera is pressed down.

二人の奇妙な女の子、花坊（日本）とシーマン（香港）が、いろいろ
な街の観光名所を一緒にまわります。彼女たちは旅行中に写真を撮り
、それにさらに手を加えて展覧会をします。

最初の観光スポットは香港。文章と写真が思い出と現実のかけ橋にな
って、どの街も新しい旅の目的地となることでしょう。

ピンクのオルゴールは、彼女の甘い思い出をとじこめていました。カ
メラのシャッターが押されたとき、その思をかいま見ることが出来ま
す。

攝影 Photography : 花坊Kabo
文字＋裝置 Text & Installation : 二犬十一咪
開幕音樂演出guest performersパフォーマンス : aniDa
開幕酒會opening reception: 5/11/2005 ,7:00pm
オープニングレセプション

展覽日期 Date: 5/11/2005 - 18/12/2005
　　　逢星期三／四／五 Every wed/ thur/ fri : 4:00 - 8:00 pm
　　　逢星期六／日　　　Every sat/sun : 2:00 - 8:00 pm

場地place: 二犬backyard(seeman backyard)
(中環卑利街43號1樓　1/F, 43 Peel Street,Central tel:35273167)

Seeman Ho

Hong Kong, China

Title: Press The Button Tour, The First Stop, Hong Kong
Type of work: Postcard, poster
Client: -
Design: ad, d// seemanho
Year: 2005

Promotional items for an exhibition of installation and photography. Two extraordinary girls, one from Japan and another from Hong Kong, travel the tourist spots in every city together. They capture all the interesting things in the photos during the journey and rework on them for the exhibition. The concept of 'two doors open into the same room' meaning the two people from two different places are looking into the same world.

Sussner Design Company

Minneapolis, USA

Title: Sussner 6 Year Anniversary Poster
Type of work: Poster
Client: Sussner Design Company
Design: ad// Derek Sussner d// CJ Marxer
Year: 2005

The designer started working on the concept for the 24" x 32.5" poster for the 5th business anniversary. The logo is his hand where the five fingers were symbolizing for five years in business. But then they were busy until a year later when they actually started to design it. They thought about starting all over again, but finally added a sixth finger to the hand instead, in which they believe it would make it funnier than with 5 fingers only. It was then a 6th anniversary poster adding with a new client lists at the end.

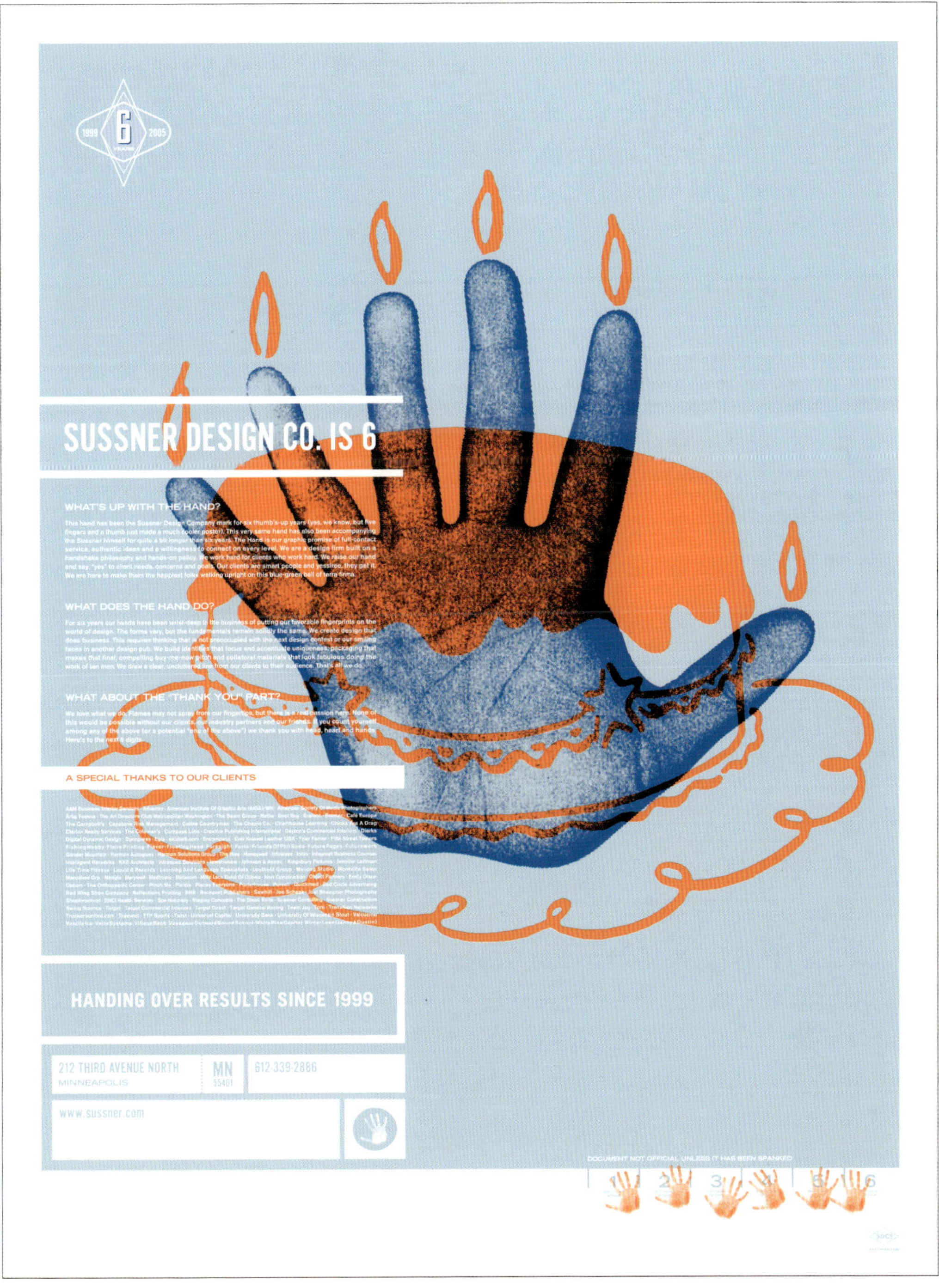

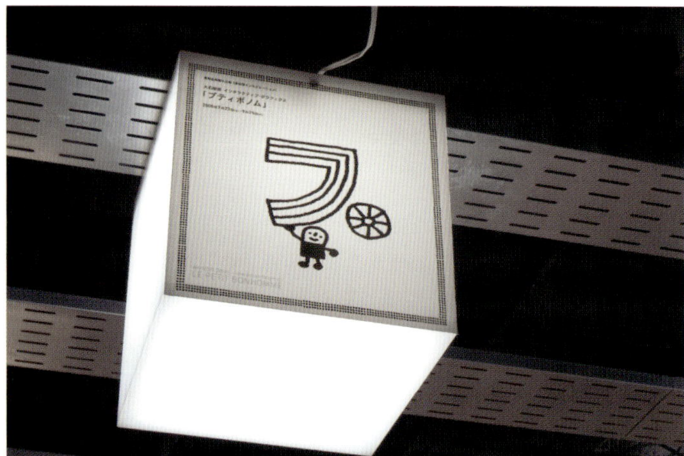

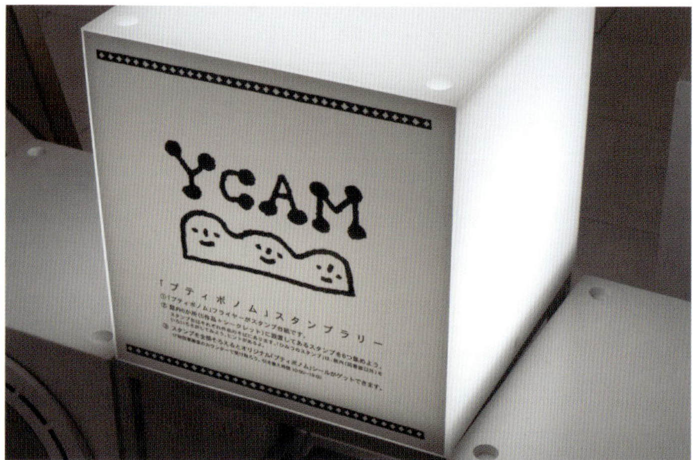

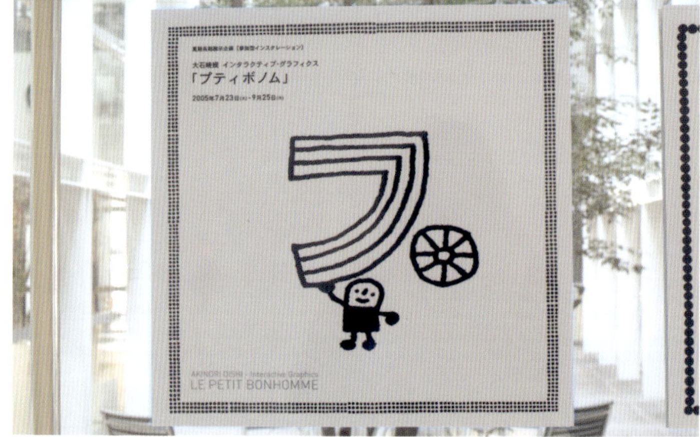

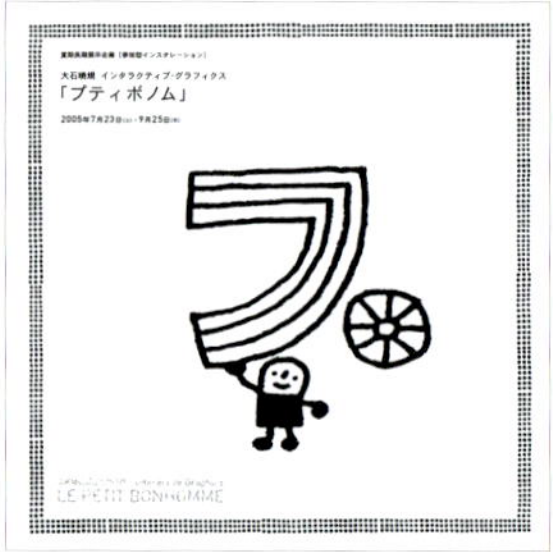

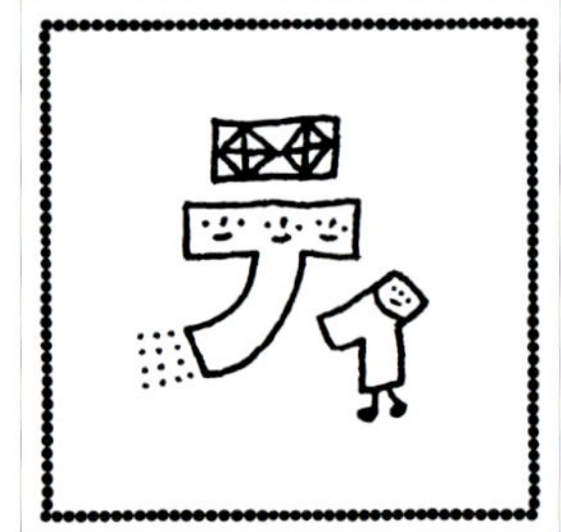

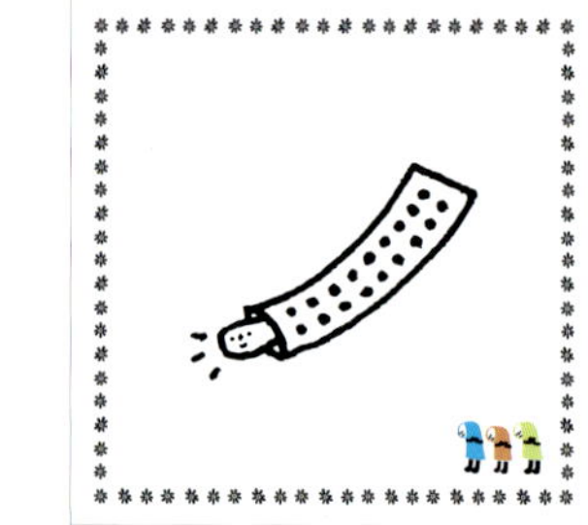

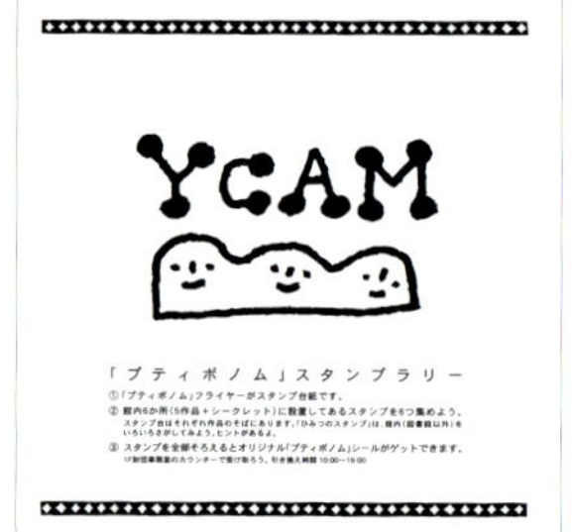

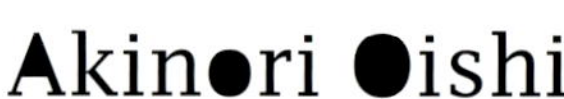

A k i n o r i   O i s h i

Nagoya, Japan

Title: Le Petit Bonhomme
Type of work: Poster
Client: YCAM (Yamaguchi Center for Arts and Media)
Design: ad, d// Akinori Oishi, YCAM
Year: 2005

This set of posters is designed for the exhibition 'Le Petit Bonhomme', meaning small people like beans in French. The concept was carried out through the promotional items. These illustrated squared size posters, with Japanese katakana character of the translation of the exihibition title 'Le Petit Bonhomme', make it easier for the visitors who are mostly children to understand the idea and concept.

④インクカラー　ピンク　　　　⑤インクカラー　グリーン　　　　⑥インクカラー　スカイブルー

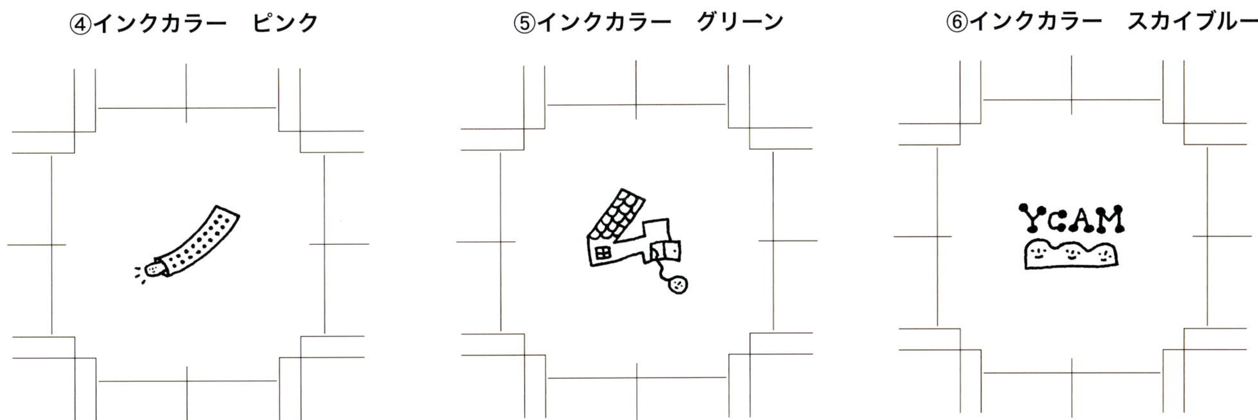

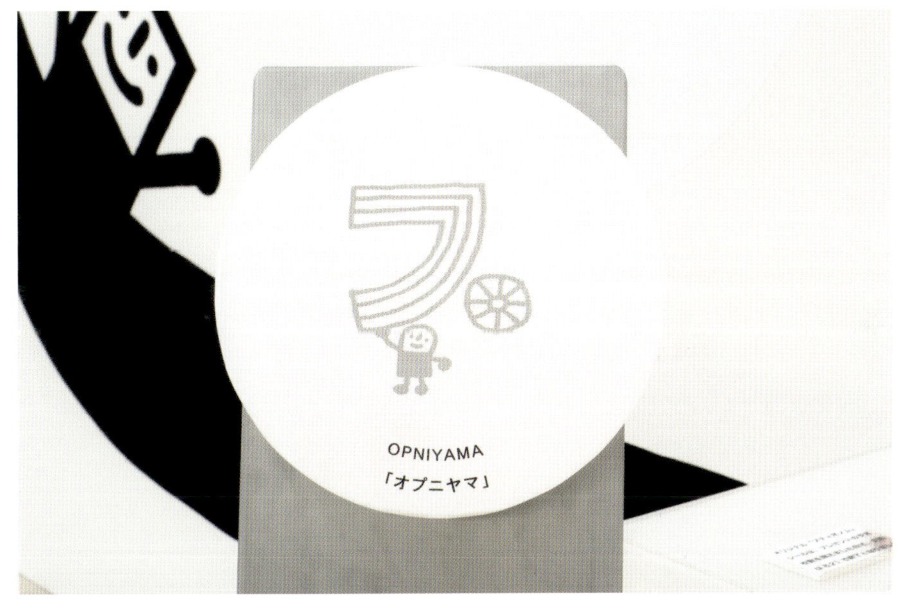

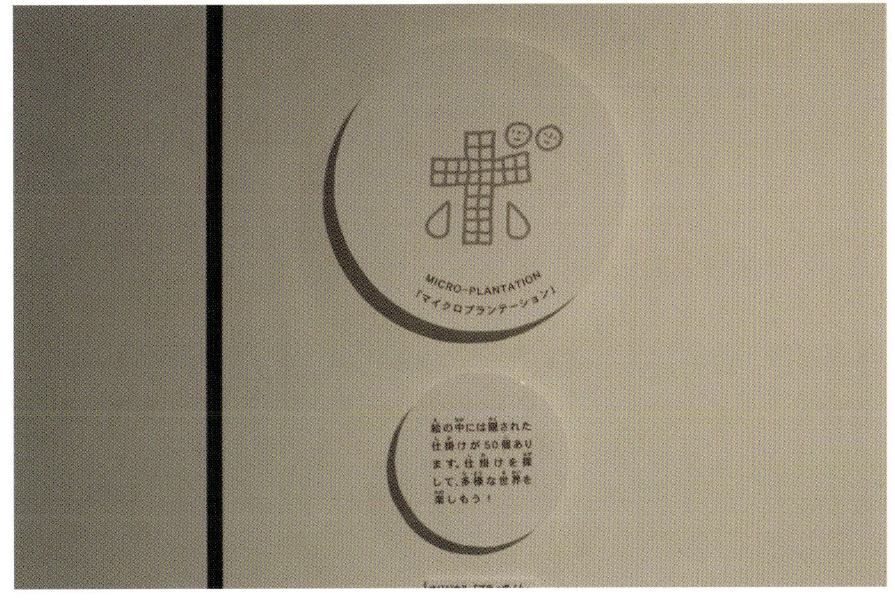

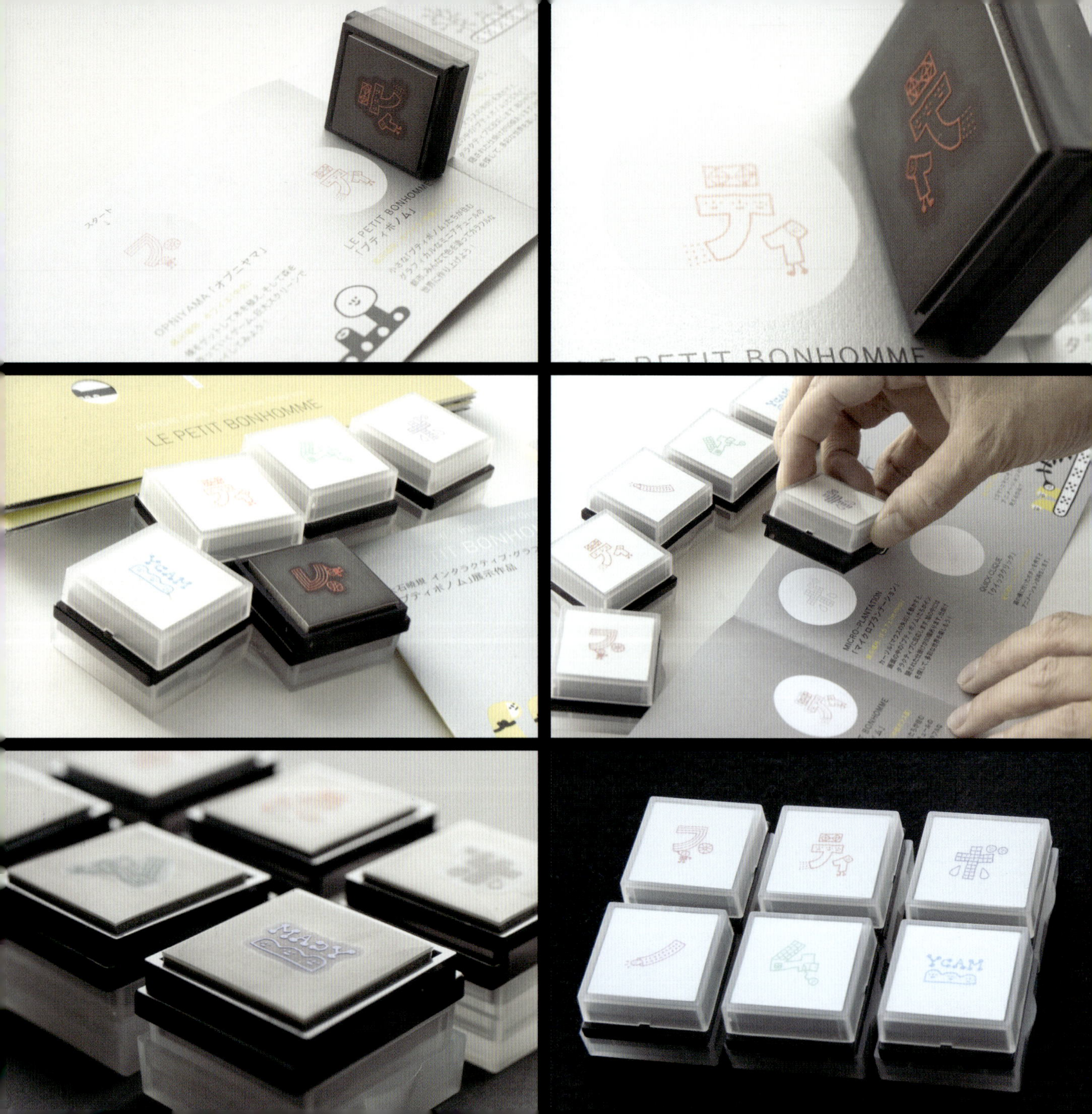

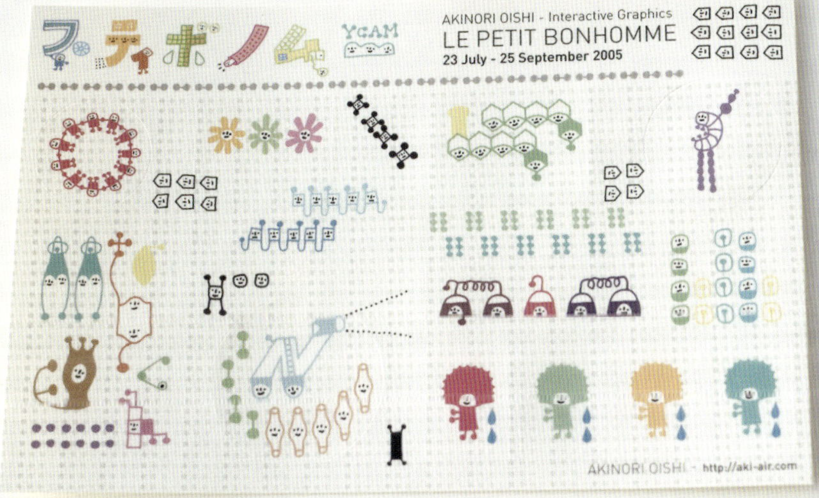
AKINORI OISHI - Interactive Graphics
LE PETIT BONHOMME
23 July - 25 September 2005
YCAM
AKINORI OISHI - http://aki-air.com

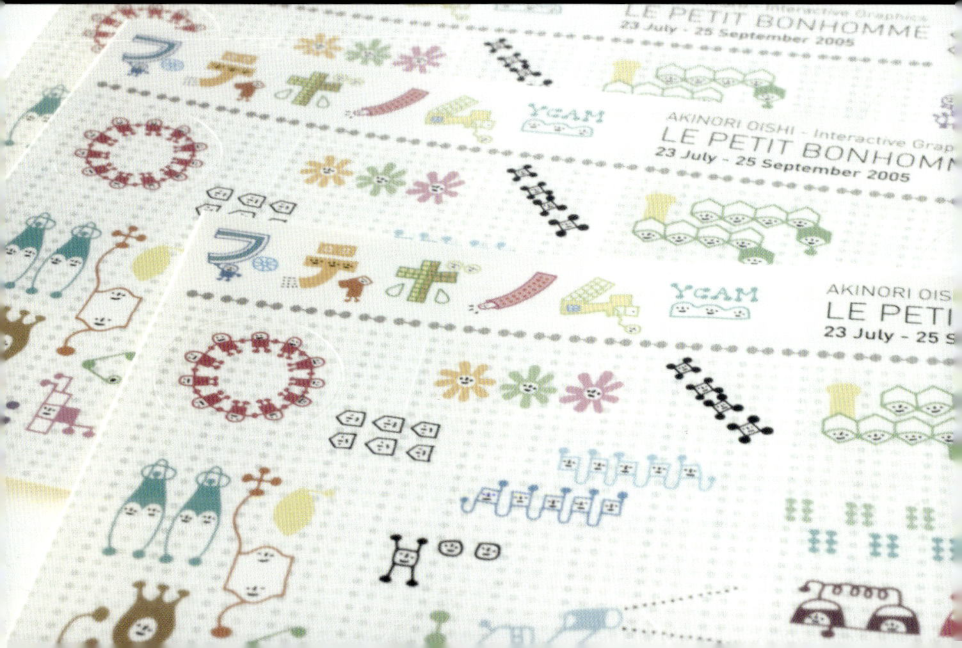

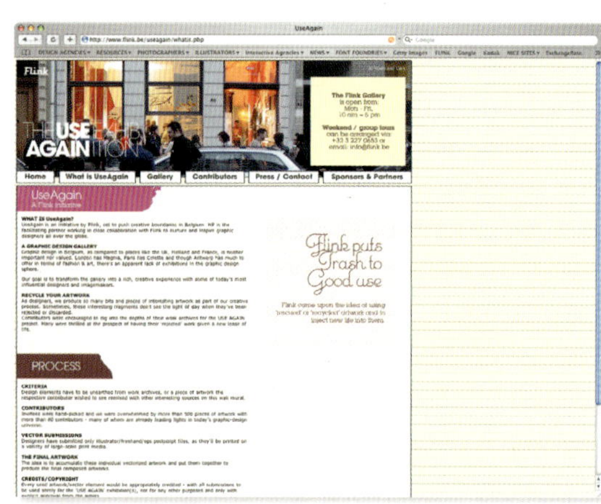

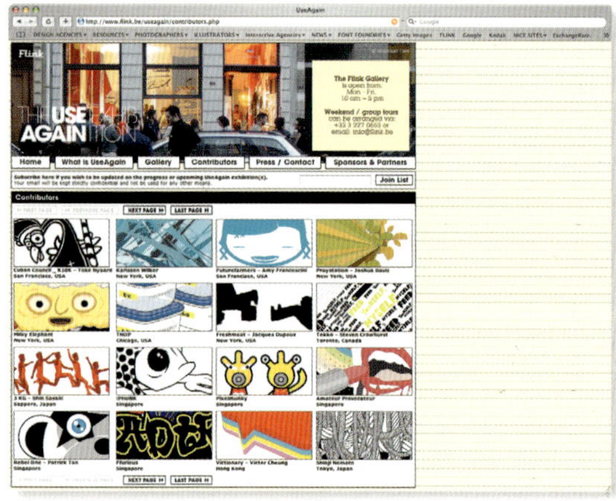

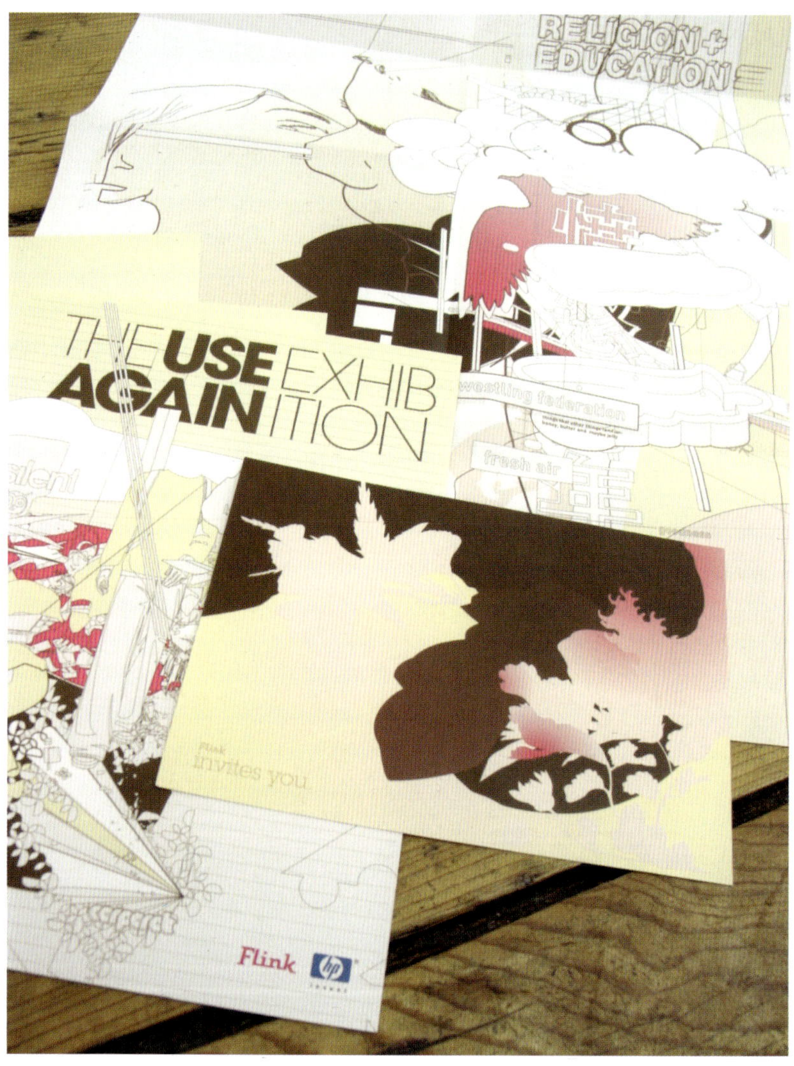

Flink

Antwerp, Belgium

Title: UseAgain Exhibition
Type of work: Exhibition
Client: Flink
Design: ad// Fanny Khoo d// Fanny Khoo & Tom Merckx
Year: 2005

UseAgain is an initiative by Flink. It is set to push creative boundaries in Belgium. As compared to places like the UK, Holland and France, there's an apparent lack of exhibitions in the graphic design sphere in Belgium. The goal is therefore to transform the gallery into a rich, creative experience with some of today's most influential designers and imagemakers from the globe. Contributors were encouraged to dig into the depths of their work archives for the USE AGAIN project. Many were thrilled at the prospect of having their 'rejected' work given a new lease of life.

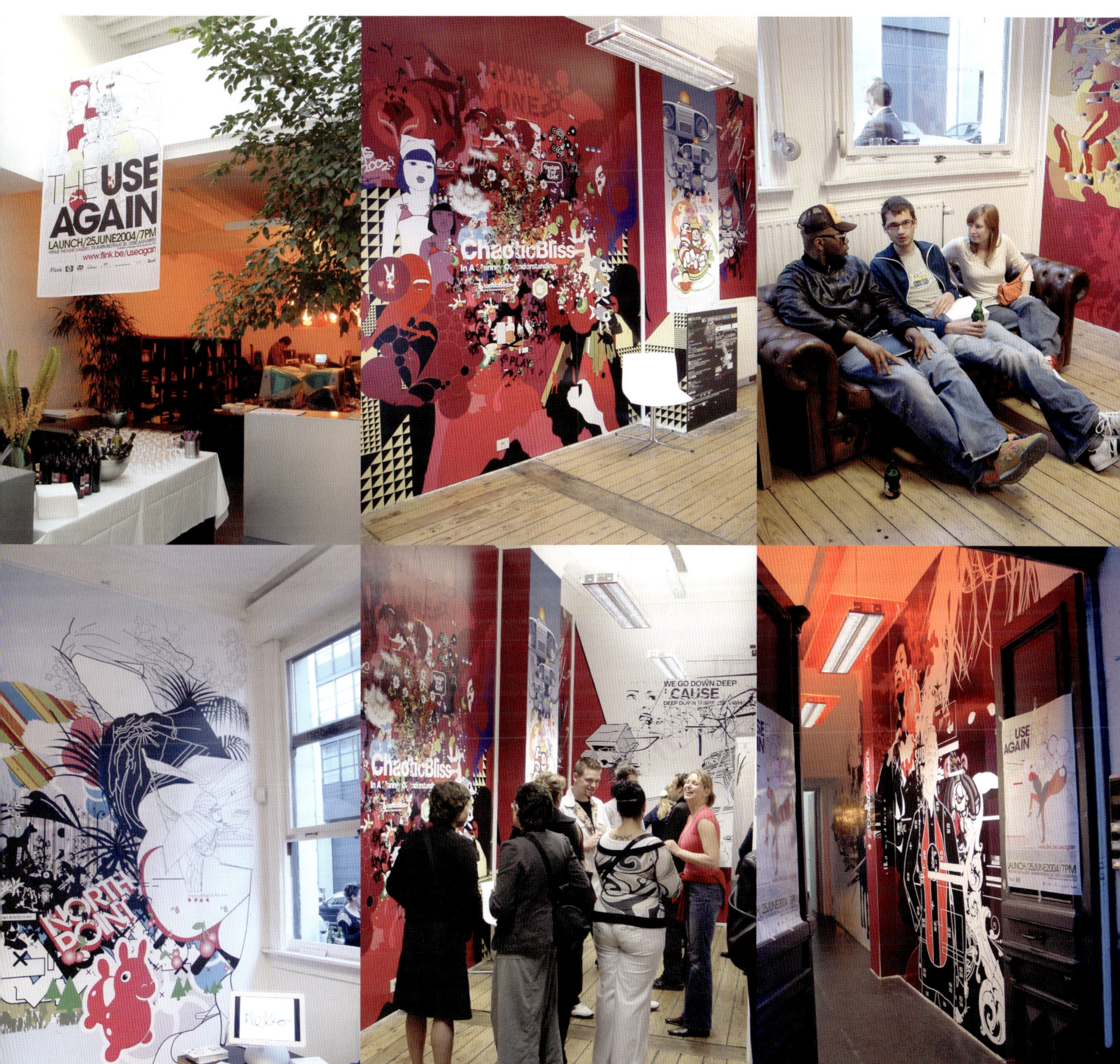
THE USE
AGAIN
LAUNCH/25JUNE2004/7PM
www.flink.be/useagain
Flink
ChaoticBliss
In A Manner Of Understanding
NORTH POINT
hello
ChaoticBliss
In A Manner Of Understanding
WE GO DOWN DEEP
CAUSE
DEEP DOWN THERE
USE
AGAIN
USE
AGAIN
LAUNCH/25JUNE2004/7PM

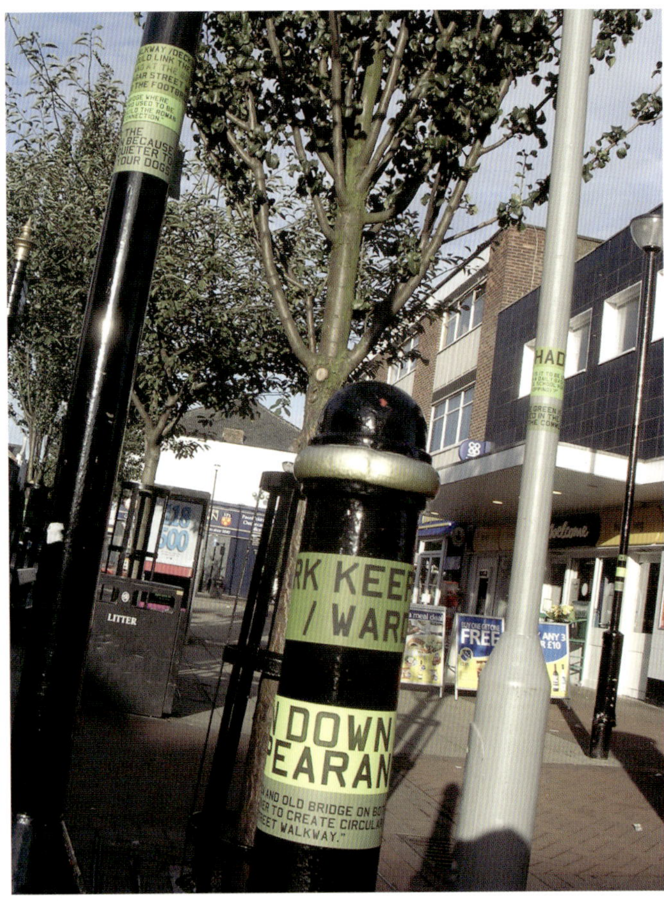
RK KEEP
/ WARE
N DOWN
PEARAN
LITTER

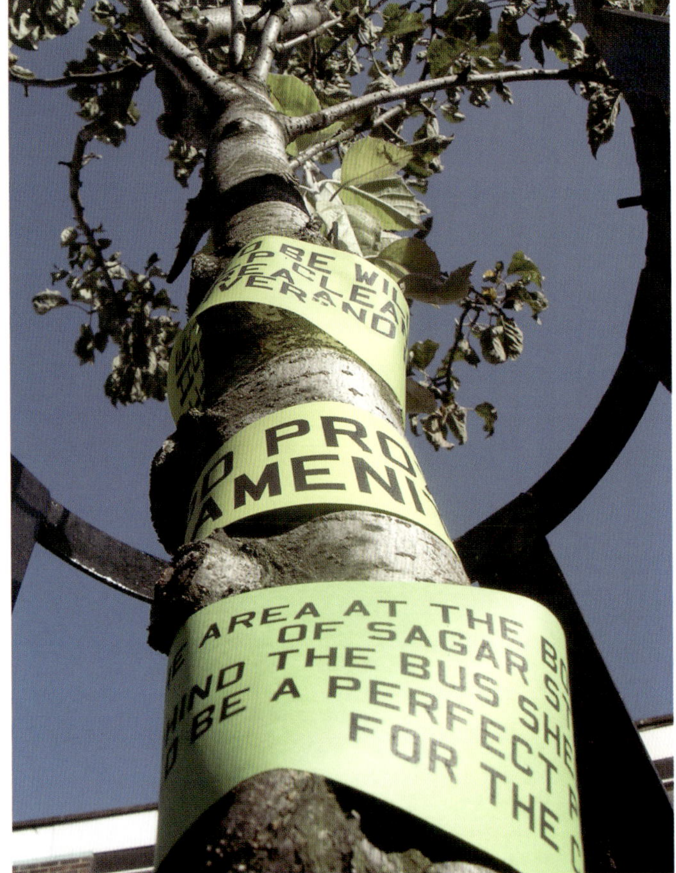
BE WI
EA CLEA
E RAND
P PRO
AMENI
E AREA AT THE B
OF SAGAR S
IND THE BUS SHE
BE A PERFECT
FOR THE C

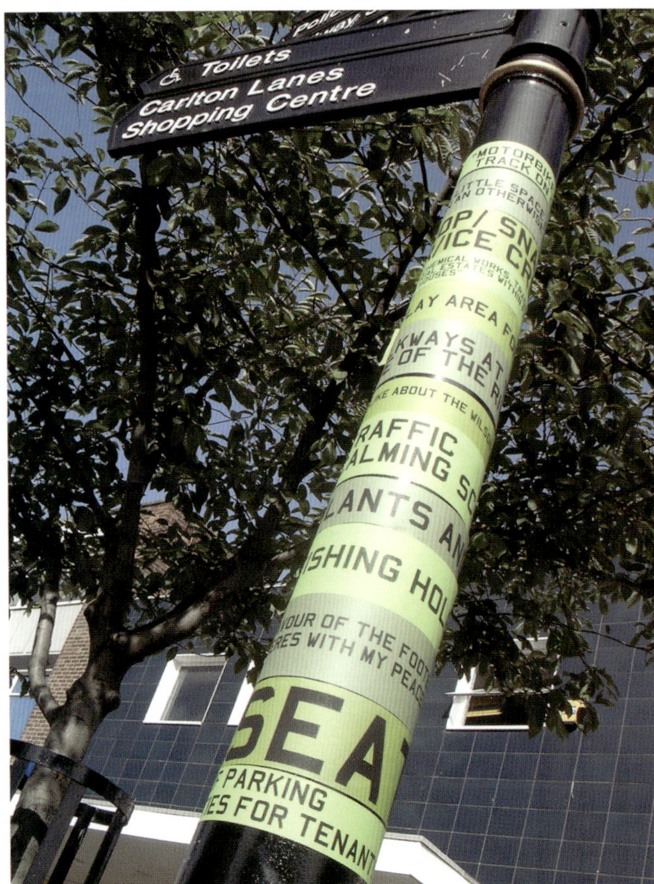
Toilets
Carlton Lanes
Shopping Centre
MOTORB
TRACK ON
OP/ SN
ICE C
LAY AREA F
KWAYS AT
OF THE R
E ABOUT THE WIL
RAFFIC
ALMING S
ANTS AN
SHING HOL
OUR OF THE FOOT
RES WITH MY PEAC
SEA
PARKING
ES FOR TENANT

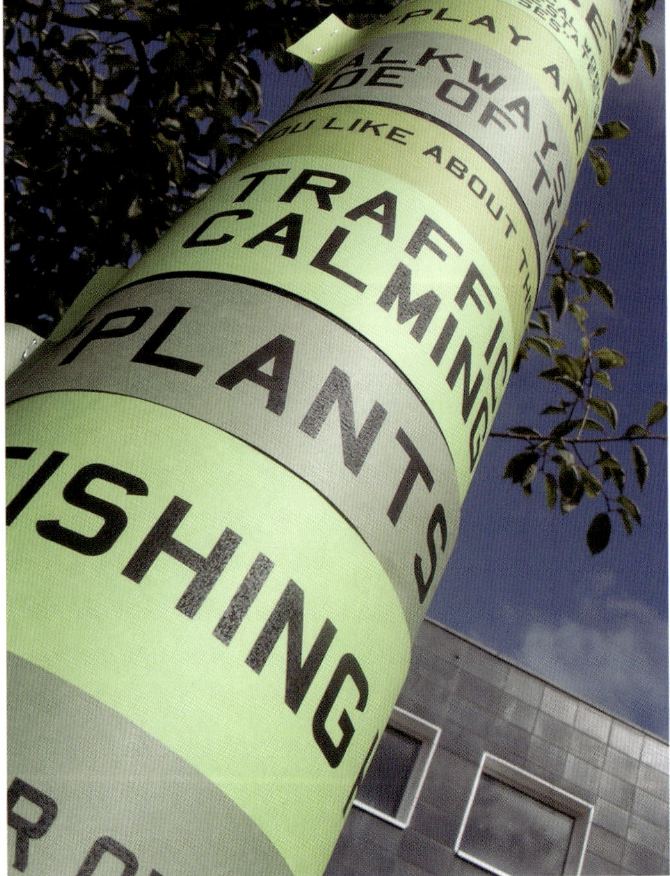
PLAY ARE
ALKWAYS
DE OF T
YOU LIKE ABOUT T
TRAFFI
CALMING
PLANTS
ISHING

Peter Anderson

London, UK

Title: The Castleford Project
Type of work: Program branding, installation
Client: David Barrie Wakefield metropolitan District Council/ talkback Thames, Channel four
Design: ad, d// Peter Anderson
Year: 2004

The graphic installation of this project took the people's view of their town, in which the information was gathered by sending out a questionnaire. Their words about what was good or bad, and what they thought could be changed in Castleford, were printed onto thousands of strips of green coloured paper and overnight the town centre was extensively covered. It resulted in a highly visual political starting point for conversation and debate.

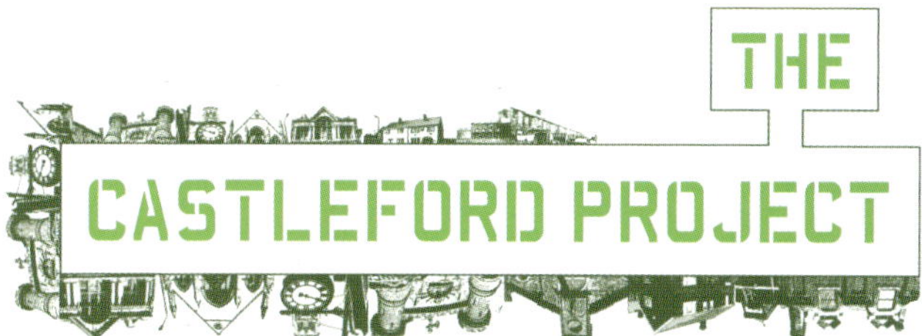

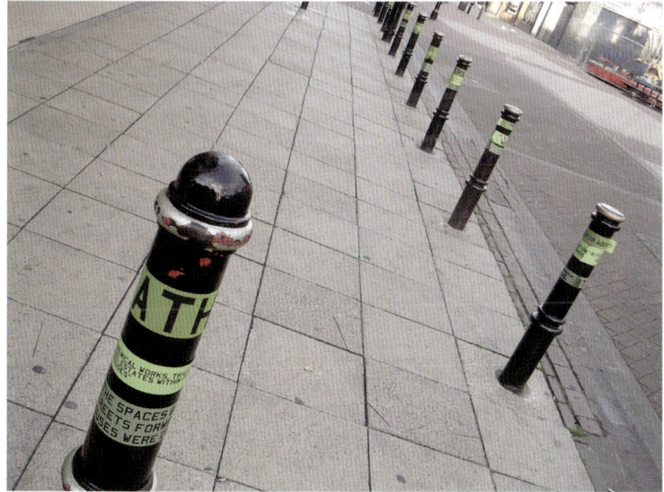

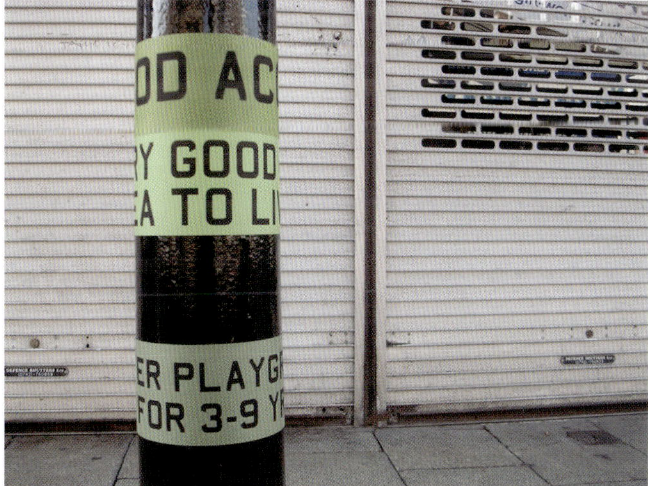

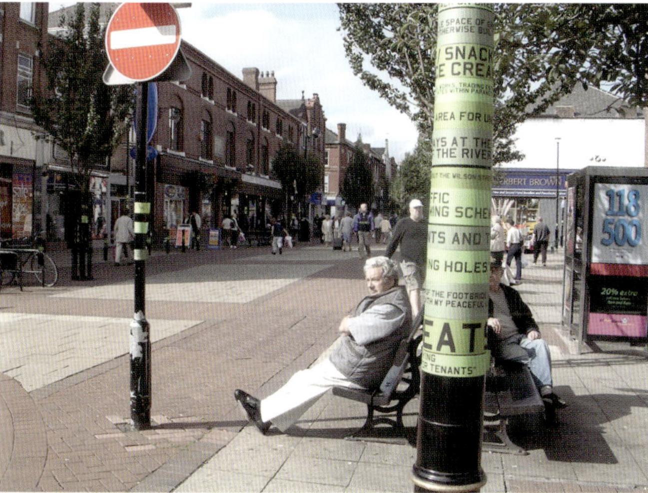

The exhibitions in this broad category share a common thread of appeal—
they aim to touch you based on your impression, or your attention to the
piece. Admittedly, this is rather a capricious method for analysis, but as
you peruse the coming pages, you'll see the way in which look different
from structure to message; these pieces were grouped based on the way
they trigger the eye, rather than the appeal of any statement they make or
the components of their construction.

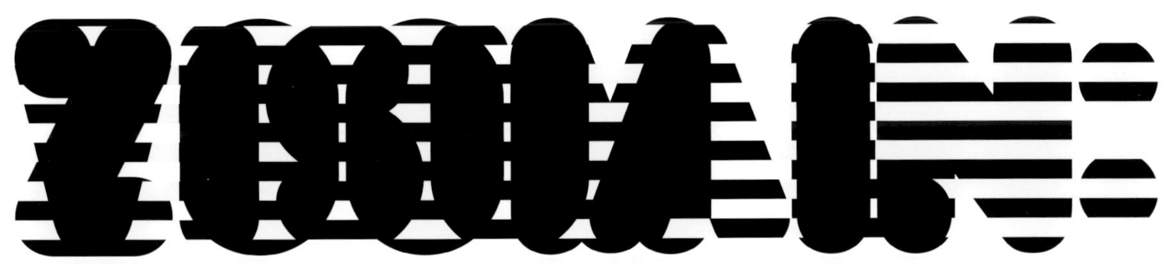

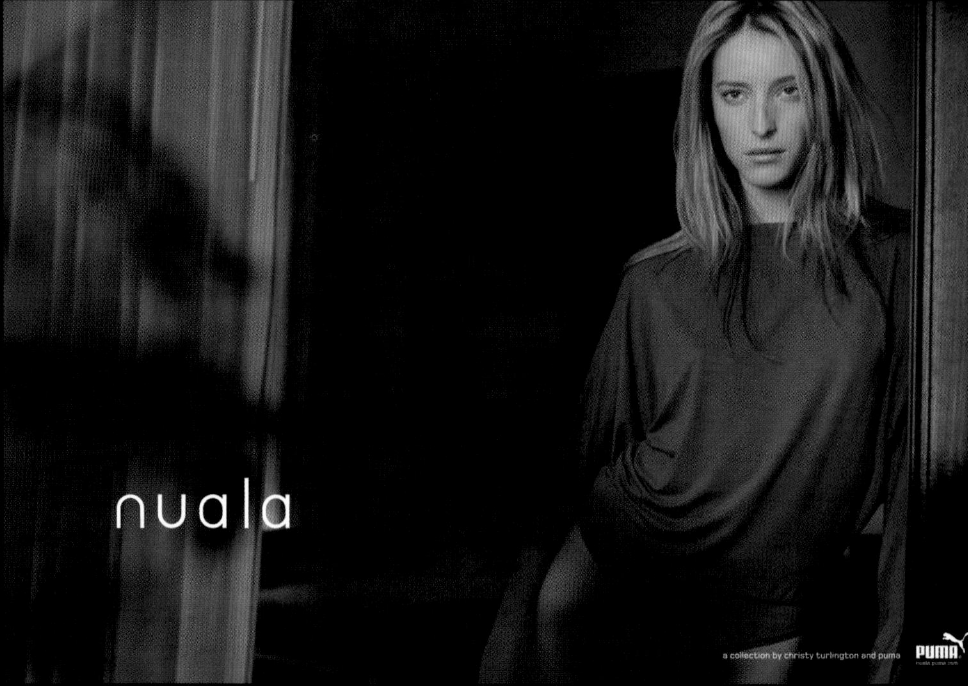

nuala
a collection by christy turlington and puma
PUMA

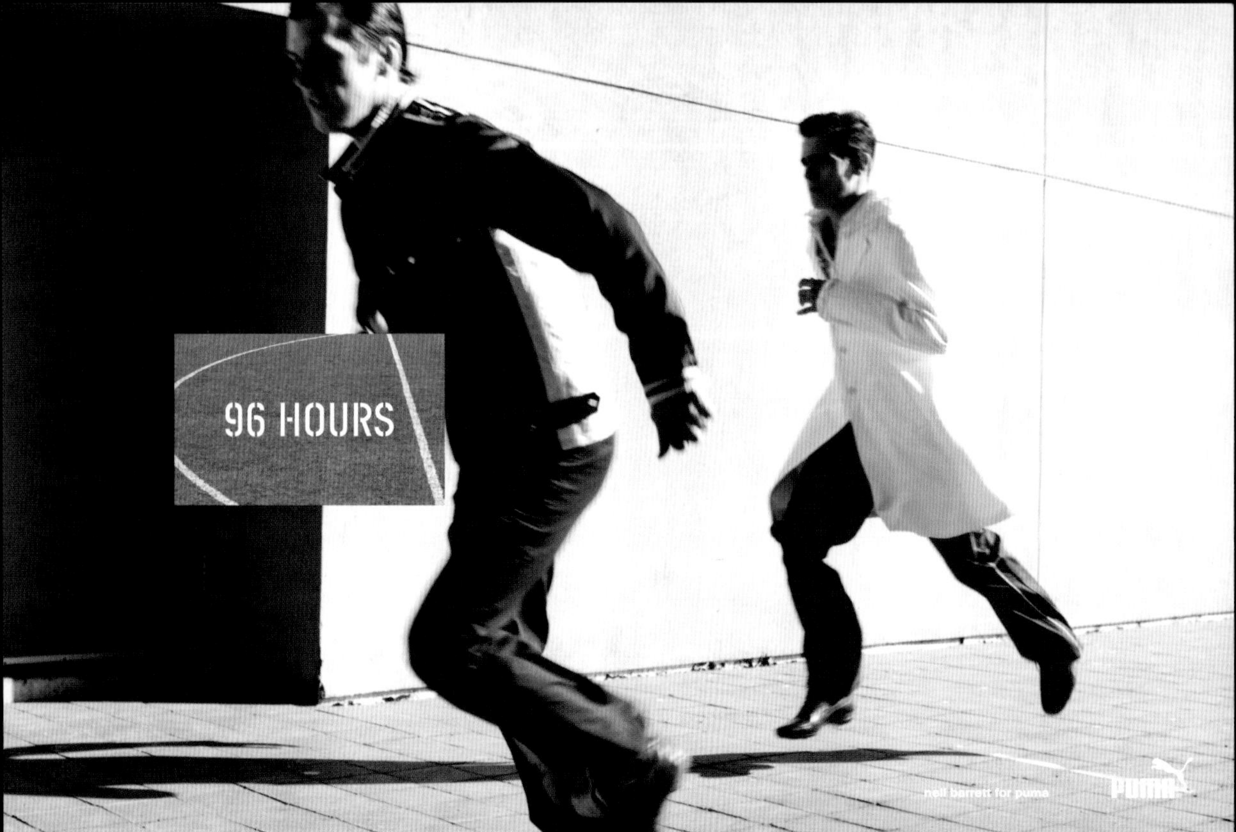

96 HOURS
neil barrett for puma
PUMA

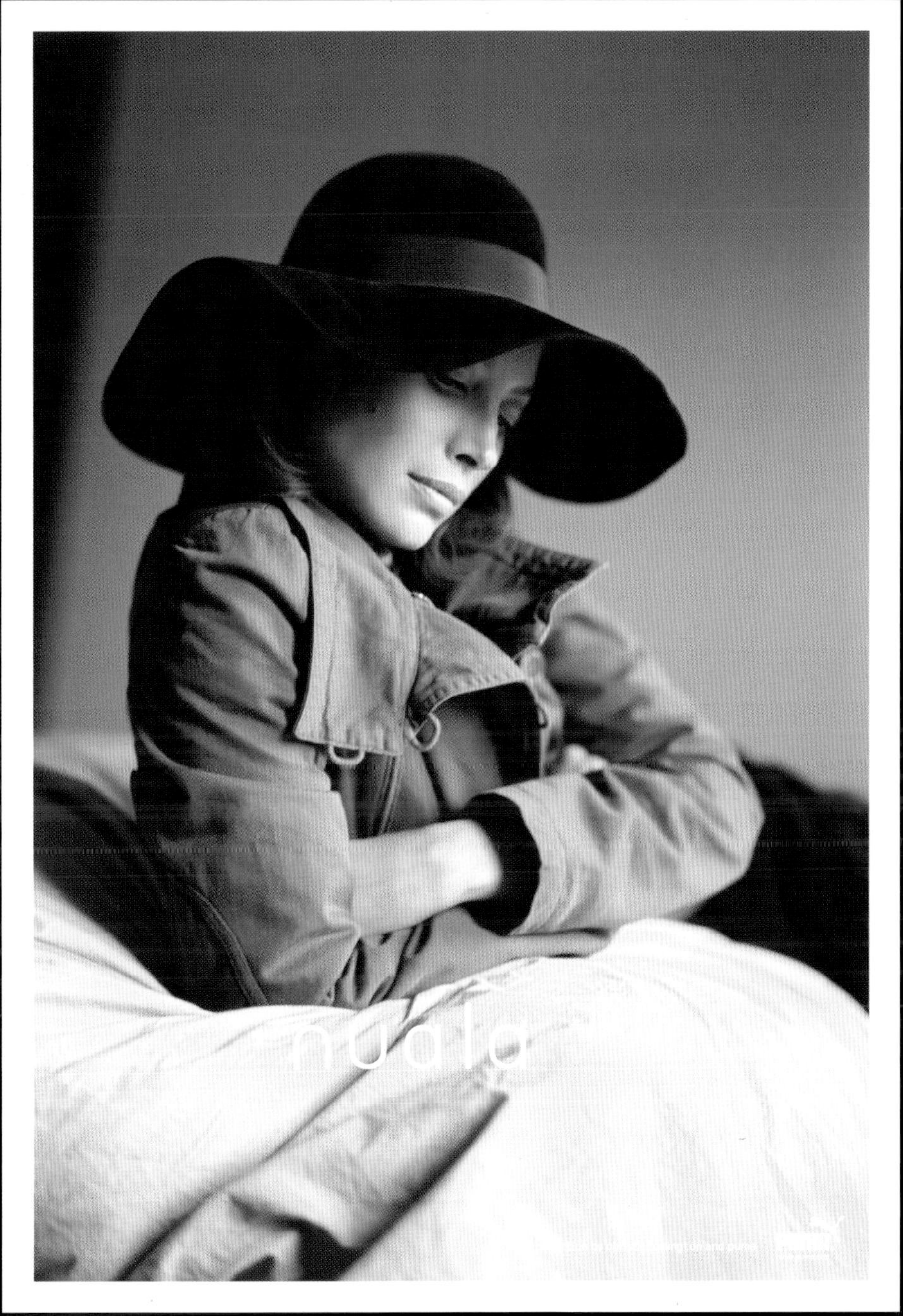

3.//

Base

New York, USA

Title: -
Type of work: Logo, catalogue, advertising, art direction
Client: 1,3.// Nuala 2.// Puma 96 Hours
Design: ad, d// Base
Year: 1.// 2005 2.// 2005 3.// 2004

2.// For this brand's campaigns, Base chose to present each season with one sport. Rather than presenting the sport explicitly, they wanted to reference Puma's comprehensive sports heritage. Imagery often gave a 'backstage' view of pre- or post-game. The result is very fashionable, with a slight retro feel, but definitely contemporary.

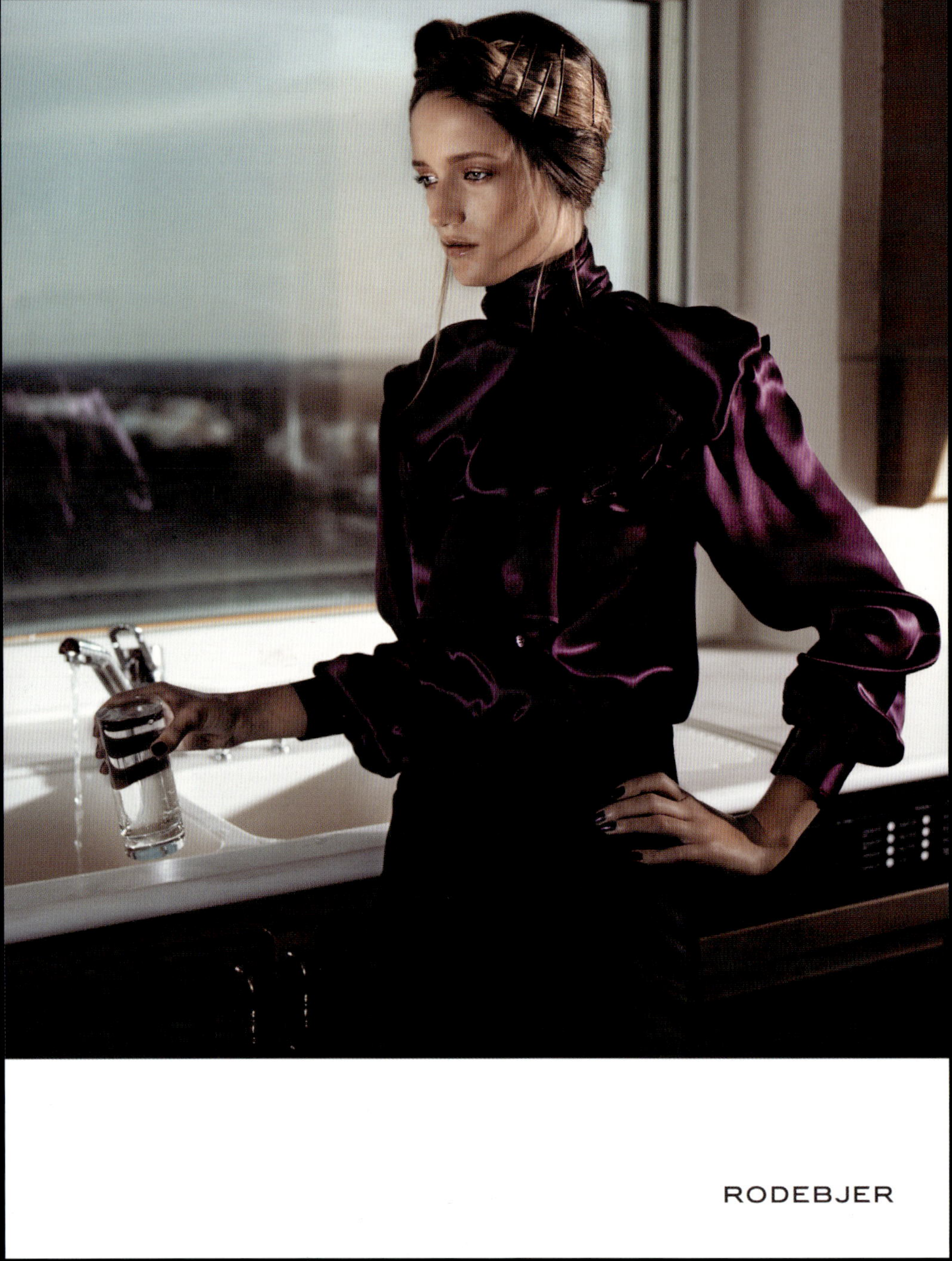

1.//

Stefania

Stockholm, Sweden

Title: -
Type of work: Advertising
Client: Rodebjer
Design: ad// Stefania Malmsten d// Jacob Huuri-

For this advertisment, graphic design and photography have been instrumental in communicating the vision of Carin Rodebjer and in the development of her company - a proper fashion design

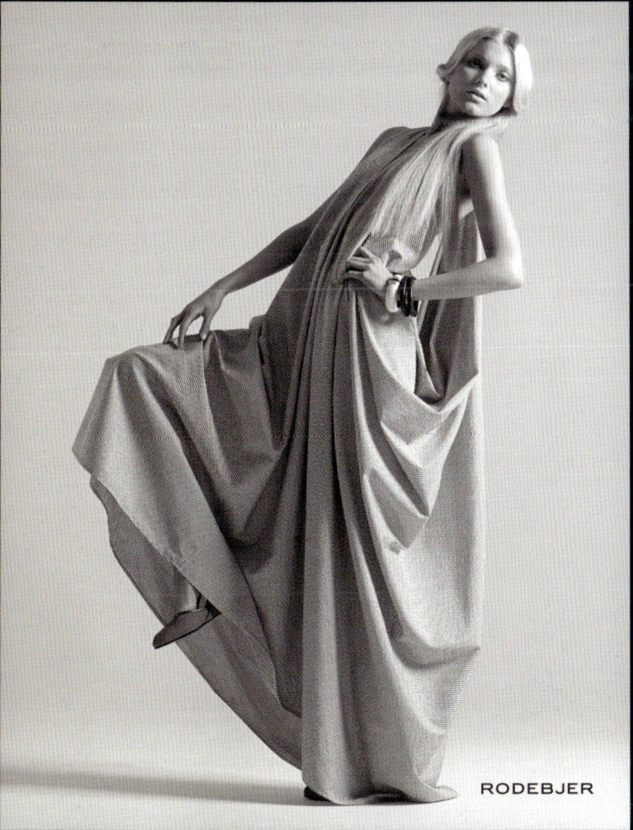

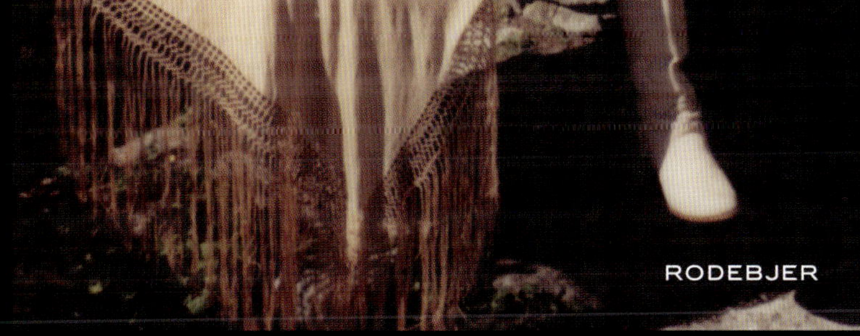

3.//

RODEBJER

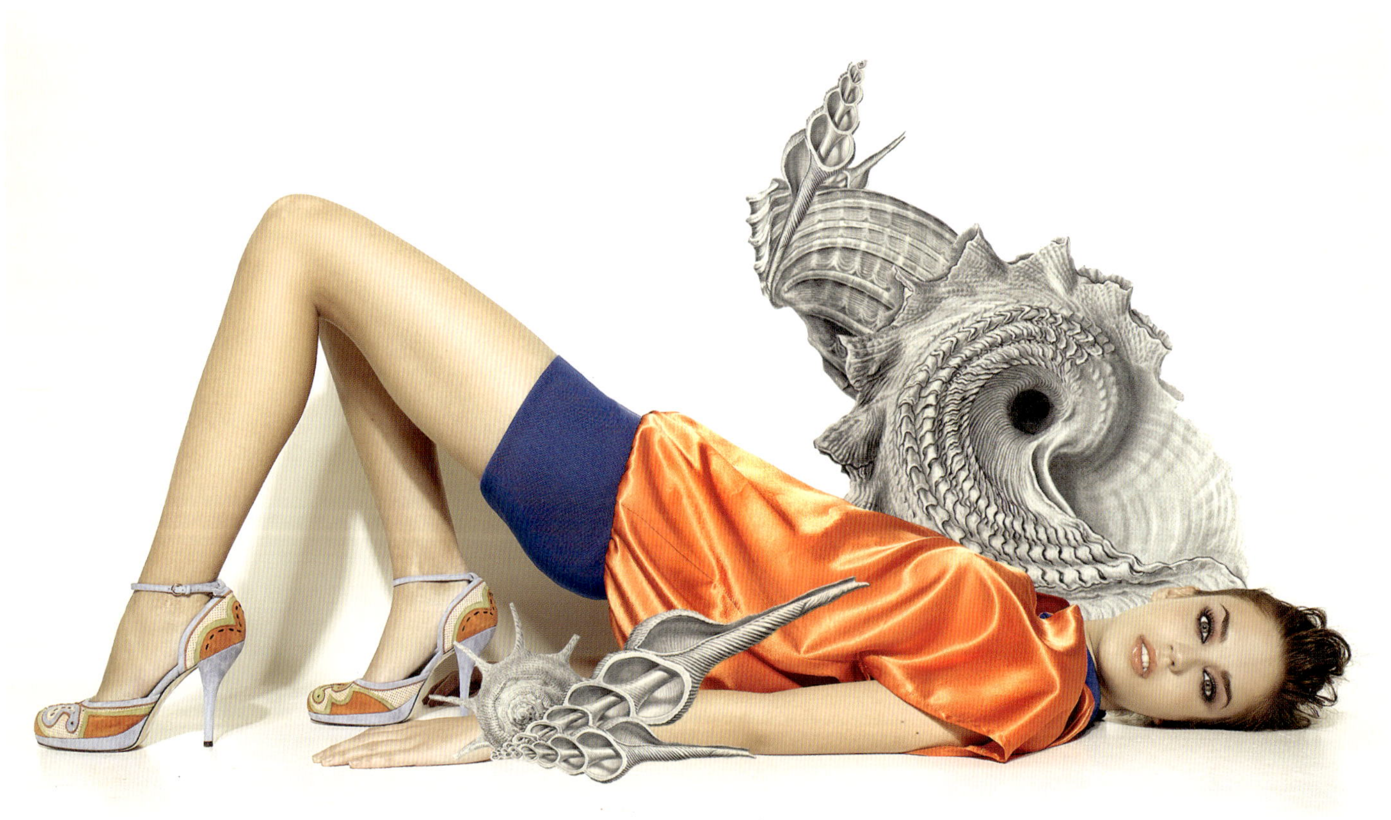

Serial Cut™

Madrid, Spain

Title: Unveiling Nature
Type of work: Fashion editorial for trends magazine
Client: *Clone Magazine*
Design: ad, d// Sergio del Puerto
Year: 2005

This piece is an enigmatic fashion editorial reinforced with the fabulous clothes by Spanish fashion designer Iñigo Aragón. Photographer Jose Oyón and stylist Pablo Torres Weist created a delicate scene which was finished off with drawings of shells, as if taken from a botanist's book.

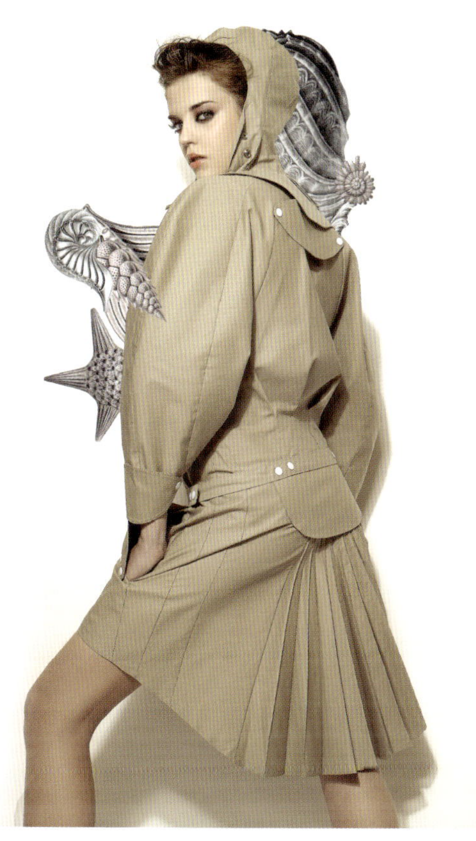

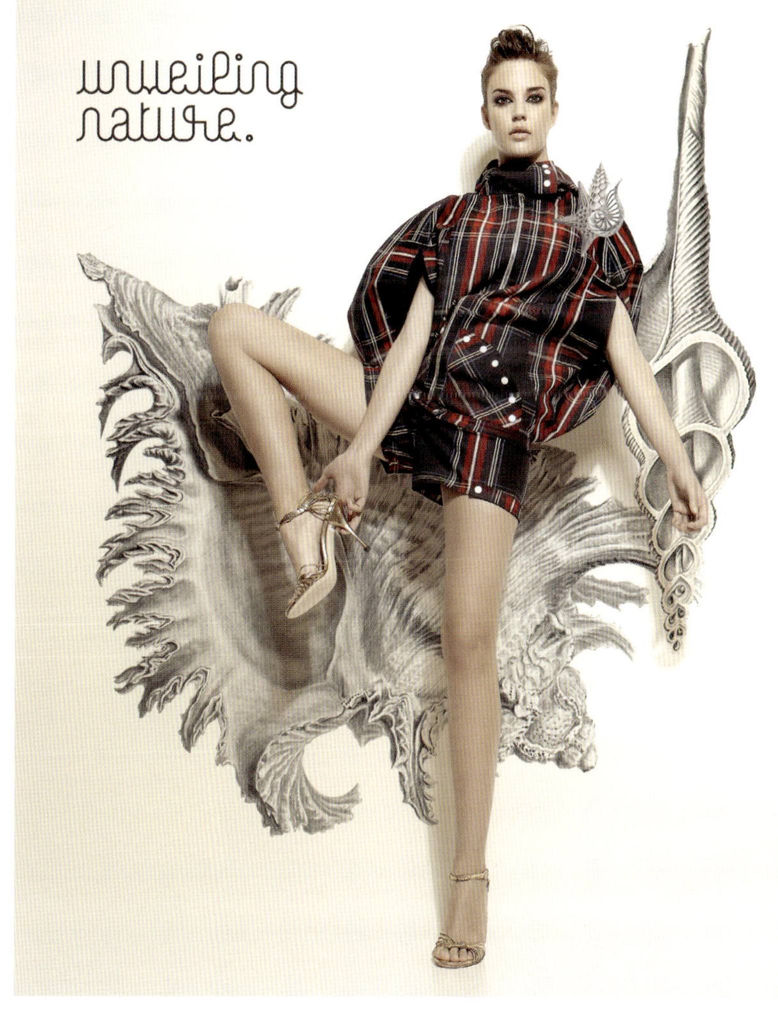
unveiling
nature.

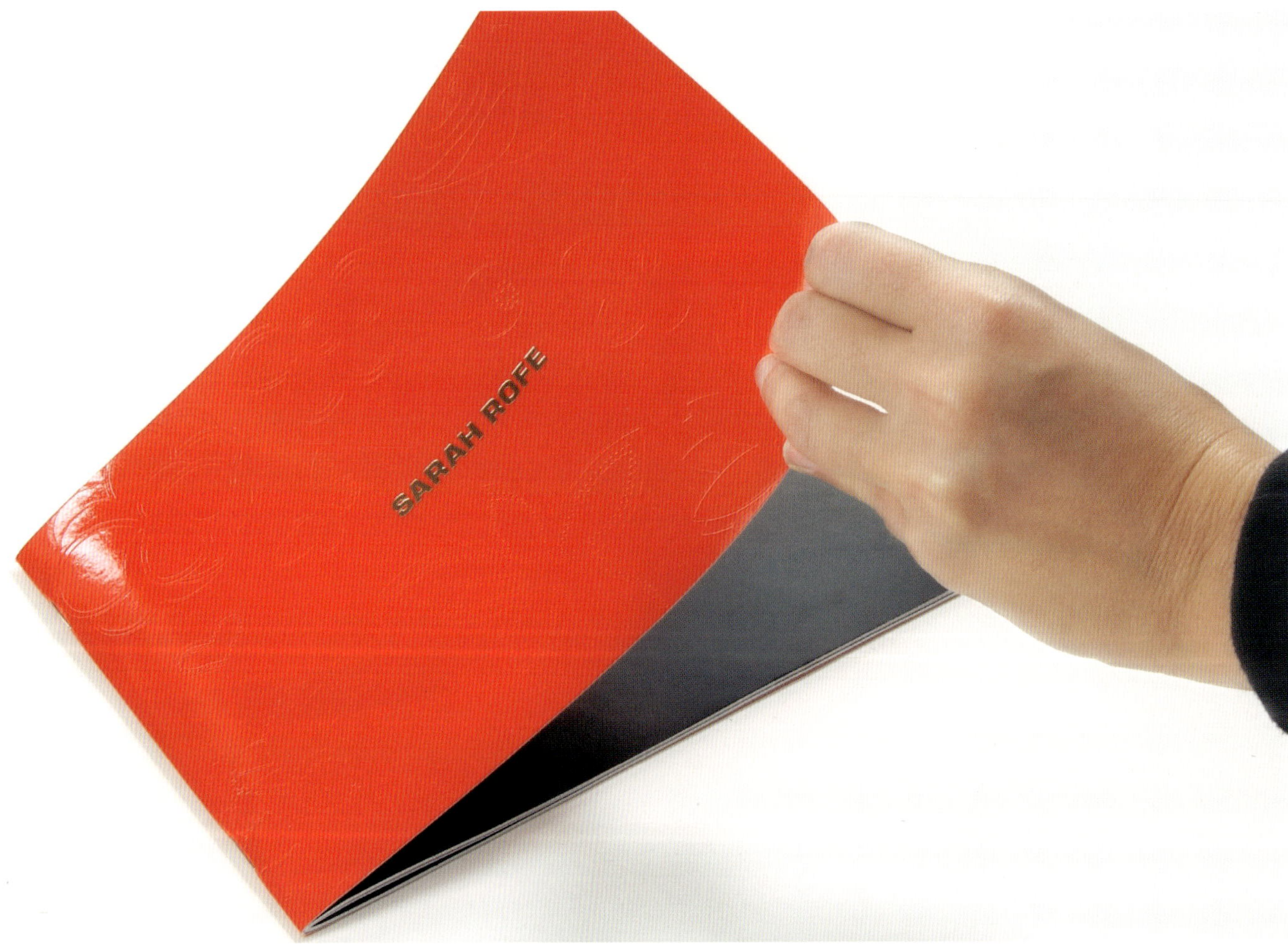

Koniak Design Studio

Madrid, SpainTel-Aviv, Israel

Title: Catalogue for Sarah Rofe – handcrafted accessories
Type of work: Catalogue
Client: Sarah Rofe
Design: ad, d// Nurit Koniak
Year: 2005

The catalogue aimed at reflecting the unique handcrafted quality of the products, by creating a graphic language combining illustration & photography. This language was very useful to create a differentiation between the accessories and the other clothing items presented in the catalogue. The graphic language played an important role to make it clear to the customer that the items being sold are the accessories only.

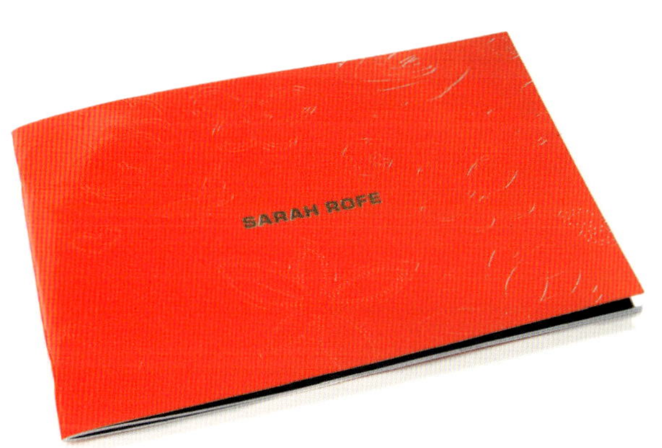

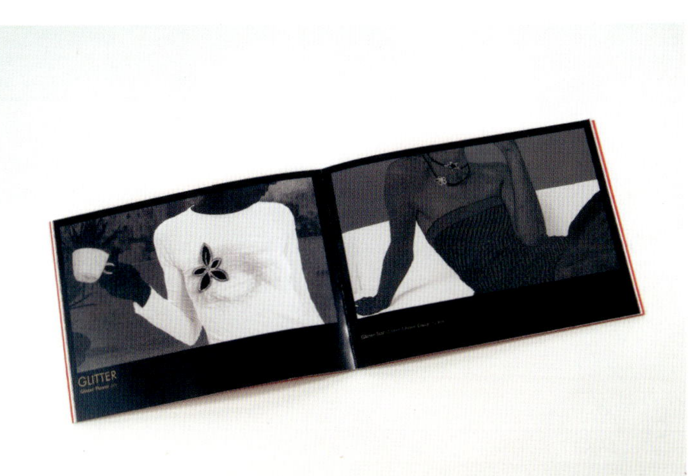

GLITTER

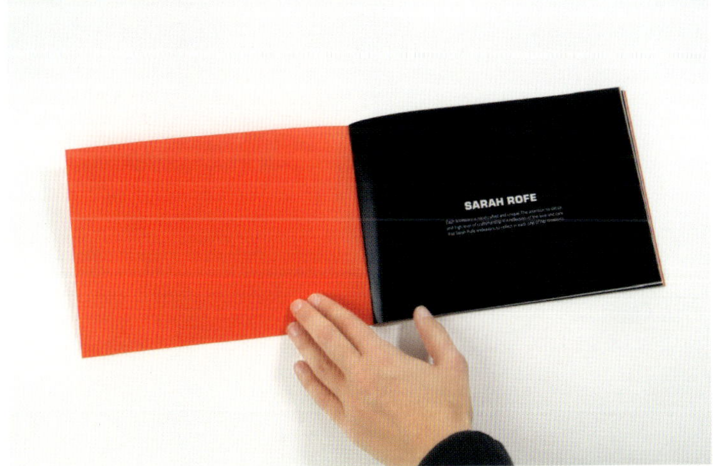

SARAH ROFE

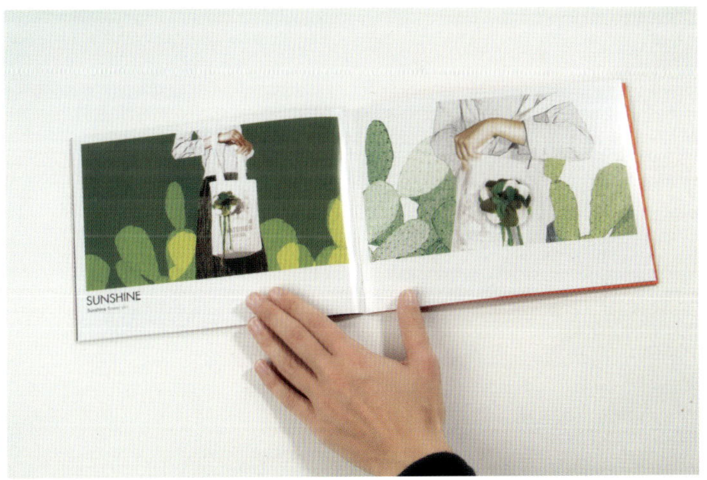

SUNSHINE

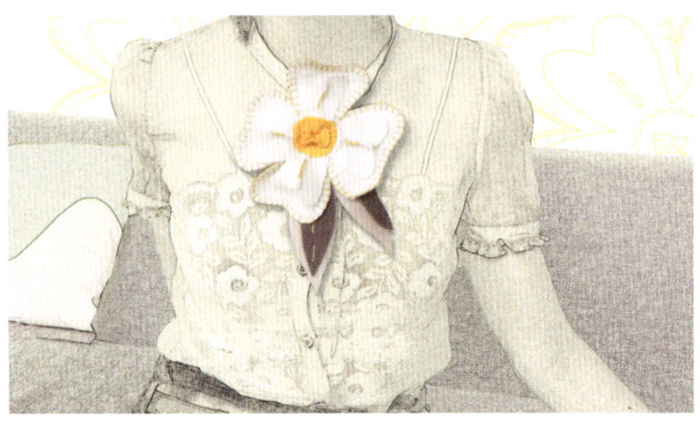

ALLURE

Allure Attraction flower pin

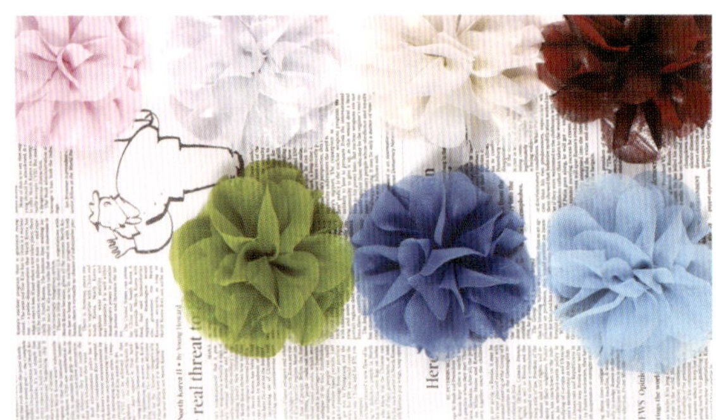

ELEGANCE

Elegance flower pins & hair clips in various colors

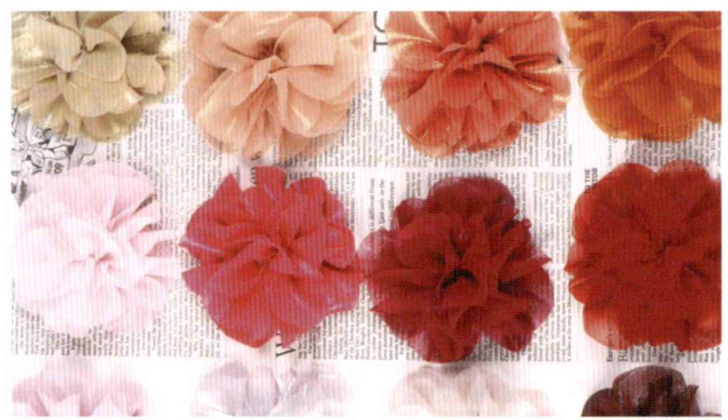

Koniak Design Studio

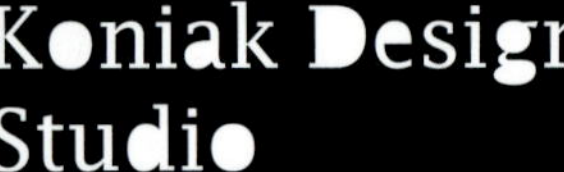

Tel-Aviv, Israel

Title: Catalogue for Sarah Rofe – handcrafted accessories
Type of work: Catalogue
Client: Sarah Rofe
Design: ad, d// Nurit Koniak
Year: 2005

The catalogue aimed at reflecting the unique handcrafted quality of the products, by creating a graphic language combining illustration & photography. This language was very useful to create a differentiation between the accessories and the other clothing items presented in the catalogue. The graphic language played an important role to make it clear to the customer that the items being sold are the accessories only.

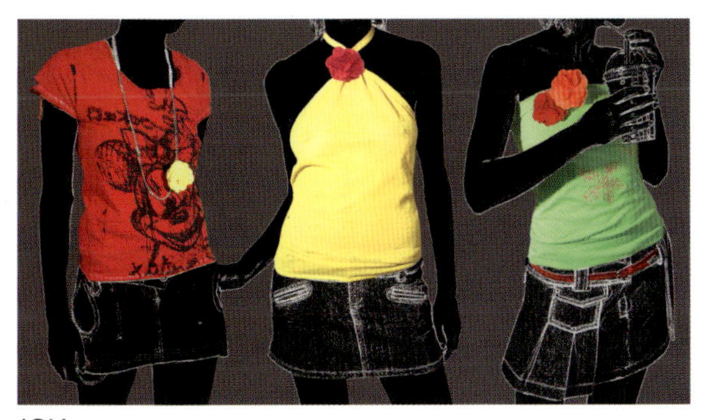

JOY

Joy *flower pins in various colors*

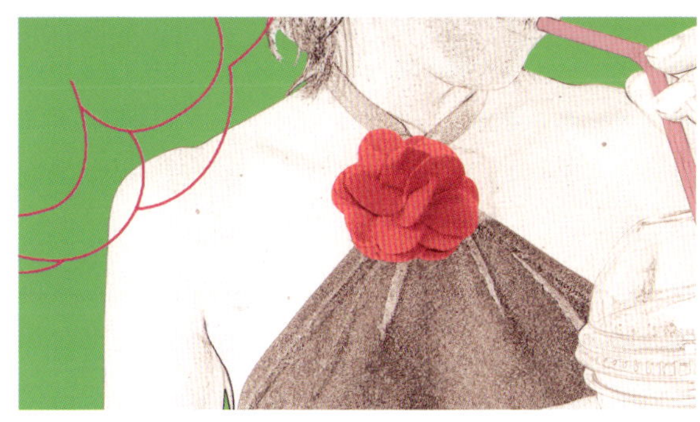

Joy *flower pin*

ALLURE

From left : **Allure Sensation** *flower pin*, **Allure Romance** *flower pin*, **Allure Love** *flower pin*

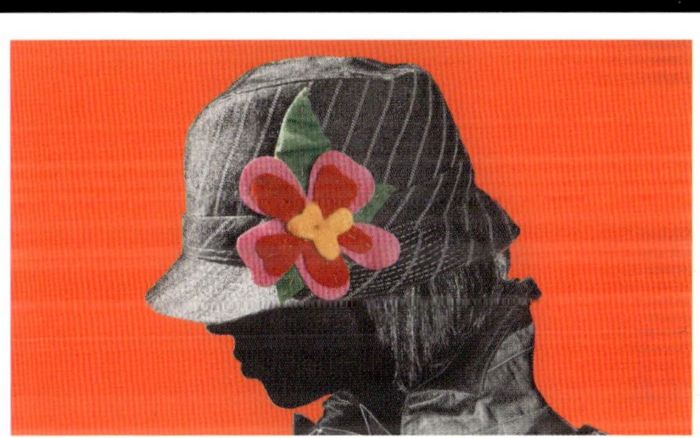

Allure Forever *flower pin*

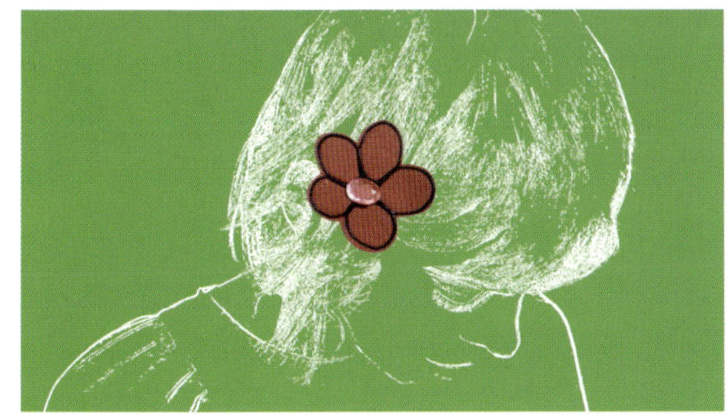

CARTOON

Cartoon *flower hair clip*

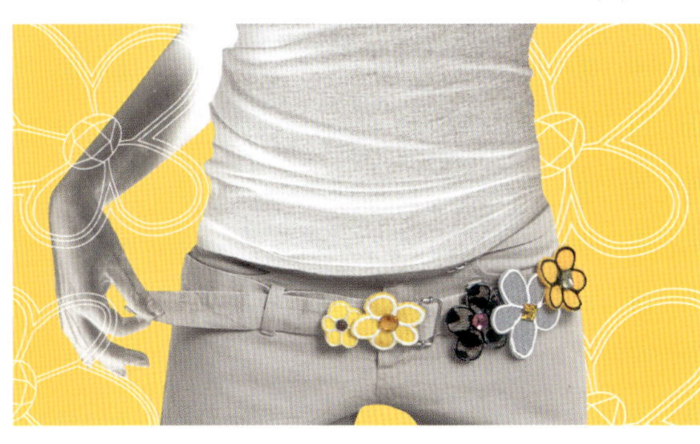

Cartoon *flower pins in various sizes*

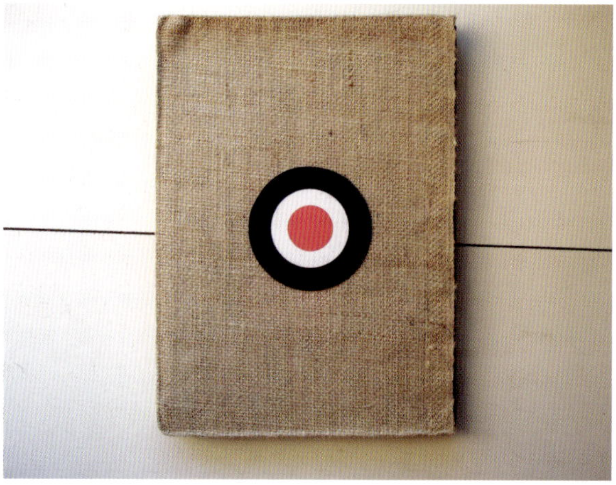

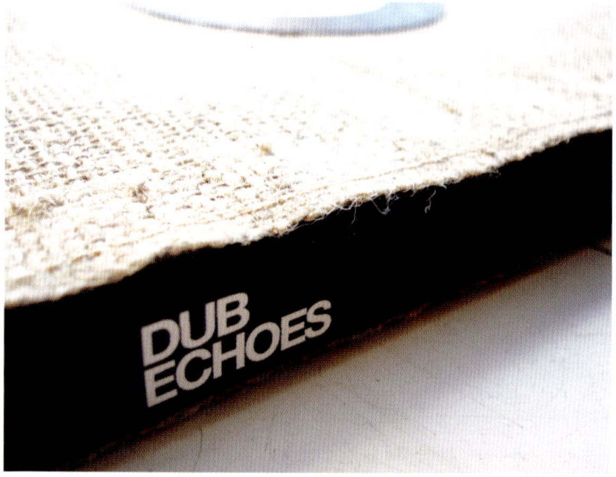

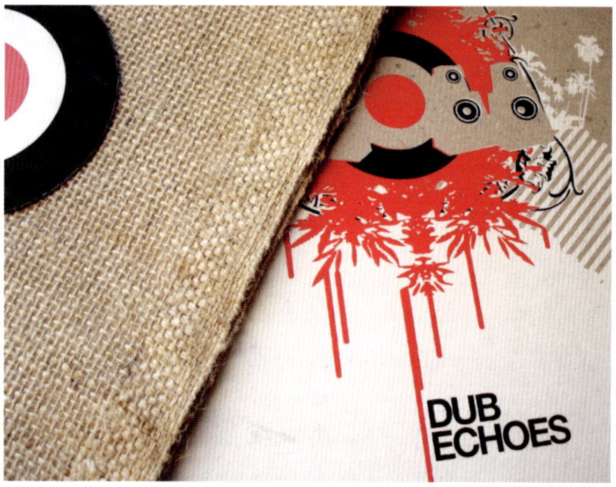

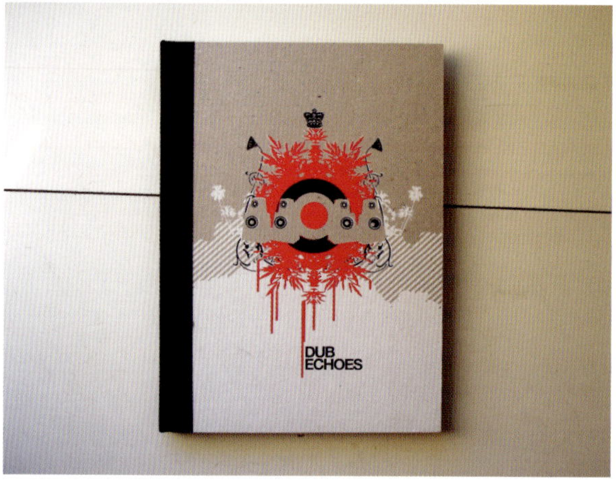

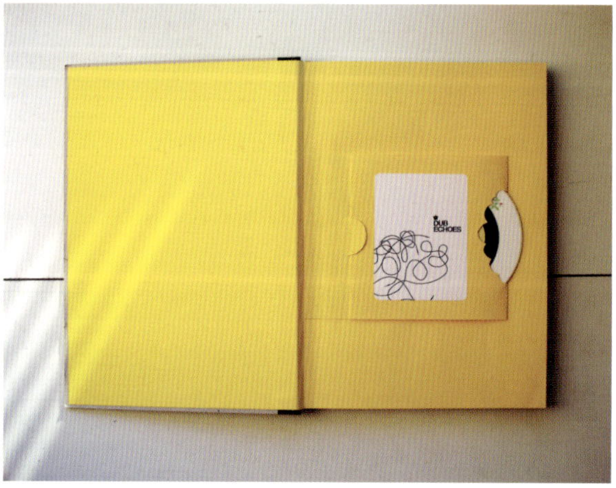

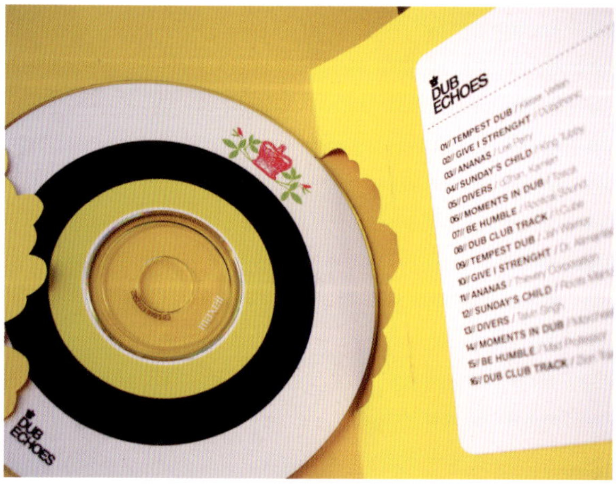

Dimaquina

Rio de Janeiro – RJ – Brazil

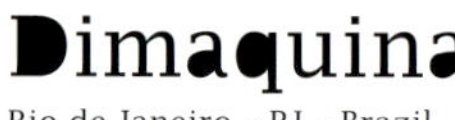

Title: Dub Echoes
Type of work: Book
Client: Dub Echoes
Design: ad// Antônio Pedro, Dimaquina
d// Antônio Pedro
Year: 2004

This piece is a book which guides the reader through the history of Jamaican music, since its beginning until the latest influence on contemporary electronic music. It shows different moments of this important trajectory with visual interpretations made from a mix of photographs and symbolic elements from the dub world. The graphic project follows the editorial concept of the book: to transform the rusticity and lack of resources of the Jamaican music into a modern language.

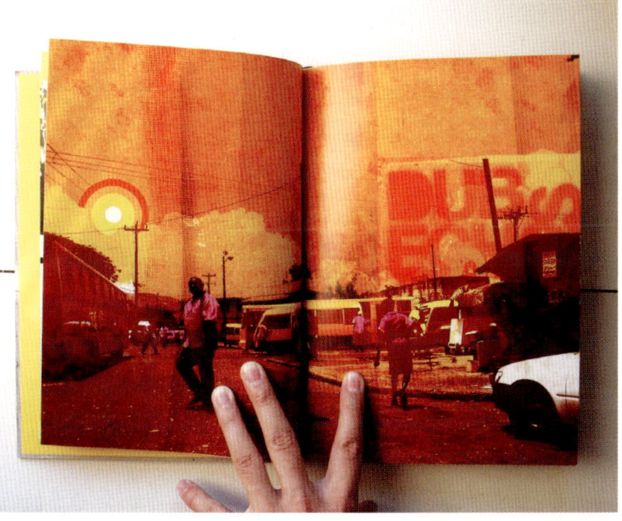

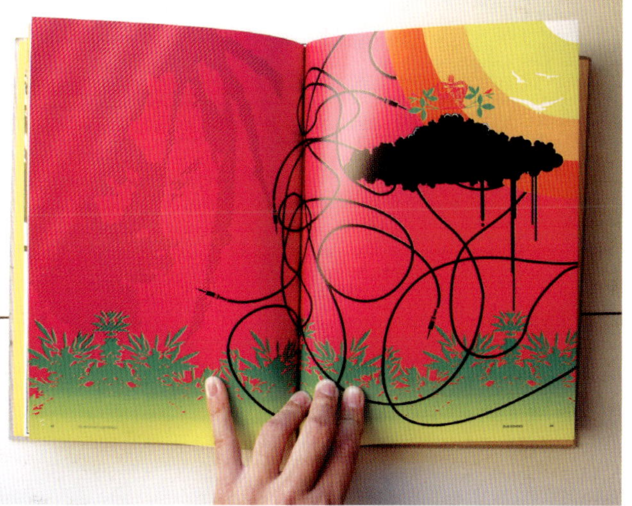

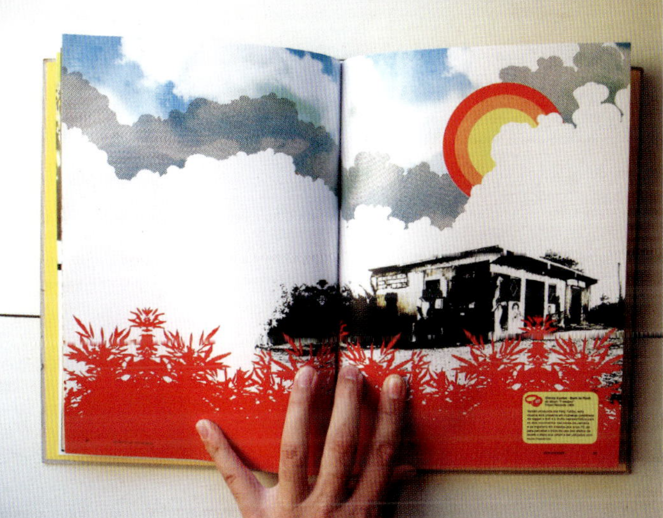

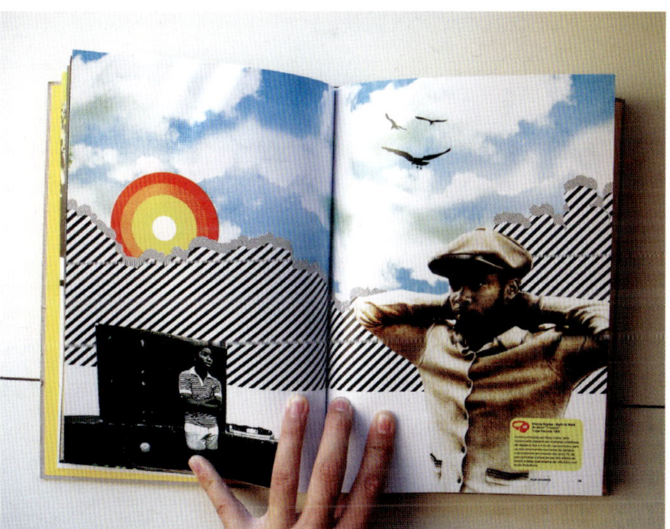

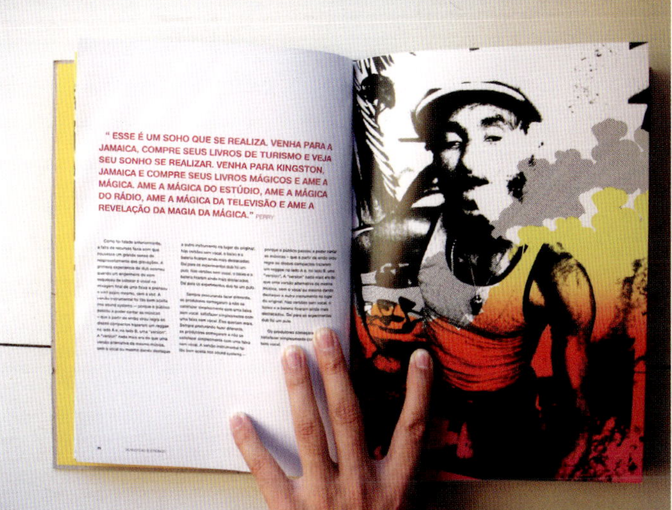
" ESSE É UM SOHO QUE SE REALIZA. VENHA PARA A JAMAICA, COMPRE SEUS LIVROS DE TURISMO E VEJA SEU SONHO SE REALIZAR. VENHA PARA KINGSTON, JAMAICA E COMPRE SEUS LIVROS MÁGICOS E AME A MÁGICA. AME A MÁGICA DO ESTÚDIO, AME A MÁGICA DO RÁDIO, AME A MÁGICA DA TELEVISÃO E AME A REVELAÇÃO DA MAGIA DA MÁGICA." PERRY

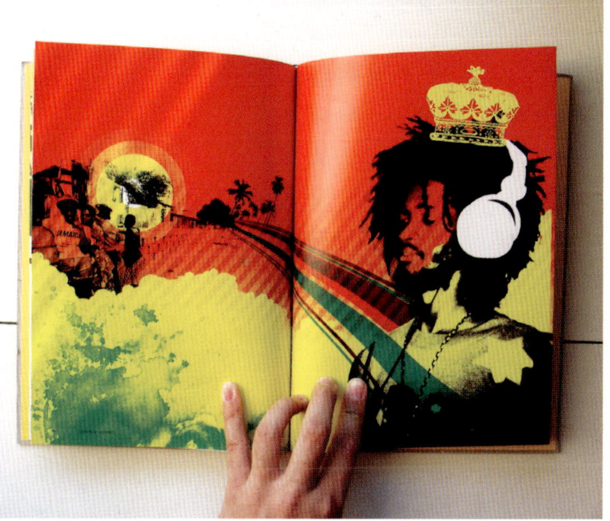

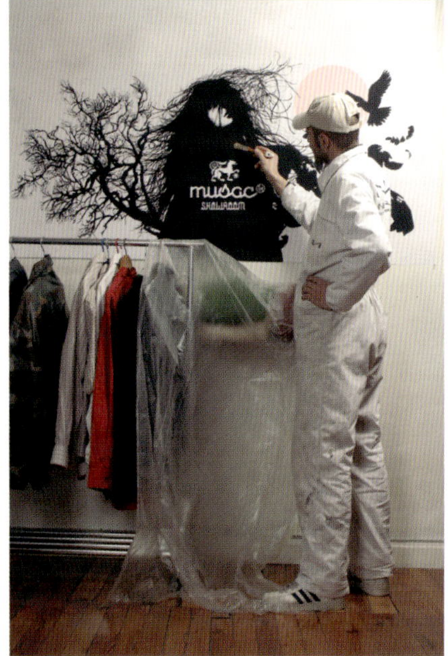

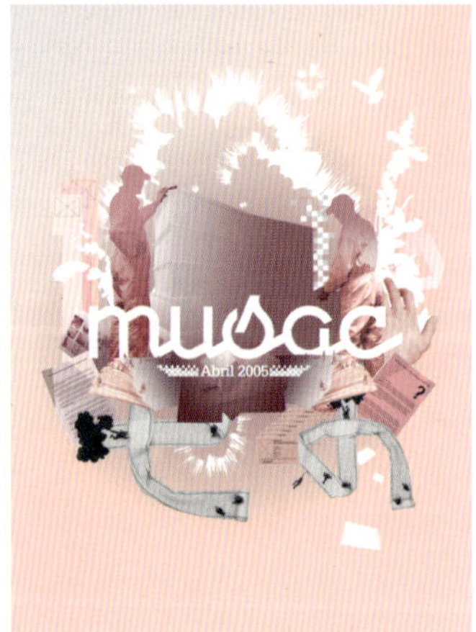

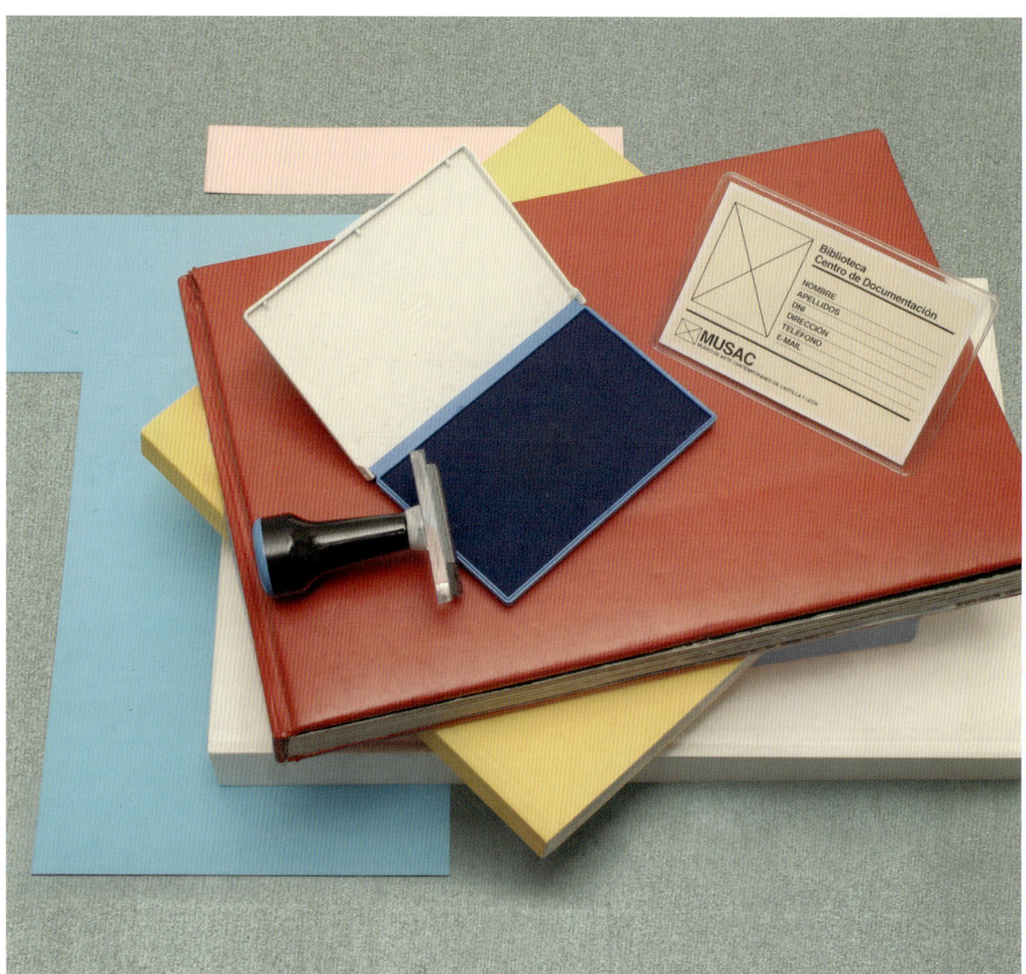

Serial Cut™

Madrid, Spain

Title: MUSAC
Type of work: Publication
Client: MUSAC (Museo Contemporáneo de Castilla y León)
Design: ad, d// Sergio del Puerto
Year: 2005

A 68-page promotional publication for the new Contemporary Art Museum of León, MUSAC, which focuses on art from the last 10 years. The only aim of this book was given out at the ARCO'05 Contemporary Art Fair in Madrid was 'to create a publication that people would keep as a collector's item'. The idea was to create a special layout with a lovely typeface and conceptual photographs to explain each area of the museum. Most of these photographs had some designed elements, which were firstly cut and put into the picture background, to be then photographed as real life elements. The art direction and the concept were definitely to make it special.

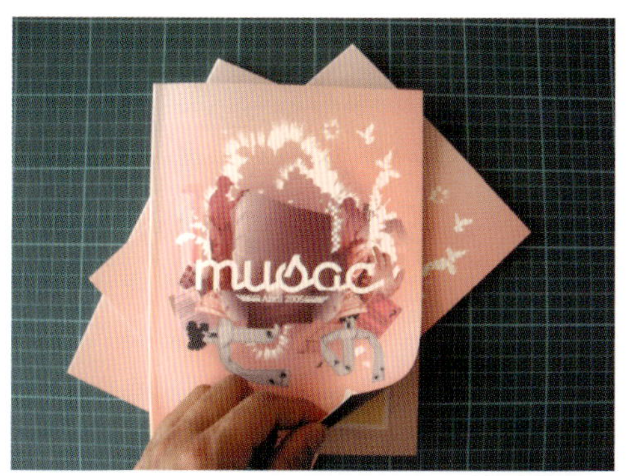
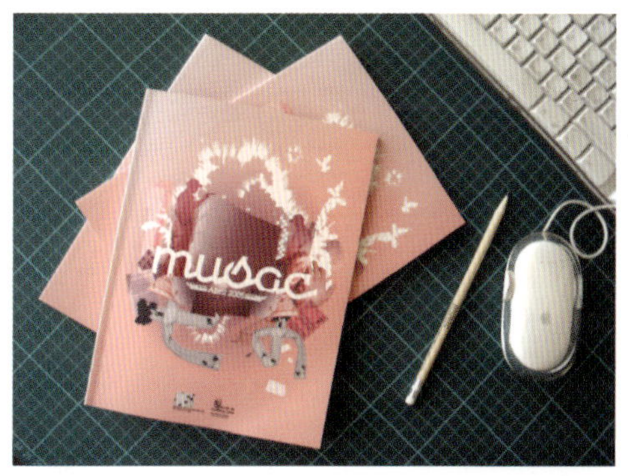
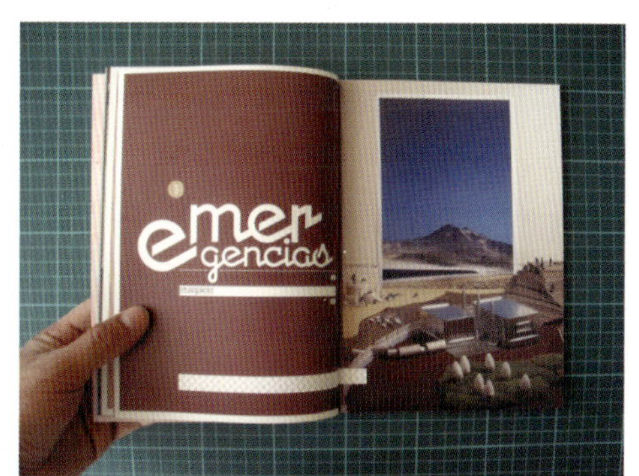
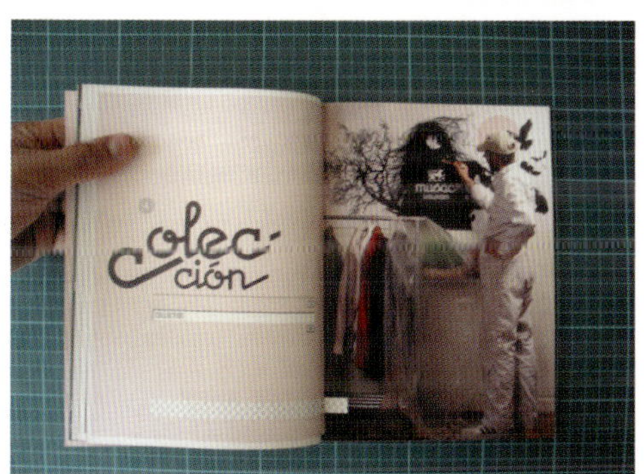
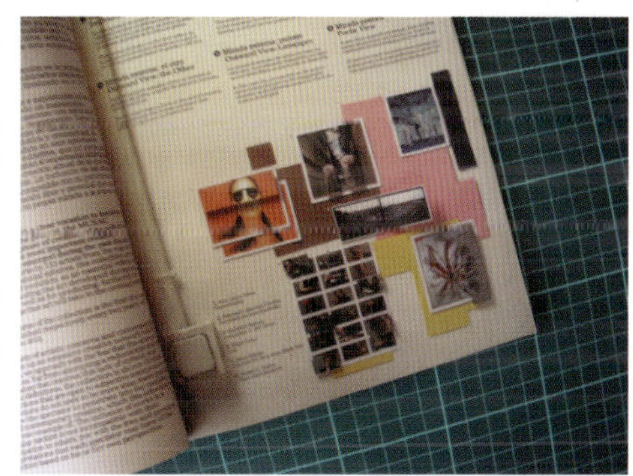
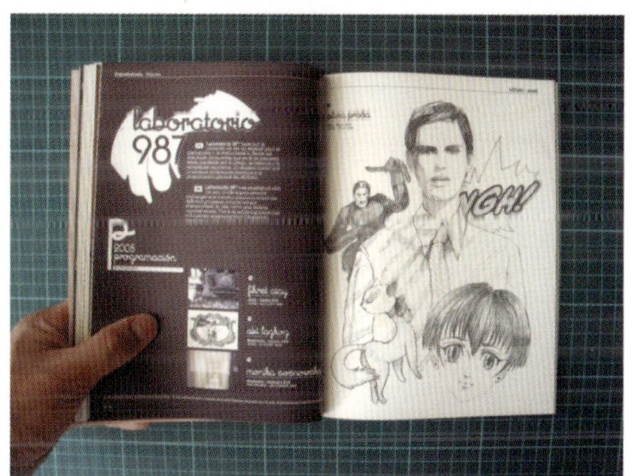
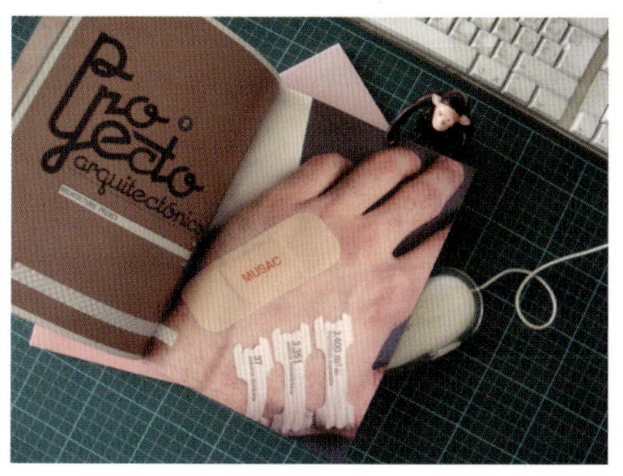
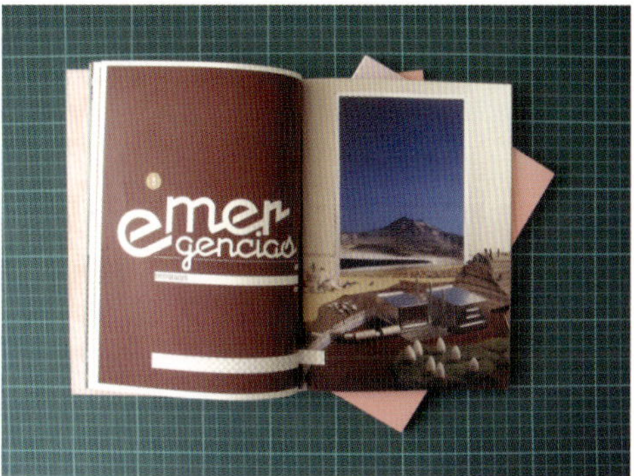
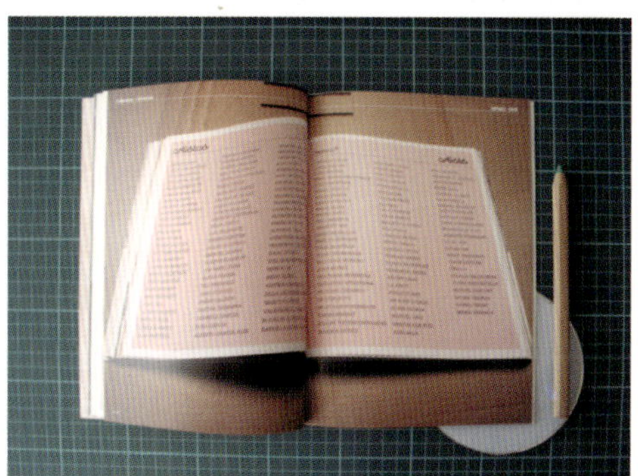

strichpunkt

Stuttgart, Germany

Title: General Directory 2004/2005, Verlag Hermann Schmidt Mainz
Type of work: Directory
Client: Verlag Herman Schmidt Mainz
Design: cd// Kirsten Dietz, Jochen Rädeker ad// Kirsten Dietz d// Kirsten Dietz, Anika Marquardsen
Year: 2004

This book appears every year to coincide with the Frankfurt Book Fair. It is the 'book of books' for graphic designers and advertisers, which, in its own right become a collectors' item. This can be put down in no small part to the regular annual change made to the design of the intermediate pages and cover. With the aid of the finest typography, high-quality cover paper, raised and lowered embossments as well as a variety of heat-seal films, the designers have turned the catalogue into a 'White Album' that lives up to its title 'For the Love of Books' in every way.

Stephen Layfield

New York, USA

Title: Floranova
Type of work: Book
Client: Random House
Design: ad, d// Stephen Layfield
Year: 2004

When photographing flowers the aim was to reduce the image to its purest form, conveying the absolute essence of a bloom or a piece of foliage. This idea of simplicity was key to the design of 'Floranova'. 600 images were distilled to 200, then divided by themes evoking a mood for each chapter. Layfield kept the typography restrained and to a minimum, respecting the balance between producing a coffee table 'art' book and something that was accessible to a larger audience, from the weekend gardener to the Christmas gift market.

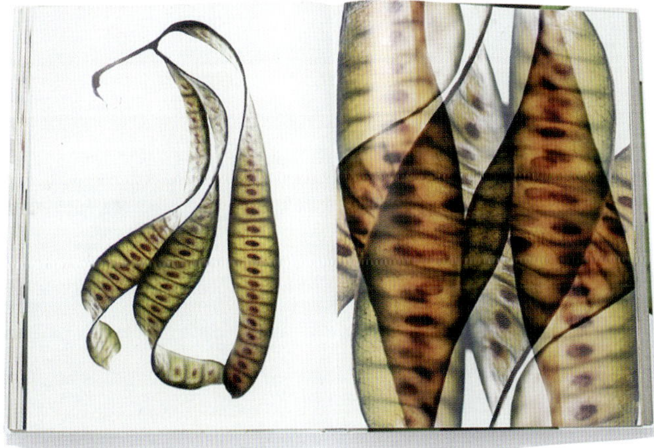

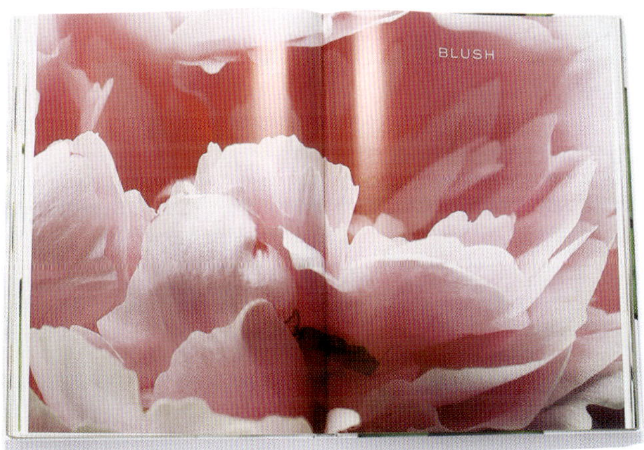

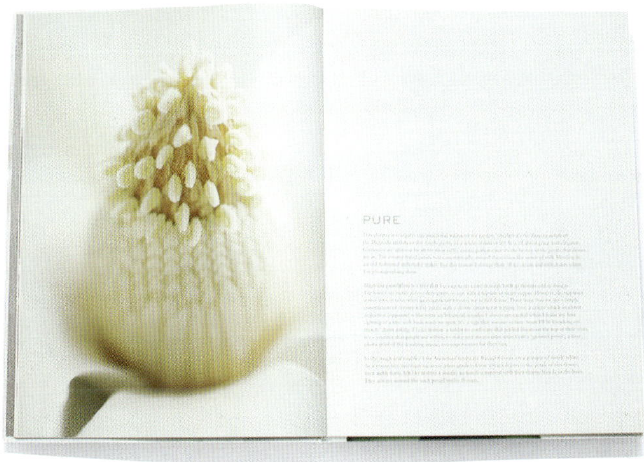

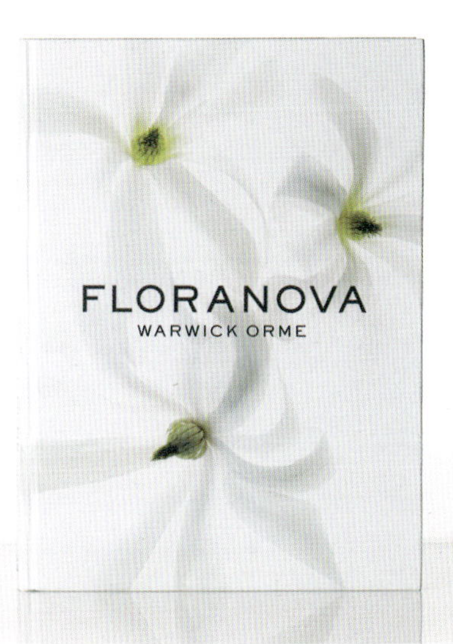

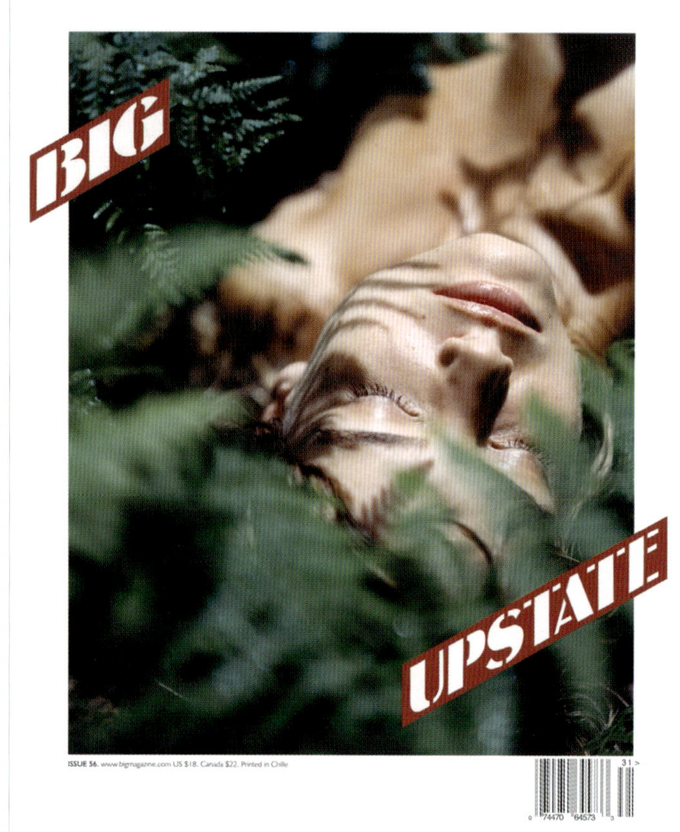

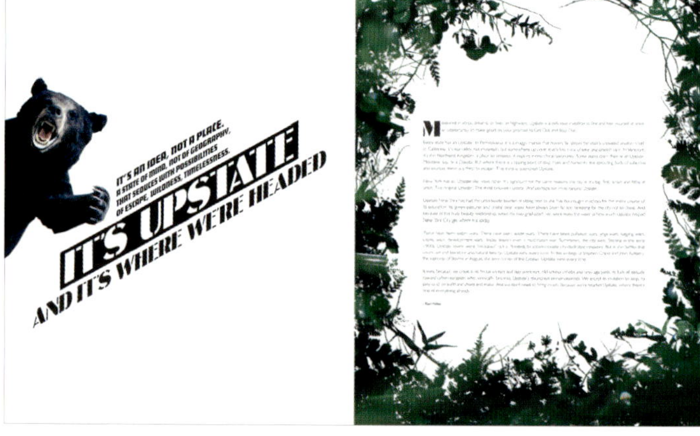

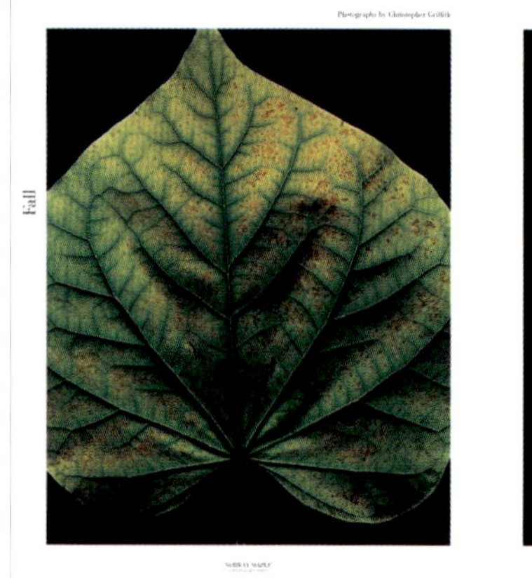

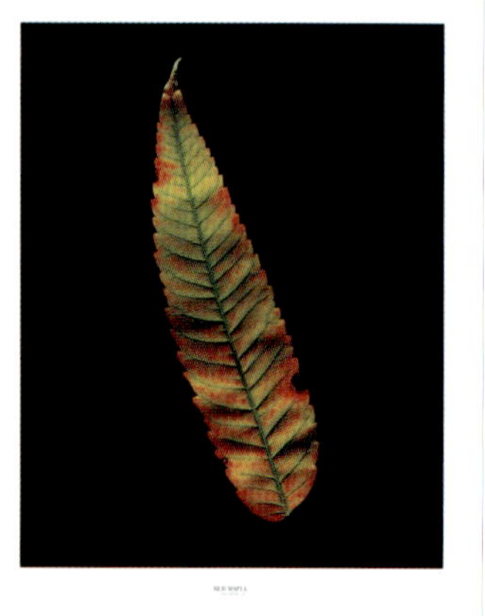

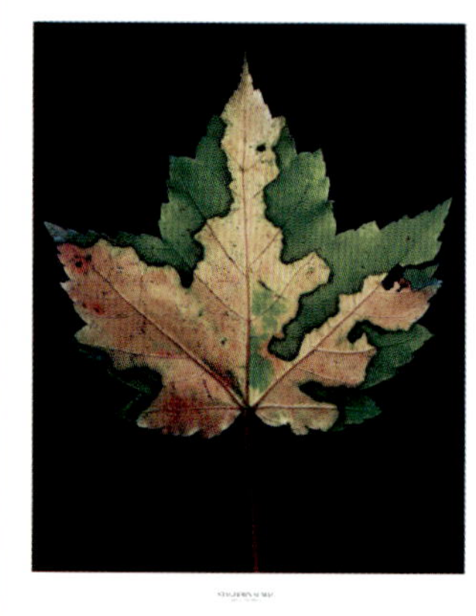

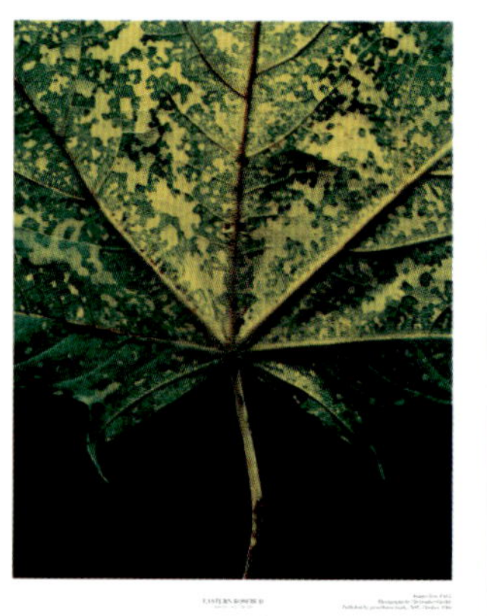

The Fold

New York, USA

Title: Big Upstate
Type of work: Editorial
Client: *Big Magazine*
Design: ad, d// John Codling, Darren Crawforth
Year: 2005

This piece focuses on the visual and cultural identities of countries, places, things and people. By collaborating with top art directors and photographers, The Fold proposed to the *Big Magazine* an issue on Upstate New York. Upstate is an idea, not a place; A state of mind, not of geography, that seduces with possibilities of escape, wildness and timelessness, in which all of that are expressed through the design.

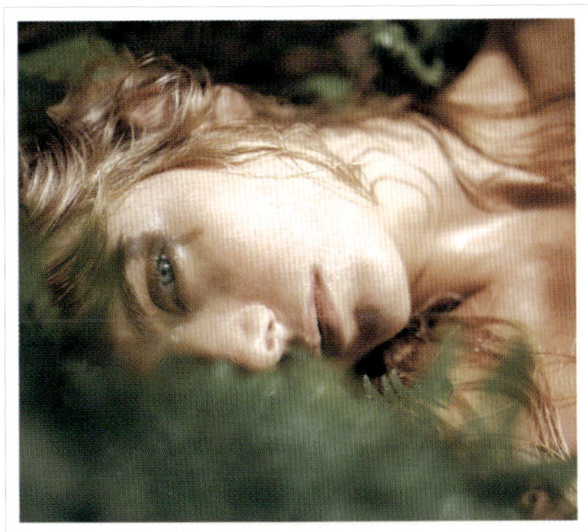

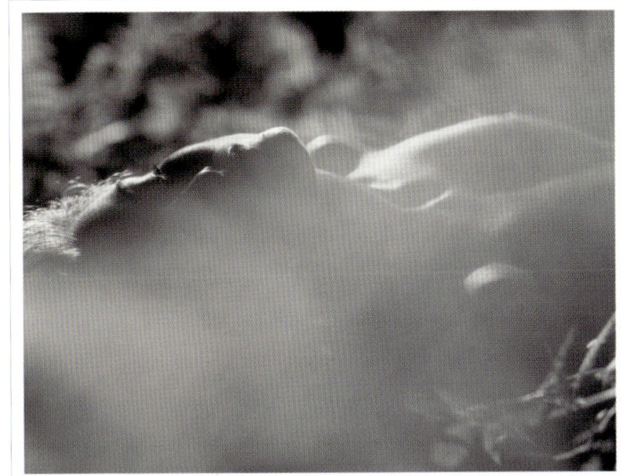

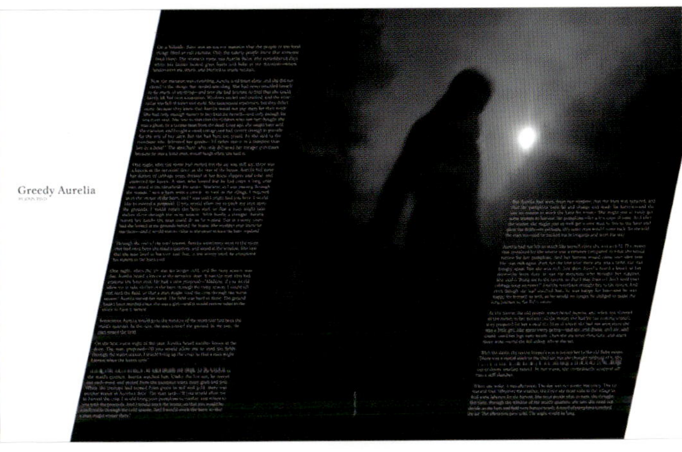

Greedy Aurelia

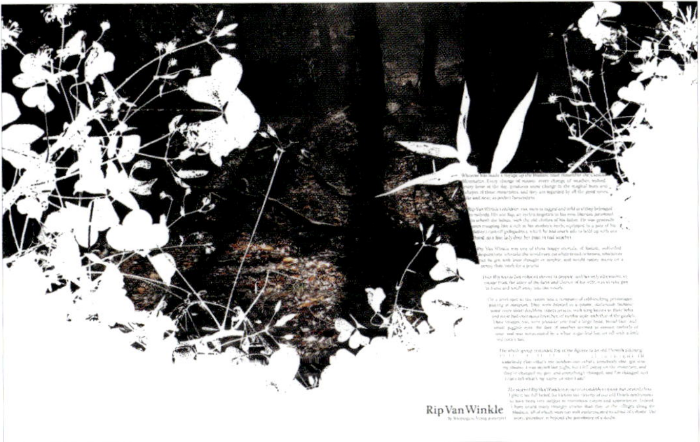

Rip Van Winkle

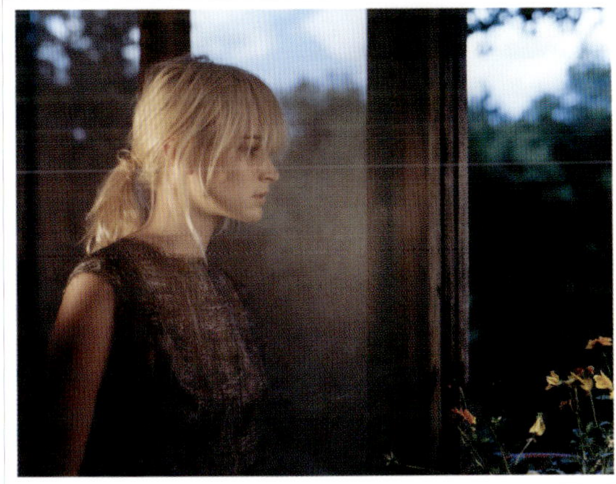

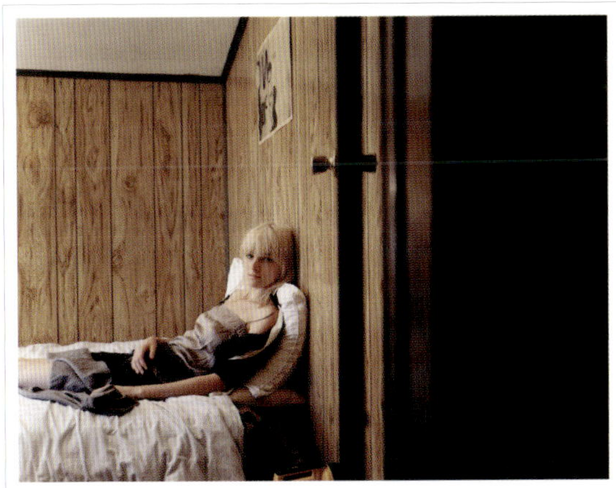

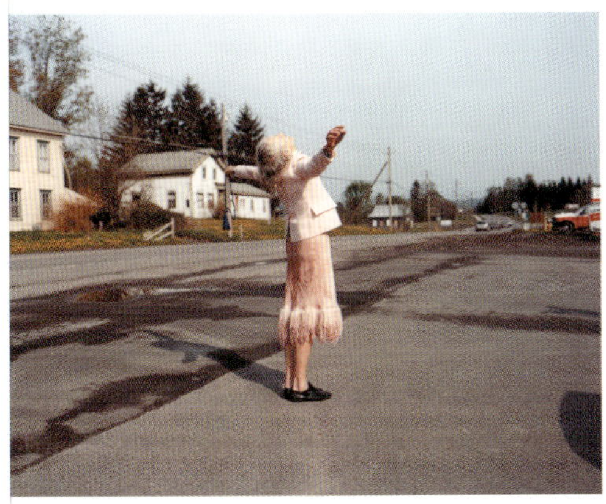

Mother

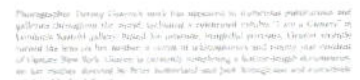

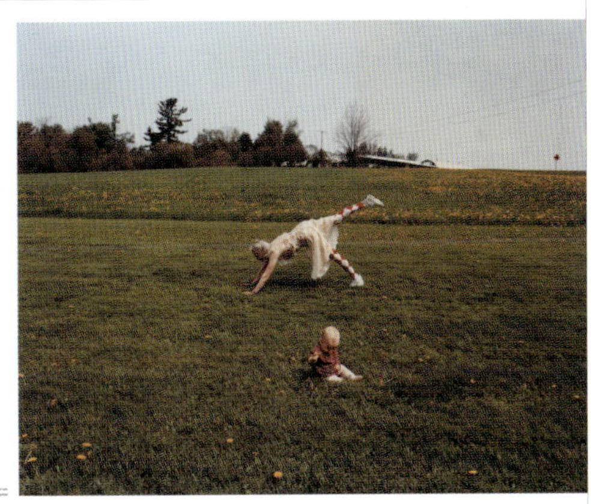

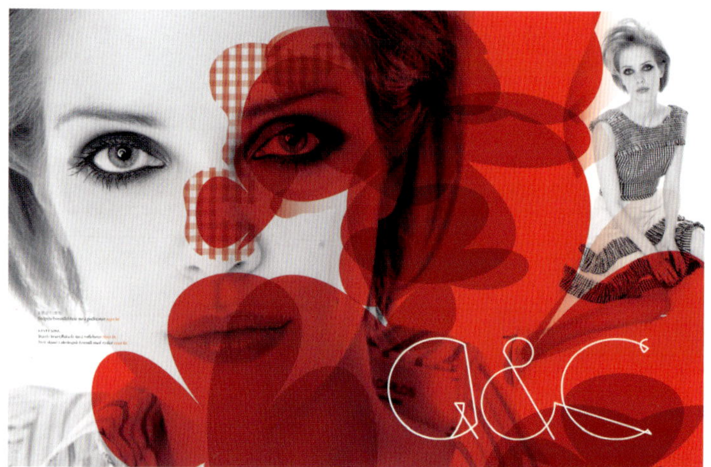

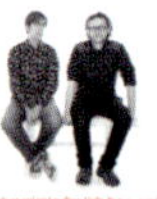

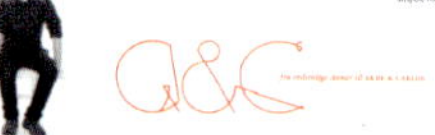

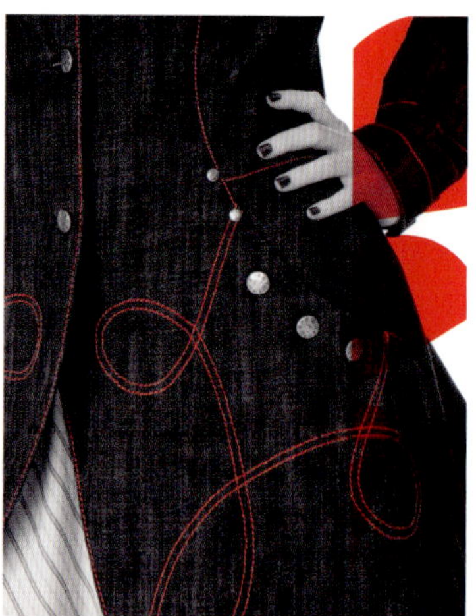

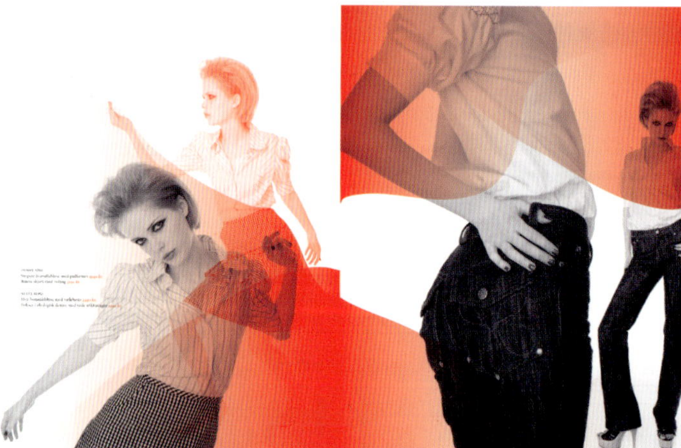

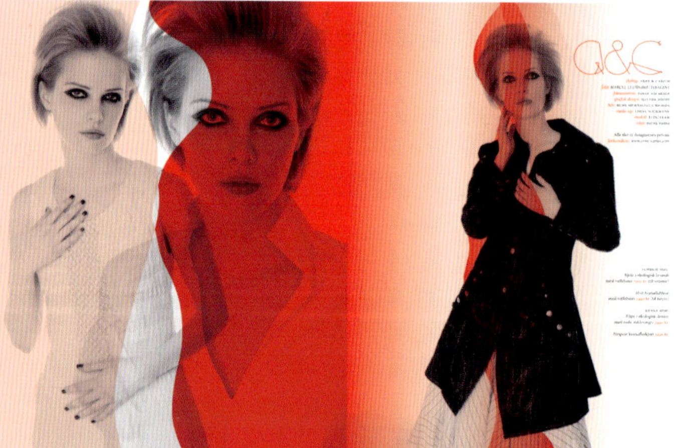

Halvor Bodin

Oslo, Norway

Title: No Magazine
Type of work: Editorial, layout illustration
Client: *No Magazine*
Design: ad, d// Halvor Bodin p// Marcel leliën-
hof, Tinagent
Year: 2005-06

No Magazine decided to use same colour tone for
every spread with transparency with patterns having a hand-written feel, two pages are therefore
look consistant and coherant like a story.

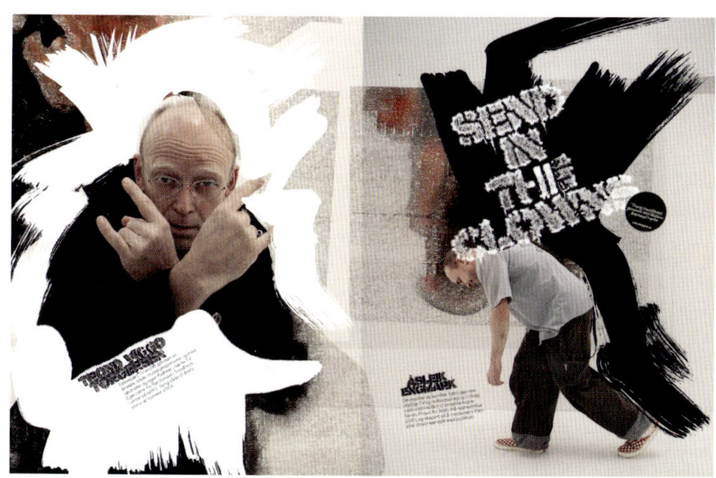

TROND VIGGO
TORGERSEN
SEND IN THE CLOWNS
ASLAK
ENGEBAK

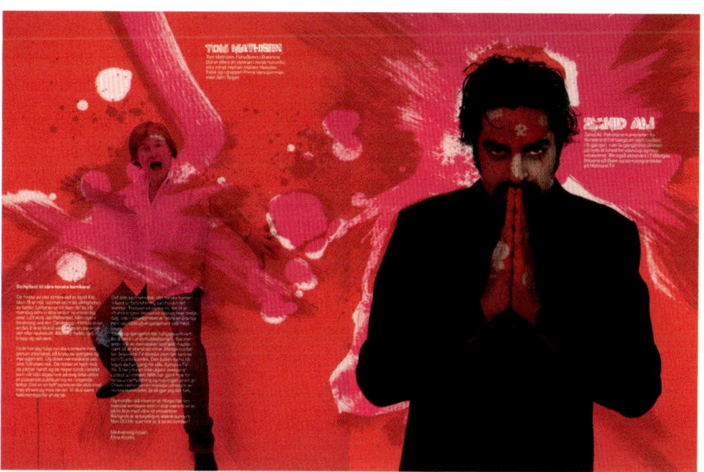

TOM MATHISEN
ZAHID ALI

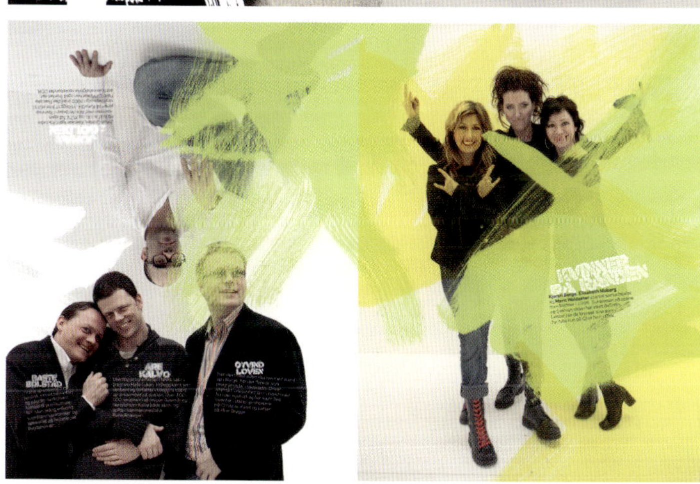

BÅRD
BULSTAD
ÅGE
KALTO
ØYVIND
LOVEN
KVINNER
PÅ KANTEN

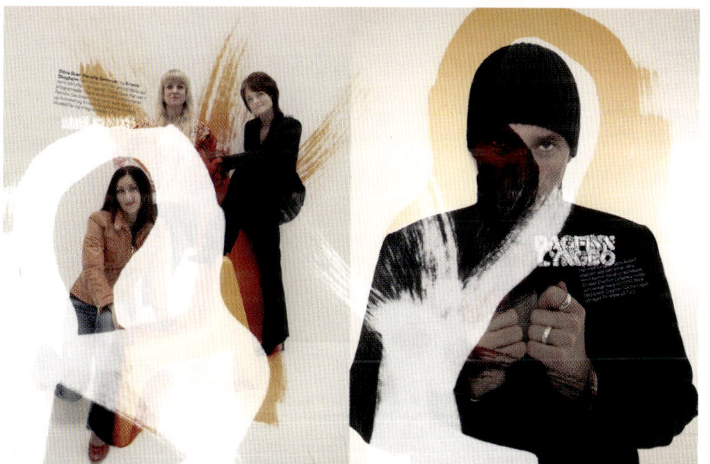

DAGFINN
LYNGBØ

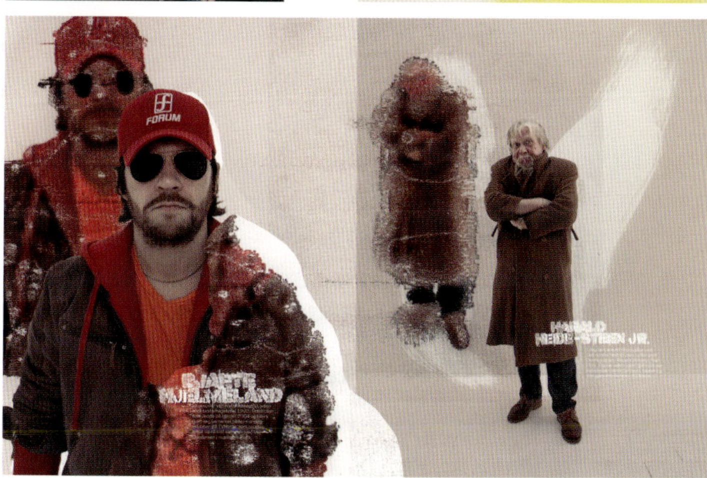

BJARTE
HJELMELAND
HARALD
HEIDE-STEEN JR.

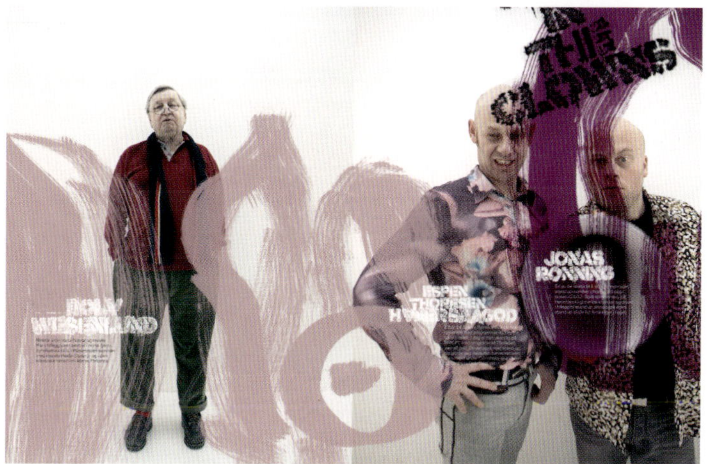

IN
THE
CLOWNS
ROLV
WESENLUND
ASPEN
THORESEN
HVEM ER GOD
JONAS
RØNNING

strichpunkt

Stuttgart, Germany

Title: The Summit Book – Diary 2005
Type of work: Diary, calendar
Client: Papierfabrik Scheufelen GmbH + Co. KG
Design: cd// Kirsten Dietz, Jochen Rädeker
ad// Kirsten Dietz d// Anika Marquardsen,
Stephanie Zehender, Felix Widmaier
Year: 2004

This Book is a journey and calendar. The 72 pages
in the first part, was divided into four chapters –
preparation, ascent, set-backs and attack featuring
a theme of personal highlights for the year. The
second part – the calendar proper, accompanies its
users on every step of their path to their personal
summit with stickers and a mood 'barometer' for
each and every day. It was all printed in outstanding quality using eleven different techniques.

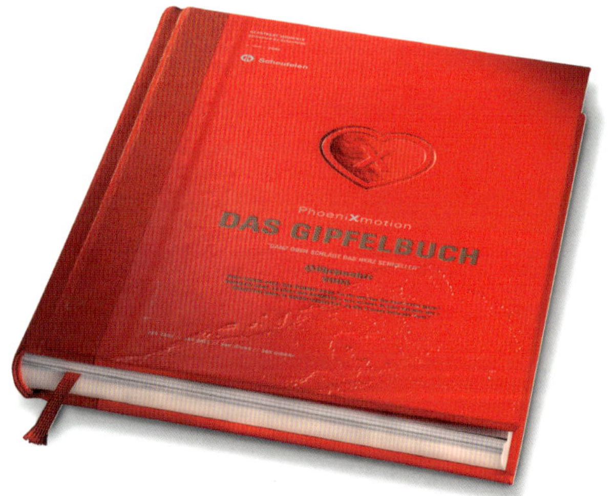

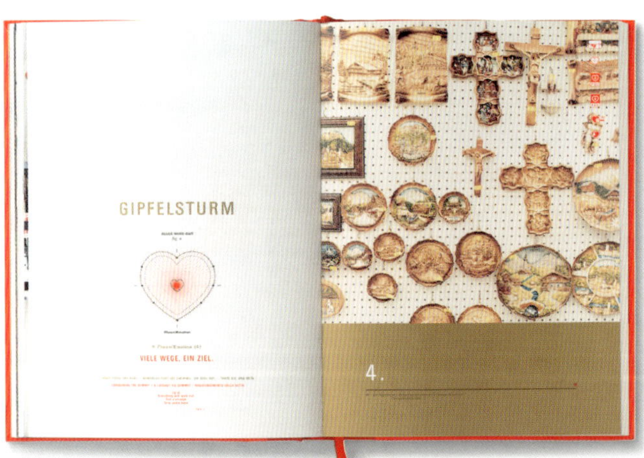

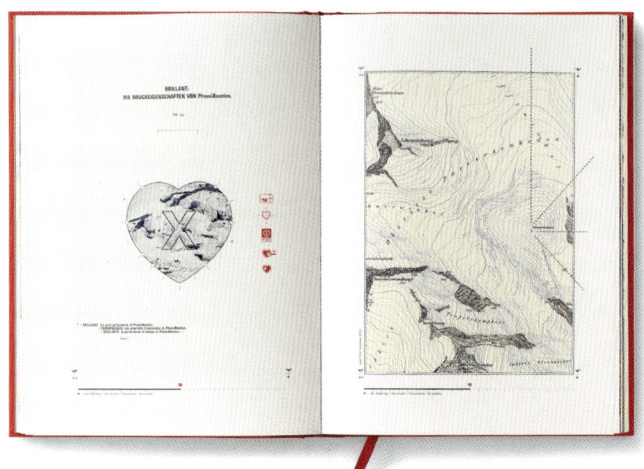

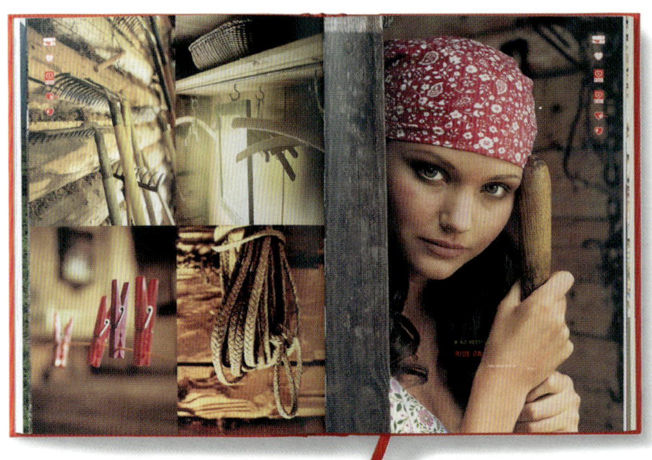

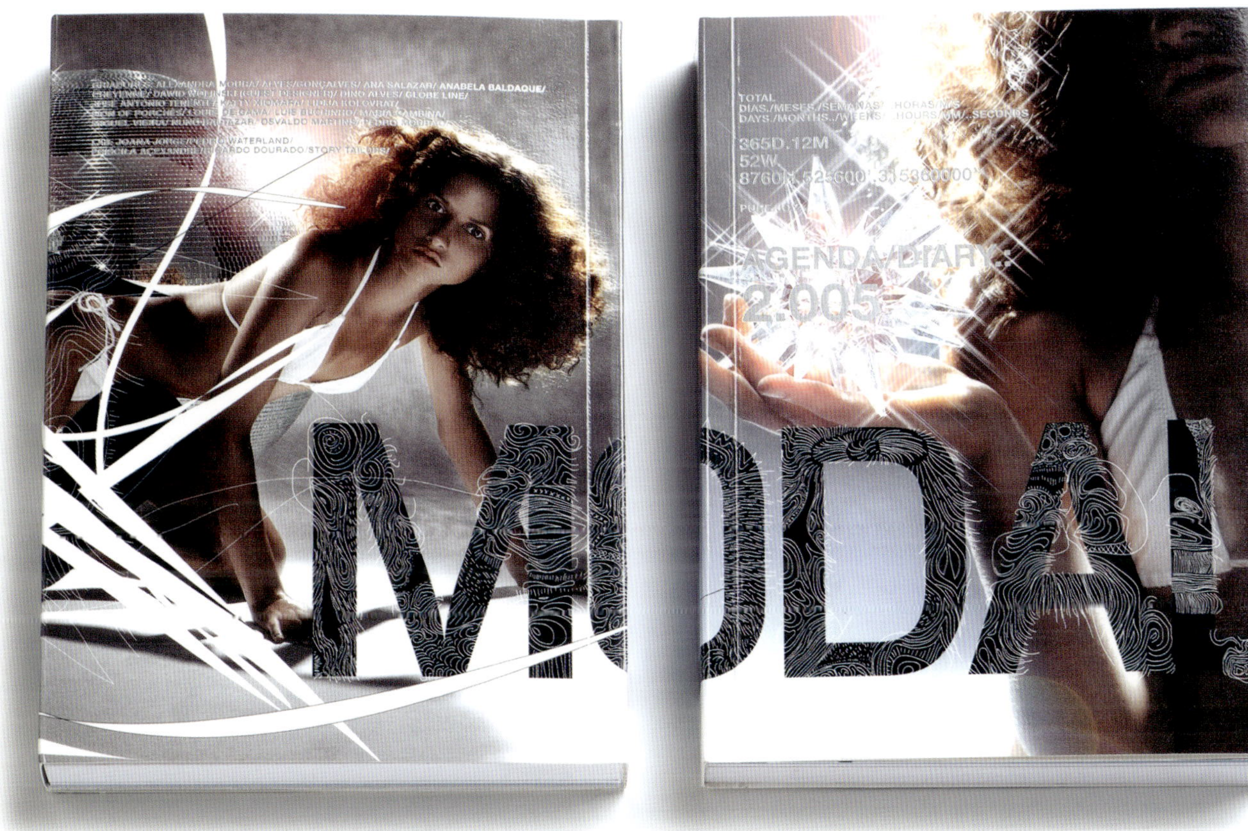

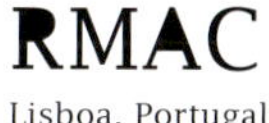

RMAC

Lisboa, Portugal

Title: 23rd Edition Modalisboa: Hi-lights
Type of work: Agenda
Client: Associação ModaLisboa
Design: ad// Ricardo Mealha, Ana Cunha
d// Ana Cunha, Diogo Potes
Year: 2005

The 23rd Edition Modalisboa is covered in elegant and sophisticated images of a bikini girl spot lighted by a star-shaped crystal. The front and back covers is also linked with the word 'MODAL'.

Styl●

London, UK

Title: Metro
Type of work: Book
Client: Philip Xavier Publishing
Design: ad, d// Tom Lancaster
Year: 2003

This book about the world's underground systems has a highly graphical transport signage concept that was implemented as a play on the subject of the book. The book is sealed by a belly band.

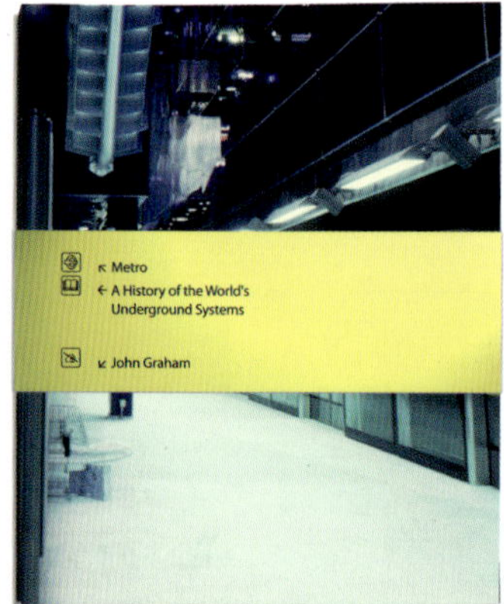

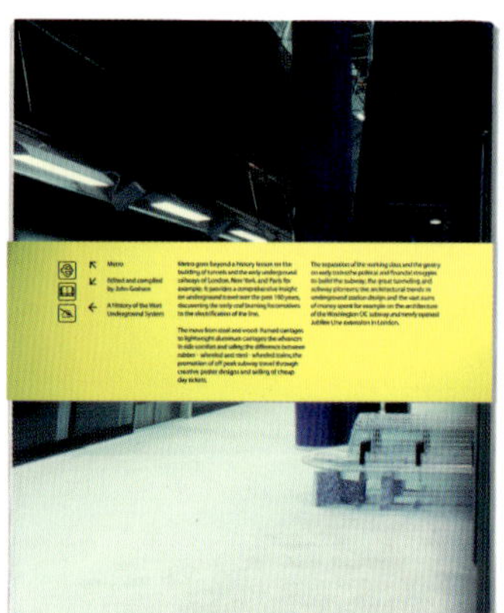

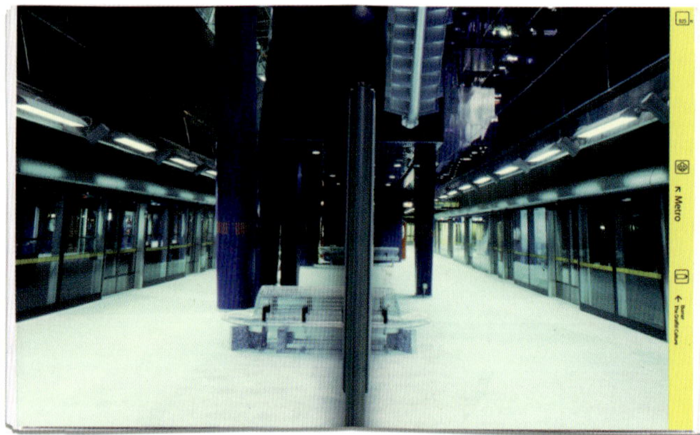

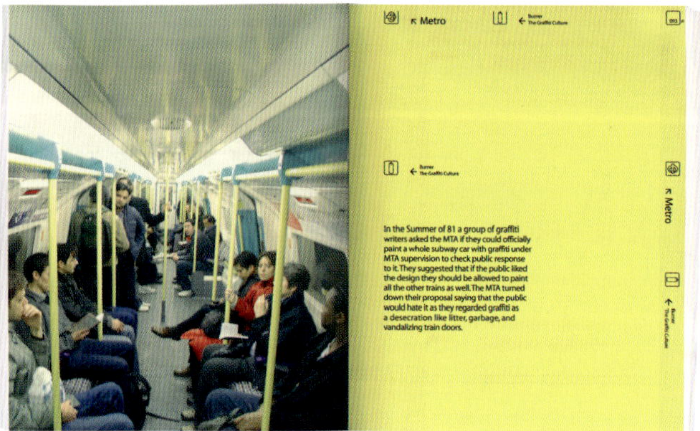

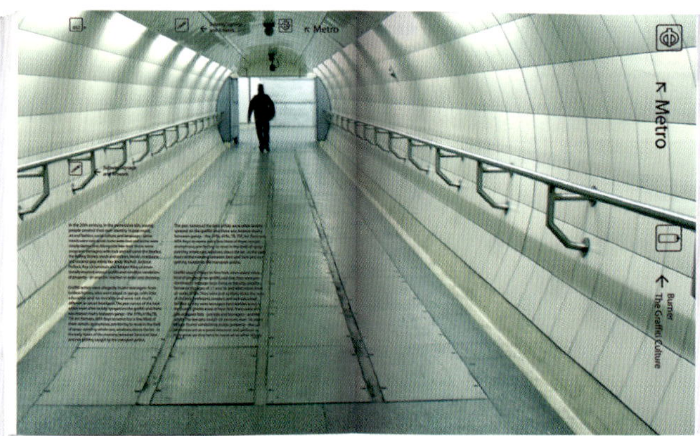

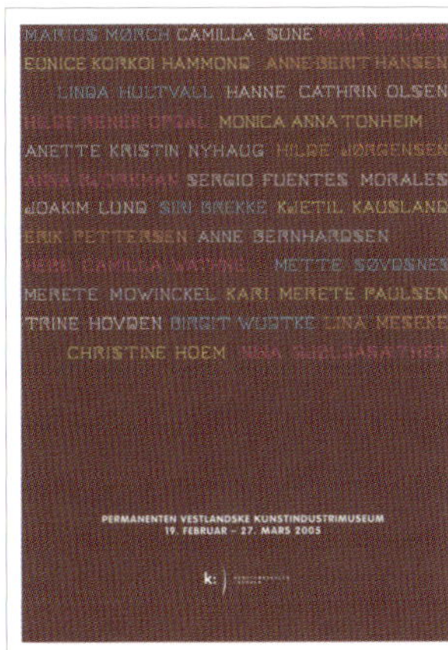
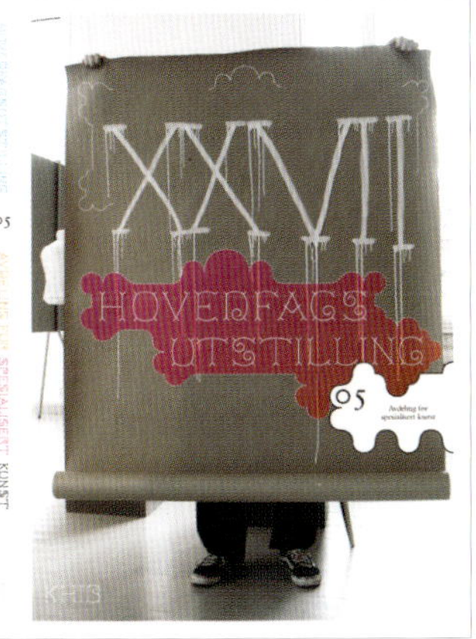
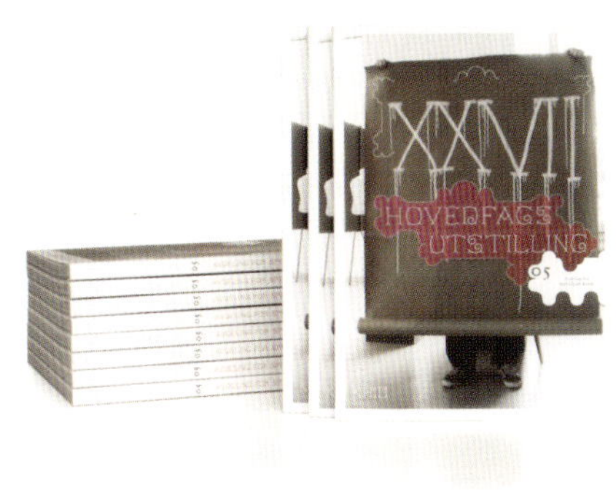

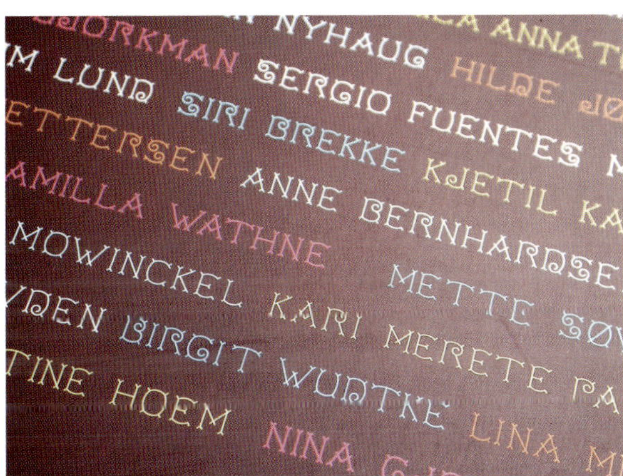
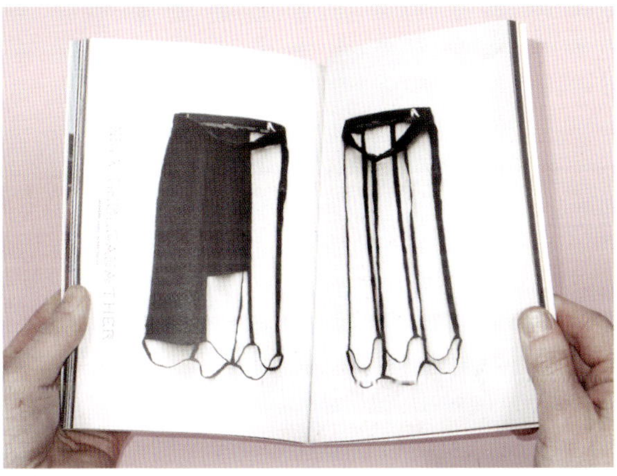

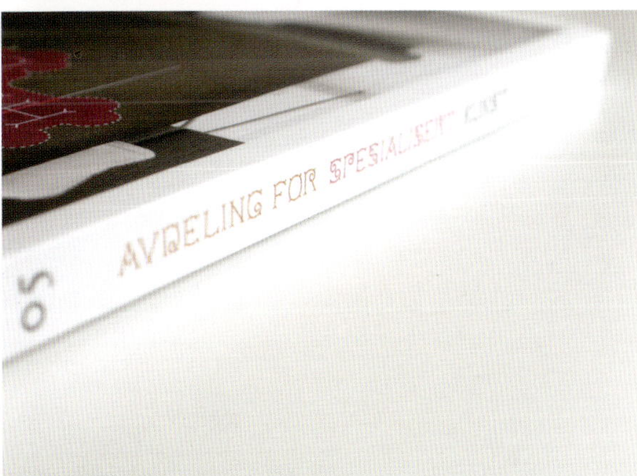
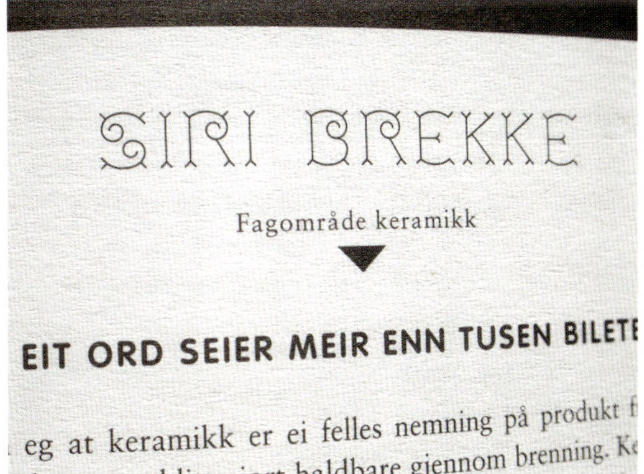

Grandpeople

Bergen, Norway

Title: XXVII – Master Exhibition
Type of work: Catalogue
Client: KHiB - Bergen National Academy of the Arts
Design: ad, d// Grandpeople
Year: 2005

For this catalogue, the challenge was to unify different imagery, as always for any catalogue design. The designers decided to focus on a strong frame which the imagery did not have to be dictated by them, their own type set Maria helped make this possible. This project was in collaboration with Thomas Dybsland.

un**do**boy

Miami, USA

Title: Portfolio Book
Type of work: Book
Client: -
Design: ad, d// undoboy
Year: 2005

The designer's own portfolio book that used rubber bend for binding allows clients to change the content easily based on their preference. A very flexible design.

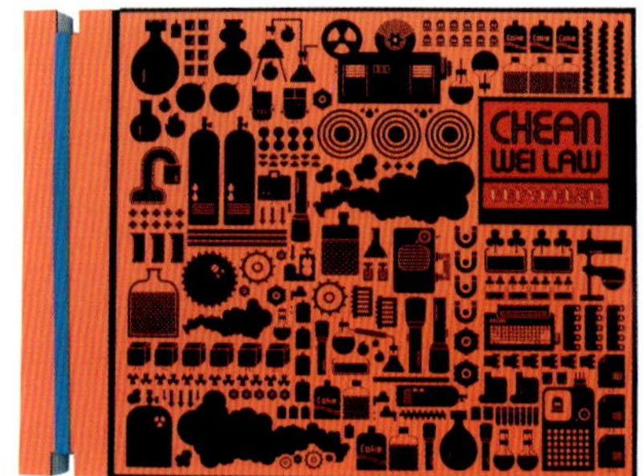

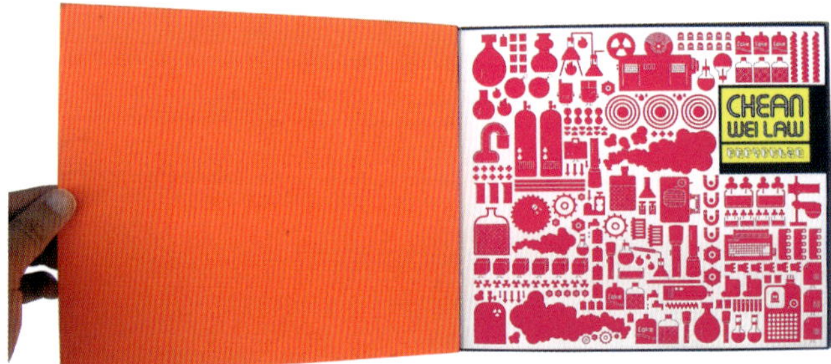

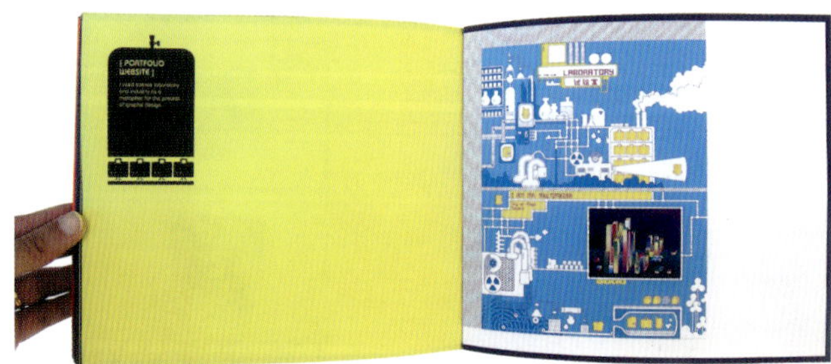

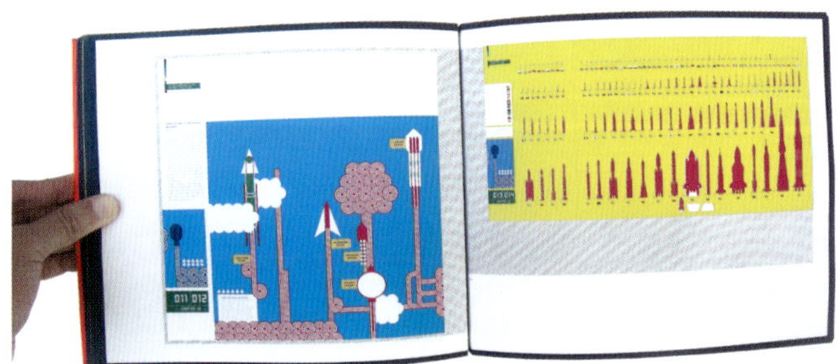

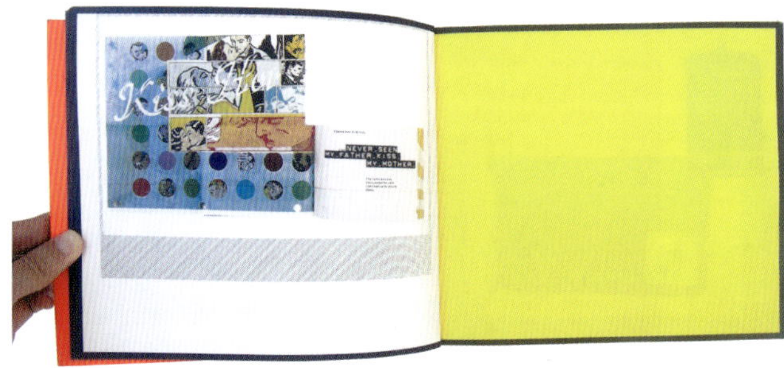

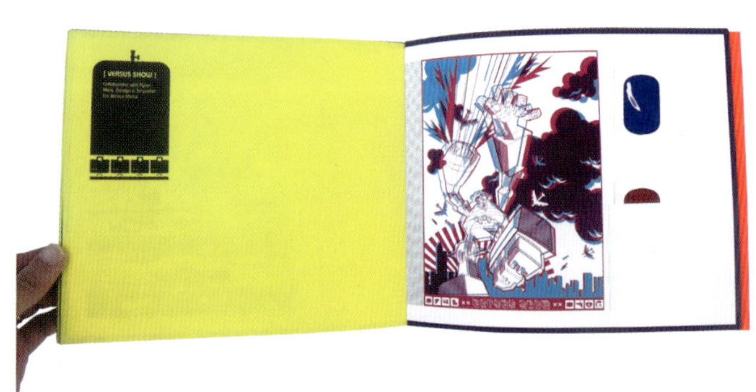

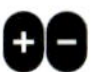

Teresa & David

Stockholm, Sweden

Title: Selma Lagerlöf
Type of work: Editorial
Client: Bonnier
Design: ad, d// Teresa & David
Year: 2005

This is a paper back covers designed for novels by Swedish author Selma Lagerlöf. Working on a tight budget, the designer used the same design for all 5 books, changing just the colour. The overall result gives a strong identity all together as well as separately. Selma Lagerlöf's oeuvre consists of many great novels and it's easy to add a new title in a new colour.

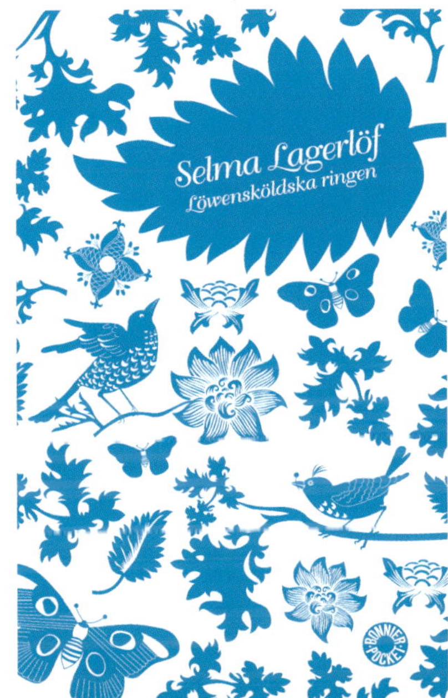

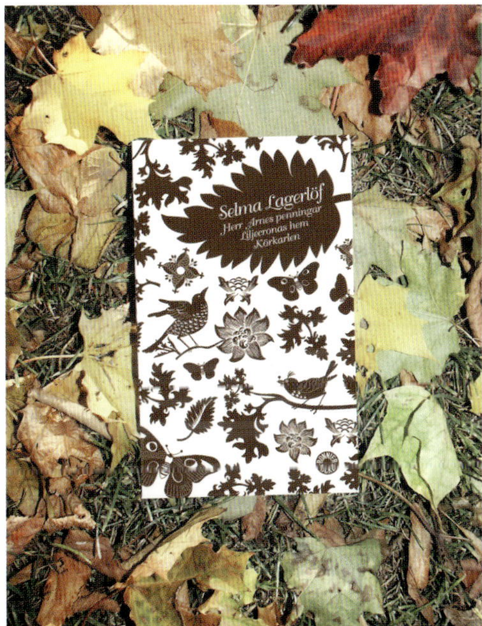

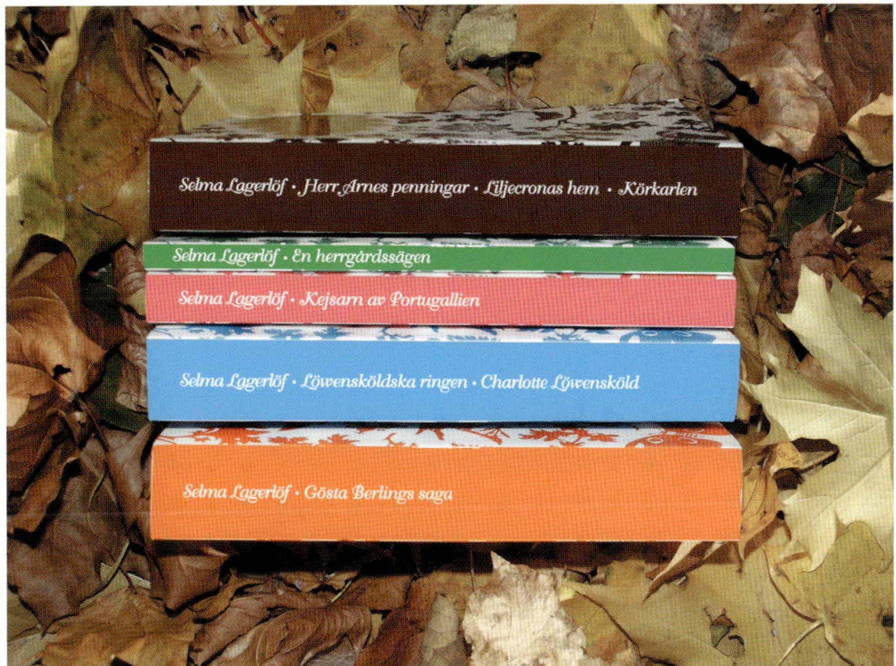

Do what you do every day, just better with a Vespa

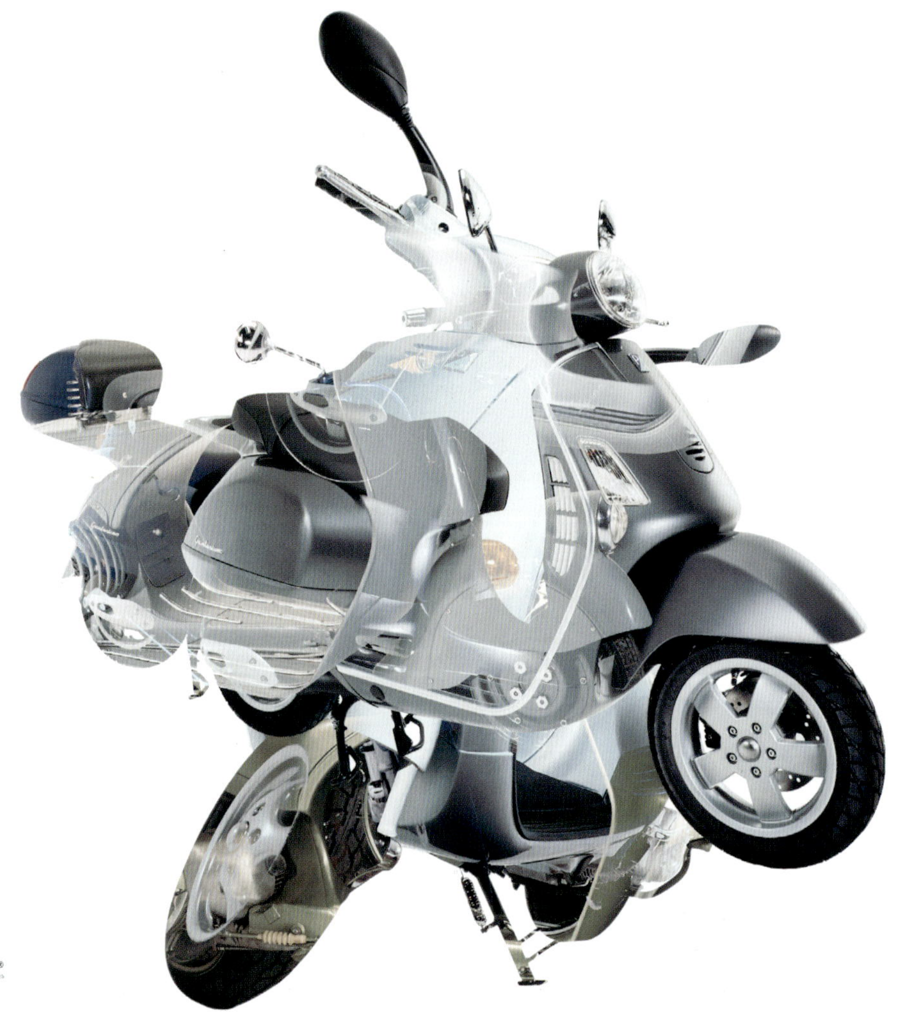

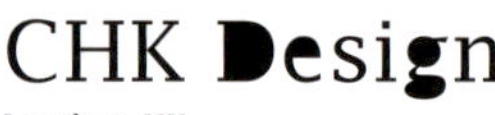

CHK **Design**
London, UK

Title: Vespa Calendar 2005
Type of work: Calendar cover
Client: Vespa
Design: cd// Evelyn Kim ad// Christian Küsters
Year: 2005

This piece illustrates the real-life values of the world's favourite scooter: style, individuality and freedom for everyone. The team has created a wholly international piece of work intended to connect with Vespa's worldwide audience. The cover is a digital collage which shows how the classic Vespa still informs and influences today's designs.

Milkxhake

Hong Kong, China

Title: FAB Magazine
Type of work: Identity, magazine
Client: FABRICA, Italy
Design: ad, d// Milkxhake, FAB Creative Team
Year: 2005

A magazine published quarterly by FABRICA, the Benetton Research and Communication centre in Italy. It is the result of different people, cultures and experiences that met by chance in FABRICA. The magazine is not for sale and it circulates among people in creative industry worldwide. Milkxhake tried to avoid too much information on the magazine's cover. The logotype is simply printed on both front and back cover vertically with Spot UV. It keeps a neat and strong image of the cover.

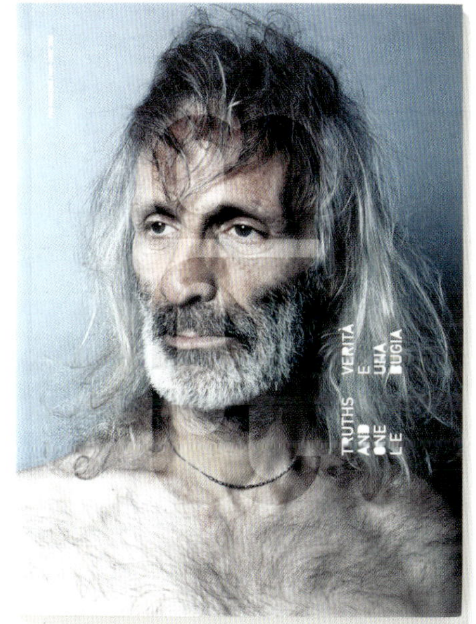

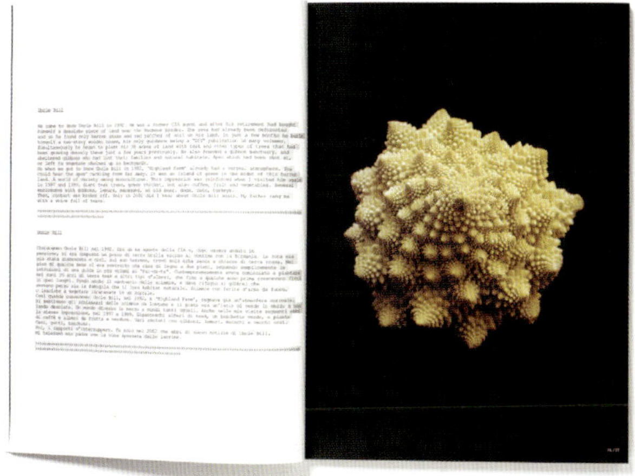

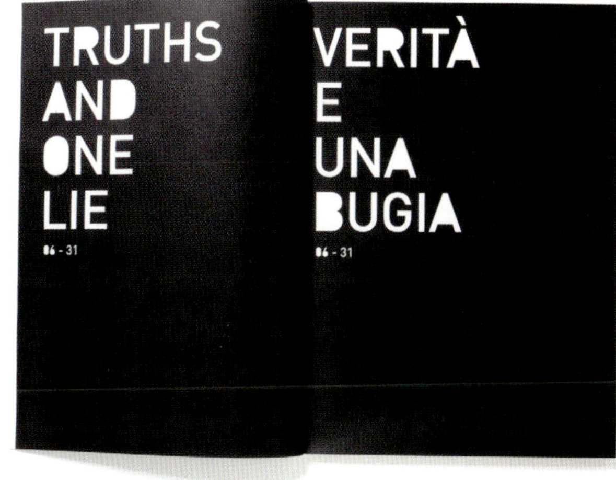

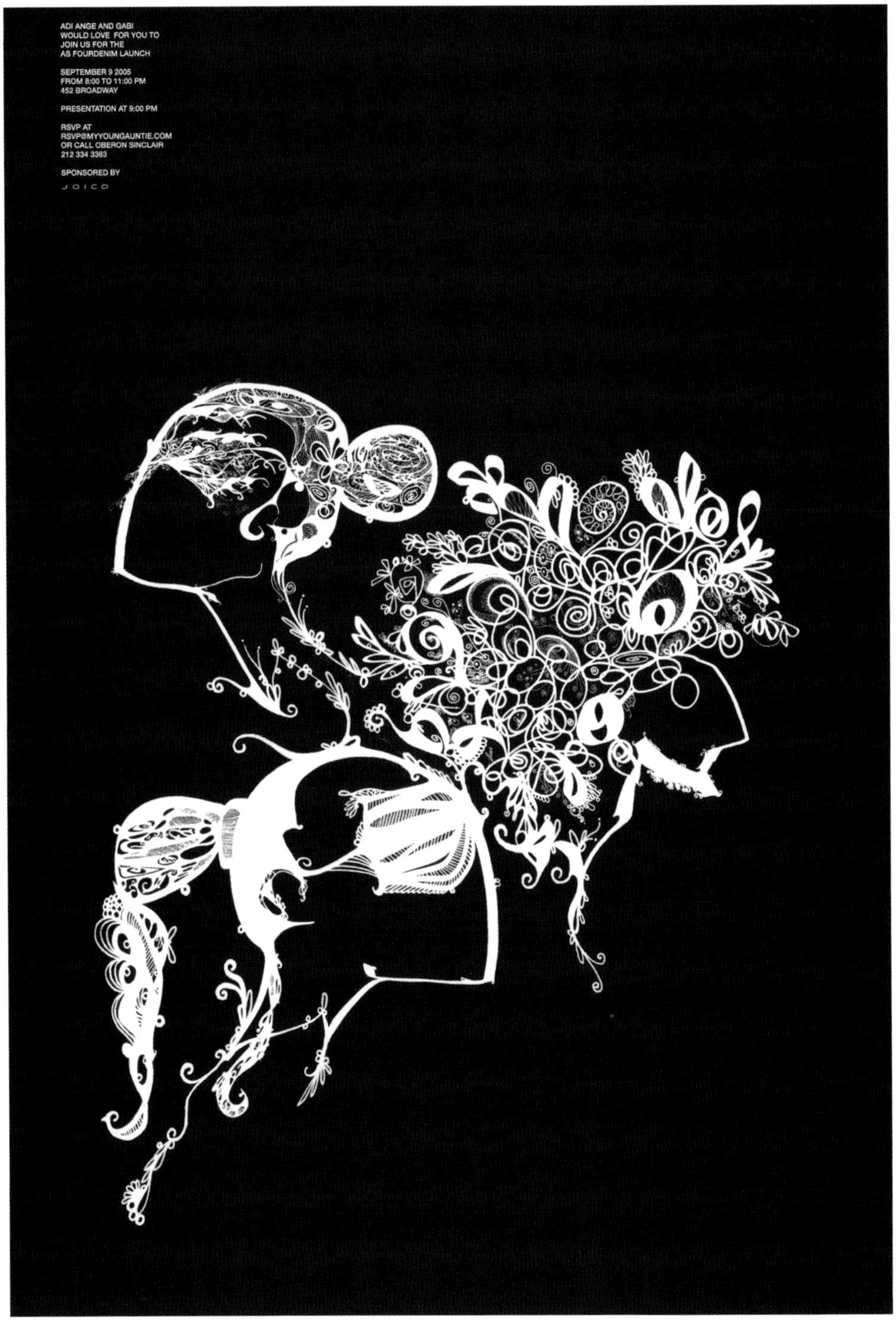

Stiletto

New York, USA

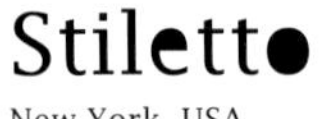

Title: As Four
Type of work: Invitation, poster, packaging
Client: As Four
Design: ad, d// Stiletto
Year: 2004-05

White outlines with plants/flowers elements which forms two shapes of lady head with hair in just plain black as the background, this design gives a sophisticated and feminine feel to the self-promotion items of As Four. It will be used for different collaterals include invitation card, poster and packaging.

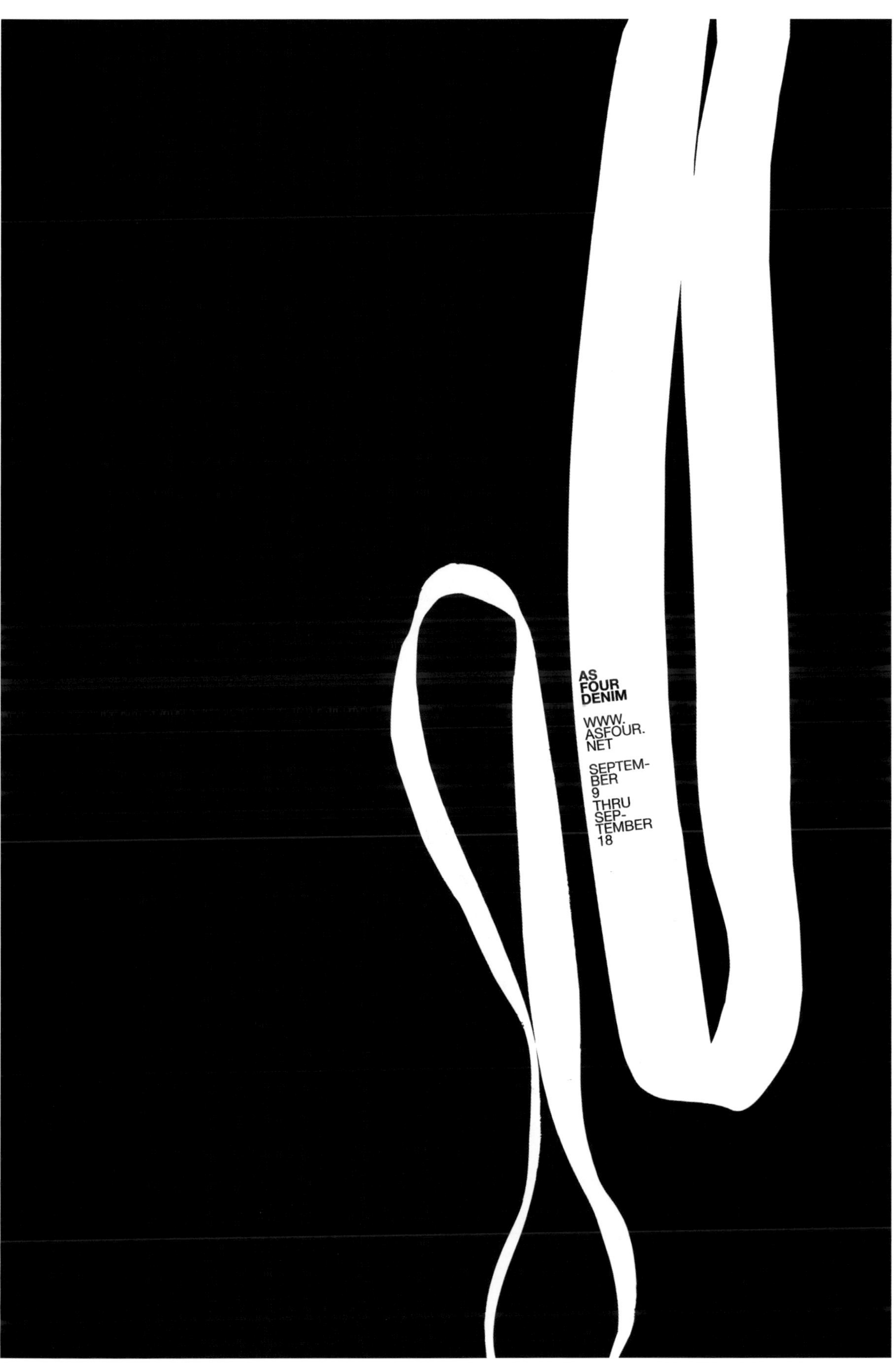
AS
FOUR
DENIM

WWW.
ASFOUR.
NET

SEPTEM-
BER
9
THRU
SEP-
TEMBER
18

RMAC

Lisboa, Portugal

Title: New Year's Invitation
Type of work: Invitation
Client: Lux Frágil
Design: ad// Ricardo Mealha , Ana Cunha
d// Ana Cunha, Diogo Potes
Year: 2004

A promotional item designed for the most important New Year's party happened in the Lux/Frágil. A Ball of Masks where the guests could not come masked since the mask was drawn and produced by Portuguese artist and creators especially for this event. The invitation is a colourful mix of shapes, a mask and a face.

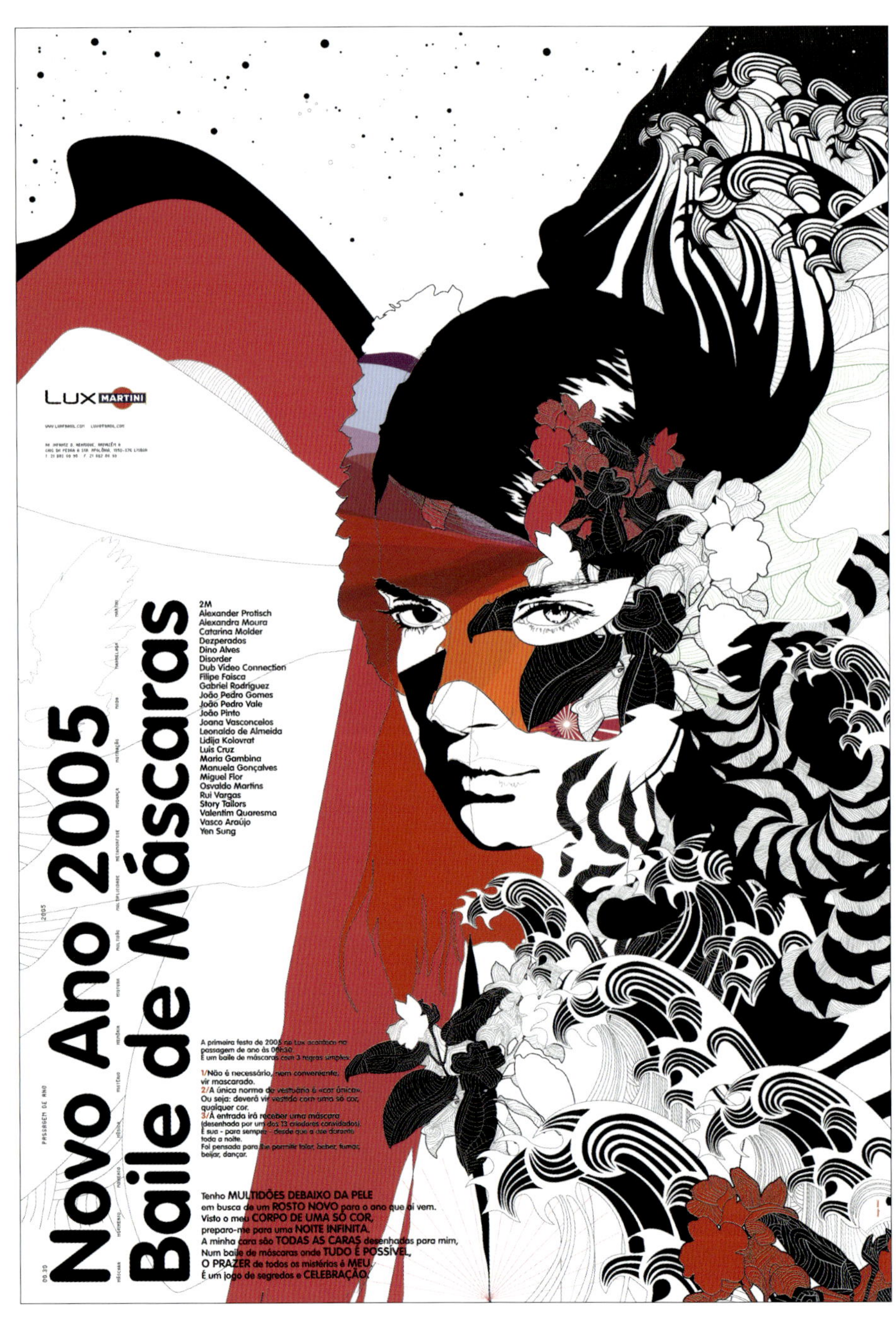

Medusateam

Spain

Title: New Year's Invitation
Type of work: Poster
Client: Ajuntament of Poal
Design: ad, d// Ajuntament of Poal
Year: 2005

A promotional item designed for New Year's party that held by Ajuntament of Poal. With illustration of old time music player, film projectors and a DJ, plus information in old fashioned font types, the poster shows you a preview of the expected party.

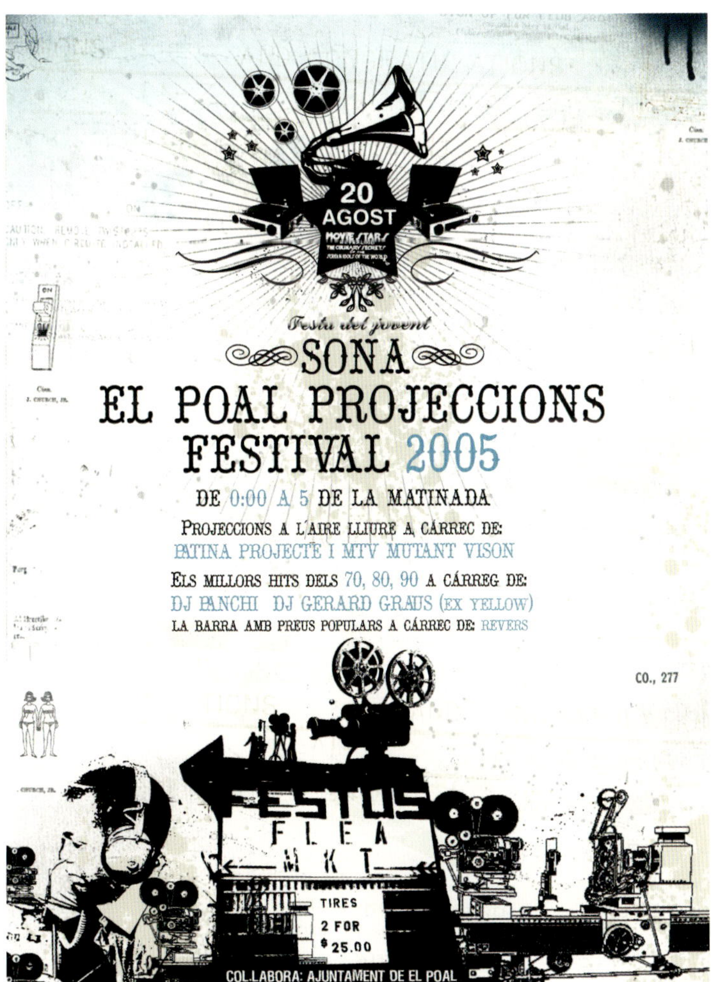

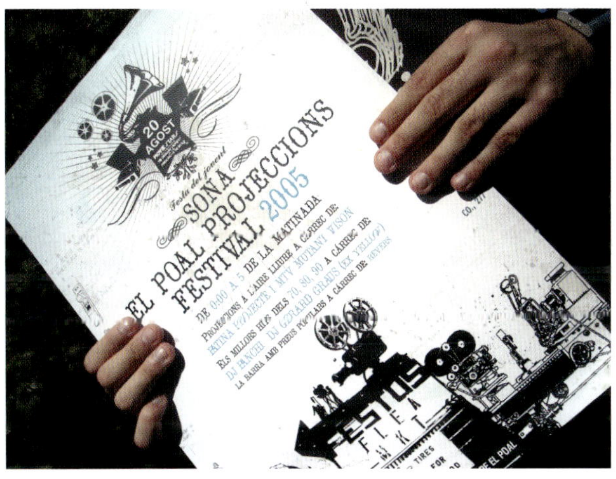

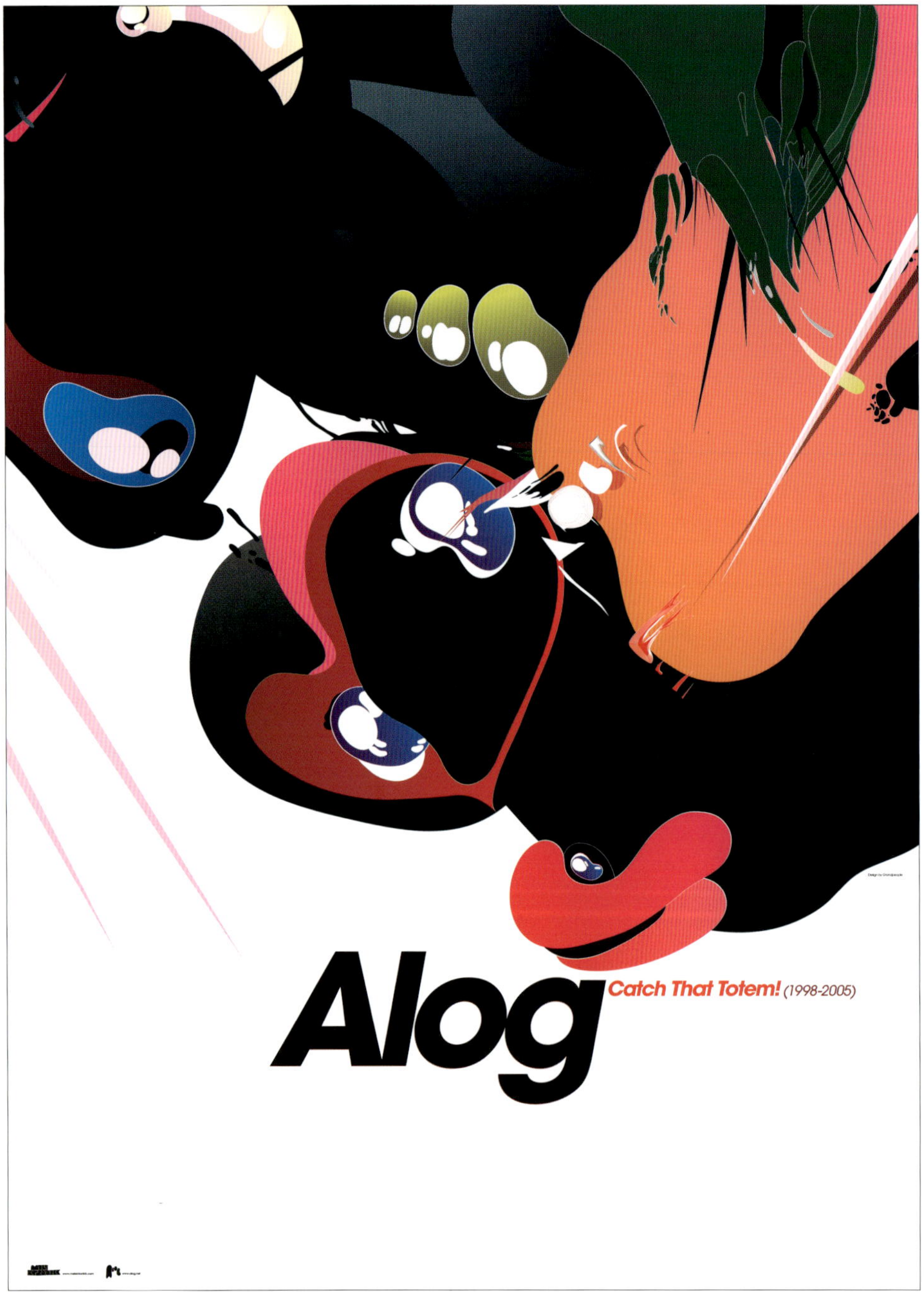

Gran**dpeo**ple

Bergen, Norway

Title: Alog – Catch That Totem
Type of work: CD Sleeve
Client: Melektronikk
Design: ad, d// Grandpeople
Year: 2005

A CD sleeve design for the highly acclaimed electronic band, Alog, who had set their aims for a release with old, new and unreleased materials from 1998 to 2005. Just like the music, they wanted to visualize the contrast. Words like "evil", "bubble gum" and "summer" was mentioned in the artwork. It turned out to be something that belongs to a twisted manga universe.

Serial Cut™

Madrid, Spain

Title: Freezer
Type of work: Flyer, poster, VIP access card
Client: Freezer Morning Club
Design: ad, d// Sergio del Puerto
Year: 2005

The picture was a combination of the two concepts: electronic music and a fresh environment with plenty of vegetation, that define Freezer®, the open-air morning club after the FIB (Festival Internacional de Benicassim) in the summer of 2005. The reflections and the aseptic set give a sophisticated feel, in line with the club's avant-garde sound.

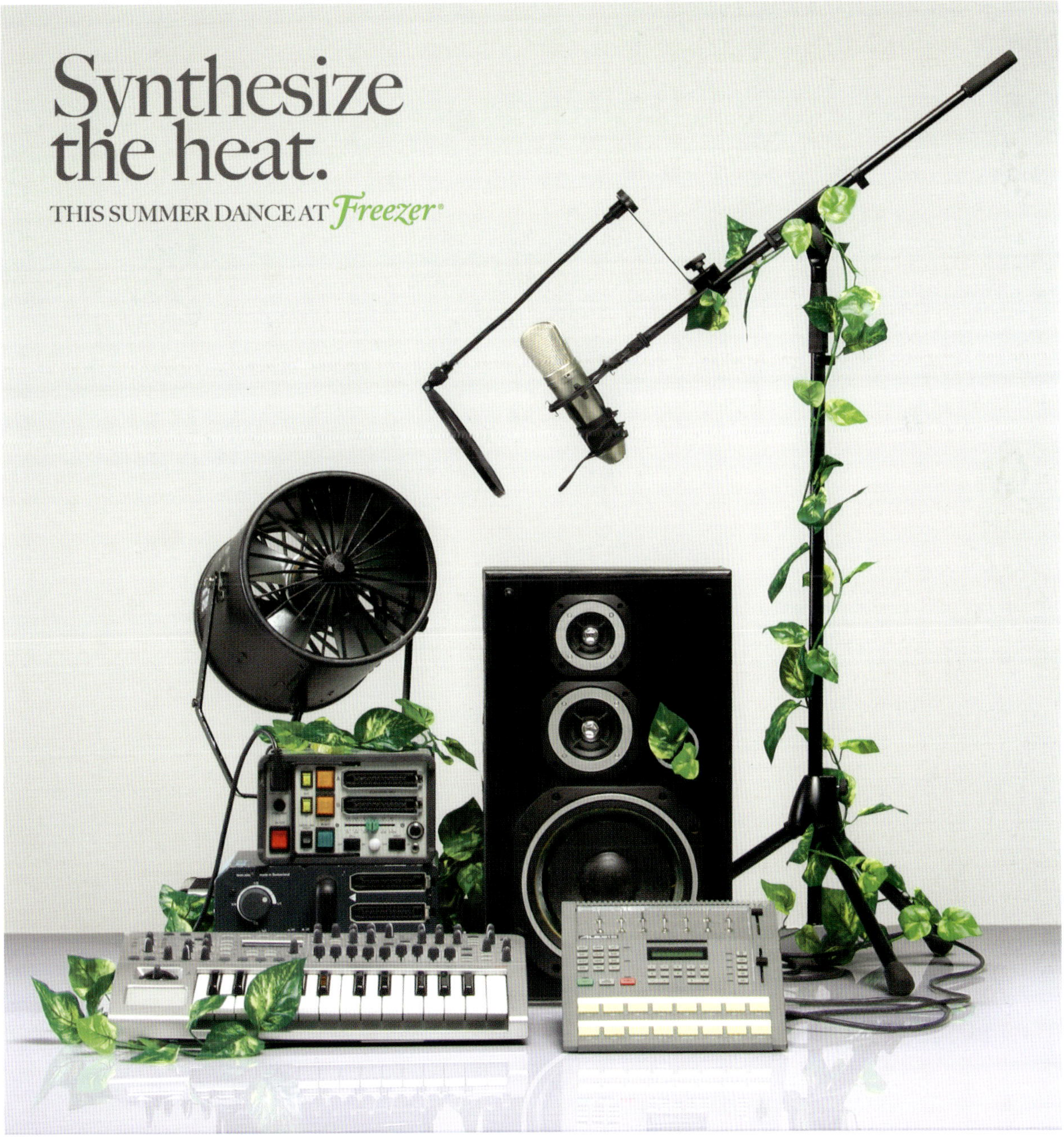

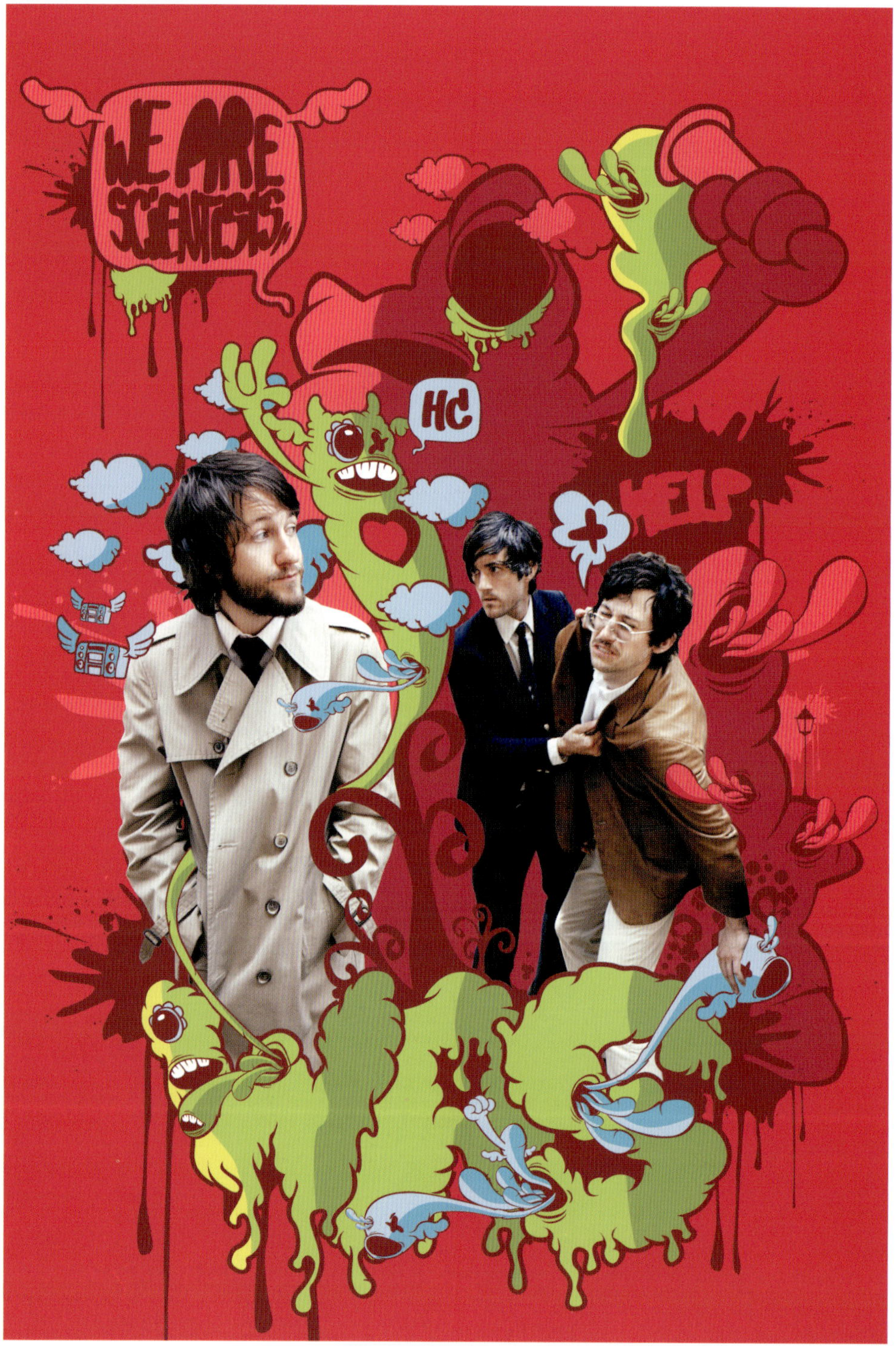

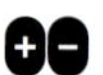

Paulo Arraiano

Cascais, Portugal

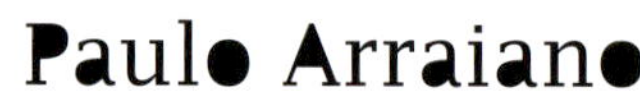

Title: W.A.S (We Are Scientists) Fused !!!!
Type of work: Editorial illustration
Client: *Fused Magazine*
Design: ad, d// Paulo Arraiano
Year: 2005

This editorial illustration for Fused Magazine show a feel of mixing nature beings and science with united illustration of birds and fishes and photographs of 3 humans on a illustrated hell-like, full of monsters and bloody background.

Electroclandestino

Portugal

Title: Abstract Natural Forms
Type of work: Single Spread Design
Client: Abstract Natural Forms
Design: ad, d// David Carvalho aka Electroclandestino
Year: 2005

This piece cellebrating the 2º anniversary, is featured in the book and on its future identity.

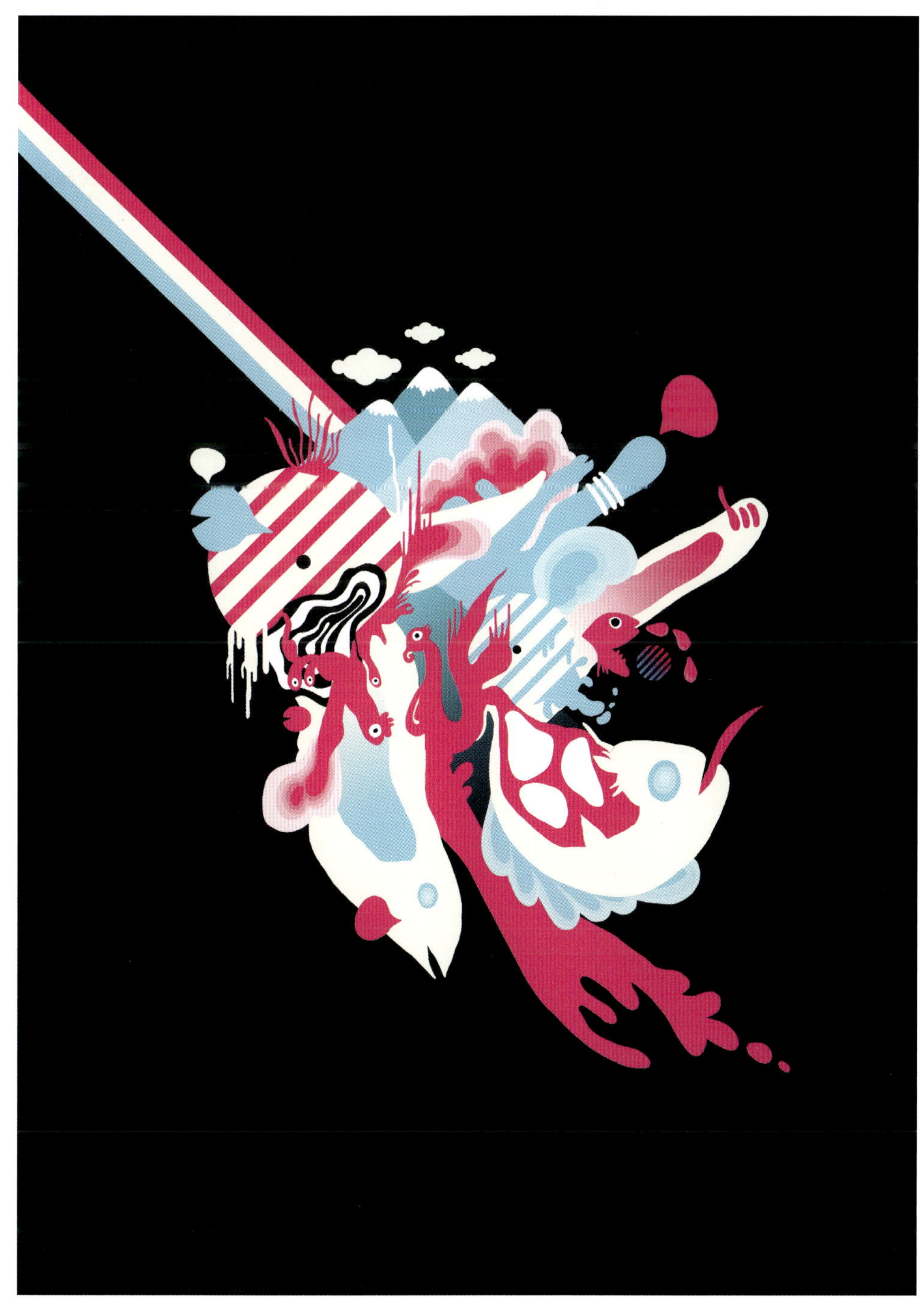

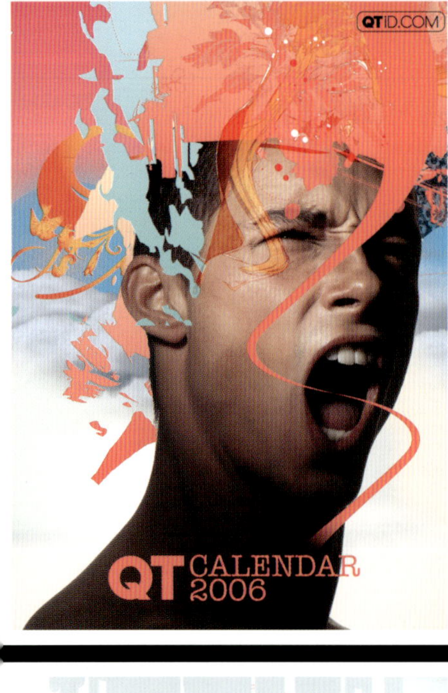

QTID.COM
QT CALENDAR 2006

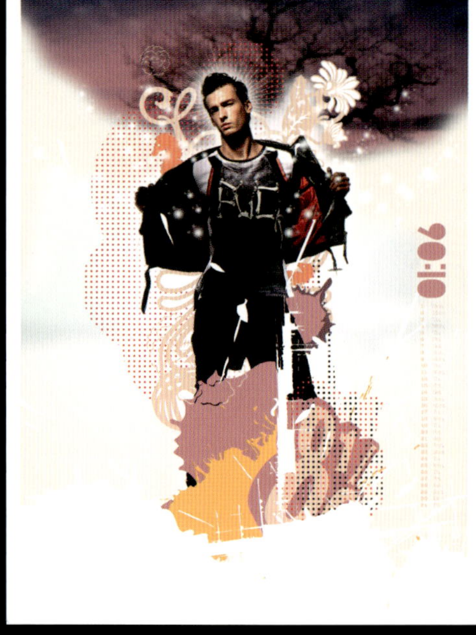

01:06

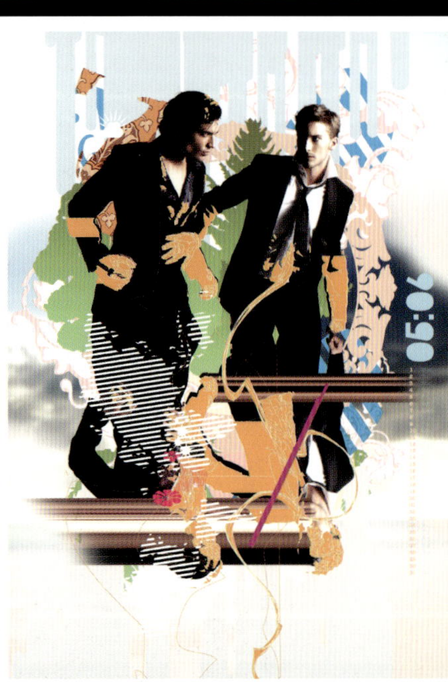

05:06

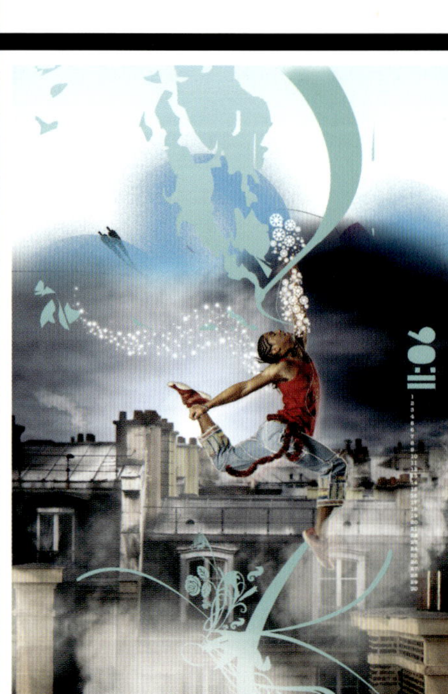

11:06

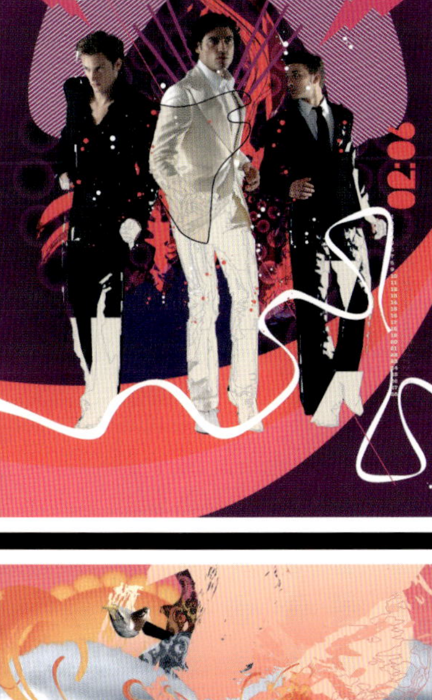
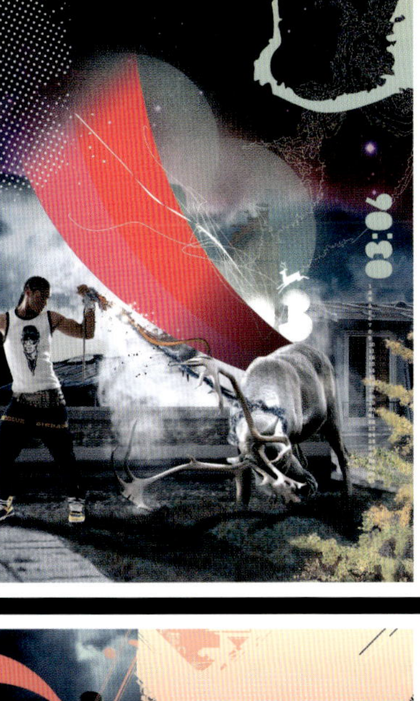
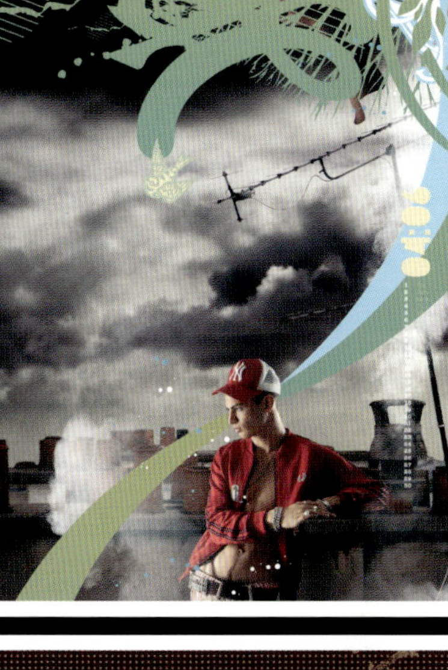
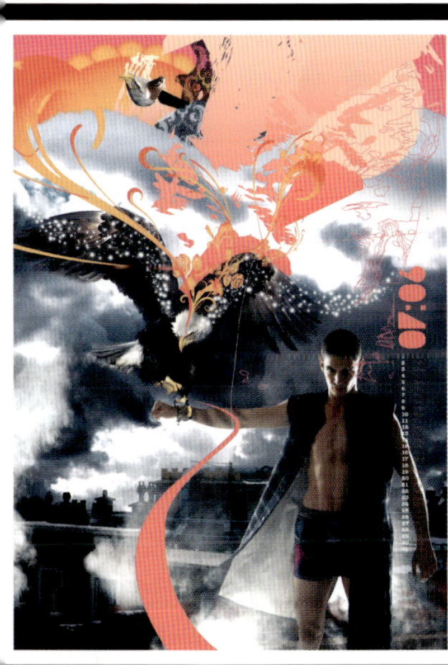
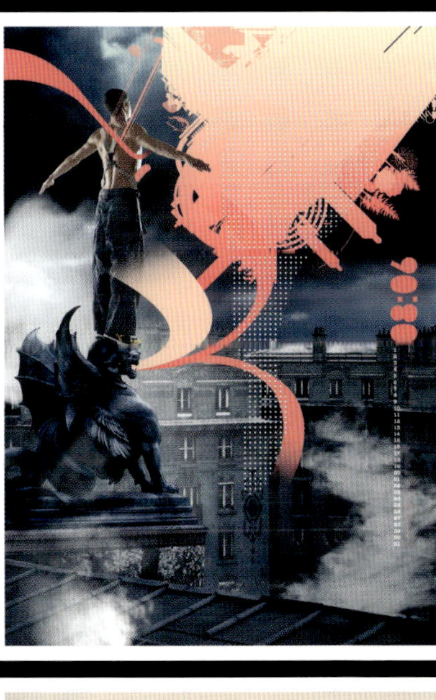
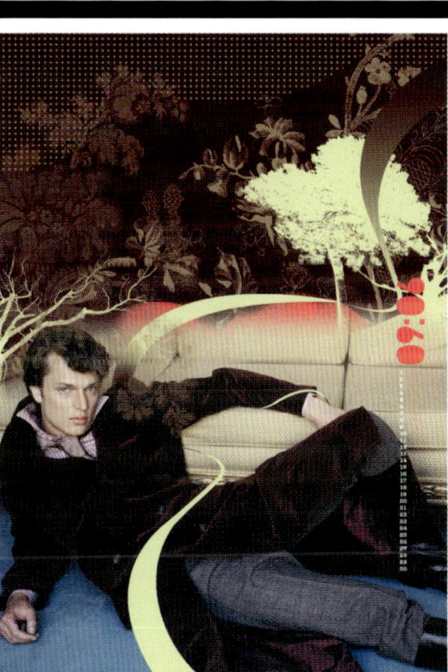
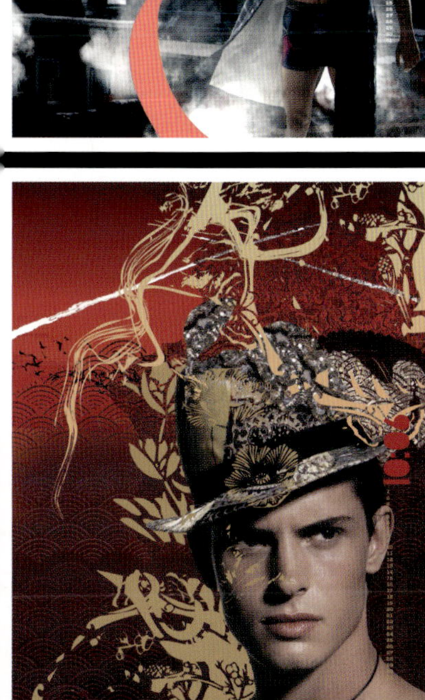
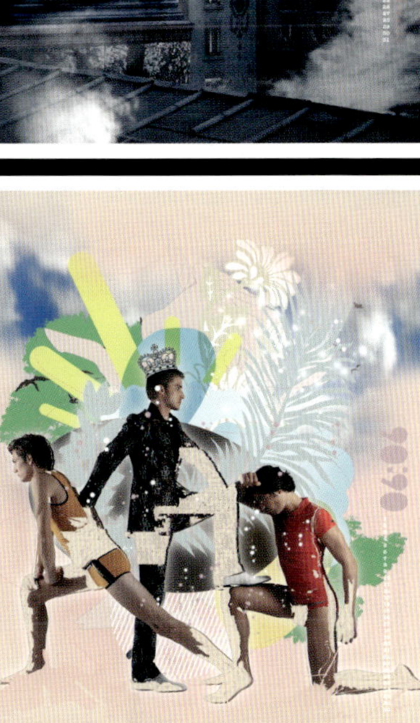
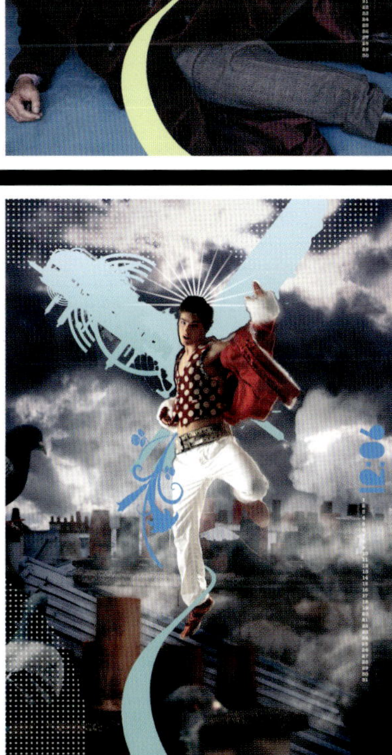

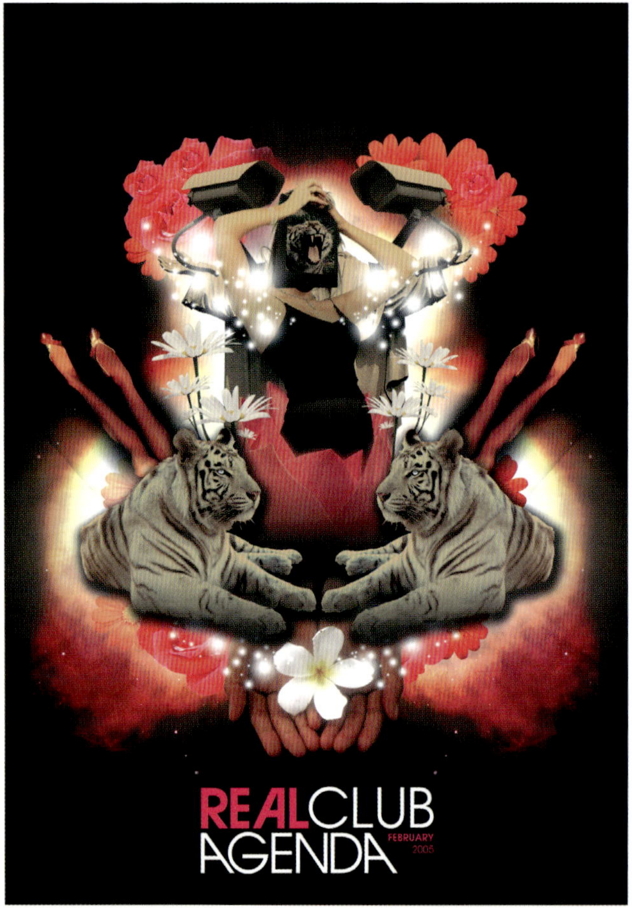

REAL CLUB
AGENDA
FEBRUARY
2005

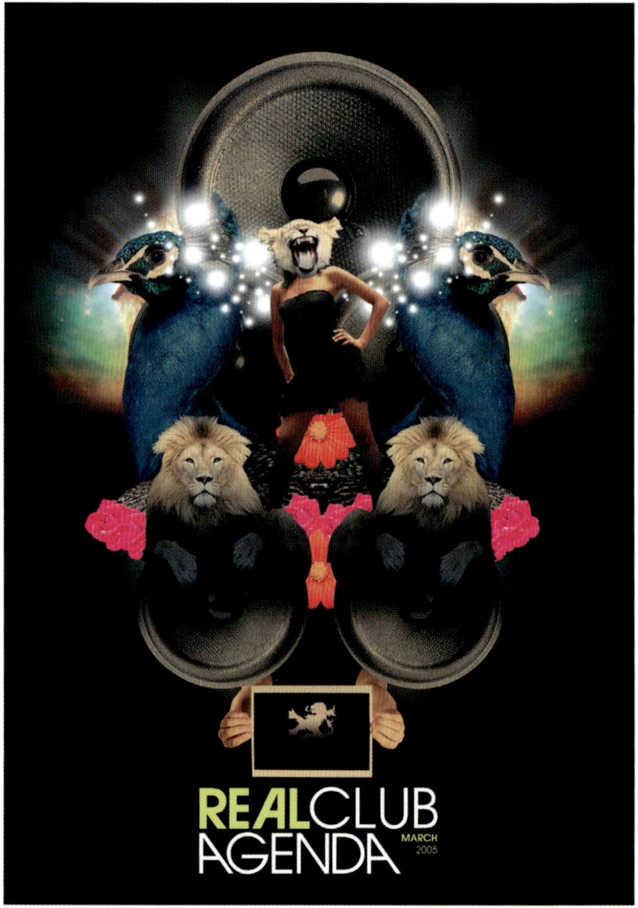

REAL CLUB
AGENDA
MARCH
2005

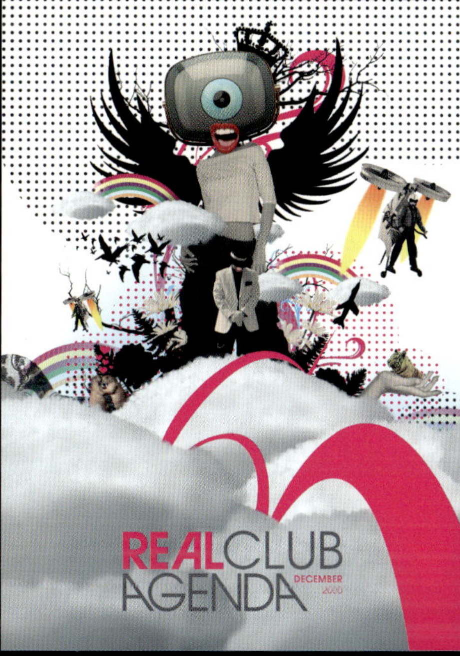

REAL CLUB
AGENDA
DECEMBER
2005

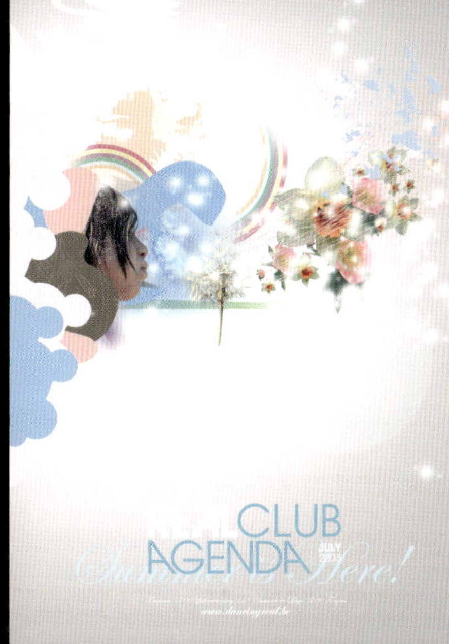

CLUB
AGENDA JULY 2005
Summer is Here!
www.dancingreal.be

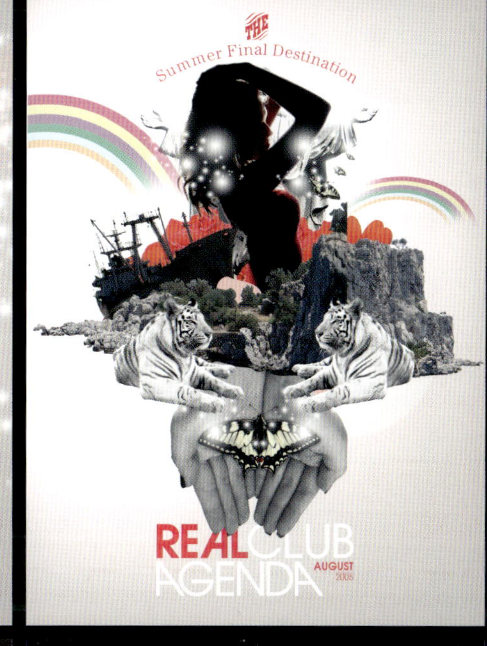

THE
Summer Final Destination
REAL CLUB
AGENDA AUGUST 2005

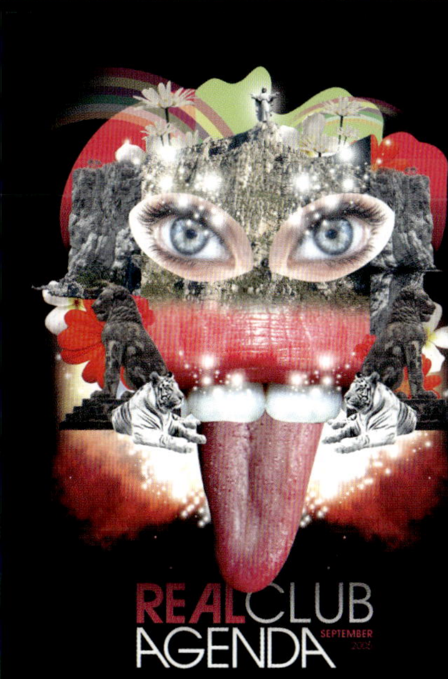

REAL CLUB
AGENDA SEPTEMBER 2005

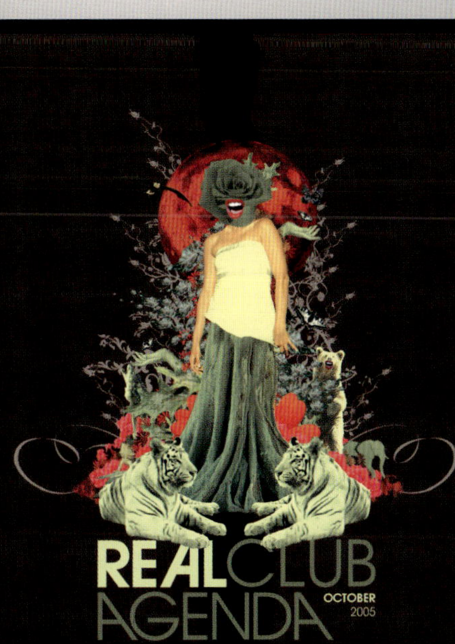

REAL CLUB
AGENDA OCTOBER 2005

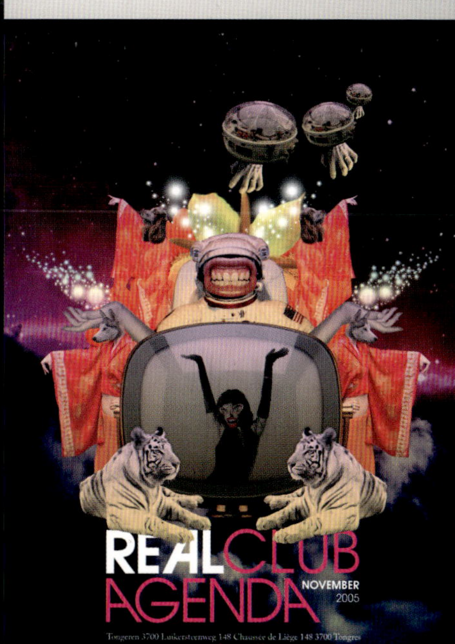

REAL CLUB
AGENDA NOVEMBER 2005
Tongeren 3700 Luikersteenweg 148 Chaussée de Liège 148 3700 Tongres

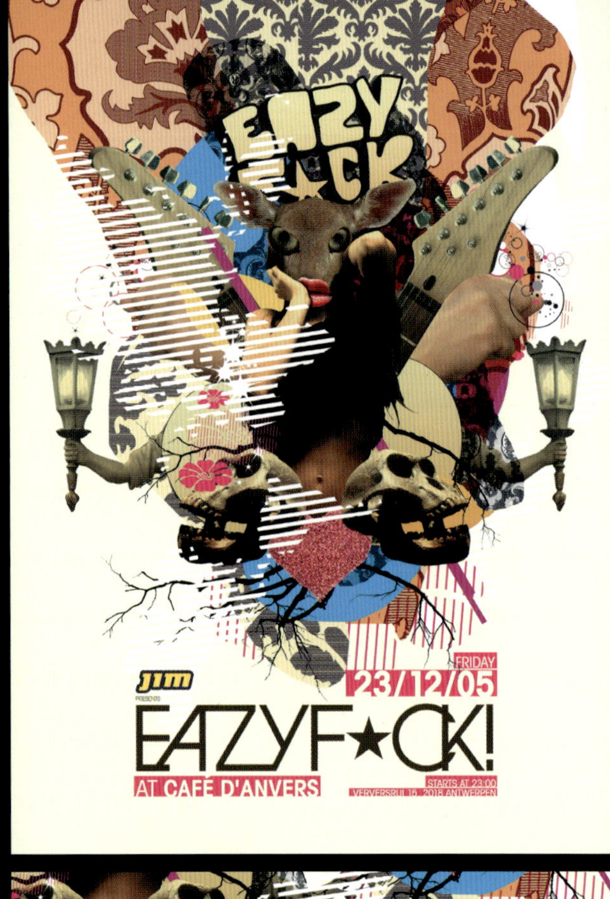

EAZY
F*CK
JIM
PRESENTS
FRIDAY
23/12/05
EAZYF★CK!
AT CAFÉ D'ANVERS
STARTS AT 23:00
VERVERSRUI 15, 2018 ANTWERPEN

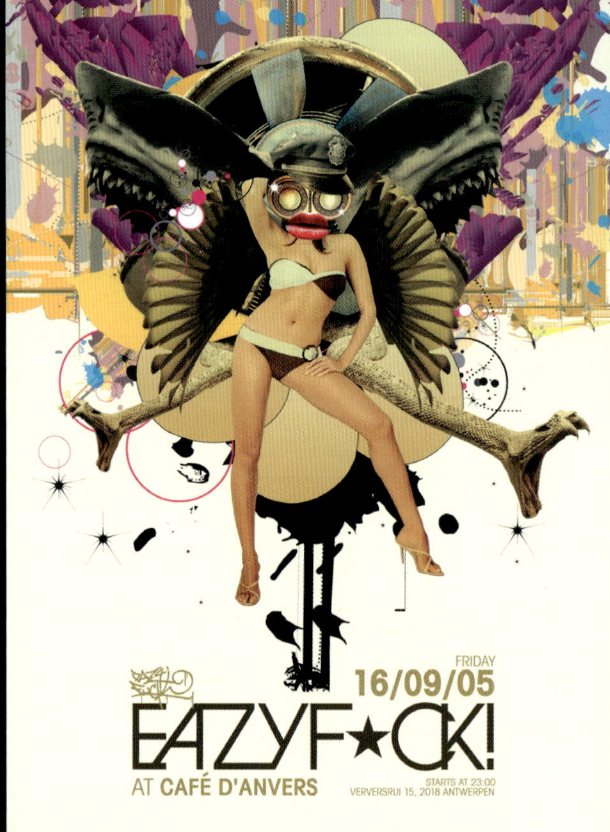

FRIDAY
16/09/05
EAZYF★CK!
AT CAFÉ D'ANVERS
STARTS AT 23:00
VERVERSRUI 15, 2018 ANTWERPEN

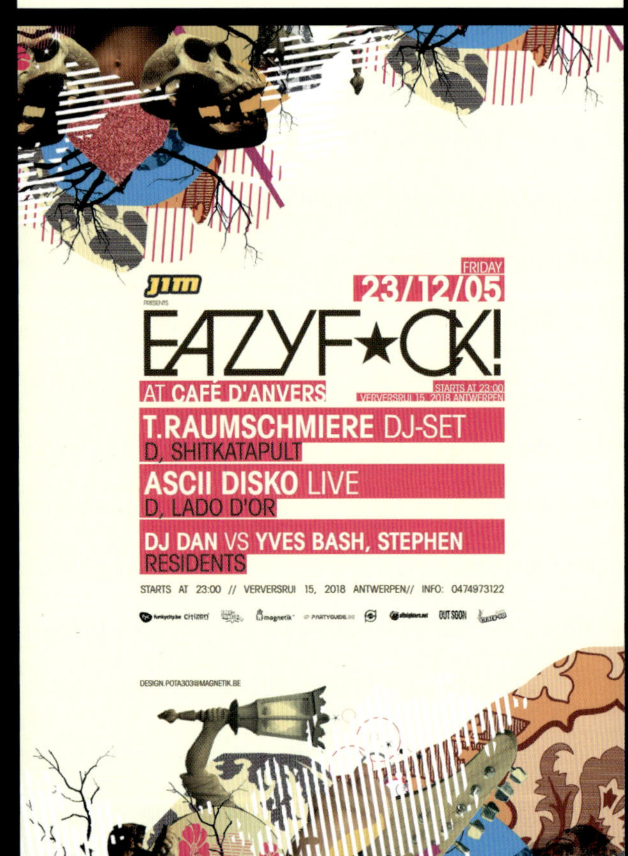

JIM
PRESENTS
FRIDAY
23/12/05
EAZYF★CK!
AT CAFÉ D'ANVERS
STARTS AT 23:00
VERVERSRUI 15, 2018 ANTWERPEN
T.RAUMSCHMIERE DJ-SET
D, SHITKATAPULT
ASCII DISKO LIVE
D, LADO D'OR
DJ DAN VS YVES BASH, STEPHEN
RESIDENTS
STARTS AT 23:00 // VERVERSRUI 15, 2018 ANTWERPEN// INFO: 0474973122
DESIGN.POTA303@MAGNETIK.BE

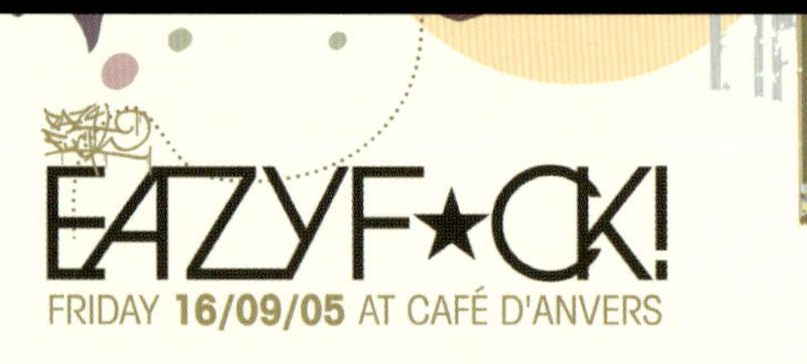

EAZYF★CK!
FRIDAY 16/09/05 AT CAFÉ D'ANVERS

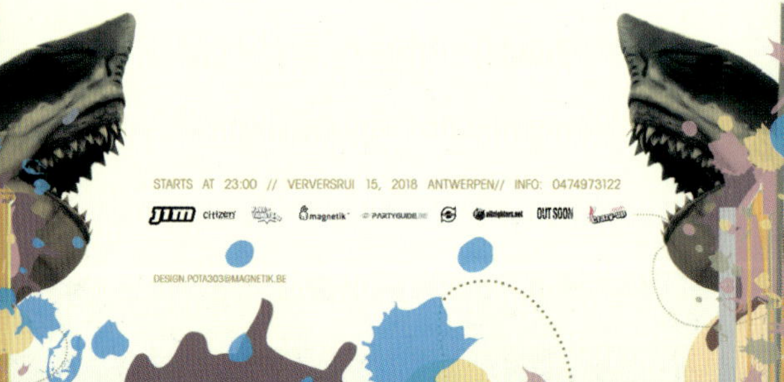

TOMAS ANDERSSON
SWE, LIVE, BPITCHCONTROL
DAMIAN LAZARUS
UK, BUGGED OUT!
ED&KIM AND DJ DAN
RESIDENT, SWITCH
RESIDENT, BODY TO BODY
STARTS AT 23:00 // VERVERSRUI 15, 2018 ANTWERPEN// INFO: 0474973122
DESIGN.POTA303@MAGNETIK.BE

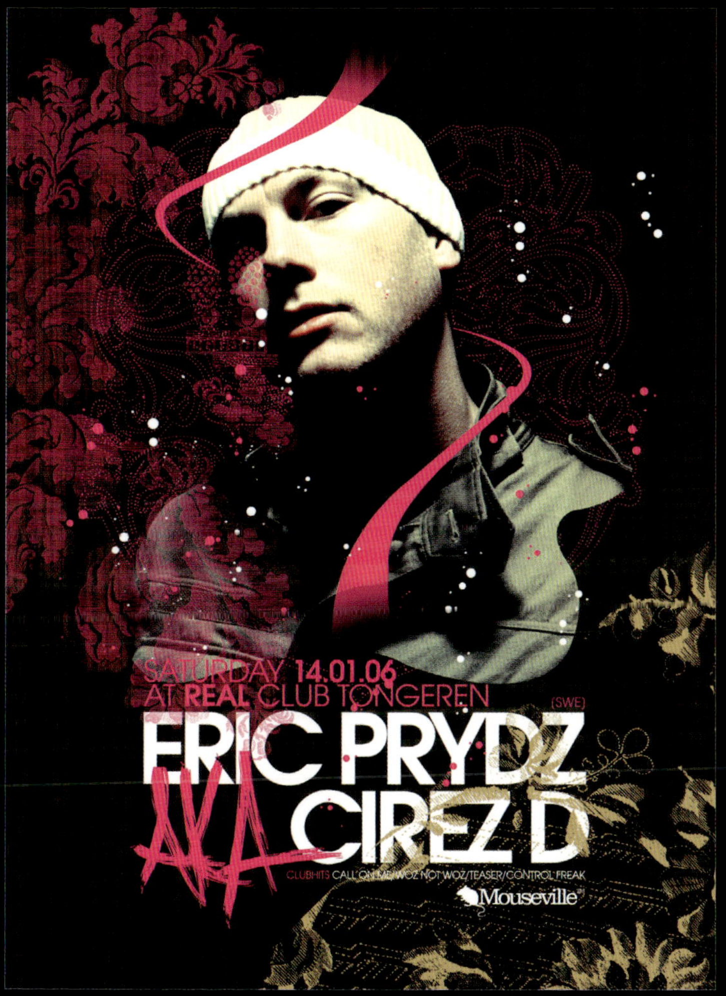

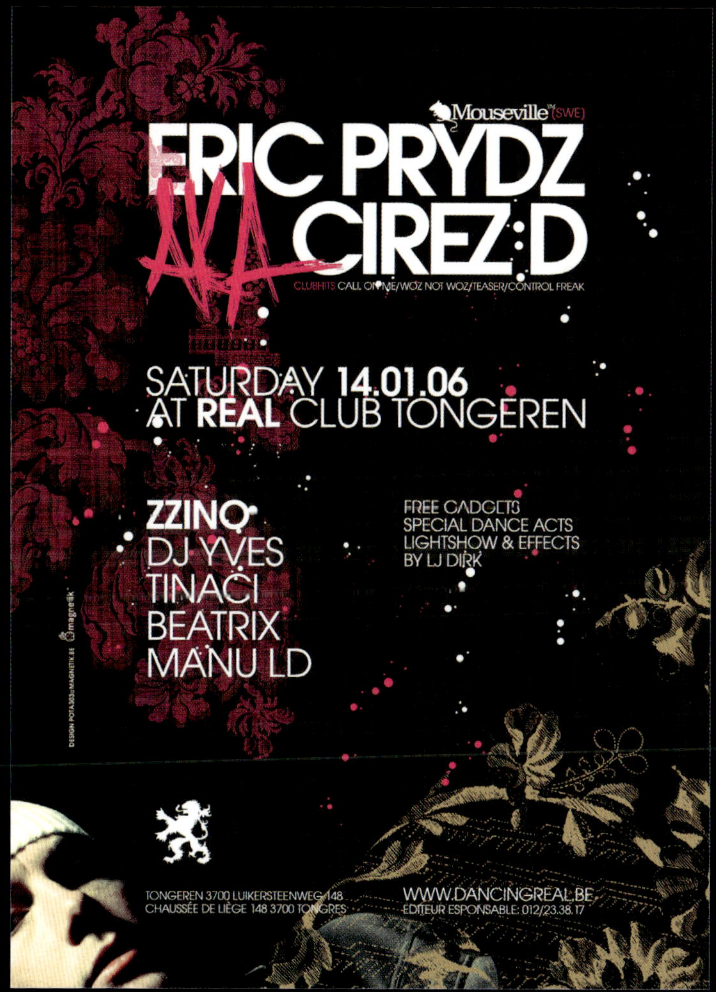

1.//

2.//

Magnetik

Liège, Belgium

Title: –
Type of work: Flyer, poster
Client: 1.// Eazy F*ck And Café D'Anvers
2.// Real
Design: ad, d// Chris Vermiglio
Year: 2005-06

Using mixed media of collage and vectorial shapes, the designers try to render the spirit of the club - classy, fun And decadent.

Grandpeople

Bergen, Norway

Title: Langz
Type of work: Front cover illustration
Client: Publishing house Gasspedal
Design: ad, d// Grandpeople
Year: 2005

A sleeve designed for the publisher, Gasspedal's sixth release, 'Langz'. The illustration tries to capture a metro-like feeling linked to the stories.

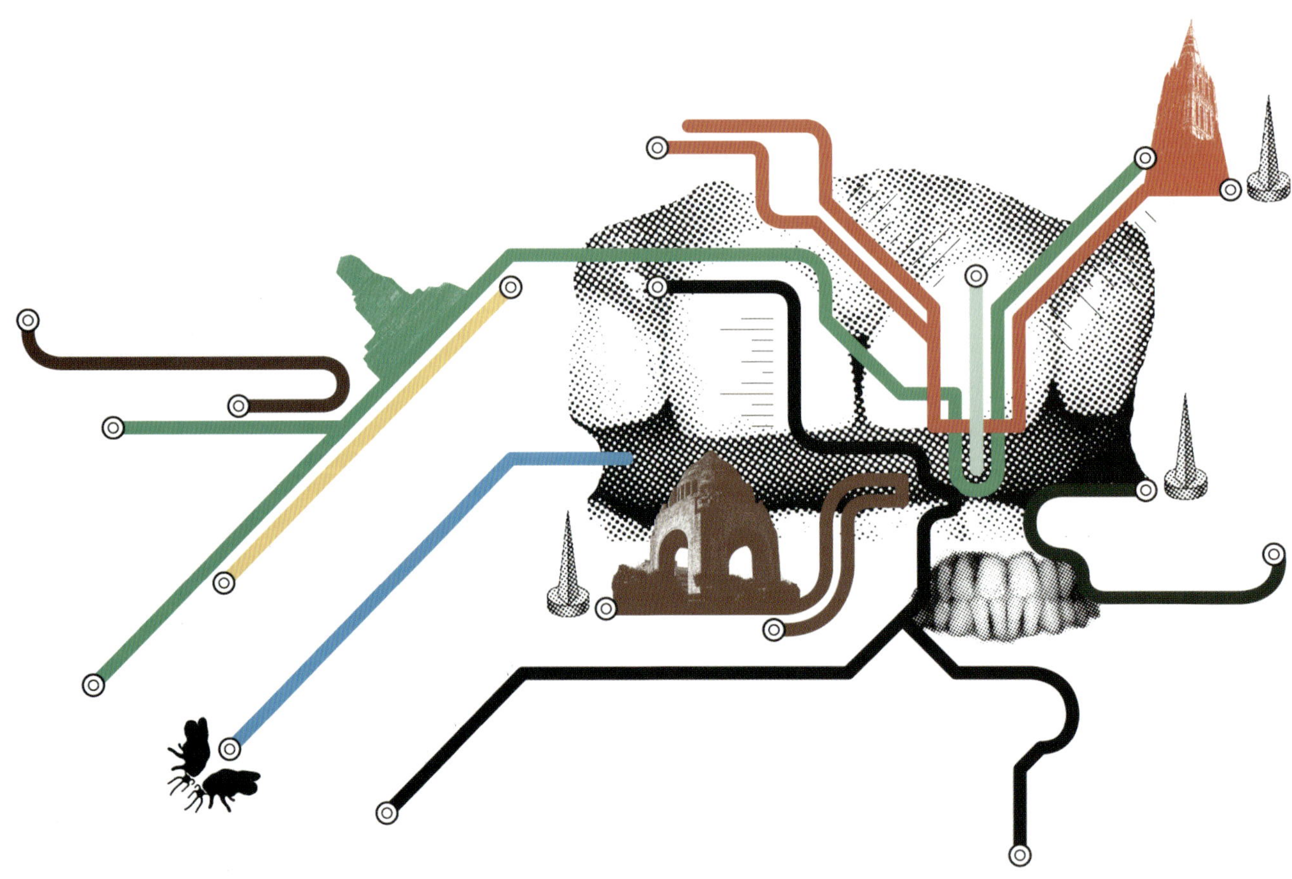

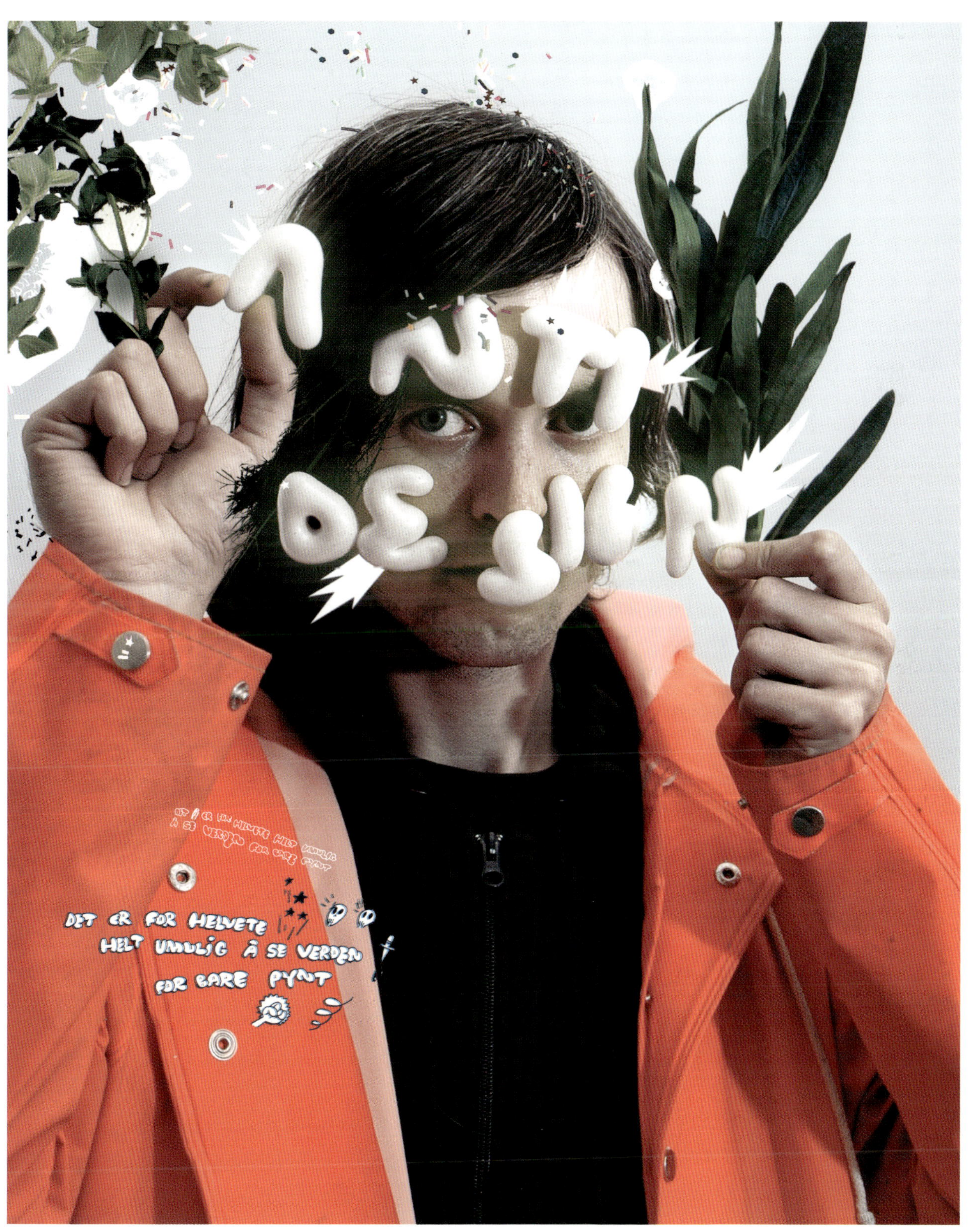

DET ER FOR HELVETE
HELT UMULIG Å SE VERDEN
FOR BARE PYNT

Dipesh Pandya

Paris, France

Title: Mike Ladd / Nostalgialator – Housewives At Play
Type of work: Album/single packaging, CD, vinyl, poster
Client: K7! Records, Like Madd Music
Design: ad, d// Dipesh Pandya
Year: 2004

The use fo lego-like figures and colourful balloons added a playful feeling of partying to the design. Yellow is used to link up the whole design package for this album promotion.

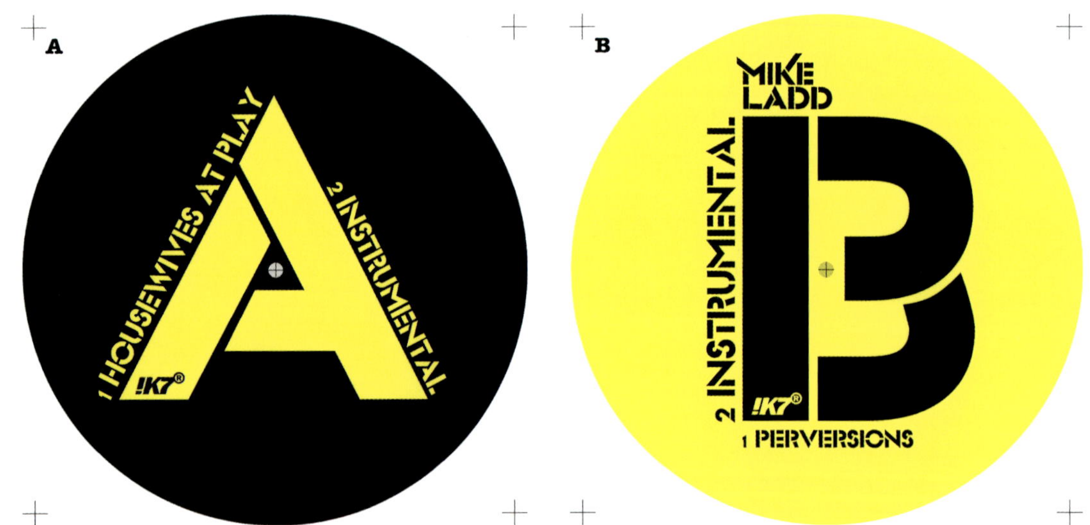

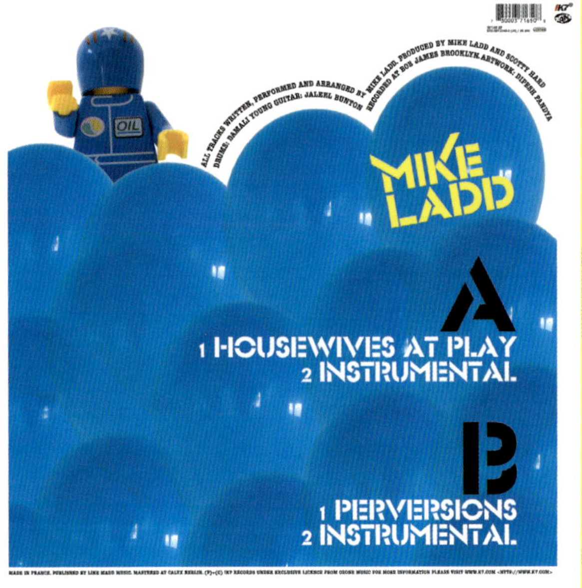

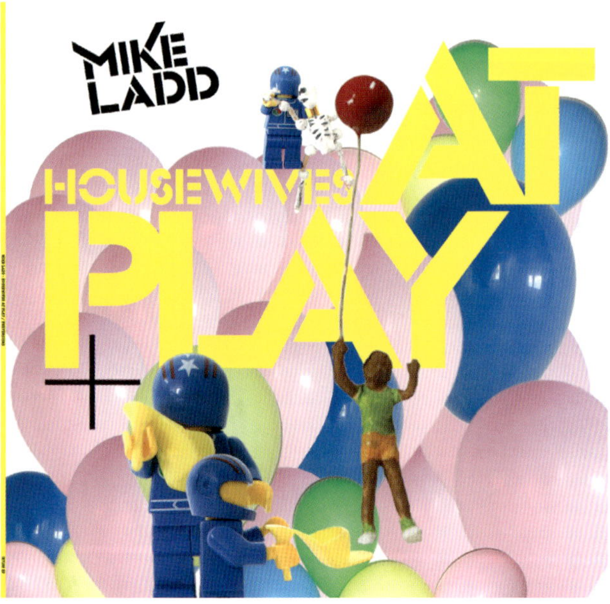

Dimaquina

Rio de Janeiro, Brazil

Title: Chico Dub – b heavy and loaded with dynamite
Type of work: CD packaging
Client: Chico Dub
Design: ad// Antônio Pedro, Dimaquina
d// Antônio Pedro
Year: 2005

A cd package for a Jamaican music DJ- Chico Dub. With a small budget, this package which would be sent to no more than 100 person is made use of only a thick sheet of offset paper, a laser printer and two cans of spray, in which the designers used stencils to get a unique look for each one of the them. The package would turn into a poster when it is opened up.

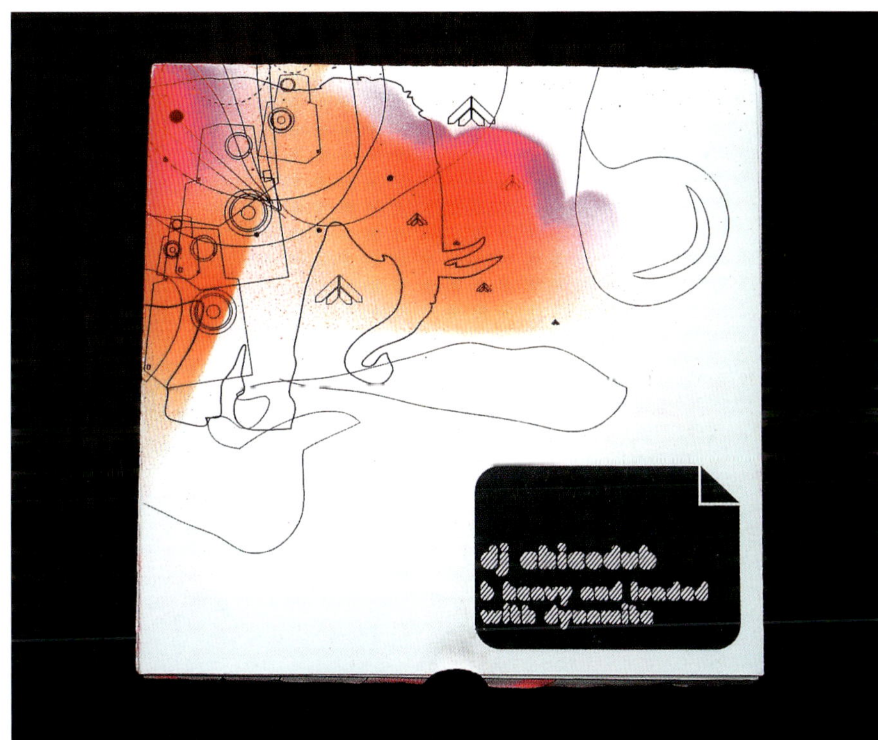
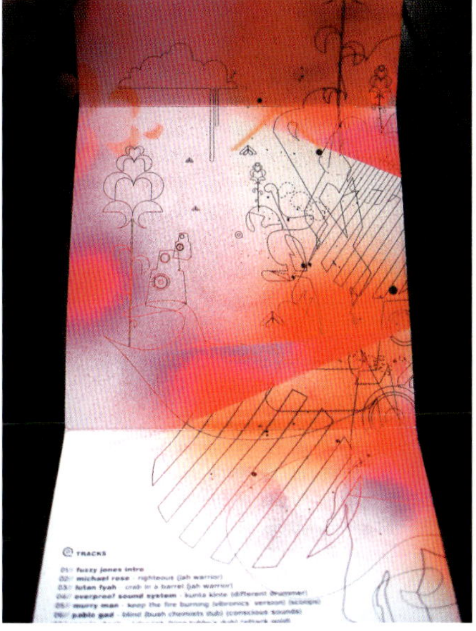
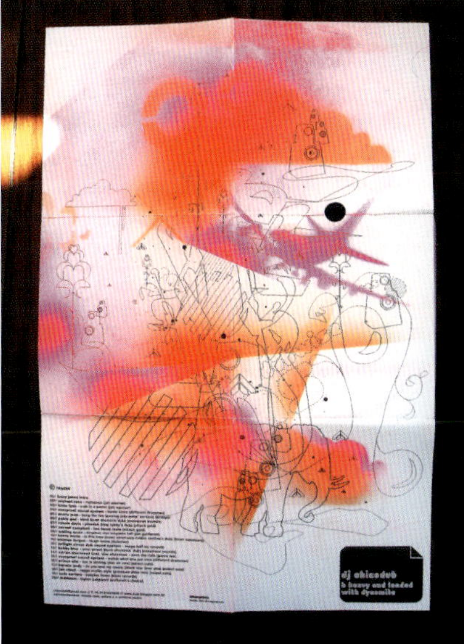
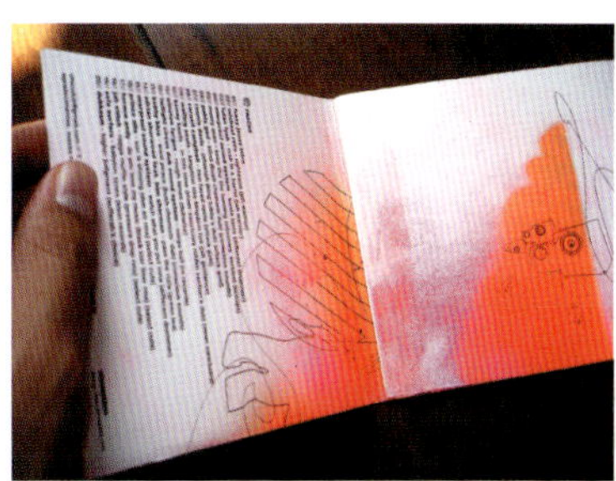
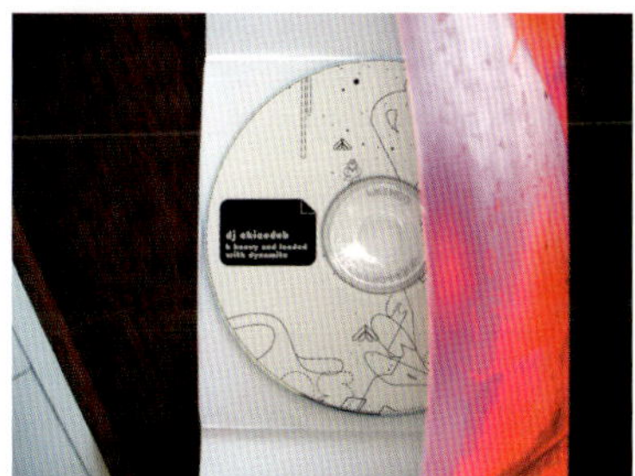

Styl●

London, UK

Title: Alright Orchid
Type of work: CD packaging
Client: X Marks Recordings
Design: ad, d// Tom Lancaster
Year: 2002

A matt dark green plastic jewel case sealed with a high gloss sticker containing all the details of the release. A simple and direct design it is.

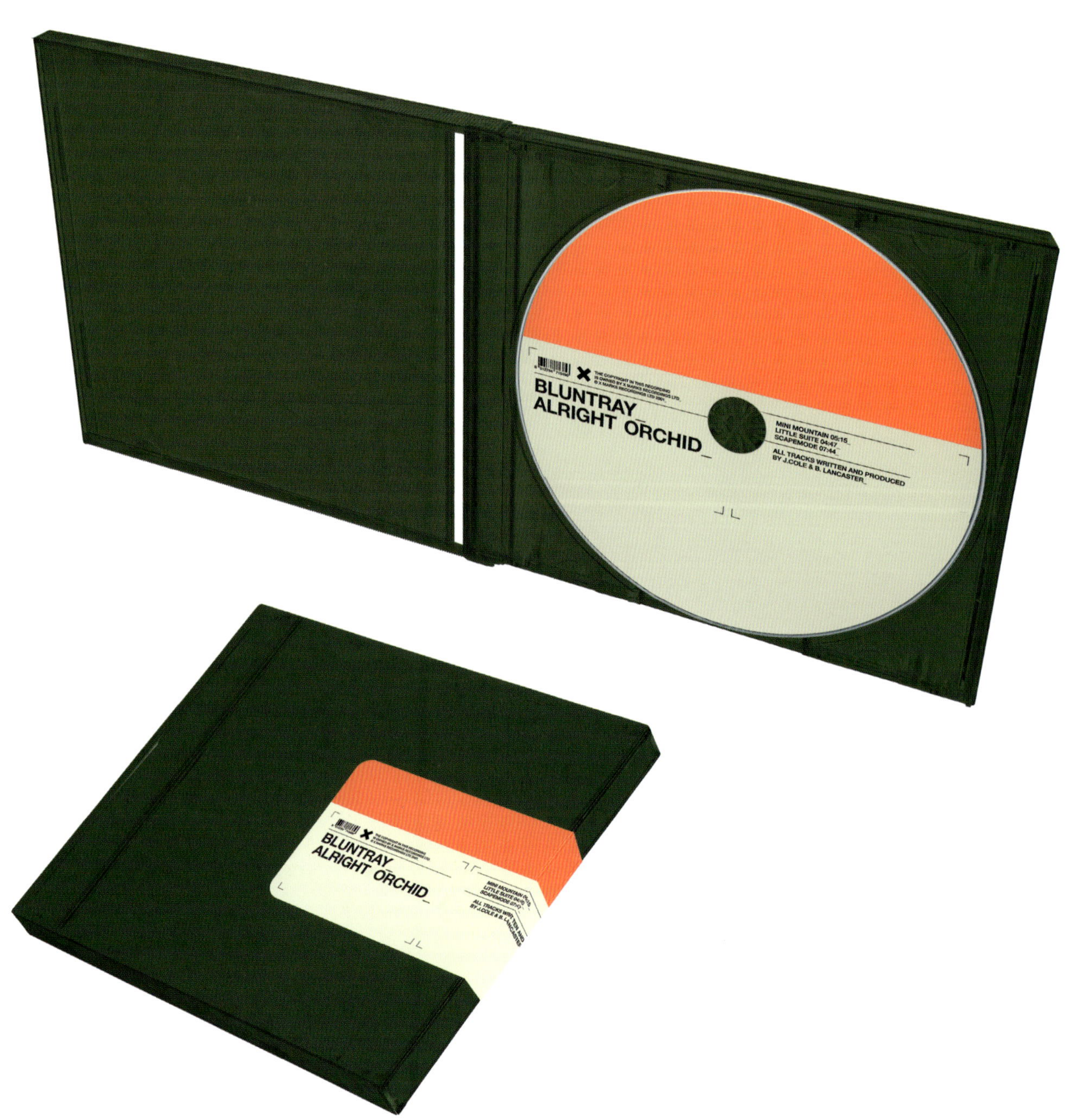

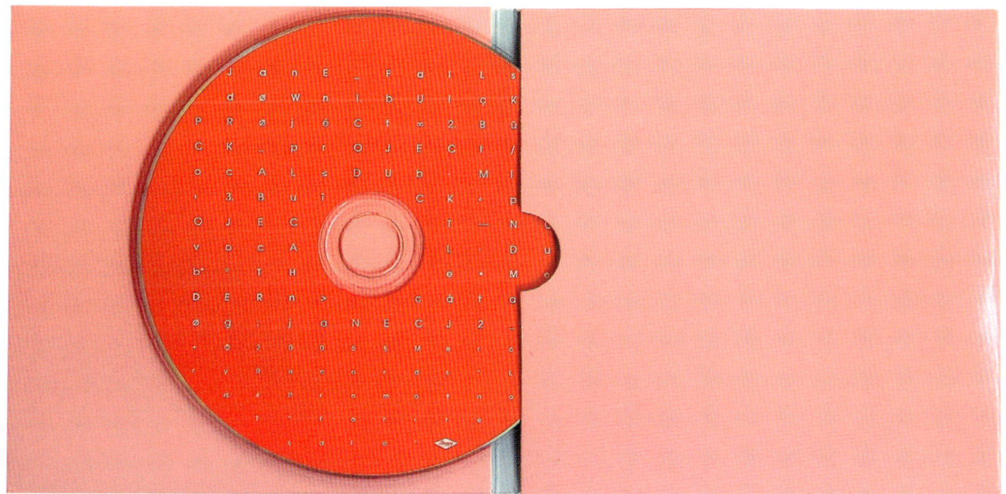

F●rm ®

London, UK

Title: The Modern single promo CD pouchette and tour poster
Type of work: CD packaging
Client: Mercury Records
Design: ad// Paul West, Paula Benson d// Paul West, Claire Warner, Andy Harvey
Year: 2005

This piece is designed for a band- The Modern, a mix of 80's electro pop and burlesque cabaret. The designers created a sense of theatrics with exaggerated posturing from the band, combined with the images from the industry such as Modernist/Bauhaus architecture, aeroplanes and machinery, and also coupled with non standard format packaging and 'neue' typographic layouts. The typography on the onbody label was inspired by a set of old photo-typesetting plates in the studio. To enhance the idea of eclectic 'found' collage materials, a 'Modern' postage stamp was designed. The logo is a redrawn vector of a logo that the designers created from bent wire.

Kerry Roper

London, UK

Title: Summer of Space
Type of work: CD Sleeve
Client: Quiet City Recordings
Design: ad, d// Kerry Roper
Year: 2005

Warm colours like yellow and red is always used to represent sunshine specially in summers. So as this design, it is used to match with the title 'Summer of Space', which the 'Space' is represented by images of blue sky with white clouds.

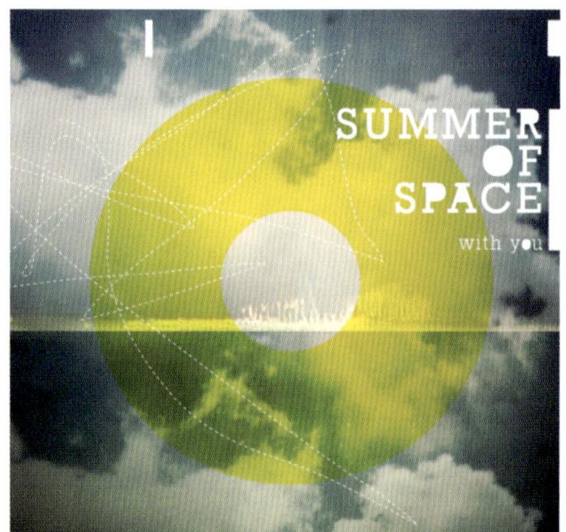

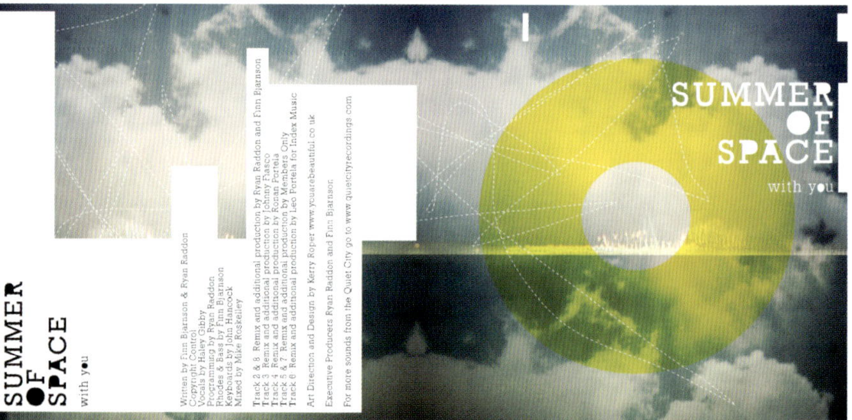

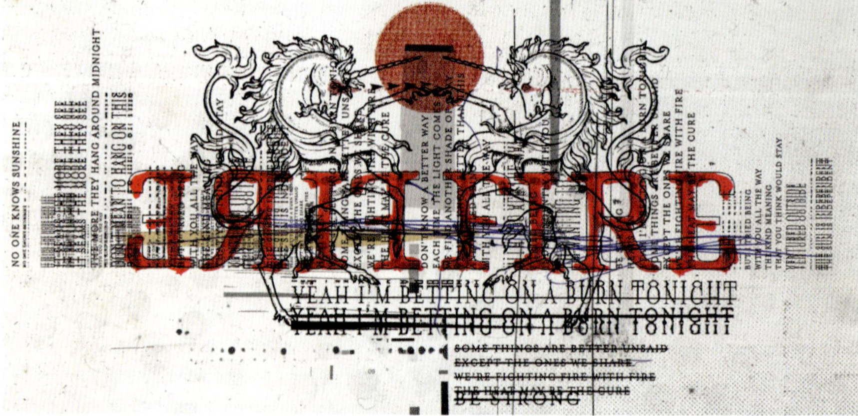

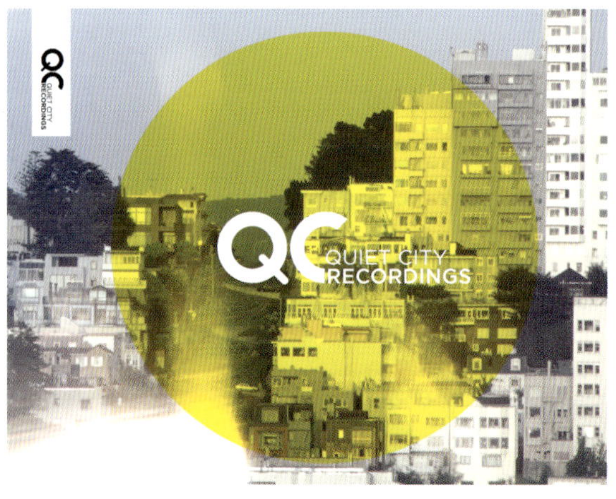

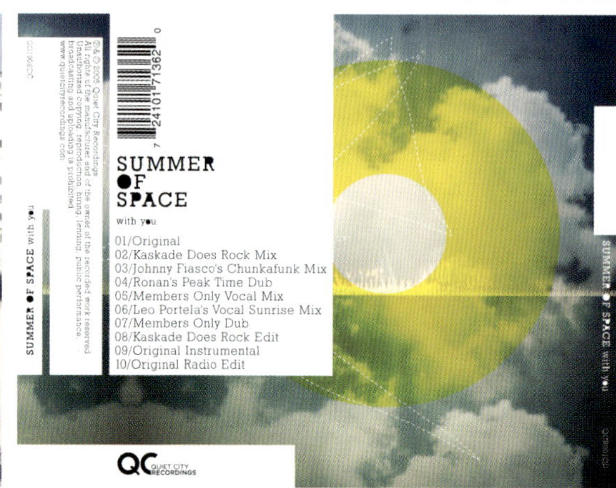

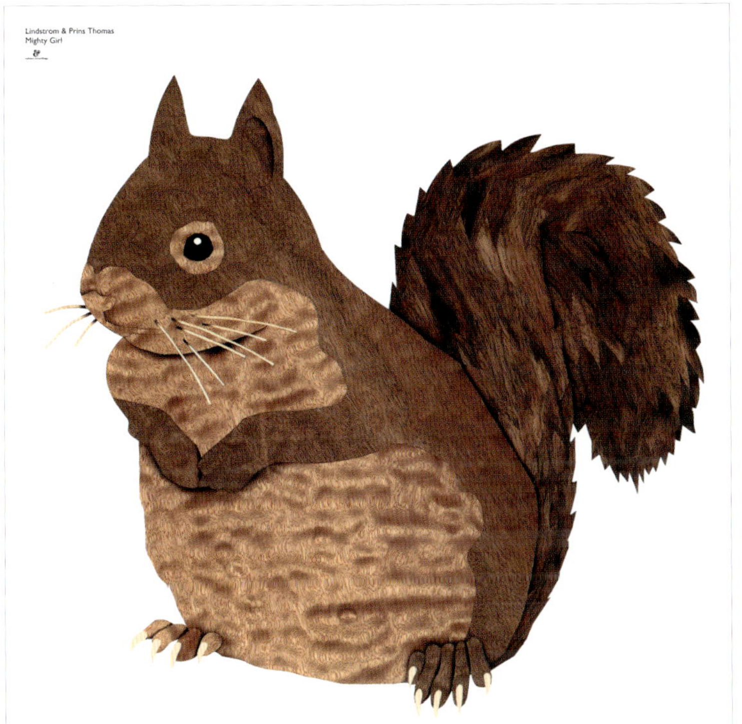

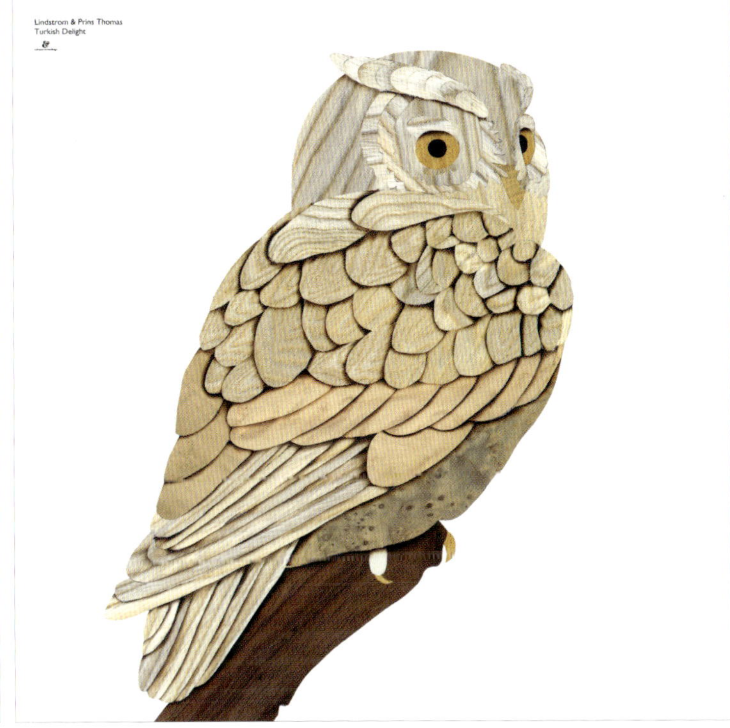

Chris Bolton

Helsinki, Finland

Title: Lindstrom & Prins Thomas 12inches 'Turkish Delight' & 'Mighty Girl'
Type of work: Record sleeve
Client: Eskimo Recordings & NEWS (Belgium)
Design: ad, d// Chris Bolton i// Juha Nuutti, Chris Bolton
Year: 2005-06

After releasing their first album 'Lindstrom & Prins thomas" and first 12" "Turkish Delight" on Eskimo Recordings, the Norwegian dance artists come up with all new tracks, which are exclusive to this 12". Again 3 excellent electronic disco tracks with strange mood and full of epic drama. The album covers is designed with wood-like squirrel and owl images on plain white background.

Dipesh Pandya

New York, USA

Title: Cerrone / Hysteria
Type of work: Album/single packaging. CD, vinyl, poster
Client: Barclay, Universal Music France
Design: ad// Dipesh Pandya d// Dipesh Pandya, Frédéric Riochet
Year: 2002

An album package designed for Cerrone, a disco kingpin specialized in club dance and house music. Colourful images of naked women in different posts indicate partying people, a vague feel is created.

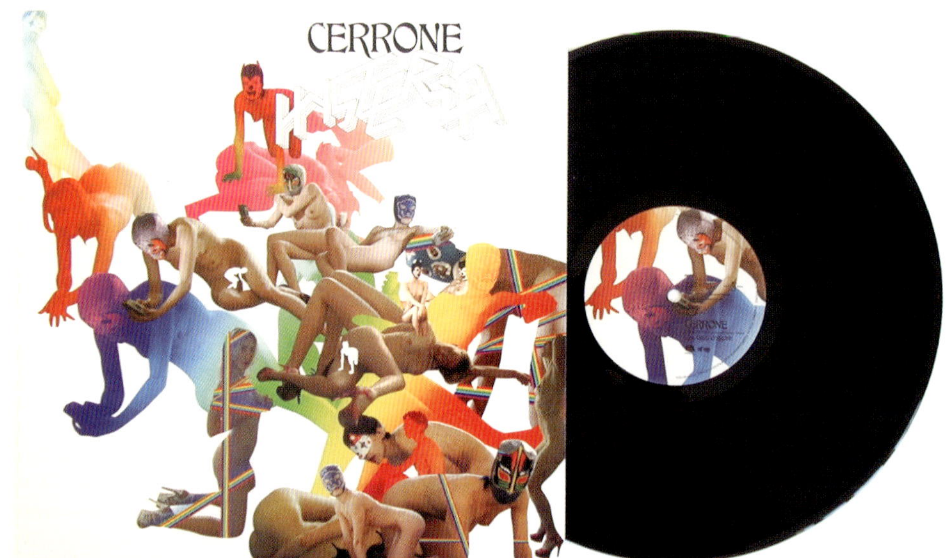

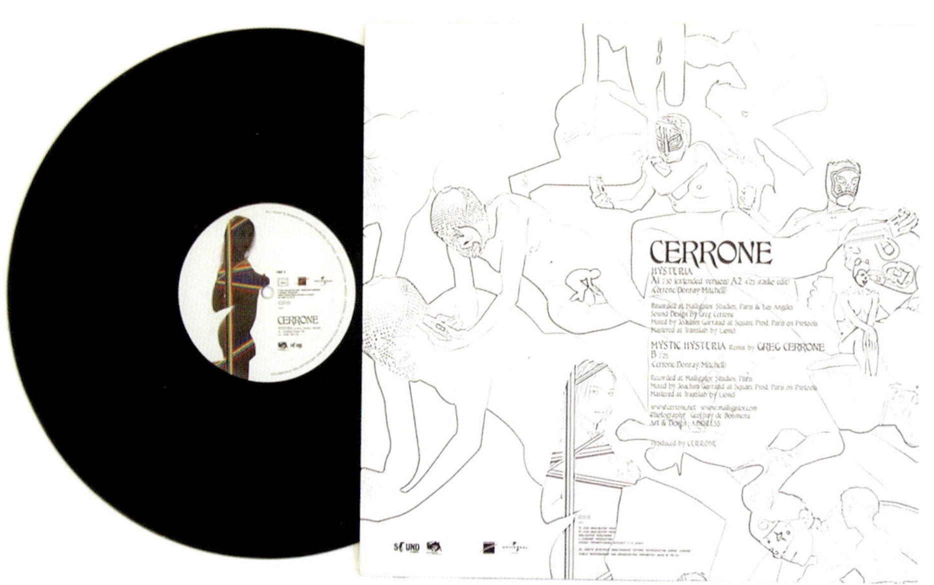

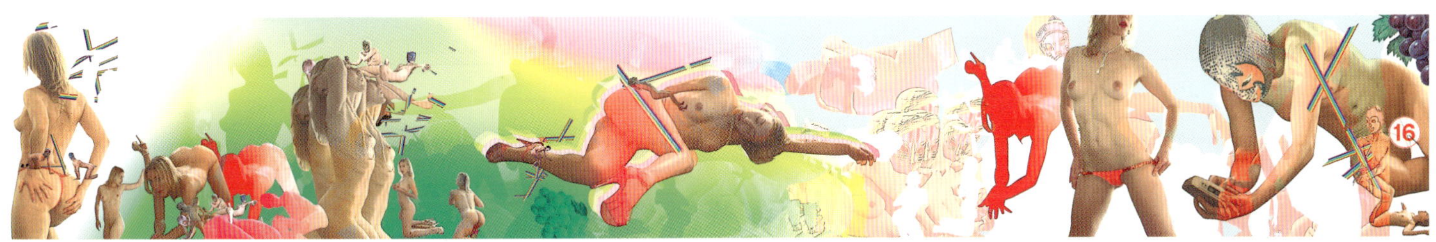

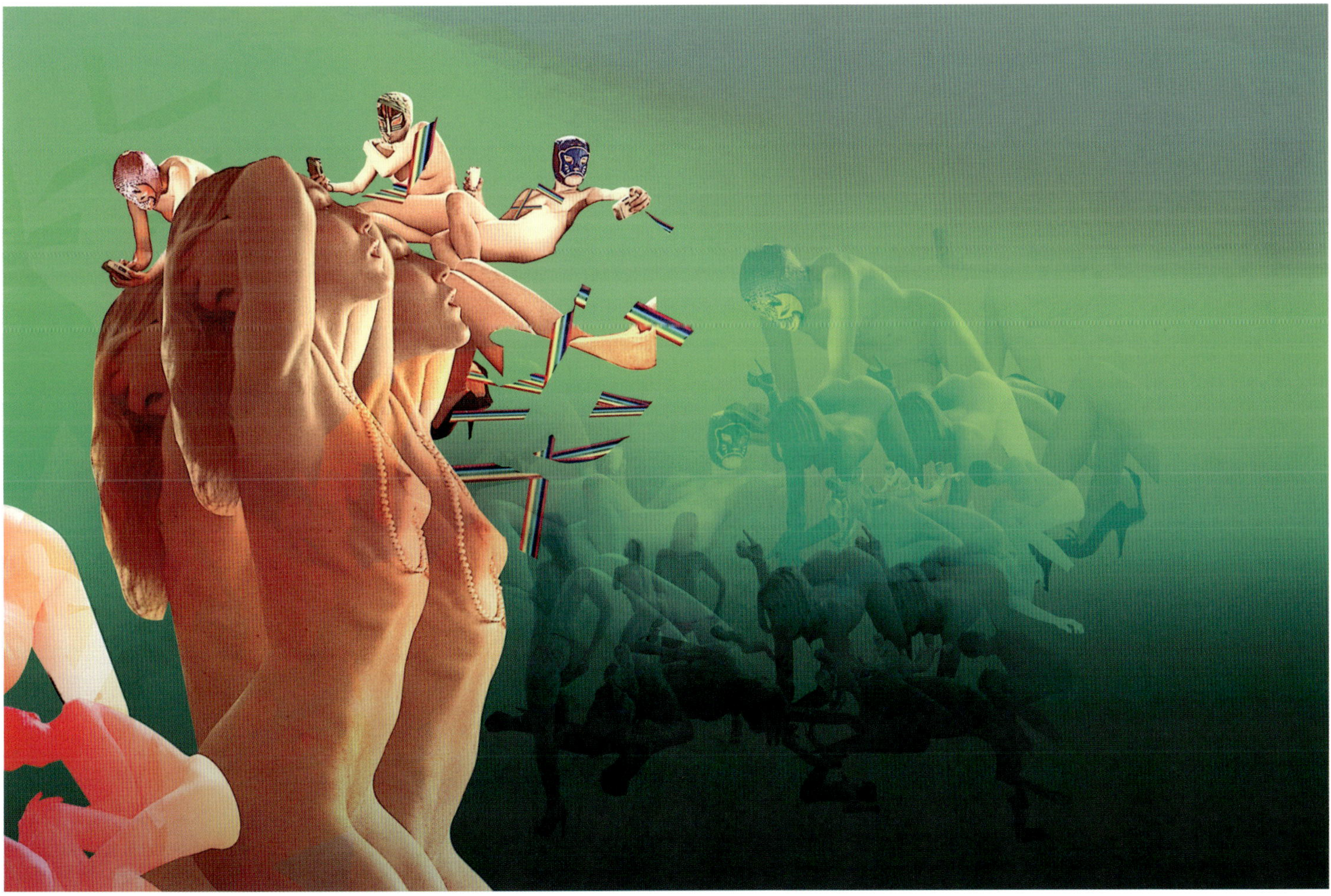

Ev●struct

Paris, France

Title: KENZO Autumn Winter Show 2005
Type of work: Motion Graphics, DVD
Client: Kenzo
Design: ad, d// Frederic Sofiyana
Year: 2005

A video animation for the Autumn / Winter 2005 show of Kenzo, in which the video takes a fresh look at the world of fashion shows with models appearing through different scenes.

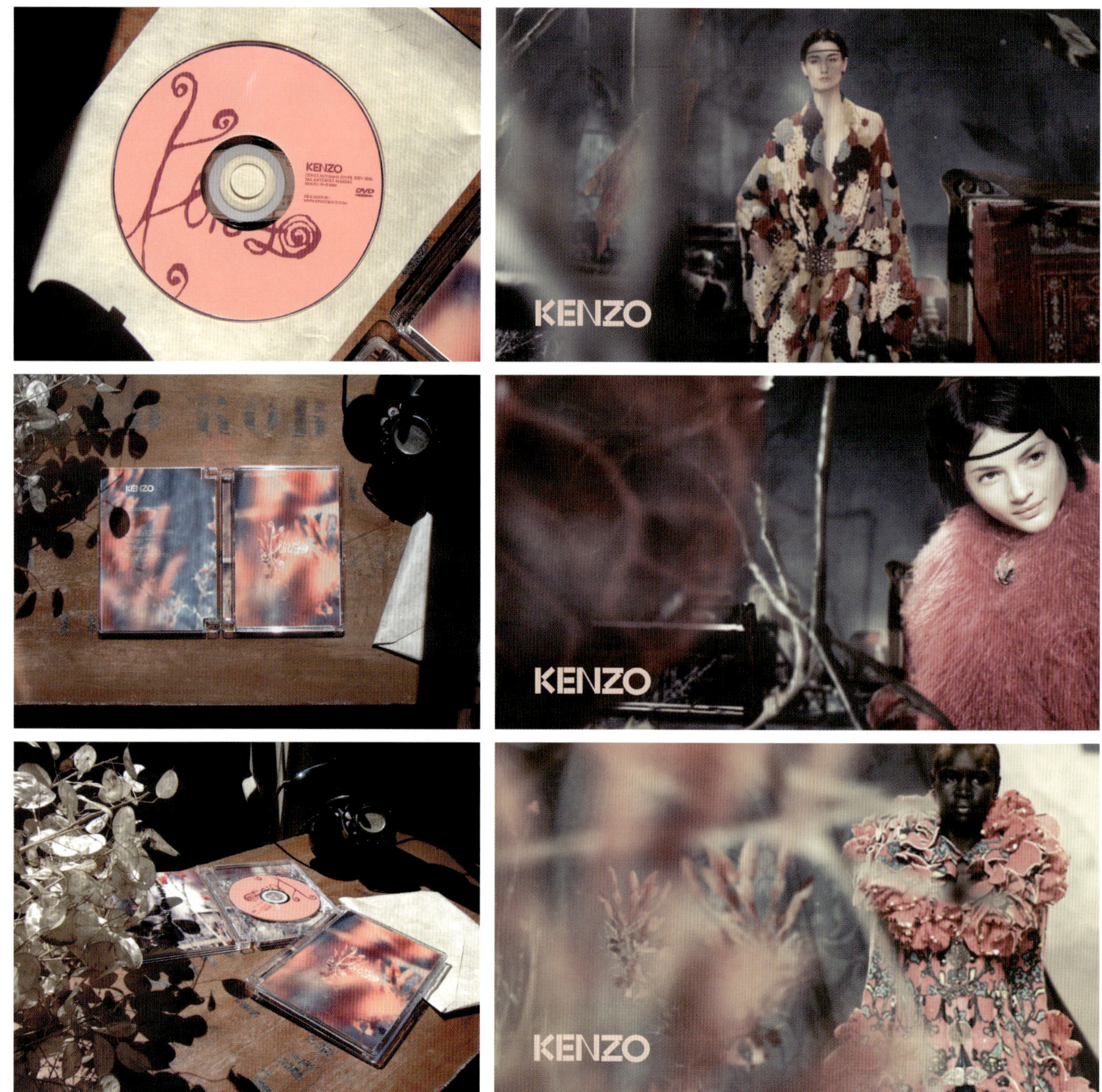

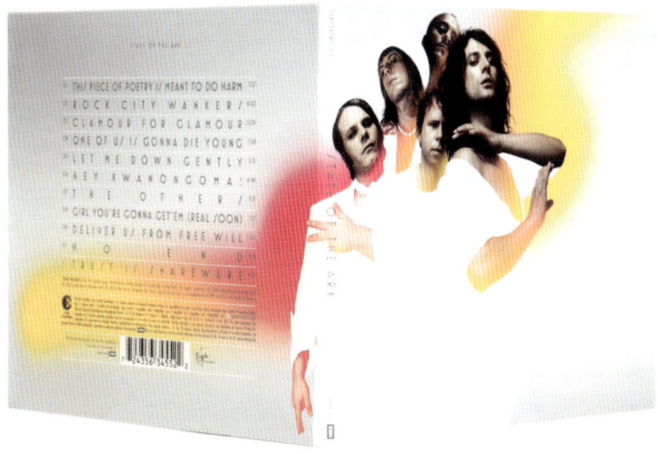
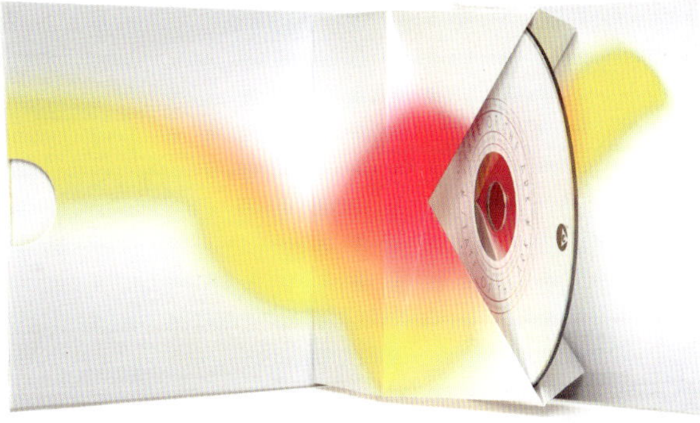
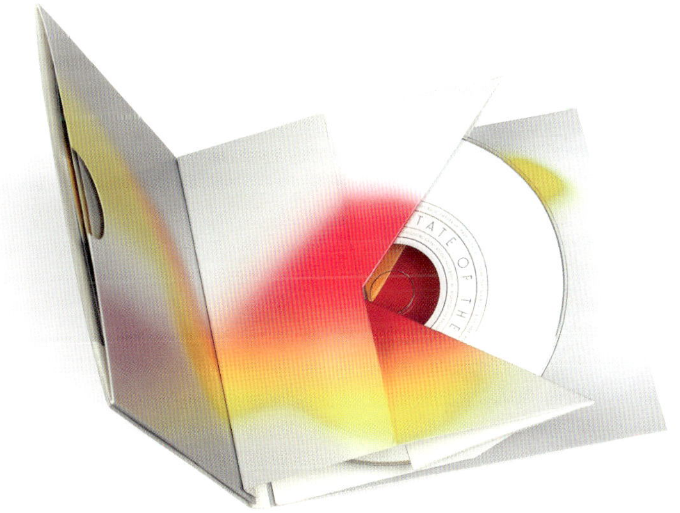

Zion Graphics

Stockholm, Sweden

Title: -
Type of work: CD Sleeve
Client: The Ark
Design: ad, d// RickyTillblad
Year: 2005

To match with the new direction of this Sweden rock band, a simple but vibrant design for the CD sleeve is created. Mainly in white, but a wave in refreshing yellow to orange to pink is placed in the middle.

Tetsuya Nagato

Tokyo, Japan

Title: 1.// Sakurai Atsushi album ainowakusei
2.// UA Live album laua
Type of work: CD
Client: 1.// Victor Entertainment 2.// Victor
Entertainment Speedstar Records
Design: 1.// ad, d: Tetsuya Nagato p: Makoto
Okuguchi 2.// ad, d, p: Tetsuya Nagato
Year: 2004

A CD package design of Sakurai Atsushi album ain-owakusei and UA Live album laua in just black and white with black and white images. It is simple but full of emotion, which is shown from the models' face and hands' gesture.

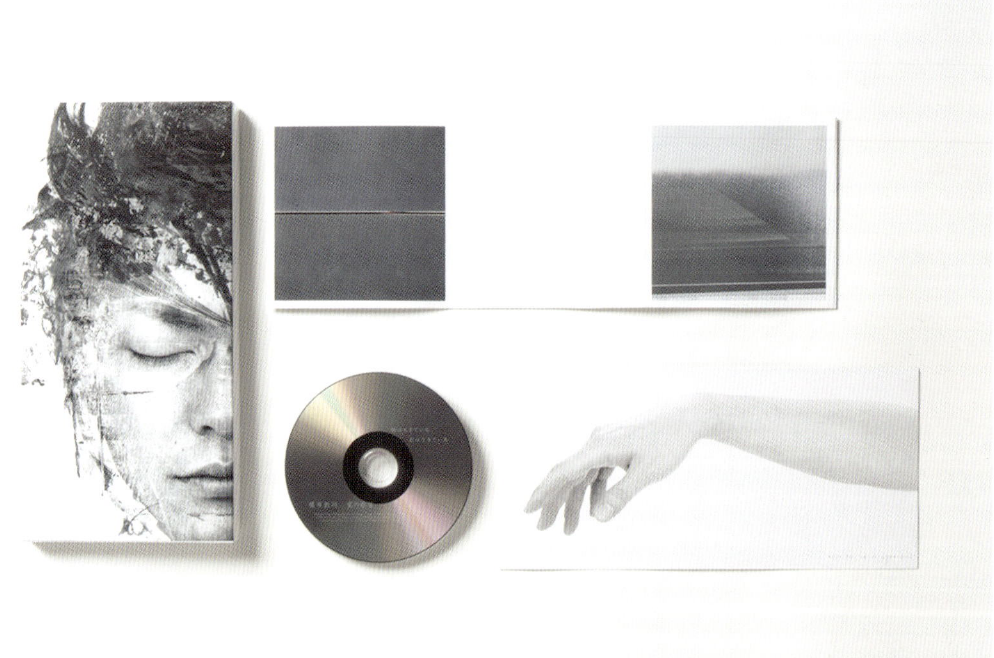

1.//

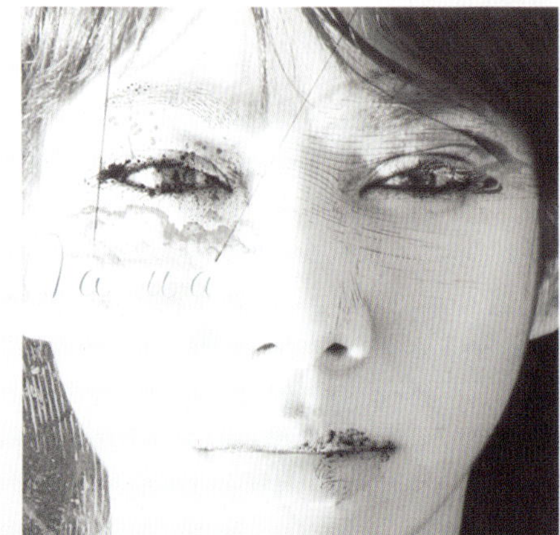

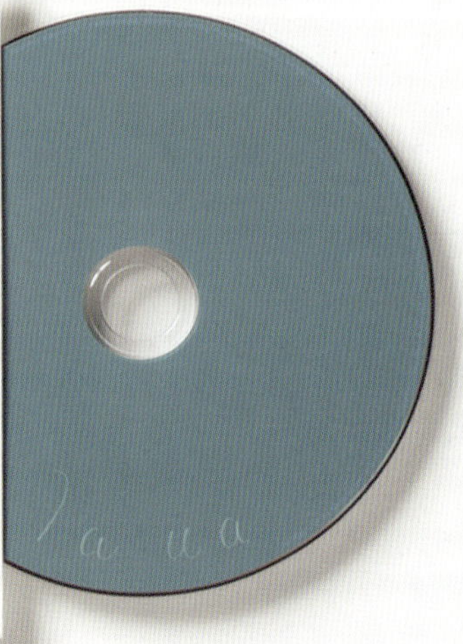

2.//

Ev●struct

Paris, France

Title: Redtenbacher's Funkestra
Type of work: Logotype, CD sleeve
Client: RSB
Design: ad// Frederic Sofiyana & Clement Dozier
d// Frederic Sofiyana
Year: 2004

This piece is designed for the British bassist, Stefan Redtenbacher and his production company-RSB, to coincide with the release of his second album 'Falling from Insanity'.

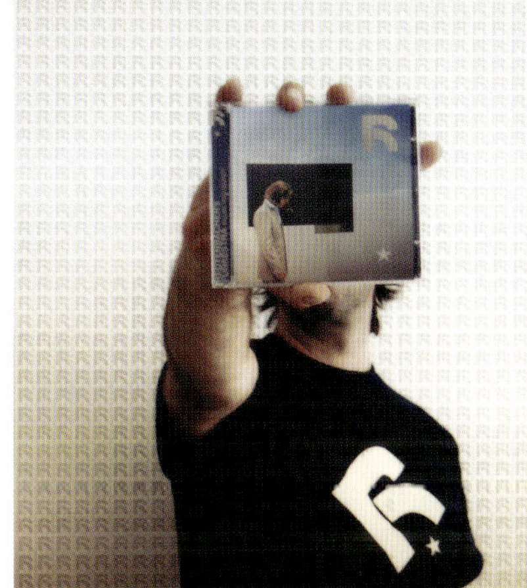

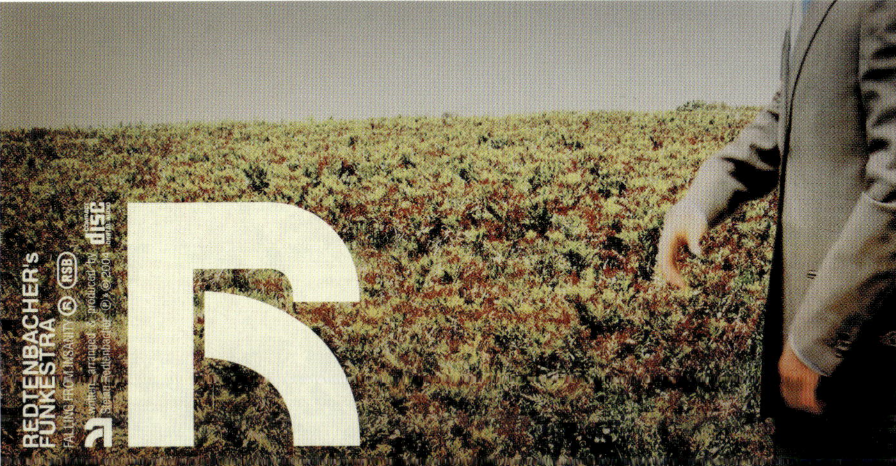

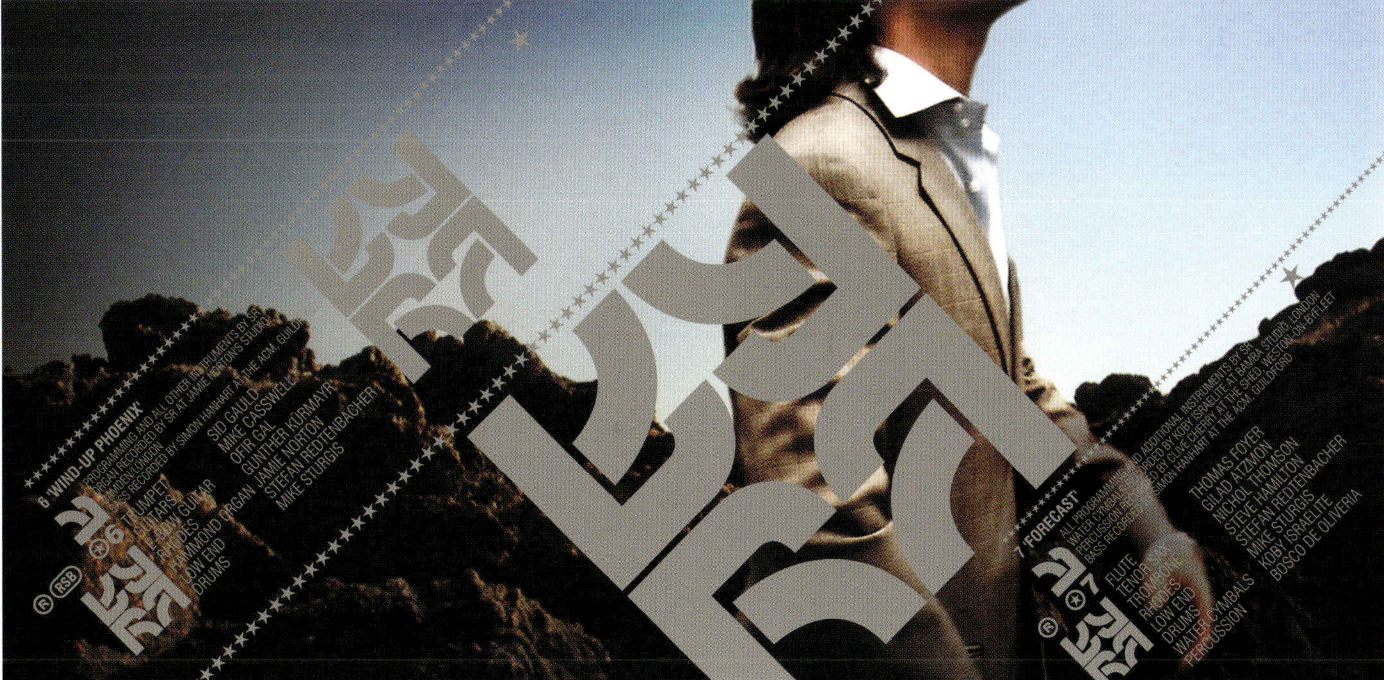

Grandpeople

Bergen, Norway

Title: Alndreas Meland & Lasse Marhaug – Brakhag
Type of work: CD sleeve
Client: Melektronikk
Design: ad, d// Grandpeople
Year: 2004

This sleeve was designed for the live music Mr Meland and Mr Marhaug played for the screenings of legendary filmmaker Stan Brakhage movies, hence the title 'Brakhage'. The films are originally silent movies and with content like autopsies, the artwork moved along dark neo-psychedelic organic skullish pathways.

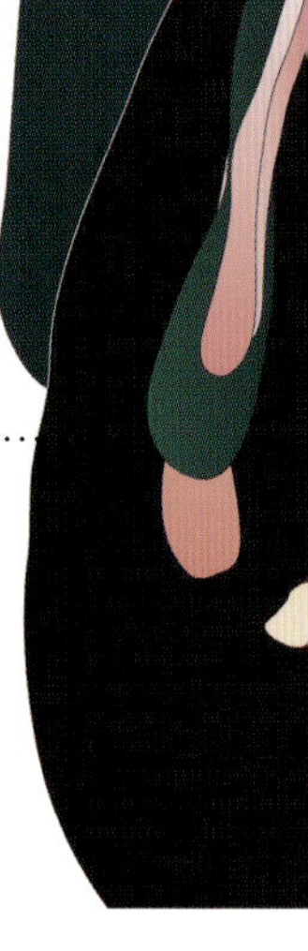

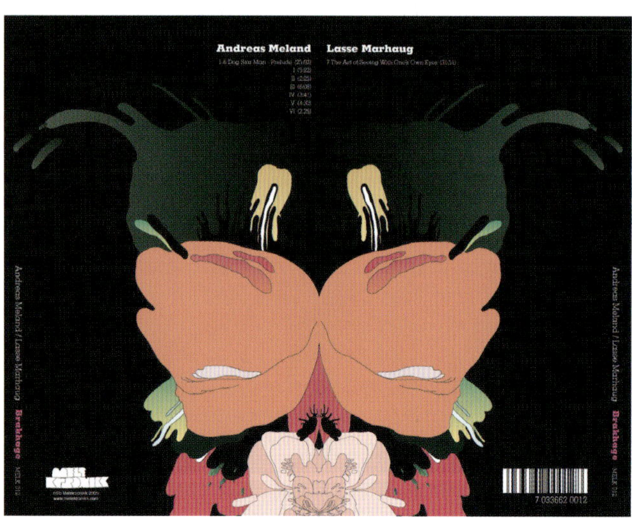

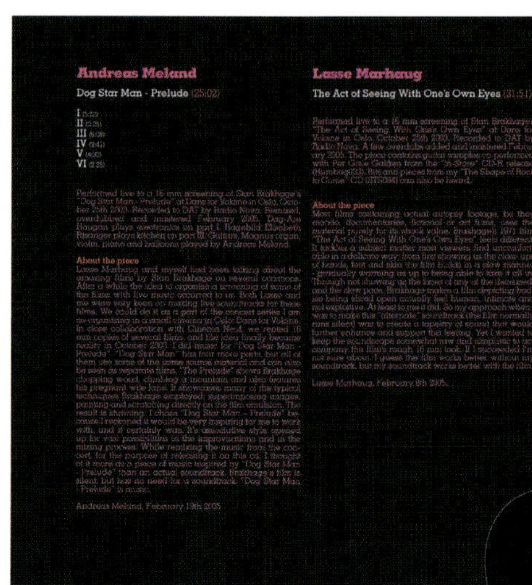

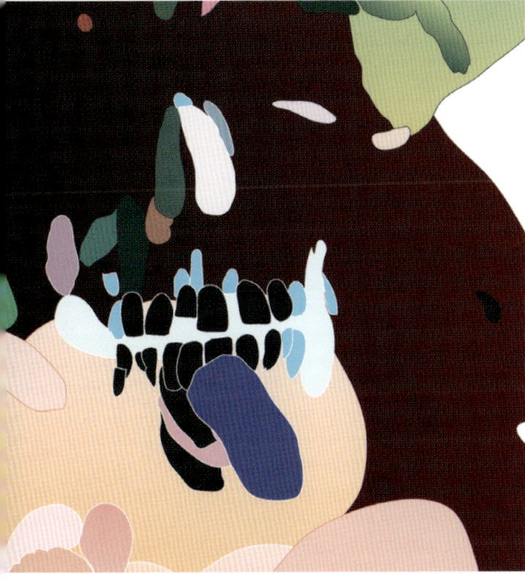
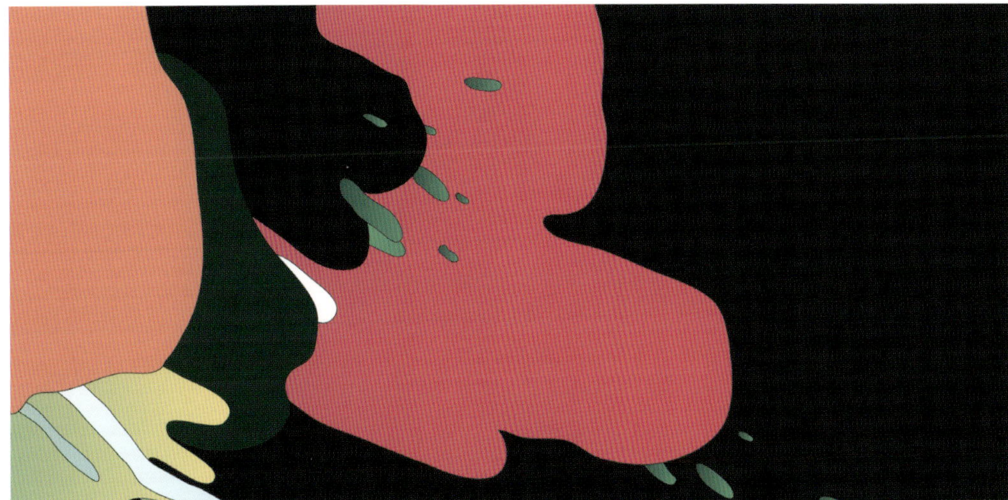

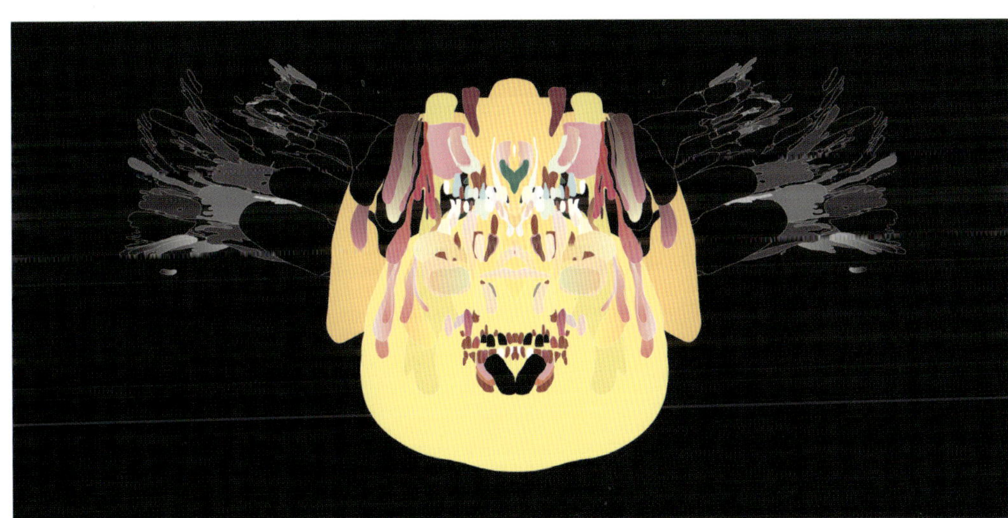
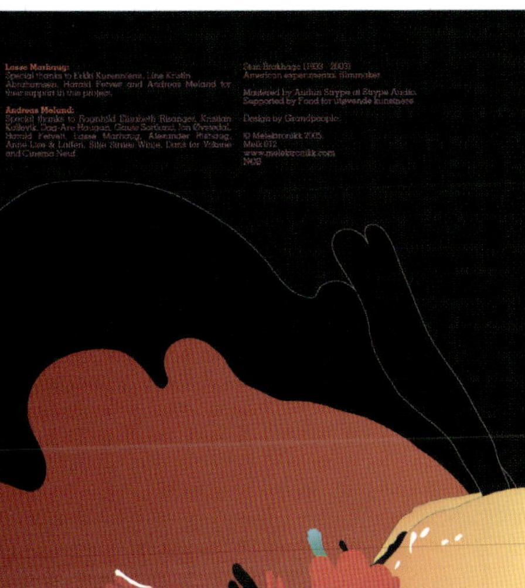

Lasse Marhaug:
Special thanks to Eddie Kuremaniens, Line Kristin Abrahamsen, Harald Fetveit and Andreas Meland for their support in this project.

Andreas Meland:
Special thanks to Rognhild Elisabeth Risanger, Kristian Kollevik, Dag-Are Haugan, Claude Sortland, Jan Kvistedal, Harald Fetveit, Lasse Marhaug, Alexander Hirsaug, André Lies & Lotten, Silje Simen Winge, Dans for Voksne and Cinema Nerd.

Stan Brakhage (1933 - 2003)
American experimental filmmaker

Mastered by Audun Strype at Strype Audio.
Supported by Fond for utøvende kunstnere

Design by Grandpeople.

© Molektronikk 2005.
Monk 012
www.molektronikk.com
MK3

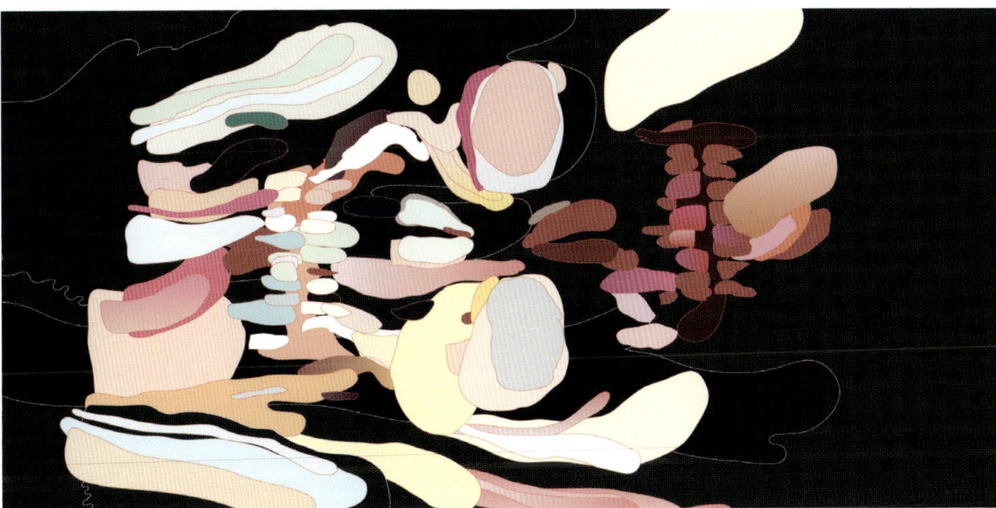

Mwmcreative

London, UK

Title: The World is Sound
Type of work: Poster
Client: Don't Panic Media
Design: ad, d// Maria da Gandra
Year: 2004

This design is developed based on a pictorial dictionary of 1290 instruments from Europe since Ancient Greece to our days. It also functions as a wallpaper.

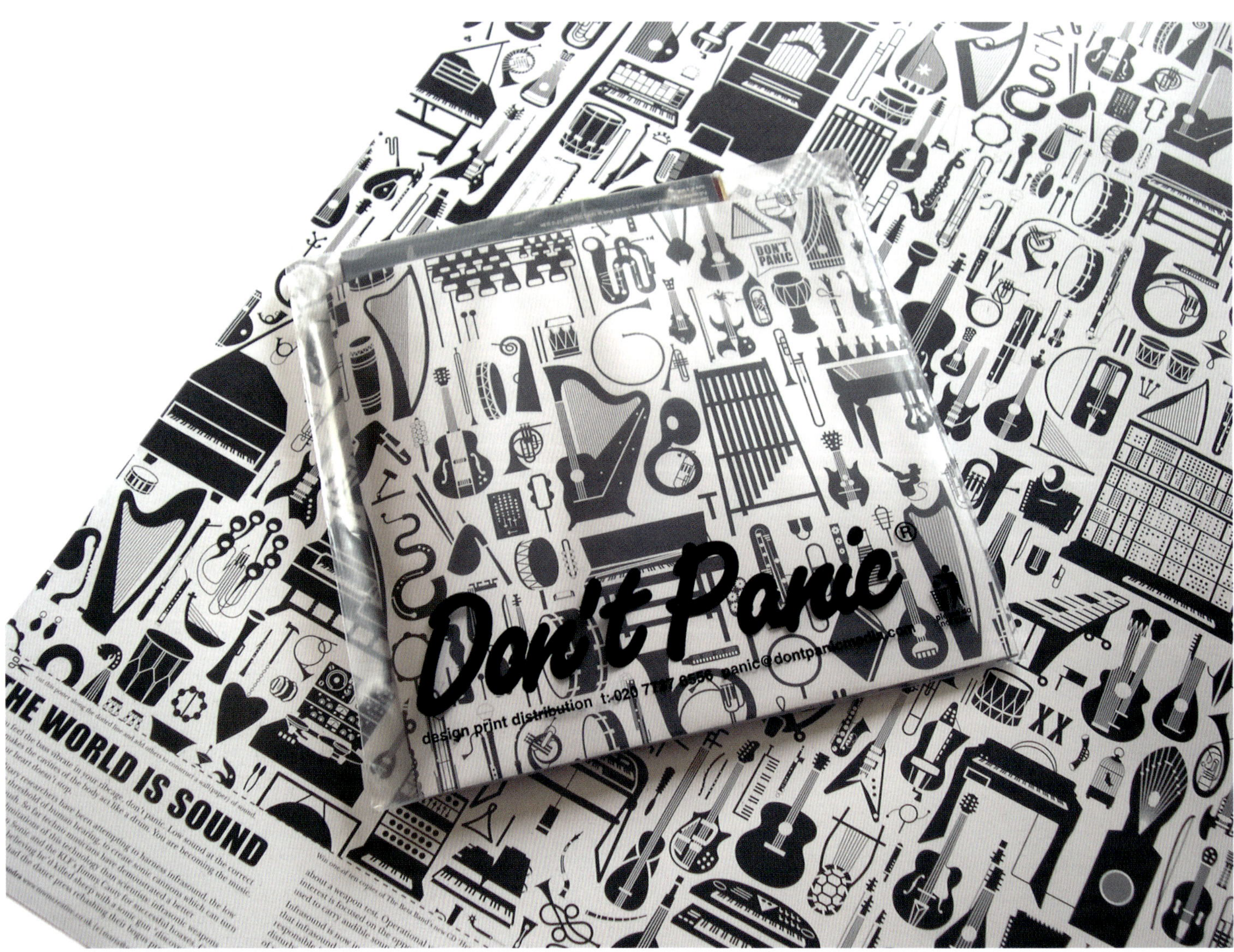

Grandpeople

Bergen, Norway

Title: Andreas – Deaf Leoppard
Type of work: CD sleeve
Client: Enlightenment
Design: ad, d// Grandpeople
Year: 2004

A sleeve design for the second follow-up in the Enlightenment 3" series released by Head of the label Melektronikk, Andreas Meland. The music is both electronic warm and electronic cold. So the design was meant to be, printed in black and white, minimalistic and with organic shapes and motifs. The label design contrasts the sleeve design and, as the title, emphasizes the humour with its bubblegummish fluorescent pink illustration.

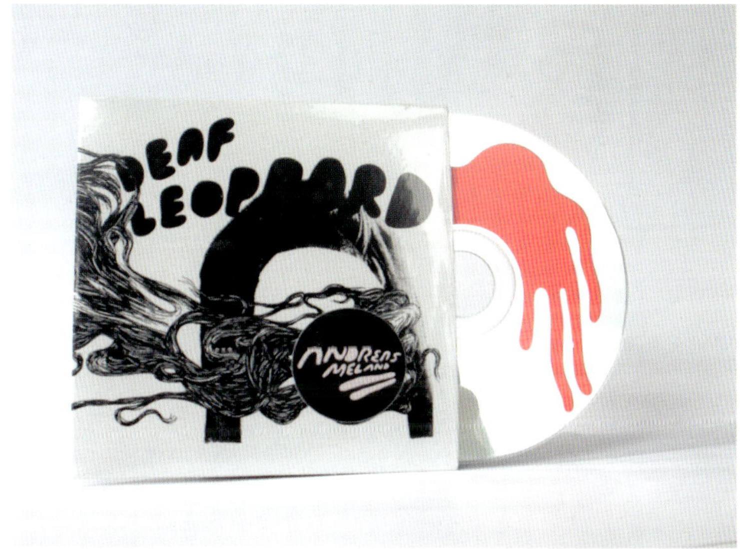

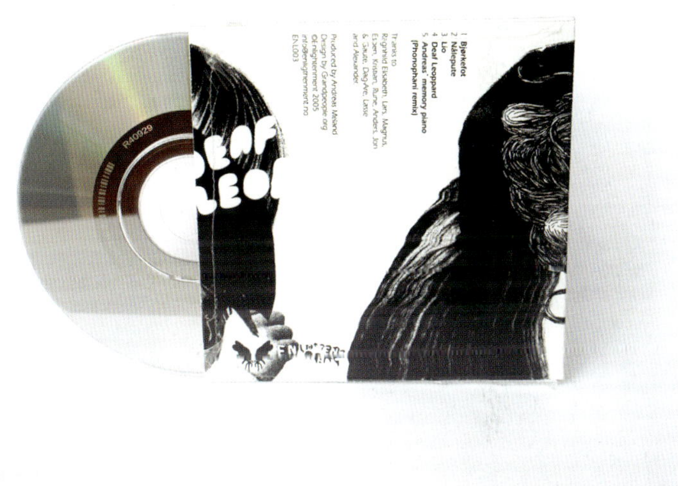

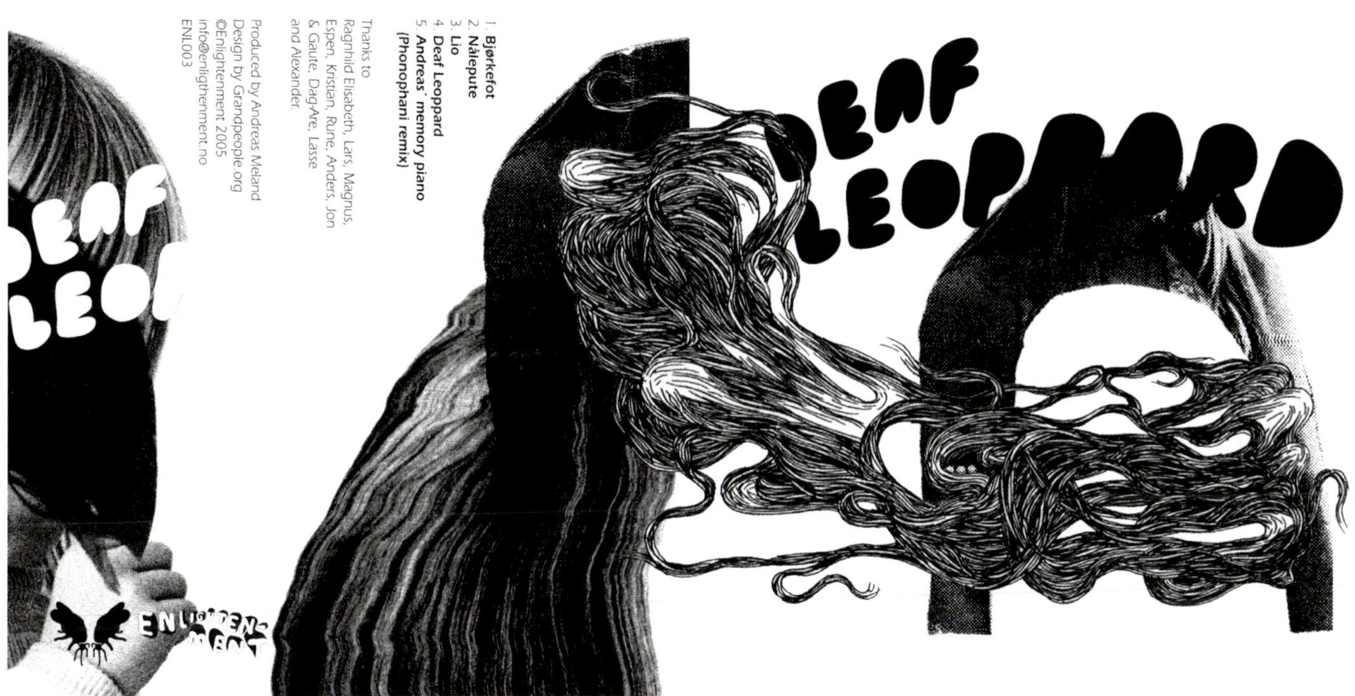

Halvor Bodin

Osly, Norway

Title: 1.// Oslo International Film Festival poster 2005 2.// Hallo Maybe
Type of work: Poster
Client: 1.// Oslo International Film Festival
2.// Bjarne Melgaard/ Haugar Art Center
Design: 1.// ad: Halvor Bodin d: Halvor Bodin, Svein Kvamme 2.// ad,d: Halvor Bodin
Year: 2005

1.// The poster designed for Oslo International Film Festival is a combination of photograph of an eye and illustration covered in blue and pink mainly. The eye image here indicates the idea of 'to watch', very suitable for the film festive. 2.// This piece is designed for Hallo Maybe. A dark, messy background, there is information in transparent white.

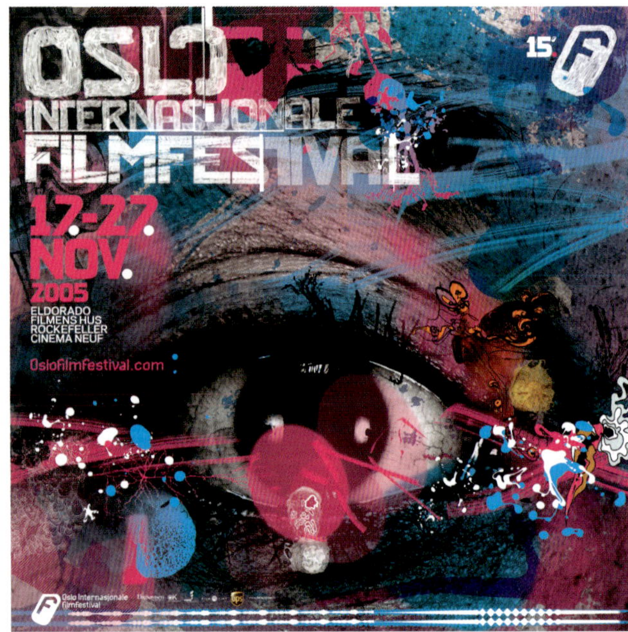

1.//

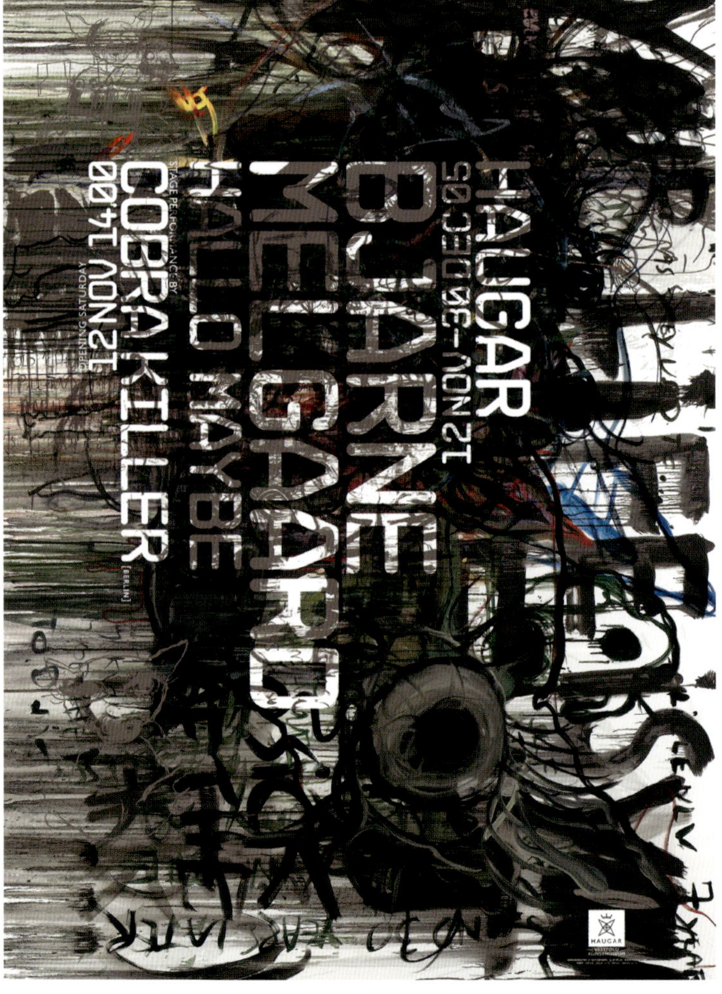

2.//

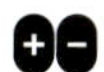

Styl●

London, UK
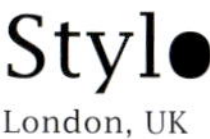

Title: Burnmurder
Type of work: CD sleeve
Client: X Marks Recordings
Design: ad, d// Tom Lancaster
Year: 2003

A double album contained within a slipcase. The card fronted jewel cases are polywrapped in 'firey' imagery which is used to match with the title 'Burnmurder'.

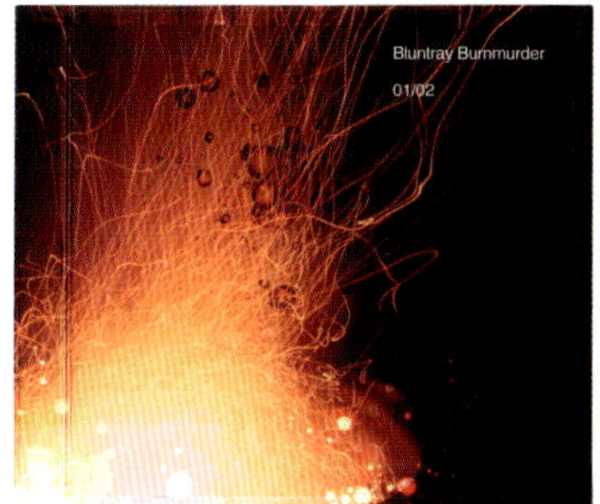
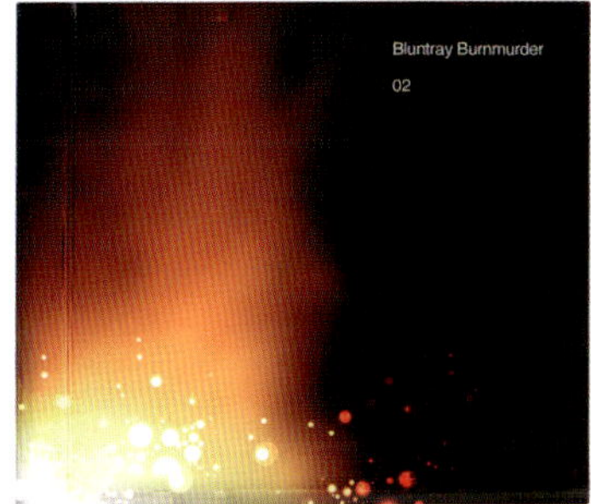
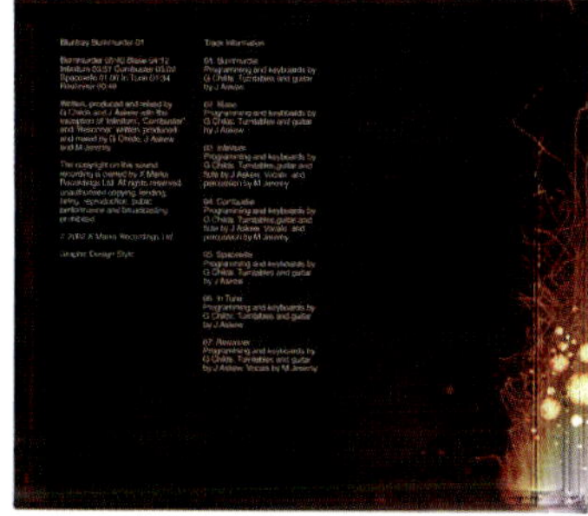
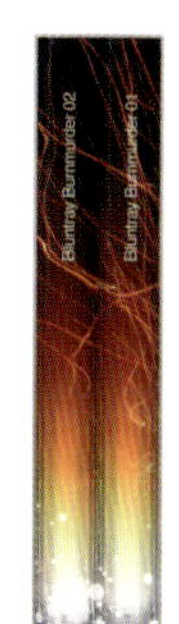
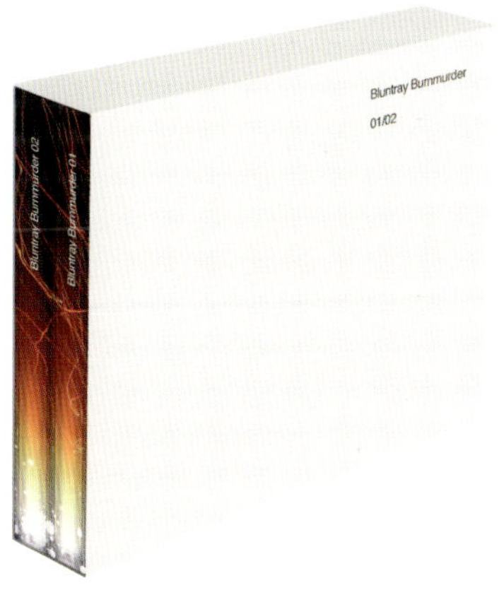
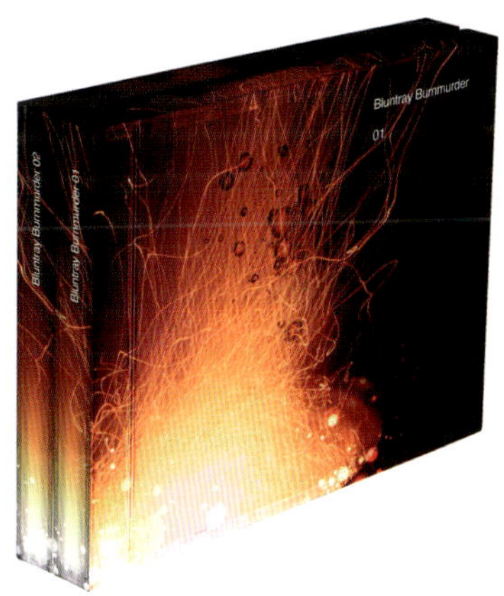
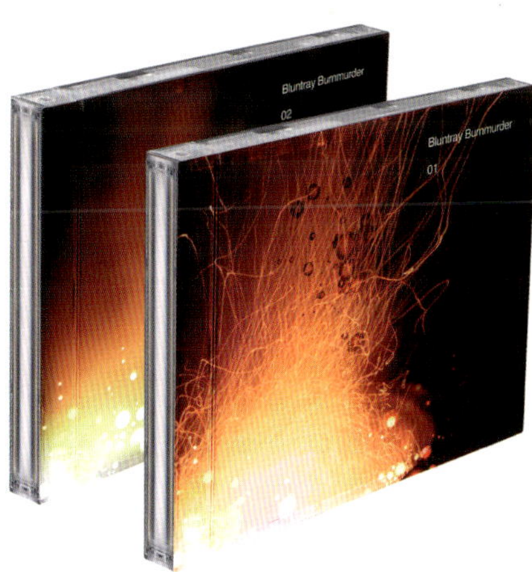
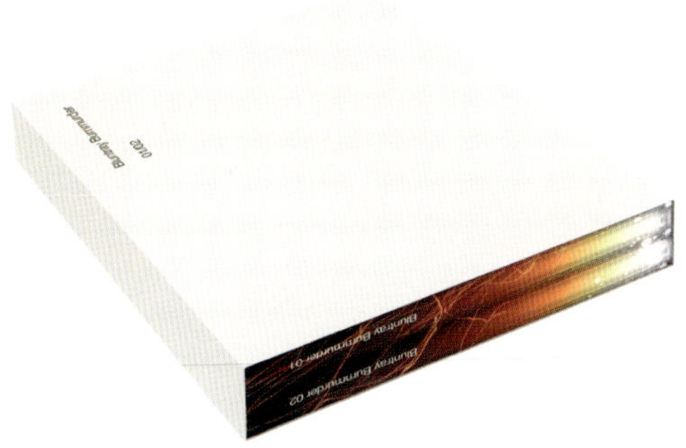

RMAC

Lisboa, Portugal

Title: Modalisboa Sport – 21st Edition
Type of work: Flyer, invitation, press ads, outdoor advertising, diary, show pass
Client: Associação Modalisboa
Design: ad// Ricardo Mealha, Ana Cunha
d// Ana Cunha, Diogo Potes
Year: 2003

This piece was designed for the theme 'ModaLisboa Sport' of ModaLisboa, the Lisbon Fashion Week, in which the 2004 Spring/ Summer collections of Portuguese fashion designers were presented on the catwalks at this edition. To convey the sense of informality, energy, movement and fun associated with the theme of 'sports', the graphic materials created for this event were colourful and witty, including the use of cutting-edge graphics. There was an interplay of images and graphic elements associated with sports: the invitations to the fashion shows resembled tickets to sports events and the fashion designers were illustrated as sports stars.

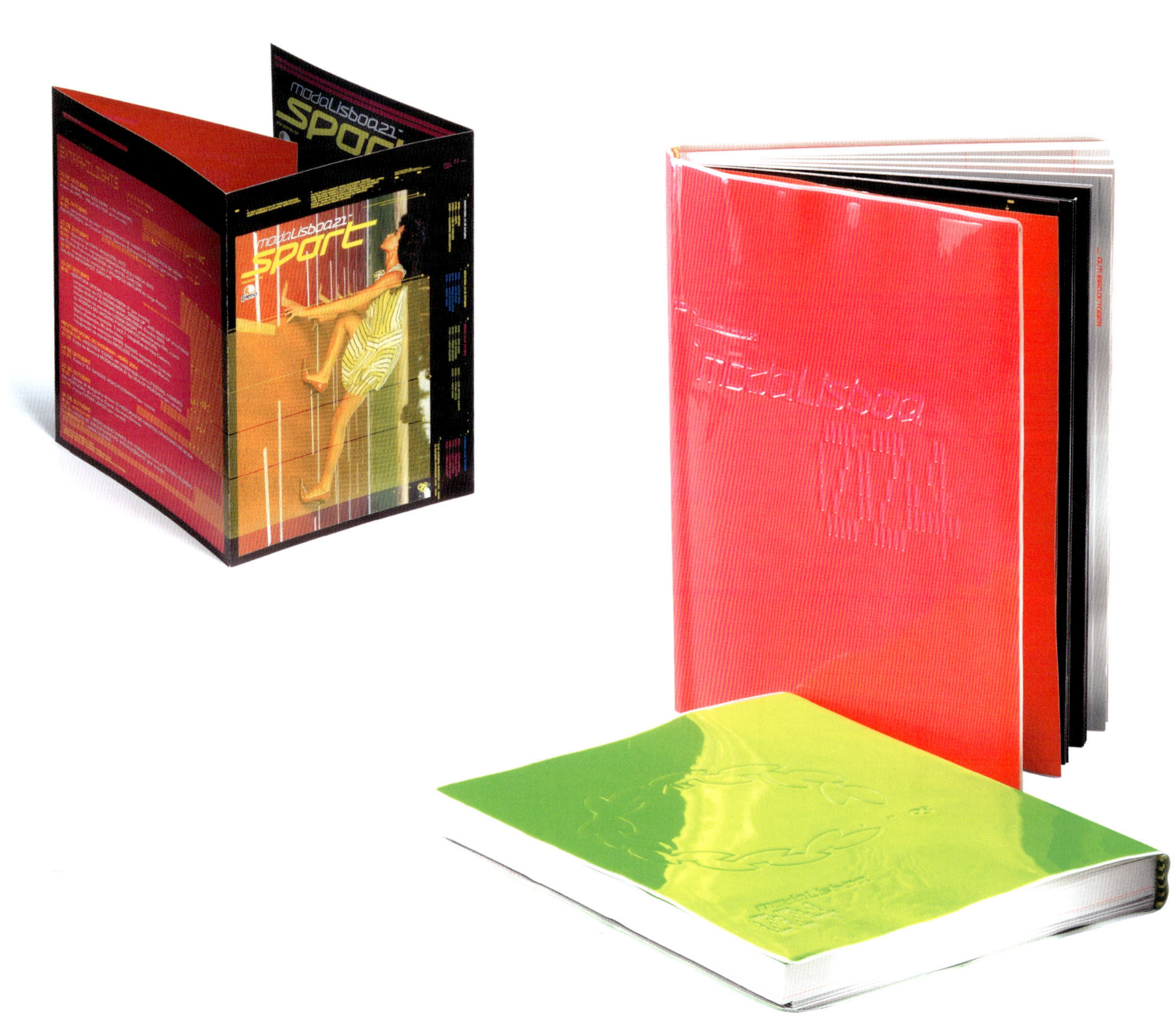

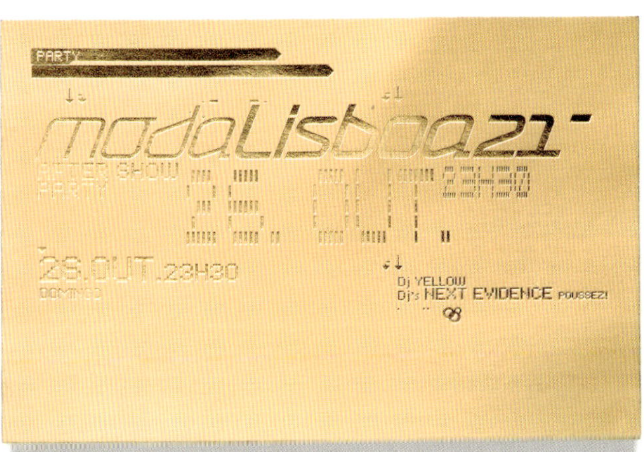

PARTY
modaLisboa21
25.OUT.23H30
25.OUT.23H30
DOMINGO
Dj YELLOW
Dj's NEXT EVIDENCE POUSSEZ!

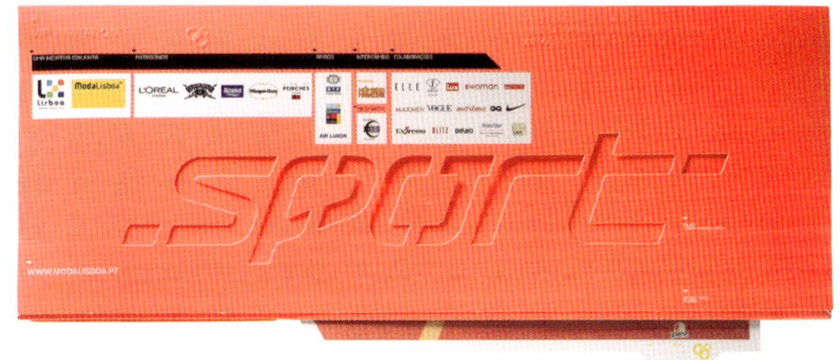

modaLisboa
L'OREAL
ELLE
VOGUE
.sport.
WWW.MODALISBOA.PT

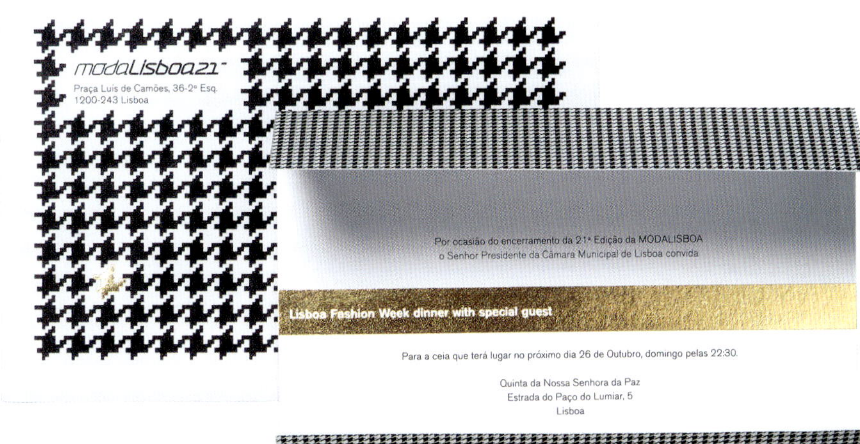

modaLisboa21
Praça Luis de Camões, 36-2º Esq.
1200-243 Lisboa
Por ocasião do encerramento da 21ª Edição da MODALISBOA
o Senhor Presidente da Câmara Municipal de Lisboa convida
Lisboa Fashion Week dinner with special guest
Para a ceia que terá lugar no próximo dia 26 de Outubro, domingo pelas 22:30.
Quinta da Nossa Senhora da Paz
Estrada do Paço do Lumiar, 5
Lisboa

Tnop™ & ®bePOS|+|VE design

Chicago, USA

Title: ®bePOS|+|VE Postcards
Type of work: Postcard
Client: ®bePOS|+|VE design, Bangkok
Design: ad, d// Tnop Wangsillapakun
Year: 2001-04

A set of self-promoting postcards for Tnop that works within their limited budgets. The materials and techniques are ranging from silk-screening on chrome paper to liquid lamination.

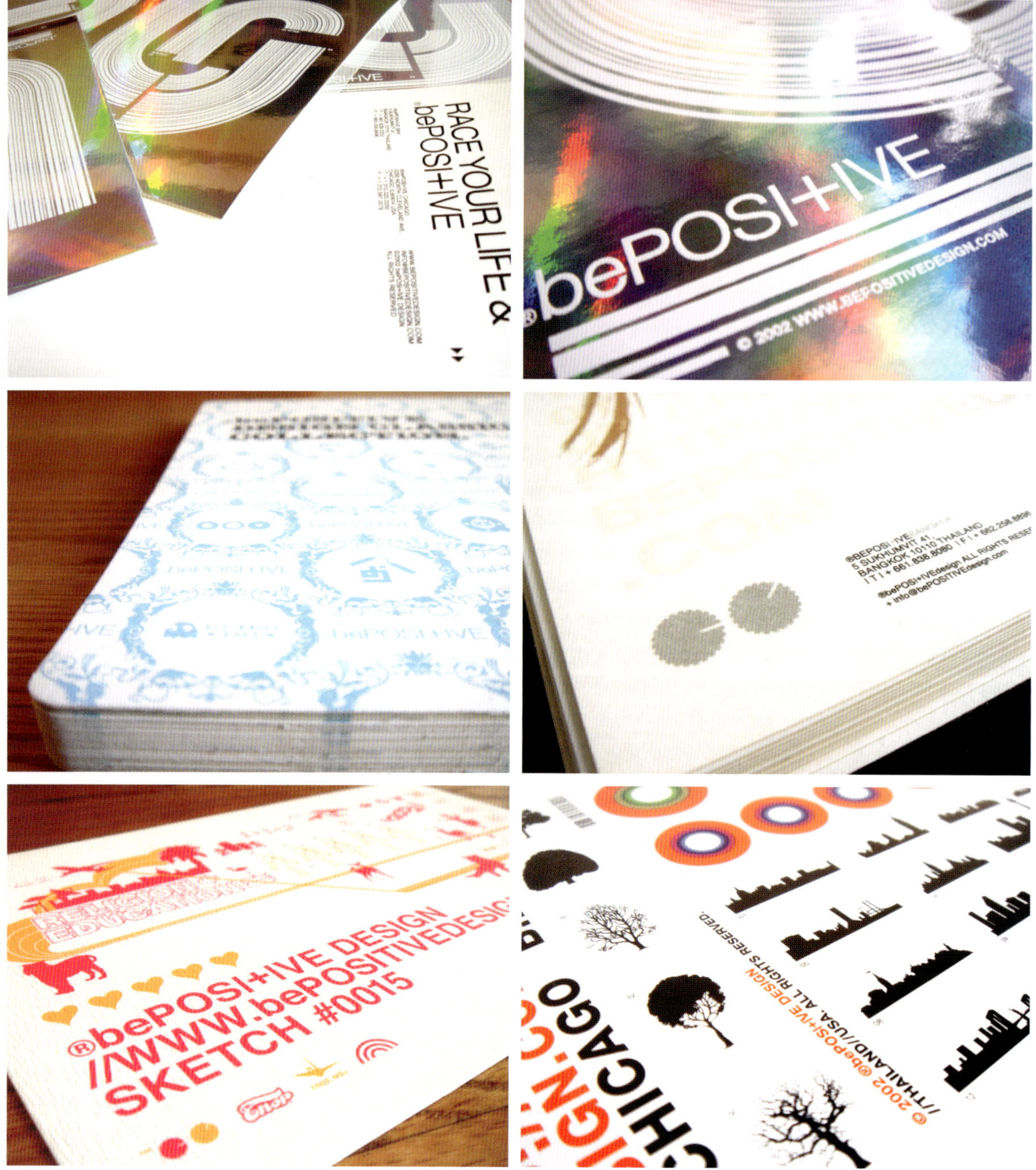

Tnop™ & ®bePOS|+|VE design

Chicago, USA

Title: Habitat® Postcards
Type of work: Postcard
Client: Habitat® Bangkok
Design: ad// Tnop Wangsillapakun d// Tnop Wangsillapakun, Akewit Vongsa-ngiam, Woottinat Wangsillapakun
Year: 2001-04

These are various promotional postcards for Habitat® furniture store in Bangkok. To be sent out throughout the year, the postcards have to be effective under limited budgets. The size for these postcards is 5"x7" and have unique design and printing techniques from 2 colours printing, fluorescence colour, foil stamping to emboss and liquid lamination.

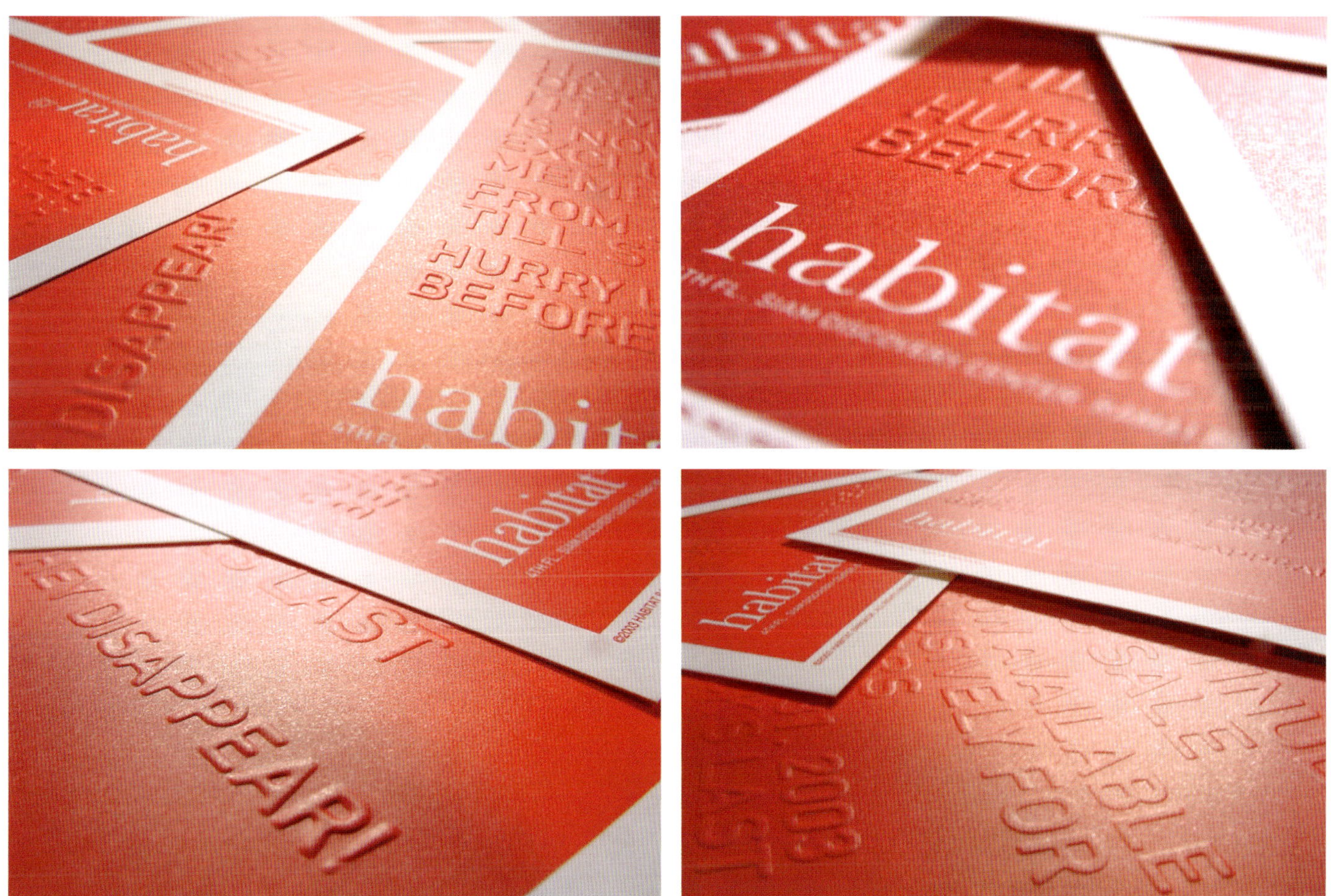

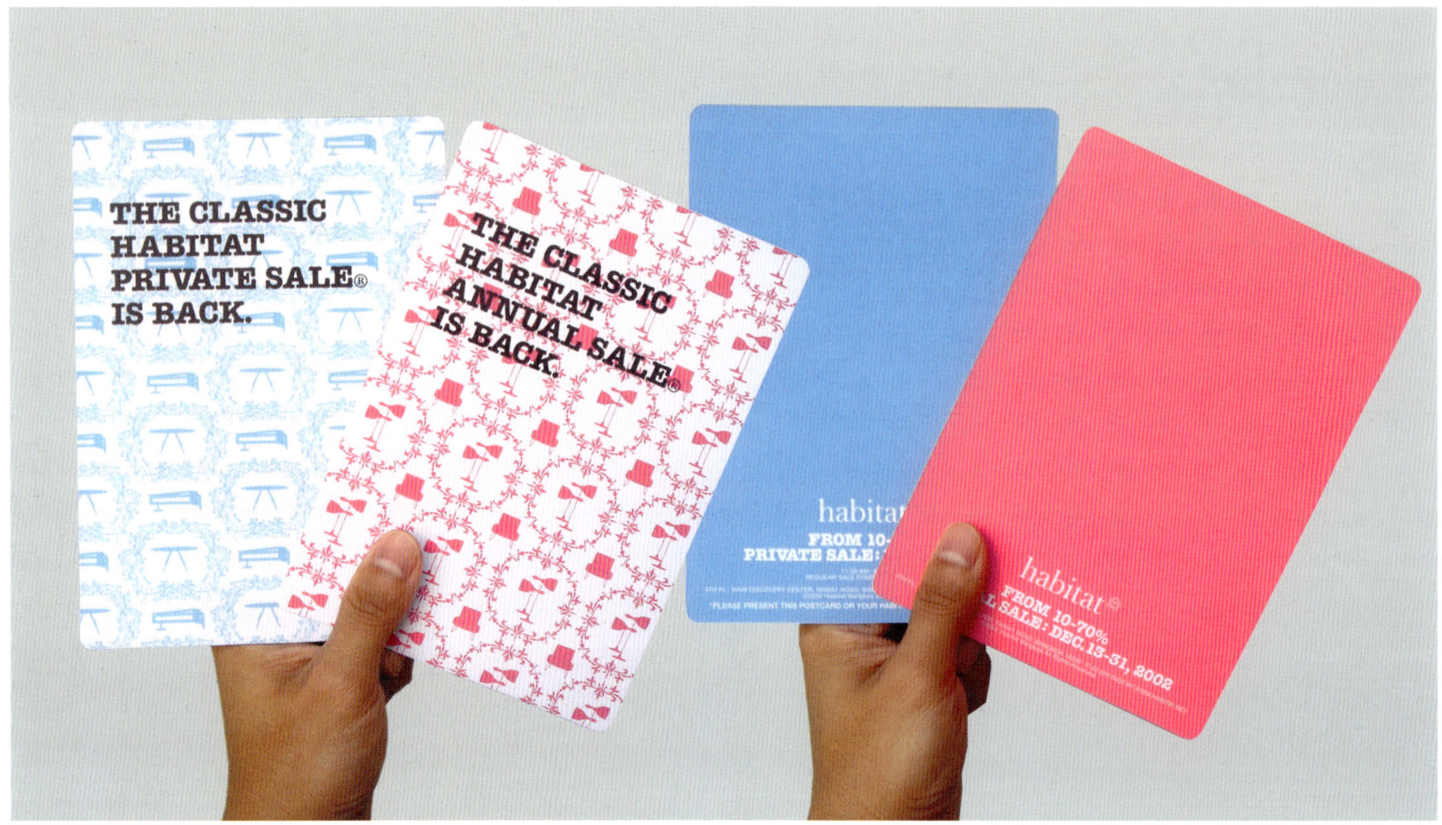

Tnop™ & ®bePOS|+|VE design

Chicago, USA

Title: Habitat® Postcards
Type of work: Postcard
Client: Habitat® Bangkok
Design: ad// Tnop Wangsillapakun d// Tnop Wangsillapakun, Akewit Vongsa-ngiam, Woottinat Wangsillapakun
Year: 2001-04

These are various promotional postcards for Habitat® furniture store in Bangkok. To be sent out throughout the year, the postcards have to be effective in the limited budgets. The size for these postcards is 5"x7" and have unique design and printing techniques from 2 colours printing, fluorescence colour, foil stamping to emboss and liquid lamination.

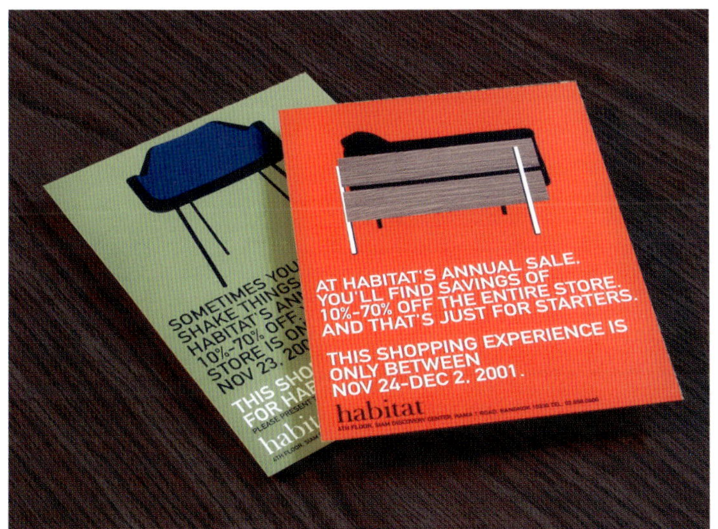

SOMETIMES YOU
SHAKE THINGS
HABITAT'S AN
10%~70% OFF
STORE IS ON
NOV 23, 200
AT HABITAT'S ANNUAL SALE.
YOU'LL FIND SAVINGS OF
10%~70% OFF THE ENTIRE STORE.
AND THAT'S JUST FOR STARTERS.
THIS SHOPPING EXPERIENCE IS
ONLY BETWEEN
NOV 24-DEC 2, 2001.
habitat

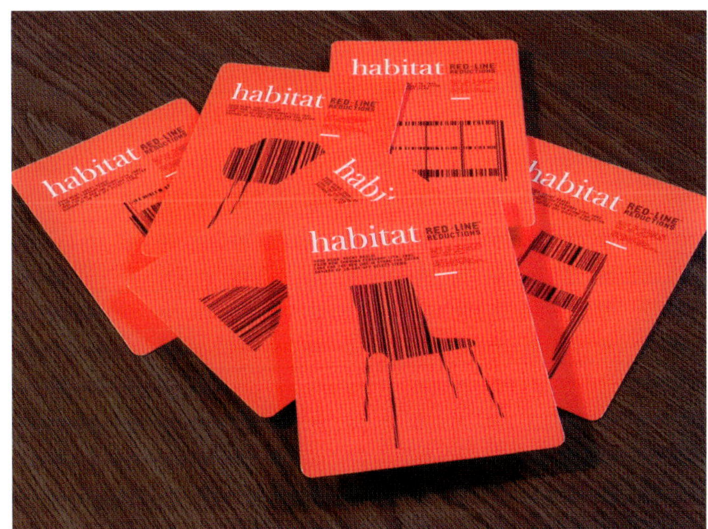

habitat
RED-LINE
COLLECTION

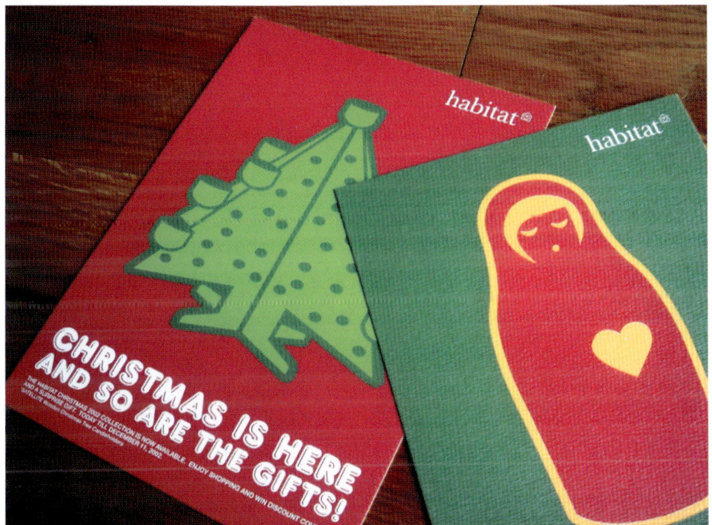

habitat
CHRISTMAS IS HERE
AND SO ARE THE GIFTS!

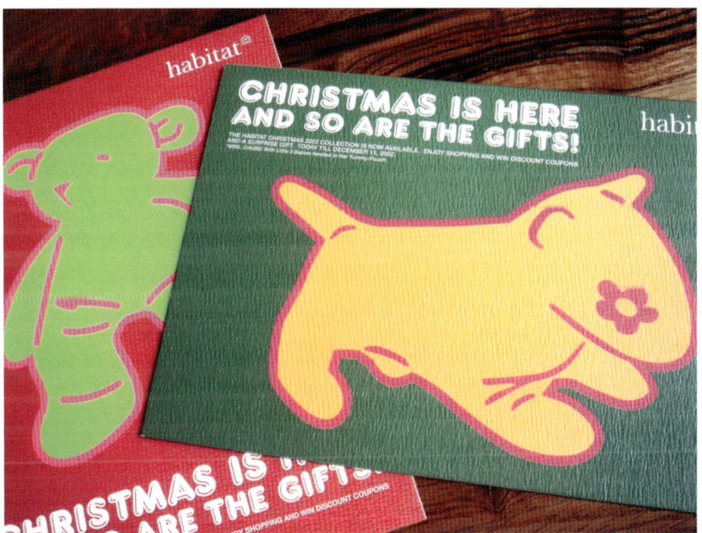

habitat
CHRISTMAS IS HERE
AND SO ARE THE GIFTS!

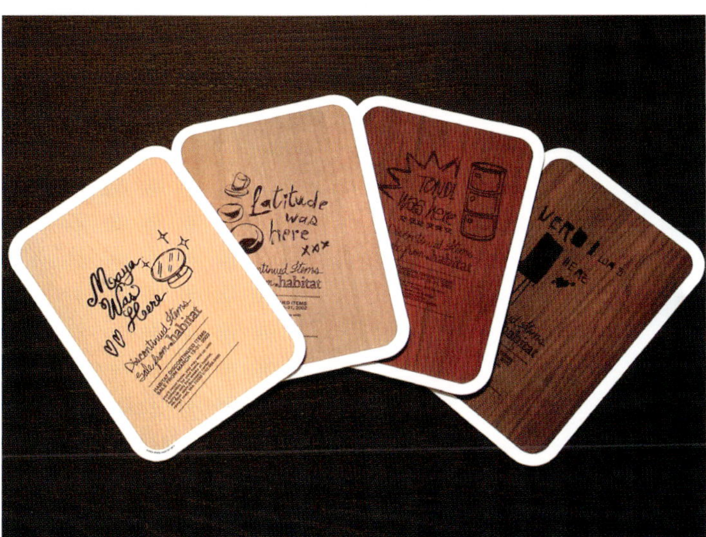

Latitude
was
here
Mona
Was
Here

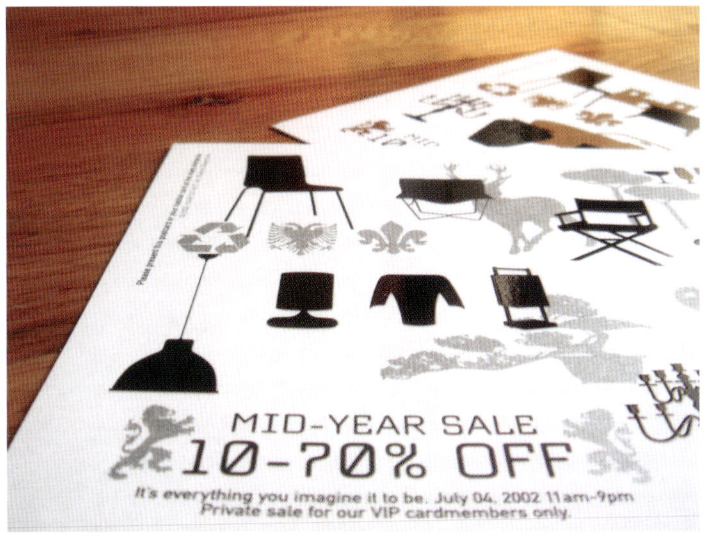

MID-YEAR SALE
10-70% OFF
It's everything you imagine it to be. July 04, 2002 11am~9pm
Private sale for our VIP cardmembers only.

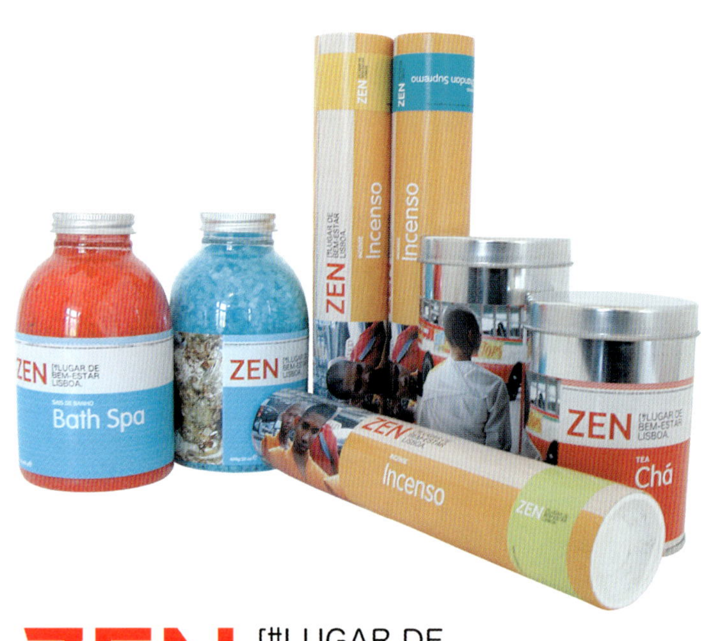

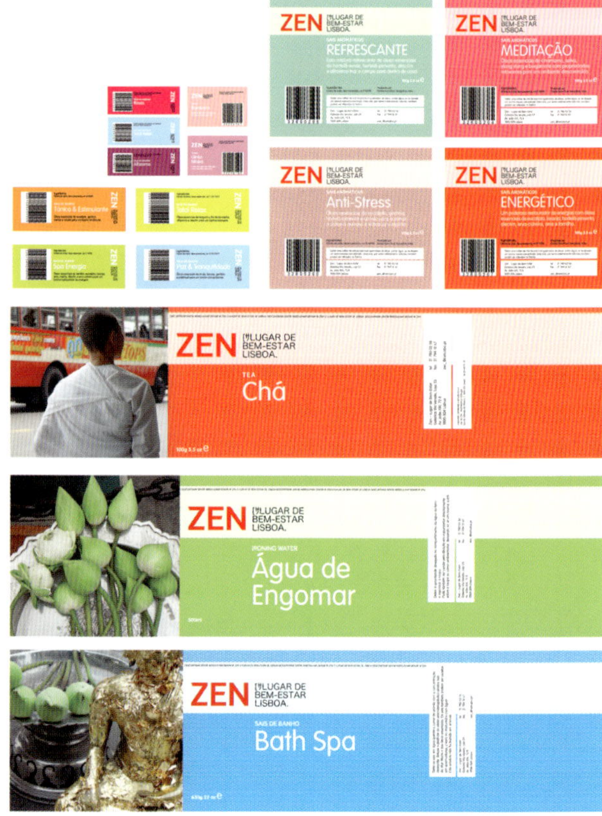

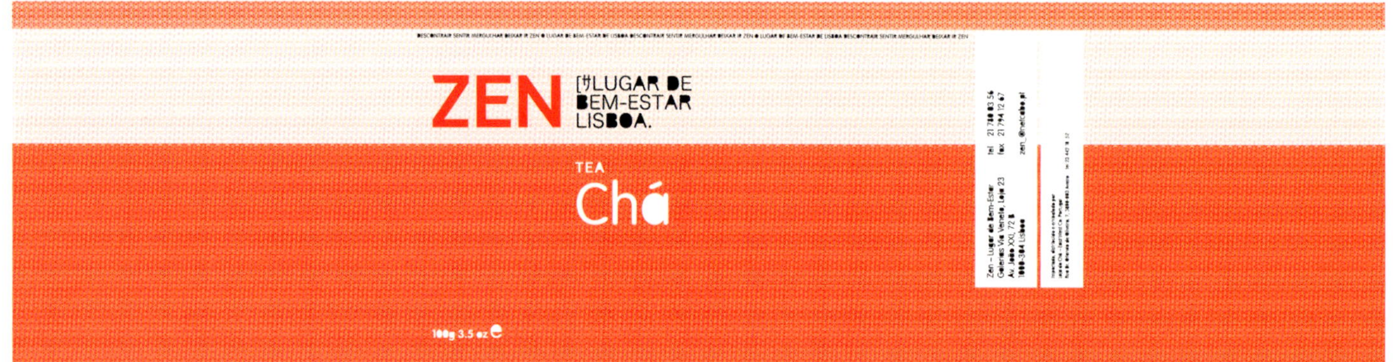

RMAC

Lisboa, Portugal

Title: Zen
Type of work: Packaging
Client: Zen
Design: ad, d// Ricardo Mealha, Ana Cunha
Year: 2004

The graphics of this design expressed the spirit of the shop, which focuses on the products that make you feel comfortable, relaxed and that fill your environment with unique ambience.

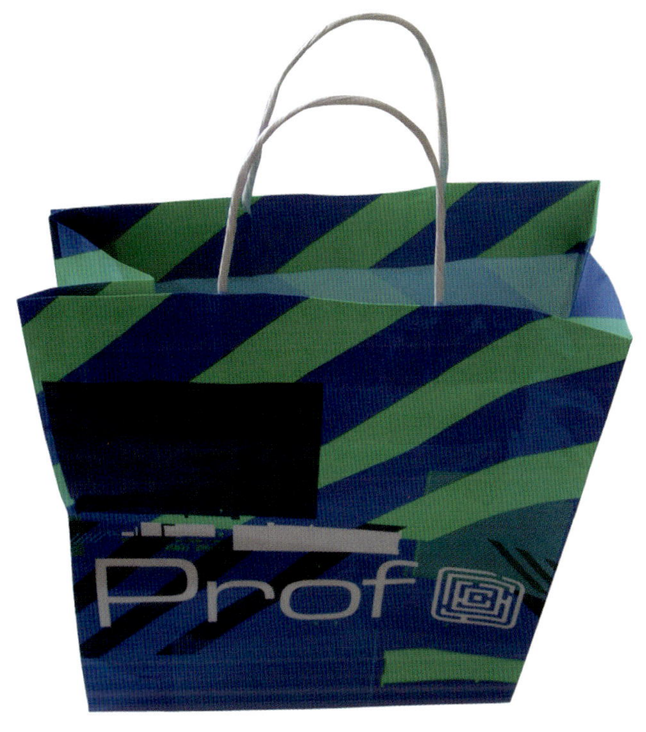

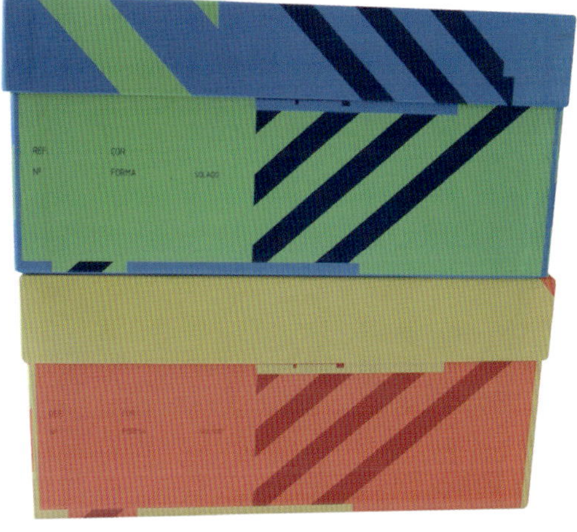

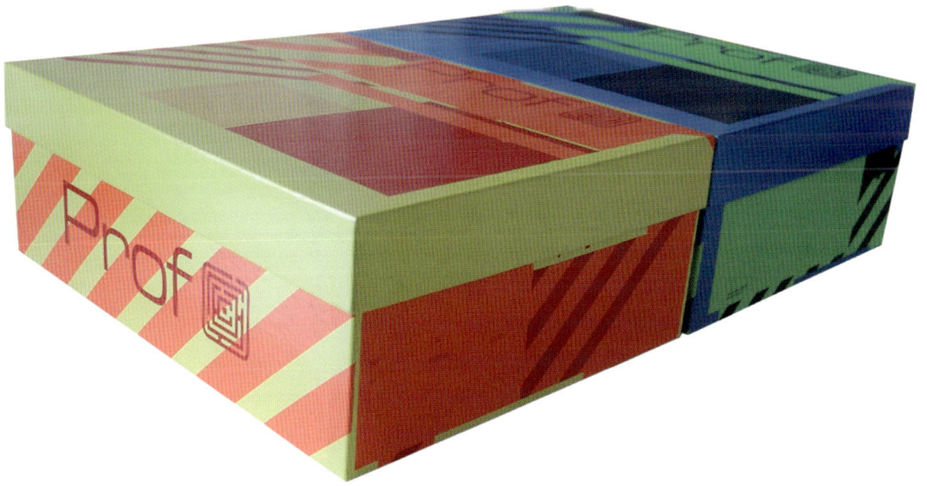

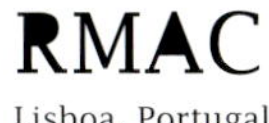

RMAC

Lisboa, Portugal

Title: Packaging Prof
Type of work: Packaging
Client: Prof
Design: ad// Ricardo Mealha, Ana Cunha
d// Diogo Potes
Year: 2004

A design for a shoe store chain that has high quality shoes with exclusive design. Following the brand's spirit: irreverence and the deeply marked contemporary presence, Prof's boxes and bags reflect strong image of style and fashion, always with colourful illustrations.

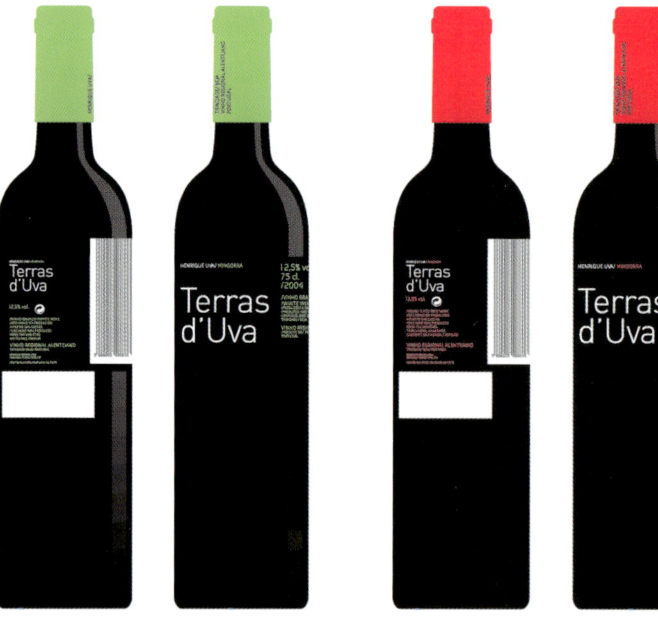

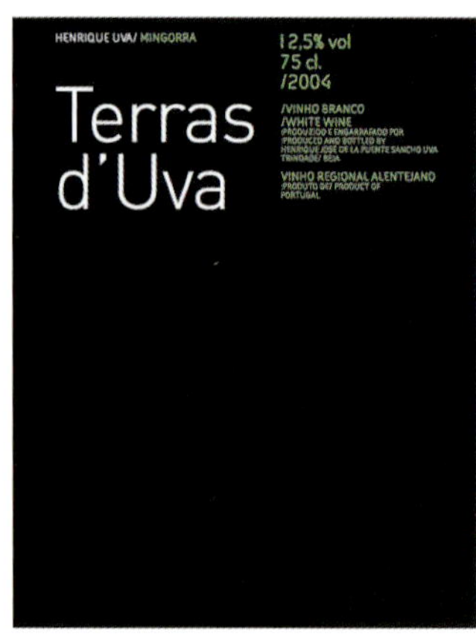

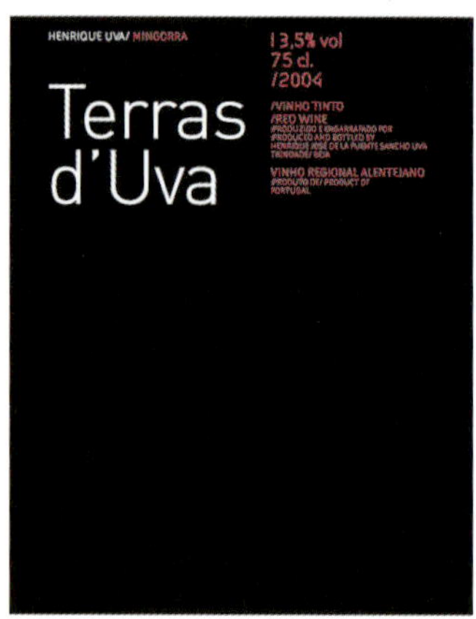

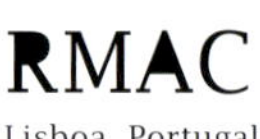

RMAC

Lisboa, Portugal

Title: Terras de Uva, Alfaraz
Type of work: Label
Client: Henrique Uva, Herdade da Mingorra
Designers: ad, d// Ricardo Mealha, Ana Cunha
Year: 2005

The Herdade da Mingorra's tags give authenticity and modernity in an original way: they flee from the usual image of an aletejano's hill, appeal to suggestive illustrations, very relaxed but also very elegant and innovating printing techniques less is used.

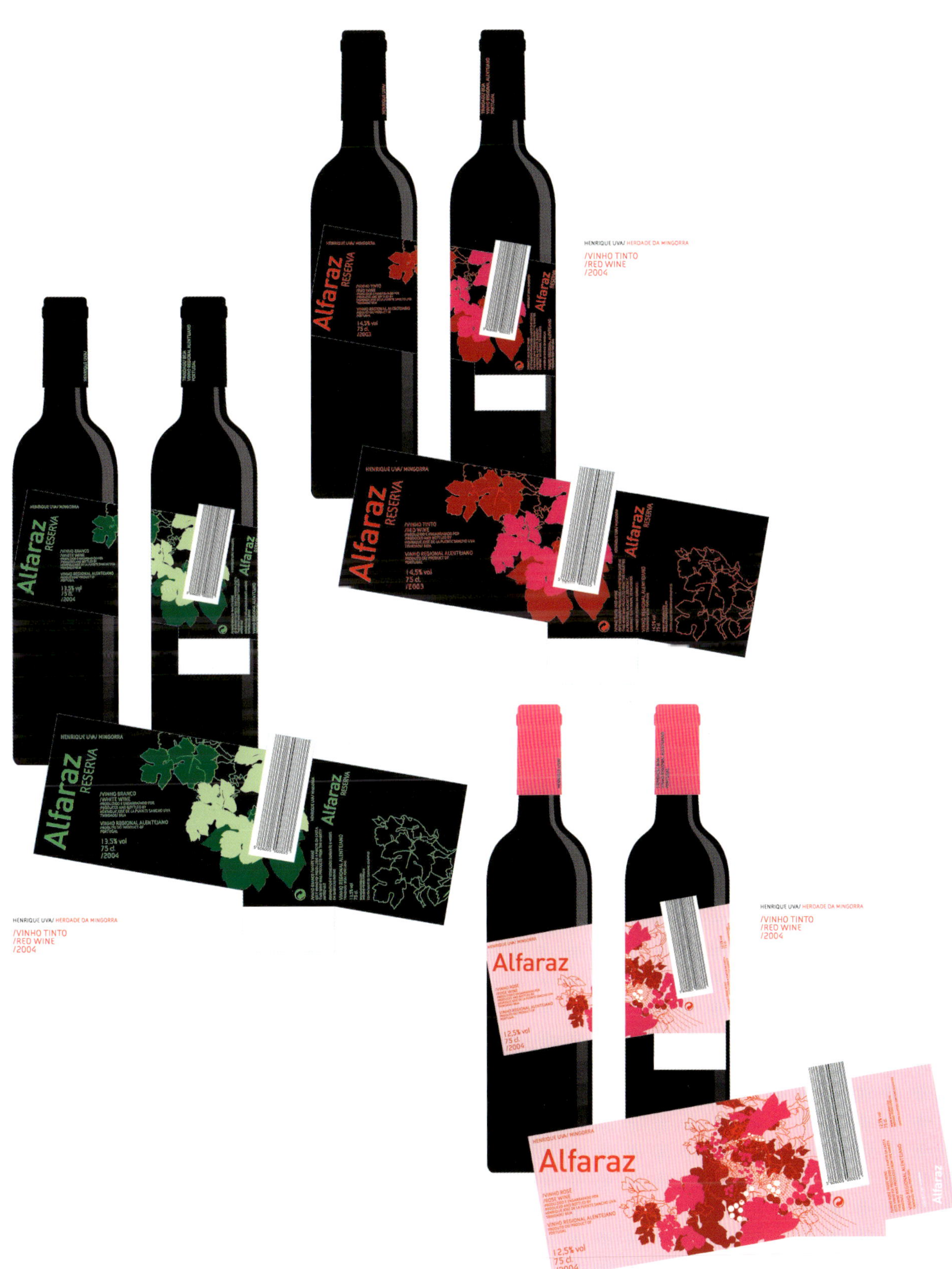
HENRIQUE UVA/ HERDADE DA MINGORRA
/VINHO TINTO
/RED WINE
/2004

Alfaraz
RESERVA

HENRIQUE UVA/ HERDADE DA MINGORRA
/VINHO TINTO
/RED WINE
/2004

Alfaraz
RESERVA

Alfaraz

HENRIQUE UVA/ HERDADE DA MINGORRA
/VINHO TINTO
/RED WINE
/2004

Alfaraz

RMAC

Lisboa, Portugal

Title: Modalisboa Five Stars – 22nd Edition
Type of work: Invitation, poster, flyer, outdoor ad, booklet, TV ad
Client: Associação Modalisboa
Design: ad, d// Ricardo Mealha, Ana Cunha
Year: 2004

This piece was designed under the theme of the ModaLisboa is Lisbon´s Official Fashion Week 22nd edition: luxury and glamour under the designation of 'Five Stars'. A picture of Sofia Loren taken by John Springer in the Fifties served as the inspiration and background for the graphic languages were utilized. The materials used to convey the message consisted of fine paper and foil stamping in eight different colours. Swarovski crystals were also used in VIP invitation.

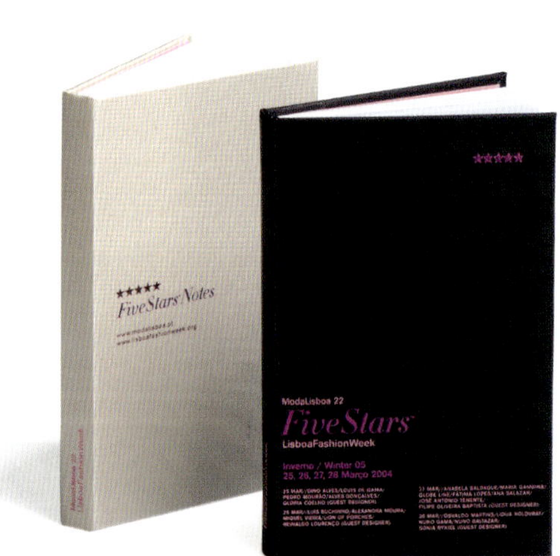

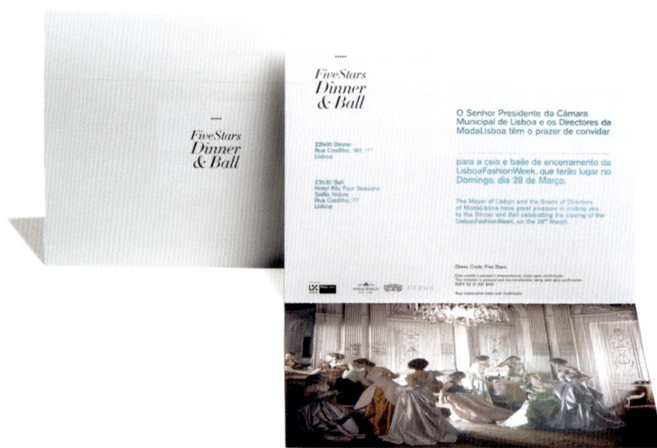

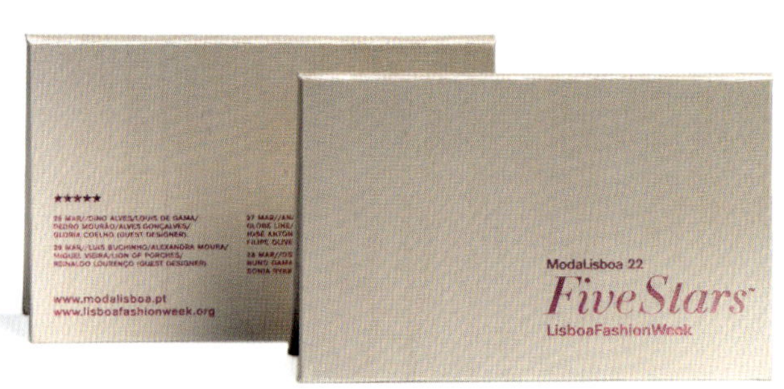

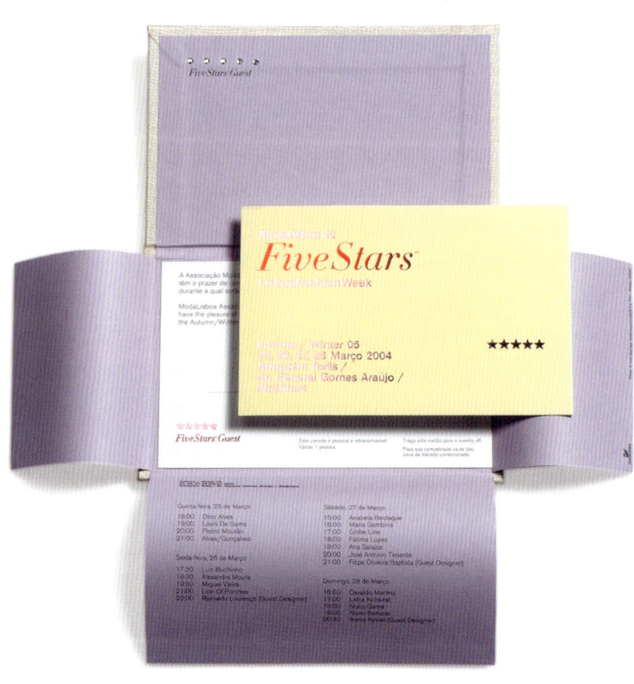

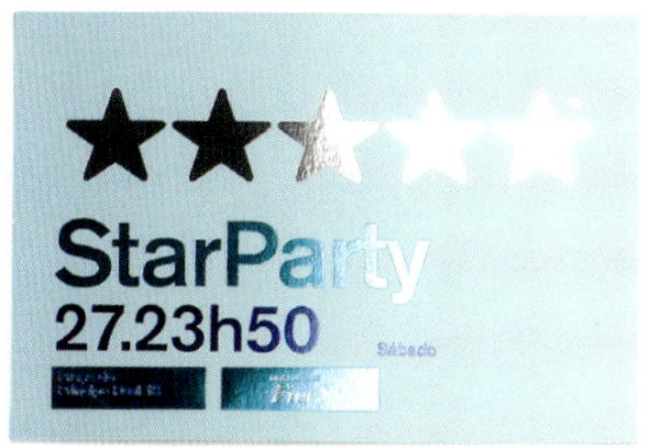
★★★☆☆
StarParty
27.23h50
Sábado

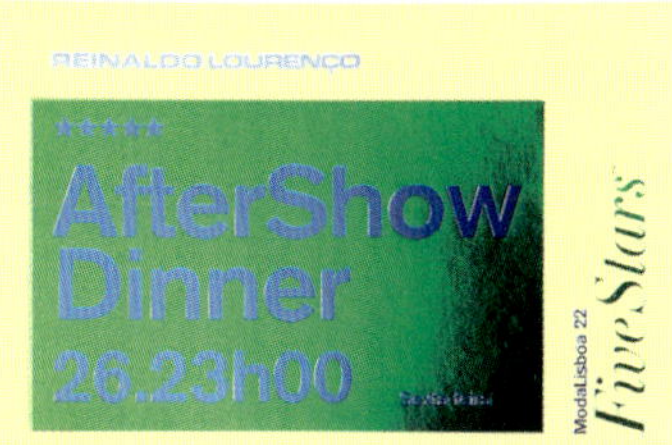
REINALDO LOURENÇO
★★★★★
AfterShow
Dinner
26.23h00
ModaLisboa 22
FiveStars

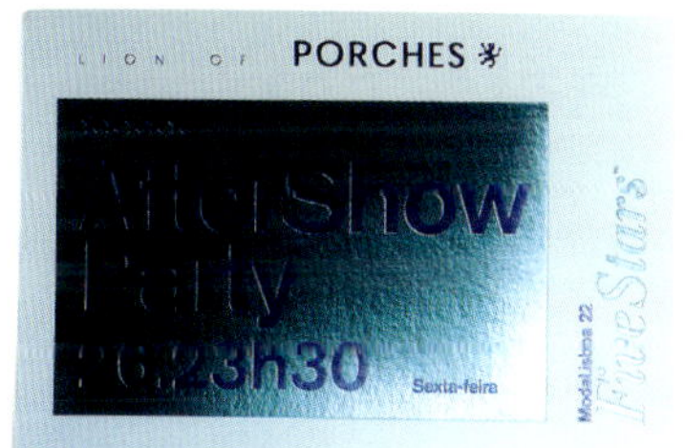
LION OF PORCHES
AfterShow
Party
26.23h30
ModaLisboa 22
FiveStars
Sexta-feira

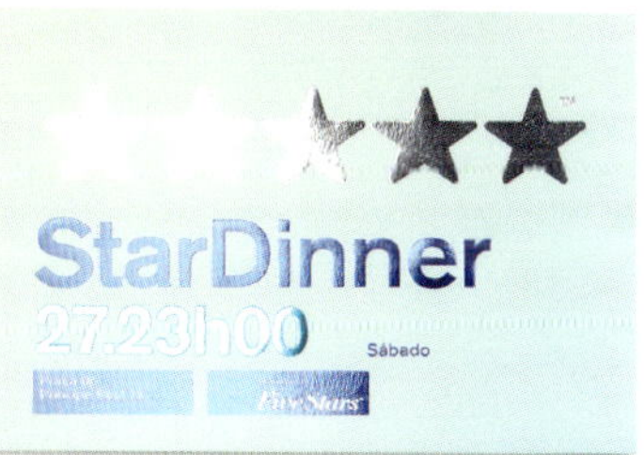
★★★★★
StarDinner
27.23h00
Sábado
FiveStars

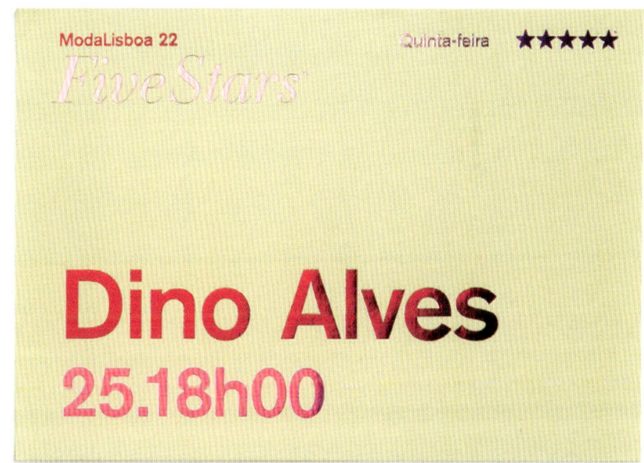
ModaLisboa 22
Quinta-feira ★★★★★
FiveStars
Dino Alves
25.18h00

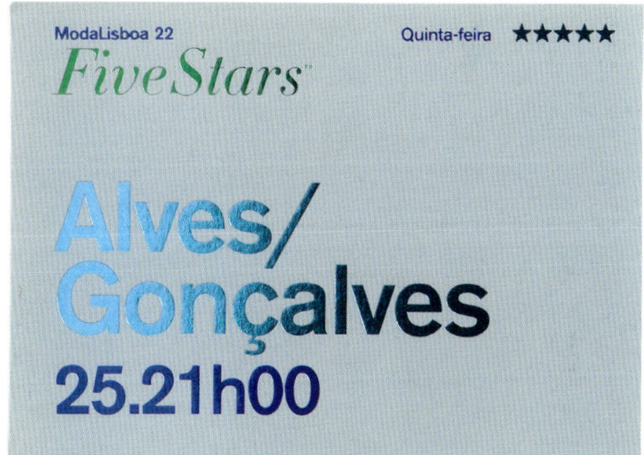
ModaLisboa 22
Quinta-feira ★★★★★
FiveStars
Alves/
Gonçalves
25.21h00

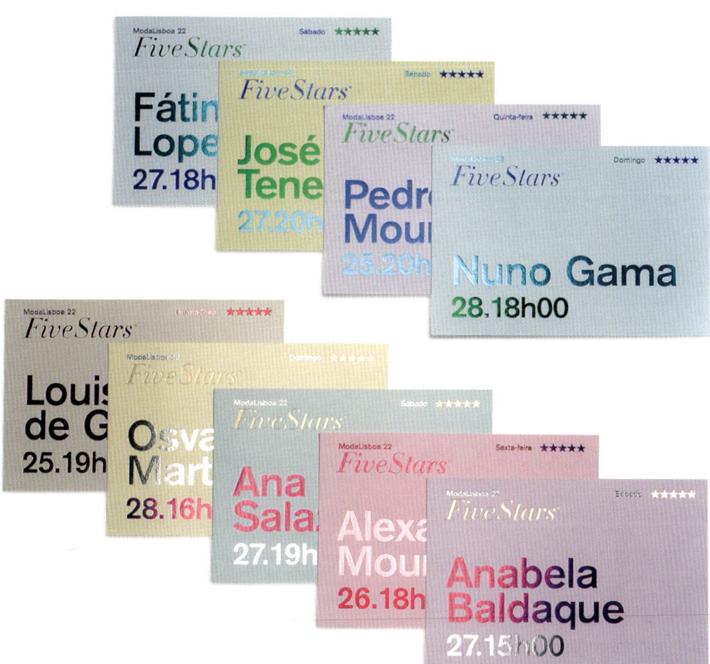
ModaLisboa 22
Sábado ★★★★★
FiveStars
Fátima
Lopes
27.18h
ModaLisboa 22
Sábado ★★★★★
FiveStars
José
Tene
27.20h
ModaLisboa 22
Quinta-feira ★★★★★
FiveStars
Pedro
Mour
25.20h
ModaLisboa 22
Domingo ★★★★★
FiveStars
Nuno Gama
28.18h00
ModaLisboa 22
★★★★★
FiveStars
Louis
de G
25.19h
ModaLisboa 22
★★★★★
FiveStars
Osva
Mart
28.16h
ModaLisboa 22
★★★★★
FiveStars
Ana
Sala
27.19h
ModaLisboa 22
Sexta-feira ★★★★★
FiveStars
Alexa
Mou
26.18h
ModaLisboa 22
★★★★★
FiveStars
Anabela
Baldaque
27.15h00

F●rm®

London, UK

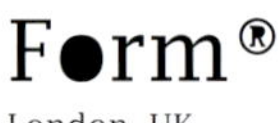

Title: MGEITF Television Festival Identity 2005
Type of work: Programme of events, delegate list, invitation
Client: MediaGuardian Edinburgh International Television Festival
Design: ad// Paul West d// Paul West, Claire Warner
Year: 2005

An identity which the existing logo was kept but with a strong and vibrant look added to run across all festival literature including invites, adverts, brochures, etc. It creates a brand that would be easily adaptable over the years, yet keeping a homogeneity. The typeface Volkswagen is used to illustrate the entertaining - yet controversial nature of the festival. Different colour blockfoils against a similar solid colour are used. The identity is constantly evolving but retains its strength and character.

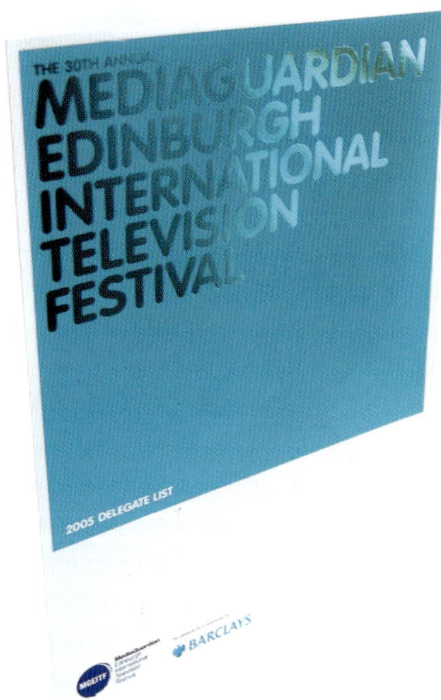

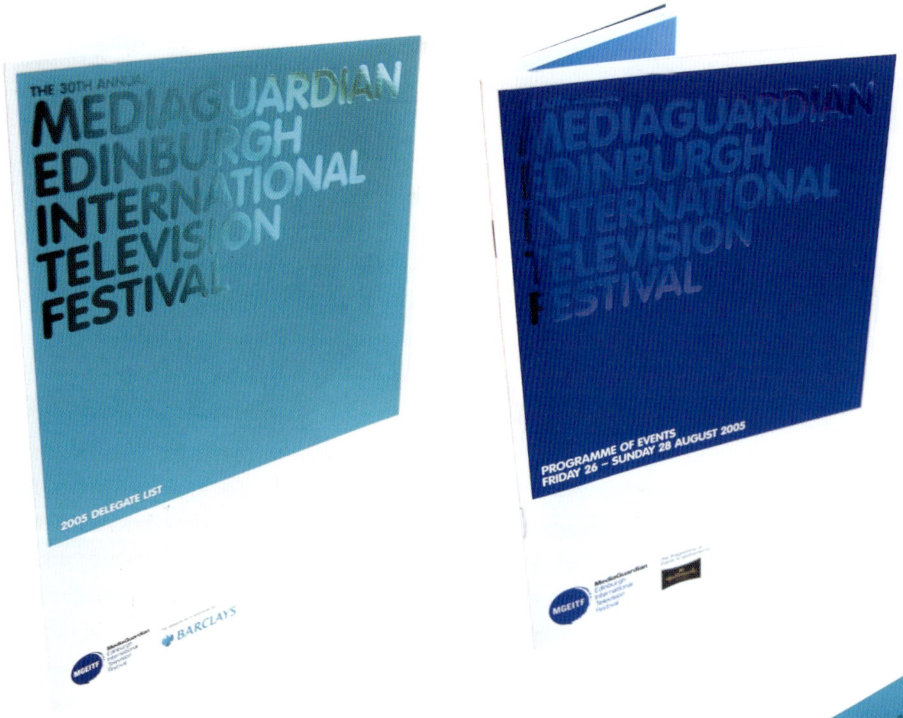

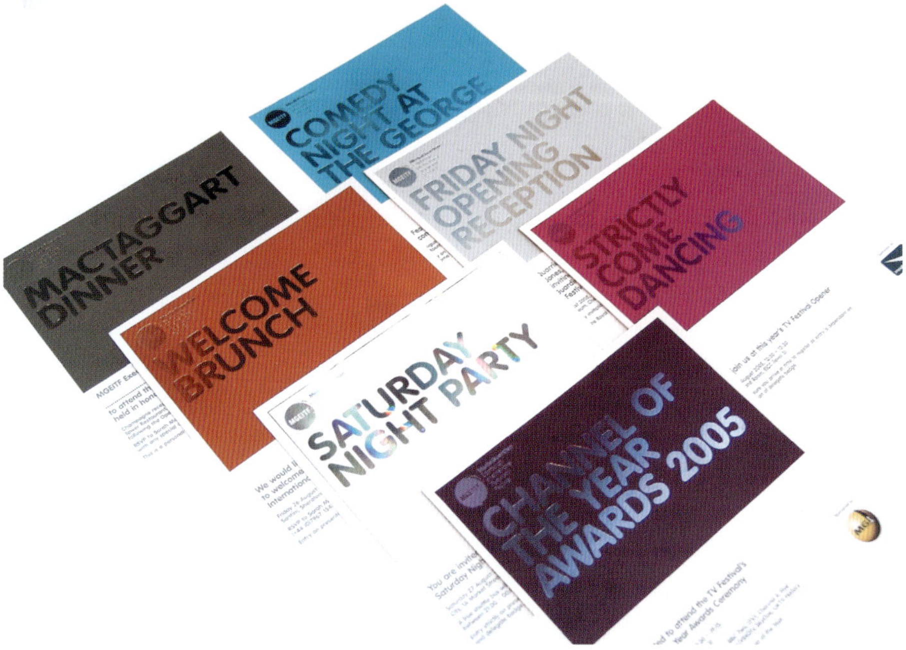

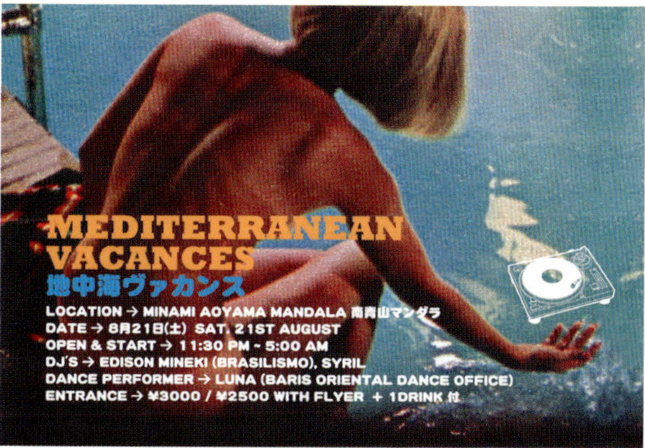

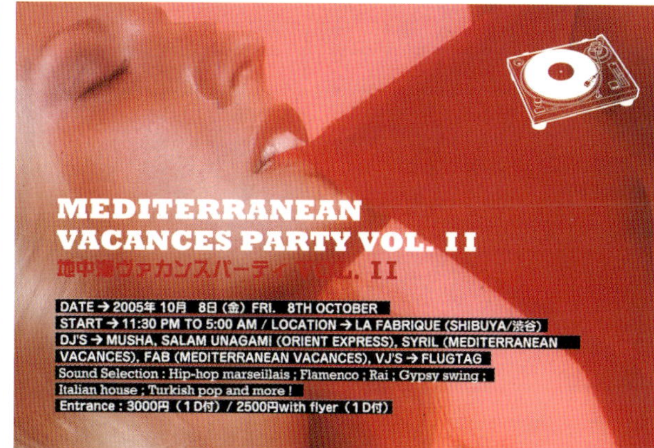

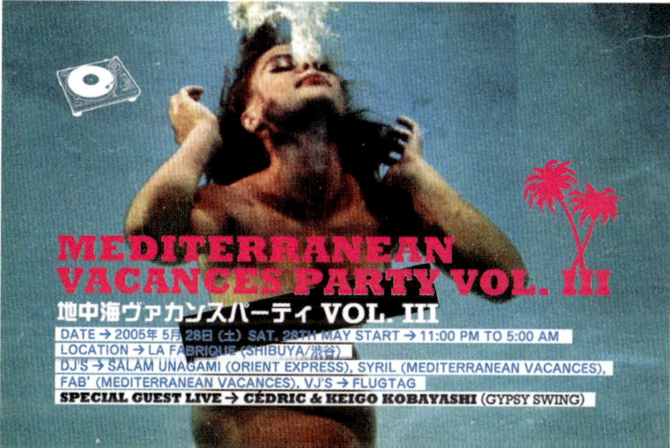

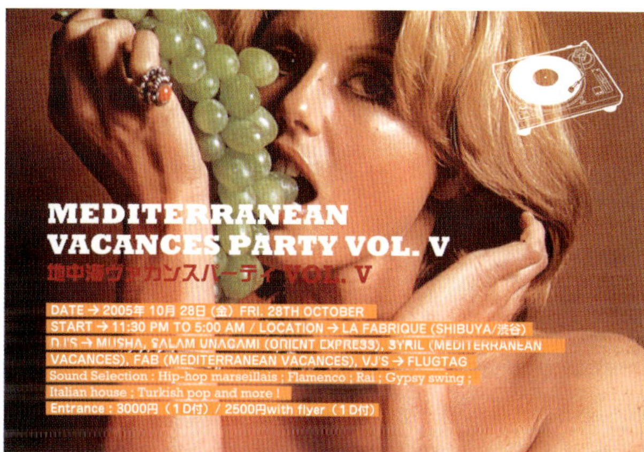

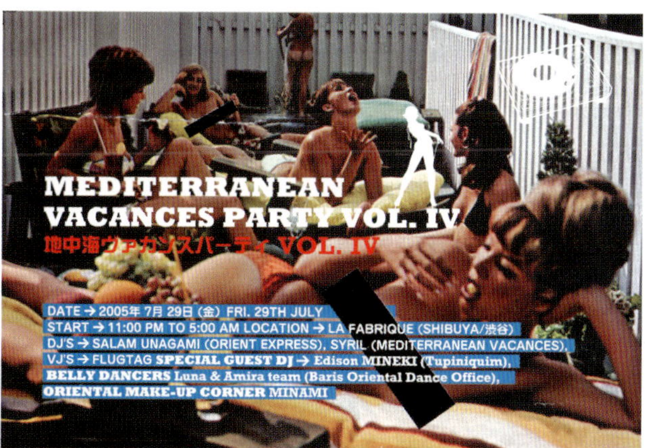

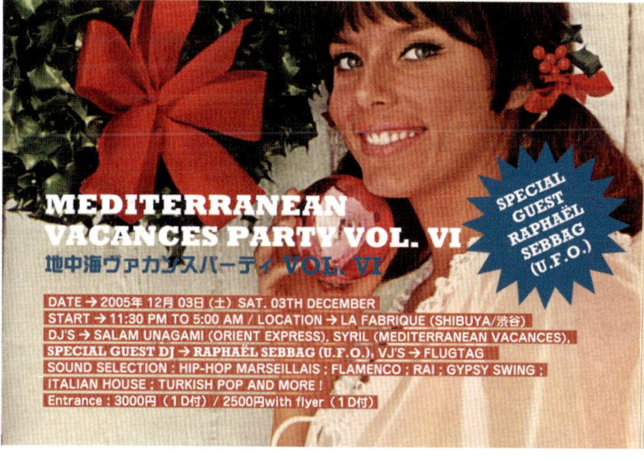

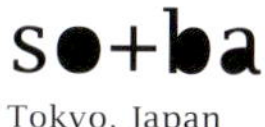

so+ba

Tokyo, Japan

Title: Med Vacance Flyers
Type of work: Flyer
Client: Cyril Coppini
Design: ad, d// so+ba
Year: 2004-05

A set of flyers designed by Cyril Coppini is in 50s, 60s style illustration with beautiful sexy women and old fashioned font type to match the title, Mediterranean Vancance.

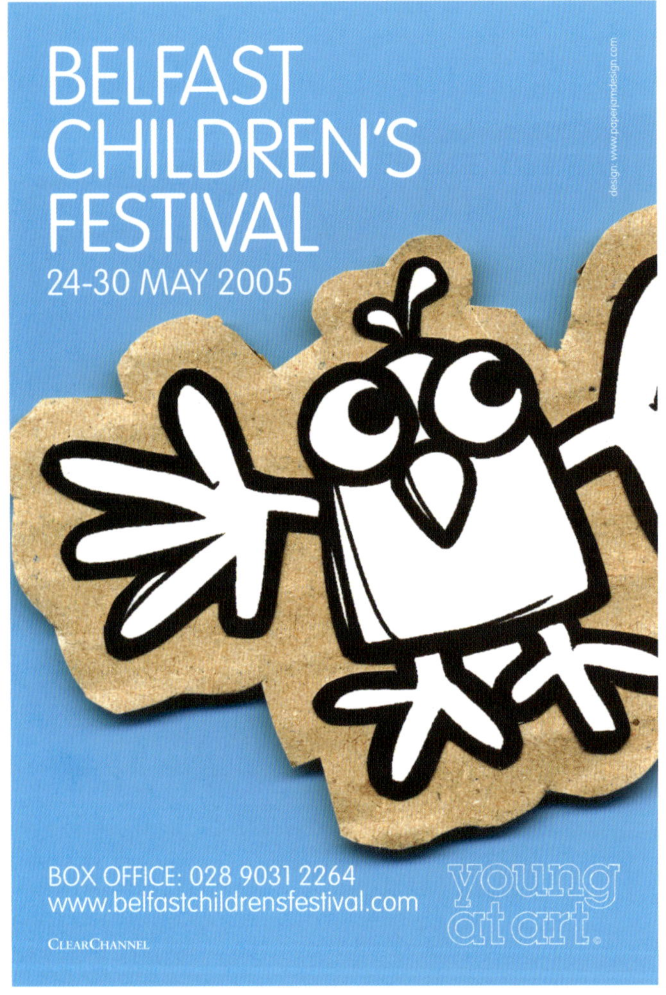

BELFAST CHILDREN'S FESTIVAL
24-30 MAY 2005
design: www.paperjamdesign.com
BOX OFFICE: 028 9031 2264
www.belfastchildrensfestival.com
young at art
CLEARCHANNEL

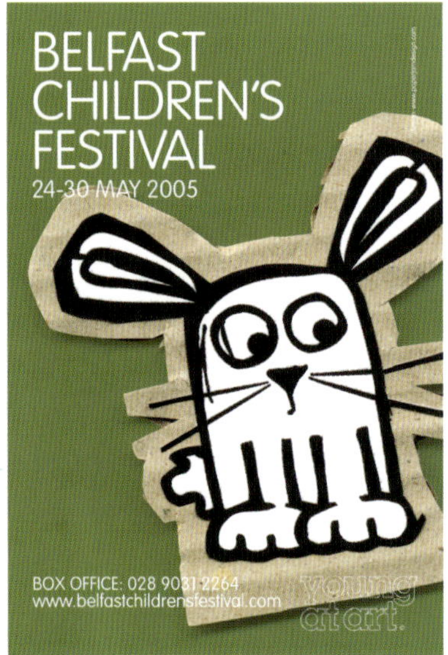

BELFAST CHILDREN'S FESTIVAL
24-30 MAY 2005
BOX OFFICE: 028 9031 2264
www.belfastchildrensfestival.com
young at art

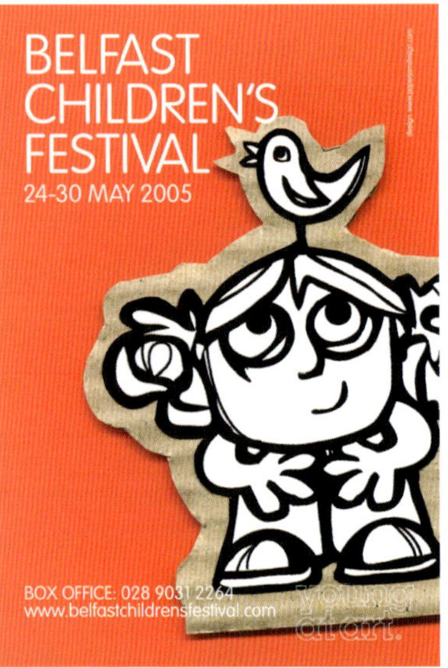

BELFAST CHILDREN'S FESTIVAL
24-30 MAY 2005
BOX OFFICE: 028 9031 2264
www.belfastchildrensfestival.com
young at art

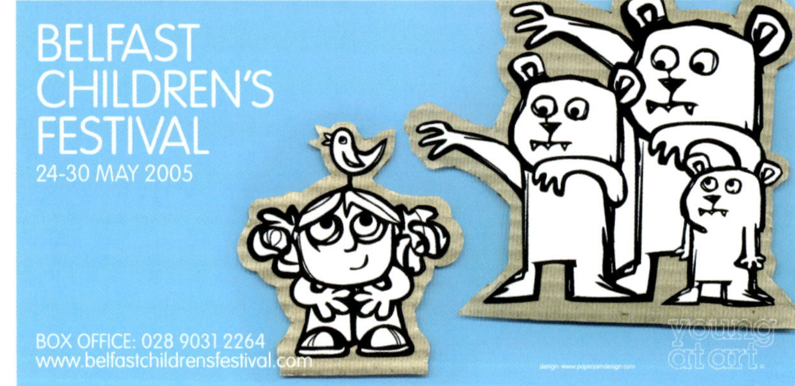

BELFAST CHILDREN'S FESTIVAL
24-30 MAY 2005
BOX OFFICE: 028 9031 2264
www.belfastchildrensfestival.com
young at art
design: www.paperjamdesign.com

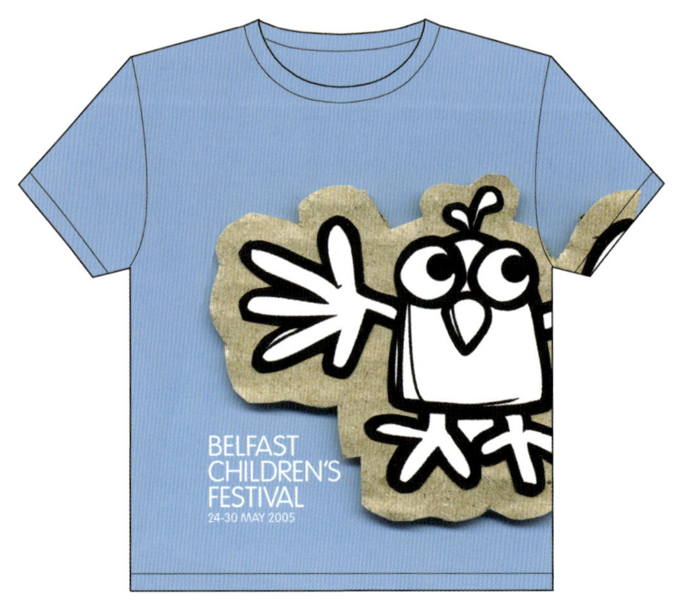

BELFAST CHILDREN'S FESTIVAL
24-30 MAY 2005

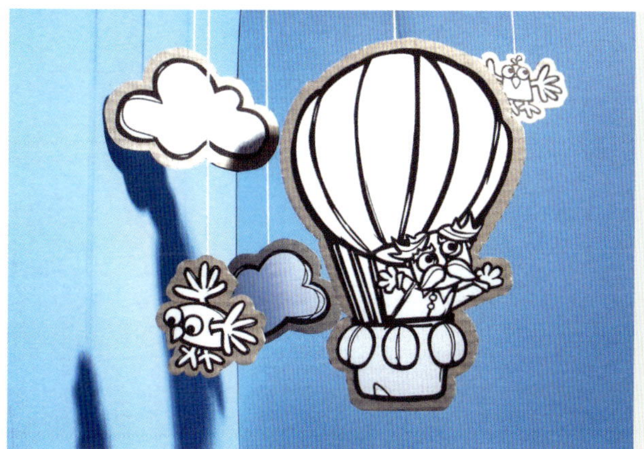

The Travelling Teller

Tales from long ago told through magic and illusion

Theatre
Cahoots NI

Festival favourite Cahoots NI celebrate the 200th anniversary of Hans Christian Andersen with a show inspired by tales from long ago. The Travelling Teller is a strange and mythical character who shares his tales of comical characters and colourful places, of magical happenings and wonderful inventions, of lands far away and times long ago.

Thur	26 May	7pm
Fri	27 May	10am, 12 noon
Sat	28 May	11am, 2.30pm

Age: 5 years +
Duration: 1 hour
Ticket: £6
Family Ticket: £20

Studio Theatre, Waterfront Hall

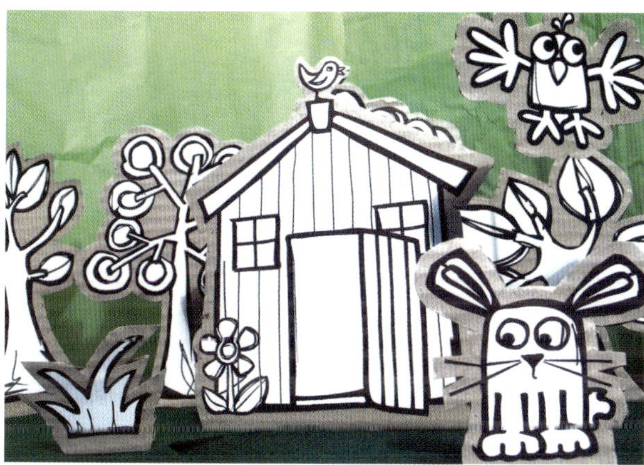

Sensor Shacks

Senses are shaken and stirred in the Sensor Shacks

Multi-Arts
Katie Blue and Young at Art

Something smells fishy about Lucy Turner's funky floral bouquets; will you come up smelling of roses... or bananas? See eye to eye with Colin McGookin's willow sculptures. Katie Blue's banquet looks incredible but is it edible? Get musical with the fusion and confusion of Stevie Noonan's orchestral junk sculpture. Stand still, shut your eyes and be touched by Angela Ginn's moving work. Each of these five outdoor shacks offers a unique experience to confuse and amuse the senses.

Tues 24 – Mon 30 May
11am, 11.45am, 12.30pm, 1.15pm, 2pm, 2.45pm, 3.30pm, 4.15pm, 5pm

Age: 5+
Duration: 30 mins
Ticket: £3

Botanic Gardens

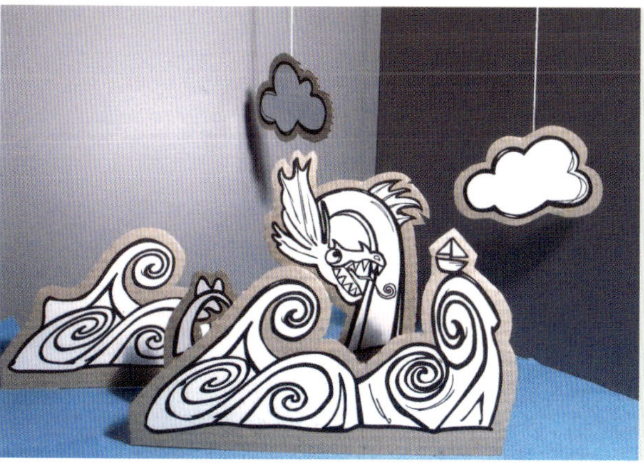

Tales from the Seashore

Giant sea serpents, magical rocks and more…

Storytelling
Niall de Burca

'When I walk into a room a story will pop up and tell me "I want to be told"'. So says leading Irish bard Niall de Burca. In his chocolate-rich tones, Niall will soothe, scare and enchant children with a selection of stories drawn from folklore. Expect sea serpents, fairy women, magical rocks and mountains, and much more. His Tales by Torchlight sold out in last year's festival so book early!

Venue: An Culturlann
English language performances:
Thur 26 May 10.30am
Fri 27 May 10.30am
As Gaeilge
Thur 26 May 12.30pm
Sat 28 May 2.30pm
Venue: Waterfront Hall
English language performances:
Sun 29 May 11am, 1pm, 3pm
Age: 7+
Duration: 1 hour
Ticket: £6
Family Ticket: £20

Festival on Tour: Niall de Burca travels to Armagh, Derry/ Londonderry and Omagh. Telephone 028 9023 0660 for details.

An Culturlann &
Waterfront Hall

Paperjam Design

Belfast, Ireland

Title: BYAA Belfast Children's festival
Type of work: Advertising campaign
Client: Young At Art (YAA)
Designers: ad// Paul Malone d// David Woods
Year: 2005

A set of promotion materials for BYAA Belfast Children's Festival is designed with a playful and joyful direction. Small animals like chicken, birds, bear, mouse etc. are illustrated and used as main figures of the design.

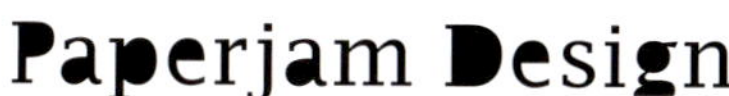

Airside

London, UK

Title: Panasonic Japan
Type of work: Mobile phone content, T-shirts
Client: Panasonic Japan
Design: ad, d// Airside
Year: 2005

Designs to decorate a new mobile phone launched in Japan in August 2005. Without a brief to adhere to, the designers let their imaginations roam free, in which it was expressed in the outcome of spunky ghosts, one-eyed monsters zapping little people to smoldering heaps, strange travelling tubes and dancing pooing monkeys. Four covers were designed for the phone as a result and they were also transferred to t-shirts, as well as an animated ring tone consisting of the four cover illustrations turned into moving images.

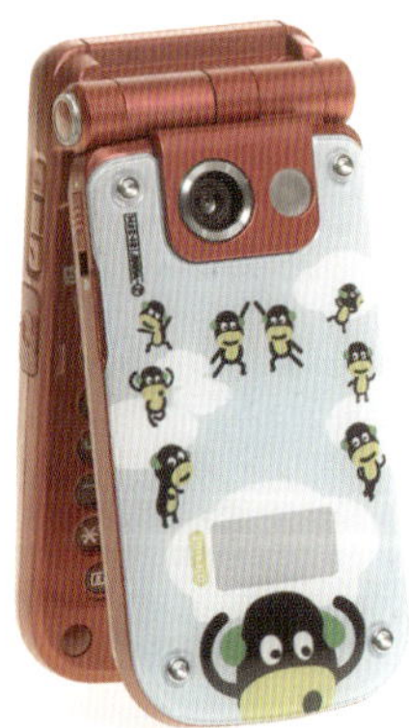
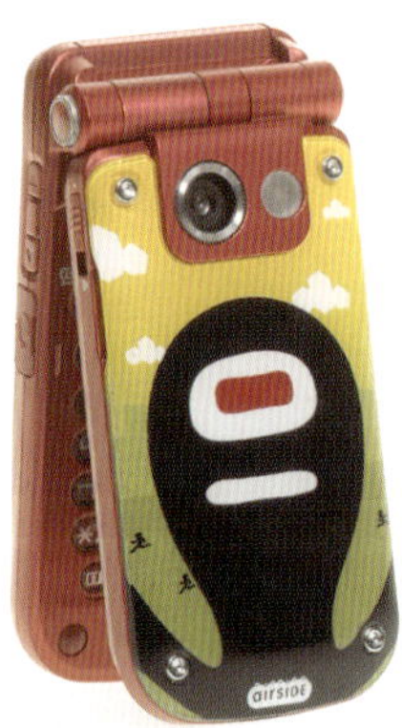
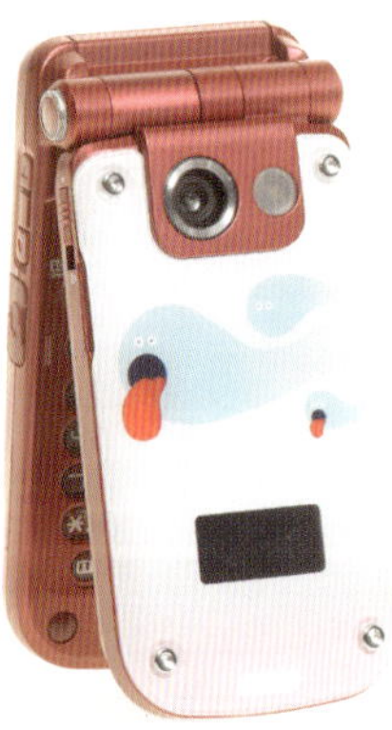
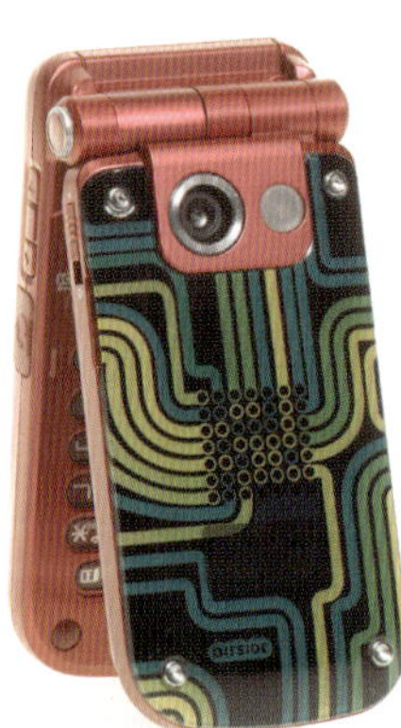

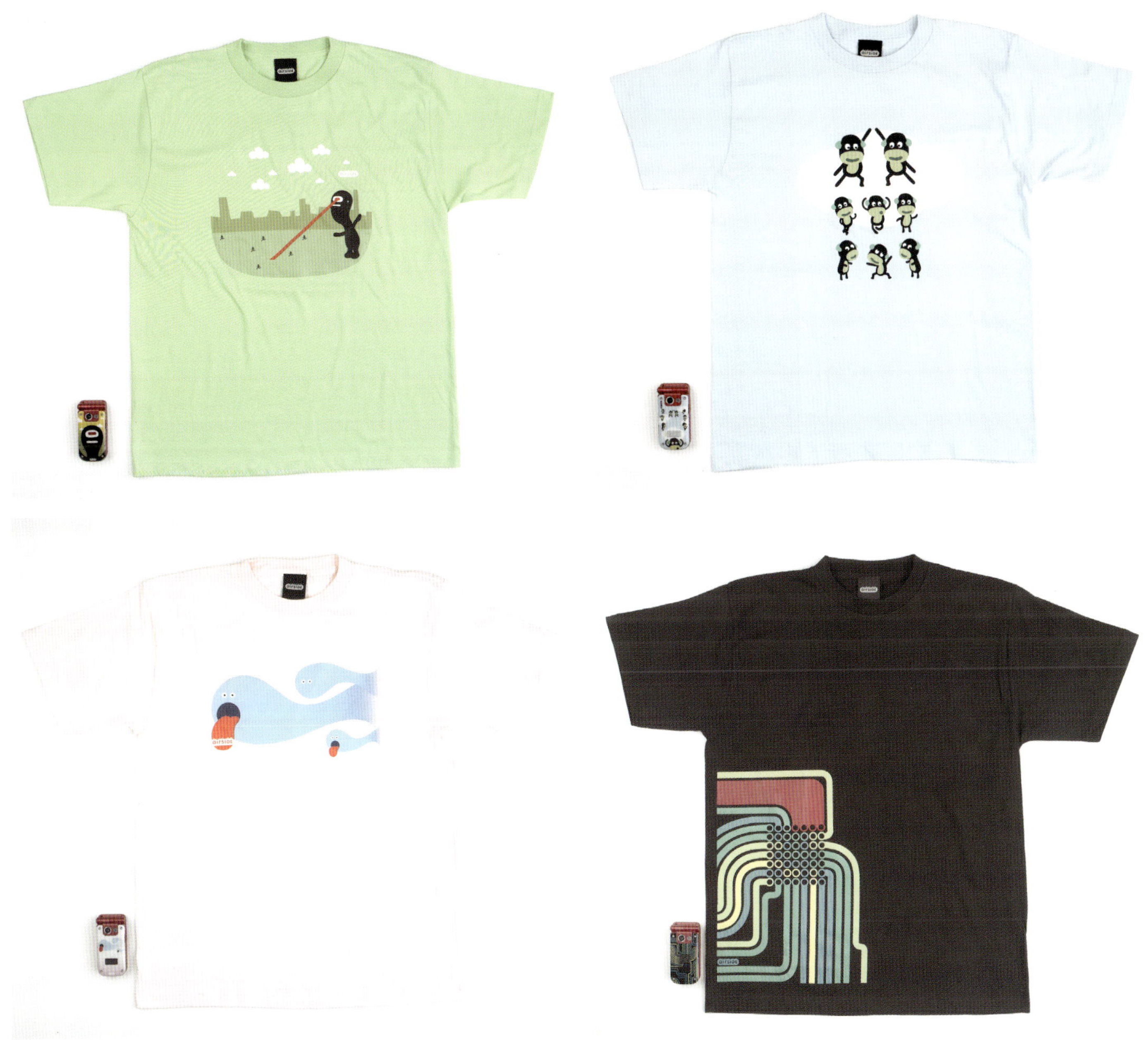

Carmen Garcia Huerta

Madrid, Spain

Title: -
Type of work: Calendar and stationery
Client: -
Design: Carman Garcia Huerta
Year: -

A set of stationery and calendar with illustration by Carmen Garcia Huerta. Mainly with sexy women in good figure on black background.

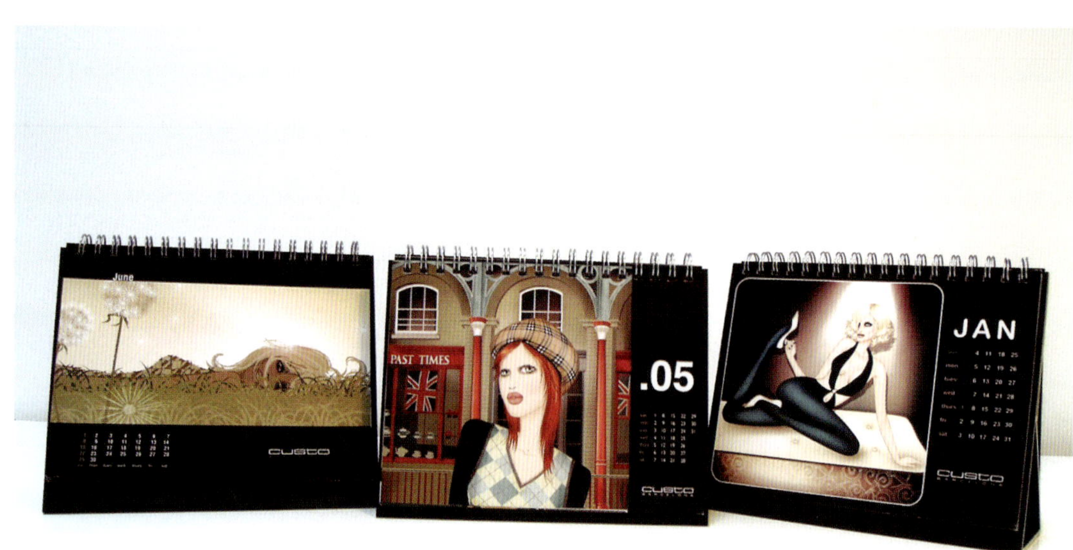

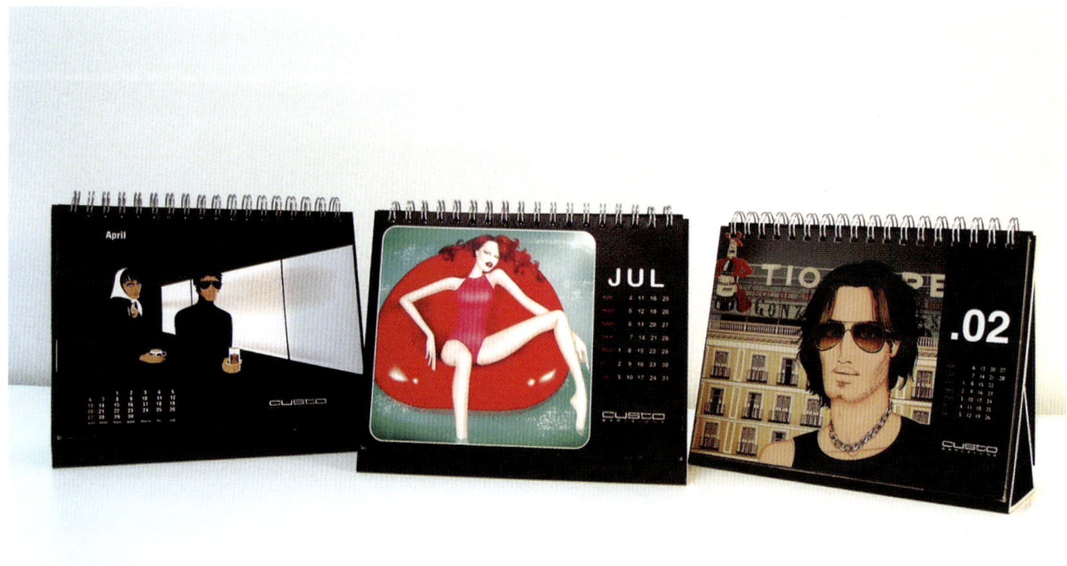

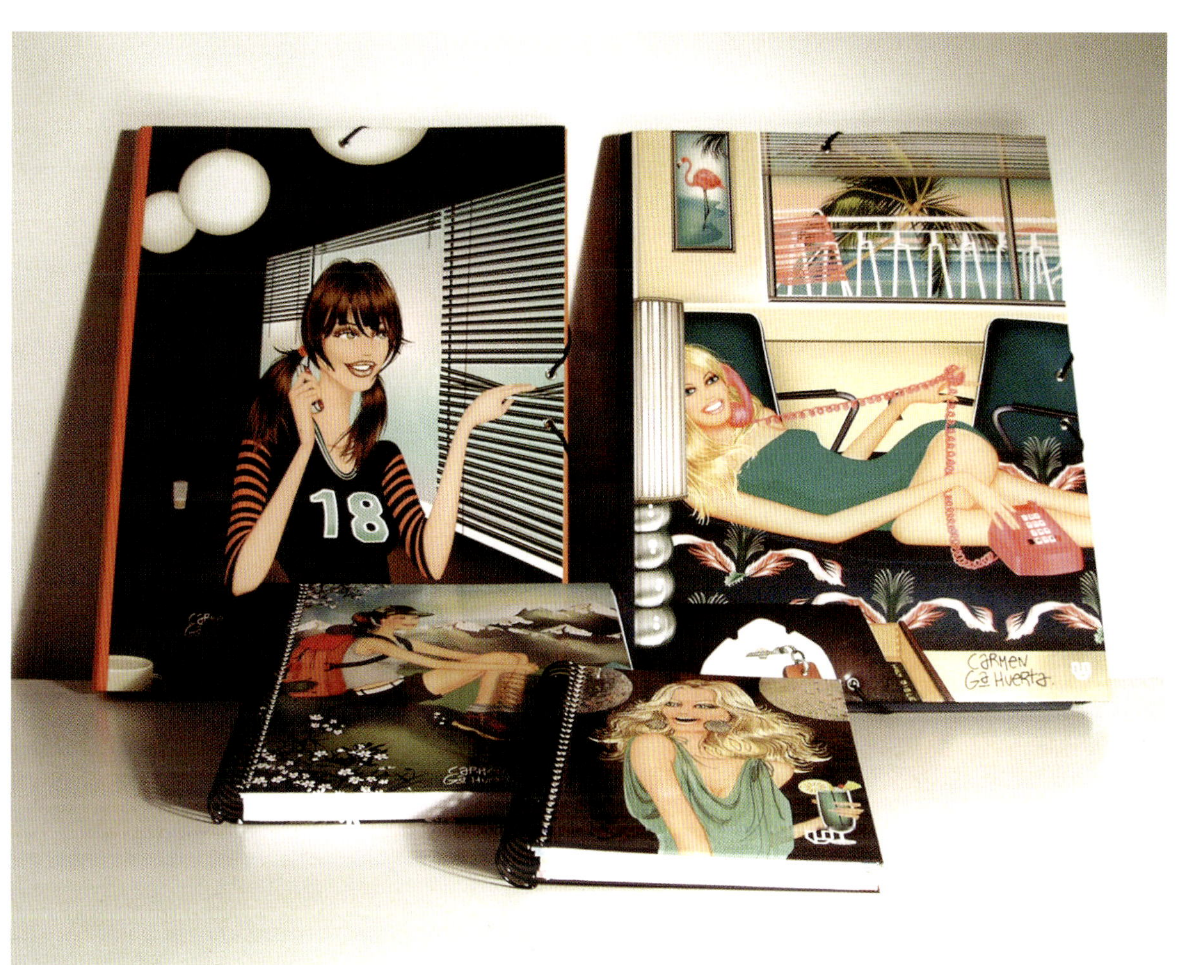

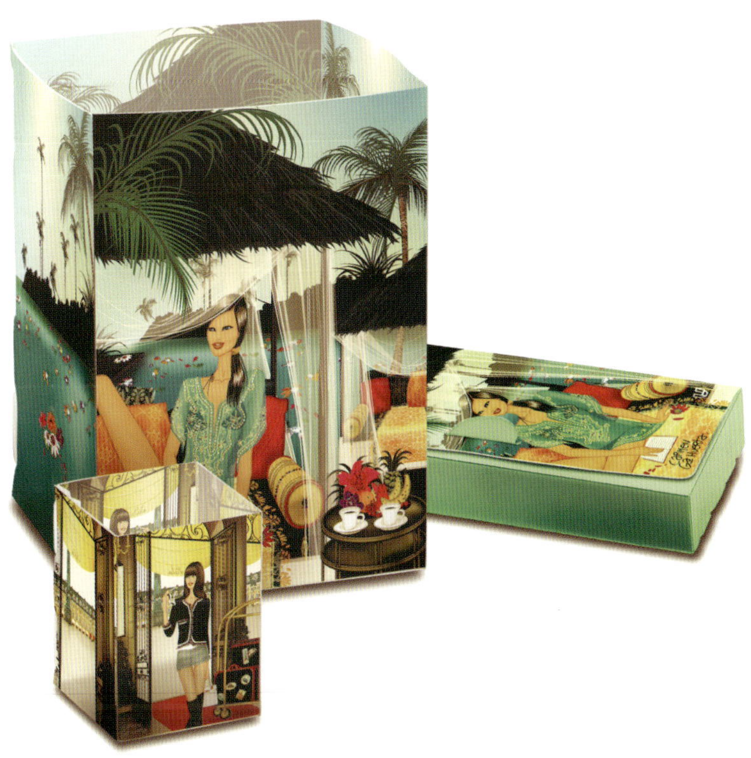

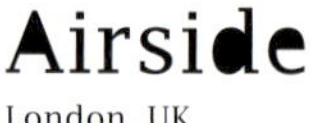

London, UK

Title: -
Type of work: Calendar
Client: Airside
Design: ad, d// Airside
Year: 2005

Calandar produced each year is a great way to show off work that is made during the year. It is also a marketing tool-cum-Christmas card to send out to everyone who they have worked with, would like to work with or care about.

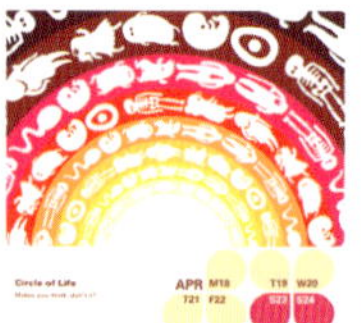 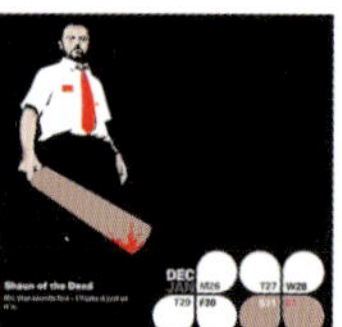 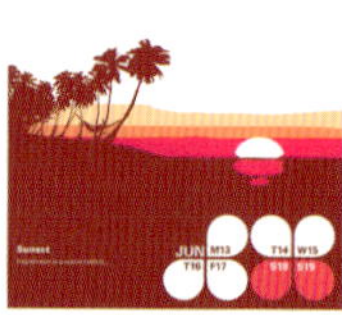 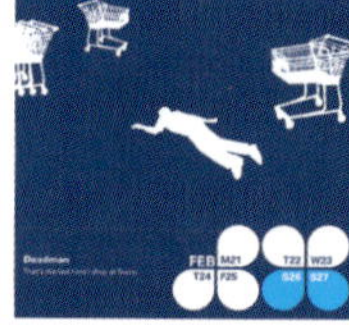 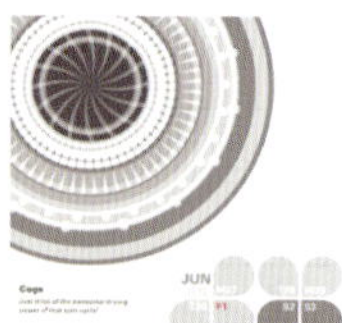

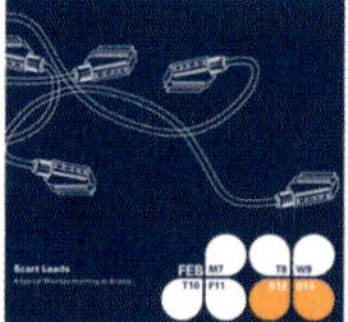 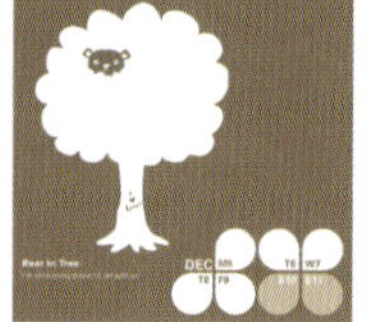 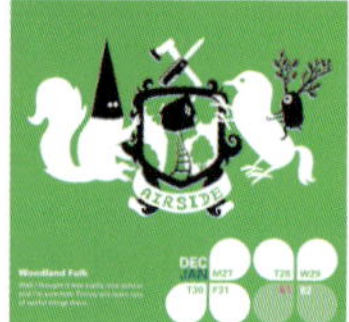 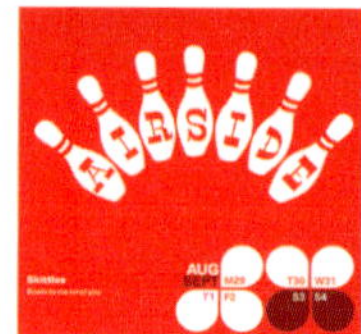 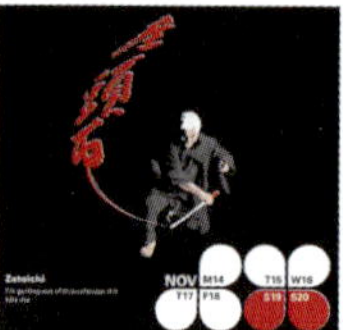

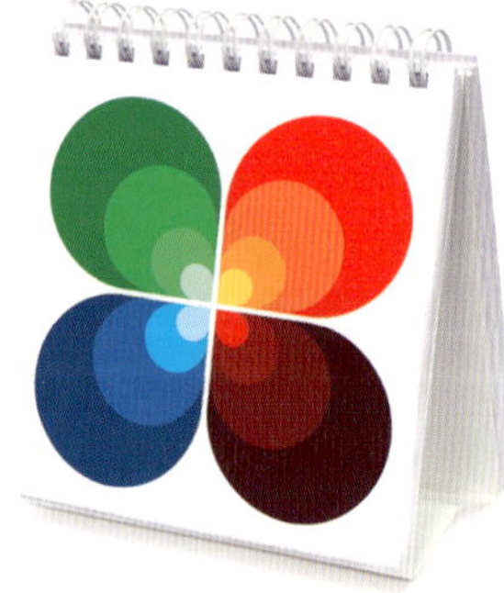

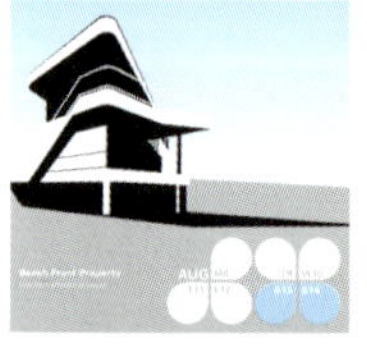 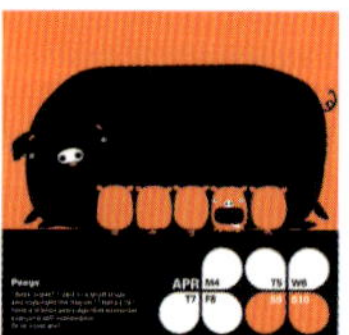 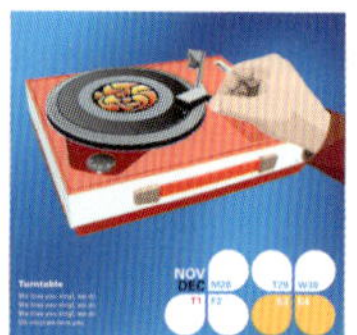 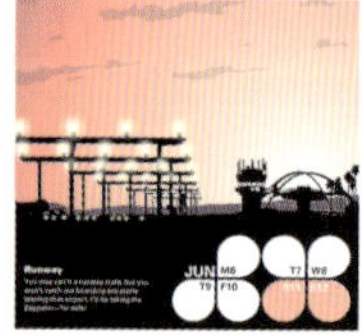 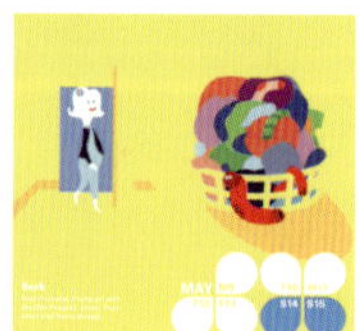

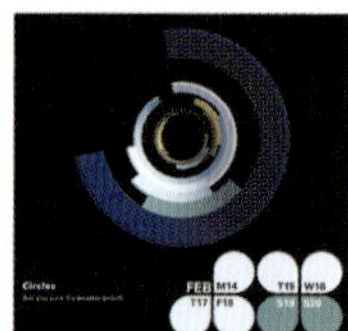

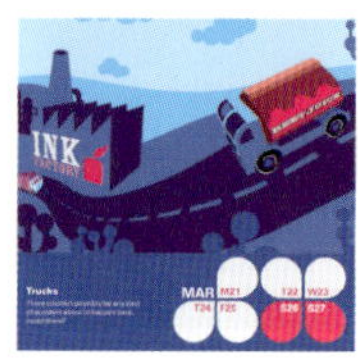

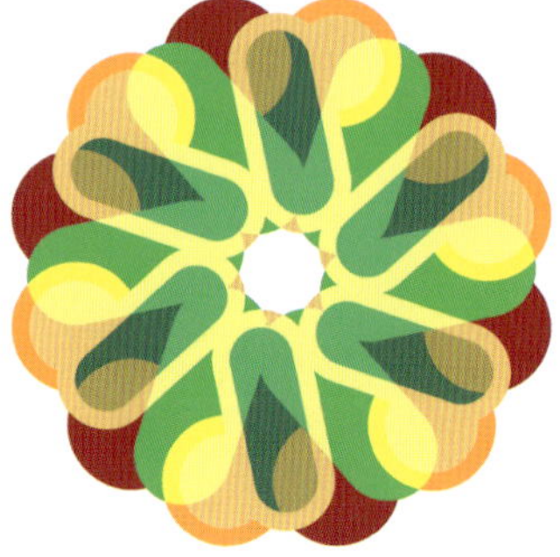

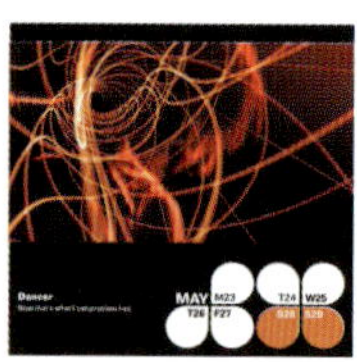 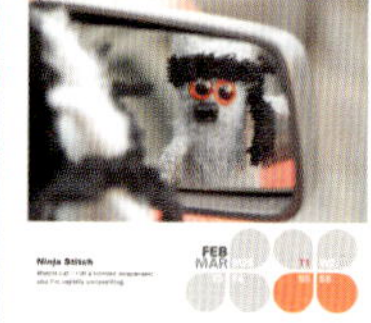

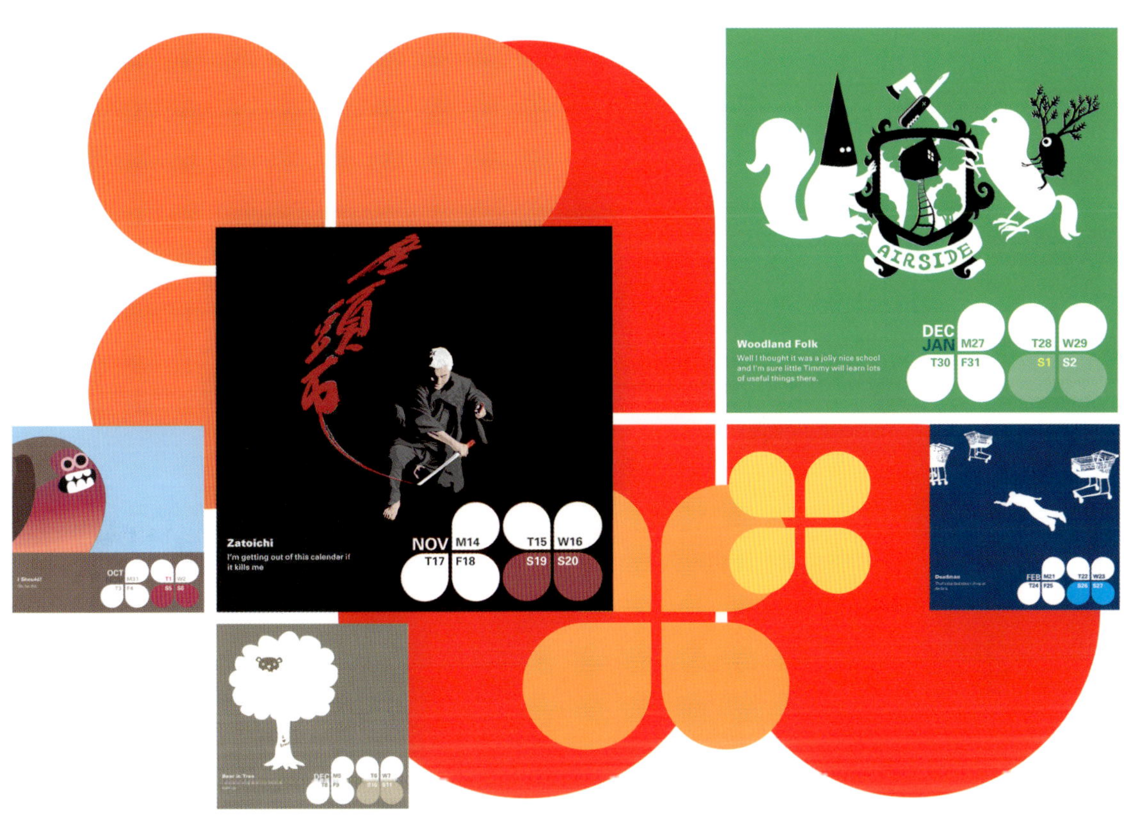

Zatoichi
I'm getting out of this calendar if it kills me
NOV M14 T15 W16 T17 F18 S19 S20
Woodland Folk
Well I thought it was a jolly nice school and I'm sure little Timmy will learn lots of useful things there.
AIRSIDE
DEC JAN M27 T28 W29 T30 F31 S1 S2
Deadman
FEB M21 T22 W23 T24 F25 S26 S27
OCT

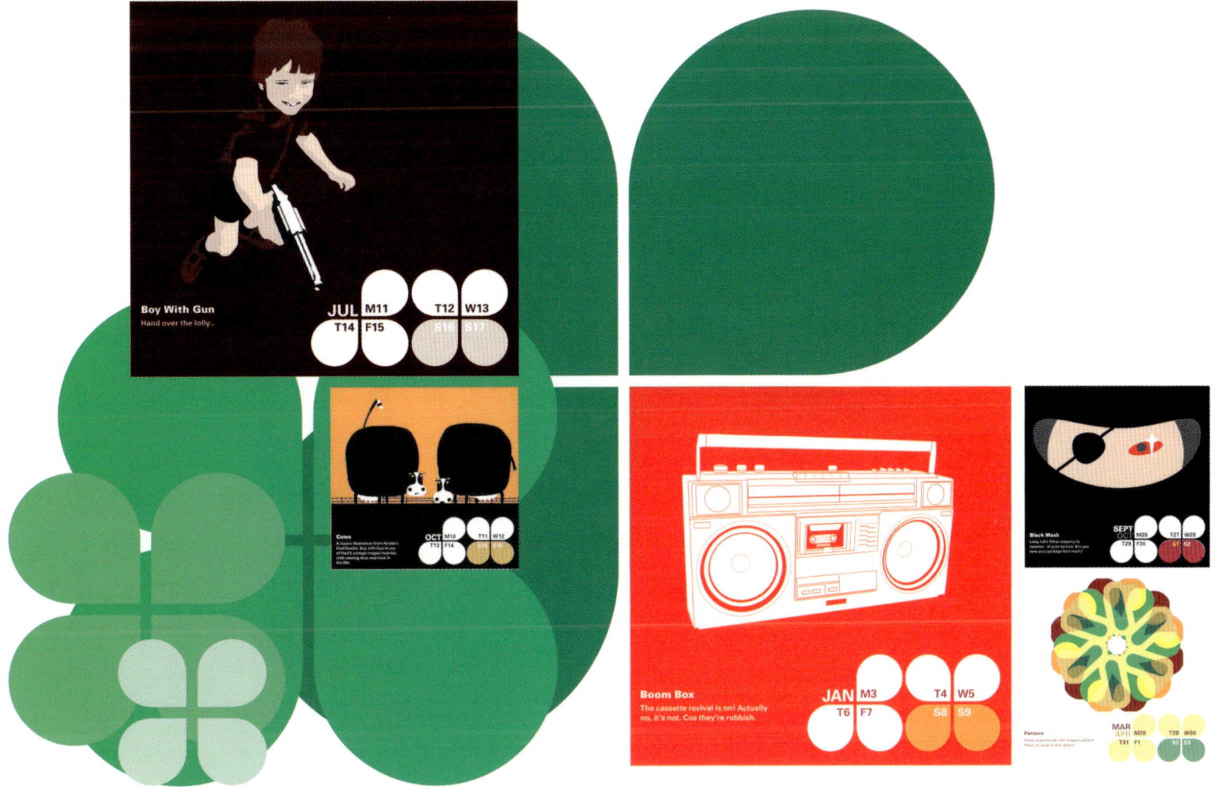

Boy With Gun
Hand over the lolly..
JUL M11 T12 W13 T14 F15 S16 S17
Cows
OCT M9 T11 W12 T13 F14
Boom Box
The cassette revival is on! Actually no, it's not. Cos they're rubbish.
JAN M3 T4 W5 T6 F7 S8 S9
Black Mask
SEPT M29 T22 W23 T29 F30 S1 S2
Pattern
MAR APR M28 F1 T29 W30 T31

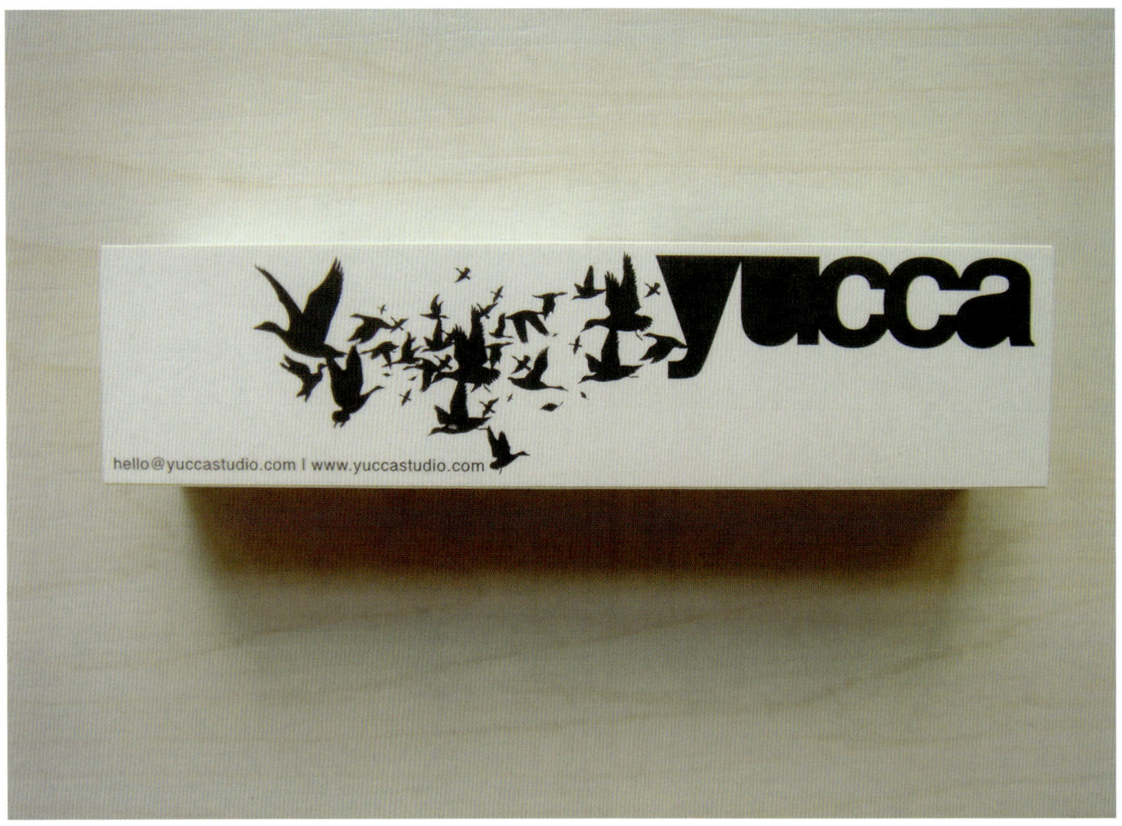

yucca
hello@yuccastudio.com I www.yuccastudio.com

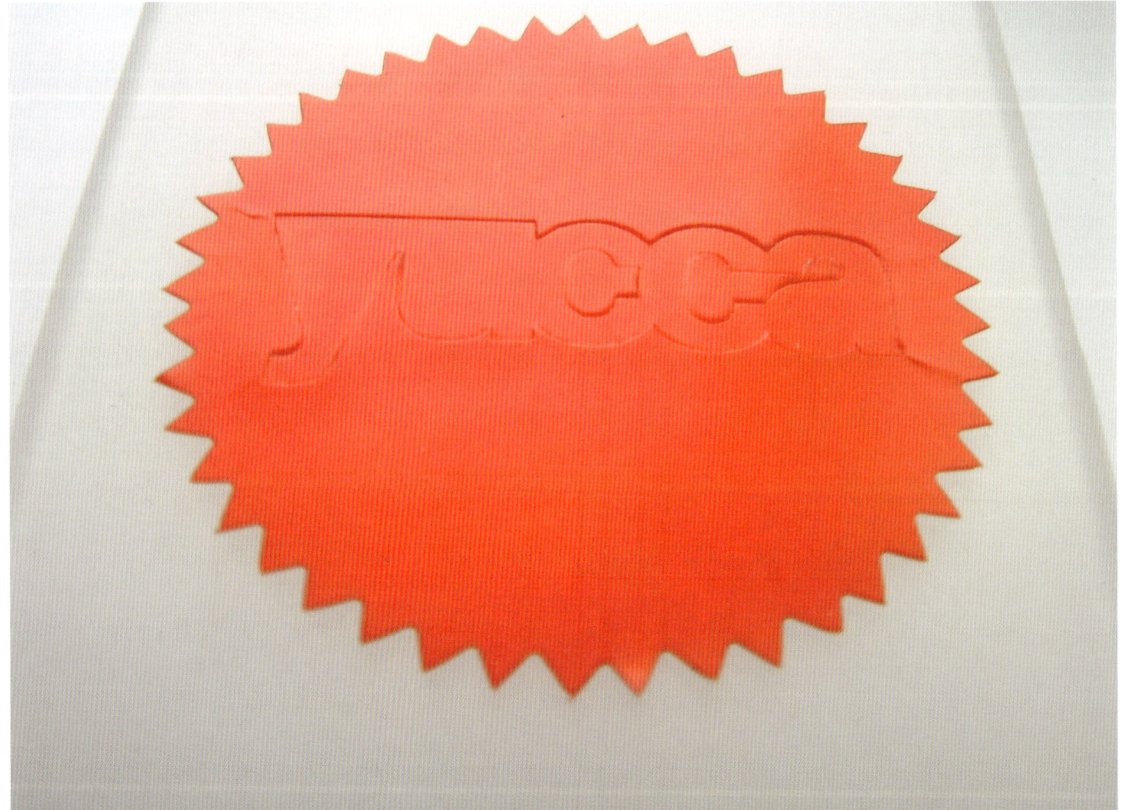

yucca

Yucca Studio

Singapore

A simple design it is, illustration with a modern oriental theme – 'Blissfullness comes from the heart' – is designed for this set of greeting cards.

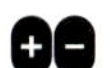

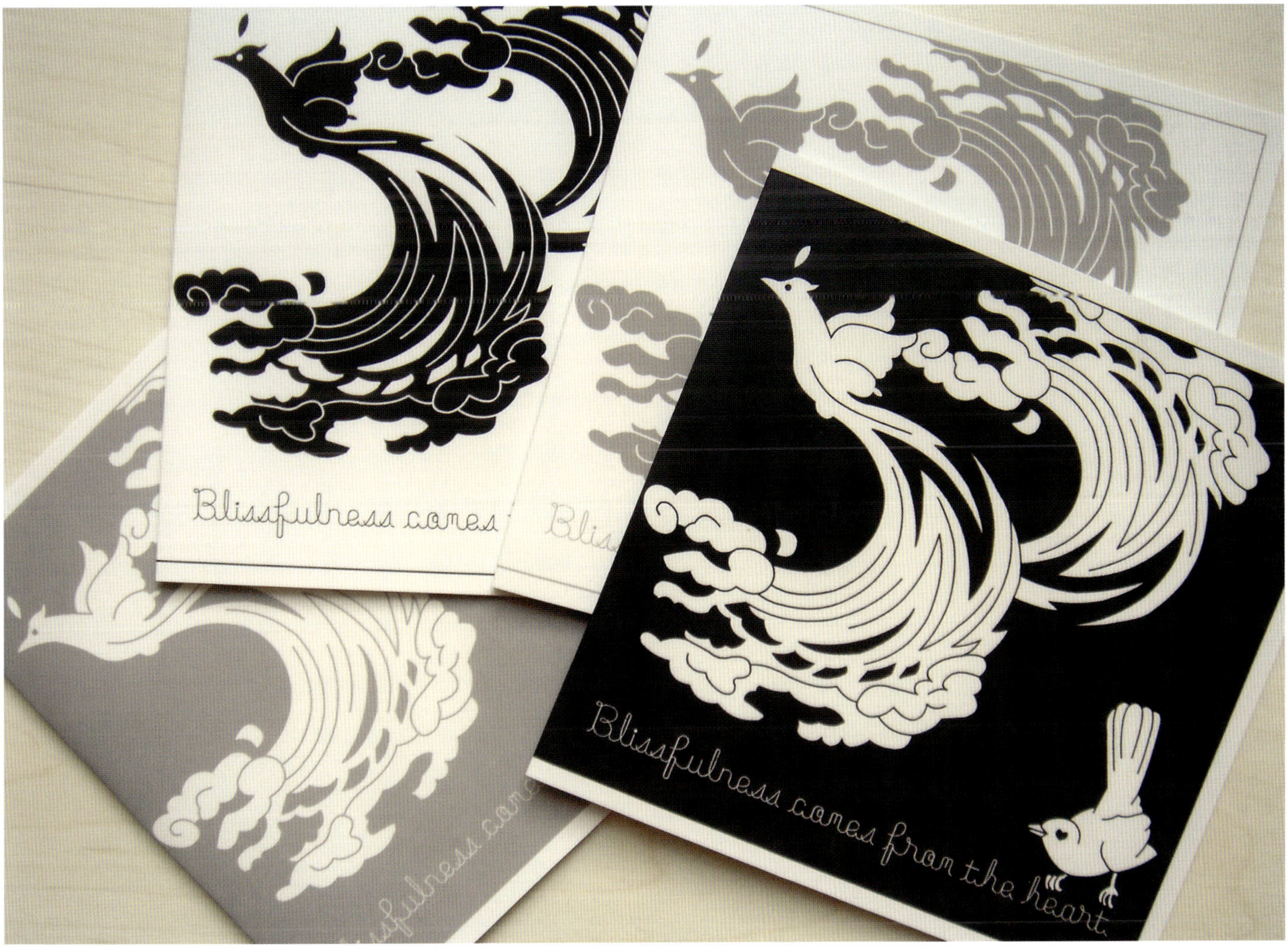

F●rm ®

London, UK

Title: Indoor Garden Design fleet of vans
Type of work: Van graphics
Client: Indoor Garden Design
Design: ad// Paula Benson d// Nick Hard, Paula Benson
Year: 2005

A design of a van fleet for Indoor Garden Design, which is one of the UK's leading interior landscaping companies who works with businesses, designers and architects. The identity is developed based on beautiful and stunning images of plants. The photography was art directed by Form and taken by Lee Funnell.

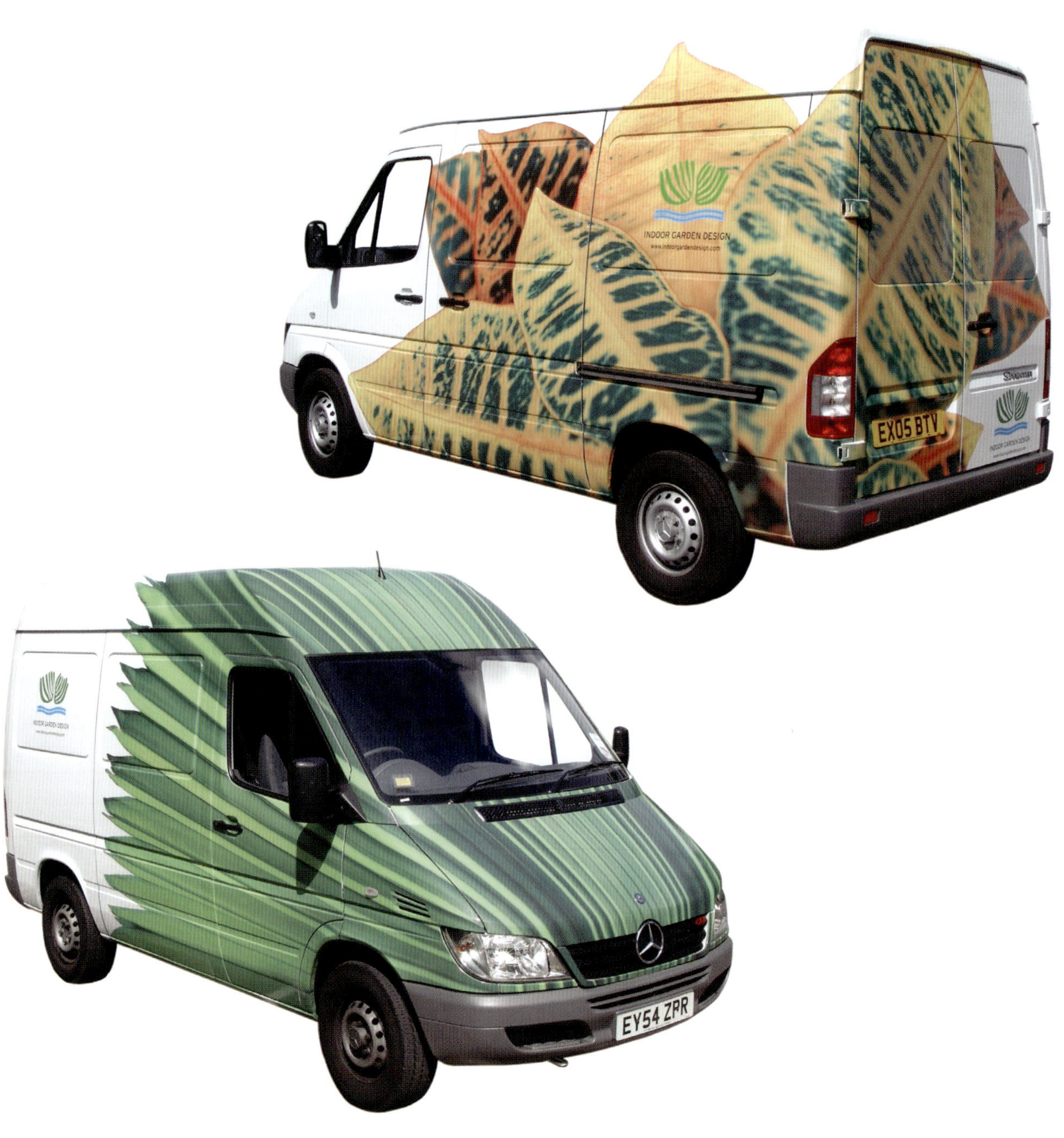

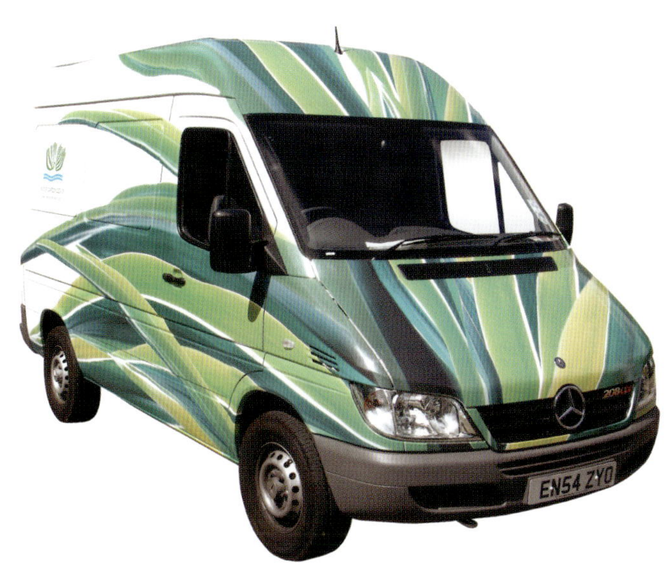
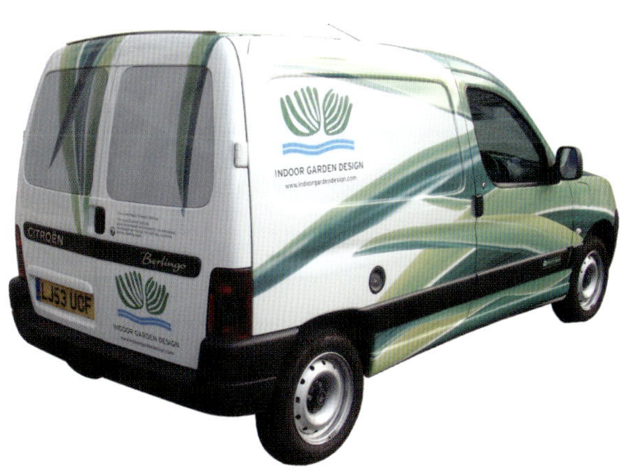
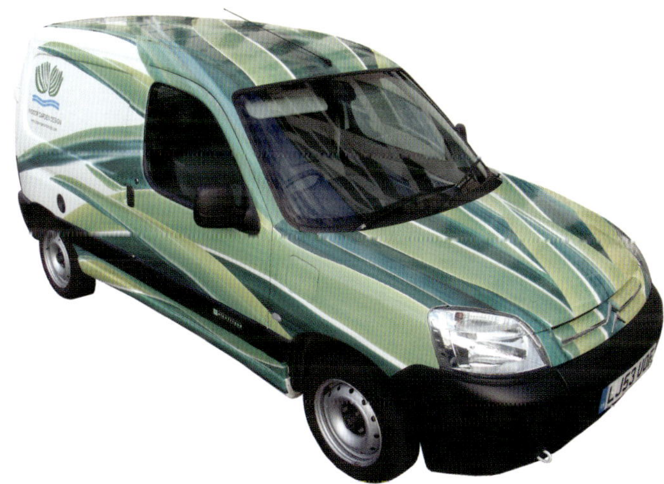
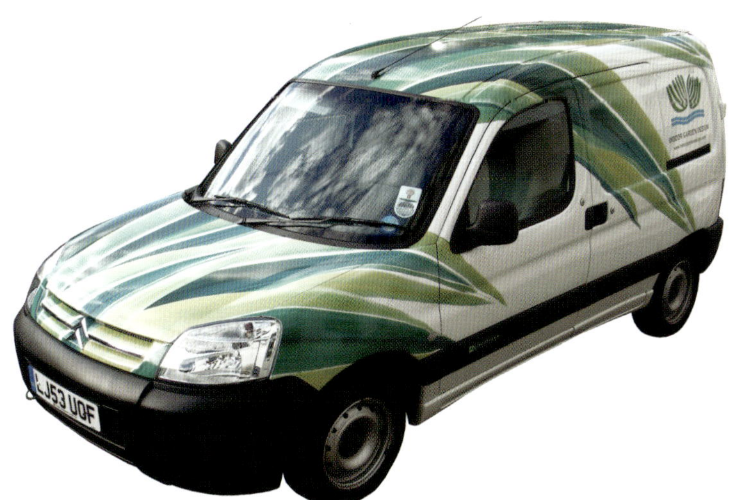
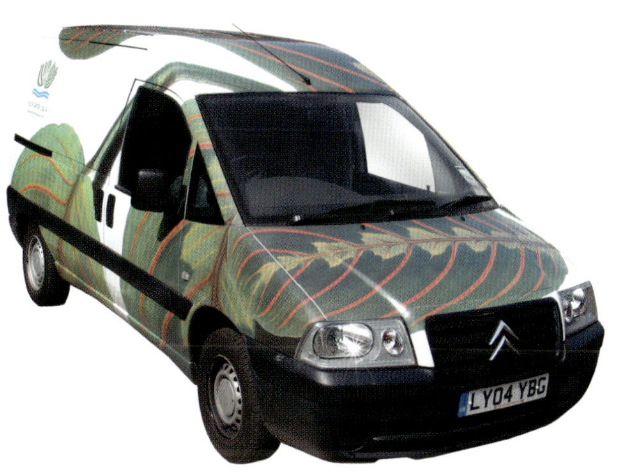

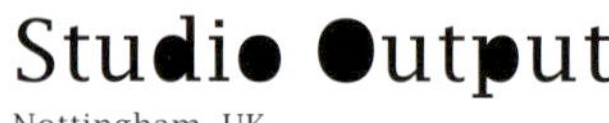

Studio Output

Nottingham, UK

Title: –
Type of work: Mural
Client: Brass Monkey
Design: Steve Payne
Year: 2005

A series of illustrations applied on a 5m x 4m mural for Brass Monkey, a Nottingham cocktail bar. They wanted to move away from the ubiquitous 'style bar' which pervades every city centre, and create something more mind-bending and thought-provoking. The inspiration came from a twisted Wizard of Oz, flying monkeys, an enchanted forest, a woodland clash and lots of stuffed animals. The aim was for the eye to be drawn up the wall, to maximize the impact of the high ceilings and encourage the viewer to explore the pictures.

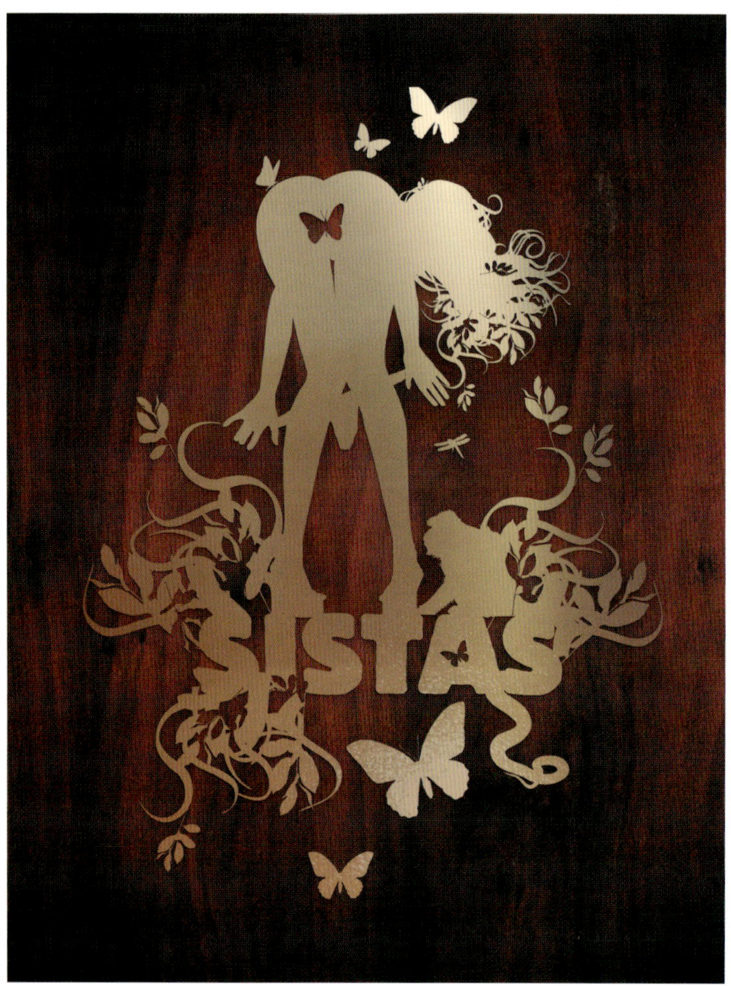

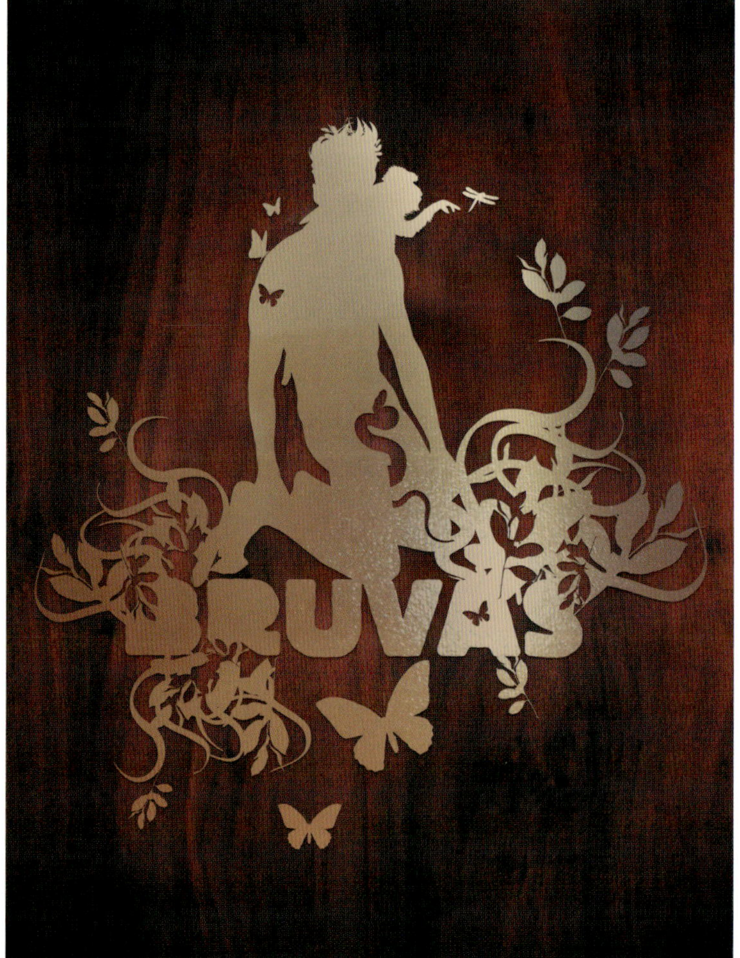

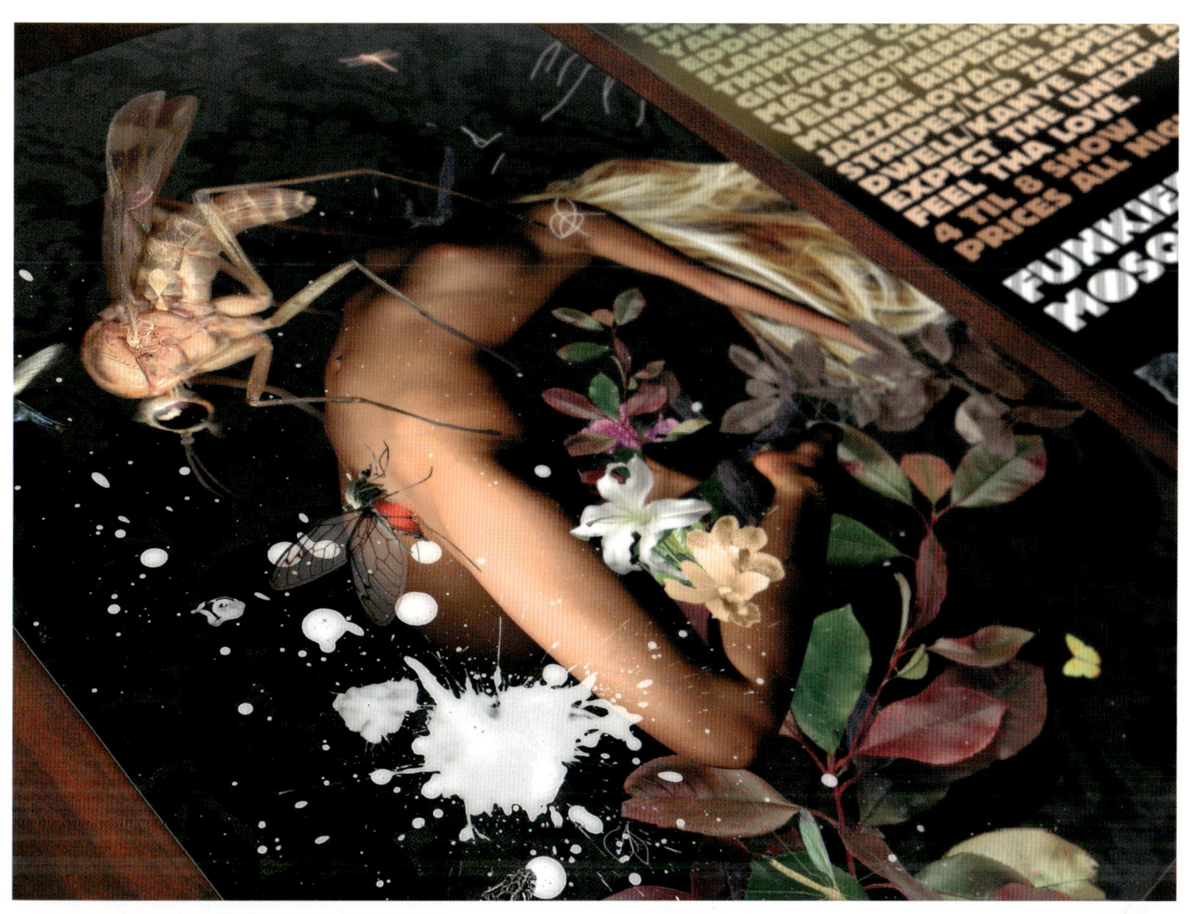

FUNKIER
MOS

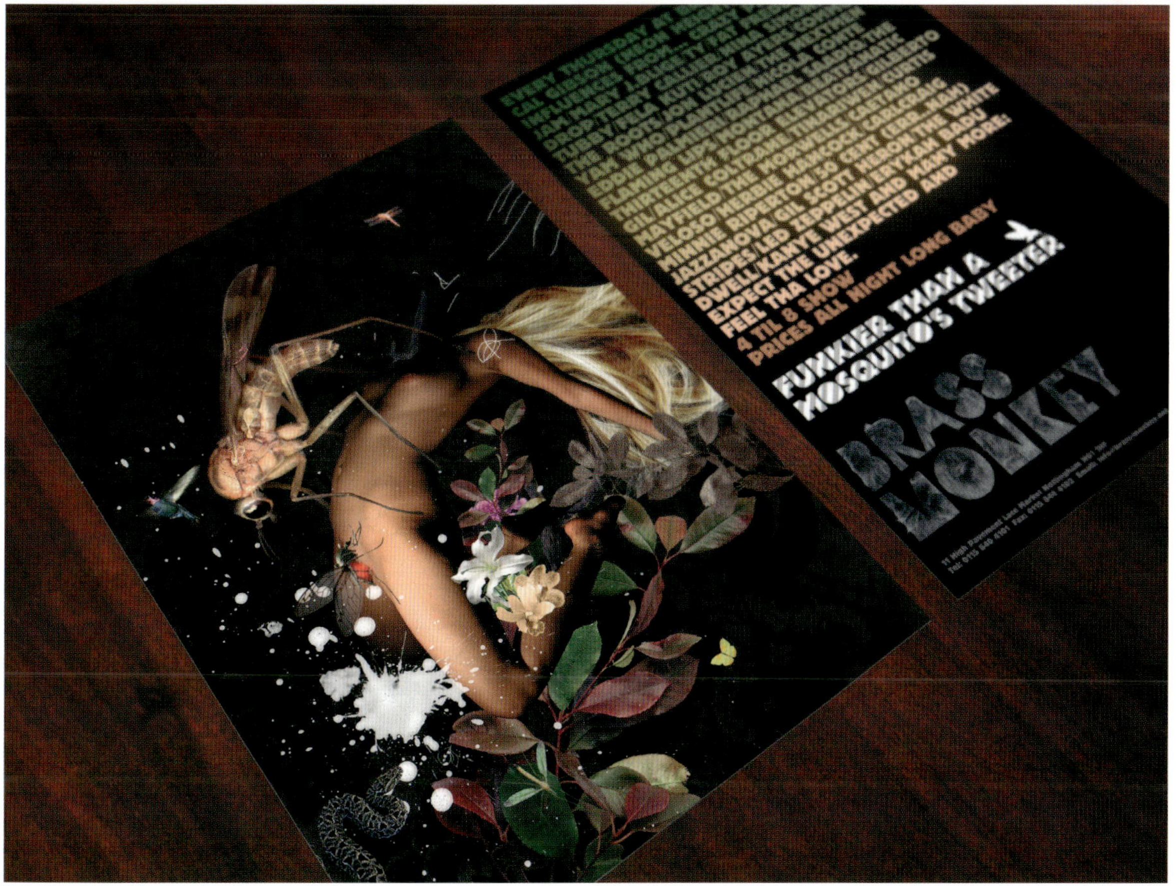

FUNKIER THAN A
MOSQUITO'S TWEETER.
BRASS
MONKEY

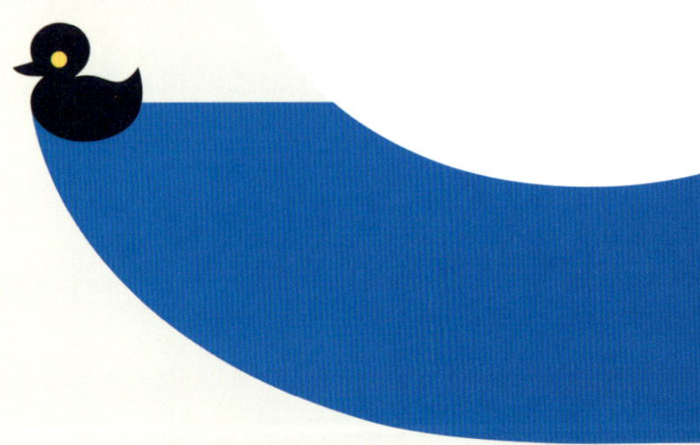

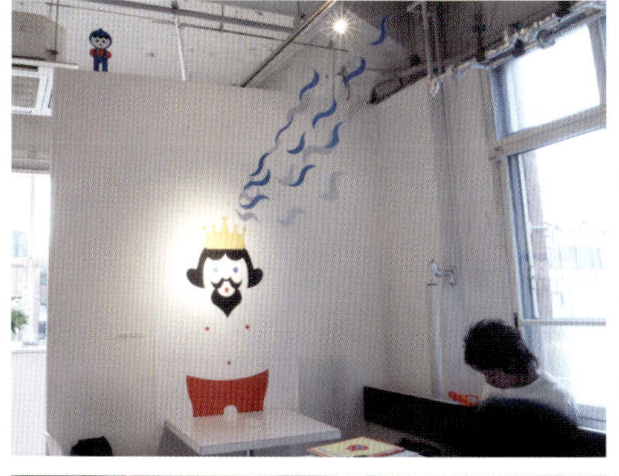 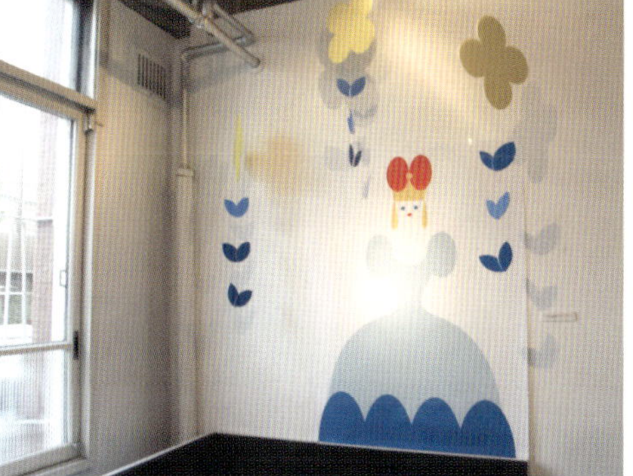 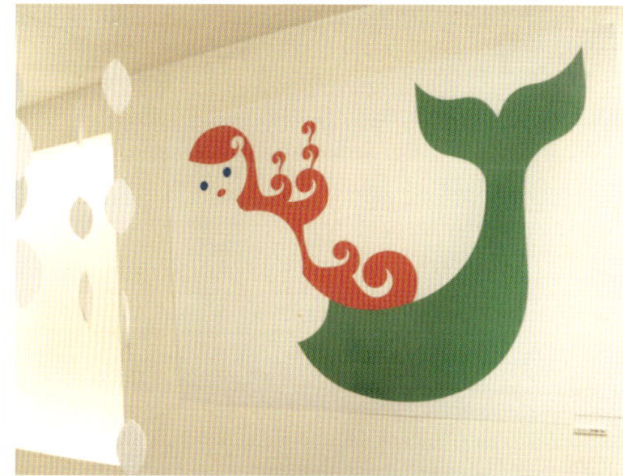

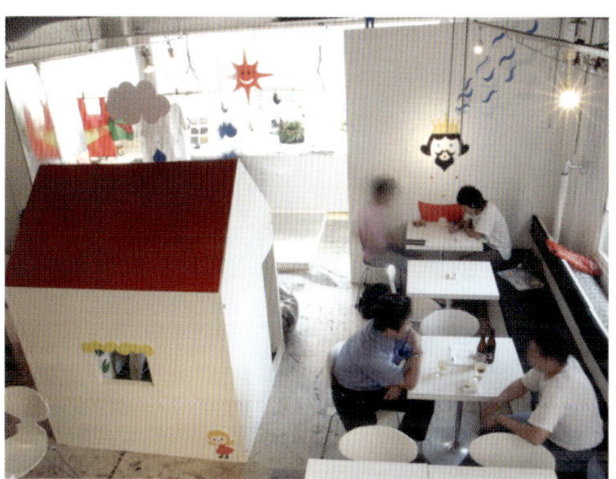 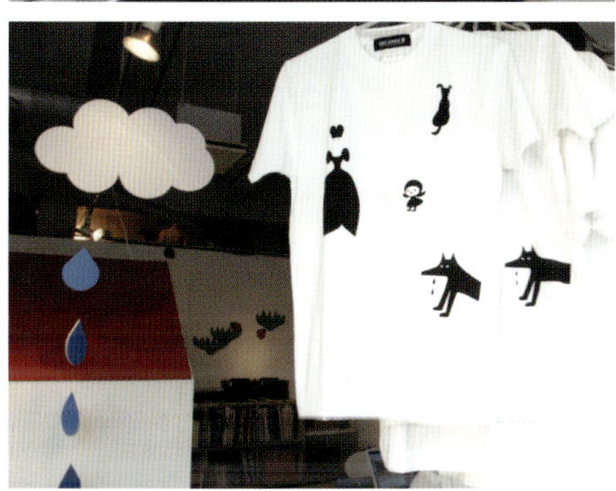 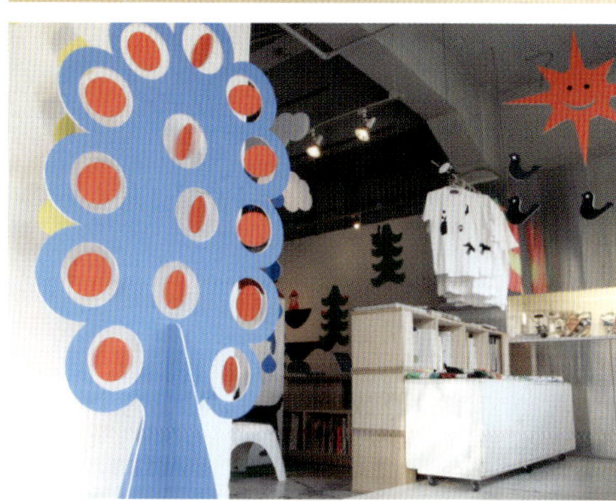

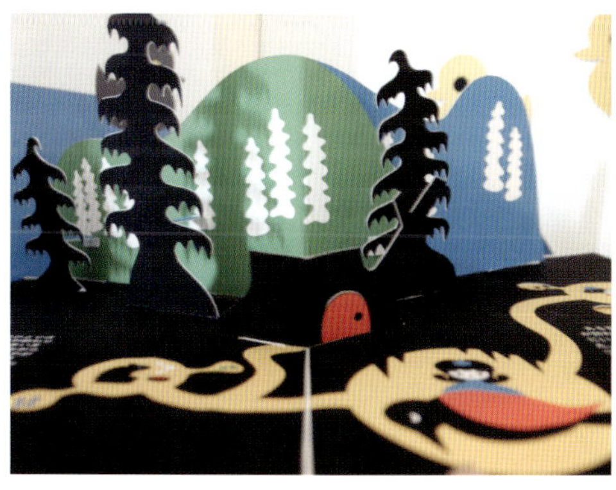 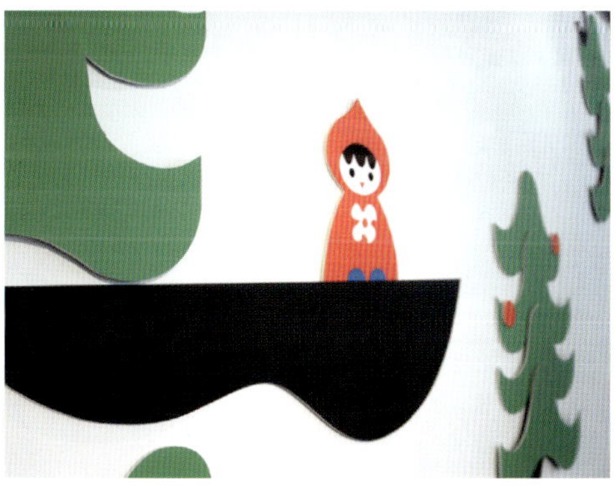 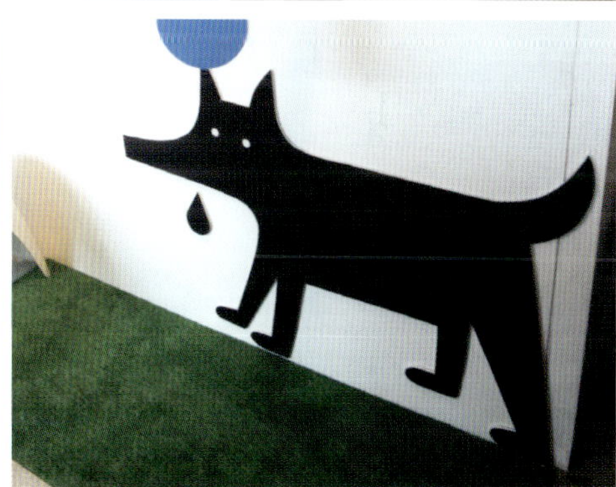

Kinpro

Japan

Title: Andersen
Type of work: Illustration, molding
Client: –
Design: ad// Shift production d// Chisato Shinya aka Kinpro
Year: 2005

Three-dimensional pieces based on illustrations that Kinpro recently offered to Die Gestalten Verlag, a publisher in Germany for The Illustrated Fairy Tales of the Brothers Grimm and Andersen. Commemorating the 200th anniversary of Hans Christian Andersen's birth in 2005, the piece is an imaginary world of him.

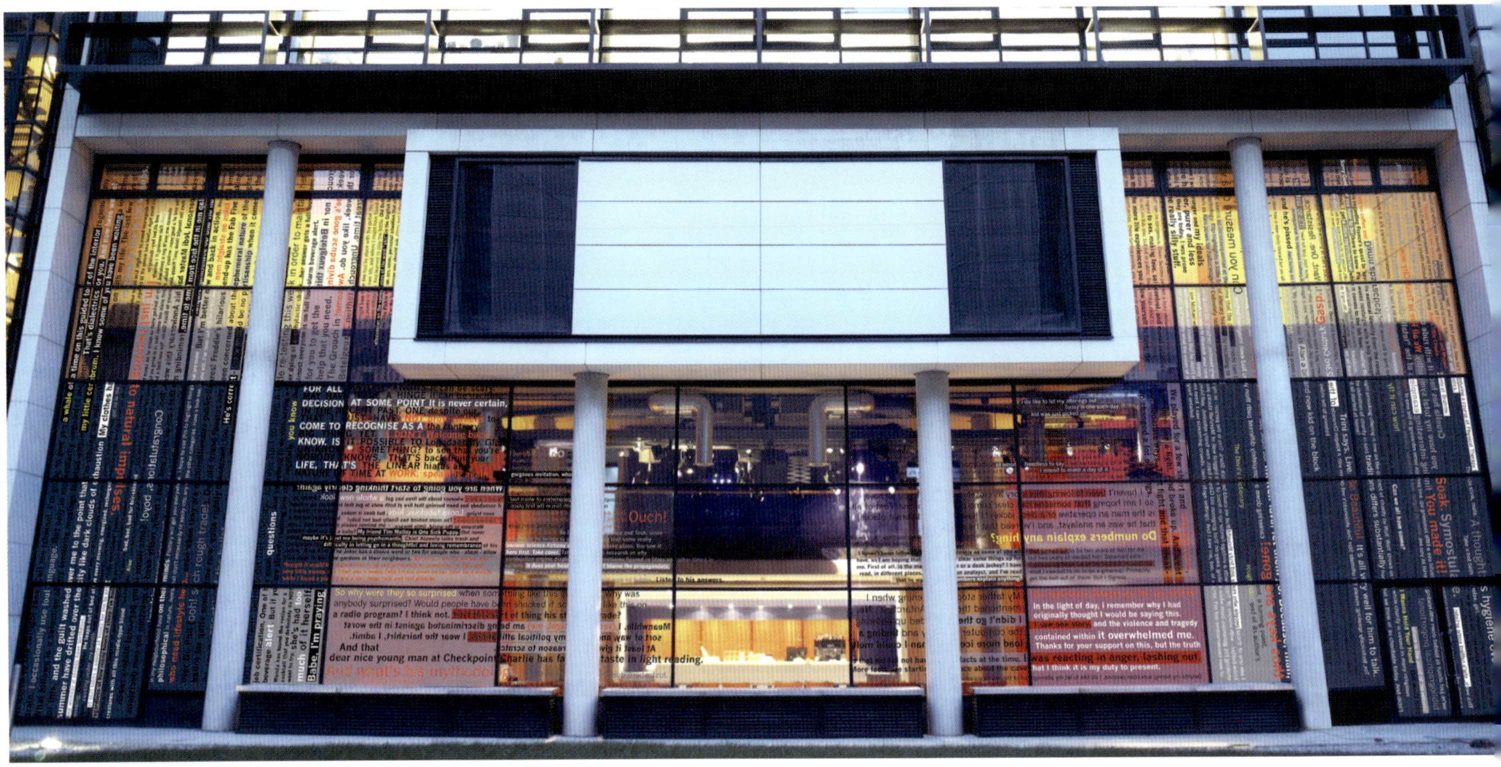

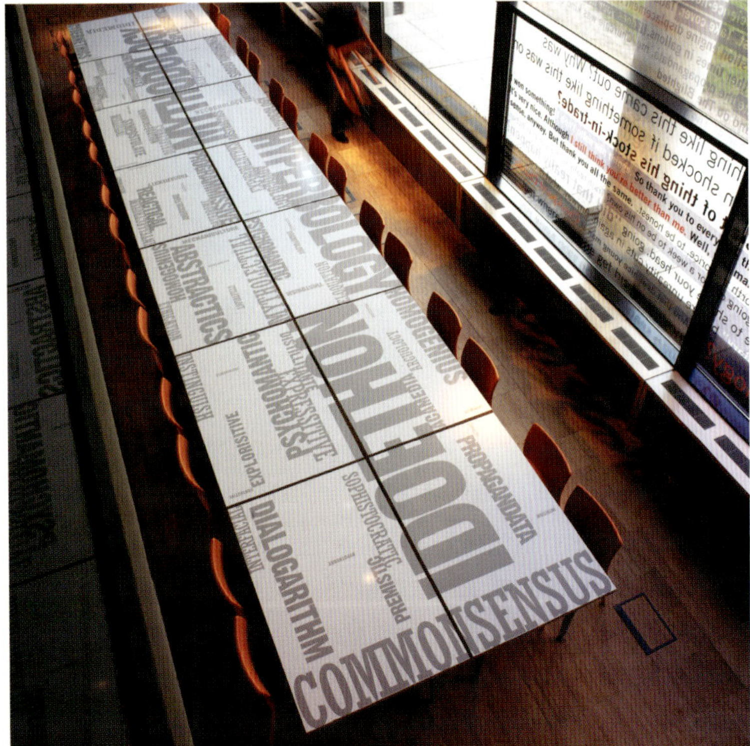

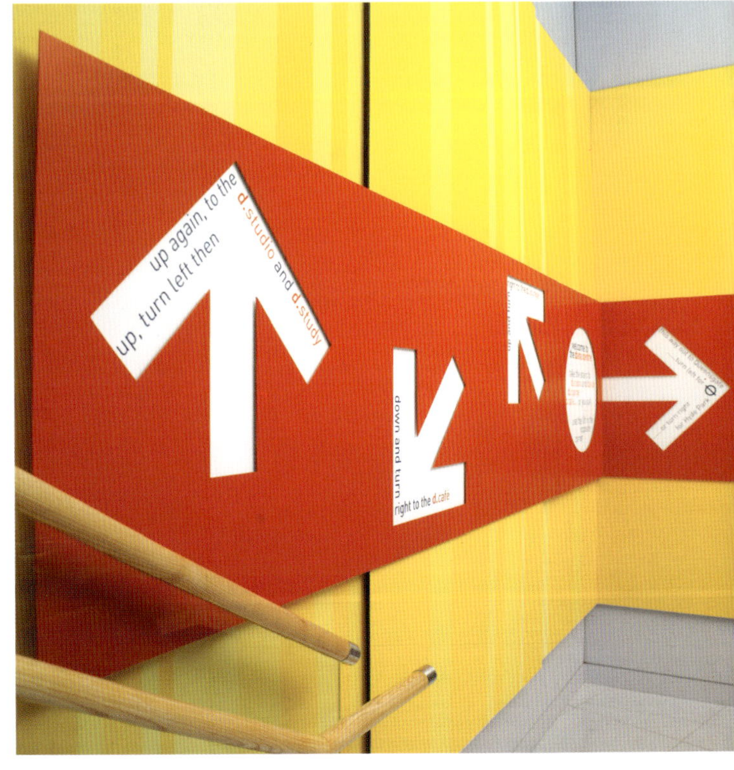

Lippa Pearce Design

London, UK

Title: The Dana Centre, Science Museum, London, UK
Type of work: Museum
Client: The Science Museum
Design: ad// Harry Pearce, Tim Molloy
d// Harry Pearce, Jeremy Roots, Nicole Forster, Richard Wilson, Joke Rasch
Year: 2004

Identity for the Science Museum's unique Dana Building – a centre for the public to enter into dialogue, about issues in contemporary science. The concept of language evolves throughout the whole building. It is essentially about conversation which is summed up by the great glass wall with textural interplay running through both sides of the glass. Typographic game play continues this theme playing with scale and the 3 dimensional space involving direction, information, conversation, rhetorical text and logotype.

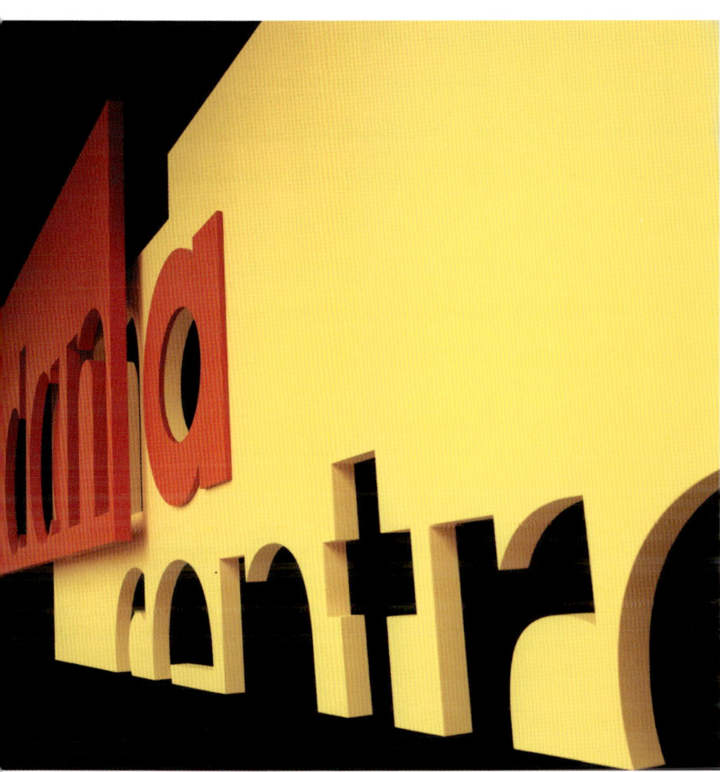

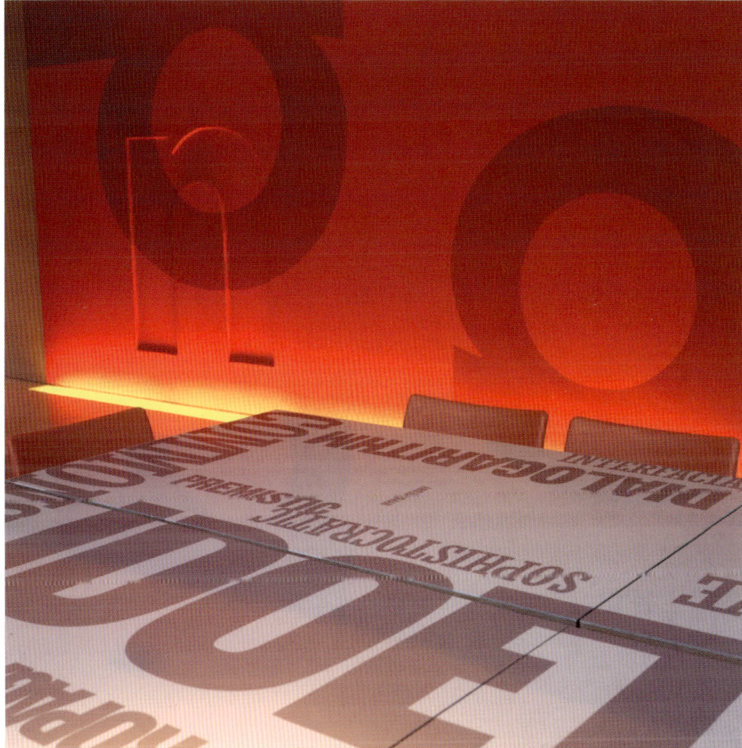

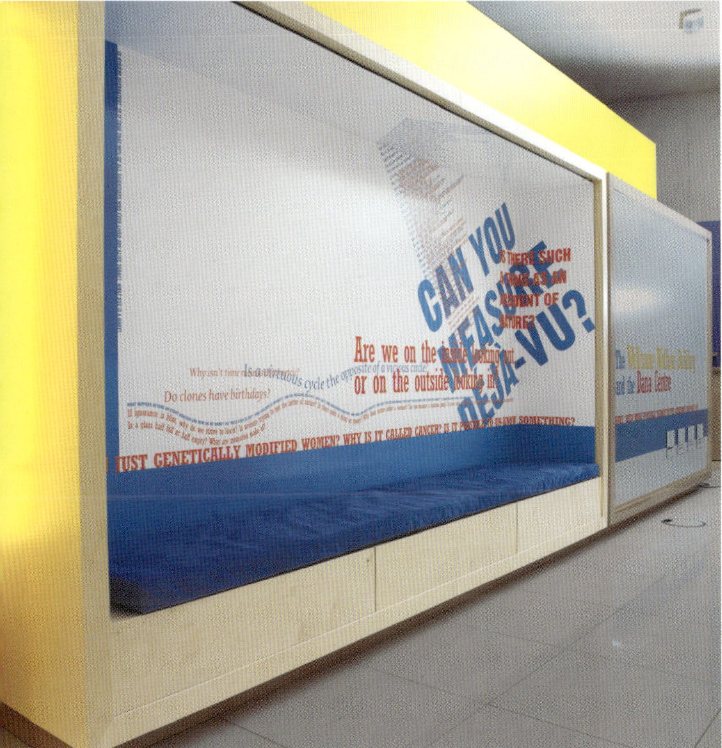

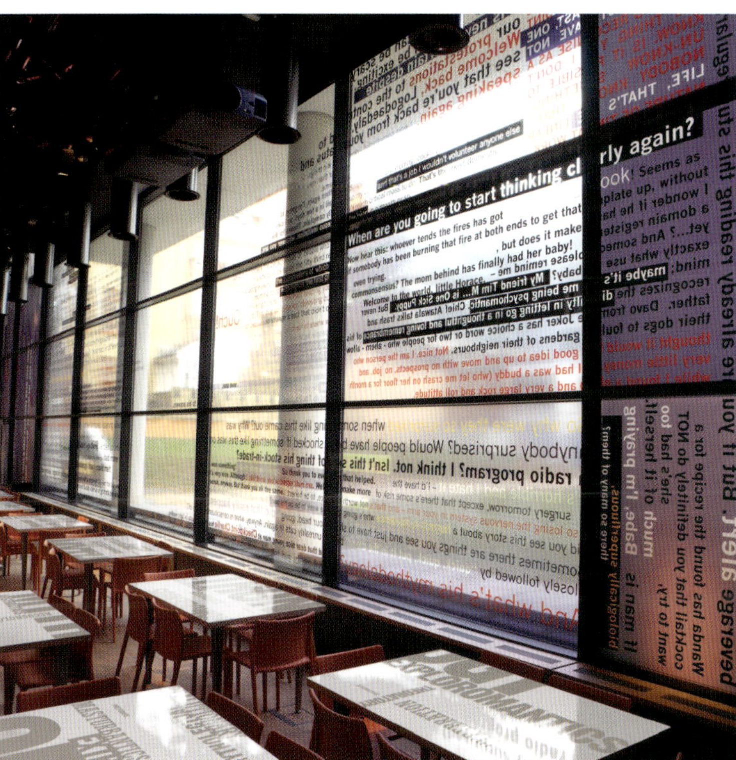

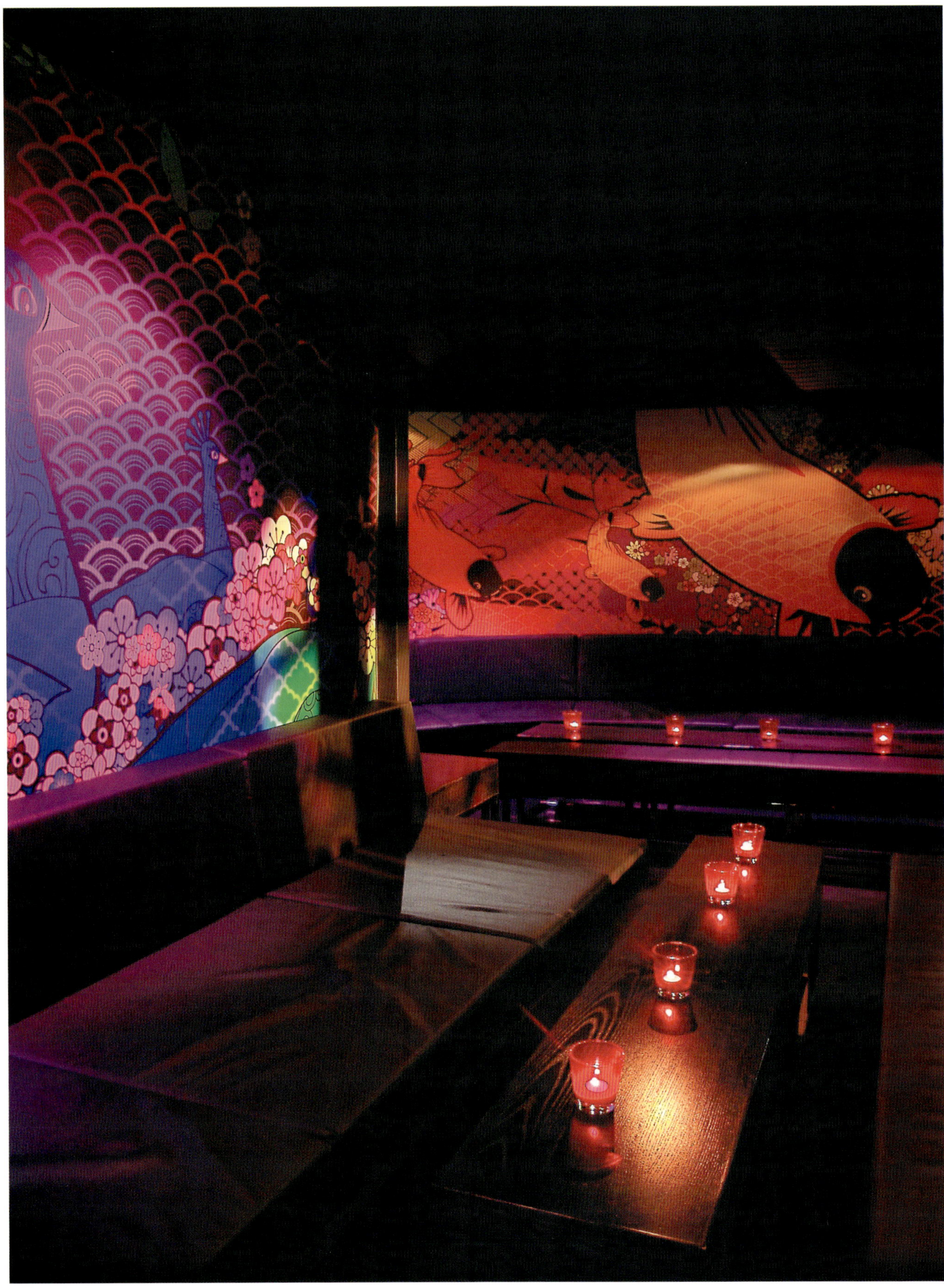

Studio Output

Nottingham, UK

Title: –
Type of work: Mural
Client: Geisha
Design: ad// Dan Moore d// Lydia Lapinski
Year: 2004

Interior graphic scheme for Geisha, a Far East-inspired restaurant and nightclub. The plum blossom or 'ume' is associated with spring and new life. Printwork in a stark two colour design scheme features rich subtle patterns achieved through overprinting magenta on black. One wall is covered with a 16 metre mural applied in Bisazza; a technique which involves mosaic tiles being individually grouted in metallic gold. Large scale graphics panels are hung in stairwells and around the walls, and are changed on a regular basis.

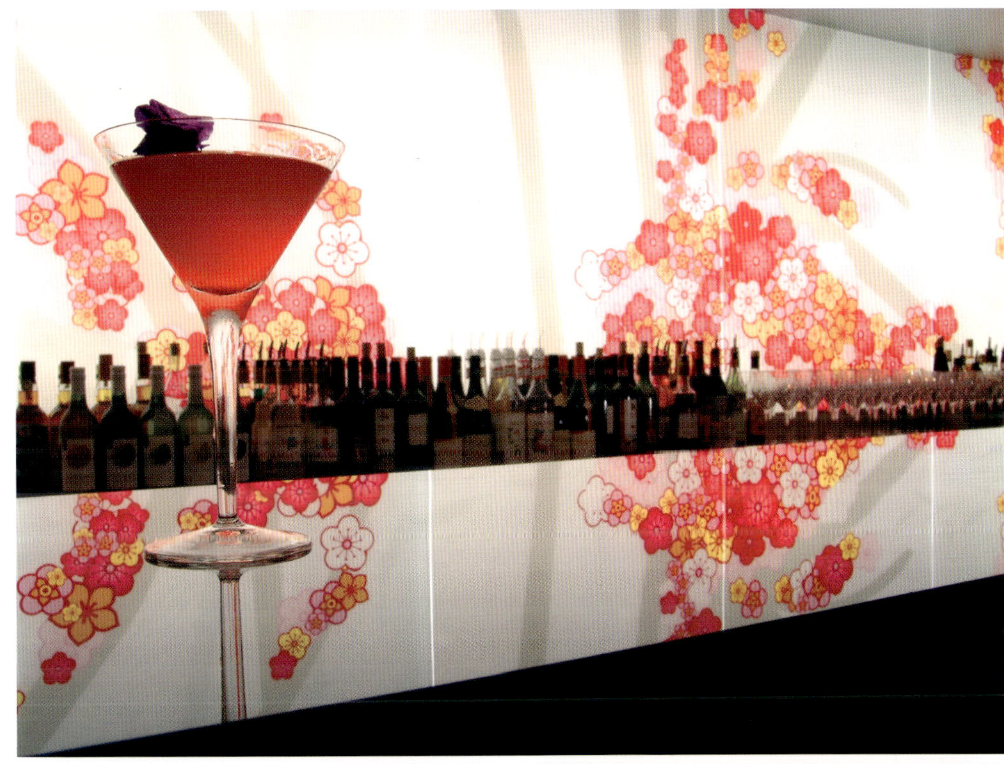

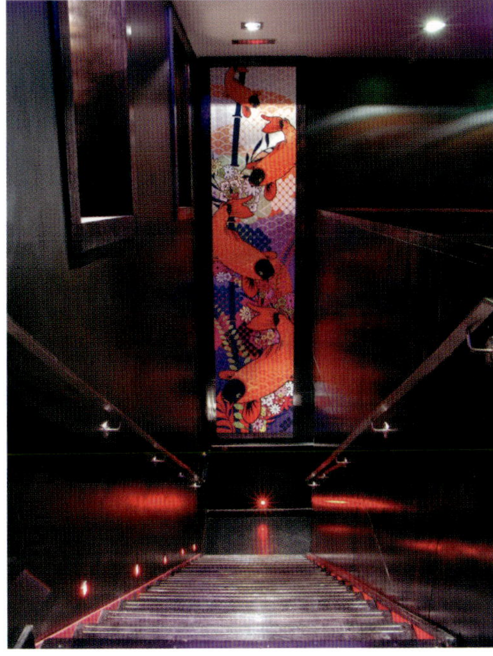

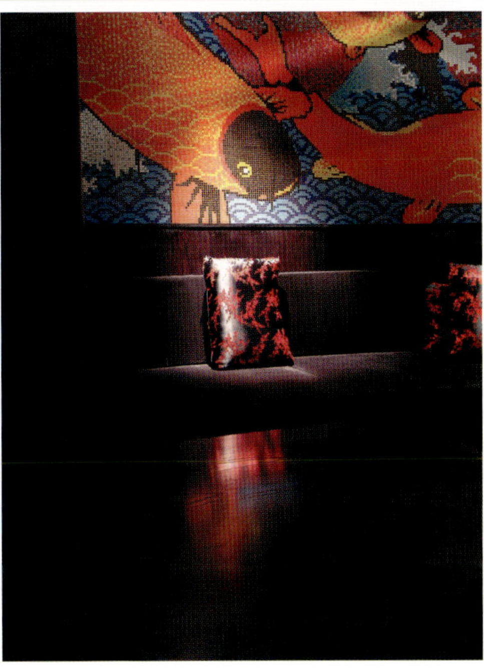

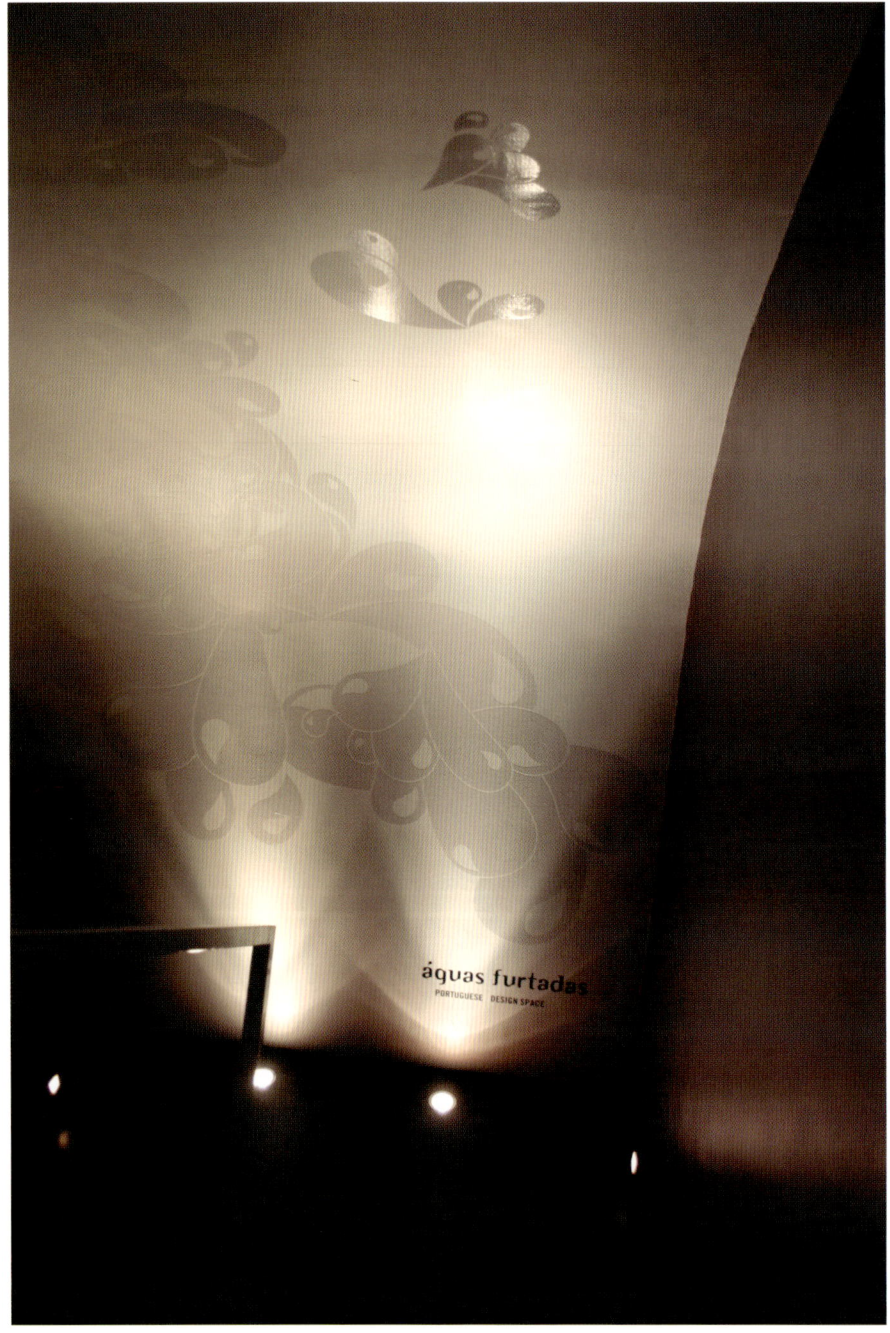

Passvite
(Filipe Mesquita,
Pedro Serrão)

Porto, Portugal

Title: Águas Furtadas
Type of work: Identity, ambient, product
Client: Águas Furtadas – Portuguese Design Space
Design: ad, d// Filipe Mesquita, Pedro Serrão
Year: 2005

Graphic concept created for a Portuguese space that combines selling of different design objects with the creation of it's own products. This space is located on the last floor of a traditional Portuguese house, typically named Águas Furtadas (stolen waters). A concept is created with this in mind not only for the main identity but also the furniture and decoration of the entire store.

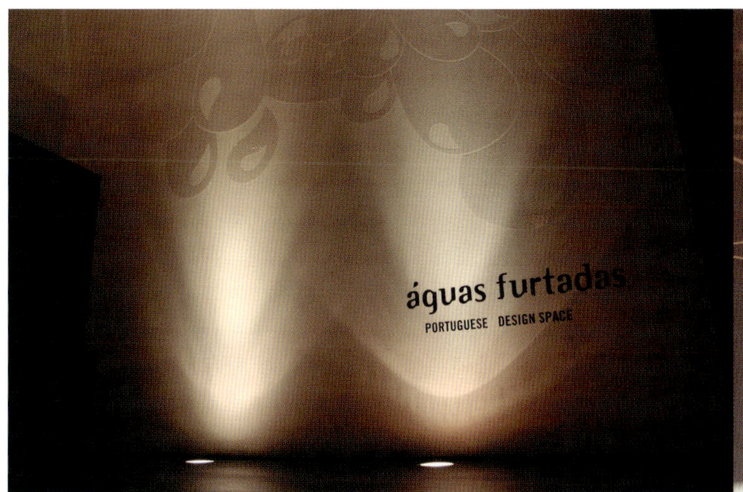

águas furtadas
PORTUGUESE DESIGN SPACE

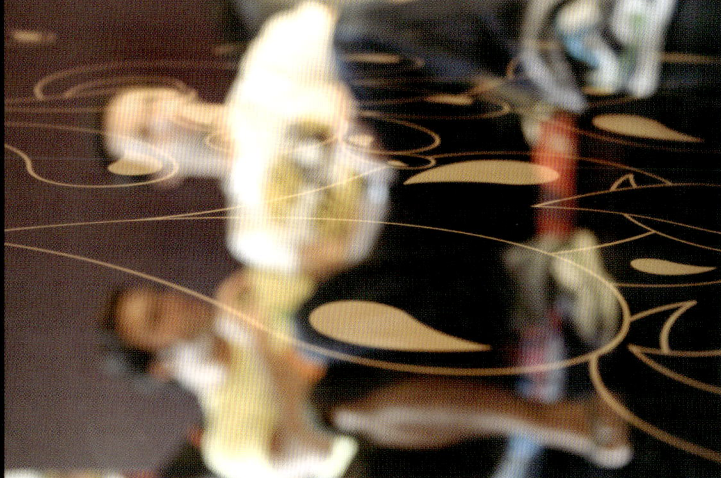

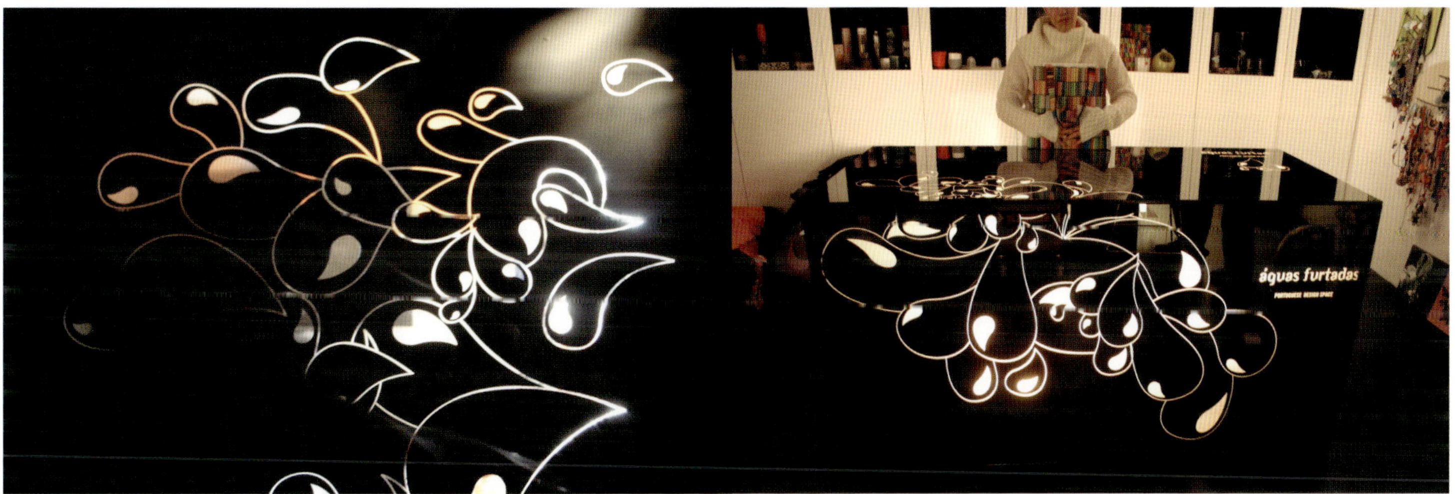

águas furtadas
PORTUGUESE DESIGN SPACE

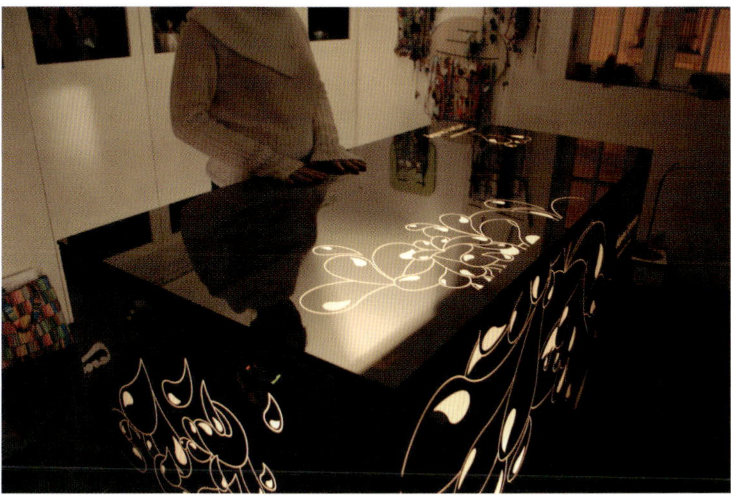

Stiletto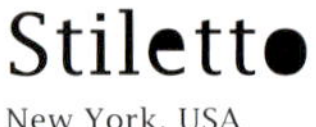

New York, USA

Title: Autumn, Bird
Type of work: Window graphics, interior canvas
Client: Lamarthe
Design: ad, d// Stiletto
Year: 2005

Illustration on birds, grasslands with fonts in classic style forms a feel as in Autumn for Lamerthe. They are therefore mainly in brown, yellow, green and even black, some dark cold colour scheme that is used.

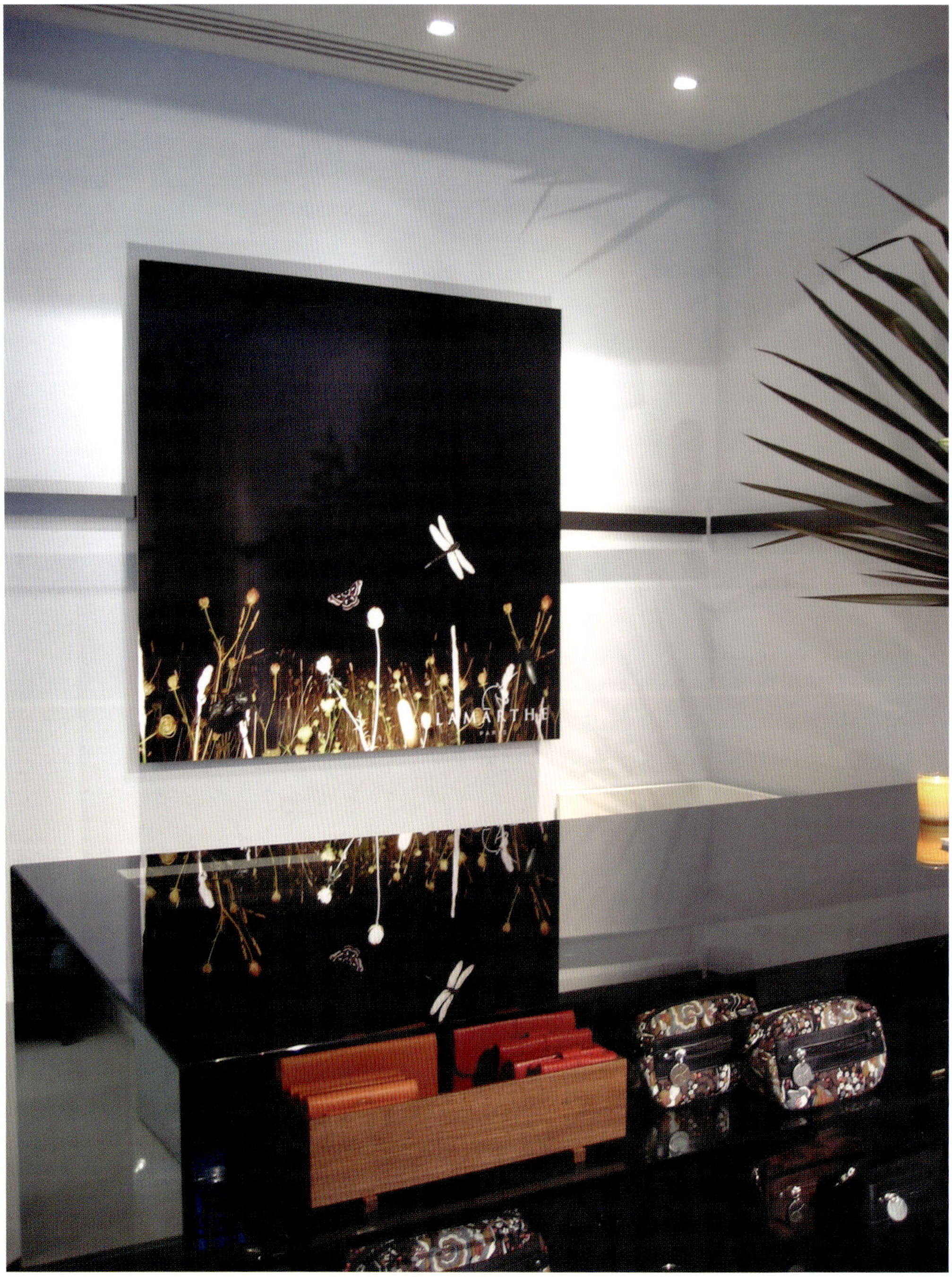

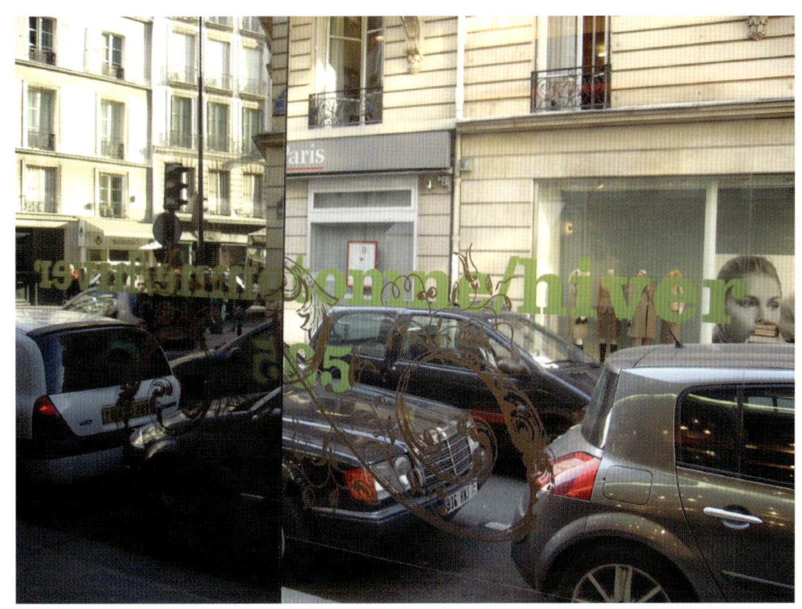
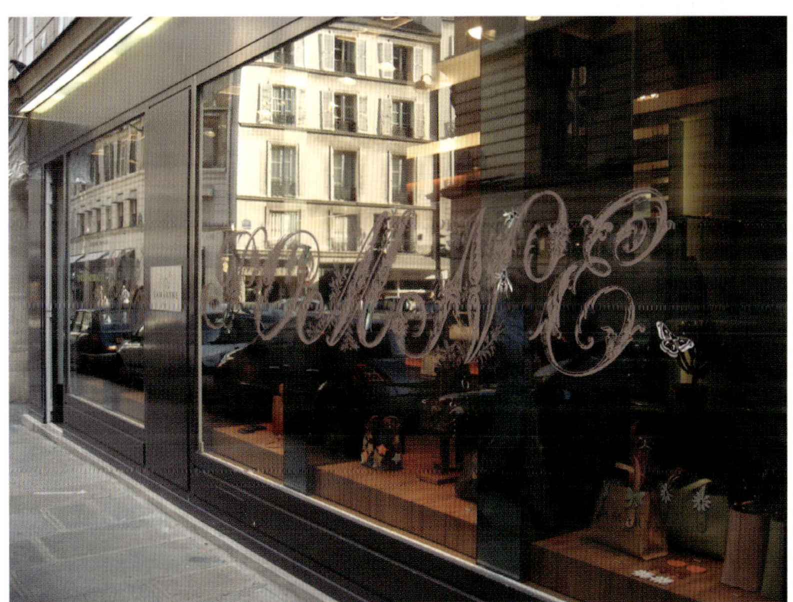
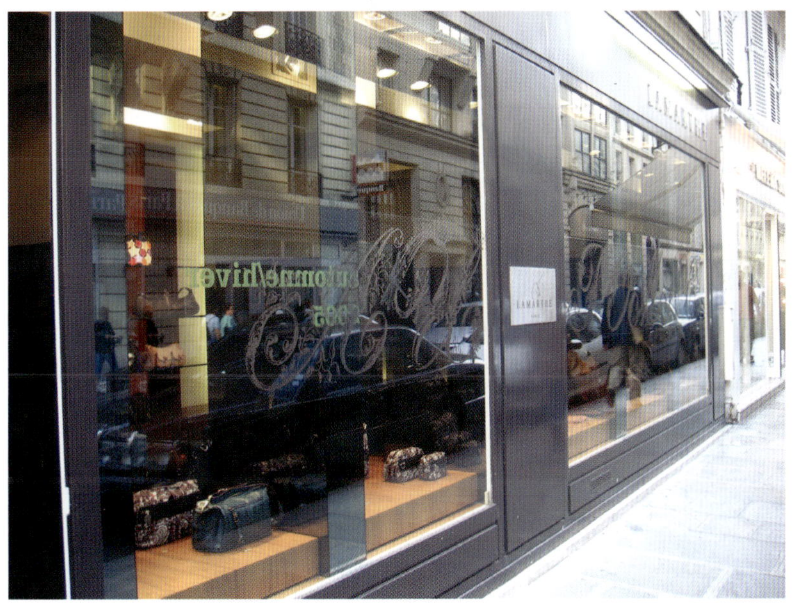

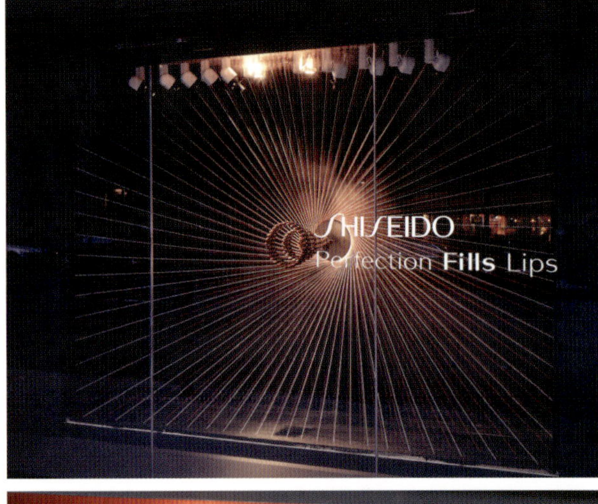

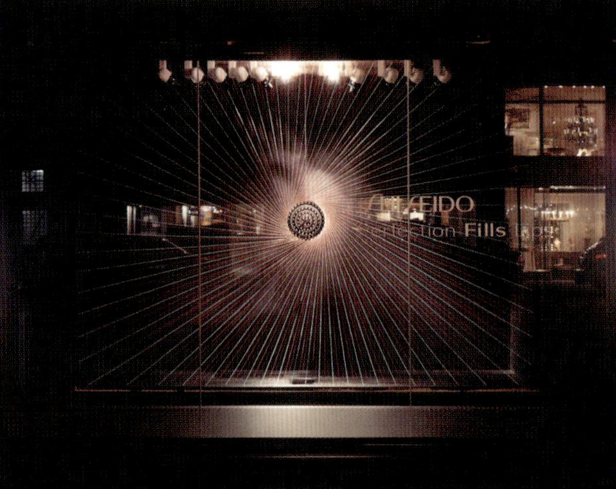

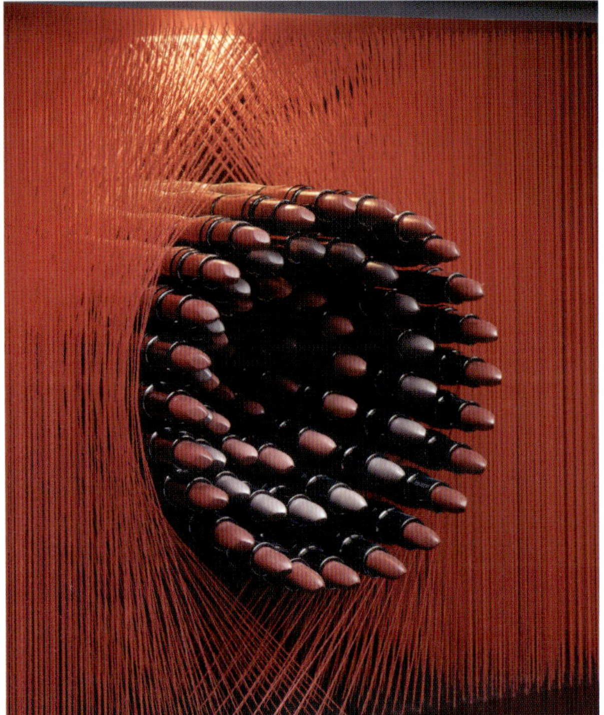

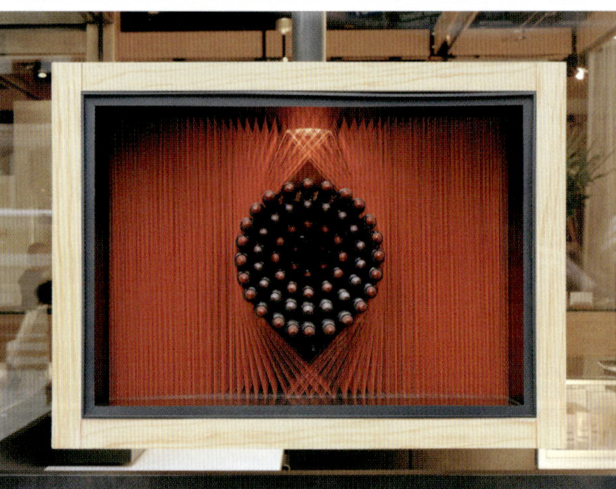

Heads Inc

New York, USA

Title: POS Display Unit for Shiseido Perfumery Store
Type of work: Display unit
Client: Shiseido Cosmetics
Design: ad, d// So Takahashi
Year: 2005

The unit has been used in more than 250 locations throughout the U.S. One of the requirements from the client was to design a unit compact enough to be able to use in the different locations yet to be stands out effectively. By combining two different angular elements to the relatively small unit, Heads Inc has successfully made the solution to the project.

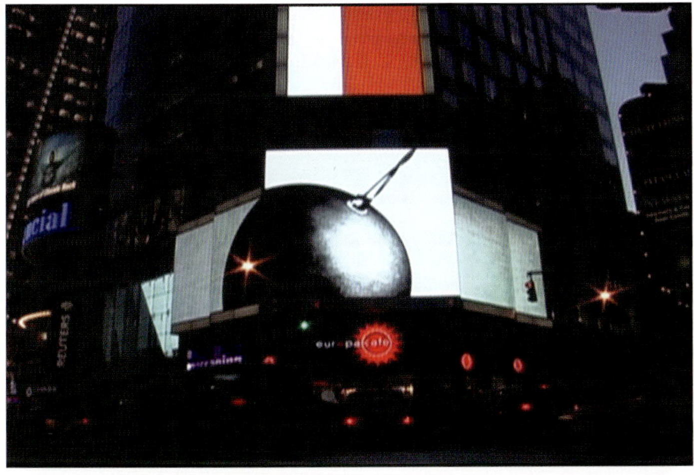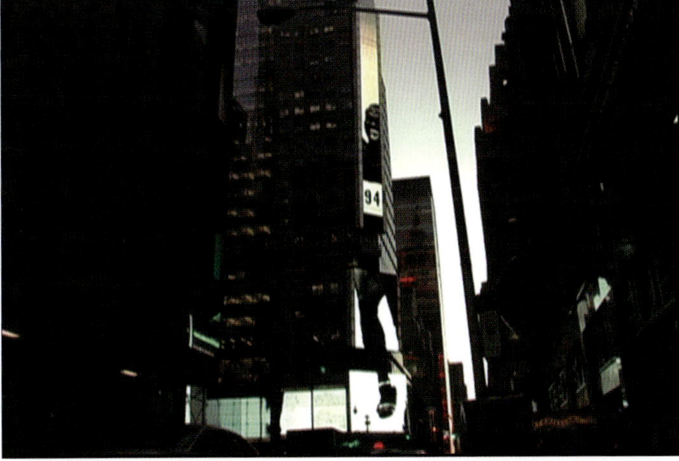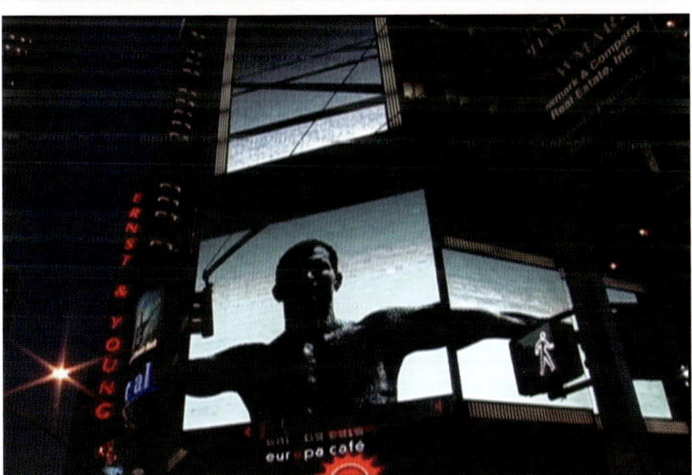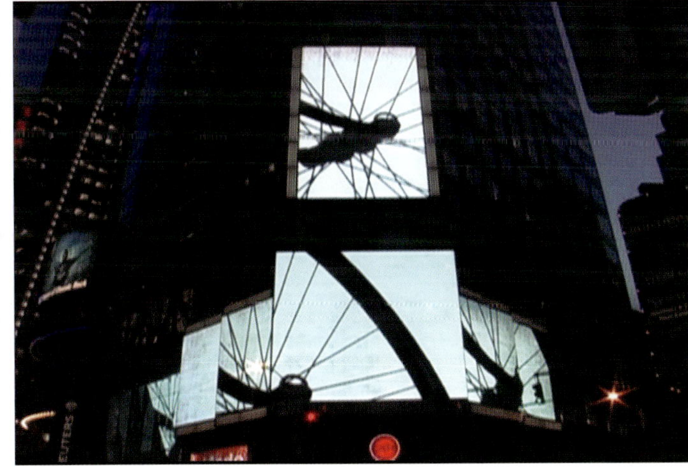

Trollbäck+ Company

New York, USA

Title: NYC 2012 Olympics Environmental Film
Type of work: Mural Design, architectural film installation
Client: NYC 2012
Design: ad// Jakob Trollbäck, Joe Wright
d// Jens Mebes, Todd Neale, Greg Hahn
Year: 2005

An environmental short film that would introduce the City to its Olympic Logo during the last year when New York City was still holding its breath with the prospect of hosting 2012's Olympics. Projected on the multi-story screens of Times Square, the film blanketed across multiple screens, wrapping the bustling intersection at 42nd street in an energetic montage of iconic sports graphics culminating in the NYC 2012 logo.

Designers

123 Buero

A Berlin-based design unit who develops and realizes contemporary graphic design projects with a strong focus on typography, image and production.

Page 60-61

Airside

A London-based design group started in 1999. They work in every possible medium, and at the moment they are working on knitting, screen-printing, badge-making, pop promos, posters, web sites, brand identities, events, tee-shirts and animations for mobile phones.

They believe that all design is experiential, and so they focus on elegant and efficient interfaces in every medium. They also believe in the concept of communities, and they create them through their work by inspiring and empowering people. In practice, this means that they like to welcome people and encourage them to make friends with each other.

Page 54-55, 94-97, 260-261, 264-265

Akinori Oishi

A graphic artist based in Paris, France. He was born in Osaka, Japan in 1972. He studied Fine Arts and Multimedia. He was the winner of the International Multimedia Prize at Cannes France, Milia 2001. He now works mainly in Europe, on Multimedia, TV commercial, Publishing, Comic, and Fine Art.

Page 86, 172-175

Alice Chan

An illustrator and graphic designer based in Hong Kong. She is active in design and illustration work for advertisements, editorials, comics, fashion, stationery, toys, and websites. She founded her own brand 'Asteria' and is now working for corporate, product and editorial clients from around the world. Her current clients are from Japan, USA, France, England, Germany, Finland and Hong Kong. They include: Canon, Anna Sui, Colette, Sakamoto, Sun Hoseki, Ito Yokado, Triiads, Pictoplasma, Die Gestalten Verlag, Web Design Index, Page One the designer's bookshop, Yakuta, Toy2R, IdN Magazine, Clutter Magazine, Milk Magazine, etc.

Page 83

Aloof Design

Aloof Design creates innovative structural packaging and develops unique marketing campaigns. Their work is distinctive, sensitive and honest. They are compulsive innovators, pushing their ideas beyond the anticipated, conscientious brand guardians, dedicated to help businesses to grow.

Their projects range from the development of brand identities for start up's, to pack designs for some of the world's best-known multi-nationals. Their disciplines include: Brand identity design, brand and product naming, brand evolution, structural packaging design, product development, marketing campaigns & promotional literature, website design, photography art direction, print and production management.

Page 84-85, 100, 160

Atelier Susana Carvalho Kai Bernau

Page 102

Base

A studio specializing in creative direction and brand development, with offices in Brussels, New York, Barcelona, Madrid, and Paris.

Page 14-15, 19, 23, 26-27, 30, 32, 126-131, 182-183

Beng

Jan Willem van den Ban and Bastiaan de Wolff met at Total Design (now Total Identity) where they worked on large to extra large identity projects. Jan Willem continued to work in London for Intro for a couple of years. There he dug his way into new media, working on interactive projects for the likes of British Airways, Ricky Martin and Metallica. In the meantime, Bas explored the boundaries between design, leading creative sessions and project management.

With the idea 'BETTER AND MORE FUN!' in mind, Jan Willem and Bas reunited. Since 1998 they form BENG and serve clients with outspoken communication concepts combined with fresh and powerful design. BENG focuses on campaigns and identities.

Page 64-67

Bleed

A graphic design agency based in Oslo, Norway. It was established in June 2000 by five individuals with background in graphic design, advertising and technology. Today Bleed counts 12 employees and stands out both nationally and internationally as a creative design agency that challenges the borders between commercial and art projects. Bleed believes that design must be based on creative ideas to stand out and that identity, function and values make the design work. Based on these values, Bleed applies graphic design as a communication tool and develops innovative design solutions for all channels.

Page 78

Brighten The Corners

An independent, multi-disciplined design and strategy consultancy with offices in London and Stuttgart. Established in 1999, they are a small organization which handles both large and small scale projects. Whether designing a book, a stamp or branding an organization, their belief is that communication should be clear and direct and that good design always makes a difference.

Page 88

Build

Founded by Michael C. Place, who was born in North Yorkshire, England in 1969 and studied at Newcastle College. He first worked in London with Trevor Jackson at Bite It! and then the Designers Republic (tDR) in Sheffield. His work includes record designs for Champion Records, Gee Street Records, R&S Records, Satoshi Tomiie, Warp Records and Sun Electric. He has produced the Wipeout series for PlayStation and the book 3D>2D Adventures In + Out of Architecture. In 2001 he returned from travelling and started 'Build' in London. It specializes mainly in design for print.

Page 13, 44-45, 74-75, 140-141

C100

A Munich-based design studio working for both national and international clients. It offers expertise in conception, creative direction and realization of print, web and art projects.

Page 69

Carmen Garcia Huerta

Born in Madrid, Spain in 1975. She graduated with a degree in Advertising and Public Relations, at Universidad Complutense de Madrid. She began soon to work in graphic design for several enterprises. In 2001 she started her career as a fashion illustrator, working ever since for Spanish and international magazines such as Vogue Spain, L'officiel Russia, FrAU Japan, Glamour Germany, Madame, Monsieur, ELLE, Woman, El Pais, Vanidad. Her regular clients are Custo Barcelona, Eric Bompard, Kellogg's, Carrera & Carrera, Unipapel and Jean Louis David.

Page 262-263

Cartlidge Levene

Chillichilly

For them, design is recognizing the art of living. Through their work, they hope to give attention to ideas that are clever and contemporary without being media and trend driven. Though they are constantly submerged in a world that claims to understand what 'lifestyle' is all about, they make no pretensions about being arbiters of how one should style one's life. Instead, they would like to think of themselves more as storytellers, who with each endeavor push to reveal, narrate, as well as discover the connections between art and living.

CHK Design

A London-based company established by Christian Küsters, who holds a degree from the London College of Printing and Yale University. He also launched Acme Fonts, a digital type foundry. Küsters teaches at Camberwell College of Arts and is an Art Director of Architectural Design magazine. He has written for magazines such as Eye, Baseline and Graphics International. He is also co-author with Emily King of Restart: New Systems in Graphic Design (Thames & Hudson, London, 2001). He curated and designed with Marcus Maurer 'Design Now – Graphics', an exhibition on contemporary graphic design for the Design Museum in London.

Chris Bolton

Born 1975, Bolton is a British/Canadian Graphic Designer based in Helsinki. He studied graphic design in England at Berkshire School of Art & Design before moving to Helsinki to work in various Advertising and Design agencies. He is now working as a freelance graphic designer for various local and international clients such as Nokia, Eskimo Recordings(Belgium), A-lehdet (Finland), Escalator Records (Japan), and Comme Des Garcons.

Deanne Cheuk

Labeled as one of the top 50 creatives in the world by The Face magazine; 'a leader' by Flaunt Magazine; and 'the fashion world's darling of the moment' by the Canadian National Post. Her clients are as diverse as Tokion Magazine, Urban Outfitters, and Levi's Strauss. She regularly compiles the graphic 'zine of inspiration' Neomu.

Deluxe

Design People Studio

Based in Madrid Spain, Design People are Alex and Maria. Alex has studied architecture and publicity. Maria first studied fashion design, then taught drawing and illustration. They have been designing together since 1990, firstly as NoLimit and since last year as Design People.

They specialize in Corporate Design, producing emotive and highly acclaimed work for customers around the globe.

DesignArbeid

A collaboration between Ruben Abels and Adam Oostenbrink which was founded in 1998. Based in Amsterdam, The Netherlands, they work for any client who leaves room for conceptual development before starting the design.

Dimaquina

A Brazilian design collective created with the intention to make innovative, defying and stimulating work. They value the creative process, where clients participate as co-authors. Design to them is not just a plain result, but a search for a unique experience; solutions that can, at the same time, inform and seduce. They believe in art as a device and that collaboration can lead to outstanding work.

Dipesh Pandya

An Art Director & Graphic Designer who was raised in England and graduated from Central Saint Martins in London. He arrived in Paris in 1993 and embarks upon an editorial journey as Associate Art Director, first at Citizen K, followed by Vogue Hommes International. It was an experience through which he developed a taste for fashion and a means of expressing it through the medium of a magazine. At the launch of the US edition of Jalouse magazine, Pandya was taken on as Art Director and has moved to New York with a position that allows him to collaborate with prestigious photographers and illustrators. He further focuses his fine-tuned approach to the world of fashion. Since the magazine was closed, Pandya has continued to explore creative mediums with recent ventures including album covers and music videos directing, fashion-oriented publications like Le Colette and contemporary arts projects like Palais de Tokyo.

Electroclandstino

The alter ego of the designer David Carvalho, who is responsible for many design and art related projects in Portugal. He is the founder of projects like Camouflage Book and Ruadebaixo. Always being involved in many collaborations and exhibitions, Carvalho has been featured in many projects like: Rojo Magazine, Dif Magazine, Orgasmik Design, Musabook, WIWP, NLF Magazine, Passvite, My Brand, Magnolia, Blank Magazine, Le Cool Magazine, Search Megazine, Nike, PALM Shirts, Dezperados, Pink boy, Karacter Models and Experimenta Design.

Elmwood

One of the Britain's leading brand and design consultancies. The company's core skills are the creation of brands with authentic attitude and their strategic development and implementation via the appropriate marketing channels. It has a diverse range of clients from the retail, financial services, sport, FMCG and cultural sectors such as ASDA, B&Q, HBOS, Boots, McCain, GNER, The BBC, and The FA. It is currently in the top 10 of the DBA's Design Effectiveness Awards league tables and has a well-earned reputation for delivering creative and commercially effective work, on time and on budget.

Emmi Salonen

Originally from Finland, Emmi Salonen moved to the UK in 1996. She graduated from University of Brighton in 2001 with a BA Hons in Graphic Design. Straight after, she moved to Italy to work at Fabrica, Benetton's controversial young designers' melt pot. After a year, she was back in London where she worked a couple of years until moving to New York in 2004. There she was with Karlssonwilker, a small company known for its wit clever designs. Earlier in 2005 she relocated again, and is now working from her studio in East London.

Enric Aguilera

A creative studio from Barcelona founded in 1986. They develop their professional activity in different areas such as graphic design, advertising and packaging.

Evostruct

A design studio set up by Frédéric Sofiyana who previously opened the Subakt studio. He acts as a consultant and is also head of creation and artistic direction, as well as developing global design activity. With 10 years experience in the visual communication field, the studio's team offers individual, personalized solutions which respect their partners' inherent values. Three words define the studio: available, creative and rigorous. Their studio is involved in many different activities such as festivals and publishing in the international graphic design field.

Flink

A multi-disciplinary creative studio based in Antwerp, Belgium. Their work crosses over vast disciplines including: brand development, corporate identity, interactive media, packaging and print. Flink has an open and flexible structure to allow organic growth: thinking with their hearts and minds has always been their greatest asset. Their ambition is to produce good work that speaks for itself.

Form®

Form® is an award-winning graphic design consultancy based in London. Established by Paul West and Paula Benson in 1991, their background focused on creating campaigns for many high profile bands in the music industry, working as art directors and designers of record sleeves, logos, POS and merchandise. Over the years their client list has expanded dramatically and in addition to the music work, they now receive regular commissions for identity and branding: book, brochure and DVD packaging design; advertising campaigns; websites; and moving image projects.

To date, Form® clients have covered the areas of music, sport, fashion, furniture, architecture, interiors, events, TV, film, video, publishing, marketing and PR, and they welcome challenges from all areas where clients require an inspiring and creative approach – they don't like to be pigeonholed!

Fundición Gráfica

A design and production company created in 2000 in Palma de Mallorca, Spain. It is a multi-disciplinary creative studio composed by David Robles (Communication & Design), Juan Chito (Art direction & Design), David Fuster (Multimedia & Web), Hector Robles (3D & Postproduction) and Rubén Casas (Video & Production). Their works include graphic design and communication, illustration, multimedia and web design, 2D/3D Animation, TV production, and TV FX.

Grandpeople

Founded in 2001 while all members were still students at the Bergen National Academy of The Arts in Norway. Since then they have been able to work with a lot of different clients that allow them to really explore the fields of design and illustration. In 2006, this willingness to experiment and play is still the single most important motivation for their work, and perhaps the hallmark of their designs.

Halvor Bodin

An independent graphic designer and visual artist based in Oslo, Norway. He runs his own practice Superlow, autodidact with only formal education in political science. He was originally a film producer, but switched to graphic design in 1993. Bodin's international work includes FUSE 17 (with Kim Hiorthøy and Marius Watz), collaborations with Alex Tylevich (Logan), Record covers for Earth and promotional work for the art gallery W139 in Amsterdam 2005. He has worked for numerous international exhibitions, books, videoes in collaboration with artist Bjarne Melgaard. He is known for working with everything from True Norwegian Black Metal to Church altar pieces, without irony. He also writes for two Norwegian design magazines.

Page 200-201, 242

Heads Inc

A design studio based in New York City run by designer So Takahashi. They specialize in art direction, graphic design, package design, product design, as well as several other fields.

Page 282

J3 Productions

Established in 1998, and located in Costa Mesa, CA, J3 is an agency of visual communications specializing in design, brand image development, marketing and photography. It is made up of a small group of art directors, designers, stylists and photographers who are dedicated to provide creative solutions. Their recent clients include: Quiksilver/ Roxy, Urban Decay Cosmetics, Modern Amusement, The Lab/ The Camp (Costa Mesa), Five Crown, Nike, and Target.

Page 51, 89

José Duarte

Born in Portugal, Duarte studied Communication Design at the Faculdade de Belas Artes of Porto (FBAUP). He is also an Erasmus student at the Facultat des Belles Arts in Barcelona. He began as a freelance graphic designer in 2001, working in the fields of publishing, corporate design and photography. One of his most recent works include designing the catalog of the photography exhibition result of a partnership between FBAUP and the Institute of Sistems and Computers Ingeniring. His project 'Fibras ópticas' was also selected to participate in the exhibition.

Page 119

Joseph Magliaro

Born in 1977 in a small town in the suburbs of New Jersey. Surrounded by housing developments, dairy cows and fast-food chains, he developed a fascination for repetition and the mundane. He studied philosophy and art at the University of Richmond, where he developed his interest in examining the 'everyday'— either by re-contextualizing common objects or by cataloging details that often go unnoticed. In 2004 Magliaro formed Es Gibt with Shu Hung. Es Gibt is a platform under which Shu and Joseph collaborate to produce clothing, products and art projects.

Page 161

Julia Hoffmann

A graphic designer who works beside her daytime job at Pentagram NY on freelance projects during nights and weekends.

Page 10-11, 71

Julian Morey

A London based designer and art director. As a protégé of Peter Saville Associates he contributed to designs for New Order, Factory Records and The Haçienda. Working independently his clients have included Diesel Jeans, Environ Records, Giorgio Armani, KesselsKramer, and Vogue. In 1999 he founded Club-21 as an outlet for his diverse collection of contemporary typefaces. Frequently profiled by the design press, they have been incorporated into advertising for the likes of Nike and stamp designs for the Dutch PTT. Recently he established Editions Eklektic as an outlet for personal work expressed through the form of silk-screen prints.

Page 12, 76-77

Kerry Roper

A London-based graphic designer and illustrator. His work combines traditional illustration with photography and typography.

Page 230

Kinetic

Their creed is to break the barriers that hinder marketing communication and to explore the creative and conceptual limits of our projects. They are driven by the passionate belief that creativity can be transformed into arresting creatives that stop people in their tracks. Their design and advertising arm enables a web campaign to be extended into the other platforms of traditional advertising and marketing and vice versa, always without losing sight of the key messages and the brand image. After all, Kinetic takes their work and their clients' welfare very seriously. And while they champion creativity, they have always ensured that their work functions well for their clients. That means they are not some flash in the pan outfit, and in which has never stopped them from having the fun that they have in the things they do.

Page 18, 104, 112, 118, 157

Kinpro

Chisato Shinya started working as an illustrator since 1989. Her first solo exhibition 'Visible shape/Invisible shape, then 'Imagine Story', and 'Peeping Navi' (also performed by Kimiyoshi Futori and Kentaro Hamasato) were all held at Soso cafe which were produced by Shift. There was also Gigei, 'Rising Sun Rock Festival 2004 in Ezo'. Chisato set up an original fashion brand 'Nozoky' with four friends. Her illustrations are published in Grimm, Anderson (both from The Illustrated Fairy Tales of the Brothers), Designed To Help published by Die Gestalten Verlag and LeBron James:Chamber Of Fear by Nike. She has participated in projects such as 'ChilliChilly' produced by ChilliChilly; 'Maxzlot Wallpaper Collection' produced by Maxalot; and 'Hotel Fox' produced by Project Fox.

Page 272-273

Koniak Design Studio

Tel-Aviv based Koniak design studio deals with small to medium scale branding projects. The studio aims at giving simple but unique solutions to the demands of corporate design. They also specialize in graphic art and illustration.

Page 188-191

Lippa Pearce Design

A broad-based graphic design consultancy based in London that specializes in corporate/brand identity, print, packaging, information graphics, and multi media design. Harry Pearce is the co-founder and Domenic Lippa the fellow designer director. The company was founded in 1990 along with Giles Calver. They hold the fundamental belief that design can have an impact whether it is for a large company or a small organization, which is reflected in its client base including Boots Company, Science Museum/London, Heal's, Unilever, Espa, The Typographic Circle and Witness, and the Human Rights Organization, NYC. Being one of the UK's most respected design companies, they also hold a long record of winning awards, for both design effectiveness and creativity, and a history of having its work published and exhibited worldwide. Both Domenic Lippa and Harry Pearce are members of the AGI.

Page 274-275

Made

A design studio from Oslo, Norway, Made consist of three healthy and bright individuals. Their clients often hire them to do design and Art Direction. Sometimes they do it at night, sometimes blindfolded, sometimes backwards and sometimes one more time with feeling.

Page 134-135

Magnetik

A one man agency by Chris Vermiglio, who has started graphic design in 1999 with the project 'Digital High cut' and in parallel a dj carreer as Mr.Magnetik. Trying to combine cutting edge design with cutting edge music, his clients include: Emporio Armani, Axe Parfums, Soma records and Muller records.

Page 218-223

Maiko Gubler

Originally from Switzerland, and now based in Berlin, Gubler used to assist Fork Unstable Media as an art director. She also co-founded the collective ALRT! She currently designs motion graphics, 3d illustration, identity and web site.

Page 108

Mark Boyce

Born in London, England in 1972, Boyce studied typography at the London College of Printing. Since graduating he has worked for several design agencies, designed and art directed a substantial and varied range of work. He designs mainly for print but is also active in interactive design, retail and exhibition environments, and art direction for photography and moving image.

Page 132-133

Martin Woodtli

Perhaps the most accomplished representative of the new design scene in Switzerland, where the joy of the design process, as opposed to monetary reward, seems to determine the direction of the studio. Swiss designers would rather work for small cultural projects to which they are often connected personally, than to fall into the trap of large advertising conglomerates. Woodtli does not subscribe to the silly adage circulated by many of his colleagues about the computer being just a tool; he sees it simply as a process. He can also actually think with the keyboard. His proficiency in various programs is such that he sketches with the keyboard as quickly and uninhibitedly as with pencil and paper.

Page 72-73

Medusateam

Page 213

Milkxhake

A new Hong Kong-based design studio founded by three designers in 2002, specializing in graphic and interactive designs. The founders started from a design project when studying Digital Graphic Communication at Hong

Kong Baptist University. Their name 'milkxhake' not only means a glass of drink, it also symbolizes the spirit of 'mixing', which is expressed through their logo.

Mwmcreative

A young and innovative graphic and screen-based design studio based in London. It was set up early in 2004 by two MA Communication Design CSM friends Maria da Gandra and Maaike van Neck.

Nuno Martins

Born in 1979 in Oporto, Portugal, where Martins lives and works today. He graduated in Communication Design from Faculdade de Belas Artes do Porto (1998-2003) and studied at Willem de Kooning Academie – Hoogeschool in Rotterdam, Netherlands.

Paperjam Design

A multi-discipline graphic design and advertising agency based in Belfast, Northern Ireland. Their process is one of the sound ideas based on directed research, actively seeking unique and engaging solutions.

Park Studio

A London-based graphic design studio founded by Linda Lundin and Nina Nägel in 2002. It is the place to come to for a solution which is friendly but sharp, challenging and always on brand, whether it is for an identity, publications, retail or exhibition graphics. Their attitude to experiment and question to create the most original result keeping their clients one step ahead of the competition.

Passvite (Filipe Mesquita, Pedro Serrão)

Filipe Mesquita and Pedro Serrão have been working together since 2003. They created a series of experimental and commercials projects such as: Passvite (an exhibition and development of an acting community to systematic facts, themes, problems of the everyday), by02 (commercials creative services), Águas Furtadas (Portuguese design shop), shortcut to unknown (personal and experimental work of Filipe Mesquite) and Antek (Pedro Serrão's personal work). In partnership or individually their work have been in some exhibitions, books and magazines such as Din magazine, Musabook, Rojo, Nlf book,etc.

Paul Swagerman

A graphic designer based in Rotterdam that specializes in new media design. He started freelancing after a 4-year study at AKI, academy for fine arts and design in Enschede. He received a grant from the Fund for Fine arts and Architecture, Amsterdam. He is interested in the field of new media within graphic design. His clients include record labels, artists and companies in the design and cultural field.

Paulo Arraiano

Aged 28, originally from Portugal, Arraiano is working as a print, editorial and multimedia designer. His has worked for serveral magazines such as Magnolia, Slang, and company like Palm, Transformadores Records, Disconnet and El Camino. His current works include Musa-book, NLF Magazine, Fused Magazine UK, Idea Magazine Taiwan, Orgasmikdesign France, Camouflage, and Le Cool Magazine.

Peter Anderson

A graphic artist hales from Belfast and studied at Central Saint Martins College, London. His clients include Moschino, BBC and The European Union. His work can also be found in the Tate Gallery, the Victoria and Albert Museum, London, The Museum of Modern Art, New York, The Sakner Collection of Concrete Poetry, Miami and The Ulster Museum. His work has branched out into grand scale commissions including a pole installation around the island's perimeter for the gallery St Lucia Fine Art, a series of recent installations for Puma Sportswear in London and more locally, interactive artworks for Paul and Jeanne Rankin's Belfast restaurants, Cayenne, Rain City, Roscoff and the ever expanding Cafe Paul Rankin. He has represented graphic design opinion in a conference on 'non space' hosted by Edinburgh University. His recent television work includes Bleak House and Mayo both for BBC1.

RMAC

Founded in 1996 based in Lisbon, Portugal, the studio altogether has about twelve people and a spontaneous and observant spirit in solving every challenge from the clients. They work on graphic, industrial and interior design projects, in which they claim 'No image lives forever. Work is always in progress. RM/Design is our life.'

Seeman Ho

A visual artist who achieves successfully in different media including installations, paintings, publications, animations and theatre productions. She is also a subtle poet with poetic artworks. Since her graduation from the Bachelor course of Fashion Design in the Hong Kong Polytechnics University in 1999, she had eight books published, nine installation exhibitions and numerous illustrations for newspapers and magazines.

Her animation work 'The circus of n_n, v_v' was one of the programs in the Hong Kong International Film Festival 2001 and Short Film Festival 2002, France. Her installation, 'A tree to be found', was awarded in the Hong Kong Arts Biennial 2003 and was collected by the Hong Kong Museum of Art. She has her own 'seeman backyard' gallery in Hong Kong.

Serial Cut™

Founded by Sergio del Puerto since 1999. Their art direction and design has always been with a 'big touch' of illustration. They became famous in Spain with the weekly Tentaciones illustrations, the supplement of El Pais, the Spainsh leading newspaper. He has a versatile style, and loves typography. He often uses a 'cut & paste' style because there is a mix of different techniques such as vectorial, hand-painting and photo collage. He takes inspiration of the visual culture of the present and past.

so+ba

Founded by Alex Sonderegger and Susanna Baer in 2001, So+ba is a dynamic creative design agency based in one of the most exciting Asian metropolitans — Tokyo, Japan.

Stefania

Based in Stockholm 2002 and founded by Stefania Malmsten, who was born in Stockholm, Sweden in 1967. She initiated and designed Pop and Bibel Magazines during the nineties, in which the core activity is printed matters for fashion houses, art institutions and other companies. The studio and sister company Pipel also work with a network of professionals in film, web design and other related fields.

Stephen Layfield

One of Australia's leading designers, Layfield was recently awarded Australia's top graphic design award - The AGDA Pinnacle. He has also won numerous international awards for his design work.

Stiletto

Founded by Julie Hirschfeld and Stefanie Barth, their clients include MTV, German VIVA Plus, USA Networks, the Gap, Arnold Advertising, RCA Records, HBO, Fujitsu Siemens, Architect Andrea Tognon, Sundance Channel and Area. Currently, they are redesigning Res, a US film, video and culture lifestyle magazine. They have been featured in The Face, Wallpaper, I.D. and in 'Restart: New Systems in Graphic Design' published by Universe. Their motion graphics for MTV had won two Art Director's Club awards. They will be featured in 'Fresh Dialogue', a book about experimental design studios, published by Princeton Architectural Press and American Institute of Graphic Arts.

strichpunkt

With a staff of seventeen, strichpunkt concentrates on strategic communication consulting and visual communication, particularly in the fields of corporate design, image media and financial market media. The co-founders of the agency, Kirsten Dietz and Jochen Rädeker (members of the TDC in New York and ADC Germany), place emphasis on high-quality typography and sensitive graphics solutions. Basic criteria in all strichpunkt projects is to have freedom for unusual approaches even when the goals are initially defined and to have fun in every creative process.

Studio Output

A design studio formed in summer 2002 by three partners. They now employ a versatile design team with a wealth of skill and experience. They combine the vision of a big agency with the efficiency of a compact and responsive team. Their sole aim is to enable their clients to communicate clearly, creatively and effectively. As well as some of the major names in broadcasting, they also work regularly with clients in all areas of fashion, PR, music, leisure and the arts.

Studio Volk

Founded by Enrico Bonafede in the summer of 2003. Bonafede was born in Rome, Italy in 1974. He graduated from college in 1995 and began a career in print design. He has worked for 7 years as a graphic designer at design agency in Rome and has been working on identity, print, typography and packaging since 1996.

Stylo

A creative design consultancy that works for public and private clients on a variety of projects in various disciplines including corporate identity, print, internet, e-commerce, moving image and sound design.

Page 152-153, 204, 228, 243

Sussner Design Company

Opened by Derek Sussner in 1999, forging a heads-up style, driven by solid, individual-oriented client service. They have worked with over 100 companies, including Best Buy, Bremer Bank, Target Commercial Interiors, Evel Knievel Leather, Life Time Fitness, Red Wing Shoes, Reflections Printing, Rockport Publishing and Voyageur Outward Bound. Their clients have benefited from a uniquely hands-on, business-based design approach, and award winning creative. A process that partners with clients to truly understand their needs and goals. While at the same time, they believes that their job is to also challenge client's notions of business-as-usual.

Page 171

Teresa & David

A design studio based in Stockholm, and established in 2001 by Teresa Holmberg, who graduated from Beckmans College of Design, and design journalist David Castenfors. They have broadly worked on graphic identity, motion graphics, book design, magazine and illustration. Variety is important to them, not just to stimulate a high level of creativity, but also to prevent getting stuck into only one certain style. Their work philosophy is based on passion, fun, patience and dignity.

Page 207

Tetsuya Nagato

Born in 1970 in Tokyo, Nagato enjoyed painting since childhood. He moved to United States after graduating from high school and returned to Japan in 1996 where he began working on digital photo-collage and illustrations. He won the 18th Annual 'The Choice Prize' in 2001, the 2002 Media Arts Festival, Agency for Cultural Affairs Award Digital Art (Non interactive) Division Excellence Prize, and the 2003 Tokyo WonderWall, WonderWall Prize. He is currently working on visual production for magazines of the fashion and the music industry.

Page 236

The Consult

An independent graphic design agency based in the UK. Their focus is to develop insightful and memorable communication that works. They engage in an exploration of thought and process in order to create inspiring concepts and beautifully styled design.

Page 154

The Fold

A New York-based design agency founded in 2000. Initially offering their skills of art direction and design for the music industry, they have rapidly built their reputation in other areas, including fashion, editorial design, and video installation.

Page 198-199

Tnop™ & ®bePOS|+|VE

Founded by Tnop Wangsillapakun, a Chicago-based designer, who received his Bachelor of Fine Art in visual communication arts from Rangsit University, Bangkok in 1993. He started working as a graphic designer at J. Walter Thompson, Bangkok. Two years later, he joined TBWA Bangkok as an art director. In 1996, he went to the United States to study graphic design at Savannah College of Art and Design, Georgia, from where he received his Master degree in 1998. He then moved to Chicago to work at Segura Inc. His works have been featured in books and renowned magazines inside and outside of the U.S. In 2000, he started ®bePOS|+|VE design in Bangkok with his friends. He left Segura Inc. in 2005 to focus on his studios in both Chicago and Bangkok.

Page 246-249

Tom Muller

A Belgian graphic designer living and working in London, UK. He studied Graphic and Advertising design at the Royal Academy for Fine Arts in Antwerp, Belgium. Since 2000 Muller has been working at Vir2L Studios and Lost In Space. In 2001 he launched ximeraLabs, his personal site, and co-founded Duolog-Visual Identity Systems and Plan B Science and Entertainment. Since March 2002 he has become the Art Director at a design consultancy, Kleber.

Page 62-63

Toxic Design Studio

Based in Rome, Italy since 1998, and founded by Fabio Lattanzi Antinori who was born in 1971. Antinori is a graphic designer and musician who has been working on visual communication through corporate identity, illustration, editorial, music graphics, title sequences, soundtracks, etc.

Page 16-17

Traffic

A small London-based design studio specializing in design for the music industry. Their types of work include creative projects, packaging, corporate identities and marketing. Their clients include EMI, Parlophone, Polydor, Island, Sony, Paramount.

Page 46

Trafik

Composed of four designers: Damien Gautier, Pierre Rodière, Lionel Michée, Julien Sappa, and one developer: Joel Rodière. Collective design and interactivity lie at the heart of their work. It enables them to go beyond the traditional representations of technicians and graphic artists. For six years now, Trafik has done projects on all types of media, either on their own work like Signotek, The Reticular writing pieces and Collekto, or for clients such as Oxbow, Salomon, Agnès B, Louis Vuitton and Habitat. Whether they are asked to design a website for an art gallery or design a pattern on a porcelain dinner set, whether their work is typographical, in image form or computer-generated, or a mix of all three, Trafik approaches the subject without compromise or preconceived ideas. Their concerns are to question themselves continuously in order to ensure the originality of the concept and, above all, to never get tired of their work.

Page 58-59

Trollbäck + Company

A bicoastal creative studio committed to develop innovative visual and branding solutions. Rooted in a strong European design sensibility, the young multi-disciplinary company works across a variety of media from film titles and trailers to TV commercials, environmental and architectural installations, network branding, outdoor advertising, magazine and book design. Their design and production studios are on Fifth Avenue and Venice Beach.

Page 283

undoboy

He loves and hates design, in which brings him happiness.

Page 90-91, 124-125, 206

Via Grafik

An art & design studio founded in late 2003, Via Grafik consists of Leo Volland (boe/bstrkt), André Nossek (mnwrks/slave), Robert Schwartz (n6), Tim Bollinger (g13), Till Heim (sign) and Lars Herzig. They are a professional design studio located in Wiesbaden, Germany, which offers a wide range of services. On one hand they specialize in print design such as logo design, corporate identities, illustration, font type design, book and catalog design, interior design and web design. On the other hand they are offering motion and animation design. Via Grafik is also an art studio. Every one of them has a background in graffiti or street art. They always try to combine their artistic skills with their design skills. They participate in exhibitions, thus share a great diversity in their artistic visions in which they combine within their projects. They love to work free.

Page 169

Warmrain

A studio that does events, installations, branding, marketing campaigns and graphics design. They think 'plinth' is a lovely word and they like the smell of a freshly opened book. They will never forget to say hello and how do you do.

Page 101

Wig-01

Two pixel punks who are passionate about creating graphic design and illustrations. They work for anyone who wants to separate himself from formulaic, mediocre design and who is prepared to take risks.

Page 33, 136-137

Yucca Studio

A multi-disciplinary creative boutique believing in a strong desire to create the best design and user experience possible. They have stayed independent, they focuse and believe in a future crafted out by passion. Their holistic approach emphasizes on critical thinking and aesthetic research, by applying simplified complicity into visual solutions and interactive media. They believe first and foremost that they are communicators, and that enables them to deliver their client's message across any communications platform.

Page 266-267

Zion Graphics

Founded in 2002, Zion Graphics specializes in design for the music and fashion industry. They work with clients such as Sony Music, EMI, Peak Performance and J. Lindeberg. Formally, Ricky Tillblad also runs the design companies, F+ and 24HR.

Page 68, 163, 235